500 BEST-EVER RECIPES APPETIZERS

The ultimate collection of first courses and finger food, snacks and starters, dips and dippers, shown in 500 stunning photographs

Editor: Anne Hildyard

HERMES HOUSE

This edition is published by Hermes House,
an imprint of Anness Publishing Ltd, Hermes House
88–89 Blackfriars Road, London SE1 8HA
tel. 020 7401 2077; fax 020 7633 9499
www.hermeshouse.com; www.annesspublishing.com

Publisher: Joanna Lorenz
Project Editor: Anne Hildyard
Copy Editor: Jay Thundercliffe
Jacket Design: Nigel Partridge
Production Controller: Wendy Lawson
Design: SMI
Recipes: Catherine Atkinson, Alex Barker, Angela Boggiano, Carla Capalbo, Kit Chan, Jacqueline Clarke, Maxine Clarke, Andi Cleverly, Roz Denny, Matthew Drennan, Joanna Farrow, Rafi Fernandez, Christine France, Silvano Franco, Sarah Gates, Shirley Gill, Brian Glover, Nicola Graimes, Rosamund Grant, Carole Handslip, Deh-Ta Hsing, Peter Jordan, Lucy Knox, Elisabeth Lambert Ortiz, Ruby Le Bois, Clare Lewis, Sara Lewis, Christine McFadden, Leslie Mackley, Norma MacMillan, Sue Maggs, Sally Mansfield, Sallie Morris, Jane Milton, Keith Richmond, Rena Salaman, Marlena Spieler, Jenny Stacey, Liz Trigg, Linda Tubby, Oona van den Berg, Hilaire Walden, Laura Washburn, Steven Wheeler, Kate Whiteman, Elizabeth Wolf-Cohen, Jeni Wright
Photographers: Karl Adamson, Edward Allwright, Caroline Arber, Steve Baxter, Martin Brigdale, Nicki Dowey, James Duncan, Gus Filgate, John Freeman, Ian Garlick, Michelle Garrett, Peter Henley, John Heseltine, Amanda Heywood, Janine Hosegood, David Jordan, Maris Kelly, Dave King, Don Last, William Lingwood, Patrick McLeavy, Michael Michaels, Roisin Neild, Thomas Odulate, Spike Powell, Craig Robertson, Simon Smith, Sam Stowell, Polly Wreford

A CIP catalogue record for this book
is available from the British Library.

Notes

Bracketed terms are intended for American readers.

For all recipes, quantities are given in both metric and imperial measures and, where appropriate, in standard cups and spoons. Follow one set of measures, but not a mixture, because they are not interchangeable.

Standard spoon and cup measures are level. 1 tsp = 5ml, 1 tbsp = 15ml, 1 cup = 250ml/8fl oz. Australian standard tablespoons are 20ml. Australian readers should use 3 tsp in place of 1 tbsp for measuring small quantities.

American pints are 16fl oz/2 cups. American readers should use 20fl oz/2.5 cups in place of 1 pint when measuring liquids.
Electric oven temperatures in this book are for conventional ovens. When using a fan oven, the temperature will probably need to be reduced by about 10–20°C/20–40°F. Since ovens vary, you should check with your manufacturer's instruction book for guidance.
The nutritional analysis given for each recipe is calculated per portion (i.e. serving or item), unless otherwise stated.
If the recipe gives a range, such as Serves 4–6, then the nutritional analysis will be for the smaller portion size, i.e. 6 servings.
Measurements for sodium do not include salt added to taste.
Medium (US large) eggs are used unless otherwise stated.

Main front cover image shows Halloumi with Rocket Salad – for recipe, see page 244

Contents

Introduction 6

Dips and Dippers 8

Finger Food 20

Pâtés, Terrines and Mousses 62

Cheese and Eggs 74

Poultry and Meat 98

Fish and Shellfish 144

Hearty Vegetable Appetizers 180

Soups 212

Salads 232

Index 252

Introduction

Appetizers can often be the best part of a meal and many people prefer them to larger courses. Indeed, they are so popular that sometimes whole dinner parties consist entirely of a variety of appetizers, or for those dining out, the temptation is often to order a variety of appetizers instead of a main course. You can see the attraction – appetizers by definition indicate small portions, which means there could be a wide and delicious selection of different and interesting dishes from which diners can pick and choose. Of course, for the cook, having to provide such a medley of diverse foods can be quite a challenge (although one you may well feel equal to), but for the guests it will be nothing less than a complete delight.

In some countries, appetizers, or starters, have become an institution. Tapas, in Spain, are a meal in their own right and are as diverse as they are delectable. Italian antipasto is so varied and delicious that you'd be forgiven for wishing to stop right there with the artichokes and superb dried hams, and forget entirely about the pasta and meat that follow.

If you're planning a dinner party, it is possible to start with a simple but tasty appetizer such as the classic and much-loved Prawn Cocktail or the deliciously messy Barbecued Mini Ribs. Your choice of appetizer should take its cue from the food you intend to serve as a main course. Choose it with care, as the appetizer will set the tone for the rest of the meal. Select something fairly light, such as French Onion Soup or a simple salad such as the popular Caesar Salad or Tuna Niçoise, if you plan to serve a roast meat or hearty stew. If, on the other hand, you are barbecuing fish or grilling (broiling) chicken, you could decide on something much more elaborate such as Smoked Salmon Pâté or Baked Gruyère and

Potato Soufflés. Fish or vegetable terrines, such as Haddock and Smoked Salmon Terrine or Asparagus and Egg Terrine, look pretty and taste wonderful. For an Asian style meal, you could serve Spicy Chicken Satay with Peanut Sauce, Crispy Spring Rolls or Duck Wontons with Mango Sauce.

However, you shouldn't feel too constrained by the ethnicity of your meal. Today, the trend is to serve foods that complement each other. A Mediterranean-style appetizer such as Charred Artichokes with Lemon Oil Dip could happily come before an Indonesian green curry. Similarly, Malayan Prawn Laksa would be fine before a French or Italian-style meal. Those rules that do exist are related to texture and taste. For example, if you're making a soufflé or roulade as a main course, choose something crunchy and fresh as a first course.

The recipes in this book are extremely versatile and can be used for a range of occasions such as a buffet party, a light lunch, as finger food for an informal dinner party or as pre-dinner nibbles. The choice of appetizers that are perfect for party snacks and canapés, such as Lamb Samosas and Savoury Pork Pies or Smoked Salmon Pancakes with Pesto and Curried Sweet Potato Balls, will ensure there is something for any gathering. There are also recipes for the popular Sushi and the traditional Angels on Horseback featuring oysters wrapped in bacon. For fans of dips and dippers, there is a variety of classic recipes including Tsatziki, Hummus and Blue Cheese Dip. The beauty of many of the dishes is that they are incredibly simple and quick to make and can look stunning with very little effort – they are ideal for getting any meal or party off to the best possible start.

The 500 deliciously tempting recipes in this book are clearly explained in steps and feature a shot of the finished dish, making it ideal for the first-time cook as well as the more experienced one, who will find lots of tempting dishes suited to his or her talents. The book is organized so that you can quickly find the kind of recipes you want, when you need them. Whatever the occasion or the season, you will be sure to find something appropriate and tempting for your guests to enjoy.

Saucy Tomato Dip

This versatile dip is delicious, and will give a lift to many dishes – from soups and salads to rice and pasta. It can be made up to 24 hours in advance.

Serves 4
1 shallot
2 garlic cloves
handful of fresh basil leaves, plus extra to garnish
500g/1¼lb ripe tomatoes
30ml/2 tbsp olive oil
2 green chillies
salt and pepper

1 Peel and halve the shallot and garlic cloves. Place in a blender or food processor with the basil leaves, then process the ingredients until they are very finely chopped.

2 Halve the tomatoes and add to the shallot mixture. Process until the mixture is well blended and the tomatoes are finely chopped.

3 With the motor still running, slowly pour in the olive oil. Add salt and pepper to taste.

4 Halve the chillies lengthways and remove their seeds. Finely slice them across into tiny strips and stir them into the tomato mixture. Serve at room temperature. Garnish with a few torn basil leaves.

Variation
This dip is best made with full-flavoured sun-ripened tomatoes. If fresh, ripe tomatoes are unavailable, use a drained 400g/14oz can of good quality plum tomatoes.

Cook's Tip
Wear gloves while preparing chillies or cut them up with a knife and fork if you find that they irritate your skin. Wash your hands in warm, soapy water after preparing the chillies.

Tamarillo Sauce

This unusual Peruvian sauce makes a delicious dip for serving with arepas – those irresistible cornmeal griddle cakes that are frequently filled with soft white cheese. Alternatively, its delicious, hot and spicy flavour contrasts beautifully with the natural sweetness of fresh grilled seafood.

Serves 4
450g/1lb fresh tamarillos
2.5ml/½ tsp ground ginger
1.5ml/¼ tsp ground cinnamon
1 fresh red chilli, seeded and chopped
1 small onion, finely chopped
5ml/1 tsp light brown sugar
105ml/7 tbsp water
30ml/2 tbsp olive oil
salt

1 Place the whole fresh tamarillos in a large pan of boiling water for about 30 seconds.

2 Drain the tamarillos, refresh in cold water, then carefully remove the peel with a sharp knife and discard it. Roughly chop the flesh.

3 Place the ginger and cinnamon in a small heavy pan over a low heat. Stir the mixture for 30 seconds, until the spices release their aromas.

4 Add the chopped tamarillos, chilli, onion, brown sugar and water to the pan containing the spices.

5 Bring the mixture to the boil, lower the heat, cover and simmer for 20 minutes.

6 Remove the lid from the pan and continue cooking the sauce until it reduces and thickens. Stir in the olive oil and season with salt to taste. Serve the sauce with grilled (broiled) seafood, if you like.

Cook's Tip
If the tamarillos feel heavier than they look, they will be ripe and juicy inside.

Saucy Tomato Dip Energy 81kcal/336kJ; Protein 2.3g; Carbohydrate 4.2g, of which sugars 4.2g; Fat 6.2g, of which saturates 0.9g; Cholesterol 0mg; Calcium 24mg; Fibre 1.3g; Sodium 15mg.
Tamarillo Sauce Energy 85kcal/355kJ; Protein 1.4g; Carbohydrate 6.6g, of which sugars 5.4g; Fat 6.2g, of which saturates 0.9g; Cholesterol 0mg; Calcium 17mg; Fibre 1.3g; Sodium 12mg.

Aubergine and Pepper Spread

This spread is a tasty mixture of rich, cooked vegetables. It can be used as an appetizer simply spread on breads, as a dip or as a delicious accompaniment to a variety of grilled meats and vegetables.

Serves 6–8

675g/1½lb aubergines (eggplants), halved lengthways
2 green (bell) peppers, seeded and quartered
45ml/3 tbsp olive oil
2 firm ripe tomatoes, halved, seeded and finely chopped
45ml/3 tbsp chopped fresh parsley or coriander (cilantro)
2 garlic cloves, crushed
30ml/2 tbsp red wine vinegar
lemon juice, to taste
salt and ground black pepper
sprigs of parsley or coriander (cilantro), to garnish
dark rye bread and lemon wedges, to serve

1 Place the aubergines and peppers under a preheated grill (broiler), skin side uppermost, and cook until the skins blister and char.

2 Turn the vegetables over and cook for a further 3 minutes. Place the vegetables in a plastic bag, seal the opening and leave for 10 minutes.

3 Peel away the blackened skin from the vegetables. Place the aubergine and pepper flesh in a food processor or blender and process until puréed.

4 With the motor of the processor or blender still running, pour in the olive oil in a continuous stream, through the feeder tube or opening in the lid.

5 Transfer the aubergine and pepper purée into a bowl and stir in the chopped tomatoes, parsley or coriander, garlic, vinegar and lemon juice. Stir thoroughly until all the ingredients are well combined.

6 Season to taste with salt and ground black pepper, garnish with fresh parsley or coriander and serve with dark rye bread and wedges of lemon.

Muhammara

This thick, roasted red pepper and walnut purée is popular in the Middle East. Serve it as a dip with spears of cos or romaine lettuce, wedges of pitta bread and chunks of tomato.

Serves 4

1½ slices Granary (whole-wheat) bread, day-old and toasted
3 red (bell) peppers, roasted, skinned and chopped
2 very mild chillies, roasted, skinned and chopped
115g/4oz/1 cup walnut pieces
3–4 garlic cloves, chopped
15–30ml/1–2 tbsp balsamic vinegar or pomegranate molasses
juice of ½ lemon
2.5–5ml/½–1 tsp ground cumin
2.5ml/½ tsp sugar, or to taste
105ml/7 tbsp olive oil, preferably extra virgin
salt

1 Break the Granary bread into small pieces and place in a food processor or blender with all the remaining ingredients except the extra virgin olive oil. Blend together until the ingredients are finely chopped.

2 With the motor running, slowly drizzle the extra virgin olive oil into the food processor or blender and process until the mixture forms a smooth paste.

3 Transfer the muhammara into a serving dish. Serve at room temperature.

Variation

For a quick and easy variation on the muhammara theme, make red pepper hummus. Drain a 400g/14oz can of chickpeas in a colander, rinse them gently under cold water and drain again. Place into the bowl of a food processor. Scoop out 2 roasted red peppers from a jar or can, remove any seeds, then add them to the food processor with 1 crushed garlic clove, 15ml/1 tbsp tahini, 2.5ml/½ tsp ground cumin and 2.5ml/½ tsp mild chilli powder. Whizz these ingredients together, then scrape the mixture into a bowl and add salt, pepper and lemon juice to taste. Serve at room temperature.

Aubergine Pepper Spread Energy 74kcal/308kJ; Protein 1g; Carbohydrate 4.7g, of which sugars 4.4g; Fat 5.9g, of which saturates 0.9g; Cholesterol 0mg; Calcium 9mg; Fibre 1.8g; Sodium 3mg.
Muhammara Energy 444kcal/1833kJ; Protein 6.8g; Carbohydrate 15.5g, of which sugars 9.9g; Fat 39.8g, of which saturates 4.6g; Cholesterol 0mg; Calcium 62mg; Fibre 3.7g; Sodium 69mg.

Artichoke and Cumin Dip

This dip is so quick and easy to make and is unbelievably tasty. Serve it with olives, hummus and wedges of pitta bread to make a summery snack selection. Canned artichokes are ideal for this recipe and are readily available in many large supermarkets, or look out for them in specialist food stores.

Serves 4
2 x 400g/14oz cans artichoke hearts, drained
2 garlic cloves, peeled
2.5ml/½ tsp ground cumin
olive oil
salt and ground black pepper
pitta bread, warmed and thickly sliced, to serve

1 Put the artichoke hearts in a food processor or blender, and add the garlic and ground cumin. Pour in a generous drizzle of olive oil.

2 Process to a smooth purée and season with plenty of salt and ground black pepper to taste.

3 Spoon the purée into a serving bowl. Drizzle a little extra olive oil in a swirl over the top of the dip and serve with slices of warm pitta bread to scoop up the purée.

Variation
You can easily vary the flavourings of this dip, if you prefer. Tasty variations to try include adding chilli powder in place of the ground cumin, or try adding a handful of basil leaves to the artichokes before blending the dip. If you prefer a more tangy dip, add a little lemon juice to taste.

Cook's Tip
Grilled artichokes are also available to buy bottled in oil. They have a fabulous flavour and can be used for this recipe instead of the canned artichokes.

Chilli Bean Dip

Substantial enough to serve for supper on a baked potato, this creamy bean dip also tastes great with triangles of lightly toasted pitta bread or a bowl of crunchy tortilla chips. Serve it warm to enjoy it at its best. If the flavours are too fiery, use sweet bell peppers instead of green chillies and omit the red chilli strips.

Serves 4
2 fresh green chillies
2 garlic cloves
1 onion
30ml/2 tbsp vegetable oil
5–10ml/1–2 tsp hot chilli powder
400g/14oz can kidney beans
75g/3oz/¾ cup grated mature (sharp) Cheddar cheese
1 fresh red chilli, seeded
salt and ground black pepper
pitta bread, warmed, to serve

1 Slit the green chillies and use a sharp knife to scrape out and discard the seeds. Chop the chilli flesh finely, then crush the garlic and finely chop the onion.

2 Heat the oil in a large pan or wok and add the garlic, onion and green chilli mixture. Stir in the chilli powder. Cook gently for 5 minutes, stirring, until the onions have softened and are transparent, but not browned.

3 Drain the kidney beans, reserving the liquid in which they were canned. Set aside 30ml/2 tbsp of the beans and purée the remainder in a food processor or blender.

4 Spoon the puréed beans into the pan or wok and stir in 30–45ml/2–3 tbsp of the reserved can liquid. Heat gently, stirring to mix all the ingredients well.

5 Stir in the reserved whole kidney beans and the Cheddar cheese. Cook gently for 2–3 minutes, stirring regularly until all the cheese has melted. Add salt and ground black pepper to taste.

6 Cut the red chilli into tiny strips. Spoon the dip into four individual serving bowls and sprinkle the chilli strips over the top. Serve the dip while still warm with plenty of slices of toasted pitta bread.

Artichoke and Cumin Dip Energy 76kcal/315kJ; Protein 2g; Carbohydrate 3.8g, of which sugars 2g; Fat 6g, of which saturates 0.8g; Cholesterol 0mg; Calcium 84mg; Fibre 2.7g; Sodium 121mg.
Chilli Bean Dip Energy 240kcal/1002kJ; Protein 12.3g; Carbohydrate 20.3g, of which sugars 5.4g; Fat 12.3g, of which saturates 4.8g; Cholesterol 18mg; Calcium 219mg; Fibre 6.6g; Sodium 527mg.

Sesame and Lemon Dip

This delightful little dip, known as tahin tarama, is from central Anatolia, where it is often served in outdoor cafés and restaurants as a meze dish on its own – a sort of whetting of the appetite while you wait for the assortment of exciting dishes to come. Sometimes you will see groups of old men drinking raki or refreshing tea, sharing a plate of tahin tarama or a bowl of roasted chickpeas while they play cards or backgammon. Sweet and tangy, it is good mopped up with chunks of crusty bread or toasted pitta bread.

Serves 2

45ml/3 tbsp light sesame paste
juice of 1 lemon
15–30ml/1–2 tbsp clear honey or grape pekmez
5–10ml/1–2 tsp dried mint
lemon wedges, to serve

1 Beat together the sesame paste and lemon juice in a bowl until well blended.

2 Add the honey and mint and beat again until thick and creamy, then spoon into a small serving dish. Serve the dip at room temperature, accompanied by lemon wedges for squeezing over.

Cook's Tip

Sesame paste, known as tahini, comes in light and dark varieties and is available from health food stores and supermarkets.

Variation

Popular for breakfast or as a sweet snack is a variation of tahin tarama known as tahin pekmez. To make it, combine 30–45ml/2–3 tbsp light sesame paste with 30ml/2 tbsp grape pekmez to form a sweet paste, then scoop up with chunks of fresh bread. If you can't find pekmez, use date syrup from Middle Eastern and health food stores.

Basil and Lemon Dip

This lovely dip is based on fresh mayonnaise flavoured with lemon juice and two types of basil, green and opal. Serve with crispy potato wedges for a delicious appetizer.

Serves 4

2 large egg yolks
15ml/1 tbsp lemon juice
150ml/¼ pint/⅔ cup olive oil
150ml/¼ pint/⅔ cup sunflower oil
4 garlic cloves
handful of fresh green basil
handful of fresh opal basil
salt and ground black pepper

1 Place the egg yolks and lemon juice into a blender or food processor and process them briefly until they are lightly blended.

2 In a jug (pitcher), stir together the oils. With the machine running, pour in the oil very slowly, a little at a time.

3 Once half of the oil has been added, the remaining oil can be incorporated more quickly. Continue processing to form a thick, creamy mayonnaise.

4 Peel and crush the garlic cloves. Alternatively, place them on a chopping board and sprinkle with salt, then flatten them with the heel of a heavy-bladed knife and chop the flesh. Flatten the garlic again to make a coarse purée.

5 Tear both types of basil into small pieces and then stir into the mayonnaise along with the crushed garlic.

6 Add salt and pepper to taste, then transfer the dip to a serving dish. Cover and chill until ready to serve.

Yogurt with Cucumber and Mint

This tasty dip is ideal as a refreshing appetizer on a hot summery day.

Serves 4

15cm/6in piece cucumber
5ml/1 tsp sea salt
300ml/½ pint/1¼ cups Greek (US strained plain) yogurt
3–4 garlic cloves, crushed
45ml/3 tbsp chopped fresh mint
ground black pepper
chopped fresh mint and/or ground toasted cumin seeds, to garnish

1 Slice the cucumber, place in a sieve (strainer) and sprinkle with half the salt. Leave over a bowl for 30 minutes.

2 Rinse the cucumber in cold water, pat dry and mix with the yogurt, garlic and mint. Season to taste. Leave for 30 minutes, stir and sprinkle with fresh mint and/or toasted cumin seeds.

Cook's Tip

To make a yogurt and garlic dressing, spoon 150ml/¼ pint/⅔ cup Greek (US strained plain) yogurt into a bowl. Beat in 1 chopped garlic clove, 5ml/1 tsp French mustard and a pinch of sugar. Season with salt and pepper, then beat in 15–30ml/1–2 tbsp olive oil and 15–30ml/1–2 tbsp chopped fresh herbs.

Sesame and Lemon Dip Energy 160kcal/664kJ; Protein 4.3g; Carbohydrate 6.4g, of which sugars 6.2g; Fat 13.3g, of which saturates 1.9g; Cholesterol 0mg; Calcium 155mg; Fibre 1.8g; Sodium 6mg.
Basil and Lemon Dip Energy 210kcal/871kJ; Protein 2.7g; Carbohydrate 12.5g, of which sugars 3.3g; Fat 17g, of which saturates 2.2g; Cholesterol 0mg; Calcium 61mg; Fibre 0.7g; Sodium 35mg.
Yogurt with Mint Energy 98kcal/408kJ; Protein 6.6g; Carbohydrate 10.3g, of which sugars 10.3g; Fat 3.8g, of which saturates 0.9g; Cholesterol 2mg; Calcium 244mg; Fibre 0.2g; Sodium 236mg.

Spicy Carrot Dip

When carrots are cooked over a gentle heat in a slow cooker their flavour intensifies and becomes deliciously sweet, making them the perfect partner for hot, spicy flavourings.

Serves 4

1 onion, finely chopped
3 carrots, grated, plus extra to garnish (optional)
grated rind and juice of 1 orange
15ml/1 tbsp hot curry paste
150ml/¼ pint/⅔ cup natural (plain) yogurt
handful of fresh basil leaves
15ml/1 tbsp fresh lemon juice
dash Tabasco sauce (optional)
salt and ground black pepper

1 Put the onion, carrots, orange rind and juice, and curry paste in the ceramic cooking pot and stir well to combine. Cover with the lid and cook on high for 2 hours, or until the carrots are soft and tender.

2 Uncover the pot and leave to cool for about 10 minutes, then transfer the mixture to a food processor or blender and process until smooth.

3 Transfer the carrot purée to a mixing bowl and leave, uncovered, for about 1 hour to cool completely.

4 Add the yogurt to the cooled carrot purée. Tear the basil leaves roughly into small pieces, then stir them into the mixture until thoroughly combined.

5 Stir in the lemon juice and Tabasco, if using, then season to taste with salt and pepper. Serve at room temperature, within a few hours of making.

Cook's Tip
Serve this versatile dip as an appetizer or on its own with wheat crackers or fiery tortilla chips, or with a variety of raw vegetables for a healthy snack.

Libyan Spicy Pumpkin Dip

This spicy dip is a beautiful warm orange colour and its flavour, spiced with paprika and ginger, is equally warming. It is great to serve at a Thanksgiving feast. It can be stored for at least a week in the refrigerator. Serve chunks of bread or raw vegetables to dip into it.

Serves 6–8

45–60ml/3–4 tbsp olive oil
1 onion, finely chopped
5–8 garlic cloves, roughly chopped
675g/1½lb pumpkin, peeled and diced
5–10ml/1–2 tsp ground cumin
5ml/1 tsp paprika
1.5–2.5ml/¼–½ tsp ground ginger
1.5–2.5ml/¼–½ tsp curry powder
75g/3oz chopped canned tomatoes or diced fresh tomatoes
15–30ml/1–2 tbsp tomato purée (paste)
½–1 red jalapeño or serrano chilli, chopped, or cayenne pepper, to taste
pinch of sugar, if necessary
juice of ½ lemon, or to taste
salt
30ml/2 tbsp chopped fresh coriander (cilantro) leaves, to garnish

1 Heat the oil in a frying pan, add the onion and half the garlic and fry until softened. Add the pieces of pumpkin, then cover the pan and cook for about 10 minutes, or until the pumpkin is half tender.

2 Add the spices to the pan and cook for 1–2 minutes. Stir in the tomatoes, tomato purée, chilli, sugar and salt and cook over a medium-high heat until the liquid has evaporated.

3 When the pumpkin is tender, mash to a coarse purée. Add the remaining garlic and taste for seasoning, then stir in the lemon juice to taste. Serve at room temperature, sprinkled with the chopped fresh coriander.

Variation
Use butternut squash, or any other winter squash, in place of the pumpkin, if you prefer.

Spicy Carrot Dip Energy 58kcal/241kJ; Protein 2.5g; Carbohydrate 9.5g, of which sugars 8.4g; Fat 1.3g, of which saturates 0.4g; Cholesterol 0mg; Calcium 80mg; Fibre 1.3g; Sodium 34mg.
Libyan Spicy Pumpkin Dip Energy 54kcal/224kJ; Protein 0.9g; Carbohydrate 2.9g, of which sugars 2.3g; Fat 4.4g, of which saturates 0.7g; Cholesterol 0mg; Calcium 37mg; Fibre 1.3g; Sodium 3mg.

Lemon and Coconut Dhal Dip

A warm spicy dish, this can be served either as a dip or as an accompaniment to cold meats.

Serves 4–6

5cm/2in piece fresh root ginger
1 onion
2 garlic cloves
2 small fresh red chillies, seeded
30ml/2 tbsp sunflower oil
5ml/1 tsp cumin seeds
150g/5oz/⅔ cup red lentils
250ml/8fl oz/1 cup water
15ml/1 tbsp hot curry paste
200ml/7fl oz/scant 1 cup coconut cream
juice of 1 lemon
handful of fresh coriander (cilantro) leaves
25g/1oz/¼ cup flaked (sliced) almonds
salt and ground black pepper

1 Use a vegetable peeler to peel the ginger, then chop it finely with the onion, garlic and chillies.

2 Heat the sunflower oil in a large, shallow pan. Add the ginger, onion, garlic, chillies and cumin. Cook over a medium heat, stirring occasionally, for about 5 minutes, until the onion is softened but not coloured.

3 Stir the lentils, measured water and curry paste into the pan. Bring to the boil, then reduce the heat to low, cover and simmer gently, stirring occasionally, for 15–20 minutes, until the lentils are just tender but have not yet broken up.

4 Stir in all but 30ml/2 tbsp of the coconut cream. Bring to the boil and cook, uncovered, for 15–20 minutes, until the mixture is thick and pulpy. Remove the pan from the heat, stir in the lemon juice and coriander leaves. Season to taste.

5 Heat a large, heavy frying pan and dry-fry the flaked almonds for about 1–2 minutes on each side, until golden brown. Stir about three-quarters of the toasted almonds into the dhal. Reserve the remainder for the garnish.

6 Transfer the dhal to a serving bowl; swirl in the remaining coconut cream. Sprinkle the reserved almonds on top and serve warm.

Tsatziki

Cool, creamy and refreshing, tsatziki is wonderfully easy to make and even easier to eat. Serve this classic Greek dip with toasted pitta bread as part of a salad spread, or with chargrilled vegetables.

Serves 4

1 mini cucumber, topped and tailed
4 spring onions (scallions)
1 garlic clove
200ml/7fl oz/scant 1 cup Greek (US strained plain) yogurt
45ml/3 tbsp chopped fresh mint
salt and ground black pepper
fresh mint sprig, to garnish
toasted pitta bread, to serve

1 Cut the cucumber into 5mm/¼ in dice. Chop the spring onions and garlic very finely.

2 Beat the yogurt in a bowl until smooth, if necessary, then gently stir in the cucumber, spring onions, garlic and mint.

3 Add salt and plenty of ground black pepper to taste, then transfer the mixture to a serving bowl. Cover and chill in the refrigerator until ready to serve.

4 Garnish with a mint sprig and serve with pitta bread.

Cook's Tip
Choose Greek-style (US strained plain) yogurt for this dip – it has a higher fat content than most yogurts, which gives the dish a deliciously rich, creamy texture.

Variation
A similar, but smoother, dip can be made in the food processor. Peel one mini cucumber and process with two garlic cloves and 75g/3oz/3 cups mixed fresh herbs to a purée. Stir the purée into 200ml/7fl oz/scant 1 cup sour cream and season to taste with salt and pepper.

Lemon Dhal Dip Energy 190kcal/791kJ; Protein 6g; Carbohydrate 12.2g, of which sugars 1.9g; Fat 13.4g, of which saturates 7.9g; Cholesterol 0mg; Calcium 22mg; Fibre 1.3g; Sodium 11mg.
Tsatziki Energy 67kcal/279kJ; Protein 4g; Carbohydrate 2.3g, of which sugars 1.6g; Fat 5.3g, of which saturates 2.6g; Cholesterol 0mg; Calcium 107mg; Fibre 0.3g; Sodium 39mg.

Cacik

This refreshing yogurt dish is served all over the Eastern Mediterranean, whether as part of a mezze with marinated olives and pitta bread, or as an accompaniment to meat dishes. Greek tsatziki is very similar.

Serves 6
1 small cucumber
300ml/½ pint/1¼ cups thick natural (plain) yogurt
3 garlic cloves, crushed
30ml/2 tbsp chopped fresh mint
30ml/2 tbsp chopped fresh dill or parsley
salt and ground black pepper
mint or parsley and dill, to garnish
olive oil, olives and pitta bread, to serve

1 Finely chop the cucumber and layer in a colander. Sprinkle with salt to cover the cucumber and position the colander over a bowl to catch the juices that run out. Leave to stand for 30 minutes.

2 Wash the cucumber in several changes of cold water to remove the salt and drain it thoroughly. Pat the diced cucumber dry on kitchen paper.

3 Mix together the natural yogurt, garlic and fresh herbs until the ingredients are thoroughly combined, and season with salt and ground black pepper. Stir in the cucumber.

4 Garnish with herbs, drizzle over a little olive oil and serve with olives and pitta bread.

Cook's Tip
The fresh herbs used in this recipe – mint, dill and parsley – are simple to grow yourself. Buy a plant of each herb and keep them on a sunny windowsill in your kitchen. Ensure they are kept moist but don't over-water them. Pull off the leaves as and when you need them. They will regrow in a matter of days. Keep any mint plants separate from other herbs in their own container as they are very invasive and will rapidly spread.

Garlic-infused Spicy Bean Dip

Broad beans, also known as fava beans, are among the oldest vegetables in cultivation, and are a staple ingredient in the cuisines of North Africa, where they are native and are eaten both fresh and dried. This delicious garlic and bean dip comes from Morocco. Sprinkled with paprika or dried thyme, it makes a tasty appetizer, and is best served with warmed flat bread or slices of toasted pitta bread.

Serves 4
350g/12oz/1¾ cups dried broad (fava) beans, soaked overnight
4 garlic cloves
10ml/2 tsp cumin seeds
60–75ml/4–5 tbsp olive oil
salt
paprika or dried thyme to garnish

1 Drain the beans, remove their wrinkly skins and place them in a large pan with the garlic and cumin seeds.

2 Add enough water to cover the beans and bring to the boil. Boil vigorously for about 10 minutes, skimming off any scum that rises to the surface.

3 Reduce the heat, cover the pan and simmer the beans gently for about 1 hour, or until they are tender.

4 Drain the beans and, while they are still warm, pound them in a mortar and pestle or use a food processor or blender to process them with the olive oil until the mixture forms a smooth dip.

5 Season to taste with salt and serve warm or at room temperature, sprinkled with paprika.

Cook's Tip
A good way of saving energy while cooking the beans is to tightly cover the pan after boiling the beans and then turn off the heat. The beans can be left to cook in the slowly cooling water in the pan for about 3–4 hours, by which time they should be tender.

Cacik Energy 33kcal/140kJ; Protein 3g; Carbohydrate 4.4g, of which sugars 4.3g; Fat 0.6g, of which saturates 0.3g; Cholesterol 1mg; Calcium 116mg; Fibre 0.6g; Sodium 45mg.
Spicy Bean Dip Energy 155kcal/650kJ; Protein 7.4g; Carbohydrate 18.4g, of which sugars 3.9g; Fat 6.3g, of which saturates 0.9g; Cholesterol 0mg; Calcium 96mg; Fibre 6.9g; Sodium 394mg.

Hummus

This classic chickpea dip from the eastern Mediterranean is a firm favourite everywhere. It is flavoured with garlic and tahini – sesame seed paste. For extra flavour, a little ground cumin can be added, and olive oil can also be stirred in to enrich the hummus, if you like. It is lovely served with wedges of toasted pitta or with crudités as a delicious dip.

Serves 4–6
400g/14oz can chickpeas, drained
60ml/4 tbsp tahini
2–3 garlic cloves, chopped
juice of $\frac{1}{2}$–1 lemon
salt and ground black pepper
a few whole chickpeas reserved, to garnish

1 Reserving a few for garnish, coarsely mash the chickpeas in a mixing bowl with a fork. If you like a smoother purée, process the chickpeas in a food processor or blender until a smooth paste is formed.

2 Mix the tahini into the bowl of chickpeas, then stir in the chopped garlic cloves and lemon juice. Season to taste and garnish the top with the reserved chickpeas. Serve the hummus at room temperature.

Variations
- *Process 2 roasted red (bell) peppers with the chickpeas, then continue as above. Serve sprinkled with lightly toasted pine nuts and paprika mixed with a little extra virgin olive oil.*
- *Add a pinch of cayenne to the mixture.*
- *Instead of chickpeas, top with a drizzle of olive oil and a dusting of paprika.*

Cook's Tip
Add more lemon juice to taste if necessary when seasoning.

Baba Ganoush with Lebanese Flatbread

Baba Ganoush is a delectable aubergine dip from the Middle East. Tahini – sesame seed paste – and ground cumin are the main flavourings, giving a subtle hint of spice.

Serves 6
2 small aubergines (eggplants)
1 garlic clove, crushed
60ml/4 tbsp tahini
25g/1oz/$\frac{1}{4}$ cup ground almonds
juice of $\frac{1}{2}$ lemon
$\frac{1}{2}$ tsp ground cumin
30ml/2 tbsp fresh mint leaves
30ml/2 tbsp olive oil
salt

For the Lebanese flatbread
4 pitta breads
45ml/3 tbsp toasted sesame seeds
45ml/3 tbsp fresh thyme leaves
45ml/3 tbsp poppy seeds
150ml/$\frac{1}{4}$ pint/$\frac{2}{3}$ cup olive oil

1 Start by making the Lebanese flatbread. Split the pitta breads horizontally through the middle and carefully open them out flat, cut side up. Mix the sesame seeds, chopped thyme and poppy seeds in a mortar. Crush them lightly with a pestle to release their flavour.

2 Stir the olive oil into the spice mixture. Spread the mixture lightly over the cut sides of the pitta bread. Grill (broil) until golden brown and crisp. When cool enough to handle, break into rough pieces and set aside.

3 Grill the aubergines, turning them frequently, until the skin is blackened and blistered. Remove the peel, chop the flesh roughly and leave to drain in a colander.

4 Squeeze out as much liquid from the aubergine as possible. Place the flesh in a blender or food processor. Add the garlic, tahini, ground almonds, lemon juice and cumin, with salt to taste and process to a smooth paste. Roughly chop half the mint and stir into the dip.

5 Spoon into a bowl, sprinkle the remaining leaves on top and drizzle with olive oil. Serve with the Lebanese flatbread.

Hummus Energy 210Kcal/880kJ; Protein 10.3g; Carbohydrate 16.9g, of which sugars 0.6g; Fat 11.8g, of which saturates 1.6g; Cholesterol 0mg; Calcium 146mg; Fibre 5.5g; Sodium 223mg.
Baba Ganoush Energy 451kcal/1878kJ; Protein 9.3g; Carbohydrate 29.5g, of which sugars 3.1g; Fat 33.8g, of which saturates 4.7g; Cholesterol 0mg; Calcium 204mg; Fibre 4.2g; Sodium 225mg.

Fiery Guacamole

One of the best loved Mexican salsas, this blend of creamy avocado, tomatoes, chillies, coriander and lime now appears on tables the world over. Bought guacamole usually contains mayonnaise, which helps to preserve the avocado, but this is not an ingredient in traditional recipes.

Serves 6–8

4 medium tomatoes
4 ripe avocados, preferably fuerte
juice of 1 lime
½ small onion
2 garlic cloves
small bunch of fresh coriander (cilantro), chopped
3 fresh red fresno chillies
salt
tortilla chips, to serve

1 Cut a cross in the base of each tomato. Place the tomatoes in a heatproof bowl and pour over boiling water to cover.

2 Leave the tomatoes in the water for 3 minutes, then lift them out using a slotted spoon and plunge them into a bowl of cold water. Drain. The skins will have begun to peel back from the crosses. Remove the skins completely. Cut the tomatoes in half, remove the seeds with a teaspoon, then chop the flesh roughly and set it aside.

3 Cut the avocados in half, then remove the stones (pits). Scoop the flesh out of the shells and place it in a food processor or blender. Process until almost smooth, then scrape into a bowl and stir in the lime juice.

4 Chop the onion finely, then crush the garlic. Add both to the avocado and mix well. Stir in the coriander.

5 Remove the stalks from the chillies, slit them and scrape out the seeds with a small sharp knife. Chop the chillies finely and add them to the avocado mixture, with the chopped tomatoes. Mix well.

6 Check the seasoning and add salt to taste. Cover closely with clear film (plastic wrap) or a tight-fitting lid and chill for 1 hour before serving as a dip with tortilla chips. If it is well covered, guacamole will keep in the refrigerator for 2–3 days.

Tapenade with Quail's Eggs and Crudités

This tasty, olive-based spread or dip makes a sociable start to a meal for friends.

Serves 6

225g/8oz/2 cups pitted black olives
2 large garlic cloves, peeled
15ml/1 tbsp salted capers, rinsed
6 canned or bottled anchovy fillets, drained
50g/2oz good-quality canned tuna
5–10ml/1–2 tsp Cognac (optional)
5ml/1 tsp chopped fresh thyme
30ml/2 tbsp chopped fresh parsley
30–60ml/2–4 tbsp extra virgin olive oil
a dash of lemon juice
30ml/2 tbsp crème fraîche or fromage frais (optional)
12–18 quail's eggs
ground black pepper

For the crudités

bunch of spring onions (scallions), halved if large
bunch of radishes, trimmed
bunch of baby fennel, trimmed and halved if large, or 1 large fennel bulb, cut into thin wedges

To serve

French bread
unsalted (sweet) butter or olive oil and sea salt to dip

1 Process the olives, garlic cloves, capers, anchovies and tuna in a food processor or blender. Transfer to a mixing bowl and stir in the Cognac, if using, the thyme, parsley and enough olive oil to make a paste. Season to taste with pepper and a dash of lemon juice. Stir in the crème fraîche or fromage frais, if using, and transfer to a serving bowl.

2 Place the quail's eggs in a pan of cold water and bring to the boil. Cook for only 2 minutes, then immediately drain and plunge the eggs into iced water to stop them from cooking any further and to help make them easier to shell. When the eggs are cold, carefully part-shell them.

3 Serve the tapenade with the eggs and crudités and offer chunks of crusty French bread, unsalted butter or olive oil and sea salt alongside.

Fiery Guacamole Energy 262kcal/1083kJ; Protein 3.2g; Carbohydrate 5g, of which sugars 3g; Fat 25.4g, of which saturates 5.4g; Cholesterol 0mg; Calcium 37mg; Fibre 5.5g; Sodium 15mg.
Tapenade Energy 157kcal/665kJ; Protein 6.3g; Carbohydrate 28.4g, of which sugars 1.8g; Fat 2.8g, of which saturates 0.6g; Cholesterol 37mg; Calcium 76mg; Fibre 1.5g; Sodium 522mg.

Taramasalata

This delicious speciality makes an excellent start to any meal, accompanied by fruity black olives and slices of warm pitta bread. This is one of the most famous Greek dips, and a central part of any meze table, home-made taramasalata is incomparably better than the ready-made versions sold in supermarkets.

Serves 4

115g/4oz smoked mullet roe or smoked cod's roe
2 garlic cloves, crushed
30ml/2 tbsp grated onion
60ml/4 tbsp olive oil
4 slices white bread, crusts removed
juice of 2 lemons
30ml/2 tbsp milk or water
ground black pepper
warm pitta bread, to serve

1 Place the smoked fish roe, garlic, grated onion, oil, bread and lemon juice in a blender or food processor and process until the mixture is smooth.

2 Scrape down the edges of the food processor or blender to ensure that all the ingredients are properly incorporated. Blend quickly again.

3 Add the milk or water and process again for a few seconds. (This will give the taramasalata a creamier texture.)

4 Pour the taramasalata into a serving bowl, cover with clear film (plastic wrap) and chill for 1–2 hours before serving. Sprinkle the dip with black pepper and serve with warm pitta bread.

Cook's Tip

The smoked roe of grey mullet is traditionally used for taramasalata, but it is expensive and can be difficult to obtain. Smoked cod's roe is often used instead to make this dish. It varies in colour and may be paler than the burnt-orange colour of mullet roe, but is still very good. When buying smoked cod's roe, make sure that it is not overcooked as this makes it hard and prevents it blending well.

Brandade of Salt Cod

There are many versions of this creamy French salt cod purée: some contain mashed potatoes, others truffles. Serve the brandade with warmed crispbread or crusty bread for a tasty appetizer, or for a light lunch serve the brandade and bread with a tomato and basil salad. You can omit the garlic from the brandade, if you prefer, and serve toasted slices of crusty French bread rubbed with garlic instead.

Serves 6

200g/7oz salt cod
250ml/8fl oz/1 cup extra virgin olive oil
4 garlic cloves, crushed
250ml/8fl oz/1 cup double (heavy) or whipping cream

1 Soak the salt cod in a bowl of cold water for 24 hours, changing the water frequently.

2 Drain the fish well. Cut the fish into pieces, place in a shallow pan and pour in enough cold water to cover. Heat the water until it is simmering and poach the fish for 8 minutes, until it is just cooked.

3 Drain the fish thoroughly, then carefully remove the skin and bones with a sharp knife.

4 Combine the extra virgin olive oil and crushed garlic cloves in a small pan and heat gently.

5 In another pan, heat the double cream or whipping cream until it just starts to simmer.

6 Put the cod into a food processor, process it briefly, then gradually add alternate amounts of the garlic-flavoured olive oil and cream, while continuing to process the mixture. The aim is to create a purée with the consistency of mashed potato.

7 Season to taste with ground black pepper, then scoop the brandade into a serving bowl or on to individual serving plates and serve with crispbread or crusty bread.

Taramasalata Energy 185Kcal/770kJ; Protein 8.4g; Carbohydrate 11.4g, of which sugars 1.7g; Fat 12.1g, of which saturates 1.8g; Cholesterol 95mg; Calcium 38mg; Fibre 0.5g; Sodium 139mg.
Brandade of Cod Energy 467kcal/1927kJ; Protein 11.7g; Carbohydrate 1.1g, of which sugars 1.1g; Fat 46.2g, of which saturates 14.8g; Cholesterol 63mg; Calcium 32mg; Fibre 0g; Sodium 144mg.

Thousand Island Dip

This variation on the classic thousand island dressing is far removed from the original version, but can be served in the same way – with shellfish laced on to bamboo skewers for dipping or with a simple salad as a tasty appetizer.

Serves 4

4 sun-dried tomatoes in oil
4 plum tomatoes, or 2 beefsteak tomatoes
150g/5oz/⅔ cup mild soft cheese, or mascarpone or fromage frais
60ml/4 tbsp mayonnaise
30ml/2 tbsp tomato purée (paste)
30ml/2 tbsp chopped fresh parsley
1 lemon
Tabasco sauce, to taste
5ml/1 tsp Worcestershire sauce or soy sauce
salt and ground black pepper

1 Drain the oil from the sun-dried tomatoes and then cut them into small pieces.

2 Cut a cross in the blossom end of each fresh tomato, place them in a heatproof bowl and pour over boiling water. Leave for 1–2 minutes, then lift them out and peel off the skins.

3 Chop the flesh finely. Put the sun-dried tomatoes and chopped fresh tomatoes in separate bowls and set aside.

4 Put the soft cheese in a bowl. Beat it until it is creamy, then gradually beat in the mayonnaise. Add the tomato purée in the same way.

5 Stir in the parsley and sun-dried tomatoes, then the fresh tomatoes. Mix well so that the dip is evenly coloured.

6 Grate the lemon finely and add the rind to the dip. Mix well. Squeeze the lemon and add the juice to the bowl, with Tabasco sauce to taste. Stir in the Worcestershire sauce or soy sauce, and salt and pepper to taste.

7 Spoon the dip into a serving bowl, swirling the surface attractively. Cover with clear film (plastic wrap) and chill in the refrigerator until ready to serve.

Salmon Dip

This creamy salmon dip can be served as an appetizer or as part of a buffet lunch.

Serves 4

115g/4oz smoked salmon, diced
250g/9oz/generous 1 cup mascarpone cheese
60ml/4 tbsp chopped fresh chives
grated rind and juice of 1 lemon
1 red (bell) pepper, seeded and cut into strips
1 yellow (bell) pepper, seeded and cut into strips
sea salt and ground black pepper

For the potato wedges

675g/1½lb potatoes, scrubbed
60ml/4 tbsp olive oil
30ml/2 tbsp chopped fresh rosemary
1 fresh red chilli, seeded and finely chopped

1 Preheat the oven to 200°C/400°F/Gas 6. To make the potato wedges, cut the potatoes into thick pieces. Pour the oil into a roasting pan and heat it in the oven for 10 minutes. Add the wedges to the pan, then sprinkle over the rosemary and chilli.

2 Coat the potatoes in the oil, rosemary and chilli. Season well with salt and black pepper. Bake for 50–60 minutes or until tender, turning occasionally to prevent the wedges from sticking to the roasting pan.

3 Put the mascarpone cheese, chives and lemon rind in a bowl and mix with a fork until thoroughly blended.

4 Add the lemon juice to the cheese mixture, a little at a time, mixing constantly, so that the mixture is thinned and given a lemony tang, but does not curdle. A reamer (a ridged, tear-shaped tool) is useful for squeezing the lemon, but watch out for any pips (seeds) that might fall into the bowl.

5 Add the salmon pieces to the cheese mixture and season with ground black pepper to taste. Transfer into a serving bowl, cover and chill until required.

6 To serve, arrange the pepper strips and potato wedges around the edge of a large serving platter and place the dip to one side or in the centre.

Thousand Island Dip Energy 194kcal/805kJ; Protein 4.7g; Carbohydrate 5.7g, of which sugars 5.6g; Fat 17.1g, of which saturates 5.2g; Cholesterol 27mg; Calcium 11mg; Fibre 1.2g; Sodium 184mg.
Salmon Dip Energy 487kcal/2030kJ; Protein 16.9g; Carbohydrate 33.2g, of which sugars 7.9g; Fat 32.7g, of which saturates 14.2g; Cholesterol 71mg; Calcium 124mg; Fibre 3.9g; Sodium 774mg.

Feta and Roast Pepper Dip with Chillies

This is a familiar meze in northern Greece, where it is eaten as a dip with pittas, with other dishes, or with toast to accompany a glass of ouzo. The strong, salty feta cheese with the smoky peppers and hot chillies makes a powerful combination to enliven the taste buds. In Greek it is known as htipiti, which literally means 'that which is beaten'.

Serves 4
1 yellow or green (bell) pepper
1–2 fresh green chillies
200g/7oz feta cheese
60ml/4 tbsp extra virgin olive oil
juice of 1 lemon
45–60ml/3–4 tbsp milk
ground black pepper
a little finely chopped fresh flat leaf parsley, to garnish
slices of toasted Greek bread or pittas, to serve

1 Thread the pepper and the chillies on metal skewers and turn them over a flame or under the grill (broiler), until the skins are charred all over.

2 Put the pepper and chillies in a plastic bag or in a covered bowl and set them aside until cool enough to handle.

3 Peel off as much of the pepper and chilli skins as possible and wipe the blackened bits off with kitchen paper. Slit the pepper and chillies and discard the seeds and stems.

4 Put the pepper and chilli flesh into a food processor. Add all the other ingredients except the parsley and blend to a fairly smooth paste. Add a little more milk if the mixture seems too stiff. Spread on slices of toast, sprinkle a hint of parsley on top and serve.

Variation
Add 75g/3oz sun-dried tomatoes bottled in oil, drained, to the mixture in the food processor.

Blue Cheese Dip

This rich and delectable dip can be mixed up in next to no time and is delicious served with pears, or with fresh vegetable crudités as an appetizer. Add extra yogurt to make a great dressing for a mixed salad.

Serves 4
150g/5oz blue cheese, such as Stilton or Danish blue
150g/5oz/⅔ cup soft cheese
75ml/5 tbsp Greek (US strained plain) yogurt
salt and ground black pepper

1 Crumble the blue cheese into a bowl. Using a wooden spoon, beat the cheese to soften it.

2 Add the soft cheese and beat well until the two cheeses are blended together.

3 Gradually beat the Greek-style yogurt into the bowl of blended cheeses, adding enough to give you the consistency you prefer.

4 Season with lots of ground black pepper and a little salt. Cover and chill the dip in the refrigerator until you are ready to serve it.

Cook's Tip
The thinner, dressing version of this dip is made by adding a little more yogurt and is the classic accompaniment to Buffalo wings. These deep-fried chicken wings are named after the city of Buffalo in the state of New York in the USA. There they will invariably come with a bowl of blue cheese dressing on the side for dipping the wings.

Variation
This is a very thick dip to which you can add a little more Greek-style yogurt, or stir in a little milk, for a softer and thinner consistency, if you prefer.

Feta Roast Pepper Dip Energy 244kcal/1010kJ; Protein 8.8g; Carbohydrate 4.4g, of which sugars 4.3g; Fat 21.4g, of which saturates 8.5g; Cholesterol 35mg; Calcium 205mg; Fibre 0.7g; Sodium 731mg.
Blue Cheese Dip Energy 267kcal/1106kJ; Protein 12.1g; Carbohydrate 0.4g, of which sugars 0.4g; Fat 24.4g, of which saturates 15.4g; Cholesterol 62mg; Calcium 253mg; Fibre 0g; Sodium 595mg.

Bread Sticks

These crispy bread sticks make a tasty snack or appetizer alongside a dip.

Serves 8–10

15ml/1 tbsp active dried yeast
300ml/½ pint/1¼ cups lukewarm water
425g/15oz/3⅔ cups strong white bread flour
10ml/2 tsp salt
5ml/1 tsp caster (superfine) sugar
30ml/2 tbsp olive oil
150g/5oz/10 tbsp sesame seeds
1 beaten egg, for glazing
coarse salt, for sprinkling

1 Combine the yeast and water, stir and leave for 15 minutes to dissolve.

2 Place the flour, salt, sugar and olive oil in a food processor. With the motor running, slowly pour in the yeast mixture, and process until the dough forms a ball. If sticky, add more flour; if dry, add more water.

3 Transfer to a floured surface and knead until smooth. Place in a bowl, cover and leave to rise in a warm place for 45 minutes.

4 Lightly toast the sesame seeds in a frying pan. Grease two baking sheets.

5 Roll small handfuls of dough into cylinders, about 30cm/12in long. Place on the baking sheets. Brush with egg glaze, sprinkle with the sesame seeds, then sprinkle over some coarse salt. Leave to rise, uncovered, until almost doubled in volume, about 20 minutes.

6 Preheat the oven to 200°C/400°F/Gas 6. Bake the bread sticks until golden, about 15 minutes. Turn off the heat but leave the bread sticks in the oven for 5 minutes more. Serve warm or leave to cool before eating.

Prosciutto and Mozzarella Parcels

Italian prosciutto crudo is a delicious raw smoked ham. Here it is baked with melting mozzarella in a pastry case.

Serves 6

a little hot chilli sauce
6 prosciutto crudo slices
200g/7oz mozzarella cheese, cut into 6 slices
6 sheets filo pastry, each measuring 45 x 28cm/18 x 11in, thawed if frozen
50g/2oz/¼ cup butter, melted
150g/5oz frisée lettuce, to serve

1 Preheat the oven to 200°C/400°F/Gas 6. Sprinkle a little chilli sauce over the prosciutto. Top with a slice of mozzarella, then fold it around the cheese so the cheese is enclosed by the ham.

2 Brush a sheet of filo pastry with melted butter and fold it in half. Place a ham and mozzarella parcel in the middle of the pastry. Brush the remaining pastry with butter, then fold it to make a neat parcel. Repeat with the remaining parcels and sheets.

3 Brush all the parcels with butter. Bake for 15 minutes, until the pastry is golden. Serve immediately.

Navajo Fried Bread

These bread rounds are great served with a salsa.

Serves 4

225g/8oz/2 cups plain (all-purpose) flour
10ml/2 tsp baking powder
2.5ml/½ tsp salt
250ml/8fl oz/1 cup lukewarm water
oil for frying

1 Sift the flour, baking powder and salt into a bowl. Pour in the lukewarm water and stir quickly with a fork until the dough gathers into a ball.

2 With floured hands, gently knead the dough by rolling it around the bowl. Be careful not to overknead; the dough should be very soft.

3 Divide the dough into eight pieces. With floured hands, pat each piece into a round about 13cm/5in in diameter. Place the rounds on a floured baking sheet.

4 Put a 2.5cm/1in layer of oil in a heavy frying pan and heat until hot but not smoking. To test the temperature, drop in a small piece of the dough; if the oil bubbles immediately, then it is ready.

5 Add the dough rounds to the hot oil and press down with a slotted spoon to submerge them. Release the dough and cook until puffed and golden on both sides, 3–5 minutes total, turning for even browning. Fry in batches, if necessary.

6 Drain the bread on kitchen paper and serve immediately. They are good as an accompaniment to a bowl of spicy chilli or with grated cheese and an assortment of home-made salsas and guacamole.

Cook's Tip
These fried bread rounds are best eaten on the day they are made as they will not keep well.

Bread Sticks Energy 128kcal/538kJ; Protein 3.4g; Carbohydrate 16.8g, of which sugars 0.6g; Fat 5.7g, of which saturates 0.8g; Cholesterol 0mg; Calcium 80mg; Fibre 1.3g; Sodium 199mg.
Prosciutto Parcels Energy 206kcal/856kJ; Protein 10g; Carbohydrate 9.9g, of which sugars 0.4g; Fat 14.3g, of which saturates 9.1g; Cholesterol 45mg; Calcium 141mg; Fibre 0.4g; Sodium 353mg.
Navajo Bread Energy 295kcal/1240kJ; Protein 5.4g; Carbohydrate 44.7g, of which sugars 0.9g; Fat 11.7g, of which saturates 1.3g; Cholesterol 0mg; Calcium 107mg; Fibre 1.8g; Sodium 542mg.

Monte Cristo Triangles

These opulent little sandwiches are stuffed with ham, cheese and turkey, dipped in egg, then fried in butter and oil. They are rich and filling.

Serves 8

16 thin slices firm-textured white bread
120g/4oz/½ cup butter, softened
8 slices oak-smoked ham
45–60ml/3–4 tbsp wholegrain mustard
8 slices Gruyère or Emmenthal cheese
45–60ml/3–4 tbsp mayonnaise
8 slices cooked turkey or chicken breast fillets
4–5 eggs
50ml/2fl oz/¼ cup milk
5ml/1 tsp Dijon mustard
vegetable oil, for frying
butter, for frying
salt and ground white pepper

For the garnish

pimiento-stuffed green olives
fresh parsley leaves

1 Arrange eight of the bread slices on a work surface and spread with half the softened butter. Lay a slice of ham on each piece of bread and spread with a little mustard. Cover with a slice of Gruyère or Emmenthal cheese and spread with a little of the mayonnaise, then cover with a slice of turkey or chicken. Butter the rest of the bread slices and use to top the sandwiches. Cut off the crusts, trimming to an even square.

2 In a large, shallow, ovenproof dish, beat the eggs with the milk and Dijon mustard until thoroughly combined. Season to taste with salt and pepper. Soak the sandwiches in the egg mixture on both sides until all the egg has been absorbed.

3 Heat about 1cm/½in of oil with a little butter in a large, heavy frying pan, until hot, but not smoking. Gently fry the sandwiches, in batches, for about 4–5 minutes, until crisp and golden, turning once. Add more oil and butter as necessary. Drain on kitchen paper.

4 Transfer the sandwiches to a chopping board and cut each into four triangles, then cut each in half again. Make 64 triangles in total. Thread an olive and parsley leaf on to a cocktail stick (toothpick), then stick into each triangle and serve while warm.

Home-made Crisp Rye Breads

These traditional crispbreads are from Sweden and were originally made with a hole in the centre so they could be hung over the oven to keep dry. Nowadays, they keep well in an airtight container. They are ideal as a snack or appetizer spread with pâté or soft cheese.

Makes 15

600ml/1 pint/2½ cups milk
50g/2oz fresh yeast
565g/1¼lb/5 cups rye flour plus 225g/8oz/2 cups, for dusting
565g/1¼lb/5 cups strong white bread flour
10ml/2 tsp caraway or cumin seeds
5ml/1 tsp salt

1 Put the milk in a pan and heat gently until warm to the touch. Remove from the heat. In a bowl, blend the yeast with a little of the warmed milk. Add the remaining milk, then add the rye flour, bread flour, caraway or cumin seeds and salt and mix together to form a dough.

2 Using the rye flour for dusting, turn the dough out on to a lightly floured surface and knead the dough for about 2 minutes. Cut the dough into 15 equal pieces, then roll out each piece into a thin, flat round. Place on baking sheets and leave to rise in a warm place for 20 minutes.

3 Preheat the oven to 150°C/300°F/Gas 2. Using the rye flour, roll out the pieces of dough again into very thin, flat rounds. Return to the baking sheets. Make a pattern on the surface using a fork or knife.

4 Bake the breads in the oven for 8–10 minutes, turning after about 5 minutes, until hard and crispy. Transfer to a wire rack and leave to cool. Store the breads in an airtight container.

Cook's Tip

The Swedes use a special rolling pin with a knobbly surface to create the distinctive texture of this hard bread. An ordinary rolling pin is a good substitute, with the speckled texture created with the head of a fork or a knife end.

Monte Cristo Triangles Energy 84kcal/351kJ; Protein 4.3g; Carbohydrate 5.1g, of which sugars 0.3g; Fat 5.3g, of which saturates 2.1g; Cholesterol 29mg; Calcium 38mg; Fibre 0.2g; Sodium 120mg.
Home-made Breads Energy 323kcal/1376kJ; Protein 9.2g; Carbohydrate 71.1g, of which sugars 2.4g; Fat 2.2g, of which saturates 0.7g; Cholesterol 2mg; Calcium 118mg; Fibre 7.3g; Sodium 19mg.

Pretzels

These breads are ideal for a buffet or picnic.

Serves 6

For the yeast sponge

10g/¼oz fresh yeast
75ml/5 tbsp water
15ml/1 tbsp unbleached plain (all-purpose) white flour

For the dough

10g/¼oz fresh yeast
150ml/¼ pint/⅔ cup lukewarm water
75ml/5 tbsp lukewarm milk
400g/14oz/3½ cups unbleached strong white bread flour
7.5ml/1½ tsp salt
25g/1oz/2 tbsp butter, melted

For the topping

1 egg yolk
15ml/1 tbsp milk
salt or caraway seeds, to sprinkle

1 Flour two baking sheets and grease two baking sheets. Cream the yeast for the yeast sponge with the water. Add the flour, cover and stand at room temperature for 2 hours.

2 Mix the yeast for the dough with the water, then stir in the milk. Sift 350g/12oz/3 cups of the flour and the salt into a bowl. Add the yeast sponge and the butter and mix for 3–4 minutes. Turn out on to a floured surface and knead in the remaining flour. Place in an oiled bowl, cover with lightly oiled clear film (plastic wrap) and leave to rise in a warm place for 30 minutes.

3 Turn out on to a floured surface and knock back (punch down) the dough. Return to the bowl, cover and leave for 30 minutes.

4 Turn out the dough on to a floured surface, divide into 12 pieces and form into balls. Roll each ball into a stick 46cm/18in long and about 1cm/½in thick in the middle and thinner at the ends. Bend each end into a horseshoe. Cross over and place the ends on top of the thick part.

5 Place on the floured baking sheets to rest for 10 minutes. Preheat the oven to 190°C/375°F/Gas 5. Bring a large pan of water to the boil, then simmer the pretzels, in batches, for about 1 minute. Drain and place on the greased baking sheets. Mix the egg yolk and milk and brush over the pretzels. Sprinkle with salt or seeds and bake the pretzels for 25 minutes.

Cheese and Potato Bread Twists

A complete ploughman's lunch, with the cheese cooked right in the bread. It makes an excellent base for a filling of smoked salmon.

Serves 4

225g/8oz potatoes, diced
225g/8oz/2 cups strong white bread flour
5ml/1 tsp easy-blend (rapid-rise) dried yeast
150ml/¼ pint/⅔ cup lukewarm water
175g/6oz/1½ cups red Leicester cheese, finely grated
10ml/2 tsp olive oil, for greasing
salt

1 Cook the potatoes in a large pan with plenty of lightly salted boiling water for 20 minutes or until tender. Drain through a colander and return to the pan. Mash until smooth and set aside to cool.

2 Meanwhile, sift the flour into a large bowl and add the yeast and a good pinch of salt. Stir in the potatoes and rub with your fingers to form a crumb consistency.

3 Make a well in the centre and pour in the water. Start by bringing the mixture together with a round-bladed knife, then use your hands. Knead for 5 minutes on a well-floured surface. Return the dough to the bowl. Cover with a damp cloth and leave to rise in a warm place for 1 hour or until doubled in size.

4 Turn the dough out and knock back the air bubbles. Knead again for a few seconds. Divide the dough into 12 pieces and shape into rounds.

5 Sprinkle the cheese over a baking sheet. Take each ball of dough and roll it in the cheese. Roll each cheese-covered roll on a dry surface to a long sausage shape. Fold the two ends together and twist the bread. Lay the bread twists on an oiled baking sheet.

6 Cover with a damp cloth and leave the bread to rise in a warm place for 30 minutes. Preheat the oven to 220°C/425°F/Gas 7. Bake the bread for 10–15 minutes. Serve hot or cold.

Pretzels Energy 281kcal/1190kJ; Protein 7.5g; Carbohydrate 53.9g, of which sugars 1.8g; Fat 5.4g, of which saturates 2.7g; Cholesterol 43mg; Calcium 119mg; Fibre 2.1g; Sodium 521mg.
Cheese Twists Energy 465kcal/1950kJ; Protein 17.4g; Carbohydrate 53.1g, of which sugars 1.6g; Fat 20.8g, of which saturates 10.5g; Cholesterol 43mg; Calcium 407mg; Fibre 2.3g; Sodium 326mg.

Pepitas

These crunchy, spicy and slightly sweet pumpkin seeds are absolutely irresistible, especially if you use hot and tasty chipotle chillies to spice them up. Serve bowls of pepitas with pre-dinner drinks as an alternative to nuts.

Serves 4–6

250g/9oz/2 cups pumpkin seeds
8 garlic cloves, crushed
2.5ml/½ tsp salt
20ml/4 tsp crushed dried chillies
10ml/2 tsp caster (superfine) sugar
2 wedges of lime

1 Heat a small, heavy frying pan, add the pumpkin seeds and dry-fry for a few minutes, stirring constantly as they swell.

2 When all the seeds have swollen, add the garlic and cook for a few minutes more, stirring constantly. Add the salt and the crushed chillies and stir to mix. Turn off the heat, but keep the pan on the stove. Sprinkle the sugar over the seeds and shake the pan to make sure that they are all coated.

3 Transfer the pepitas into a bowl and serve with the wedges of lime for squeezing over the seeds. If the lime is omitted, the seeds can be cooled and stored in an airtight container for serving cold or reheating later, but they are best served fresh and warm.

Cook's Tips

- *It is important to keep the pumpkin seeds moving as they cook. Watch them carefully and do not let them burn, or they will taste bitter.*
- *Chipotle chillies are smoke-dried jalapeño chillies.*

Variation

If you are serving the pepitas cold, they can be mixed with cashew nuts and dried cranberries to make a spicy and fruity bowl of nibbles.

Roasted Coconut Cashew Nuts

Serve these hot and sweet cashew nuts in paper or cellophane cones at parties. Not only do they look enticing and taste terrific, but the cones help to keep clothes and hands clean and can simply be thrown away after eating the contents.

Serves 6–8

15ml/1 tbsp groundnut (peanut) oil
30ml/2 tbsp clear honey
225g/8oz/2 cups cashew nuts
115g/4oz/1⅓ cups desiccated (dry unsweetened shredded) coconut
2 small fresh red chillies, seeded and finely chopped
salt and ground black pepper

1 Heat the oil in a wok or large frying pan and then stir in the honey. After a few seconds add the nuts and coconut, and stir-fry until both are golden brown.

2 Add the chillies, with salt and pepper to taste. Toss until all the ingredients are well mixed. Serve warm or cooled in paper cones or on saucers.

Cook's Tip

For Deep-fried Cashew Nuts, mix 225g/8oz cashew nuts with 2.5ml/½ tsp paprika, 2.5ml/½ tsp turmeric, 2.5ml/½ tsp salt and 5ml/1 tsp water in a bowl. Leave the nuts to soak in the spices for 1 hour. Heat oil for deep-frying in a large pan or wok and fry the nuts until evenly browned. Remove with a slotted spoon and drain on kitchen paper. Transfer to a serving dish and sprinkle with a little chilli powder.

Variation

Almonds also work well, or choose peanuts for a more economical snack.

Pepitas Energy 299kcal/1242kJ; Protein 10.3g; Carbohydrate 11.2g, of which sugars 2g; Fat 23.8g, of which saturates 2.3g; Cholesterol 0mg; Calcium 57mg; Fibre 3.2g; Sodium 2mg.
Roasted Nuts Energy 301kcal/1247kJ; Protein 7.2g; Carbohydrate 9.7g, of which sugars 5.5g; Fat 26.2g, of which saturates 11.1g; Cholesterol 0mg; Calcium 14mg; Fibre 3g; Sodium 95mg.

Spiced Noodle Pancakes

The delicate rice noodles puff up in the hot oil to give a fabulous crunchy bite that melts in the mouth. For maximum enjoyment, serve the golden pancakes as soon as they are cooked and savour the subtle blend of spices and wonderfully crisp texture.

Serves 4

150g/5oz dried thin rice noodles
1 fresh red chilli, finely diced
10ml/2 tsp garlic salt
5ml/1 tsp ground ginger
¼ small red onion, very finely diced
5ml/1 tsp finely chopped lemon grass
5ml/1 tsp ground cumin
5ml/1 tsp ground coriander
large pinch of ground turmeric
salt
vegetable oil, for frying
sweet chilli sauce, for dipping

1 Roughly break up the noodles and place in a large bowl. Pour over enough boiling water to cover, and soak for about 4–5 minutes. Drain and rinse under cold water. Dry on kitchen paper.

2 Transfer the noodles to a bowl and add the chilli, garlic salt, ground ginger, red onion, lemon grass, ground cumin, coriander and turmeric. Toss well to mix, and season with salt.

3 Heat 5–6cm/2–2½in oil in a wok. Working in batches, drop tablespoons of the noodle mixture into the oil. Flatten using the back of a skimmer and cook for 1–2 minutes on each side until crisp and golden. Lift out from the wok.

4 Drain the noodle pancakes on kitchen paper and carefully transfer to a plate or deep bowl. Serve immediately with the chilli sauce for dipping.

Cook's Tip
For deep-frying, choose very thin rice noodles. These can be cooked dry, but here are soaked and seasoned first.

Coconut Chips

Coconut chips are a tasty nibble to serve with drinks. The chips can be sliced ahead of time and frozen (without salt), on open trays. When frozen, simply shake into plastic boxes. You can then take out as many as you wish for the party.

Serves 8

1 fresh coconut
salt

1 Preheat the oven to 160°C/325°F/Gas 3. First drain the coconut juice, either by piercing one of the coconut eyes with a sharp instrument or by breaking it carefully.

2 Lay the coconut on a board and hit the centre sharply with a hammer. The shell should break cleanly in two.

3 Having opened the coconut, use a broad-bladed knife to ease the flesh away from the hard outer shell. Taste a piece of the flesh just to make sure it is fresh. Peel away the brown skin with a potato peeler, if you like.

4 Slice the coconut flesh into wafer-thin shavings, using a food processor, mandoline or sharp knife. Sprinkle the shavings evenly all over one or two baking sheets and sprinkle with salt.

5 Bake for about 25–30 minutes or until crisp, turning them from time to time. Cool and serve. Any leftovers can be stored in airtight containers.

Cook's Tip
This is the kind of recipe where the slicing blade on a food processor comes into its own. It is worth preparing two or three coconuts at a time, and freezing surplus chips. The chips can be cooked from frozen, but will need to be spread out well on the baking sheets, before being salted. Allow a little longer for frozen chips to cook.

Noodle Pancakes Energy 248kcal/1031kJ; Protein 2.4g; Carbohydrate 32.7g, of which sugars 0.9g; Fat 11.5g, of which saturates 1.3g; Cholesterol 0mg; Calcium 32mg; Fibre 1.1g; Sodium 22mg.
Coconut Chips Energy 41kcal/178kJ; Protein 0.6g; Carbohydrate 9.2g, of which sugars 9.2g; Fat 0.6g, of which saturates 0.4g; Cholesterol 0mg; Calcium 54mg; Fibre 0g; Sodium 206mg.

Curry Crackers

Crisp curry-flavoured crackers are very good with creamy cheese or yogurt dips and make an unusual nibble with pre-dinner drinks. Add a pinch of cayenne pepper for an extra kick.

Serves 6–8

175g/6oz/1½ cups self-raising (self-rising) flour
pinch of salt
10ml/2 tsp garam masala
75g/3oz/6 tbsp butter, diced
5ml/1 tsp finely chopped fresh coriander (cilantro)
1 egg, beaten

For the topping

beaten egg
black onion seeds
garam masala

1 Preheat the oven to 200°C/400°F/Gas 6. Put the flour, salt and garam masala into a bowl. Rub in the butter until the mixture resembles fine breadcrumbs. Stir in the coriander, add the egg and mix to a soft dough.

2 Turn out on to a lightly floured surface and knead gently until smooth. Roll out to a thickness of about 3mm/⅛in.

3 Using a fluted biscuit (cookie) wheel, knife or pizza wheel, cut the dough into neat rectangles measuring about 7.5 × 2.5cm/3 × 1in. Brush with a little beaten egg and sprinkle each cracker with a few black onion seeds. Place on non-stick baking sheets and bake in the oven for about 12 minutes until the crackers are light golden brown all over.

4 Remove from the oven and transfer to a wire rack using a metal spatula. Put a little garam masala in a saucer and, with a dry pastry brush, dust each cracker with a little of the spice mixture. Leave to cool before serving.

Cook's Tip
Garam masala is a mixture of Indian spices that usually contains a blend of cinnamon, cloves, peppercorns, cardamom seeds and cumin seeds. You can buy it ready-made or make your own.

Sweet and Salty Beetroot Crisps

The Spanish love new and colourful snacks. Try these brightly coloured crisps, which make an appealing alternative to potato crisps (US potato chips). Serve them with a bowl of creamy, garlicky mayonnaise, and use the crisps to scoop it up.

Serves 4

1 small fresh beetroot (beet)
caster (superfine) sugar and fine salt, for sprinkling
olive oil, for frying
coarse sea salt, to serve

1 Peel the beetroot and, using a mandoline or a vegetable peeler, cut it into very thin slices.

2 Place the beetroot slices on kitchen paper. Spread them out, then sprinkle them with sugar and fine salt.

3 Pour oil into a deep pan to a depth of 5cm/2in. Heat to 180°C/350°F or until a bread cube, added to the hot oil, turns golden in 1 minute. Cook the slices in batches, until they float to the surface and turn golden at the edges. Drain on kitchen paper and sprinkle with sea salt when cool.

Cook's Tip
Don't fry too many beetroot (beet) slices at once, or they may stick together and not become crisp. If you use a chip basket, it will be easy to lift the cooked crisps out so they can be drained on kitchen paper. Keep each batch hot while cooking the remainder.

Variation
Beetroot crisps are particularly flavoursome, but other naturally sweet root vegetables, such as carrots and sweet potato, also taste delicious when cooked in this way. You might like to make several different varieties, using a mixture of different vegetables, and serve them heaped in separate small bowls.

Curry Crackers Energy 14Kcal/60kJ; Protein 0.4g; Carbohydrate 3.2g, of which sugars 0.1g; Fat 0.1g, of which saturates 0g; Cholesterol 0mg; Calcium 6mg; Fibre 0.1g; Sodium 49mg.
Beetroot Crisps Energy 113kcal/466kJ; Protein 0.4g; Carbohydrate 3.2g, of which sugars 3.1g; Fat 11g, of which saturates 1.6g; Cholesterol 0mg; Calcium 6mg; Fibre 0.5g; Sodium 508mg.

Peanut Crackers

These tasty, nutty crackers are ideal as a welcoming appetizer to take the edge off your hunger while you wait for your meal.

Serves 4–5

225g/8oz/1 ¼ cups rice flour
5ml/1 tsp baking powder
5ml/1 tsp ground turmeric
5ml/1 tsp ground coriander
300ml/½ pint/1 ¼ cups coconut milk
115g/4oz/¾ cup unsalted peanuts, coarsely chopped or crushed
2–3 candlenuts, crushed
2–3 garlic cloves, crushed
corn or groundnut (peanut) oil, for shallow frying
salt and ground black pepper
chilli sambal, for dipping (optional)

To season

5ml/1 tsp paprika or fine chilli flakes
salt

1 Put the rice flour, baking powder, ground turmeric and ground coriander into a bowl. Make a well in the centre, pour in the coconut milk and stir to mix well, drawing in the flour from the sides. Beat well to make a smooth batter.

2 Add the peanuts, candlenuts and garlic and mix well together. Season with salt and pepper, then put aside for 30 minutes.

3 Meanwhile, in a small bowl, prepare the seasoning by mixing the paprika or fine chilli flakes with a little salt.

4 Heat a thin layer of oil in a wok or large frying pan and drop in a spoonful of batter for each cracker – the size of spoon doesn't matter as the crackers are supposed to vary in size.

5 Work in batches, flipping the crackers over when the lacy edges become crispy and golden brown. Drain on kitchen paper and toss them into a basket.

6 Sprinkle the paprika and salt over the crackers and toss them lightly for an even dusting of seasoning.

7 Serve the peanut crackers immediately, while they are still warm and crisp. Dip them into some chilli sauce, if you like.

Parmesan Thins

These thin, crisp, savoury snacks will melt in the mouth, so make plenty for guests. They are a great treat at any time of the day, so don't just keep them for parties and picnics.

Serves 8–10

50g/2oz/½ cup plain (all-purpose) flour
40g/1 ½oz/3 tbsp butter, softened
1 egg yolk
40g/1 ½oz/⅔ cup freshly grated Parmesan cheese
pinch of salt
pinch of mustard powder

1 Rub together the flour and the butter in a bowl using your fingertips, then work in the egg yolk.

2 Add the Parmesan cheese, salt and mustard to the flour mixture. Mix the ingredients thoroughly and then bring the dough together into a ball.

3 Shape the dough mixture into a log. Wrap the dough log tightly in foil or clear film (plastic wrap) and chill in the refrigerator for 10 minutes.

4 Preheat the oven to 200°C/400°F/Gas 6. Cut the Parmesan log into very thin slices, 3–6mm/⅛–¼in maximum, and arrange on a baking sheet.

5 Flatten each thin with a fork to give a pretty ridged pattern. Bake for about 10 minutes, or until the crackers are crisp, but not changing colour.

Cook's Tip
The quality of the Parmesan cheese is essential in this recipe. Although Parmesan is made in various countries, such as Australia and the USA, the best by far is the Italian version called Parmigiano Reggiano. It may be more expensive than other varieties but it is well worth the extra cost.

Peanut Crackers Energy 403kcal/1679kJ; Protein 9.7g; Carbohydrate 42.2g, of which sugars 4.6g; Fat 21.3g, of which saturates 3.4g; Cholesterol 0mg; Calcium 44mg; Fibre 2.5g; Sodium 69mg.
Parmesan Thins Energy 36kcal/148kJ; Protein 1.2g; Carbohydrate 2g, of which sugars 0.1g; Fat 2.6g, of which saturates 1.5g; Cholesterol 16mg; Calcium 29mg; Fibre 0.1g; Sodium 34mg.

Prawn Toasts with Sesame Seeds

This healthy version of the ever-popular appetizer has lost none of its classic crunch and taste. Serve it as a snack, too. It is great for getting a party off to a good start.

Serves 4–6

6 slices medium-cut white bread, crusts removed
225g/8oz raw tiger prawns (jumbo shrimp), peeled and deveined
50g/2oz/⅓ cup drained, canned water chestnuts
1 egg white
5ml/1 tsp sesame oil
2.5ml/½ tsp salt
2 spring onions (scallions), finely chopped
10ml/2 tsp dry sherry
15ml/1 tbsp sesame seeds, toasted (see Cook's Tip)
shredded spring onion (scallion), to garnish

1 Preheat the oven to 120°C/250°F/Gas ½. Cut each slice of bread into four triangles. Spread out on a baking sheet and bake for 25 minutes or until crisp.

2 Meanwhile, put the prawns in a food processor with the water chestnuts, egg white, oil and salt. Process the mixture, using the pulse facility, until a coarse purée is formed.

3 Scrape the mixture into a bowl, stir in the chopped spring onions and sherry, and set aside for 10 minutes at room temperature to allow the flavours to blend.

4 Remove the toast from the oven and raise the temperature to 200°C/400°F/Gas 6. Spread the prawn mixture on the toast, sprinkle with the sesame seeds and bake for 12 minutes. Garnish the prawn toasts with spring onion and serve hot or warm.

Cook's Tip
To toast sesame seeds, put them in a dry frying pan and place over medium heat until the seeds change colour. Shake the pan constantly so the seeds brown evenly and do not burn.

Spicy Moroccan Olives

Green olives, marinated in these two spicy herbal concoctions, are simple and quick to prepare and absolutely delicious.

Serves 6–8

450g/1lb/2⅔ cups green or tan olives (unpitted) for each marinade

For the spicy herbal marinade
45ml/3 tbsp chopped fresh coriander (cilantro)
45ml/3 tbsp chopped fresh flat leaf parsley
1 garlic clove, finely chopped
good pinch of cayenne pepper
good pinch of ground cumin
30–45ml/2–3 tbsp olive oil, plus extra if necessary
30–45ml/2–3 tbsp lemon juice, plus extra if necessary

For the hot chilli marinade
60ml/4 tbsp chopped fresh coriander (cilantro)
60ml/4 tbsp chopped fresh flat leaf parsley
1 garlic clove, finely chopped
5ml/1 tsp grated fresh root ginger
1 red chilli, seeded and sliced
¼ preserved lemon, cut into thin strips

1 Crack the olives, hard enough to break the flesh but taking care not to crack the pits. Place in a bowl of cold water and leave overnight to remove the excess brine. Drain thoroughly and divide the olives between two jars.

2 Mix all the ingredients for the spicy herbal marinade in a jug (pitcher). Pour over the olives in one of the jars, adding more olive oil and lemon juice to cover, if necessary.

3 To make the hot chilli marinade, mix all the ingredients. Pour over the olives in the second jar. Store both the jars in the refrigerator for at least 1 week, shaking them occasionally.

Variation
A jar of marinated olives makes a perfect present for anyone who appreciates their flavour. Experiment with herbs and spices in the marinade – try oregano and basil, and substitute lime juice for the lemon juice, or even use flavoured vinegars.

Prawn Toasts Energy 392kcal/1635kJ; Protein 19.1g; Carbohydrate 21.1g, of which sugars 1.2g; Fat 25.9g, of which saturates 3.4g; Cholesterol 110mg; Calcium 270mg; Fibre 2.7g; Sodium 558mg.
Moroccan Olives Energy 99kcal/406kJ; Protein 0.6g; Carbohydrate 0.2g, of which sugars 0.2g; Fat 10.6g, of which saturates 1.6g; Cholesterol 0mg; Calcium 38mg; Fibre 1.5g; Sodium 846mg.

Tapas of Almonds, Olives and Cheese

Serving a few choice nibbles with drinks is the perfect way to get an evening off to a good start, and when you can get everything ready ahead of time, life's easier all round.

Serves 6–8

For the marinated olives
2.5ml/½ tsp coriander seeds
2.5ml/½ tsp fennel seeds
2 garlic cloves, crushed
5ml/1 tsp chopped fresh rosemary
10ml/2 tsp chopped fresh parsley
15ml/1 tbsp sherry vinegar
30ml/2 tbsp olive oil
115g/4oz/⅔ cup black olives
115g/4oz/⅔ cup green olives

For the marinated cheese
150g/5oz Manchego or other firm cheese
90ml/6 tbsp olive oil
15ml/1 tbsp white wine vinegar
5ml/1 tsp black peppercorns
1 garlic clove, sliced
fresh thyme or tarragon sprigs
fresh flat leaf parsley or tarragon sprigs, to garnish (optional)

For the salted almonds
1.5ml/¼ tsp cayenne pepper
30ml/2 tbsp sea salt
25g/1oz/2 tbsp butter
60ml/4 tbsp olive oil
200g/7oz/1¾ cups blanched almonds

1 To make the marinated olives, crush the coriander and fennel seeds in a mortar with a pestle. Work in the garlic, then add the rosemary, parsley, vinegar and olive oil. Mix well. Put the olives in a small bowl and pour over the marinade. Cover with clear film (plastic wrap) and chill for up to 1 week.

2 To make the marinated cheese, cut the Manchego or other firm cheese into bitesize pieces, removing any rind, and put in a small bowl. Combine the oil, vinegar, peppercorns, garlic, thyme or tarragon and pour over the cheese. Cover with clear film and chill for up to 3 days.

3 To make the salted almonds, combine the cayenne pepper and salt in a bowl. Melt the butter with the oil in a frying pan. Add the almonds and fry them, stirring, for 5 minutes. Transfer the almonds into the salt mixture and toss until they are evenly coated. Leave to cool, then store in an airtight container for up to 1 week. Serve the almonds, olives and cheese in separate dishes.

Tapenade and Aioli with Vegetables

These summer vegetables with tapenade and aioli make an excellent appetizer.

Serves 6

For the tapenade
175g/6oz/1½ cups pitted black olives
50g/2oz can anchovy fillets, drained
30ml/2 tbsp capers
120ml/4fl oz/½ cup olive oil
finely grated rind of 1 lemon
15ml/1 tbsp brandy (optional)
ground black pepper

For the herb aioli
2 egg yolks
5ml/1 tsp Dijon mustard
10ml/2 tsp white wine vinegar
250ml/8fl oz/1 cup light olive oil
45ml/3 tbsp chopped mixed fresh herbs, such as chervil, parsley or tarragon
30ml/2 tbsp chopped watercress
5 garlic cloves, crushed
salt and ground black pepper

To serve
2 red (bell) peppers, seeded and cut into wide strips
30ml/2 tbsp olive oil
225g/8oz new potatoes
115g/4oz green beans
225g/8oz baby carrots
225g/8oz young asparagus
12 quail's eggs (optional)
fresh herbs, to garnish
coarse salt for sprinkling

1 Make the tapenade. Finely chop the olives, anchovies and capers and beat with the oil, lemon rind and brandy, if using.

2 To make the aioli, beat together the egg yolks, mustard and vinegar. Whisk in the oil, a trickle at a time, until thick and smooth. Season and add the herbs, watercress and garlic. Cover and chill.

3 Put the peppers on a foil-lined grill (broiler) rack and brush with the oil. Cook under high heat until just beginning to char.

4 Cook the potatoes in boiling water until tender. Add the beans and carrots and cook for 1 minute. Add the asparagus and cook for 30 seconds. Drain the vegetables.

5 Cook the quail's eggs in boiling water for 2 minutes. Drain and remove half of each shell. Arrange all the vegetables, eggs and sauces on a serving platter. Garnish with fresh herbs and serve with coarse salt for sprinkling.

Tapas Energy 383kcal/1580kJ; Protein 10.3g; Carbohydrate 1.8g, of which sugars 1.1g; Fat 36.8g, of which saturates 8.9g; Cholesterol 25mg; Calcium 217mg; Fibre 2.7g; Sodium 1051mg.
Tapenade Energy 583kcal/2408kJ; Protein 10.7g; Carbohydrate 14.6g, of which sugars 8g; Fat 54g, of which saturates 8.6g; Cholesterol 199mg; Calcium 104mg; Fibre 4.3g; Sodium 1050mg.

Olive and Anchovy Bites

These little melt-in-the-mouth morsels are very moreish, and are perfect accompaniments for drinks. They are made from two ingredients that are forever associated with tapas and are included in many traditional recipes – olives and anchovies. The reason for this is that both contain plenty of salt, which helps to stimulate thirst and therefore drinking.

Makes 40–45

115g/4oz/1 cup plain (all-purpose) flour
115g/4oz/½ cup chilled butter, diced
115g/4oz/1 cup finely grated Manchego, mature (sharp) Cheddar or Gruyère cheese
50g/2oz can anchovy fillets in oil, drained and roughly chopped
50g/2oz/½ cup pitted black olives, roughly chopped
2.5ml/½ tsp cayenne pepper
sea salt, to serve

1 Place the flour, butter, cheese, anchovies, olives and cayenne pepper in a food processor and process to a firm dough.

2 Wrap the dough loosely in clear film (plastic wrap). Chill for 20 minutes.

3 Preheat the oven to 200°C/400°F/Gas 6. Roll out the dough thinly on a lightly floured surface.

4 Cut the dough into 5cm/2in wide strips, then cut across each strip in alternate directions, to make triangles. Transfer to baking sheets anc bake for 8–10 minutes until golden. Cool on a wire rack. Sprinkle with sea salt before serving.

Variations

- *To add a little extra spice, dust the olive and anchovy bites lightly with cayenne pepper before baking.*
- *Crisp little nibbles set off most drinks. Serve these bites alongside little bowls of seeds and nuts, such as sunflower seeds and pistachios. These come in the shell, the opening of which provides a diversion while chatting and gossiping. Toasted chickpeas are another popular tapas snack.*

Anchovy and Caper Bites

These miniature skewers are very popular in Spain, where they are called *pinchos*, which literally means 'stuck on a thorn'. Taste, colour and shape guide the choice of ingredients that are speared together on cocktail sticks. The selection may also include pieces of cold or cured meat, pickled tuna, salted fish or even hard-boiled eggs. In the south of the country, piquant pickled vegetables are the most popular combination. In that region, the resemblance of the little sticks to a bullfighter's dart was noticed and so the dish was renamed *pinchos*.

Serves 4

12 small capers
12 canned anchovy fillets in oil, drained
12 pitted black olives
12 cornichons or small gherkins
12 silverskin pickled onions

1 Using your fingers, place a caper at the thicker end of each anchovy fillet and carefully roll it up, so that the caper is completely enclosed.

2 Thread one caper-filled anchovy, one olive, one cornichon or gherkin and one pickled onion on to each of 12 cocktail sticks (toothpicks). Chill and serve.

Cook's Tip

If the anchovies you are using are extremely salty, try soaking them in a little milk before using them. Salted capers should also be rinsed before use.

Variations

- *Add a chunk of canned tuna in oil to each stick.*
- *You can vary the ingredients if you like, using slices of cold meats, chunks of cheese and pickled vegetables. Choose a selection of three or four ingredients to give contrasting textures, flavours and colours.*

Bites Energy 145Kcal/602kJ; Protein 4.7g; Carbohydrate 6.3g, of which sugars 0.6g; Fat 11.4g, of which saturates 7.4g; Cholesterol 33mg; Calcium 108mg; Fibre 0.4g; Sodium 407mg.
Anchovy and Caper Bites Energy 41kcal/169kJ; Protein 2.8g; Carbohydrate 2.2g, of which sugars 1.6g; Fat 2.4g, of which saturates 0.4g; Cholesterol 6mg; Calcium 44mg; Fibre 0.8g; Sodium 636mg.

Butterfly Prawn Skewers with Chilli and Raspberry Dip

The success of this dish depends upon the quality of the prawns, so it is worthwhile getting really good ones, which have a fine flavour and firm texture. A fruity, slightly spicy dip is a very easy, but fabulous accompaniment.

Serves 4–6

30 raw king prawns (jumbo shrimp), peeled
15ml/1 tbsp sunflower oil
sea salt

For the chilli and raspberry dip
30ml/2 tbsp raspberry vinegar
15ml/1 tbsp sugar
115g/4oz/2/3 cup raspberries
1 large fresh red chilli, seeded and finely chopped

1 Soak 30 wooden skewers in cold water for 30 minutes. Make the dip by mixing the vinegar and sugar in a small pan. Heat gently until the sugar has dissolved, stirring constantly, then add the raspberries.

2 When the raspberry juices start to flow, transfer the mixture into a sieve (strainer) set over a bowl. Push the raspberries through the sieve using the back of a ladle or wooden spoon. Discard the seeds left in the sieve. Stir the chilli into the purée and leave to cool. When the dip is cold, cover and place in a cool place until it is needed.

3 Preheat the grill (broiler). Remove the dark spinal vein from the prawns using a small, sharp knife. Make an incision down the curved back and butterfly each prawn.

4 Mix the sunflower oil with a little sea salt in a bowl. Add the prawns and toss to coat them completely. Thread the prawns on to the drained skewers, spearing them head first.

5 Grill (broil) the prawns for about 5 minutes, depending on their size, turning them over once. Serve hot, with the chilli and raspberry dip.

Angels on Horseback

This recipe dates back to the 19th century, when oysters were plentiful and cheap. It became fashionable in England to serve a savoury – a small, strongly flavoured dish – at the end of a meal, mainly to revive the palates of the gentlemen after dessert and before the arrival of the port. Nowadays, this little dish makes a delicious appetizer.

Serves 4

16 oysters, removed from shells
fresh lemon juice
8 rindless rashers (strips) of streaky (fatty) bacon
8 small slices of bread
butter, for spreading
paprika (optional)

1 Preheat the oven to 200°C/400°F/Gas 6. Sprinkle the oysters with a little lemon juice.

2 Lay the streaky bacon rashers on a chopping board, slide the back of a knife along each one to stretch it and then cut each in half crossways.

3 Wrap a piece of bacon around each oyster and secure with a wooden cocktail stick (toothpick). Arrange on a baking sheet.

4 Place the oysters and bacon into the hot oven for about 8–10 minutes until the bacon is just cooked through.

5 Meanwhile, toast the bread. When the bacon is cooked, butter the hot toast and serve the bacon-wrapped oysters on top. Sprinkle with a little paprika, if using.

Cook's Tip

To shell an oyster, wrap a dish towel around your hand then grip the oyster in the same hand, with the cupped shell down in the palm and the hinge pointing towards you. Insert a shucking knife (or a short, sharp knife) into the gap in the hinge and twist it from side to side until the hinge breaks. Lever open the top shell, then run the knife along the edges to free the oyster, then cut it away from the muscle that binds it to the bottom shell.

Butterfly Prawns Energy 156kcal/635kJ; Protein 12.5g; Carbohydrate 7.3g, of which sugars 0.5g; Fat 8g, of which saturates 1.3g; Cholesterol 157mg; Calcium 64mg; Fibre 0.3g; Sodium 316mg.
Angels on Horseback Energy 326kcal/1365kJ; Protein 20.3g; Carbohydrate 26.4g, of which sugars 1.4g; Fat 16.2g, of which saturates 6.9g; Cholesterol 79mg; Calcium 147mg; Fibre 0.8g; Sodium 1483mg.

Devils on Horseback

This is another popular savoury, designed to be served at the end of a lavish dinner, that makes a good appetizer. These tasty morsels will go down a treat at any gathering. They can be served on crisp, fried bread instead of buttered toast, if you prefer.

Serves 4
16 pitted prunes
fruit chutney, such as mango
8 rindless rashers (strips) of streaky (fatty) bacon
8 small slices of bread
butter, for spreading

1 Preheat the oven to 200°C/400°F/Gas 6. Ease open the prunes and spoon a small amount of the fruit chutney into each cavity.

2 Lay the streaky bacon rashers on a chopping board, slide the back of a knife along each one to stretch it out and then cut each in half crossways.

3 Wrap a piece of bacon around each prune, secure with a cocktail stick (toothpick) and place on a baking sheet. (Alternatively, omit the cocktail sticks and lay them close together on the baking sheet so that they won't unroll in the oven.)

4 Place the wrapped prunes into the hot oven for about 8–10 minutes until the bacon is just cooked through.

5 Meanwhile, toast the bread. When the bacon is cooked, butter the hot toast and top each piece with a bacon-wrapped prune. Serve immediately.

Variations
- *Instead of filling the prunes with fruit chutney, why not try some variations. If you prefer, the prunes can be stuffed with pâté, olives, whole almonds or nuggets of cured meat.*
- *For an adult version, soak the prunes in a glass of red wine for 3–4 hours before stuffing and wrapping with the bacon.*

Bruschetta with Anchovies, Quail's Eggs and Roasted Cumin

All over the Middle East and North Africa, hard-boiled eggs are enjoyed as a snack or appetizer: they may be dipped in salt and paprika, in the thyme and sumac mixture, zahtar, or in roasted cumin. Bitesize quail's eggs dipped in warm, aromatic, freshly roasted cumin make great picnic food. They also marry well with anchovies to make this tasty bruschetta.

Serves 4–6
1 ciabatta loaf
2–3 garlic cloves
30–45ml/2–3 tbsp olive oil
1 red onion, halved and finely sliced
12 quail's eggs, boiled for about 4 minutes, shelled and halved
50g/2oz anchovy fillets
10–15ml/2–3 tsp cumin seeds, roasted and ground
small bunch of flat leaf parsley, roughly chopped
coarse salt

1 Preheat the grill (broiler) on the hottest setting. Slice the loaf of bread horizontally in half and toast the cut side until golden.

2 Smash the garlic cloves with the flat blade of a knife to remove their skins and crush the flesh slightly. Rub the garlic over the toasted bread. Drizzle the olive oil over the bread and sprinkle with a little salt (not too much as the anchovies will be salty).

3 Cut each length of bread into four to six equal pieces. Pile the onion slices, quail's egg halves and anchovy fillets on the pieces of bread. Sprinkle liberally with the ground roasted cumin and chopped parsley and serve immediately while the bread is still warm.

Cook's Tip
Select anchovy fillets preserved in salt or oil. Soak anchovy fillets preserved in salt in a little milk for about 15 minutes to reduce the salty flavour, then drain (discarding the milk) and pat dry on kitchen paper. Drain fillets preserved in oil.

Devils on Horseback Energy 309kcal/1303kJ; Protein 14.7g; Carbohydrate 41.7g, of which sugars 18.3g; Fat 10.4g, of which saturates 3.5g; Cholesterol 30mg; Calcium 75mg; Fibre 3.6g; Sodium 1132mg
Bruschetta Energy 181kcal/761kJ; Protein 8.8g; Carbohydrate 18.2g, of which sugars 1.7g; Fat 8.6g, of which saturates 1.6g; Cholesterol 100mg; Calcium 87mg; Fibre 1g; Sodium 543mg.

Cannellini Bean and Rosemary Bruschetta

This variation on the theme of beans on toast makes a sophisticated appetizer.

Serves 6

150g/5oz/⅔ cup dried cannellini beans
5 tomatoes
45ml/3 tbsp olive oil, plus extra for drizzling
2 sun-dried tomatoes in oil, drained and finely chopped
1 garlic clove, crushed
30ml/2 tbsp chopped fresh rosemary
12 slices Italian-style bread, such as ciabatta
1 large garlic clove
salt and ground black pepper
handful of fresh basil leaves, to garnish

1 Place the dried beans in a bowl, cover with cold water and leave to soak overnight.

2 Drain and rinse the beans, then place in a pan and cover with fresh water. Bring to the boil and boil rapidly for about 10 minutes, then simmer for 50–60 minutes or until tender. Drain, return to the pan and keep warm.

3 Meanwhile, place the tomatoes in a bowl, cover with boiling water, leave for 30 seconds, then peel, seed and chop the flesh.

4 Heat the oil in a frying pan, add the fresh and sun-dried tomatoes, garlic and rosemary. Cook for 2 minutes until the tomatoes begin to break down and soften.

5 Add the tomato mixture to the cannellini beans and season to taste. Mix together well. Keep the bean mixture warm.

6 Rub the cut sides of the bread slices with the garlic clove, then toast them lightly.

7 Spoon the cannellini bean mixture on top of the toast. Sprinkle with basil leaves and drizzle each bruschetta with a little extra olive oil before serving.

Spicy Toasts

These crunchy toasts make an ideal snack, appetizer or part of a brunch. They are especially delicious served with grilled tomatoes.

Serves 4

4 eggs
300ml/½ pint/1¼ cups milk
2 fresh green chillies, finely chopped
30ml/2 tbsp chopped fresh coriander (cilantro)
75g/3oz/¾ cup grated Cheddar or mozzarella cheese
2.5ml/½ tsp salt
1.5ml/¼ tsp ground black pepper
4 slices bread
corn oil, for frying

1 Break the eggs into a medium bowl and whisk together. Slowly add the milk and whisk again. Add the chopped chillies, coriander and grated cheese. Add the salt and ground black pepper, and mix well.

2 Cut the bread slices in half diagonally, and soak them, one at a time, in the egg mixture.

3 Heat the oil in a medium frying pan and fry the bread slices over medium heat, turning them once or twice, until they are golden brown.

4 Drain off any excess oil as you remove the toasts from the pan, and serve immediately.

Variations

- *You can also use these ingredients to make a spicy topping for toasted bread. Toast the sliced and halved bread on one side. Mix 115g/4oz cheese with the flavourings and spread on the untoasted side. Grill (broil) until bubbling and golden.*
- *Try using garlic and wholegrain mustard in place of the chillies for toasting.*
- *Make it a creamy spread for toasting by adding 75g/3oz cubed and steamed butternut squash mashed with the cheese and flavourings.*

Cannellini Bean Energy 499kcal/2111kJ; Protein 20.2g; Carbohydrate 84.3g, of which sugars 8.5g; Fat 11.3g, of which saturates 1.7g; Cholesterol 0mg; Calcium 195mg; Fibre 8.1g; Sodium 749mg.
Spicy Toasts Energy 355kcal/1479kJ; Protein 16.6g; Carbohydrate 17.3g, of which sugars 4.4g; Fat 24.6g, of which saturates 7.7g; Cholesterol 213mg; Calcium 295mg; Fibre 0.4g; Sodium 383mg.

Crostini with Tomato, Red Pepper and Mozzarella Toppings

This Italian appetizer was originally a way of using up an over-abundance of tomatoes at harvest time.

Makes 16

1 ciabatta loaf

For the tomato, pepper and anchovy topping

400g/14oz can or bottle Italian roasted red (bell) peppers and tomatoes, in vinegar or brine

50g/2oz can anchovy fillets

15ml/1 tbsp extra virgin olive oil

15–30ml/1–2 tbsp balsamic vinegar

1 garlic clove

25ml/1½ tbsp red pesto

30ml/2 tbsp chopped fresh chives, oregano or sage, to garnish

15ml/1 tbsp capers, to garnish

For the mozzarella and tomato topping

25ml/1½ tbsp green pesto

120ml/4fl oz/½ cup thick home-made or bottled tomato sauce

75g/3oz reduced-fat mozzarella cheese, cut into 8 thin slices

2–3 ripe plum tomatoes, seeded and cut into strips

fresh basil leaves, to garnish

1 Preheat the grill (broiler) to high. Cut the ciabatta into 16 slices. Toast until golden on both sides. Cool on a wire rack.

2 For the tomato, pepper and anchovy topping, drain the tomatoes and peppers and wipe dry with kitchen paper. Cut into 1cm/½in strips and place in a shallow dish. Rinse and dry the anchovy fillets and add to the peppers and tomatoes. Drizzle with the olive oil and sprinkle with the balsamic vinegar.

3 Using a sharp knife, peel and halve the garlic clove. Rub eight toasts with the cut edge of the clove and lightly brush the toasts with a little red pesto. Arrange the tomatoes, peppers and anchovies decoratively on the toasts and sprinkle with chopped herbs and capers.

4 For the mozzarella and tomato topping, lightly brush the remaining toasts with the green pesto and spoon on some tomato sauce. Arrange a slice of mozzarella on each and cover with the tomato strips. Garnish with basil leaves.

Egg Crostini with Rouille

Crostini are extremely quick to make so are perfect for brunch parties or a speedy appetizer. The spicy rouille gives them a hint of a Mediterranean flavour, providing the perfect complement to the lightly fried eggs.

Serves 8

8 slices of ciabatta bread

extra virgin olive oil, for brushing

90ml/6 tbsp home-made mayonnaise

10ml/2 tsp harissa

8 eggs

8 small slices smoked ham

watercress or salad leaves, to serve

1 Preheat the oven to 200°C/400°F/Gas 6. Use a pastry brush to brush each slice of ciabatta bread lightly with a little olive oil. Place the bread on a baking sheet and bake for 10 minutes, or until crisp and turning golden brown.

2 Meanwhile, make the rouille. Put the mayonnaise and harissa in a small bowl and mix well together.

3 Fry the eggs lightly in a little oil in a large non-stick frying pan until cooked.

4 Top the bread with the ham, eggs and a small spoonful of rouille. Serve immediately with watercress or salad leaves.

Cook's Tip

Harissa is a fiery North African chilli paste made from dried red chillies, cumin, garlic, coriander, caraway and olive oil.

Variation

You can use four small portions of smoked haddock instead of ham and poach them for 5–7 minutes.

Crostini Energy 116kcal/488kJ; Protein 4.8g; Carbohydrate 15.9g, of which sugars 3.2g; Fat 4.1g, of which saturates 1g; Cholesterol 5mg; Calcium 60mg; Fibre 1.3g; Sodium 301mg.
Egg Crostini Energy 259kcal/1083kJ; Protein 15.8g; Carbohydrate 13.6g, of which sugars 1.3g; Fat 16.3g, of which saturates 3.4g; Cholesterol 220mg; Calcium 62mg; Fibre 0.6g; Sodium 705mg.

Paprika-spiced Black Pudding Crostini

Spanish morcilla – a version of black pudding – is flavoured with spices and herbs, usually including garlic and oregano, and has a wonderfully rich taste. These delicious bites are ideal at a party or as a tasty appetizer.

Serves 4

15ml/1 tbsp olive oil
1 onion, thinly sliced
2 garlic cloves, thinly sliced
5ml/1 tsp dried oregano
5ml/1 tsp paprika
225g/8oz black pudding (blood sausage), cut into 12 thick slices
1 thin French stick, cut into 12 rounds
30ml/2 tbsp fino sherry
sugar, to taste
salt and ground black pepper
chopped fresh oregano, to garnish

1 Heat the olive oil in a large frying pan and fry the onion, garlic, oregano and paprika for about 7–8 minutes until the onion is softened and has turned golden brown.

2 Add the slices of black pudding, then increase the heat and cook them for 3 minutes, without stirring. Turn the slices over carefully with a metal spatula and cook on the other side for a further 3 minutes until crisp.

3 Arrange the rounds of bread on a large serving plate and top each with a slice of black pudding.

4 Stir the sherry into the onions and add a little sugar to taste. Heat, swirling the mixture around the pan until it is bubbling, then season with salt and black pepper.

5 Spoon a little of the onion mixture on top of each slice of black pudding. Sprinkle the oregano over and serve.

Cook's Tip
If you are able to find real morcilla, serve it neat to make the most of its subtle flavour: simply fry the slices in olive oil and use to top little rounds of bread. If you cannot find black pudding, you can use red chorizo instead.

Prawn and Vegetable Crostini

Use bottled carciofini (tiny artichoke hearts preserved in olive oil) for this simple Italian appetizer, which can be prepared very quickly.

Serves 4

450g/1lb whole cooked prawns (shrimp), in the shell
4 thick slices of ciabatta, cut diagonally across
3 garlic cloves, peeled and 2 garlic cloves halved lengthwise
60ml/4 tbsp extra virgin olive oil
200g/7oz/2 cups small button (white) mushrooms, trimmed
12 bottled carciofini, drained
60ml/4 tbsp chopped flat leaf parsley
salt and ground black pepper

1 Peel the shells from the cooked prawns and remove the heads with a sharp knife.

2 Rub the ciabatta slices on both sides with the cut sides of the halved garlic cloves, drizzle with a little of the olive oil and toast in the oven or grill (broil) until lightly browned. Keep hot.

3 Finely chop the remaining garlic. Heat the remaining oil in a frying pan and gently fry the chopped garlic until golden, but do not allow it to brown.

4 Add the mushrooms and stir to coat with oil. Season with salt and pepper and fry for about 2–3 minutes. Gently stir in the drained carciofini, then add the chopped flat leaf parsley.

5 Adjust the seasoning, then stir in the prawns and cook briefly to warm through.

6 Pile the prawn mixture on top of the toasted ciabatta slices, pouring over any remaining cooking juices from the pan, and serve immediately.

Cook's Tip
Don't use frozen peeled prawns (shrimp) in this recipe: freshly cooked prawns in their shells are infinitely tastier.

Black Pudding Energy 538kcal/2268kJ; Protein 17.4g; Carbohydrate 81.2g, of which sugars 6.4g; Fat 17.4g, of which saturates 5.6g; Cholesterol 38mg; Calcium 228mg; Fibre 3.7g; Sodium 1271mg.
Prawn Crostini Energy 264kcal/1104kJ; Protein 23.7g; Carbohydrate 13.6g, of which sugars 1.2g; Fat 13.1g, of which saturates 1.9g; Cholesterol 219mg; Calcium 152mg; Fibre 1.9g; Sodium 356mg.

Pea and Potato Pakoras with Coconut and Mint Chutney

These delicious bites make a wonderful appetizer drizzled with the fragrant chutney.

Makes 25

15ml/1 tbsp sunflower oil
20ml/4 tsp cumin seeds
5ml/1 tsp black mustard seeds
1 small onion, finely chopped
10ml/2 tsp grated fresh root ginger
2 fresh green chillies, seeded and chopped
600g/1lb 5oz potatoes, cooked
200g/7oz fresh peas
juice of 1 lemon
90ml/6 tbsp chopped fresh coriander (cilantro) leaves
vegetable oil, for frying
salt and ground black pepper

For the batter

115g/4oz/1 cup gram flour
25g/1oz/¼ cup self-raising (self-rising) flour
40g/1½oz/⅓ cup rice flour
large pinch of turmeric
10ml/2 tsp coriander seeds, finely crushed
350ml/12fl oz/1½ cups water

For the chutney

105ml/7 tbsp coconut cream
200ml/7fl oz/scant 1 cup natural (plain) yogurt
50g/2oz mint leaves, finely chopped
5ml/1 tsp golden caster (superfine) sugar
juice of 1 lime

1 Heat a wok and add the sunflower oil. When hot, fry the cumin and mustard seeds for 1–2 minutes. Add the onion, ginger and chillies and cook for another 3–4 minutes. Add the potatoes and peas and stir-fry for a further 5–6 minutes. Season, then add the lemon juice and coriander leaves. Cool, then divide into 25 portions. Shape each into a ball and chill.

2 To make the chutney, place all the ingredients in a blender and process until smooth. Season, then chill. To make the batter, put the gram flour, self-raising flour and rice flour in a bowl. Season and add the turmeric and coriander seeds. Gradually whisk in the water to make a smooth batter.

3 Fill a wok one-third full of oil and heat to 180°C/350°F. Working in batches, dip the chilled balls in the batter, then drop into the oil and deep-fry for 1–2 minutes, or until golden. Drain on kitchen paper, and serve immediately with the chutney.

Curried Sweet Potato Balls

These sweet potato balls, with roots in Chinese and South-east Asian cooking, are delicious dipped in a fiery red chilli sauce, fried black chilli sauce or hot peanut dipping sauce. Simple to make, they are ideal for serving as a nibble with a drink.

Serves 4

450g/1lb sweet potatoes or taro root, boiled or baked, and peeled
30ml/2 tbsp sugar
15ml/1 tbsp Indian curry powder or spice blend of your choice
25g/1oz fresh root ginger, peeled and grated
150g/5oz/1¼ cups glutinous rice flour or plain (all-purpose) flour
salt
sesame seeds or poppy seeds
vegetable oil, for deep-frying
dipping sauce, to serve

1 In a bowl, mash the cooked sweet potatoes or taro root. Beat in the sugar, curry powder and ginger. Add the rice flour (sift it if you are using plain flour) and salt, and work into a stiff dough – add more flour if necessary.

2 Pull off lumps of the dough and mould them into small balls – you should be able to make roughly 24 balls. Roll the balls on a bed of sesame seeds or poppy seeds until they are completely coated.

3 Heat enough oil for deep-frying in a wok. Fry the sweet potato balls in batches, until golden. Drain on kitchen paper. Serve the balls with wooden skewers to make it easier to dip them into a dipping sauce of your choice.

Cook's Tip

Also known as 'dasheen', taro root is a starchy tuber cultivated in many parts of Asia. If you opt to use it instead of the sweet potato in this recipe, you may need to add more sugar as it has a much nuttier taste when cooked.

Potato Pakoras Energy 125kcal/525kJ; Protein 4.1g; Carbohydrate 8.3g, of which sugars 2.6g; Fat 8.8g, of which saturates 5.2g; Cholesterol 0mg; Calcium 35mg; Fibre 1.3g; Sodium 16mg.
Curried Balls Energy 354kcal/1495kJ; Protein 4.9g; Carbohydrate 61g, of which sugars 14.8g; Fat 11.8g, of which saturates 1.5g; Cholesterol 0mg; Calcium 84mg; Fibre 3.9g; Sodium 47mg.

Deep-fried Tofu Balls

These tasty tofu balls are ideal to serve as snacks at a party or as an appetizer.

Makes 16

2 x 300g/11oz packets firm tofu
½ small carrot, diced
6 green beans, chopped
2 large (US extra large) eggs
30ml/2 tbsp sake
10ml/2 tsp mirin (sweet rice wine)
5ml/1 tsp salt
10ml/2 tsp soy sauce
pinch of caster (superfine) sugar
vegetable oil, for deep-frying

For the lime sauce
45ml/3 tbsp soy sauce
juice of ½ lime
5ml/1 tsp rice vinegar

To garnish
300g/11oz mooli (daikon), peeled
2 dried red chillies, halved and seeded
4 chives, finely chopped

1 Drain the tofu and wrap it in kitchen paper. Set a large plate with a weight on top and leave for 2 hours, or until it loses most of its liquid. Make the lime sauce by mixing all the ingredients in a bowl.

2 Cut the mooli for the garnish into 4cm/1½in thick slices. Make 3–4 holes in each slice with a skewer and insert chilli pieces into the holes. Leave for 15 minutes, then grate the mooli finely. Cook the carrot and beans for 1 minute in boiling water, then drain well.

3 In a food processor, process the tofu, eggs, sake, mirin, salt, soy sauce and sugar until smooth. Transfer to a bowl and mix in the carrot and beans. Oil your hands and shape the mixture into 16 little balls.

4 Deep-fry the tofu balls in oil until they are crisp and golden. Drain on kitchen paper.

5 Arrange on a serving plate and sprinkle with chives. Put 30ml/2 tbsp grated mooli in each of four small bowls. Mix the lime sauce ingredients in a serving bowl. Serve the balls with the lime sauce to be mixed with grated mooli by each guest.

Chicken and Sticky Rice Balls

These balls can either be steamed or deep-fried. The fried versions are crunchy and are excellent for serving at drinks parties.

Serves 6

450g/1lb minced (ground) chicken
1 egg
15ml/1 tbsp tapioca flour
4 spring onions (scallions), finely chopped
30ml/2 tbsp chopped fresh coriander (cilantro)
30ml/2 tbsp Thai fish sauce
pinch of sugar
225g/8oz cooked sticky rice
banana leaves
oil, for brushing
ground black pepper
shredded carrot, strips of red (bell) pepper and chopped chives, to garnish
sweet chilli sauce, to serve

1 In a bowl, combine the chicken, egg, flour, spring onions and coriander. Mix and season with fish sauce, sugar and pepper. Spread the cooked sticky rice on a large plate or flat tray.

2 Place 5ml/1 tsp of the chicken mixture on the bed of rice. With damp hands, roll and shape the mixture in the rice to make a ball about the size of a walnut. Repeat using the rest of the chicken mixture and rice.

3 Line a bamboo steamer with banana leaves and lightly brush them with oil. Place the chicken balls on the leaves, spacing them well apart to prevent them sticking together as they cook. Steam the balls over a high heat for 10 minutes or until cooked.

4 Remove the balls from the steamer and arrange on serving plates. Garnish with shredded carrot, red pepper strips and chopped chives. Serve with sweet chilli sauce for dipping.

Cook's Tip
Sticky rice, also known as glutinous rice, has a very high starch content. It is so called because the grains stick together when it is cooked. It is very popular in Thailand and can be eaten both as a savoury and as a sweet dish.

Deep-fried Tofu Balls Energy 40kcal/164kJ; Protein 3.9g; Carbohydrate 1.1g, of which sugars 0.9g; Fat 2.2g, of which saturates 0.4g; Cholesterol 24mg; Calcium 187mg; Fibre 0.3g; Sodium 380mg.
Sticky Rice Balls Energy 249kcal/1044kJ; Protein 20.8g; Carbohydrate 32.9g, of which sugars 0.4g; Fat 3.7g, of which saturates 1g; Cholesterol 64mg; Calcium 39mg; Fibre 0.5g; Sodium 212mg.

Crispy Pork Balls

These crispy balls made from pork and Asian spices are the perfect food to serve at a party.

Serves 4–6

4 slices of white bread, crusts removed
5ml/1 tsp olive oil
225g/8oz skinless, boneless pork meat, roughly chopped
50g/2oz/⅓ cup drained, canned water chestnuts
2 fresh red chillies, seeded and roughly chopped
1 egg white
10g/¼ oz/¼ cup fresh coriander (cilantro) leaves
5ml/1 tsp cornflour (cornstarch)
2.5ml/½ tsp salt
1.5ml/¼ tsp ground white pepper
30ml/2 tbsp light soy sauce
5ml/1 tsp caster (superfine) sugar
30ml/2 tbsp rice vinegar
2.5ml/½ tsp chilli oil
shredded red chillies and fresh coriander (cilantro) sprigs

1 Preheat the oven to 120°C/250°F/Gas ½. Brush the bread slices with olive oil and cut them into 5mm/¼in cubes. Spread over a baking sheet and bake for 15 minutes until dry and crisp.

2 Meanwhile, mix together the pork meat, water chestnuts and chillies in a food processor. Process to a coarse paste.

3 Add the egg white, coriander, cornflour, salt, pepper and half the soy sauce. Process for 30 seconds. Scrape into a bowl, cover and set aside.

4 Remove the toasted bread cubes from the oven and set them aside. Raise the oven temperature to 200°C/400°F/Gas 6. Shape the pork mixture into 12 balls.

5 Crush the toasted bread cubes and coat the pork balls in the crumbs. Place on a baking sheet and bake for about 20 minutes or until the pork filling is cooked.

6 In a small bowl, mix the remaining soy sauce with the caster sugar, rice vinegar and chilli oil. Serve the sauce with the pork balls, garnished with shredded chillies and coriander sprigs.

Spicy Koftas

These delectable meatballs are popular throughout parts of Europe, the Middle East and South Asia. Serve as part of a party buffet or as an appetizer with your choice of dip – a chilli and tomato dip or a minty yogurt sauce would be ideal.

Serves 6–8

450g/1lb lean minced (ground) beef
30ml/2 tbsp finely ground ginger
30ml/2 tbsp finely chopped garlic
4 fresh green chillies, seeded finely chopped
1 small onion, finely chopped
1 egg
2.5ml/½ tsp ground turmeric
5ml/1 tsp garam masala
50g/2oz/2 cups coriander (cilantro) leaves, chopped
4–6 mint leaves, chopped, or 2.5ml/½ tsp mint sauce
175g/6oz raw potato
salt
vegetable oil, for deep-frying

1 Place the minced beef in a large bowl with the ground ginger, garlic, chillies, onion, egg, turmeric, garam masala and herbs. Mix well to combine the ingredients.

2 Grate the potato into the bowl, and season with salt. Knead together to blend well and form a soft dough.

3 Using your hands, shape the kofta mixture into portions the size of golf balls. You should be able to make about 20–25 koftas. Set the balls aside at room temperature to rest for about 25 minutes.

4 In a wok or frying pan, heat the oil to medium-hot and deep-fry the koftas, in small batches, until they are golden brown in colour. Drain well and serve hot.

Cook's Tips

- *Any leftover koftas can be coarsely chopped and packed into pitta bread spread with chutney or relish for a quick and delicious snack.*
- *If the mixture is too sticky while shaping the koftas, then moisten your hands with a little water or dust them with flour.*

Crispy Pork Balls Energy 161kcal/676kJ; Protein 12.9g; Carbohydrate 15g, of which sugars 7.1g; Fat 5.9g, of which saturates 1.3g; Cholesterol 55mg; Calcium 19mg; Fibre 0.4g; Sodium 446mg.
Spicy Koftas Energy 96kcal/404kJ; Protein 5.2g; Carbohydrate 11.8g, of which sugars 1.2g; Fat 3.4g, of which saturates 1.4g; Cholesterol 18mg; Calcium 16mg; Fibre 1g; Sodium 28mg.

Bacon-rolled Enokitake Mushrooms

The Japanese name for this dish is obimaki enoki. An obi (belt or sash) is made from bacon and wrapped around enokitake mushrooms before they are cooked. The strong, smoky flavour of the bacon complements the subtle, delicate flavour of the mushrooms.

Serves 4

450g/1lb fresh enokitake mushrooms
6 rindless smoked streaky (fatty) bacon rashers (strips)
4 lemon wedges, to serve

1 Cut off the root part of each enokitake cluster 2cm/¾in from the end. Do not separate the stems. Cut the bacon rashers in half lengthways.

2 Divide the enokitake into 12 equal bunches. Take one bunch, then place the middle of the enokitake near the edge of one bacon rasher, with 2.5–4cm/1–1½in of enokitake protruding at each end.

3 Carefully roll up the bunch of enokitake in the bacon. Tuck any straying short stems into the bacon and slide the bacon slightly upwards at each roll to cover about 4cm/1½in of the enokitake.

4 Secure the end of the bacon roll with a cocktail stick (toothpick). Repeat using the remaining enokitake and bacon to make 11 more rolls.

5 Preheat the grill (broiler) to a high temperature. Place the enokitake rolls on an oiled wire rack. Grill (broil) both sides until the bacon is crisp and the enokitake start to char. This takes about 10–13 minutes.

6 Remove the enokitake rolls and place on a board. Using a fork and knife, chop each roll in half in the middle of the bacon belt. Arrange the top part of the enokitake roll standing upright, the bottom part lying down next to it. Add a wedge of lemon to each portion and serve.

Sushi

The preparation of sushi in Japan is almost an artform, so revered are these delicious and healthy bites. They make the ideal snack or appetizer. The fish is not cooked but rather rolled up raw so ensure that it is the freshest fish available.

Serves 4

For the tuna sushi
3 sheets nori (paper-thin seaweed)
150g/5oz freshest tuna fillet, cut into fingers
5ml/1 tsp wasabi paste, thinned with a little water
6 young carrots, blanched
450g/1lb/6 cups cooked sushi rice

For the salmon sushi
2 eggs
2.5ml/½ tsp salt
10ml/2 tsp sugar
5 sheets nori
450g/1lb/6 cups cooked sushi rice
150g/5oz freshest salmon fillet, cut into fingers
5ml/1 tsp wasabi paste, thinned with a little water
½ small cucumber, cut into strips

1 To make the tuna sushi, spread half a sheet of nori on to a bamboo mat, lay strips of tuna across the full length and season with the thinned wasabi. Place a line of blanched carrot next to the tuna and roll tightly. Moisten the edge with water and seal.

2 Place a square of wet baking parchment on the bamboo mat, then spread evenly with rice. Place the nori-wrapped tuna along the centre and wrap tightly, enclosing the nori completely. Remove the paper and cut into neat rounds with a wet knife.

3 To make the salmon sushi, make a simple flat omelette by beating together the eggs, salt and sugar. Heat a large non-stick pan, pour in the egg mixture, stir briefly and allow to set. Transfer to a clean dish towel and cool.

4 Place the nori on a bamboo mat, cover with the omelette and trim to size. Spread a layer of rice over the omelette, then lay strips of salmon across the width.

5 Season the salmon with the thinned wasabi, then place a strip of cucumber next to the salmon. Fold the bamboo mat in half. Cut into neat rounds with a wet knife. Serve immediately.

Bacon-rolled Enokitake Energy 84kcal/348kJ; Protein 6g; Carbohydrate 0.5g, of which sugars 0.2g; Fat 6.5g, of which saturates 2.2g; Cholesterol 16mg; Calcium 8mg; Fibre 1.3g; Sodium 321mg.
Sushi Energy 183kcal/768kJ; Protein 10.2g; Carbohydrate 28.7g, of which sugars 2.1g; Fat 2.9g, of which saturates 0.5g; Cholesterol 13mg; Calcium 25mg; Fibre 0.4g; Sodium 17mg.

Fried Prawn Balls

When the moon waxes in September, the Japanese celebrate the arrival of autumn by making an offering to the moon. The dishes offered, such as tiny rice dumplings, sweet chestnuts and these shinjyo, should all be round in shape.

Makes about 14
150g/5oz raw prawns (shrimp), peeled
75ml/5 tbsp freshly made dashi (kombu and bonito stock) or instant dashi
1 large (US extra large) egg white, well beaten
30ml/2 tbsp sake
15ml/1 tbsp cornflour (cornstarch)
1.5ml/¼ tsp salt
vegetable oil, for deep-frying

To serve
25ml/1½ tbsp ground sea salt
2.5ml/½ tsp sansho
½ lemon, cut into 4 wedges

1 Mix the prawns, dashi stock, beaten egg white, sake, cornflour and salt in a food processor or blender, and process until smooth. Scrape the mixture into a small mixing bowl.

2 In a wok or small, heavy pan, heat the vegetable oil until it reaches 175°C/347°F.

3 Take two dessertspoons and wet them with a little vegetable oil. Use them to scoop 30ml/2 tbsp prawn-ball paste to form a small ball. Carefully plunge the ball into the oil and deep-fry until lightly browned. Drain on a wire rack. Repeat this process, one at a time, until all the prawn-ball paste is used.

4 Mix the salt and sansho on a small plate. Serve the fried prawn balls on a large serving platter or on four serving plates. Garnish with lemon wedges and serve hot with the sansho salt.

Cook's Tip
Sansho is ground spice made from the dried pod of the prickly ash. Serve the sansho and salt in separate mounds, if you like.

Seaweed-wrapped Prawn Rolls

Japanese nori seaweed is used to enclose the fragrant filling of prawns, water chestnuts, and fresh herbs and spices in these pretty steamed rolls. Ideal for entertaining, the rolls can be prepared in advance and stored in the refrigerator until ready to steam.

Serves 4
675g/1½lb raw tiger prawns (jumbo shrimp), peeled and deveined
5ml/1 tsp finely chopped kaffir lime leaves
1 red chilli, seeded and chopped
5ml/1 tsp finely grated garlic clove
5ml/1 tsp finely grated root ginger
5ml/1 tsp finely grated lime rind
60ml/4 tbsp very finely chopped fresh coriander (cilantro)
1 egg white, lightly beaten
30ml/2 tbsp chopped water chestnuts
4 sheets of nori
salt and ground black pepper
kecap manis or soy sauce, to serve

1 Place the prawns in a food processor with the lime leaves, red chilli, garlic, ginger, lime rind and coriander. Process the mixture until smooth.

2 Add the egg white and water chestnuts to the food processor, season and process again until combined. Transfer the mixture to a bowl, cover and chill for 3–4 hours.

3 Lay the nori sheets on a clean, dry surface and spread the prawn mixture over each sheet, leaving a 2cm/¾in border at one end. Roll up to form tight rolls, wrap in clear film (plastic wrap) and chill for 2–3 hours.

4 Unwrap the rolls and place on a board. Cut each roll into 2cm/¾in lengths. Place the slices in a baking parchment-lined bamboo steamer, cover and place over a wok of simmering water (making sure the water does not touch the steamer).

5 Steam the rolls for 6–8 minutes, or until cooked through. Serve warm or at room temperature with a dish of kecap manis or soy sauce for dipping.

Fried Prawn Balls Energy 41kcal/170kJ; Protein 2.1g; Carbohydrate 1g, of which sugars 0g; Fat 3.2g, of which saturates 0.4g; Cholesterol 21mg; Calcium 9mg; Fibre 0g; Sodium 446mg.
Seaweed Rolls Energy 136Kcal/574kJ; Protein 30.8g; Carbohydrate 0.4g, of which sugars 0.4g; Fat 1.2g, of which saturates 0.2g; Cholesterol 329mg; Calcium 162mg; Fibre 0.7g; Sodium 345mg.

Tuna in Rolled Red Peppers

This lovely savoury combination originated in southern Italy. Grilled peppers have a deliciously sweet, smoky taste that combines particularly well with a robust-tasting fish such as tuna. You could use canned mackerel instead.

Serves 8–10

3 large red (bell) peppers
200g/7oz can tuna, drained
30ml/2 tbsp lemon juice
45ml/3 tbsp olive oil
6 green or black olives, pitted and chopped
30ml/2 tbsp chopped fresh parsley
1 garlic clove, finely chopped
1 celery stick, very finely chopped
salt and ground black pepper

1 Arrange the peppers on a baking sheet and place under a hot grill (broiler). Cook, turning them occasionally, until they are charred and blistered on all sides.

2 Remove the peppers from the heat with tongs and place them in a plastic bag. Tie the top.

3 Leave the peppers for 5 minutes until they are cool enough to handle, then remove from the bag and peel off the skins.

4 Cut the peppers into quarters and remove and discard the stems, seeds and membranes.

5 Meanwhile, flake the tuna and combine it with the lemon juice and oil. Stir in the olives, parsley, garlic and celery. Season with salt and plenty of ground black pepper.

6 Lay the pepper segments out flat, skin side down on a chopping board. Divide the tuna mixture equally among them. Spread it out, pressing it into an even layer. Roll the peppers up around the tuna filling.

7 Place the pepper rolls in the refrigerator for at least 1 hour. Just before serving, cut each roll in half with a sharp knife, then arrange on a large serving platter.

Salmon Rolls with Asparagus and Butter Sauce

The green asparagus contrasts beautifully with the pink of the salmon in this recipe and each has a sweetness of flavour that marries perfectly. This dish will make a particularly sophisticated appetizer at a dinner party.

Serves 4

4 thick or 8 thin asparagus spears
4 very thin slices salmon fillet, each weighing about 115g/4oz
juice 1 lemon
1 bunch fresh parsley, chopped, to serve
salt and ground black pepper

For the butter sauce

1 shallot, finely chopped
6 peppercorns
120ml/4fl oz/½ cup dry white wine
60ml/4 tbsp double (heavy) cream
200g/7oz/scant 1 cup butter, cut into small cubes
salt and ground black pepper

1 Steam the asparagus spears for 6–8 minutes, according to their size. Refresh under cold running water, drain and set aside.

2 The salmon slices should be wide enough to roll around the asparagus. Don't worry if they have to be patched together. Season the salmon with salt and pepper, lay one or two asparagus spears across each slice and then roll the salmon around them. Place on a rack over a pan of boiling water, sprinkle with lemon juice, and cover and steam for 3–4 minutes until tender.

3 To make the butter sauce, put the shallot, peppercorns and wine in a small pan and heat gently until the wine has reduced to a tablespoonful. Strain and return to the pan. Add the cream, bring to the boil, and then lower the heat.

4 Add the butter to the sauce in small pieces, whisking all the time until well incorporated before adding another piece. Do not allow the sauce to boil or it will separate. Season the sauce with salt and pepper to taste, if necessary.

5 Stir the chopped fresh parsley into the sauce and serve immediately with the salmon rolls.

Tuna in Red Peppers Energy 90kcal/374kJ; Protein 6.1g; Carbohydrate 3.8g, of which sugars 3.6g; Fat 5.7g, of which saturates 0.9g; Cholesterol 10mg; Calcium 16mg; Fibre 1.2g; Sodium 119mg.
Salmon Rolls Energy 694kcal/2867kJ; Protein 25.7g; Carbohydrate 2.4g, of which sugars 2.1g; Fat 62.5g, of which saturates 33.4g; Cholesterol 187mg; Calcium 55mg; Fibre 0.6g; Sodium 362mg.

Crab Egg Rolls

These appetizers are similar to Chinese spring rolls, and are ideal for buffets, parties and summer picnics.

Serves 4–6

3 eggs
450ml/¾ pint/scant 2 cups water
175g/6oz/1½ cups plain (all-purpose) flour, sifted
2.5ml/½ tsp salt
vegetable oil, for deep-frying
45ml/3 tbsp light soy sauce mixed with 5ml/1 tsp sesame oil, for dipping
lime wedges, to serve

For the filling

225g/8oz/1⅓ cups white crab meat or small prawns (shrimp)
3 large spring onions (scallions), shredded
2.5cm/1in piece fresh root ginger, grated
2 large garlic cloves, chopped
115g/4oz bamboo shoots, chopped, or beansprouts
15ml/1 tbsp soy sauce
10–15ml/2–3 tsp cornflour (cornstarch) blended with 15ml/1 tbsp water
1 egg, separated
salt and ground black pepper

1 Lightly beat the eggs and gradually stir in the water. Put the flour and salt into another bowl and work in the egg mixture. Blend to a smooth batter, then leave to rest for 20 minutes.

2 Grease a 25cm/10in frying pan and heat gently. Whisk the batter, then pour 45ml/3 tbsp into the pan and spread it very thinly. Cook for 2 minutes, or until set underneath. There is no need to cook the pancake on the other side. Make a further 11 pancakes. Stack the pancakes, cooked side upwards, between sheets of baking parchment. Set aside until ready to use.

3 To make the filling, combine the crab or prawns, spring onions, ginger, garlic, bamboo shoots or beansprouts, soy sauce, cornflour and water, egg yolk and seasoning. Lightly beat the egg white. Place a spoonful of filling in the middle of each pancake, brush the edges with egg white and fold into parcels, tucking in the ends.

4 Heat the oil in a deep-frying pan. When a cube of bread turns golden in 1 minute, carefully add four of the parcels. Cook for 1–2 minutes, or until golden. Remove and place on kitchen paper and cook the remaining egg rolls. Serve with the soy sauce and sesame oil dipping sauce and wedges of lime.

Shiitake and Scallop Bundles

A wok does double duty for making these delicate mushroom and seafood treats, first for steaming and then for deep-frying.

Serves 4

4 scallops
8 large fresh shiitake mushrooms
225g/8oz long yam, unpeeled
20ml/4 tsp miso
50g/2oz/1 cup fresh breadcrumbs
cornflour (cornstarch), for dusting
2 eggs, beaten
vegetable oil, for deep-frying
salt
4 lemon wedges, to serve

1 Slice the scallops in two horizontally, then sprinkle with salt. Remove the stalks from the shiitake and discard them. Cut shallow slits on the top of the shiitake to form a 'hash' symbol. Sprinkle with a little salt.

2 Heat a steamer and steam the long yam for 10–15 minutes, or until soft. Test with a skewer. Leave to cool, then remove the skin. Mash the flesh in a bowl, add the miso and mix well. Take the breadcrumbs into your hands and break them down finely. Mix half into the mashed long yam, keeping the rest on a small plate.

3 Fill the underneath of the shiitake caps with a scoop of mashed long yam. Smooth down with the flat edge of a knife and dust the mash with cornflour. Add a little mash to a slice of scallop and place on top.

4 Spread another 5ml/1 tsp mashed long yam on to the scallop and shape to completely cover. Make sure that all of the ingredients are clinging together. Repeat to make eight little mounds.

5 Place the beaten eggs in a shallow container. Dust the shiitake and scallop mounds with cornflour, then dip into the egg. Handle with care as the mash and scallop are quite soft. Coat well with the remaining breadcrumbs and deep-fry in hot oil until golden. Drain well on kitchen paper. Serve hot on individual plates with a wedge of lemon.

Crab Egg Rolls Energy 313kcal/1309kJ; Protein 15.1g; Carbohydrate 26.1g, of which sugars 1g; Fat 17.3g, of which saturates 2.5g; Cholesterol 154mg; Calcium 67mg; Fibre 1.3g; Sodium 351mg.
Shiitake Bundles Energy 812kcal/3396kJ; Protein 45.8g; Carbohydrate 54g, of which sugars 12.6g; Fat 47.8g, of which saturates 7.5g; Cholesterol 428mg; Calcium 279mg; Fibre 7g; Sodium 741mg.

Thai Fish Cakes with Cucumber Relish

These wonderful little nibbles are a very familiar and popular appetizer.

Serves 4

300g/11oz white fish fillet, such as cod, cut into chunks
30ml/2 tbsp Thai red curry paste
1 egg
30ml/2 tbsp Thai fish sauce
5ml/1 tsp granulated (white) sugar
30ml/2 tbsp cornflour (cornstarch)
3 kaffir lime leaves, shredded
15ml/1 tbsp chopped fresh coriander (cilantro)
50g/2oz green beans, thinly sliced
vegetable oil, for frying
Chinese mustard cress, to garnish

For the cucumber relish
60ml/4 tbsp rice vinegar
60ml/4 tbsp water
50g/2oz/¼ cup sugar
1 whole bulb pickled garlic
1 cucumber, quartered and sliced
4 shallots, thinly sliced
15ml/1 tbsp chopped fresh root ginger

1 To make the cucumber relish, bring the vinegar, water and sugar to the boil. Stir until the sugar dissolves, then remove from the heat and leave to cool.

2 Combine the rest of the relish ingredients together in a bowl and pour the vinegar mixture over.

3 Combine the fish, curry paste and egg in a food processor and process until combined. Transfer the mixture to a bowl, add the Thai fish sauce, sugar, cornflour, lime leaves, coriander and green beans and mix well.

4 Mould and shape the mixture into patties about 5cm/2in in diameter and 5mm/¼in thick.

5 Heat the oil in a wok or deep-fryer. Add the fish cakes, in small batches, and deep-fry for about 4–5 minutes, or until golden brown. Remove and drain well on kitchen paper. Keep the cooked fish cakes warm in a low oven while you cook the remainder. Garnish with Chinese mustard cress and serve immediately with a little cucumber relish spooned on the side.

Eggy Thai Fish Cakes

These tangy little fish cakes, with a kick of Eastern spice, make great party food, dipped in an Asian-style sauce. If they are made slightly larger, they are a great appetizer, too.

Serves 4–6

225g/8oz smoked cod or haddock (undyed)
225g/8oz fresh cod or haddock
1 small fresh red chilli
2 garlic cloves, grated
1 lemon grass stalk, very finely chopped
2 large spring onions (scallions), chopped
30ml/2 tbsp Thai fish sauce or 30ml/2 tbsp soy sauce and a few drops anchovy essence (paste)
60ml/4 tbsp thick coconut milk
2 large (US extra large) eggs, lightly beaten
15ml/1 tbsp chopped fresh coriander (cilantro)
15ml/1 tbsp cornflour (cornstarch)
oil, for frying
soy sauce, rice vinegar or Thai fish sauce, for dipping

1 Place the smoked fish in a bowl of cold water and leave to soak for 10 minutes. Dry thoroughly on kitchen paper. Roughly chop the smoked and fresh fish and place in a food processor or blender.

2 Seed and finely chop the chilli, then add with the garlic, lemon grass, spring onions, the sauce and the coconut milk, and process until well blended with the fish. Add the eggs and coriander and process for a few more seconds. Cover with clear film (plastic wrap) and chill in the refrigerator for 1 hour.

3 To make the fish cakes, flour your hands with cornflour and shape teaspoonfuls of the mixture into neat balls, then coat them with flour.

4 Heat 5–7.5cm/2–3in oil in a medium pan until a crust of bread turns golden in about 1 minute. Fry the fish balls 5 or 6 at a time, turning them carefully for 2–3 minutes, until they turn golden all over. Remove with a slotted spoon and drain on kitchen paper. Keep the fish cakes warm until all are cooked. Serve with dipping sauces.

Thai Fish Cakes Energy 86kcal/361kJ; Protein 6.2g; Carbohydrate 8.1g, of which sugars 5.4g; Fat 3.4g, of which saturates 0.5g; Cholesterol 27mg; Calcium 16mg; Fibre 0.2g; Sodium 2040mg.
Eggy Thai Fish Cakes Energy 60kcal/250kJ; Protein 6.2g; Carbohydrate 0.9g, of which sugars 0.2g; Fat 3.5g, of which saturates 0.5g; Cholesterol 29mg; Calcium 15mg; Fibre 0.1g; Sodium 152mg.

Mini Saffron Fish Cakes

A scented cucumber salad makes a superbly refreshing accompaniment for these fish cakes. Both the fish cakes and salad include sweet and spicy flavours. If you can't buy fresh fish, tuna canned in spring water or brine (drained) is a good substitute.

Serves 6

450g/1lb white fish fillets, such as sea bass, ling or haddock, skinned and cut into chunks
10ml/2 tsp harissa
rind of ½ preserved lemon, finely chopped
small bunch of fresh coriander (cilantro), finely chopped
1 egg
5ml/1 tsp clear honey
pinch of saffron threads, soaked in 5ml/1 tsp hot water
15ml/1 tbsp sunflower oil
salt and ground black pepper

For the salad
2 cucumbers, peeled and grated
juice of 1 orange
juice of ½ lemon
15–30ml/1–2 tbsp orange flower water
15–20ml/3–4 tsp caster (superfine) sugar
2.5ml/½ tsp ground cinnamon

1 Make the salad in advance so that it has time to chill. Place the cucumber in a colander over a bowl and sprinkle with salt. Leave to drain for about 10 minutes. Squeeze out the excess liquid and place the cucumber in a bowl. To make the dressing, combine the orange and lemon juice, orange flower water and sugar and pour over the cucumber. Toss well to mix, sprinkle with cinnamon and chill for at least 1 hour.

2 To make the fish cakes, put the fish in a food processor. Add the harissa, preserved lemon, chopped coriander, egg, honey, saffron with its soaking water, and seasoning, and whizz until smooth. Divide the mixture into 18 equal portions. Wet your hands under cold water to prevent the mixture from sticking to them, then roll each portion into a ball and flatten in the palm of your hand.

3 Heat the oil in a large non-stick frying pan and fry the fish cakes in batches, until golden brown on each side. Drain on kitchen paper and keep hot until all the fish cakes are cooked. Serve with the chilled cucumber salad.

Pimiento Tartlets

These pretty Spanish tartlets are filled with strips of roasted sweet peppers and a creamy, cheesy custard. They make a perfect snack to serve with drinks.

Serves 4

1 red (bell) pepper
1 yellow (bell) pepper
175g/6oz/1½ cups plain (all-purpose) flour
75g/3oz/6 tbsp chilled butter, diced
30–45ml/2–3 tbsp cold water
60ml/4 tbsp double (heavy) cream
1 egg
15ml/1 tbsp grated Parmesan cheese
salt and ground black pepper

1 Preheat the oven to 200°C/400°F/Gas 6, and heat the grill (broiler). Place the peppers on a baking sheet and grill (broil) for 10 minutes, turning occasionally, until blackened. Cover with a dish towel and leave for 5 minutes. Peel away the skin, then discard the seeds and cut the flesh into very thin strips.

2 Sift the flour and a pinch of salt into a bowl. Add the butter and rub it in until the mixture resembles fine breadcrumbs. Stir in enough of the water to make a firm, not sticky, dough.

3 Roll the dough out thinly on a lightly floured surface and line 12 individual moulds or a 12-hole tartlet tin (muffin pan). Prick the bases with a fork and fill the pastry cases with crumpled foil. Bake for 10 minutes, then remove the foil and divide the pepper strips among the pastry cases.

4 Whisk the cream and egg in a bowl. Season and pour over the peppers. Sprinkle each tartlet with Parmesan and bake for 15–20 minutes until firm. Cool for 2 minutes, then remove from the moulds and transfer to a wire rack. Serve warm or cold.

Variation
Use strips of grilled aubergine (eggplant) mixed with sun-dried tomatoes in place of the roasted (bell) peppers.

Saffron Fish Cakes Energy 115kcal/481kJ; Protein 15.6g; Carbohydrate 5.6g, of which sugars 5.5g; Fat 3.5g, of which saturates 0.6g; Cholesterol 66mg; Calcium 42mg; Fibre 0.8g; Sodium 63mg.
Pimiento Tartlets Energy 427kcal/1778kJ; Protein 8.4g; Carbohydrate 40g, of which sugars 6.4g; Fat 27g, of which saturates 16.1g; Cholesterol 112mg; Calcium 131mg; Fibre 2.8g; Sodium 180mg.

Smoked Chicken with Peach Mayonnaise in Filo Tartlets

The filling for these tartlets can be prepared a day in advance and chilled, but only fill the pastry cases when you are ready to serve.

Makes 12

25g/1oz/2 tbsp butter
3 sheets of filo pastry, each measuring 45 x 28cm/ 18 x 11in, thawed if frozen
2 skinless, boneless smoked chicken breast portions, finely sliced
150ml/¼ pint/⅔ cup mayonnaise
grated (shredded) rind of 1 lime
30ml/2 tbsp lime juice
2 ripe peaches, peeled, stoned (pitted) and chopped
salt and ground black pepper
fresh tarragon sprigs, lime slices and salad leaves, to garnish

1 Preheat the oven to 200°C/400°F/Gas 6. Place the butter in a small pan and heat gently until melted. Lightly brush 12 mini flan rings with a little melted butter.

2 Cut each sheet of filo pastry into 12 equal rounds large enough to line the tins and stand above the rims. Place a round of pastry in each tin and brush with a little butter, then add another round of pastry. Brush each with more butter and add a third round of pastry.

3 Bake the tartlets for 5 minutes. Leave in the tins for a few moments before transferring to a wire rack to cool. Once cool, store in a tin until ready to use.

4 Mix together the chicken, mayonnaise, lime rind and peaches and season with salt and pepper. Chill for at least 30 minutes, preferably overnight. Just before serving, spoon the chicken mixture into the filo pastry cases and garnish with tarragon, lime slices and salad leaves.

Cook's Tip
You can use small tartlet tins (muffin pans) if you do not have any mini flan rings.

Leek, Saffron and Mussel Tartlets

Serve these vividly coloured little tarts with cherry tomatoes and salad leaves.

Makes 12

4 large yellow (bell) peppers, halved
2kg/4½lb mussels, scrubbed and beards removed
large pinch of saffron threads
30ml/2 tbsp hot water
4 large leeks, sliced
60ml/4 tbsp olive oil
4 large (US extra large) eggs
600ml/1 pint/2½ cups single (light) cream
60ml/4 tbsp chopped fresh parsley
salt and ground black pepper

For the pastry
450g/1lb/4 cups plain (all-purpose) flour
5ml/1 tsp salt
250g/8oz/1 cup butter, diced
30–45ml/2–3 tbsp water

1 To make the pastry, mix together the flour and salt and rub in the butter. Mix in the water and knead lightly. Wrap the dough in clear film (plastic wrap) and chill for 30 minutes.

2 Grill (broil) the pepper halves, skin sides uppermost, until blackened. Place them in a plastic bag and leave for 10 minutes, then peel and cut the flesh into thin strips.

3 Preheat the oven to 190°C/375°F/Gas 5. Use the pastry to line twelve 10cm/4in tartlet tins (muffin pans), 2.5cm/1in deep. Prick the bases and line with foil. Bake for 10 minutes. Remove the foil and bake for another 5–8 minutes, or until lightly coloured. Reduce the oven temperature to 180°C/350°F/Gas 4.

4 Soak the saffron in the hot water for 10 minutes. Fry the leeks in the oil for 6–8 minutes until beginning to brown. Add the pepper strips and cook for another 2 minutes.

5 Put the mussels in a large pan and discard any open mussels that do not shut when tapped sharply. Cover and cook, shaking the pan occasionally, for 3–4 minutes, or until the mussels open. Discard any mussels that do not open. Shell the remainder. Beat the eggs, cream, saffron liquid and parsley together and season. Arrange the leeks, peppers and mussels in the pastry, add the egg mixture and bake for 20–25 minutes, until just firm.

Chicken in Filo Tartlets Energy 246kcal/1021kJ; Protein 7g; Carbohydrate 6.3g, of which sugars 1.4g; Fat 21.7g, of which saturates 4.5g; Cholesterol 42mg; Calcium 13mg; Fibre 0.4g; Sodium 146mg.
Leek Tartlets Energy 506kcal/2112kJ; Protein 17.2g; Carbohydrate 35.1g, of which sugars 6.1g; Fat 34.1g, of which saturates 18.3g; Cholesterol 155mg; Calcium 221mg; Fibre 2.8g; Sodium 273mg.

Crab and Ricotta Tartlets

Use the meat from a freshly cooked crab, weighing about 450g/1lb, if you can. Otherwise, look out for frozen brown and white crab meat as an alternative.

Serves 4

225g/8oz/2 cups plain (all-purpose) flour
pinch of salt
115g/4oz/½ cup butter, diced
225g/8oz/1 cup ricotta cheese
15ml/1 tbsp grated onion
30ml/2 tbsp grated Parmesan cheese
2.5ml/½ tsp mustard powder
2 eggs, plus 1 egg yolk
225g/8oz crab meat
30ml/2 tbsp chopped fresh parsley
2.5–5ml/½–1 tsp anchovy essence (paste)
5–10ml/1–2 tsp lemon juice
salt and cayenne pepper
salad leaves, to garnish

1 Preheat the oven to 200°C/400°F/Gas 6. Sift the flour and salt into a bowl, add the butter and rub it in until it resembles fine breadcrumbs. Stir in about 60ml/4 tbsp cold water.

2 Turn the dough on to a floured surface and knead lightly. Roll out and line four 10cm/4in tartlet tins (muffin pans). Prick the bases with a fork, then chill for 30 minutes.

3 Line the bases with baking parchment and fill with baking beans. Bake for 10 minutes, remove the paper and beans and bake for another 10 minutes.

4 Place the ricotta cheese, onion, Parmesan and mustard powder in a bowl and beat until soft. Gradually beat in the eggs and egg yolk.

5 Stir in the crab meat and chopped fresh parsley, then add the anchovy essence and lemon juice. Season to taste with salt and cayenne pepper.

6 Remove the tartlet cases from the oven and reduce the temperature to 180°C/350°F/Gas 4. Spoon the filling into the cases and bake for 20 minutes, until set and golden. Serve hot, garnished with salad leaves.

Garlic Prawns in Filo Tartlets

Tartlets made with crisp golden layers of filo pastry and filled with spicy garlic and chilli prawns make a tempting appetizer. They will be ideal for any occasion such as a buffet or party.

Serves 4

For the tartlets
50g/2oz/¼ cup butter, melted
2–3 large sheets filo pastry

For the filling
115g/4oz/½ cup butter
2–3 garlic cloves, crushed
1 red chilli, seeded and finely shredded
350g/12oz/3 cups cooked peeled prawns (shrimp)
30ml/2 tbsp chopped fresh parsley
salt and ground black pepper
salad leaves, to serve

1 Preheat the oven to 200°C/400°F/Gas 6. Lightly brush four individual 7.5cm/3in flan tins (pans) with the melted butter.

2 Cut the filo pastry into twelve 10cm/4in squares and brush with the melted butter. Place three squares of pastry inside each tin, overlapping them at slight angles and carefully frilling the edges and points while forming a good hollow in the centre of each case.

3 Bake the pastry in the oven for 10–15 minutes, until crisp and golden. Leave to cool slightly, then carefully remove the pastry cases from the tins, taking care not to break off the points of the pastry cases.

4 Meanwhile, make the filling. Melt the butter in a frying pan, then add the garlic, chilli and prawns and fry quickly for about 1–2 minutes to warm through. Stir in the parsley and season with salt and plenty of pepper. Spoon the prawn filling into the tartlets and serve immediately, with a few green salad leaves on the side.

Cook's Tip
If you prefer your spicy food with a little more heat, then simply add another fresh chilli, or choose a hotter variety.

Crab Tartlets Energy 644kcal/2685kJ; Protein 28.1g; Carbohydrate 46.3g, of which sugars 3.3g; Fat 39.8g, of which saturates 23g; Cholesterol 278mg; Calcium 288mg; Fibre 2.4g; Sodium 609mg.
Garlic Prawns Energy 440kcal/1825kJ; Protein 17.6g; Carbohydrate 15g, of which sugars 0.7g; Fat 34.8g, of which saturates 21.6g; Cholesterol 259mg; Calcium 118mg; Fibre 1g; Sodium 419mg.

Filo Cigars Filled with Feta, Parsley, Mint and Dill

These classic cigar-shaped Turkish pastries are popular snack and meze food, and they are also good as nibbles with drinks. In this version they are filled with cheese and herbs, but other popular fillings include aromatic minced meat, baked aubergine and cheese, or pumpkin, cheese and dill. The filo pastry can be folded into triangles, but cigars are the most traditional shape. They can be prepared in advance and kept under a damp dish towel in the refrigerator until you are ready to fry them at the last minute.

Serves 3–4

225g/8oz feta cheese
1 egg, lightly beaten
1 small bunch each of fresh flat leaf parsley, mint and dill, finely chopped
4–5 sheets of filo pastry
sunflower oil, for deep-frying
dill fronds, to garnish (optional)

1 In a bowl, mash the feta with a fork. Beat in the egg and fold in the herbs. Working with one sheet at a time, cut the filo into strips about 10–13cm/4–5in wide, and pile them on top of each other. Keep the strips covered with a damp dish towel.

2 Place a heaped teaspoon of the cheese filling along one of the short ends of a strip. Roll the end over the filling, quite tightly to keep it in place, then tuck in the sides to seal in the filling and continue to roll until you get to the other end.

3 Brush the tip with a little water to help seal the roll. Place the filled cigar, join side down, on a plate and cover with a damp dish towel to keep it moist. Continue with the remaining sheets of filo and filling.

4 Heat enough oil for deep-frying in a wok or other heavy, deep-sided pan, and deep-fry the filo cigars in batches for about 5–6 minutes until crisp and golden brown. Lift out of the oil with a slotted spoon and drain on kitchen paper. Serve immediately, garnished with dill fronds, if you like.

Tung Tong

Popularly called 'gold bags', these crisp pastry purses from Thailand have a coriander-flavoured filling based on water chestnuts and corn. They are the perfect vegetarian snack and look very impressive.

Serves 6

18 spring roll wrappers, about 8cm/3¼in square, thawed if frozen
oil, for deep-frying
plum sauce, to serve

For the filling

4 baby corn cobs
130g/4½oz can water chestnuts, drained and chopped
1 shallot, coarsely chopped
1 egg, separated
30ml/2 tbsp cornflour (cornstarch)
60ml/4 tbsp water
small bunch fresh coriander (cilantro), chopped
salt and ground black pepper

1 Make the filling. Place the baby corn, water chestnuts, shallot and egg yolk in a food processor or blender. Process to a coarse paste. Place the egg white in a cup and whisk it lightly with a fork.

2 Put the cornflour in a small pan and stir in the water until smooth. Add the corn mixture and chopped coriander and season with salt and pepper to taste. Cook over a low heat, stirring constantly, until thickened.

3 Leave the filling to cool slightly, then place 5ml/1 tsp in the centre of a spring roll wrapper. Brush the edges with the beaten egg white, then gather up the points and press them firmly together to make a pouch or bag.

4 Repeat with remaining wrappers and filling, keeping the finished bags and the wrappers covered until needed so they do not dry out.

5 Heat the oil in a deep-fryer or wok until a cube of bread browns in about 45 seconds. Fry the bags, in batches, for about 5 minutes, until golden brown and crispy. Drain thoroughly on kitchen paper and serve hot, with the plum sauce.

Filo Cigars Energy 311kcal/1291kJ; Protein 12.4g; Carbohydrate 11.2g, of which sugars 1.6g; Fat 24.4g, of which saturates 9.5g; Cholesterol 92mg; Calcium 278mg; Fibre 1.7g; Sodium 838mg.
Tung Tong Energy 55kcal/229kJ; Protein 1.2g; Carbohydrate 6.3g, of which sugars 0.4g; Fat 2.9g, of which saturates 0.4g; Cholesterol 12mg; Calcium 19mg; Fibre 0.5g; Sodium 42mg.

Green Curry Puffs

Shrimp paste and green curry sauce, used judiciously, give these puffs their distinctive, spicy, savoury flavour, and the addition of chilli steps up the heat.

Serves 6–8

24 small wonton wrappers, about 8cm/3¼in square, thawed if frozen
15ml/1 tbsp cornflour (cornstarch), mixed to a paste with 30ml/2 tbsp water
oil, for deep-frying
few chives, to garnish

For the filling

1 small potato, about 115g/4oz, boiled and mashed
25g/1oz/¼ cup cooked petits pois (baby peas)
25g/1oz/¼ cup cooked corn
few sprigs fresh coriander (cilantro), chopped
1 small fresh red chilli, seeded and finely chopped
½ lemon grass stalk, finely chopped
15ml/1 tbsp soy sauce
5ml/1 tsp Thai fish sauce
5ml/1 tsp Thai green curry paste
chives, to garnish

1 Mix together the filling ingredients until well combined. Lay out one wonton wrapper and place a teaspoon of the filling in the centre. Wonton wrappers dry out quickly, so keep them covered using clear film (plastic wrap) until you need them.

2 Brush a little of the cornflour paste along two sides of the square. Fold the other two sides over to meet them, then press together to make a triangular pastry and seal in the filling. Make more pastries in the same way.

3 Heat the oil in a karahi, wok or deep-fryer to a temperature of 190°C/375°F or until a cube of bread, dropped in the oil, browns in about 45 seconds.

4 Add the pastries to the oil, a few at a time, and fry them for about 5 minutes, until golden brown.

5 Remove the puffs from the karahi, wok or deep-fryer and drain on kitchen paper. If you intend to serve the puffs hot, place them in a low oven to keep warm while cooking successive batches. The puffs also taste good cold. Garnish with chives before serving.

Mini Sausage Rolls

These miniature versions of sausage rolls are always popular – the Parmesan gives them an extra special flavour.

Serves 8–10

15g/½oz/1 tbsp butter
1 onion, finely chopped
350g/12oz good quality sausage meat (bulk sausage)
15ml/1 tbsp dried mixed herbs such as oregano, thyme, sage, tarragon or dill
25g/1oz finely chopped pistachio nuts (optional)
350g/12oz puff pastry, thawed if frozen
60–90ml/4–6 tbsp freshly grated Parmesan cheese
salt and ground black pepper
1 egg, lightly beaten, for glazing
poppy seeds, sesame seeds, fennel seeds and aniseeds, for sprinkling

1 In a small frying pan, over medium heat, melt the butter. Add the onion and cook for about 5 minutes, until softened. Remove from the heat and cool. Put the onion, sausage meat, herbs, salt and pepper and nuts, if using, in a mixing bowl and stir together until completely blended.

2 Divide the sausage mixture into four equal portions and roll into thin sausages measuring about 25cm/10in long. Set aside.

3 On a lightly floured surface, roll out the pastry to about 3mm/⅛in thick. Cut the pastry into four strips 25 x 7.5cm/10 x 3in long. Place a long sausage on each pastry strip and sprinkle each with a little Parmesan cheese.

4 Brush one long edge of each of the pastry strips with the egg glaze and roll up to enclose each sausage. Set them seam side down and press gently to seal. Brush each with the egg glaze and sprinkle with one type of seeds. Repeat with remaining pastry strips, using different seeds.

5 Preheat the oven to 220°C/425°F/Gas 7. Lightly grease a large baking sheet. Cut each of the pastry logs into 2.5cm/1in lengths and arrange on the baking sheet. Bake for about 15 minutes until the pastry is crisp and brown. Serve warm or allow to cool before serving.

Green Curry Puffs Energy 32kcal/134kJ; Protein 1g; Carbohydrate 6.7g, of which sugars 0.4g; Fat 0.3g, of which saturates 0g; Cholesterol 1mg; Calcium 16mg; Fibre 0.4g; Sodium 58mg.
Mini Sausage Rolls Energy 59kcal/245kJ; Protein 1.8g; Carbohydrate 3.7g, of which sugars 0.3g; Fat 4.3g, of which saturates 1.2g; Cholesterol 9mg; Calcium 24mg; Fibre 0.1g; Sodium 99mg.

Chorizo Pastry Puffs

These flaky pastry puffs make a really superb accompaniment to a glass of cold sherry or beer. For best results, choose a mild cheese, as the chorizo has plenty of flavour.

Serves 8

225g/8oz puff pastry, thawed if frozen
115g/4oz cured chorizo sausage, finely chopped
50g/2oz/½ cup grated cheese
1 small (US medium) egg, beaten
5ml/1 tsp paprika

1 Roll out the pastry thinly on a floured work surface. Using a 7.5cm/3in cutter, stamp out 16 rounds.

2 Preheat the oven to 230°C/450°F/Gas 8. Put the chopped chorizo sausage and grated cheese in a bowl and toss together lightly until combined.

3 Lay one of the pastry rounds in the palm of your hand and place a little of the chorizo mixture across the centre. Using your other hand, pinch the edges of the pastry together along the top to seal. Repeat the process with the remaining rounds to make 16 puffs in all.

4 Place the pastries on a non-stick baking sheet and brush lightly with the beaten egg. Dust the tops of the pastries lightly with a little paprika.

5 Bake the pastries in the oven for 10–12 minutes, until puffed and golden. Serve the chorizo pastry puffs warm, dusted with the remaining paprika.

Cook's Tip
Chorizo is a spicy pork sausage flavoured with garlic, chilli and other spices. It is popular in Mexican and Spanish cuisine. Remove the casing on the sausage before cooking.

Duck Egg Nests

These attractive parcels are usually made using a conical dispenser, but a thin funnel also works well.

Makes about 12–15

4 coriander (cilantro) roots
2 garlic cloves
10 white peppercorns
pinch of salt
45ml/3 tbsp oil
1 small onion, finely chopped
115g/4oz minced (ground) pork
75g/3oz shelled prawns (shrimp), chopped
50g/2oz/½ cup roasted peanuts, ground
5ml/1 tsp palm sugar (jaggery)
Thai fish sauce, to taste
6 duck eggs
coriander (cilantro) leaves
spring onion (scallion) tassels and sliced red chillies, to garnish

1 Using a mortar and pestle, grind the coriander roots, garlic, white peppercorns and salt into a paste.

2 Heat 30ml/2 tbsp of the oil, add the paste and fry until fragrant. Add the onion and cook, stirring, until softened. Add the pork and prawns and continue to stir-fry until the meat is cooked through.

3 Add the peanuts, palm sugar, salt and fish sauce, to taste. Stir the mixture and continue to cook until it becomes a little sticky. Remove from the heat. Transfer the mixture to a small bowl and set aside.

4 Beat the duck eggs in a bowl. Grease a non-stick frying pan with the remaining oil and heat. Using a small hole funnel or squeezy bottle, trail the eggs across the pan to make a net pattern, about 13cm/5in in diameter.

5 When the net is set, carefully remove it from the pan, and repeat until all the eggs have been used up.

6 To assemble, lay a few coriander leaves on each nest and top with a spoonful of the filling. Turn in the edges to make neat square shapes. Repeat with the rest of the nests. Arrange on a serving dish, garnish and serve immediately.

Chorizo Pastry Puffs Energy 183kcal/763kJ; Protein 5.4g; Carbohydrate 12.1g, of which sugars 0.6g; Fat 13.1g, of which saturates 3g; Cholesterol 36mg; Calcium 73mg; Fibre 0.1g; Sodium 258mg.
Duck Egg Nests Energy 90kcal/376kJ; Protein 6.1g; Carbohydrate 1.1g, of which sugars 0.8g; Fat 6.9g, of which saturates 1.4g; Cholesterol 151mg; Calcium 23mg; Fibre 0.3g; Sodium 43mg.

Crackling Rice Paper Seafood Rolls

The wrappers hold their shape during cooking, yet dissolve in your mouth when eaten.

Makes 12

12 rice paper sheets, each about 20 x 10cm/8 x 4in
45ml/3 tbsp flour mixed to a paste with 45ml/3 tbsp water
vegetable oil, for deep-frying
fresh herbs, to garnish

For the filling

24 young asparagus spears, trimmed
225g/8oz raw prawns (shrimp), peeled and deveined
25ml/1½ tbsp olive oil
6 spring onions (scallions), finely chopped
1 garlic clove, crushed
2cm/¾in piece of fresh root ginger, grated
30ml/2 tbsp chopped fresh coriander (cilantro)
5ml/1 tsp five-spice powder
5ml/1 tsp finely grated lime or lemon rind
salt and ground black pepper

1 Make the filling. Bring a pan of lightly salted water to the boil; cook the asparagus for 3–4 minutes until tender. Drain, refresh under cold water and drain again. Cut the prawns into thirds.

2 Heat half of the oil in a small frying pan or wok and stir-fry the spring onions and garlic over a low heat for 2–3 minutes until soft. Transfer to a bowl and set aside.

3 Heat the remaining oil in the pan and stir-fry the prawns until they start to go pink. Add to the spring onion mixture with the remaining ingredients. Stir to mix.

4 To make each roll, brush a sheet of rice paper liberally with water and lay it on a clean surface. Place two asparagus spears and a spoonful of the prawn mixture just off centre. Fold in the sides and roll up to make a fat cigar. Seal the ends with a little of the flour paste.

5 Heat the oil in a deep-fryer and fry the rolls in batches until pale golden. Drain well, garnish with herbs and serve.

Popiah

This delectable creation is a great do-it-yourself dish to serve as an appetizer.

Serves 4–6

45ml/3 tbsp vegetable oil
225g/8oz firm tofu, rinsed, drained and diced
4 garlic cloves, finely chopped
4 rashers (strips) streaky (fatty) bacon, finely sliced
45ml/3 tbsp fermented soya beans, mashed
450g/1lb fresh prawns (shrimp), peeled and deveined
225g/8oz jicama (sweet turnip), peeled and shredded
450g/1lb bamboo shoots, grated
15ml/1 tbsp dark soy sauce
10ml/2 tsp sugar
4–6 fresh red chillies, seeded and pounded
6–8 garlic cloves, crushed
kecap manis
12 cos or romaine lettuce leaves
1 small cucumber, peeled, seeded and finely shredded
225g/8oz/1 cup beansprouts
2 Chinese sausages, fried and sliced
225g/8oz cooked prawns (shrimp), peeled
225g/8oz cooked crab meat
1 omelette, sliced into thin ribbons
fresh coriander (cilantro) leaves, roughly chopped
12 popiah wraps or Mexican corn tortillas
coriander (cilantro) leaves, to garnish

1 Heat the oil in a wok or heavy pan. Fry the tofu until golden brown. Remove from the oil and pat dry on kitchen paper.

2 Fry the garlic and bacon in the oil until they begin to colour. Stir in the fermented soya beans and fresh prawns. Add the jicama, bamboo shoots, soy sauce and sugar. Fry over a high heat to reduce the liquid. Toss in the fried tofu and cook the mixture gently until almost dry. Transfer to a serving dish.

3 Put the remaining ingredients in separate bowls on the table. Place the wraps on a serving plate. To serve, let everyone help themselves to a wrap. Smear the wrap with the chilli and garlic pastes, followed by the kecap manis, a lettuce leaf, a layer of cucumber and beansprouts, and a spoonful of the cooked filling. Add Chinese sausage, prawns and crab meat to the wrap. Place a few strips of omelette on top with a sprinkling of coriander, then fold the edge of the wrap over the filling, tuck in the ends and roll it up. Garnish with coriander and serve.

Crackling Rice Energy 105kcal/438kJ; Protein 5g; Carbohydrate 8.8g, of which sugars 0.7g; Fat 5.6g, of which saturates 0.7g; Cholesterol 37mg; Calcium 36mg; Fibre 0.8g; Sodium 38mg.
Popiah Energy 457kcal/1916kJ; Protein 32.3g; Carbohydrate 39.3g, of which sugars 5.8g; Fat 20.1g, of which saturates 4.9g; Cholesterol 213mg; Calcium 396mg; Fibre 4.5g; Sodium 989mg.

Pork and Peanut Wontons with Plum Sauce

These crispy filled wontons are delicious served with a sweet plum dipping sauce. The wontons can be filled and set aside for up to eight hours before they are cooked.

Makes 40–50

175g/6oz/1 ½ cups minced (ground) pork or 175g/6oz pork sausages, skinned
2 spring onions (scallions), finely chopped
30ml/2 tbsp peanut butter
10ml/2 tsp oyster sauce (optional)
40–50 wonton skins
30ml/2 tbsp flour paste
vegetable oil, for deep-frying
salt and ground black pepper
lettuce and radishes, to garnish

For the plum sauce
225g/8oz/generous ¾ cup dark plum jam
15ml/1 tbsp rice or white wine vinegar
15ml/1 tbsp dark soy sauce
2.5ml/½ tsp chilli sauce

1 Combine the minced pork or skinned sausages, spring onions, peanut butter, oyster sauce, if using, and seasoning, and then set aside.

2 For the sauce, combine the plum jam, vinegar, soy and chilli sauces in a serving bowl and set aside.

3 To fill the wonton skins, place eight wrappers at a time on a work surface, moisten the edges with the flour paste and place 2.5ml/½ tsp of the filling on each one. Fold in half, corner to corner, and twist.

4 Fill a wok or deep frying pan one-third with vegetable oil and heat to 190°C/375°F. Have ready a wire strainer or frying basket and a tray lined with kitchen paper. Drop the wontons, eight at a time, into the hot fat and then fry until they are golden all over, for about 1–2 minutes. Lift out on to the paper-lined tray, using a slotted spoon, and sprinkle with fine salt.

5 Serve the wontons with the plum sauce, garnished with the lettuce and radishes.

Five-spice and Ginger Pork Wontons

Fresh ginger and Chinese five-spice powder flavour this version of steamed open dumplings – a favourite appetizer in many Chinese teahouses.

Makes 36

2 large Chinese leaves (Chinese cabbage), plus extra for lining the steamer
2 spring onions (scallions), finely chopped
1cm/½in piece fresh root ginger, finely chopped
50g/2oz canned water chestnuts (drained weight), rinsed and finely chopped
225g/8oz minced (ground) pork
2.5ml/½ tsp Chinese five-spice powder
15ml/1 tbsp cornflour (cornstarch)
15ml/1 tbsp light soy sauce
15ml/1 tbsp Chinese rice wine
10ml/2 tsp sesame oil
pinch of caster (superfine) sugar
about 36 wonton wrappers, each 7.5cm/3in square
light soy sauce and hot chilli oil, for dipping

1 Place the Chinese leaves one on top of another. Cut them lengthways into quarters and then across into thin shreds.

2 Place the shredded Chinese leaves in a bowl. Mix in the spring onions, ginger, water chestnuts, pork, five-spice powder, cornflour, soy sauce, rice wine, sesame oil and sugar.

3 Set one wonton wrapper on a work surface. Place a heaped teaspoon of the filling in the centre of the wrapper, then lightly dampen the edges with water.

4 Lift the wrapper up around the filling, gathering to form a purse. Squeeze the wrapper firmly around the middle, then tap on the bottom to make a flat base. The top should be open. Place the wonton on a tray and cover with a damp dish towel.

5 Line the steamer with Chinese leaves and steam the dumplings for 12–15 minutes until tender. Remove each batch from the steamer as soon as they are cooked, cover with foil and keep warm. Serve the dumplings hot with soy sauce and chilli oil for dipping.

Pork and Peanut Wontons Energy 56kcal/236kJ; Protein 1.5g; Carbohydrate 7.9g, of which sugars 4.1g; Fat 2.3g, of which saturates 0.4g; Cholesterol 3mg; Calcium 8mg; Fibre 0.2g; Sodium 35mg.
Five-spice Wontons Energy 23kcal/96kJ; Protein 1.8g; Carbohydrate 2.9g, of which sugars 0.4g; Fat 0.5g, of which saturates 0.1g; Cholesterol 4mg; Calcium 9mg; Fibre 0.2g; Sodium 35mg.

Duck Wontons with Mango Sauce

These Chinese-style wontons are easy to make using ready-cooked smoked duck or chicken, or you could even use leftovers from the Sunday roast.

Makes about 40

15ml/1 tbsp light soy sauce
5ml/1 tsp sesame oil
2 spring onions (scallions), finely chopped
grated rind of ½ orange
5ml/1 tsp brown sugar
275g/10oz/1½ cups chopped smoked duck
about 40 small wonton wrappers
15ml/1 tbsp vegetable oil
whole fresh chives, to garnish (optional)

For the mango sauce
30ml/2 tbsp vegetable oil
5ml/1 tsp ground cumin
2.5ml/½ tsp ground cardamom
1.5ml/¼ tsp ground cinnamon
250ml/8fl oz/1 cup mango purée (made from 1 large mango)
15ml/1 tbsp clear honey
2.5ml/½ tsp Chinese chilli sauce (or to taste)
15ml/1 tbsp cider vinegar
chopped fresh chives, to garnish

1 First prepare the sauce. In a medium pan, heat the oil over a medium-low heat. Add the ground cumin, cardamom and cinnamon and cook for about 3 minutes, stirring constantly.

2 Stir in the mango purée, honey, chilli sauce and vinegar. Remove from the heat and leave to cool. Pour into a bowl and cover until ready to serve.

3 Prepare the wonton filling. In a large bowl, mix together the soy sauce, sesame oil, spring onions, orange rind and brown sugar until well blended. Add the duck and toss to coat well.

4 Place a teaspoonful of the duck mixture in the centre of each wonton wrapper. Brush the edges with water and then draw them up to the centre, twisting to seal and form a pouch shape.

5 Preheat the oven to 190°F/375°C/Gas 5. Line a large baking sheet with foil and brush lightly with oil. Arrange the wontons on the baking sheet and bake for 10–12 minutes until crisp and golden. Serve with the mango sauce garnished with chopped fresh chives. If you wish, tie each wonton with a fresh chive.

Pork-stuffed Steamed Buns

These treats are just one example of dim sum, featherlight steamed buns with a range of tasty fillings. They are now a popular snack the world over.

Serves 4

For the basic dough
15ml/1 tbsp sugar
about 300ml/½ pint/1¼ cups warm water
25ml/1½ tbsp dried yeast
450g/1lb/4 cups strong white flour
5ml/1 tsp salt
15g/½oz/1 tbsp lard or white cooking fat
chives, to garnish

For the filling
30ml/2 tbsp oil
1 garlic clove, crushed
225g/8oz roast pork, very finely chopped
2 spring onions (scallions), chopped
10ml/2 tsp yellow bean sauce, crushed
10ml/2 tsp sugar
5ml/1 tsp cornflour (cornstarch) mixed to a paste with water

1 Make the dough. Dissolve the sugar in half the water. Sprinkle in the yeast. Stir well, then leave for 10–15 minutes until frothy. Sift the flour and salt into a bowl and rub in the lard. Stir in the yeast mixture with enough of the remaining water to make a soft dough. Knead on a floured surface for 10 minutes. Transfer to an oiled bowl and cover. Leave in a warm place for 1 hour until doubled in bulk.

2 Meanwhile, make the filling. Heat the oil and fry the garlic until golden. Add the pork, spring onions, sauce and sugar. Stir in the cornflour paste and cook, stirring, until thickened. Leave to cool.

3 Knock back (punch down) the dough. Knead it for 2 minutes, then divide into 16 pieces. Roll out each piece on a floured work surface to a 7.5–10cm/3–4in round.

4 Place a spoonful of filling in the centre of each, gather up the sides and twist the top to seal. Secure with string.

5 Set the buns on baking parchment in a large steamer and leave in a warm place until they have doubled in size. Steam over boiling water for 30–35 minutes. Serve hot, garnished with chives.

Duck Wontons Energy 95kcal/404kJ; Protein 6.8g; Carbohydrate 14.7g, of which sugars 0.4g; Fat 1.9g, of which saturates 0.4g; Cholesterol 28mg; Calcium 35mg; Fibre 0.7g; Sodium 36mg.
Pork-stuffed Buns Energy 588kcal/2468kJ; Protein 14g; Carbohydrate 76.4g, of which sugars 14g; Fat 27.3g, of which saturates 8.5g; Cholesterol 29mg; Calcium 137mg; Fibre 2.8g; Sodium 722mg.

Crab Dim Sum with Chinese Chives

These delectable Chinese-style dumplings have a wonderfully sticky texture and make a perfect appetizer. You can make these in advance, storing them in the refrigerator until ready to cook. Steam them just before serving, then enjoy the sensation as your teeth sink through the soft wrapper into the savoury crab filling.

Serves 4

150g/5oz fresh white crab meat
115g/4oz minced (ground) pork
30ml/2 tbsp chopped Chinese chives
15ml/1 tbsp finely chopped red (bell) pepper
30ml/2 tbsp sweet chilli sauce
30ml/2 tbsp hoisin sauce
24 fresh dumpling wrappers (available from Asian stores)
Chinese chives, to garnish
chilli oil and soy sauce, to serve

1 Place the crab meat, pork and chopped chives in a bowl. Add the red pepper and mix well, then pour in the sweet chilli and hoisin sauces. Stir until thoroughly combined.

2 Working with two or three wrappers at a time, put a spoonful of the mixture on to each wrapper. Brush the edges of a wrapper with water and fold over to form a half-moon shape. Press and pleat the edges to seal, and flatten. Cover with a clean, damp dish towel and make the rest.

3 Arrange the dumplings on three lightly oiled plates and fit inside three tiers of a bamboo steamer. Alternatively, use a stainless steel steamer or an electric steamer.

4 Cover the bamboo steamer and place over a wok of simmering water (making sure the water does not touch the steamer). Steam for about 8–10 minutes, or until the dumplings are cooked through and they have become slightly translucent. If cooking the dumplings in an electric steamer follow the manufacturer's instructions.

5 Divide the dumplings among four plates. Garnish with Chinese chives and serve immediately with chilli oil and soy sauce for dipping.

Crab and Tofu Dumplings

These little crab and ginger-flavoured dumplings are usually served as a side dish but they are just as good as an appetizer or snack.

Serves 4–6

115g/4oz frozen white crab meat, thawed
115g/4oz tofu
1 egg yolk
30ml/2 tbsp rice flour or wheat flour
30ml/2 tbsp finely chopped spring onion (scallion), green part only
2cm/¾in fresh root ginger, grated
10ml/2 tsp light soy sauce
salt
vegetable oil, for deep-frying
50g/2oz mooli (daikon), very finely grated, to serve

For the dipping sauce

120ml/4fl oz/½ cup vegetable stock
15ml/1 tbsp sugar
45ml/3 tbsp dark soy sauce

1 Using your hands, squeeze as much moisture out of the crab meat as you can. Press the tofu through a fine strainer with the back of a tablespoon. Mix together the tofu and crab meat in a bowl until combined.

2 Add the egg yolk, rice or wheat flour, spring onion, ginger and soy sauce and season to taste with salt. Mix thoroughly with a metal spoon to form a light paste.

3 To make the dipping sauce, combine the vegetable stock, sugar and soy sauce in a serving bowl.

4 Line a baking sheet with kitchen paper. Heat the vegetable oil in a wok or frying pan to 190°C/375°F. Meanwhile, shape the crab and tofu mixture into thumb-sized pieces. Fry in batches of three at a time for 1–2 minutes. Drain on the kitchen paper and serve with the sauce and mooli.

Cook's Tip
Grate the mooli (daikon) before serving and press it in a sieve or strainer to remove excess liquid.

Crab Dim Sum Energy 166kcal/700kJ; Protein 14.7g; Carbohydrate 20.5g, of which sugars 1.4g; Fat 3.3g, of which saturates 1.1g; Cholesterol 46mg; Calcium 83mg; Fibre 0.8g; Sodium 287mg.
Crab and Tofu Dumplings Energy 74kcal/310kJ; Protein 6.3g; Carbohydrate 7.8g, of which sugars 3.6g; Fat 2g, of which saturates 0.4g; Cholesterol 47mg; Calcium 132mg; Fibre 0.3g; Sodium 762mg.

Crab Meat and Water Chestnut Wontons

Serve these mouthwatering parcels as part of a dim sum selection, or as snacks and appetizers at a party.

Serves 4

50g/2oz/⅓ cup canned water chestnuts
115g/4oz/generous ½ cup fresh white crab meat
12 wonton wrappers
salt and ground black pepper

1 Drain the water chestnuts, rinse under cold running water and drain again.

2 Finely chop the water chestnuts, mix them with the crab meat in a bowl and season with plenty of salt and black pepper.

3 Lay the wonton wrappers on a chopping board. Place about 5ml/1 tsp of the filling on each wrapper and roll up to enclose the filling. Place the filled wontons in a steamer over simmering water and steam for 5–8 minutes. Serve immediately.

Variation

If you are feel like treating yourself, these wontons can be made with lobster meat instead of the crab meat. It will bump up the cost of this dish but the taste will be worth it.

Cook's Tip

The water chestnut is the edible bulb of the Chinese water plant that has been cultivated for thousands of years. It is starchy and somewhat sweet, and provides the crisp crunch in many Chinese dishes. Most water chestnuts available outside of Asia are canned, although they can be found fresh in some Asian markets. Water chestnuts are a good source of carbohydrates as well as vitamin B6 and riboflavin.

Seafood Wontons

These tasty wontons make excellent snacks for a party.

Serves 4

225g/8oz cooked prawns (shrimp), peeled and deveined
115g/4oz white crab meat
4 canned water chestnuts, diced
1 spring onion (scallion), chopped
1 green chilli, seeded and chopped
1.5ml/¼ tsp grated fresh root ginger
1 egg, separated
20–24 wonton wrappers, thawed if frozen
salt and ground black pepper
fresh coriander (cilantro) leaves, to garnish

For the dressing

30ml/2 tbsp rice vinegar
15ml/1 tbsp chopped, pickled ginger
90ml/6 tbsp olive oil
15ml/1 tbsp soy sauce
45ml/3 tbsp chopped fresh coriander (cilantro)
30ml/2 tbsp finely diced red (bell) pepper

1 Finely dice the prawns and combine with the crab meat, water chestnuts, spring onion, chilli, ginger, egg white and seasoning.

2 Place a wonton wrapper on a board. Put about 5ml/1 tsp of the filling just above the centre of the wrapper. Moisten the edges of the wrapper with a little egg yolk. Bring the bottom of the wrapper up over the filling. Press gently and seal the edges neatly to form a triangle. Fill the remaining wrappers.

3 Half fill a large pan with water. Bring to the boil, then lower the heat to a simmer. Add the filled wontons, a few at a time, and simmer for about 2–3 minutes, or until the wontons float to the surface. When ready, the wrappers will be translucent and the filling should be cooked. Using a large slotted spoon, remove the wontons and drain them briefly, then spread them on trays. Keep warm while you cook the remaining wontons.

4 Make the coriander dressing by whisking all the ingredients together in a bowl using a balloon whisk or a fork.

5 Divide the wontons among individual serving dishes, drizzle with the coriander dressing and serve immediately, garnished with a handful of coriander leaves.

Crab Wontons Energy 88kcal/374kJ; Protein 7g; Carbohydrate 14.7g, of which sugars 0.4g; Fat 0.5g, of which saturates 0.1g; Cholesterol 21mg; Calcium 66mg; Fibre 0.7g; Sodium 166mg.
Seafood Wontons Energy 239kcal/1011kJ; Protein 16.9g; Carbohydrate 36.7g, of which sugars 1g; Fat 4.8g, of which saturates 0.9g; Cholesterol 69mg; Calcium 86mg; Fibre 1.8g; Sodium 89mg.

Firecrackers

It's easy to see how these snacks got their name. They whizz round the wok like rockets, and when you take a bite, they explode with flavour.

Makes 16

16 large, raw king prawns (jumbo shrimp), heads and shells removed but tails left on
5ml/1 tsp red curry paste
15ml/1 tbsp Thai fish sauce
16 small wonton wrappers, about 8cm/3¼in square, thawed if frozen
16 fine egg noodles, soaked in water until soft
oil, for deep-frying
lime wedges, for squeezing

1 Place the prawns on their sides and cut two slits through the underbelly of each, one about 1cm/½in from the head end and the other about 1cm/½in from the first cut, cutting across the prawn. This will prevent the prawns from curling when they are cooking.

2 Mix the curry paste with the fish sauce in a shallow dish. Add the prawns and turn them in the mixture until they are well coated. Cover and leave to marinate for 10 minutes.

3 Place a wonton wrapper on the work surface at an angle so that it forms a diamond shape, then fold the top corner over so that the point is in the centre. Place a prawn, slit side down, on the wrapper, with the tail projecting from the folded end, then fold the bottom corner of the wrapper over the other end of the prawn.

4 Fold each side of the wrapper over in turn to make a tightly folded roll. Tie a noodle in a bow around the roll and set it aside. Repeat with the remaining prawns and wrappers.

5 Heat the oil in a wok to 190°C/375°F or until a cube of bread, added to the oil, browns in 40 seconds. Fry the prawns, a few at a time, for 5–8 minutes, until golden brown and cooked through. Drain well on kitchen paper and keep hot while you cook the remaining batches. Serve the firecrackers immediately, with lime wedges.

Crisp Fried Aubergine

The spicy gram flour coating on these slices is deliciously crisp, revealing the succulent aubergine beneath. Choose a firm aubergine with a glossy skin.

Serves 4

50g/2oz/½ cup gram flour
15ml/1 tbsp semolina or ground rice
2.5ml/½ tsp onion seeds
5ml/1 tsp cumin seeds
2.5ml/½ tsp fennel seeds or aniseed
2.5–5ml/½–1 tsp hot chilli powder
2.5ml/½ tsp salt, or to taste
1 large aubergine (eggplant)
vegetable oil, for deep-frying

1 Sift the gram flour into a large mixing bowl and add the semolina or ground rice with the onion and cumin seeds, fennel seeds or aniseed, and the hot chilli powder and salt.

2 Halve the aubergine lengthways and cut each half into 5mm/¼in thick slices. Rinse them and shake off the excess water, but do not pat dry. With some of the water still clinging to the slices, add them to the spiced gram flour mixture. Toss them around until they are evenly coated with the flour. Use a spoon if necessary to ensure that all the flour is used.

3 Heat the oil in a karahi, wok or deep-fryer to a temperature of 190°C/375°F, or until a cube of bread dropped in the oil browns in about 45 seconds. If it floats immediately, the oil has reached the right temperature.

4 Fry the spice-coated aubergine slices in a single layer. Avoid overcrowding the pan as this will lower the oil temperature, resulting in a soggy texture. Fry until the aubergines are crisp and well browned. Drain well on kitchen paper and serve with a chutney.

Cook's Tip
Fennel and aniseed aid digestion, and most deep-fried Indian recipes use them.

Firecrackers Energy 71kcal/298kJ; Protein 3.2g; Carbohydrate 7.1g, of which sugars 0.2g; Fat 3.5g, of which saturates 0.5g; Cholesterol 25mg; Calcium 20mg; Fibre 0.3g; Sodium 30mg.
Fried Aubergine Energy 288kcal/1192kJ; Protein 1.5g; Carbohydrate 13.7g, of which sugars 4.6g; Fat 25.4g, of which saturates 3.1g; Cholesterol 0 mg; Calcium 17 mg; Fibre 1.4g; Sodium 45mg..

Vegetable Tempura

These deep-fried fritters are perfect for parties or make a tasty start to a meal.

Serves 4

2 medium courgettes (zucchini)
½ medium aubergine (eggplant)
1 large carrot
½ small Spanish (Bermuda) onion
1 egg
120ml/4fl oz/½ cup iced water
115g/4oz/1 cup plain (all-purpose) flour
salt and ground black pepper
vegetable oil, for deep-frying
sea salt flakes, lemon slices and Japanese soy sauce (shoyu), to serve

1 Using a potato peeler, pare strips of peel from the courgettes and aubergine to give a striped effect.

2 Cut the courgettes, aubergine and carrot into strips about 7.5–10cm/3–4in long and 3mm/⅛in wide.

3 Put the courgettes, aubergine and carrot into a colander and sprinkle liberally with salt. Leave for about 30 minutes, then rinse thoroughly under cold running water. Drain well.

4 Thinly slice the onion from top to base, discarding the plump pieces in the middle. Separate the layers so that there are lots of fine, long strips. Mix all the vegetables together and season with salt and pepper.

5 Make the batter immediately before frying. Mix the egg and iced water in a bowl, then sift in the flour. Mix briefly with a fork or chopsticks. Do not overmix; the batter should remain lumpy. Add the vegetables to the batter and mix to combine.

6 Half-fill a wok with oil and heat to 180°C/350°F. Scoop up one heaped tablespoon of the mixture at a time and carefully lower it into the oil. Deep-fry in batches for approximately 3 minutes, until golden brown and crisp.

7 Drain the cooked tempura on kitchen paper. Serve each portion with salt, slices of lemon and a tiny bowl of Japanese soy sauce for dipping.

Asian-style Courgette Fritters

This is an excellent cultural fusion: a twist on Japanese tempura, using Indian spices and gram flour in the batter. Also known as besan, gram flour is more commonly used in Indian cooking and gives a wonderfully crisp texture, while the courgette baton inside becomes meltingly tender. If you're feeling adventurous, vary the vegetable content by dipping some thinly sliced squash or pumpkin batons with the courgettes. This is an ideal treat for kids.

Serves 4

90g/3½oz/¾ cup gram flour
5ml/1 tsp baking powder
2.5ml/½ tsp ground turmeric
10ml/2 tsp ground coriander
5ml/1 tsp ground cumin
5ml/1 tsp chilli powder
250ml/8fl oz/1 cup beer
600g/1lb 6oz courgettes (zucchini), cut into batons
sunflower oil, for deep-frying
salt
steamed basmati rice, natural (plain) yogurt and pickles, to serve

1 Sift the gram flour, baking powder, turmeric, coriander, cumin and chilli powder into a large bowl. Stir lightly until the ingredients are combined.

2 Season the mixture with salt and make a hollow in the centre. Pour in a little of the beer, and gradually mix in all of the surrounding dry ingredients. Add more beer, mixing gently, to make a thick batter. Be careful not to overmix.

3 Fill a large wok, one-third full with sunflower oil and heat to 180°C/350°F or until a cube of bread, dropped into the oil, browns in 45 seconds.

4 Working in batches, dip the courgette batons in the spiced batter and then deep-fry for 1–2 minutes, or until crisp and golden. Lift out of the wok using a slotted spoon. Drain on kitchen paper and keep warm.

5 Serve the courgette fritters on heated plates, or on banana leaves if these are available, with steamed basmati rice, yogurt and pickles.

Vegetable Tempura Energy 313kcal/1305kJ; Protein 7.1g; Carbohydrate 30.6g, of which sugars 7.3g; Fat 18.9g, of which saturates 2.5g; Cholesterol 48mg; Calcium 94mg; Fibre 3.6g; Sodium 28mg.
Asian-style Fritters Energy 241kcal/999kJ; Protein 7.3g; Carbohydrate 15.3g, of which sugars 4.6g; Fat 15.6g, of which saturates 1.9g; Cholesterol 0mg; Calcium 83mg; Fibre 3.8g; Sodium 15mg.

Celeriac Fritters with Mustard Dip

Celeriac is an unusual vegetable with a deliciously subtle flavour. Here it is used to make hot, crispy fritters which taste fabulous combined with a cold mustard dip.

Serves 4

1 egg
115g/4oz/1½ cups ground almonds
45ml/3 tbsp freshly grated Parmesan cheese
45ml/3 tbsp chopped fresh parsley
1 celeriac, about 450g/1lb
lemon juice
oil, for deep-frying
salt and ground black pepper
sea salt flakes, to garnish

For the dip

150ml/¼ pint/⅔ cup sour cream
15–30ml/1–2 tbsp wholegrain mustard

1 Beat the egg well and pour into a shallow dish. Mix together the almonds, Parmesan cheese and parsley in a separate dish. Season well with salt and pepper.

2 Peel and cut the celeriac into batons about 1cm/½in wide and 5cm/2in long. Drop them into a bowl of water with a little lemon juice added to prevent discoloration.

3 Heat the oil to 180°C/350°F. Drain and then pat dry half the celeriac batons. Dip them into the beaten egg, then into the almond mixture, coating the pieces completely and evenly.

4 Deep-fry the fritters, in batches, for 2–3 minutes until golden. Drain on kitchen paper. Keep warm while you cook the remaining fritters.

5 Mix the dip ingredients together with salt to taste. Spoon into a bowl. Sprinkle the fritters with sea salt flakes and serve.

Cook's Tip
To check the oil is hot enough, drop a piece of bread into the pan – it should turn light brown in about 45 seconds.

Chicken Croquettes

Croquettes are very popular snacks and there are many different variations. This one is based on béchamel sauce, which is perfect for taking on different flavours such as ham or chopped peppers.

Serves 4

25g/1oz/2 tbsp butter
25g/1oz/¼ cup plain (all-purpose) flour
150ml/¼ pint/⅔ cup milk
15ml/1 tbsp olive oil, plus extra for deep-frying
1 boneless chicken breast portion with skin, diced
1 garlic clove, finely chopped
1 small egg, beaten
50g/2oz/1 cup stale white breadcrumbs
salt and ground black pepper
fresh flat leaf parsley, to garnish
lemon wedges, to serve

1 Melt the butter in a pan. Add the flour and cook gently, stirring, for 1 minute. Gradually stir in the milk and cook until smooth and thick. Cover the surface closely to prevent the formation of a skin, and set aside.

2 Heat the oil in a medium frying pan and fry the piece of chicken with the garlic for 5 minutes.

3 When the chicken is lightly browned and cooked through, transfer the contents of the frying pan into a food processor and process until finely chopped. Transfer the mixture into the sauce and stir to combine. Season with plenty of salt and pepper to taste, then set aside to cool completely.

4 Once cooled and firm, shape the mixture into eight small sausage shapes. Dip each one in beaten egg, then roll in breadcrumbs to coat.

5 Heat the oil in a large pan, until a cube of bread dropped in the oil browns in 1 minute. Lower the croquettes into the oil and cook for 4 minutes until crisp and golden. Lift out using a slotted spoon and drain on kitchen paper. Serve with lemon wedges and garnish with fresh flat leaf parsley.

Celeriac Fritters Energy 514kcal/2123kJ; Protein 14.3g; Carbohydrate 4.7g, of which sugars 4g; Fat 48.8g, of which saturates 11g; Cholesterol 81mg; Calcium 301mg; Fibre 3.7g; Sodium 349mg.
Chicken Croquettes Energy 286kcal/1195kJ; Protein 13.9g; Carbohydrate 16.4g, of which sugars 2.2g; Fat 18.9g, of which saturates 5.8g; Cholesterol 89mg; Calcium 80mg; Fibre 0.5g; Sodium 189mg.

Golden Parmesan Chicken

These tasty Parmesan-coated chicken bites can be served hot as part of a buffet or as an appetizer to a dinner party. Or, if you prefer, offer them cold with a garlic mayonnaise.

Serves 4

4 chicken breast fillets, skinned
75g/3oz/1½ cups fresh white breadcrumbs
40g/1½ oz Parmesan cheese, finely grated
30ml/2 tbsp chopped fresh parsley
2 eggs, beaten
50g/2oz/¼ cup butter, melted
salt and ground black pepper

For the garlic mayonnaise
120ml/4fl oz/½ cup mayonnaise
120ml/4fl oz/½ cup fromage frais or low-fat cream cheese
1–2 garlic cloves, crushed

1 Cut each fillet into four or five chunks. Mix together the breadcrumbs, Parmesan, parsley and seasoning in a shallow dish. Dip the chicken pieces in the egg, then into the breadcrumb mixture. Place in a single layer on a baking sheet and chill in the refrigerator for 30 minutes.

2 To make the garlic mayonnaise, mix together the mayonnaise, fromage frais or cream cheese and garlic, and season to taste with salt and pepper. Spoon into a small serving bowl and chill.

3 Preheat the oven to 180°C/350°F/Gas 4. Place the chicken pieces in an ovenproof dish, arranging them so that they are not touching. Drizzle the melted butter over the chicken pieces, place the dish in the oven and cook them for about 20 minutes, until crisp and golden. Serve the chicken accompanied by the garlic mayonnaise for dipping.

Cook's Tip
When making fresh breadcrumbs it is best to use bread that is just turning stale but not dried out. If you have a food processor or blender then simply process the bread until the breadcrumbs are the correct size.

Meat Croquettes

These tasty appetizers are ideal for parties and buffets.

Makes 8

200g/7oz lean veal, cut into pieces
2.5ml/½ tsp salt
40g/1½ oz/3 tbsp margarine
1 onion, cut into wedges
1 carrot, halved
1 fresh parsley sprig
1 fresh thyme sprig
1 bay leaf
1 mace blade
6 black peppercorns
250ml/8fl oz/1 cup hot water
25g/1oz/¼ cup plain (all-purpose) flour
1 egg yolk
5ml/1 tsp finely chopped fresh parsley
few drops of lemon juice
vegetable oil for deep-frying
salt and ground black pepper
deep-fried parsley sprigs, to garnish
ready-made mustard, to serve

For the coating
115g/4oz/2 cups fine breadcrumbs
2 eggs
10ml/2 tsp olive oil

1 Melt 10g/¼oz/1½ tsp of the margarine in a large pan. Cook the veal over medium heat for 5 minutes. Add the onion, carrot, parsley, thyme, bay leaf, mace, peppercorns and hot water, bring to the boil, then cover and simmer for 1–2 hours, until the meat is tender. Remove the veal and dice it finely. Strain the stock into a bowl and reserve 200ml/7fl oz/scant 1 cup.

2 Melt the remaining margarine in a pan. Stir in the flour and cook for 2 minutes, then stir in the stock. Cook until thickened. Beat the egg yolk with a little of the sauce in a bowl, then stir into the pan. Stir constantly until thickened. Add the meat, season and stir in the parsley and lemon juice. Spread evenly over a plate, leave to cool and chill for at least 2 hours.

3 Divide the meat mixture into eight portions and shape into cylindrical croquettes. Spread out the breadcrumbs in a shallow dish. Beat the eggs with the oil in another dish and season. Roll the croquettes in the breadcrumbs, dip them in the beaten egg mixture and roll them in the breadcrumbs again. Flatten the ends.

4 Heat the vegetable oil in a deep-fryer or pan to 180°C/350°F. Cook the croquettes in batches for 5–6 minutes, until golden brown. Drain on kitchen paper. Serve with mustard and parsley.

Golden Parmesan Energy 591kcal/2460kJ; Protein 35.7g; Carbohydrate 16.7g, of which sugars 2.4g; Fat 43g, of which saturates 14.7g; Cholesterol 227mg; Calcium 216mg; Fibre 0.8g; Sodium 571mg.
Meat Croquettes Energy 247kcal/1028kJ; Protein 9.3g; Carbohydrate 14.3g, of which sugars 1g; Fat 17.4g, of which saturates 1.7g; Cholesterol 94mg; Calcium 41mg; Fibre 0.6g; Sodium 344mg.

Crisp-fried Crab Claws

Crab claws are readily available from the freezer of many Asian stores and supermarkets. Thaw them thoroughly and dry on kitchen paper before coating them.

Serves 4

50g/2oz/⅓ cup rice flour
15ml/1 tbsp cornflour (cornstarch)
2.5ml/½ tsp sugar
1 egg
60ml/4 tbsp cold water
1 lemon grass stalk
2 garlic cloves, finely chopped
15ml/1 tbsp chopped fresh coriander (cilantro)
1–2 fresh red chillies, seeded and finely chopped
5ml/1 tsp fish sauce
vegetable oil, for deep-frying
12 half-shelled crab claws, thawed if frozen
ground black pepper

For the chilli vinegar dip
45ml/3 tbsp sugar
120ml/4fl oz/½ cup water
120ml/4fl oz/½ cup red wine vinegar
15ml/1 tbsp fish sauce
2–4 fresh red chillies, seeded and chopped

1 First make the chilli vinegar dip. Mix the sugar and water in a pan. Heat gently, stirring until the sugar has dissolved, then bring to the boil. Lower the heat and simmer for 5–7 minutes. Stir in the red wine vinegar, fish sauce and chopped chillies, pour into a serving bowl and set aside.

2 Combine the rice flour, cornflour and sugar in a bowl. Beat the egg with the cold water, then stir the egg and water mixture into the flour mixture and beat well until it forms a light batter without any lumps.

3 Cut off the lower 5cm/2in of the lemon grass stalk and chop it finely. Add the lemon grass to the batter, with the garlic, coriander, red chillies and fish sauce. Stir in pepper to taste.

4 Heat the oil in a wok or deep-fryer to 190°C/375°F or until a cube of bread browns in 40 seconds. Dip the crab claws into the batter, then fry, in batches, until golden. Serve with the dip.

Salt Cod and Potato Fritters

These little fritters are extremely easy to make and taste delicious. Serve them simply with a wedge of fresh lemon and some watercress or green salad. They are great at parties skewered on to cocktail sticks so your guests won't get messy. Offer a bowl of garlic mayonnaise for dipping.

Makes about 24

450g/1lb salt cod fillets
500g/1¼lb floury potatoes, unpeeled
plain (all-purpose) flour, for coating
vegetable oil, for deep-frying
salt and ground black pepper

1 Place the salt cod in a bowl, pour over cold water to cover the fish and leave to soak for 24 hours, changing the water every 6–8 hours.

2 Drain the fish, rinse and place in a pan of cold water. Slowly bring to the boil and simmer for 5 minutes, then drain and cool. When cooled, remove any bones and skin and mash the fish with a fork.

3 Cook the potatoes in their skins in a pan of salted boiling water for about 20–25 minutes, or until just tender. Leave to cool slightly, then peel and mash.

4 Add the salt cod to the mashed potato and mix until they are well combined. Season to taste with salt and plenty of ground black pepper.

5 Break off walnut-sized pieces of the mixture and roll into balls with your hands. Place on a floured plate, cover and chill in the refrigerator for 20–30 minutes. Roll each ball lightly in flour, dusting off any excess.

6 Heat enough vegetable oil for deep-frying in a large pan or deep-fryer and fry the balls for 5–6 minutes, or until golden. Remove the cooked balls with a slotted spoon and drain on kitchen paper. Serve hot or warm, skewered on to cocktail sticks (toothpicks).

Crisp-fried Crab Claws Energy 224kcal/933kJ; Protein 10.1g; Carbohydrate 16.9g, of which sugars 0g; Fat 12.9g, of which saturates 1.7g; Cholesterol 78mg; Calcium 62mg; Fibre 0.3g; Sodium 256mg.
Salt Cod Fritters Energy 92kcal/386kJ; Protein 6.8g; Carbohydrate 6.6g, of which sugars 0.3g; Fat 4.5g, of which saturates 0.6g; Cholesterol 11mg; Calcium 11mg; Fibre 0.3g; Sodium 77mg.

Pork and Prawn Dumplings

These little dumplings, known as dim sum, are filled with a tasty pork and shrimp mixture. If you prefer, you can make a seafood version. Whichever you decide, the bitesize morsels are perfect for serving as an appetizer.

Serves 4

100g/3¾oz raw prawns (shrimp), peeled and deveined
2 spring onions (scallions)
225g/8oz/1 cup minced (ground) pork
30ml/2 tbsp light soy sauce
15ml/1 tbsp sesame oil
2.5ml/½ tsp ground black pepper
15ml/1 tbsp cornflour (cornstarch)
16 round wonton wrappers
16 large garden peas, thawed if frozen
chilli sauce, for dipping

1 Chop the prawns finely to make a coarse paste. This can be done using a sharp knife or in a food processor, but if you chop them in a food processor, use the pulse button, or the prawns will become rubbery. Scrape into a bowl.

2 Chop the spring onions very finely. Add them to the puréed prawns, with the pork, soy sauce, sesame oil, pepper and cornflour. Mix well.

3 Holding a wonton wrapper on the palm of one hand, spoon a heaped teaspoon of the filling into the centre. Cup your hand so that the wrapper enfolds the filling to make the classic dumpling shape. Leave the top slightly open. Top each gap with a pea. Fill the remaining wonton wrappers in the same way.

4 Place the dumplings on a lightly oiled plate and steam over a wok of rapidly boiling water for 10 minutes. Serve with a chilli sauce dip.

Cook's tip
If you can only find square wonton wrappers, trim off the corners to make a rough circle before filling them.

Breaded Sole Batons

Crisp, crumbed fish strips are almost as speedy as fish fingers, but much smarter.

Serves 4

275g/10oz lemon sole fillets, skin removed
2 eggs
115g/4oz/2 cups fine fresh breadcrumbs
75g/3oz/¾ cup plain (all-purpose) flour
salt and ground black pepper
oil, for frying
lemon wedges and tartare sauce, to serve

1 Cut the fish fillets into long diagonal strips each measuring about 2cm/¾in wide.

2 Break the eggs into a shallow dish and beat well with a fork. Place the fresh breadcrumbs in another shallow dish. Put the flour in a large plastic bag and season with plenty of salt and ground black pepper. Shake to mix.

3 Dip the fish strips in the egg, turning to coat well. Place on a plate and then shake a few at a time in the bag of seasoned flour.

4 Dip the fish strips in the egg again and then in the breadcrumbs, turning to coat well. Place on a tray in a single layer, making sure that none of the breaded strips touches its neighbour. Let the coating set for at least 5 minutes.

5 Heat 1cm/½in oil in a large frying pan over medium-high heat. When the oil is hot (a cube of bread will sizzle) fry the fish strips in batches for about 2–2½ minutes, turning once, taking care not to overcrowd the pan. Drain on kitchen paper and keep warm. Serve the fish on a platter, with the tartare sauce and lemon wedges.

Variation
Instead of lemon sole, use fillets of plaice, flounder or cod. Pollock would also work well.

Pork Dumplings Energy 228kcal/957kJ; Protein 18.2g; Carbohydrate 20.2g, of which sugars 1.3g; Fat 8.8g, of which saturates 2.5g; Cholesterol 86mg; Calcium 57mg; Fibre 1.3g; Sodium 622mg.
Breaded Sole Batons Energy 334kcal/1405kJ; Protein 20.2g; Carbohydrate 36.9g, of which sugars 1g; Fat 12.9g, of which saturates 2.1g; Cholesterol 136mg; Calcium 90mg; Fibre 1.2g; Sodium 320mg.

Paella Croquettes

Paella is probably Spain's most famous dish, and here it is used for a tasty fried tapas. In this recipe, the paella is cooked from scratch, but you could, of course, use left-over paella instead.

Serves 4

pinch of saffron threads
150ml/¼ pint/⅔ cup white wine
30ml/2 tbsp olive oil
1 small onion, finely chopped
1 garlic clove, finely chopped
150g/5oz/⅔ cup risotto rice
300ml/½ pint/1¼ cups hot chicken stock
50g/2oz/½ cup cooked prawns (shrimp), peeled, deveined and coarsely chopped
50g/2oz cooked chicken, chopped
75g/3oz/⅔ cup petits pois (baby peas), thawed if frozen
30ml/2 tbsp grated Parmesan cheese
1 egg, beaten
30ml/2 tbsp milk
75g/3oz/1½ cups fresh white breadcrumbs
vegetable or olive oil, for shallow-frying
salt and ground black pepper
flat leaf parsley, to garnish
lemon wedge

1 Stir the saffron into the wine in a small bowl; set aside. Heat the oil in a pan and fry the onion and garlic for 5 minutes until soft. Stir in the rice and cook, stirring, for 1 minute. Keeping the heat fairly high, add the wine and saffron mixture to the pan, stirring until it is all absorbed.

2 Gradually add the stock, stirring until the liquid is absorbed and the rice is cooked – about 20 minutes. Stir in the prawns, chicken, petits pois and Parmesan cheese. Season.

3 Cool the mixture slightly, then use spoons to shape the mixture into 16 lozenges.

4 Mix the egg and milk in a shallow bowl. Spread out the breadcrumbs on a sheet of foil. Dip the croquettes in the egg mixture, then coat them evenly in the breadcrumbs.

5 Heat the oil in a frying pan, then shallow fry the croquettes for 4–5 minutes until crisp and golden. Work in batches. Drain on kitchen paper and keep hot. Serve garnished with a sprig of flat leaf parsley and a lemon wedge.

Salmon Tartare

The base for this dish is a lightly salted version of gravlax, the Scandinavian dish of salmon marinated with dill.

Serves 4

400g/14oz gravlax (salmon marinated with dill)
grated rind of ½ lime or lemon
2.5ml/½ tsp ground black pepper
60ml/4 tbsp crème fraîche
15ml/1 tbsp chopped fresh dill, plus a few sprigs to garnish
60ml/4 tbsp cream cheese, to serve
rye bread, to serve
lemon wedges

1 Thinly slice the gravlax into strips, reserving four small slices for a garnish. Arrange these thin strips of salmon in a line on a large chopping board and, using a large, sharp knife, cut them crossways into the finest small dice that you can. Do not be tempted to use a food processor to do this, or you will end up with salmon paste.

2 Put the chopped salmon in a large bowl and add the lime or lemon rind and the pepper, then mix in half the crème fraîche.

3 Mould the salmon mixture into small burger-shaped patties, either by pushing the mixture into round pastry cutters with a spoon to make neat rounds, or by shaping it with wet hands for a more rustic finish.

4 Spread a thin coating of the remaining crème fraîche across the top of each salmon mound. Top with one of the reserved salmon slices and add a sprig of dill to garnish. Serve with cream cheese, rye bread and lemon wedges.

Cook's Tips

- *Greek (US strained plain) yogurt can be used in place of crème fraîche and, conversely, sour cream can be used for those who prefer a sharper, less rich flavour.*
- *Raw fish, meat and eggs should not be eaten by pregnant women, the elderly, young children, or anyone with an impaired immune system. Ensure the fish for this recipe is very fresh.*

Paella Croquettes Energy 524kcal/2183kJ; Protein 16.2g; Carbohydrate 48.4g, of which sugars 2.3g; Fat 27.3g, of which saturates 4.9g; Cholesterol 85mg; Calcium 160mg; Fibre 1.5g; Sodium 280mg.
Salmon Tartare Energy 253kcal/1050kJ; Protein 20.8g; Carbohydrate 0.1g, of which sugars 0.1g; Fat 18.8g, of which saturates 6.8g; Cholesterol 66mg; Calcium 44mg; Fibre 0.2g; Sodium 92mg.

Parmesan Fish Goujons

These goujons are light and crisp, just like authentic fish-and-chip shop batter.

Serves 4

375g/13oz plaice or sole fillets, or thicker fish such as cod or haddock
a little plain (all-purpose) flour
oil, for deep-frying
salt and ground black pepper
dill sprigs, to garnish

For the cream sauce

60ml/4 tbsp sour cream
60ml/4 tbsp mayonnaise
2.5ml/½ tsp grated lemon rind
30ml/2 tbsp chopped gherkins or capers
15ml/1 tbsp chopped mixed fresh herbs, or 5ml/1 tsp dried

For the batter

75g/3oz/¾ cup plain (all-purpose) flour
25g/1oz/¼ cup grated Parmesan cheese
5ml/1 tsp bicarbonate of soda (baking soda)
1 egg, separated
150ml/¼ pint/⅔ cup milk

1 To make the sauce, combine the cream, mayonnaise, lemon rind, gherkins or capers, herbs and seasoning, then chill.

2 To make the batter, sift the flour into a bowl. Mix in the other dry ingredients and some salt, and then whisk in the egg yolk and milk to give a thick yet smooth batter. Then gradually whisk in 90ml/6 tbsp water. Season and chill in the refrigerator.

3 Skin the fish and cut into thin strips of similar length. Dip the fish lightly in seasoned flour.

4 Heat at least 5cm/2in oil in a large, heavy pan with a lid. Whisk the egg white until stiff and gently fold into the batter until just blended. Dip the floured fish into the batter, drain off any excess and then drop gently into the hot fat.

5 Cook the fish in batches, so that the goujons don't stick to one another, for only 3–4 minutes, turning once. When the batter is golden and crisp, remove the fish with a slotted spoon. Place the goujons or kitchen paper on a plate and keep warm while cooking the rest. Serve hot, garnished with sprigs of dill and accompanied by the cream sauce.

Calamari with Two-tomato Stuffing

Calamari, or baby squid, are quick and easy to cook, but do turn and baste them often and take care not to overcook them.

Serves 4

500g/1¼lb baby squid, cleaned
1 garlic clove, crushed
3 plum tomatoes, skinned and chopped
8 sun-dried tomatoes in oil, drained and chopped
60ml/4 tbsp chopped fresh basil, plus extra, to serve
60ml/4 tbsp fresh white breadcrumbs
45ml/3 tbsp olive oil
15ml/1 tbsp red wine vinegar
salt and ground black pepper
lemon juice, to serve

1 Remove the tentacles from the squid and roughly chop them; leave the main part of the squid whole.

2 Mix together the crushed garlic, plum tomatoes, sun-dried tomatoes, chopped fresh basil and breadcrumbs. Stir in 15ml/1 tbsp of the olive oil and the vinegar. Season well with plenty of salt and ground black pepper. Soak some wooden cocktail sticks (toothpicks) in water for 10 minutes before use, to prevent them burning during cooking.

3 Using a teaspoon, fill the squid with the stuffing mixture. Secure the open ends with the cocktail sticks to hold the stuffing mixture in place.

4 Brush the squid with the remaining olive oil and cook over a medium-hot barbecue for 4–5 minutes, turning often. Alternatively, cook them under a preheated grill (broiler). Sprinkle with lemon juice and extra chopped basil to serve.

Cook's Tip

To prepare squid yourself, get a firm hold of the head and pull it from the body. Reach inside the body sac and pull out the transparent back bone, as well as any stringy parts. Rinse the sac inside and out and pat dry. Cut the tentacles off above the eyes and add to the pile of squid. Discard everything else.

Parmesan Fish Energy 358kcal/1497kJ; Protein 24.2g; Carbohydrate 21.4g, of which sugars 3.2g; Fat 20.2g, of which saturates 5.9g; Cholesterol 116mg; Calcium 243mg; Fibre 1.4g; Sodium 293mg.
Stuffed Calamari Energy 356kcal/1486kJ; Protein 21.8g; Carbohydrate 15.2g, of which sugars 3.6g; Fat 23.6g, of which saturates 11.1g; Cholesterol 321mg; Calcium 55mg; Fibre 1.9g; Sodium 352mg.

Spiced Pork Pâté

This pâté has an Asian twist: it is steamed in banana leaves, which are available in African and Asian markets. However, if you cannot find them you can use large spring green leaves or several Savoy cabbage leaves instead.

Serves 6

45ml/3 tbsp nuoc mam
30ml/2 tbsp sesame oil
15ml/1 tbsp sugar
10ml/2 tsp five-spice powder
2 shallots, peeled and finely chopped
2 garlic cloves, crushed
750g/1lb 10oz/3¼ cups minced (ground) pork
25g/1oz/¼ cup potato starch
7.5ml/1½ tsp baking powder
1 banana leaf, trimmed into a strip 25cm/10in wide
vegetable oil, for brushing
salt and ground black pepper
nuoc cham and a baguette or salad, to serve

1 In a bowl, beat the nuoc mam and oil with the sugar and five-spice powder. Once the sugar has dissolved, stir in the shallots and garlic. Add the pork and seasoning, and knead well until thoroughly combined. Cover and chill for 2–3 hours.

2 Knead the mixture again, thumping it down into the bowl to remove any air. Add the potato starch and baking powder and knead until smooth and pasty. Mould the pork mixture into a fat sausage, about 18cm/7in long, and place it on an oiled dish.

3 Lay the banana leaf on a flat surface, brush it with a little vegetable oil, and place the pork sausage across it. Lift up the edge of the banana leaf nearest to you and fold it over the sausage mixture, tuck in the sides, and roll it up into a firm, tight bundle. Secure the bundle with a piece of string, so that it doesn't unravel during cooking.

4 Fill a wok one-third full with water. Balance a bamboo steamer, with its lid on, above the level of the water. Bring to the boil, lift the lid and place the banana leaf bundle on the rack, being careful not to burn yourself. Re-cover and steam for 45 minutes. Leave the pâté to cool in the leaf, then open it up and cut it into slices. Drizzle with nuoc cham, and serve with a baguette or salad.

Smoked Salmon Pâté

This pâté is made in individual ramekins lined with smoked salmon so that it looks really special. It is the ideal appetizer for an elaborate dinner party or special feast. Taste the mousse as you are making it, and add more lemon juice and seasoning if necessary.

Serves 4

350g/12oz thinly sliced smoked salmon (wild if possible)
150ml/¼ pint/⅔ cup double (heavy) cream
finely grated rind and juice of 1 lemon
salt and ground black pepper
Melba toast, to serve

1 Line four small ramekin dishes with clear film (plastic wrap), then line the dishes with 115g/4oz of the smoked salmon cut into strips long enough to flop over the edges.

2 In a food processor fitted with a metal blade, process the rest of the salmon with the double cream, lemon rind and juice, salt and plenty of ground black pepper.

3 Pack the lined ramekins with the smoked salmon pâté, pressing it down gently. Wrap the loose strips of salmon over the top of the pâté.

4 Cover the ramekins with clear film and chill for 30 minutes in the refrigerator.

5 To serve the pâtés, invert the ramekins on to plates. Serve with Melba toast.

Cook's Tip

Melba toast was created by the celebrated chef Auguste Escoffier for opera singer Dame Nellie Melba. It is sold packaged in most supermarkets but is easy to make at home. Simply toast a slice of bread under a grill (broiler), cut off the crusts and then carefully cut it in half to make two slices of half the thickness. Return the halved slices of bread to the grill to brown the untoasted sides.

Spiced Pork Pâté Energy 234kcal/978kJ; Protein 28g; Carbohydrate 8g, of which sugars 3g; Fat 10g, of which saturates 2g; Cholesterol 79mg; Calcium 46mg; Fibre 0.4g; Sodium 700mg.
Smoked Salmon Pâté Energy 311kcal/1293kJ; Protein 22.9g; Carbohydrate 0.8g, of which sugars 0.8g; Fat 24.1g, of which saturates 13.2g; Cholesterol 82mg; Calcium 36mg; Fibre 0g; Sodium 1654mg.

Smoked Haddock Pâté

Arbroath smokies are small haddock that are beheaded and gutted, but not split, before being salted and hot-smoked, creating a fantastic flavour, which is perfect for this appetizer.

Serves 6

butter, for greasing
3 large Arbroath smokies, about 225g/8oz each
275g/10oz/1¼ cups soft white (farmer's) cheese
3 eggs, beaten
30–45ml/2–3 tbsp lemon juice
ground black pepper
chervil sprigs, to garnish
lemon wedges and lettuce leaves, to serve

1 Preheat the oven to 160°C/325°F/Gas 3. Carefully butter six ramekin dishes. Lay the smokies in an ovenproof dish and heat through in the oven for 10 minutes.

2 Carefully remove the skin and bones from the smokies, then flake the flesh into a bowl.

3 Mash the fish with a fork and work in the cheese, then the eggs. Add lemon juice and pepper.

4 Divide the fish mixture equally among the ramekins and place in a roasting pan. Pour hot water into the roasting pan to come halfway up the dishes. Bake for 30 minutes, until just set.

5 Allow to cool for 2–3 minutes, then run a knife point around the edge of each dish and invert on to a warmed plate. Garnish with chervil sprigs and serve with the lemon wedges and lettuce.

Cook's Tip
The traditional Arbroath method of smoking haddock has earned it the Protected Geographical Indication status, granted by the European Commission. As with Parma ham and Champagne, the name 'Arbroath smokie' can only be used to describe the genuine article, made within an 8km/5-mile radius of Arbroath.

Cannellini Bean Pâté

Serve this simple bean pâté with slices of melba toast or toasted wholegrain bread as an appetizer or snack. It is a great alternative to meat-based pâtés, and any vegetarian guests will love it.

Serves 4

2 x 400g/14oz cans cannellini beans, drained and rinsed
45ml/3 tbsp olive oil
50g/2oz mature (sharp) Cheddar cheese, finely grated
30ml/2 tbsp chopped fresh parsley
salt and ground black pepper

1 Put the cannellini beans in a food processor or blender with the olive oil, and process to a chunky paste.

2 Transfer the paste to a bowl and stir in the cheese and chopped fresh parsley. Season to taste with salt and pepper.

3 Spoon the pâté into a serving dish and sprinkle a little paprika on top, if you like.

Cook's Tips
- *Canned beans are usually in a sugar, salt and water solution so always drain and rinse them thoroughly before use – otherwise the finished pâté may be rather too salty.*
- *Dried beans can be used instead of canned, if you prefer. Soak them overnight before boiling in plenty of water for about 10 minutes, skimming off any scum that rises to the surface. Reduce the heat and then simmer the beans until tender – about 1 to 2 hours.*

Variations
- *A liberal dusting of paprika will give the pâté an extra kick.*
- *You can also use other types of canned beans, if you like, such as kidney beans.*

Smoked Haddock Pâté Energy 307kcal/1274kJ; Protein 22.2g; Carbohydrate 1.5g, of which sugars 1.5g; Fat 23.7g, of which saturates 7.3g; Cholesterol 166mg; Calcium 59mg; Fibre 0g; Sodium 723mg.
Bean Pâté Energy 155kcal/650kJ; Protein 7.4g; Carbohydrate 18.4g, of which sugars 3.9g; Fat 6.3g, of which saturates 0.9g; Cholesterol 0mg; Calcium 96mg; Fibre 6.9g; Sodium 394mg.

Chicken Liver and Brandy Pâté

This rich pâté is quick and easy to make and tastes so much better than anything you can buy in the supermarkets. Serve as an appetizer with Melba toast or crackers.

Serves 4
350g/12oz chicken livers
50g/2oz/¼ cup butter
30ml/2 tbsp brandy
30ml/2 tbsp double (heavy) cream
salt and ground black pepper

1 Trim any fat from the chicken livers and discard. Roughly chop the livers. Heat the butter in a large frying pan.

2 Add the chicken livers to the pan and cook over medium heat for 3–4 minutes, or until evenly browned all over and cooked through. Add the brandy to the pan and allow to bubble for a few minutes. Remove from the heat and set aside to cool slightly.

3 Place the livers and brandy in a food processor or blender. Pour in the double cream and season with salt and plenty of ground black pepper.

4 Process the mixture until smooth and then spoon it into ramekin dishes. Level the surface of each dish and chill overnight in the refrigerator to set. Serve garnished with sprigs of fresh parsley to add a little colour.

Cook's Tips
- *If you can't find any fresh chicken livers, look out for them in the freezer section of large supermarkets. Ensure that they are fully defrosted before using.*
- *If you are making the pâté more than 1 day ahead, seal the surface of each portion in the ramekin dish with a layer of melted butter.*

Smoked Mackerel Pâté

The pâté can be given extra flavour by adding a spoonful of creamed horseradish, if you like.

Serves 4
275g/10oz smoked mackerel fillet, skinned
90ml/6 tbsp sour cream
75g/3oz unsalted (sweet) butter, softened
30ml/2 tbsp chopped fresh parsley
15–30ml/1–2 tbsp lemon juice
ground black pepper
chicory (Belgian endive) leaves and fresh parsley, to garnish
fingers of toast, to serve

1 Remove any fine bones from the mackerel fillet, then mash it well with a fork.

2 Work the sour cream and butter into the mackerel until smooth and thoroughly combined. Stir in the chopped parsley and add lemon juice and pepper to taste.

3 Spoon the mackerel mixture evenly into a dish or bowl, packing it down well. Cover the surface tightly with clear film (plastic wrap) and chill in the refrigerator for at least 8 hours or overnight.

4 About 30 minutes before serving, remove the pâté from the refrigerator to allow it to return to room temperature.

5 To serve, spoon the pâté on to individual plates and garnish with chicory leaves and parsley. Serve with fingers of toast.

Variations
- *For a less rich (and lower-calorie) version of this pâté, substitute 200g/7oz/scant 1 cup low-fat soft cheese or sieved cottage cheese for the sour cream.*
- *This pâté is also great made with kippers (smoked herrings). If you like, you can cook them first by placing them in a jug (pitcher), filling it with freshly boiled water and then leaving it to stand for about 10 minutes. This is not essential, as kippers may also be eaten raw.*

Chicken Liver Pâté Energy 227kcal/942kJ; Protein 15.7g; Carbohydrate 0.2g, of which sugars 0.2g; Fat 16.3g, of which saturates 9.6g; Cholesterol 369mg; Calcium 13mg; Fibre 0g; Sodium 144mg.
Mackerel Pâté Energy 344kcal/1421kJ; Protein 10.7g; Carbohydrate 0.5g, of which sugars 0.4g; Fat 33.3g, of which saturates 14.3g; Cholesterol 88mg; Calcium 57mg; Fibre 0.1g; Sodium 518mg.

Mushroom and Bean Pâté

Making pâté in the slow cooker results in this light and tasty version. It is delicious served on triangles of wholemeal toast for a vegetarian appetizer, or with crusty French bread as a light lunch served with salad.

Serves 8
450g/1lb/6 cups mushrooms, sliced
1 onion, finely chopped
2 garlic cloves, crushed
1 red (bell) pepper, seeded and diced
30ml/2 tbsp vegetable stock
30ml/2 tbsp dry white wine
400g/14oz can red kidney beans, rinsed and drained
1 egg, beaten
50g/2oz/1 cup fresh wholemeal (whole-wheat) breadcrumbs
10ml/2 tsp chopped fresh thyme
10ml/2 tsp chopped fresh rosemary
salt and ground black pepper
salad leaves, fresh herbs and tomato wedges, to garnish

1 Put the mushrooms, onion, garlic, red pepper, stock and wine in the ceramic cooking pot. Cover and cook on high for 2 hours, then set aside for about 10 minutes to cool.

2 Transfer the mixture to a food processor or blender and add the beans. Process to make a smooth purée, stopping the machine once or twice to scrape down the sides.

3 Lightly grease and line a 900g/2lb loaf tin (pan). Put an inverted saucer or metal pastry ring in the bottom of the ceramic cooking pot. Pour in about 2.5cm/1in of hot water, and set to high.

4 Transfer the vegetable mixture to a bowl. Add the egg, breadcrumbs and herbs, and season. Mix thoroughly, then spoon into the loaf tin and cover with cling film (plastic wrap) or foil.

5 Put the tin in the slow cooker and pour in enough boiling water to come just over halfway up the sides of the tin. Cover with the lid and cook on high for 4 hours, or until lightly set.

6 Remove the tin and place on a wire rack until cool. Chill for several hours, or overnight. Turn the pâté out of the tin, remove the lining paper and serve garnished with salad leaves, herbs and tomato wedges.

Duck Liver Pâté and Redcurrant Sauce

This tasty pâté is easy to prepare and will keep for about a week in the refrigerator if the butter seal is not broken.

Serves 4–6
1 onion, finely chopped
1 large garlic clove, crushed
115g/4oz/½ cup butter
225g/8oz duck livers
10–15ml/2–3 tsp chopped fresh mixed herbs, such as parsley, thyme or rosemary
15–30ml/1–2 tbsp brandy
50–115g/2–4oz/¼–½ cup clarified butter, or melted unsalted butter
salt and ground black pepper
a sprig of flat leaf parsley, to garnish

For the redcurrant sauce
30ml/2 tbsp redcurrant jelly
15–30ml/1–2 tbsp port
30ml/2 tbsp redcurrants

For the Melba toast
8 slices white bread, crusts removed

1 Cook the onion and garlic in 25g/1oz/2 tbsp of the butter in a pan over gentle heat, until just turning colour.

2 Add the duck livers to the pan with the herbs and cook together for about 3 minutes, or until the livers have browned on the outside but are still pink in the centre. Allow to cool.

3 Dice the remaining butter, then process the liver mixture in a food processor, gradually working in the cubes of butter by dropping them down the chute, to make a smooth purée.

4 Add the brandy, then check the seasoning and transfer to a 450–600ml/¾–1 pint dish. Seal the pâté with clarified or unsalted butter. Cool, and then chill until required.

5 For the sauce, put the jelly, port and redcurrants into a pan. Bring to the boil, then simmer to reduce a little. Leave to cool.

6 To make the Melba toast, toast the bread on both sides, then slice vertically to make 16 very thin slices. Place the untoasted side up on a grill (broiler) rack and grill (broil) until browned. Serve the chilled pâté garnished with parsley and accompanied by Melba toast and the redcurrant sauce.

Mushroom and Bean Pâté Energy 85kcal/358kJ; Protein 5.5g; Carbohydrate 12.3g, of which sugars 3.8g; Fat 1.6g, of which saturates 0.4g; Cholesterol 28mg; Calcium 47mg; Fibre 3.7g; Sodium 187mg.
Duck Liver Energy 794Kcal/3312kJ; Protein 101.3g; Carbohydrate 11.3g, of which sugars 9.9g; Fat 36.8g, of which saturates 19g; Cholesterol 2213mg; Calcium 73mg; Fibre 1.3g; Sodium 608mg.

Mallard Pâté

Mallard ducks are shot during the game season. This recipe needs two days to prepare, as the birds need to be briefly cooked and then allowed to rest overnight before making the rest of the pâté.

Serves 4

2 young mallards
a little groundnut (peanut) oil
185g/6½oz streaky (fatty) bacon
300g/11oz wild duck livers
10ml/2 tsp salt
ground black pepper
pinch each of grated nutmeg, ground ginger and ground cloves
275ml/9fl oz/generous 1 cup double (heavy) cream
4 egg yolks
37.5ml/2½ tbsp brandy
50g/2oz/scant ⅓ cup sultanas (golden raisins)

1 Preheat the oven to 240°C/475°F/Gas 9. Remove the legs from the ducks. Season the birds and sprinkle with oil. Roast in the preheated oven for 15 minutes, then remove from the oven and leave to rest, overnight if possible.

2 The next day, preheat the oven to 190°C/375°F/Gas 5. Put the bacon, livers, salt, pepper and spices into a blender and purée to a smooth cream. Add the cream, egg yolks and brandy, and purée for a further 30 seconds. Push the mixture through a sieve (strainer) into a bowl and add the sultanas.

3 Remove the breast fillets from the ducks and skin them. Dice the meat finely then mix into the liver mixture.

4 Put the mixture in a terrine, cover with foil and cook in the oven in a roasting pan of hot water for 40–50 minutes. The centre should be slightly wobbly. Cool, then chill for at least 4 hours. Serve with toast.

Cook's Tip

If game livers are not available then use chicken livers, trimming off any fat or connective tissue. This makes it easier to pass them through the sieve later.

Herbed Liver Pâté Pie

Serve this highly flavoured pâté with a glass of Pilsner beer for a change from wine, and some spicy dill pickles to complement the strong tastes.

Serves 10

675g/1½lb minced (ground) pork
350g/12oz pork liver
350g/12oz/2 cups diced cooked ham
1 small onion, finely chopped
30ml/2 tbsp chopped fresh parsley
5ml/1 tsp German mustard
30ml/2 tbsp Kirsch
5ml/1 tsp salt
beaten egg, for sealing and glazing
25g/1oz sachet aspic jelly
250ml/8fl oz/1 cup boiling water
ground black pepper
mustard, bread and dill pickles, to serve

For the pastry

450g/1lb/4 cups plain (all-purpose) flour
275g/10oz/1¼ cups butter
2 eggs plus 1 egg yolk
30ml/2 tbsp water

1 Preheat the oven to 200°C/400°F/Gas 6. For the pastry, sift the flour and salt and rub in the butter. Beat the eggs, egg yolk and water, and mix into the flour. Knead the pastry dough until it becomes smooth. Roll out two-thirds on a lightly floured surface and use to line a 10 x 25cm/4 x 10in hinged loaf tin (pan). Trim any excess pastry.

2 Process half the pork and all of the liver until fairly smooth. Stir in the remaining pork, ham, onion, parsley, mustard, Kirsch, salt and black pepper. Spoon into the tin and level the surface.

3 Roll out the remaining pastry and use it to top the pie. Seal the edges with egg. Decorate with pastry trimmings and glaze with egg. Make four holes in the top. Bake for 40 minutes, then reduce the oven temperature down to 180°C/350°F/Gas 4 and cook for another hour. Cover with foil and cool in the tin.

4 Dissolve the aspic jelly in the boiling water, then leave to cool slightly. Make a small hole near the pie edge and pour in the aspic. Chill for 2 hours. Serve in slices with mustard, bread and dill pickles.

Mallard Pâté Energy 771kcal/3203kJ; Protein 48.5g; Carbohydrate 9.8g, of which sugars 9.8g; Fat 59.3g, of which saturates 28.4g; Cholesterol 636mg; Calcium 81mg; Fibre 0.3g; Sodium 1782mg.
Herbed Liver Energy 576kcal/2407kJ; Protein 32.9g; Carbohydrate 36g, of which sugars 1.6g; Fat 33.7g, of which saturates 18.1g; Cholesterol 273mg; Calcium 87mg; Fibre 1.5g; Sodium 888mg.

Turkey, Juniper and Green Peppercorn Terrine

This is an ideal dish for entertaining as it can be made in advance. If you prefer, arrange some of the pancetta and pistachios as a layer in the middle.

Serves 10–12

225g/8oz chicken livers, trimmed
450g/1lb minced (ground) turkey
450g/1lb minced (ground) pork
225g/8oz pancetta, cubed
50g/2oz/½ cup shelled pistachio nuts, roughly chopped
5ml/1 tsp salt
2.5ml/½ tsp ground mace
2 garlic cloves, crushed
5ml/1 tsp drained green peppercorns in brine
5ml/1 tsp juniper berries
120ml/4fl oz/½ cup dry white wine
30ml/2 tbsp gin
finely grated rind of 1 orange
8 large vacuum-packed vine leaves in brine
oil, for greasing
spicy chutney, to serve

1 Chop the chicken livers finely. Put them in a bowl and mix in the turkey, pork, pancetta, pistachio nuts, salt, mace and garlic.

2 Lightly crush the peppercorns and juniper berries and add them to the mixture. Stir in the white wine, gin and orange rind. Cover and chill overnight to allow the flavours to mingle.

3 Preheat the oven to 160°C/325°F/Gas 3. Rinse the vine leaves under cold running water. Drain and pat dry. Lightly oil a 1.2 litre/2 pint/5 cup loaf tin (pan). Line the tin with the leaves, letting the ends hang over the sides. Pack the mixture into the tin and fold the leaves over to enclose the filling. Brush the top lightly with oil.

4 Cover the terrine with foil. Place it in a roasting pan and pour in boiling water to come halfway up the sides of the terrine. Bake for 1¾ hours, checking the level of the water occasionally.

5 Leave the terrine to cool, then pour off the surface juices. Cover with clear film (plastic wrap), then with foil and place weights on top. Chill overnight. Serve at room temperature with spicy chutney.

Grilled Vegetable Terrine

A colourful, layered terrine, this appetizer uses a variety of Mediterranean vegetables.

Serves 6

2 large red (bell) peppers, quartered, cored, seeded
2 large yellow (bell) peppers, quartered, cored, seeded
1 large aubergine (eggplant), sliced lengthways
2 courgettes (zucchini), sliced lengthways
90ml/6 tbsp olive oil
1 large red onion, thinly sliced
75g/3oz/½ cup raisins
15ml/1 tbsp tomato purée (paste)
15ml/1 tbsp red wine vinegar
400ml/14fl oz/1⅔ cups tomato juice
15g/½oz/2 tbsp powdered gelatine
fresh basil leaves, to garnish

For the dressing

90ml/6 tbsp extra virgin olive oil
30ml/2 tbsp red wine vinegar
salt and ground black pepper

1 Place the peppers skin side up under a hot grill (broiler) and cook until the skins are blackened. Transfer to a bowl and cover. Leave to cool. Arrange the aubergine and courgette slices on separate baking sheets. Brush them with oil and cook under the grill, turning occasionally, until they are tender and golden.

2 Heat the remaining olive oil in a frying pan, and add the onion, raisins, tomato purée and red wine vinegar. Cook gently until the mixture is syrupy. Set aside and leave to cool.

3 Lightly oil a 1.75 litre/3 pint/7½ cup terrine, then line it with clear film (plastic wrap), leaving a little hanging over the sides. Pour half the tomato juice into a pan, and sprinkle with the gelatine. Dissolve over a low heat, stirring frequently.

4 Place a layer of red peppers in the base of the terrine, and pour in enough tomato juice with gelatine to cover. Continue layering the vegetables, pouring tomato juice over each layer. Finish with a layer of red peppers. Pour the remaining tomato juice into the terrine. Cover and chill until set.

5 To make the dressing, whisk together the oil and vinegar, and season. Turn out the terrine and remove the clear film. Serve in slices, drizzled with dressing and garnished with basil leaves.

Turkey Terrine Energy 240kcal/1003kJ; Protein 25.3g; Carbohydrate 1.7g, of which sugars 1.5g; Fat 13.4g, of which saturates 4.1g; Cholesterol 153mg; Calcium 29mg; Fibre 0.8g; Sodium 316mg.
Grilled Vegetable Energy 296kcal/1229kJ; Protein 3.5g; Carbohydrate 20.2g, of which sugars 19.7g; Fat 22.9g, of which saturates 3.4g; Cholesterol 0mg; Calcium 42mg; Fibre 3.8g; Sodium 169mg.

Anchovy Terrine

This dish is based on a traditional Swedish recipe called Old Man's Mix. Just like the English speciality, Gentleman's Relish, it uses anchovies as the main ingredient, in this case the sweet, Swedish variety that are flavoured with cinnamon, cloves and allspice.

Serves 6–8

5 hard-boiled eggs
100g/3½oz can Swedish or matjes anchovies
2 gelatine leaves
200ml/7fl oz/scant 1 cup sour cream
½ red onion, chopped
1 bunch fresh dill, chopped
15ml/1 tbsp Swedish or German mustard
salt and ground black pepper
peeled prawns (shrimp) or lumpfish roe and dill fronds, to garnish
Melba toast or rye bread, to serve

1 Line a 20cm/8in terrine with clear film (plastic wrap). Mash the hard-boiled eggs in a bowl. Drain the juice from the anchovy can and add to the eggs. In a large, separate bowl, mash the anchovies.

2 Melt the gelatine as directed on the packet and add to the mashed eggs with the sour cream, mashed anchovies, chopped onion, dill and mustard. Season with salt and ground black pepper to taste and stir thoroughly together. Pour the mixture into the prepared terrine and chill in the refrigerator for about 2 hours.

3 To serve, turn out the terrine and garnish with freshly peeled prawns or lumpfish roe and dill fronds. Serve with Melba toast or rye bread.

Cook's Tip
If you have neither Swedish nor matjes anchovies, soak normal, salted canned anchovies in milk for 2–3 hours before you use them, adding a final sprinkling of ground cinnamon and cloves.

Haddock and Smoked Salmon Terrine

This substantial terrine makes a superb appetizer for a summer buffet.

Serves 10–12

15ml/1 tbsp sunflower oil, for greasing
350g/12oz oak-smoked salmon
900g/2lb haddock fillets, skinned
2 eggs, lightly beaten
105ml/7 tbsp crème fraîche
30ml/2 tbsp drained capers
30ml/2 tbsp drained soft green or pink peppercorns
salt and ground white pepper
crème fraîche, peppercorns, fresh dill and rocket (arugula), to garnish

1 Preheat the oven to 200°C/400°F/Gas 6. Grease a 1 litre/1¾ pint/4 cup loaf tin (pan) or terrine with the oil. Use half of the salmon to line the tin or terrine, letting some of the ends overhang the mould. Reserve the remaining smoked salmon.

2 Cut two long slices of haddock the length of the tin or terrine and set aside. Cut the rest of the haddock into small pieces. Season all the haddock.

3 Combine the eggs, crème fraîche, capers and peppercorns in a bowl. Season, then stir in the small pieces of haddock. Spoon into the tin or terrine until one-third full. Smooth the surface. Wrap the reserved long haddock fillets in the reserved salmon. Lay them on top of the fish mixture in the tin or terrine.

4 Fill the tin or terrine with the rest of the fish mixture, smooth the surface and fold over the overhanging pieces of salmon. Cover with a double thickness of foil. Stand the terrine in a roasting pan and pour in boiling water to come halfway up the sides. Place in the oven and cook for 45 minutes to 1 hour.

5 Take the terrine out of the roasting pan, but do not remove the foil cover. Place two or three large heavy tins on the foil to weight it and leave until cold. Chill in the refrigerator for 24 hours.

6 About 1 hour before serving, lift off the weights and remove the foil. Carefully invert the terrine on to a serving plate and lift off the terrine. Serve the terrine in thick slices with crème fraîche, peppercorns, fronds of dill and rocket leaves.

Anchovy Terrine Energy 127kcal/529kJ; Protein 8.1g; Carbohydrate 1.8g, of which sugars 1.6g; Fat 9.9g, of which saturates 4.3g; Cholesterol 142mg; Calcium 88mg; Fibre 0.3g; Sodium 602mg.
Haddock Terrine Energy 187kcal/785kJ; Protein 27.5g; Carbohydrate 0.3g, of which sugars 0.2g; Fat 8.5g, of which saturates 3.7g; Cholesterol 95mg; Calcium 31mg; Fibre 0g; Sodium 735mg.

Three-fish Terrine

This striped terrine uses haddock, salmon and turbot and is slowly baked in the oven. Serve with a small salad, brown bread or Melba toast and butter.

Serves 8–10

450g/1lb spinach
350–450g/12oz–1lb haddock, cod or other white fish, skinned and chopped
3 eggs
115g/4oz/2 cups fresh breadcrumbs
300ml/½ pint/1¼ cups fromage blanc or low-fat cream cheese
a little freshly grated nutmeg
350–450g/12oz–1lb salmon fillet
350–450g/12oz–1lb fresh turbot fillet, or other flat fish
oil, for greasing
salt and ground black pepper
lemon wedges and rocket (arugula), to serve

1 Preheat the oven to 160°C/325°F/Gas 3. Remove the stalks from the spinach and cook the leaves briskly in a pan without any added water, shaking the pan occasionally, until the spinach is just tender. Drain and squeeze out the water.

2 Put the spinach into a food processor or blender with the haddock or other white fish, eggs, breadcrumbs, fromage blanc or cream cheese, salt, pepper and nutmeg to taste. Process until smooth. Skin and bone the salmon fillet and cut into long thin strips. Repeat with the turbot.

3 Oil a 900g/2lb loaf tin (pan) and line the base with baking parchment or foil. Make layers from the spinach mixture and the strips of salmon and turbot, starting and finishing with spinach.

4 Press down carefully and cover with oiled baking parchment. Prick a few holes in it, then put the terrine into a roasting tin and pour boiling water around it to come two-thirds of the way up the sides.

5 Bake in the preheated oven for 1–1½ hours, or until risen, firm and set. Leave to cool, then chill well before serving.

6 To serve, ease a sharp knife down the sides to loosen the terrine and turn out on to a flat serving dish. Slice the terrine and serve with lemon wedges and fresh rocket.

Baked Sausage Terrine with Fruity Conserve

This unusual appetizer can be made with ready-made sausage meat, or if you prefer you can make your own, as shown here, using a mixture of oatmeal, pig's liver, pork and raisins. The oatmeal gives a texture just like the sausage meat. A sweet fruit conserve is a perfect accompaniment.

Serves 6–8

115g/4oz/1 cup oatmeal
750ml/1¼ pints/3 cups water
750ml/1¼ pints/3 cups milk
15g/½oz/1 tbsp butter
1 red onion, finely chopped
200g/7oz pig's liver, minced (ground)
200g/7oz minced (ground) pork
150g/5oz/1 cup raisins
5ml/1 tsp chopped fresh marjoram
5ml/1 tsp ground allspice
salt and ground black pepper
fruit conserve, such as lingonberrry, and toast, to serve

1 Preheat the oven to 180°C/350°F/Gas 4. Line the base and the sides of a 20cm/8in loaf tin (pan) with a sheet of baking parchment.

2 Put the oatmeal, water and milk in a large pan, bring to the boil, then reduce the heat and cook for 3–4 minutes until soft. Leave to cool.

3 Melt the butter in a separate pan, add the finely chopped onion and fry, stirring occasionally, for 5–10 minutes until softened.

4 Transfer the cooked onion to a large mixing bowl, add the cooled oatmeal, minced pig's liver, minced pork, raisins, marjoram and allspice. Season with salt and ground black pepper and mix well together.

5 Pour the mixture into the prepared tin, level the top and bake in the preheated oven for 40 minutes to 1 hour, until lightly browned on top and cooked through. Serve the sausage terrine, either hot or cold, with fruit conserve and toast.

Three-fish Terrine Energy 290kcal/1216kJ; Protein 32.5g; Carbohydrate 13.7g, of which sugars 2.8g; Fat 12.1g, of which saturates 3.9g; Cholesterol 112mg; Calcium 203mg; Fibre 1.5g; Sodium 306mg.
Baked Sausage Energy 238kcal/1003kJ; Protein 15.6g; Carbohydrate 28.5g, of which sugars 17.8g; Fat 7.7g, of which saturates 3.1g; Cholesterol 91mg; Calcium 134mg; Fibre 1.5g; Sodium 105mg.

Leek Terrine with Deli Meats

This attractive appetizer is very simple to make yet looks spectacular. You can make the terrine a day ahead and keep it covered in the refrigerator.

Serves 6

20–24 small young leeks
about 225g/8oz mixed sliced meats, such as prosciutto, coppa or pancetta
50g/2oz/⅔ cup walnuts, toasted and chopped
60ml/4 tbsp walnut oil
60ml/4 tbsp olive oil
30ml/2 tbsp white wine vinegar
5ml/1 tsp wholegrain mustard
salt and black pepper

1 Cut off the roots and most of the green part from the leeks. Wash them under cold running water to get rid of any dirt.

2 Bring a large pan of salted water to the boil. Add the leeks, bring back to the boil, then reduce the heat and simmer for 6–8 minutes, until the leeks are just tender. Drain well.

3 Fill a 450g/1lb loaf tin (pan) with the leeks, placing them alternately head to tail and seasoning each layer as you go.

4 Put another loaf tin inside the first and gently press down on the leeks. Carefully invert both tins and let any water drain out.

5 Place one or two weights on top of the tins and chill the terrine for at least 4 hours, or overnight.

6 Meanwhile, make the dressing. Whisk together the walnut and olive oils, vinegar and wholegrain mustard in a small bowl. Add seasoning to taste.

7 Carefully turn out the terrine on to a board and cut into slices using a large sharp knife. Lay the slices of leek terrine on serving plates and arrange the slices of meat alongside.

8 Spoon the dressing over the slices of terrine and sprinkle over the chopped walnuts. Serve immediately.

Asparagus and Egg Terrine

For a special occasion, this terrine is a delicious choice.

Serves 8

150ml/¼ pint/⅔ cup milk
150ml/¼ pint/⅔ cup double (heavy) cream
40g/1½oz/3 tbsp butter
40g/1½oz/3 tbsp plain (all-purpose) flour
75g/3oz herbed or garlic cream cheese
675g/1½lb asparagus, cooked
vegetable oil, for brushing
2 eggs, separated
15ml/1 tbsp chopped fresh chives
30ml/2 tbsp chopped fresh dill
salt and ground black pepper
fresh dill sprigs, to garnish

For the hollandaise sauce

15ml/1 tbsp white wine vinegar
15ml/1 tbsp fresh orange juice
4 black peppercorns
1 bay leaf
2 egg yolks
115g/4oz/½ cup butter, melted and cooled slightly

1 Heat the milk and cream in a small pan to just below boiling point. Melt the butter in a medium pan, stir in the flour and cook over low heat, stirring constantly, to a thick paste. Gradually stir in the milk, whisking as it thickens. Stir in the cream cheese, season to taste and leave to cool slightly.

2 Trim the asparagus to fit the width of a 1.2 litre/2 pint/5 cup loaf tin (pan) or terrine. Lightly oil the tin and then base line with baking parchment. Preheat the oven to 180°C/350°F/Gas 4.

3 Beat the egg yolks into the sauce. Whisk the whites until stiff. Fold in with the chives, dill and seasoning. Layer the asparagus and egg mixture in the tin, starting and finishing with the asparagus. Cover with foil, place in a roasting pan and half fill with hot water. Cook for 45–55 minutes, until firm. Cool, then chill.

4 To make the sauce, put the vinegar, orange juice, peppercorns and bay leaf in a pan and heat gently until reduced by half. Cool the sauce slightly, then whisk in the egg yolks, then the butter, over a very gentle heat. Season to taste and continue whisking until thick. Keep the sauce warm over a pan of hot water.

5 Invert the terrine on to a serving dish, remove the paper and garnish with the dill. Serve in slices with the warmed sauce.

Leek Terrine Energy 244kcal/1010kJ; Protein 9.2g; Carbohydrate 2.6g, of which sugars 2.1g; Fat 21.9g, of which saturates 2.6g; Cholesterol 22mg; Calcium 27mg; Fibre 1.8g; Sodium 452mg.
Asparagus Terrine Energy 359kcal/1483kJ; Protein 6.6g; Carbohydrate 7.1g, of which sugars 3.2g; Fat 34.1g, of which saturates 20.2g; Cholesterol 175mg; Calcium 87mg; Fibre 1.6g; Sodium 179mg.

Cardamom Chicken Mousselines

These mousselines are made in the slow cooker and make an elegant appetizer. They should be served warm not hot, so when they are cooked, turn off the slow cooker and leave to cool for half an hour before eating.

Serves 6

350g/12oz skinless chicken breast fillets
1 shallot, finely chopped
115g/4oz/1 cup full-fat soft cheese
1 egg, lightly beaten
2 egg whites
crushed seeds of 2 cardamom pods
60ml/4 tbsp white wine
150ml/¼ pint/⅔ cup double (heavy) cream
oregano sprigs, to serve

For the tomato vinaigrette

350g/12oz ripe tomatoes
10ml/2 tsp balsamic vinegar
30ml/2 tbsp olive oil
sea salt and ground black pepper

1 Chop the chicken and put in a food processor with the shallot. Process until fairly smooth. Add the cheese, beaten egg, egg whites, cardamom seeds and wine and season with salt and pepper. Process again until the ingredients are blended.

2 Gradually add the cream, using the pulsing action, until the mixture has a smooth and creamy texture. Transfer to a bowl, cover with clear film (plastic wrap) and chill for 30 minutes.

3 Meanwhile, prepare six 150ml/¼ pint/⅔ cup ramekins or dariole moulds that will all fit in the slow cooker. Lightly grease the base of each one, then line. Pour about 2cm/¾ in hot water into the ceramic cooking pot and switch the cooker to high.

4 Divide the mixture among the dishes. Cover with foil and put in the ceramic cooking pot. Add more hot water to come halfway up the dishes. Cover and cook for 2½–3 hours until firm.

5 Meanwhile, peel, quarter, seed and dice the tomatoes. Place in a bowl and sprinkle with the vinegar and salt. Stir well.

6 To serve, unmould the mousselines on to warmed plates. Place tomato vinaigrette around each, then drizzle over a little olive oil and add black pepper. Garnish with sprigs of oregano.

Sea Trout Mousse

This deliciously creamy mousse makes a little trout go a long way. Serve with Melba toast or pitta bread.

Serves 6

250g/9oz sea trout fillet
120ml/4fl oz/½ cup fish stock
2 gelatine leaves, or 15ml/1 tbsp powdered gelatine
juice of ½ lemon
30ml/2 tbsp dry sherry or dry vermouth
30ml/2 tbsp freshly grated Parmesan
300ml/½ pint/1¼ cups whipping cream
2 egg whites
15ml/1 tbsp sunflower oil, for greasing
salt and ground white pepper

For the garnish

5cm/2in piece cucumber, with peel, thinly sliced and halved
fresh dill or chervil

1 Put the sea trout in a large, shallow pan. Pour in the stock and heat gently to simmering point. Poach the fish for about 3–4 minutes, until it is lightly cooked. Strain the stock into a bowl and leave the fish to cool slightly. Add the gelatine to the stock and stir until dissolved. Cover and set aside until required.

2 Remove and discard the skin and any stray bones from the fish, then flake the flesh. Pour the stock into a food processor or blender. Process briefly, then gradually add the fish, lemon juice, sherry or vermouth and Parmesan through the feeder tube, processing until the mixture is smooth. Leave to cool.

3 Lightly whip the cream in a bowl, then fold it into the cold trout mixture. Season to taste with salt and pepper, then cover with clear film (plastic wrap) and chill until the mousse is just starting to set. It should have the consistency of mayonnaise.

4 In a clean, grease-free bowl, beat the egg whites with a pinch of salt until they form soft peaks. Stir about one-third of the egg whites into the fish mixture, then carefully fold in the remainder.

5 Grease six ramekins or similar dishes and divide the mousse among them. Place in the refrigerator for 2–3 hours, until set. To serve, arrange a few cucumber slices and a herb sprig on top of each mousse and, finally, sprinkle over a little dill or chervil.

Mousselines Energy 191kcal/795kJ; Protein 18.1g; Carbohydrate 2g, of which sugars 2g; Fat 11.6g, of which saturates 5g; Cholesterol 96mg; Calcium 30mg; Fibre 0.7g; Sodium 130mg.
Sea Trout Mousse Energy 241kcal/999kJ; Protein 12.3g; Carbohydrate 1.8g, of which sugars 1.8g; Fat 20g, of which saturates 14.5g; Cholesterol 9mg; Calcium 104mg; Fibre 0.1g; Sodium 127mg.

Salmon and Pike Mousse

When sliced, this light-textured mousse loaf reveals a pretty layer of pink salmon. For a special occasion, serve topped with red salmon roe.

Serves 8

10ml/2 tsp oil
225g/8oz salmon fillet, skinned
600ml/1 pint/2½ cups fish stock
finely grated rind and juice of ½ lemon
900g/2lb pike fillets, skinned
4 egg whites
475ml/16fl oz/2 cups double (heavy) cream
30ml/2 tbsp chopped fresh dill
salt and ground black pepper
red salmon roe or a fresh dill sprig, to garnish (optional)

1 Preheat the oven to 180°C/350°F/Gas 4. Brush a 900g/2lb loaf tin (pan) with oil and line with baking parchment.

2 Cut the salmon into 5cm/2in strips. Pour the stock and lemon juice into a pan and bring to the boil, then turn off the heat. Add the salmon strips, cover and leave for 2 minutes. Remove with a slotted spoon.

3 Cut the pike into cubes and process in a food processor or blender until smooth. Lightly whisk the egg whites with a fork. With the motor of the food processor or blender running, slowly pour in the egg whites, then the cream through the feeder tube or lid. Finally, add the lemon rind and dill. Taste the mixture and add a little salt and pepper if you think more seasoning is needed.

4 Spoon half of the pike mixture into the prepared loaf tin. Arrange the poached salmon strips on top, then carefully spoon in the remaining pike mixture.

5 Cover the loaf tin with foil and put in a roasting pan. Add enough boiling water to come halfway up the sides of the loaf tin. Bake for 45–50 minutes, or until firm.

6 Leave on a wire rack to cool, then chill for at least 3 hours. Invert on to a serving plate and remove the lining paper. Serve the mousse in slices. Garnish with red salmon roe or a sprig of fresh dill, if you like.

Smoked Fish and Asparagus Mousse

This elegant mousse looks good with its studding of asparagus and smoked salmon. Serve a mustard and dill dressing separately, if you like.

Serves 8

15ml/1 tbsp powdered gelatine
juice of 1 lemon
105ml/7 tbsp fish stock
50g/2oz/¼ cup butter, plus extra for greasing
2 shallots, finely chopped
225g/8oz smoked trout fillets
105ml/7 tbsp sour cream
225g/8oz/1 cup soft white (farmer's) cheese
1 egg white
12 spinach leaves, blanched
12 fresh asparagus spears, lightly cooked
115g/4oz smoked salmon, cut in strips
salt
shredded beetroot (beet) and beetroot leaves, to garnish

1 Sprinkle the gelatine over the lemon juice and leave until spongy. In a small pan, heat the fish stock, then add the soaked gelatine and stir to dissolve completely. Set aside. Melt the butter in a pan, add the shallots and cook gently until softened but not coloured.

2 Break up the smoked trout fillets and put them in a food processor with the shallots, sour cream, stock mixture and cheese. Process until smooth, then spoon into a bowl.

3 In a clean bowl, beat the egg white with a pinch of salt to soft peaks. Fold into the fish. Cover the bowl; chill for 30 minutes, or until starting to set.

4 Grease a 1 litre/1¾ pint/4 cup loaf tin (pan) or terrine with butter, then line it with the spinach leaves. Carefully spread half the trout mousse over the spinach-covered base, arrange the asparagus spears on top, then cover with the remaining mousse.

5 Arrange the smoked salmon strips lengthways on the mousse and fold over the overhanging spinach leaves. Cover with clear film (plastic wrap) and chill for 4 hours, until set. To serve, remove the clear film, turn out on to a serving dish and garnish with the shredded beetroot and leaves.

Salmon Mousse Energy 477kcal/1977kJ; Protein 27.8g; Carbohydrate 1g, of which sugars 1g; Fat 40.3g, of which saturates 21.4g; Cholesterol 171mg; Calcium 89mg; Fibre 0g; Sodium 105mg.
Smoked Fish Energy 174kcal/723kJ; Protein 15.8g; Carbohydrate 2.8g, of which sugars 2.6g; Fat 11g, of which saturates 6g; Cholesterol 58mg; Calcium 75mg; Fibre 0.8g; Sodium 432mg.

Shrimp, Egg and Avocado Mousses

A light creamy mousse with lots of texture and a great mix of flavours. Serve chilled on the day you make it.

Serves 6

a little olive oil
20ml/4 tsp powdered gelatine
juice and rind of 1 lemon
60ml/4 tbsp mayonnaise
60ml/4 tbsp chopped fresh dill
5ml/1 tsp anchovy essence (paste)
5ml/1 tsp Worcestershire sauce
1 large avocado, ripe but just firm
4 hard-boiled eggs, peeled and chopped
175g/6oz/1 cup cooked peeled prawns (shrimp), coarsely chopped if large
250ml/8fl oz/1 cup double (heavy) or whipping cream, lightly whipped
2 egg whites, whisked
salt and ground black pepper
fresh dill or parsley sprigs, to garnish
warmed multigrain bread or toast, to serve

1 Prepare six small ramekins. Lightly grease the dishes with olive oil, then wrap a baking parchment collar around the top of each and secure with tape. This makes sure that you can fill the dishes as high as you like and that the extra mixture will be supported while it is setting. The mousses will, therefore, look really dramatic when you remove the paper. Alternatively, prepare just one small soufflé dish.

2 Dissolve the gelatine in the lemon juice with 15ml/1 tbsp hot water in a small bowl set over hot water, until clear, stirring occasionally. Allow to cool slightly, then blend in the lemon rind, mayonnaise, dill, anchovy essence and Worcestershire sauce.

3 In a medium bowl, mash the avocado flesh. Add the eggs and prawns. Stir in the gelatine mixture and then fold in the cream, egg whites and seasoning to taste. When evenly blended, spoon into the ramekins or soufflé dish and chill for 3–4 hours. Garnish with the herbs and serve with bread.

Cook's Tip
Other fish can make a good alternative to prawns. Try using the same quantity of smoked trout or salmon, or cooked crab meat.

Hot Crab Soufflés

These delicious little soufflés must be served as soon as they are ready, so seat your guests at the table before taking the soufflés out of the oven.

Serves 6

50g/2oz/¼ cup butter
45ml/3 tbsp fine wholemeal (whole-wheat) breadcrumbs
4 spring onions (scallions), finely chopped
15ml/1 tbsp Malayan or mild Madras curry powder
25g/1oz/2 tbsp plain (all-purpose) flour
105ml/7 tbsp coconut milk or milk
150ml/¼ pint/⅔ cup whipping cream
4 egg yolks
225g/8oz white crab meat
mild green Tabasco sauce
6 egg whites
salt and ground black pepper

1 Use some of the butter to grease six ramekins or a 1.75 litre/3 pint/7½ cup soufflé dish. Sprinkle the breadcrumbs in the dishes or dish and roll them around to coat the base and sides completely, then tip out the excess breadcrumbs. Preheat the oven to 200°C/400°F/Gas 6.

2 Melt the remaining butter in a pan, add the spring onions and Malayan or mild Madras curry powder and cook over a low heat, stirring frequently, for about 1 minute, until softened. Stir in the flour and cook, stirring constantly, for 1 minute more.

3 Gradually add the coconut milk or milk and the cream, stirring constantly. Cook over a low heat, still stirring, until smooth and thick. Remove the pan from the heat, stir in the egg yolks, then the crab. Season to taste with salt, black pepper and Tabasco sauce.

4 In a clean, grease-free bowl, whisk the egg whites with a pinch of salt until they are stiff. Using a metal spoon, stir one-third of the whites into the crab mixture to slacken, then fold in the remainder. Spoon into the dishes or dish.

5 Bake the soufflés until well risen, golden brown and just firm to the touch. Individual soufflés will take about 8 minutes, while a large soufflé will take 15–20 minutes. Serve immediately.

Shrimp Mousses Energy 384kcal/1589kJ; Protein 12g; Carbohydrate 2.1g, of which sugars 1.7g; Fat 38.9g, of which saturates 15.7g; Cholesterol 245mg; Calcium 88mg; Fibre 1.3g; Sodium 230mg.
Crab Soufflés Energy 270kcal/1122kJ; Protein 14g; Carbohydrate 11.6g, of which sugars 2.2g; Fat 18.9g, of which saturates 12.1g; Cholesterol 181mg; Calcium 123mg; Fibre 1g; Sodium 426mg.

Melting Cheese Dip

This is a classic fondue in true Swiss style. It should be served with cubes of crusty, day-old bread, speared on long-handled forks, but it is also good with chunks of spicy, cured sausage such as chorizo, or with vegetable batons of carrot or celery.

Serves 2

1 garlic clove, finely chopped
150ml/¼ pint/⅔ cup dry white wine
150g/5oz Gruyère cheese
5ml/1 tsp cornflour (cornstarch)
15ml/1 tbsp Kirsch
salt and ground black pepper
bread or chorizo cubes, to serve

1 Place the chopped garlic and white wine in a small pan and bring gently to the boil. Lower the heat and simmer for about 3–4 minutes.

2 Coarsely grate the cheese and stir it into the wine. Continue to stir as the cheese melts.

3 Blend the cornflour to a smooth paste with the Kirsch and pour into the pan, stirring. Bring to the boil, stirring constantly until the sauce is smooth and thickened.

4 Add salt and pepper to taste. Serve immediately in heated bowls or transfer to a fondue pan and keep hot over a spirit burner. Garnish with black pepper and serve with bread or chorizo cubes.

Cook's Tips

- *In the 1960s this was a favourite centrepiece for a dinner party, usually kept warm in a pottery pot set over a burner. Using long-handled forks, guests speared cubes of bread and dunked them in the cheese, twirling the forks until the bread was thoroughly coated. This activity could be hazardous and cubes of bread were often lost. When this happened, the individual concerned had to pay a forfeit.*
- *Gruyère is a tasty cheese that melts incredibly well. Don't substitute other cheeses in this dip.*

Fonduta

Fontina is an Italian medium-fat cheese with a mild nutty flavour, which melts easily and smoothly. It is a little like Gruyère, which makes a good substitute. This delicious cheese dip needs only some warm ciabatta bread or focaccia, a crisp salad and some robust red wine to complete a tasty appetizer.

Serves 4

225g/8oz/2 cups diced Fontina cheese
250ml/8fl oz/1 cup milk
15g/½oz/1 tbsp butter
2 eggs, lightly beaten
ground black pepper

1 Put the diced cheese in a bowl with the milk and leave to soak for about 2–3 hours.

2 Transfer the cheese and milk mixture to a double boiler or a heatproof bowl, which is set over a pan of simmering water.

3 Add the butter and eggs to the cheese and milk and cook gently, stirring until the cheese has melted to a smooth sauce with the consistency of custard.

4 Remove the bowl or double boiler from the heat and season with ground black pepper. Transfer the fonduta to a serving dish and serve immediately.

Cook's Tip

Ensure that you don't overheat the sauce, or the eggs in it might curdle. A very gentle simmering heat will produce a lovely smooth sauce.

Variation

Pour the Fonduta over hot pasta or polenta for a really satisfying main dish.

Melting Cheese Dip Energy 390kcal/1617kJ; Protein 19.4g; Carbohydrate 3.3g, of which sugars 0.6g; Fat 24.6g, of which saturates 16.3g; Cholesterol 73mg; Calcium 562mg; Fibre 0.1g; Sodium 547mg.
Fonduta Energy 250kcal/1039kJ; Protein 15.6g; Carbohydrate 3g, of which sugars 3g; Fat 19.7g, of which saturates 12g; Cholesterol 145mg; Calcium 290mg; Fibre 0g; Sodium 320mg.

Cheese and Guinness Fondue

This simple dish can be made with any melting cheese – richly flavoured farmhouse cheeses are the most interesting. It can be used as a hot dip for drinks parties, or as an appetizer for a smaller number, perhaps served with crusty bread cubes and followed by a green salad.

Serves 8

300ml/½ pint/1¼ cups stout, such as Guinness
5ml/1 tsp lemon juice
15ml/1 tbsp cornflour (cornstarch)
450g/1lb Irish 'melting' cheese(s), grated or finely diced
salt and ground black pepper
selection of crudités, such as celery, cauliflower and broccoli florets, carrot sticks, button (white) mushrooms, and chunks of sweet (bell) pepper, to serve

1 Heat the stout and lemon juice gently in a heavy pan, until it is just reaching boiling point.

2 Mix together the cornflour and cheese. Add to the pan of stout gradually, over a gentle heat, stirring until the cheese has melted. Season to taste with salt and ground black pepper and cook gently until the fondue thickens.

3 Transfer the dip to a fondue pot and place over a burner at the table. To serve, spear the crudités with a fork and dip them into the fondue.

Cook's Tips

- *The fondue will thicken as it cools, so it is necessary to keep it warm over a flame, or serve it in a preheated electric slow cooker, if you prefer.*
- *Choose cheeses such as a mature (sharp) farmhouse Cheddar and other semi-hard melting cheeses such as Gabriel and Desmond, and Ardrahan, a vegetarian washed-rind cheese from west Cork in Ireland.*

Chilli Yogurt Cheese in Olive Oil

Yogurt, hung in muslin to drain off the whey, makes a superb soft cheese. Here it is bottled in olive oil with chilli and herbs, ready for serving on toast or crackers as a quick and tasty appetizer.

Fills 2 x 450g/1lb jars

800g/1¾lb/about 4 cups Greek (US strained plain) yogurt
2.5ml/½ tsp salt
10ml/2 tsp crushed dried chillies or chilli powder
15ml/1 tbsp chopped fresh rosemary
15ml/1 tbsp chopped fresh thyme or oregano
about 300ml/½ pint/1¼ cups olive oil, preferably garlic-flavoured
lightly toasted country bread, to serve

1 Sterilize a 30cm/12in square of muslin (cheesecloth) by steeping it in boiling water. Drain and lay over a large plate. Mix the yogurt with the salt and place on to the centre of the cloth. Bring up the sides of the cloth and tie firmly.

2 Hang the bag from a kitchen cabinet handle or in any convenient, cool position that allows a bowl to be placed underneath to catch the whey. Leave for 2–3 days until the yogurt stops dripping.

3 Sterilize two 450g/1lb clean glass preserving or jam jars by heating them in the oven at 150°C/300°F/Gas 2 for about 15 minutes. Alternatively, put them through a hot wash cycle in a dishwasher.

4 Mix the dried chillies and herbs in a bowl. Take teaspoonfuls of the cheese and roll into balls between the palms of your hands. Lower into jars, sprinkling each layer with the herb and chilli mixture.

5 Pour the oil over the cheese until the balls are completely covered. Close the jars tightly and store in the refrigerator for up to 3 weeks. To serve the cheese, spoon out of the jars with a little of the flavoured olive oil and spread on to fresh or lightly toasted farmhouse bread.

Cheese Fondue Energy 250Kcal/1036kJ; Protein 14.5g; Carbohydrate 1.8g, of which sugars 0.6g; Fat 18.4g, of which saturates 12.2g; Cholesterol 55mg; Calcium 417mg; Fibre 0g; Sodium 410mg.
Chilli Yogurt Energy 1331kcal/5488kJ; Protein 24g; Carbohydrate 7.5g, of which sugars 7.5g; Fat 138.2g, of which saturates 33.8g; Cholesterol 0mg; Calcium 563mg; Fibre 0g; Sodium 758mg.

Goat's Cheese Soufflé

This simple, elegant soufflé makes an ideal appetizer.

Serves 6–8

4 large heads of garlic
6 fresh thyme sprigs
30ml/2 tbsp olive oil
475ml/16fl oz/2 cups milk
2 fresh bay leaves
4 × 1cm/½in thick onion slices
4 cloves
115g/4oz/½ cup butter
75g/3oz/⅔ cup plain (all-purpose) flour, sifted
cayenne pepper
6 eggs, separated, plus 1 egg white
300g/11oz goat's cheese, crumbled
115g/4oz/1⅓ cups freshly grated Parmesan cheese
10ml/2 tsp chopped fresh thyme
5ml/1 tsp cream of tartar
salt and ground black pepper

1 Preheat the oven to 180°C/350°F/Gas 4. Place the garlic and thyme sprigs on a piece of foil. Sprinkle with the oil and close the foil. Bake for 1 hour, until the garlic is soft. Leave to cool. Squeeze the garlic out of its skin. Discard the thyme and garlic skins, then purée the garlic flesh with the oil.

2 Meanwhile, boil the milk, bay leaves, onion and cloves in a pan. Remove from the heat, cover and leave for 30 minutes. Melt 75g/3oz/6 tbsp of the butter in another pan. Stir in the flour and cook gently for 2 minutes. Reheat and strain the milk, then gradually stir it into the flour and butter.

3 Cook the sauce gently for 10 minutes, stirring frequently. Season with salt, pepper and a little cayenne. Cool slightly. Preheat the oven to 200°C/400°F/Gas 6. Beat the egg yolks into the sauce, then beat in the goat's cheese, all but 30ml/2 tbsp of the Parmesan and the thyme. Grease eight small ramekins.

4 Whisk the egg whites and cream of tartar in a clean, grease-free bowl until firm. Stir 90ml/6 tbsp of the whites into the sauce, then gently fold in the remainder using a rubber spatula.

5 Pour the mixture into the ramekins. Run a knife around the edge of each to push the mixture away from the rim. Sprinkle with the reserved Parmesan. Place on a baking sheet and cook for 20 minutes. The mixture should be risen and firm to a light touch in the centre. Serve immediately.

Corn Griddle Cakes

Known as arepas, these are a staple bread in several Latin American countries. Eat them filled with soft white cheese, as here, or plain as an accompaniment. With their crisp crust and chewy interior, arepas can become stale very quickly, so are best eaten piping hot.

Serves 4–6

200g/7oz/1¾ cups masarepa (or masa harina)
2.5ml/½ tsp salt
300ml/½ pint/1¼ cups water
15ml/1 tbsp oil
200g/7oz fresh white cheese, such as queso fresco or mozzarella, roughly chopped

1 Combine the masarepa or masa harina and salt in a bowl. Gradually stir in the water to make a soft dough, then set aside for about 20 minutes.

2 Divide the dough into 15 equal balls, then, using your fingers, flatten each ball into a circle, approximately 1cm/½in thick.

3 Heat 5ml/1 tsp of the oil in a large, heavy frying pan over a medium heat. Using a piece of kitchen paper, gently wipe the surface of the frying pan, leaving it just lightly greased.

4 Place five of the arepas in the frying pan. Cook for about 4 minutes, then flip over and cook for a further 4 minutes. The arepas should be lightly blistered on both sides. Open the arepas and fill each with a few small pieces of cheese. Return to the pan to cook until the cheese melts. Remove and and keep warm.

5 Cook the remaining arepas in the same way, oiling the pan and wiping with kitchen paper, to ensure it is always lightly greased. Serve the arepas warm so that the cheese is runny.

Cook's Tip
Masarepa is a flour made with the white corn grown in the Andes. Look for it in Latin American food stores. If not available, replace it with masa harina, the flour used to make tamales. The result will not be quite as delicate, but will be equally tasty.

Soufflé Energy 563kcal/2339kJ; Protein 28.8g; Carbohydrate 16.5g, of which sugars 5.8g; Fat 42.9g, of which saturates 24.1g; Cholesterol 294mg; Calcium 422mg; Fibre 0.7g; Sodium 710mg.
Corn Griddle Cakes Energy 110kcal/463kJ; Protein 4.8g; Carbohydrate 13.2g, of which sugars 0.3g; Fat 4.6g, of which saturates 2.5g; Cholesterol 10mg; Calcium 86mg; Fibre 0.5g; Sodium 68mg.

Cheese Scrolls

These delicious Bulgarian savouries are traditionally served warm as a first course, or else as a snack in cafés, restaurants and homes at any time of the day.

Serves 4–6

450g/1lb/2 cups feta cheese, well drained and finely crumbled
90ml/6 tbsp natural Greek (US strained plain) yogurt
2 eggs, beaten
14–16 sheets 40 × 30cm/16 × 12in ready-made filo pastry, thawed if frozen
225g/8oz/1 cup unsalted butter, melted
sea salt and chopped spring onions (scallions), to garnish

1 Preheat the oven to 200°C/400°F/Gas 6. In a large bowl, mix together the feta cheese, yogurt and eggs, beating well until the mixture is smooth.

2 Fit a piping (pastry) bag with a large 1cm/½in plain round nozzle and fill with half of the cheese mixture.

3 Lay out one sheet of pastry, fold into a 30 × 20cm/12 × 8in rectangle and brush with a little melted butter. Along one long edge pipe the cheese mixture 5mm/¼in away from the edge.

4 Roll up the pastry to form a sausage shape and tuck in each end, to prevent the filling escaping. Brush with more melted butter.

5 Form the 'sausage' into a tight 'S' or a crescent shape. Repeat with the remaining ingredients, refilling the piping bag as necessary.

6 Place the scrolls on a greased baking sheet and sprinkle with a little salt and chopped spring onion. Bake for 20 minutes, or until golden brown and crispy. Cool on a wire rack, before serving.

Cook's Tip

If possible, use the locally made sheep's cheese, bryndza. Made throughout Eastern Europe, it is a subtly flavoured, crumbly and moist cheese that resembles feta, but it is not as salty. It is increasingly available in Middle Eastern or Cypriot delicatessens.

Bitesize Cheese Brioches

These mouthfuls of golden, buttery dough have a nugget of melting cheese in the middle, so be sure to serve them warm.

Makes about 40

450g/1lb/4 cups plain (all-purpose) or strong white bread flour, plus extra for dusting
5ml/1 tsp salt
5ml/1 tsp ground turmeric
1 sachet easy-blend (rapid-rise) dried yeast
150ml/¼ pint/⅔ cup warm milk
2 eggs, plus 2 egg yolks
75g/3oz/6 tbsp butter, melted and slightly cooled
50g/2oz/½ cup grated Cheddar cheese
oil, for greasing
50g/2oz/½ cup cubed cheese, such as Cheshire, Gouda or Port Salut

1 Sift the dry ingredients into a large bowl with the yeast and make a hollow in the middle. Mix the milk, eggs and one yolk with the butter and Cheddar.

2 Pour the liquid into the well in the dry ingredients and blend the mixture together. Continue mixing until it is well combined. Turn out on to a lightly floured surface and knead, working in as little flour as possible, until the surface is smooth and dry.

3 Place the dough in a lightly oiled bowl. Lightly oil the top of the dough, cover with a clean dish towel and leave in a warm place for at least 1 hour, until the dough has doubled in bulk.

4 Turn out on to a floured surface and knead the dough until it becomes firm and elastic. Divide into four batches, then divide each into eight to ten pieces. Knead each piece until smooth.

5 Press a cheese cube into the middle of each piece of dough, then shape into a round and place in paper sweet (candy) cases. Place the paper cases in mini muffin trays to support the soft dough during baking. Set the brioches aside in a warm place until they are well risen and have almost doubled in size.

6 Preheat the oven to 200°C/400°F/Gas 6. Mix the remaining yolk with 15ml/1 tbsp water and glaze the brioches. Bake for 15 minutes, or until golden brown, risen and firm underneath.

Cheese Scrolls Energy 586kcal/2425kJ; Protein 17.1g; Carbohydrate 15.1g, of which sugars 2g; Fat 51.4g, of which saturates 32.3g; Cholesterol 203mg; Calcium 344mg; Fibre 0.5g; Sodium 1390mg.
Bitesize Cheese Brioches Energy 64kcal/270kJ; Protein 2.1g; Carbohydrate 9g, of which sugars 0.4g; Fat 2.5g, of which saturates 1.3g; Cholesterol 25mg; Calcium 27mg; Fibre 0.3g; Sodium 75mg.

Stilton Croquettes

These are perfect little party bites or appetizers, which you can make in advance and reheat at the last minute.

Serves 4–6

350g/12oz floury potatoes, peeled and cut into chunks
75g/3oz creamy Stilton, crumbled
3 eggs, hard-boiled, peeled and chopped
few drops of Worcestershire sauce
a little plain (all-purpose) flour
1 egg, beaten
45–60ml/3–4 tbsp fine breadcrumbs
vegetable oil, for deep frying
salt and ground black pepper
dipping sauce, to serve

1 Put the potatoes in a large pan. Add water to cover and bring to the boil. Add salt, then simmer for about 15 minutes, or until the potatoes are tender, but do not let them get too soft. Drain thoroughly and leave to cool.

2 Mash the potatoes until quite smooth. Work in the crumbled Stilton cheese, chopped egg and Worcestershire sauce. Add seasoning to taste.

3 Divide the potato and cheese mixture into approximately 20 pieces and shape into small sausage or cork shapes, no longer than 2.5cm/1in.

4 Coat in flour, then dip into the beaten egg and coat evenly in breadcrumbs. Reshape, if necessary. Chill for about 30 minutes.

5 Deep-fry, seven or eight croquettes at a time, in hot oil, turning frequently until they are golden brown all over. Drain on kitchen paper, transfer to a serving dish and keep warm for up to 30 minutes. Serve with a dipping sauce.

Cook's Tip
You can make these croquettes in advance and freeze them before frying. To defrost, leave them to stand in a warm place for 1 hour before frying.

Blue Cheese and Chive Pennies

These tasty nibbles are ideal for serving before a meal, to whet the appetite, or as appetizers with drinks. The blue cheese gives them a deliciously tangy taste.

Serves 6

225g/8oz blue cheese, such as Oregon Blue, crumbled
115g/4oz/½ cup unsalted butter, at room temperature
1 egg plus 1 egg yolk
45ml/3 tbsp chopped fresh chives
ground black pepper
225g/8oz/2 cups plain (all-purpose) flour, sifted

1 The day before serving, beat the crumbled cheese and butter together until well blended. Add the egg, egg yolk, chopped chives and a little ground black pepper and beat until the ingredients are just blended.

2 Add the flour to the mixture in three batches, folding in well between each addition.

3 Divide the mixture in half and shape each half into a log with your hands, about 5cm/2in in diameter. Tightly wrap both the rolled logs in a sheet of baking parchment and chill in the refrigerator overnight.

4 Preheat the oven to 190°C/375°F/Gas 5. Lightly grease two baking sheets.

5 Cut the logs across into slices about 3mm/⅛ in thick. Place on the prepared sheets.

6 Bake in the preheated oven until the pennies have just turned golden around the edges, about 10–12 minutes. Transfer to a wire rack to cool.

Cook's Tip
The cheese pennies will keep for up to 10 days in an airtight container in the refrigerator.

Croquettes Energy 264kcal/1095kJ; Protein 7.4g; Carbohydrate 12.7g, of which sugars 0.8g; Fat 20.6g, of which saturates 4.7g; Cholesterol 117mg; Calcium 60mg; Fibre 0.6g; Sodium 189mg.
Cheese Pennies Energy 431kcal/1794kJ; Protein 13.1g; Carbohydrate 29.9g, of which sugars 0.7g; Fat 29.6g, of which saturates 18.2g; Cholesterol 137mg; Calcium 253mg; Fibre 1.2g; Sodium 601mg.

Cheese Aigrettes

These choux buns, flavoured with mature Gruyère and dusted with grated Parmesan, are a bit fiddly to make, but the dough can be prepared ahead and then deep-fried.

Makes 30

100g/3¾oz/scant 1 cup strong plain (all-purpose) flour
2.5ml/½ tsp paprika
2.5ml/½ tsp salt
75g/3oz/6 tbsp cold butter, diced
200ml/7fl oz/scant 1 cup water
3 eggs, beaten
75g/3oz/¾ cup coarsely grated mature (sharp) Gruyère cheese
corn or vegetable oil, for deep-frying
50g/2oz piece of Parmesan cheese, finely grated
ground black pepper
sprigs of flat leaf parsley, to garnish

1 Sift the flour, paprika and salt on to a large sheet of foil or baking parchment. Add a generous grinding of black pepper.

2 Put the butter and water into a medium pan and heat gently. As soon as the butter has melted and the liquid starts to boil, add in all the seasoned flour at once and beat hard with a wooden spoon until the dough forms a ball and comes away from the sides of the pan.

3 Remove the pan from the heat and cool the paste for about 5 minutes. This step is important if the aigrettes are to rise well. Gradually beat in enough of the beaten egg to give a stiff dropping consistency that still holds a shape on the spoon. Mix in the Gruyère.

4 Heat the oil for deep-frying to 180°C/350°F or until a cube of bread, added to the hot oil, browns in about 1 minute. Take a teaspoonful of the choux paste and use a second spoon to slide it into the oil. Make more aigrettes in the same way. Fry for 3–4 minutes until golden brown. Drain on kitchen paper and keep warm while cooking successive batches.

5 To serve, pile the aigrettes on a warmed serving dish, sprinkle with Parmesan and garnish with sprigs of parsley.

Cheese and Chilli Tortillas

These cheese-filled tortillas are the Mexican equivalent of toasted sandwiches. Serve them as soon as they are cooked, or they will become chewy. If you are making them for a crowd, fill and fold the tortillas ahead of time, but only cook them to order.

Serves 4

200g/7oz mozzarella, Monterey Jack or mild Cheddar cheese
1 fresh fresno chilli (optional)
8 wheat flour tortillas, about 15cm/6in across
tomato salsa, to serve

1 If using mozzarella cheese, it must be drained thoroughly and then patted dry and sliced into thin strips. Monterey Jack and Cheddar should both be coarsely grated, as finely grated cheese will melt and ooze away when cooking. Set the cheese aside in a bowl.

2 If using the chilli, spear it on a long-handled metal skewer and roast it over the flame of a gas burner until the skin blisters and darkens. Do not let the flesh burn. Alternatively, dry fry it in a griddle pan until the skin is scorched. Place the roasted chilli in a strong plastic bag and tie the top to keep the steam in. Set aside for 20 minutes.

3 Remove the chilli from the bag and peel off the skin. Cut off the stalk, then slit the chilli and scrape out the seeds. Cut the flesh into eight thin strips.

4 Warm a large frying pan or griddle. Place one tortilla on the pan or griddle at a time, sprinkle about an eighth of the cheese on to one half and add a strip of chilli, if using. Fold the tortilla over the cheese and press the edges together gently to seal. Cook the filled tortilla for about 1 minute until the cheese is beginning to melt, then carefully turn over and cook the other side for 1 minute.

5 Remove the filled tortilla from the pan or griddle, cut it into three triangles or four strips and serve immediately, with the tomato salsa. Cook the remaining tortillas in the same way.

Cheese Aigrettes Energy 84kcal/348kJ; Protein 2.2g; Carbohydrate 2.4g, of which sugars 0.1g; Fat 7.3g, of which saturates 2.7g; Cholesterol 28mg; Calcium 46mg; Fibre 0.1g; Sodium 58mg.
Cheese and Chilli Tortillas Energy 418kcal/1764kJ; Protein 17g; Carbohydrate 66g, of which sugars 7g; Fat 11g, of which saturates 7g; Cholesterol 29mg; Calcium 303mg; Fibre 2.6g; Sodium 0.5mg.

Cheese Fritters in Wonton Wrappers

These crisp fritters owe their inspiration to Italy although the wrappers are strictly Chinese – a fine example of fusion food. A note of caution – do be careful not to burn your mouth when you take your first bite, as the soft, rich cheese filling will be very hot and the fritters are so irresistible that waiting for them to cool down is well nigh impossible.

Makes 16

115g/4oz/½ cup ricotta cheese
50g/2oz/½ cup grated fontina cheese
25g/1oz/⅓ cup finely grated Parmesan cheese
pinch of cayenne pepper
1 egg, beaten, plus a little extra to seal the wontons
16 wonton wrappers
vegetable oil, for deep-frying

1 Line a large baking sheet with baking parchment or sprinkle it lightly with flour. Set aside. Combine the cheeses in a bowl, then add the cayenne and beaten egg and mix well.

2 Place one wonton wrapper at a time on a board. Brush the edges with egg. Spoon a little filling in the centre. Pull the top corner down to the bottom corner, to make a triangle.

3 Carefully transfer the filled wontons to the prepared baking sheet, keeping them well spaced apart.

4 Heat the oil in a deep-fryer or large pan. Slip in as many wontons at one time as can be accommodated without overcrowding. Fry them for 2–3 minutes on each side or until the fritters are golden. Remove with a slotted spoon and keep warm while you make the remaining fritters. Drain well on kitchen paper and serve immediately.

Cook's Tip
The optimum temperature for frying wontons is 190°C/375°F. If you do not have a thermometer, drop a cube of stale bread into the oil; it should brown in 30–40 seconds.

Cheese Tamales

Cornmeal dumplings steamed in corn husks are to be found throughout South America, and make excellent appetizers.

Serves 5

10 large dried corn husks or baking parchment
75g/3oz/6 tbsp lard or white cooking fat, at room temperature
225g/8oz/2 cups cornmeal
5ml/1 tsp salt
5ml/1 tsp baking powder
250–300ml/8–10fl oz/1–1¼ cups warm light vegetable stock
200g/7oz fresh white cheese, such as feta, roughly chopped

1 Place the corn husks in a bowl and pour over boiling water to cover. Soak for 30 minutes, until the husks become soft and pliable. Remove from the water and pat dry with a dish towel.

2 Meanwhile put the lard or white cooking fat in a mixing bowl and beat with an electric whisk until light and fluffy. Combine the cornmeal, salt and baking powder in a separate bowl. Gradually add to the lard, beating in 45ml/3 tbsp at a time. As the mixture thickens, start adding the stock, alternating the dry mixture and the stock until the mixture is light and spreadable. If it feels tough or dry, beat in a little warm water, but don't add more stock, as the dough will already be flavoursome enough.

3 To assemble, lay the prepared corn husks on a board and spread about one-tenth of the dough mixture in the centre of each, leaving a small border at either side, with a larger border at the top and bottom.

4 Place a piece of cheese in the centre of the dough mixture. Fold one of the longer lengths of husk over, so that it covers the filling, then repeat with the opposite end. Close the package by folding over the two remaining sides, to make a neat parcel. Secure by tying with a piece of string or strip of corn husk.

5 Pile the tamales in a steamer basket placed over a pan of simmering water. Cover and steam for 1 hour. Check the level of the water occasionally, topping up if necessary. The tamales are ready when the dough comes away from the corn husk cleanly. Allow to stand for 10 minutes, then serve.

Cheese Fritters Energy 112kcal/467kJ; Protein 3.5g; Carbohydrate 8.7g, of which sugars 0.4g; Fat 7.2g, of which saturates 2.3g; Cholesterol 20mg; Calcium 59mg; Fibre 0.3g; Sodium 44mg.
Tamales Energy 399kcal/1657kJ; Protein 10.5g; Carbohydrate 33.5g, of which sugars 0.6g; Fat 24.4g, of which saturates 11.6g; Cholesterol 42mg; Calcium 146mg; Fibre 1g; Sodium 969mg.

Polpettes

Yummy little fried mouthfuls of potato and tangy-sharp Greek feta cheese, flavoured with dill and lemon juice. Serve as an appetizer or party bite.

Serves 4

500g/1¼lb floury potatoes
115g/4oz/1 cup feta cheese
4 spring onions (scallions), finely chopped
45ml/3 tbsp chopped fresh dill
1 egg, beaten
15ml/1 tbsp lemon juice
plain (all-purpose) flour, for dredging
45ml/3 tbsp olive oil
salt and ground black pepper
dill sprigs, to garnish
shredded spring onions (scallions), to garnish
lemon wedges, to serve

1 Cook the potatoes in their skins in boiling, lightly salted water until soft. Drain and leave to cool slightly, then chop them in half and peel while still warm.

2 Place the potatoes in a bowl and mash. Crumble the feta cheese into the potatoes and add the spring onions, dill, egg and lemon juice and season with salt and pepper. (The cheese is salty, so taste before you add salt.) Stir well.

3 Cover the bowl and chill in the refrigerator until the mixture is firm. Divide the mixture into walnut-size balls, then flatten them slightly. Dredge with flour, shaking off the excess.

4 Heat the oil in a heavy frying pan and fry the cakes in batches until golden brown, about 3–5 minutes on both sides. Keep the cooked cakes warm while you finish the mixture. Drain well on kitchen paper and serve hot, garnished with spring onions, dill and lemon wedges.

Cook's Tip

Ensure that you use floury varieties of potatoes for this dish rather than waxy potatoes, such as new or salad potatoes. Look out for varieties such as Golden Wonder, Maris Piper, Estima and King Edward.

Stuffed Mushrooms with Spinach

Use fresh ceps, if you can find them, to achieve the traditional flavour of this dish. Large, flat mushrooms work very well too.

Serves 6

12 large flat mushrooms
450g/1lb young spinach leaves
4 large sun-dried tomatoes preserved in oil, cut into 5mm/¼in dice
1 onion, finely chopped
2 egg yolks, beaten
40g/1½ oz/¾ cup fresh breadcrumbs
5ml/1 tsp chopped fresh marjoram
45ml/3 tbsp olive oil or vegetable oil
115g/4oz feta cheese, crumbled
salt and ground black pepper

1 Wipe the mushrooms, peeling them only if necessary. Remove the stalks and chop them finely.

2 Blanch the spinach by dropping it into boiling water for 1–2 minutes, then plunge into cold water. Squeeze dry in kitchen paper, then chop.

3 Dry fry the onion until golden, then add the mushroom stalks. Remove from the heat. Stir in the spinach, egg yolks, tomatoes, breadcrumbs and marjoram, and season to taste.

4 Place the mushrooms, undersides up, on a baking sheet and brush with a little extra virgin olive oil. Do not add too much olive oil as the mushrooms will produce moisture while they are cooking.

5 Place heaped tablespoons of the spinach mixture on to the mushroom caps. Sprinkle over the cheese and cook the mushrooms under a preheated grill (broiler) for 10 minutes, or until golden brown.

Variations

Try different combinations for the stuffing: ham and cheese, sausage and onion or crab and red (bell) pepper.

Polpettes Energy 230kcal/960kJ; Protein 8.4g; Carbohydrate 20.9g, of which sugars 2.3g; Fat 13.1g, of which saturates 5.3g; Cholesterol 68mg; Calcium 122mg; Fibre 1.4g; Sodium 446mg.
Stuffed Mushrooms Energy 212kcal/882kJ; Protein 12g; Carbohydrate 8.1g, of which sugars 2.5g; Fat 14.8g, of which saturates 4.8g; Cholesterol 87mg; Calcium 226mg; Fibre 3.7g; Sodium 636mg.

Fried Rice Balls Stuffed with Mozzarella

These deep-fried balls are very popular snacks, which is hardly surprising as they are quite delicious.

Serves 4
1 quantity risotto with Parmesan cheese or mushroom risotto
3 eggs
breadcrumbs and plain (all-purpose) flour, to coat
115g/4oz/⅔ cup mozzarella cheese, cut into small cubes
oil, for deep-frying
dressed curly endive and cherry tomatoes, to serve

1 Put the risotto in a bowl and allow it to cool completely. Beat two of the eggs, and stir them into the bowl of cold risotto until the ingredients are well mixed.

2 Use your hands to form the rice mixture into balls the size of a large egg. If the mixture is too moist to hold its shape well, stir in a few tablespoons of breadcrumbs.

3 Poke a hole in the centre of each ball with your finger, then fill it with a few small cubes of mozzarella, and close the hole over again with the rice mixture.

4 Heat the oil for deep-frying in a wok or deep-fryer to a temperature of 190°C/375°F or until a small piece of bread sizzles as soon as it is dropped in.

5 Spread some of the flour on a plate. Beat the remaining egg in a shallow bowl and pour on to another plate. Sprinkle another plate with the breadcrumbs. Roll the balls in the flour, then in the egg, and finally in the breadcrumbs, making sure they are coated all over.

6 Fry the coated rice balls a few at a time in the hot oil until golden and crisp. Drain on kitchen paper while the remaining balls are being fried. Pile on to a serving platter and serve hot, with a simple salad of dressed curly endive leaves and cherry tomatoes.

Spinach and Cheese Pancakes

These tasty pancakes are filled with feta and Parmesan cheese and spinach.

Serves 4–6
4 eggs, beaten
40g/1½oz/3 tbsp butter, melted
250ml/8fl oz/1 cup single (light) cream
250ml/8fl oz/1 cup soda water
175g/6oz/1½ cups plain (all-purpose) flour, sifted
pinch of salt
1 egg white, lightly beaten
oil, for frying

For the filling
350g/12oz/1½ cups feta cheese, crumbled
50g/2oz/⅔ cup Parmesan cheese, grated
40g/1½oz/3 tbsp butter
1 garlic clove, crushed
450g/1lb frozen spinach, thawed
shavings of Parmesan, to garnish

1 Blend the eggs, butter, cream and water in a food processor or blender. With the motor running, spoon in the flour and salt through the feeder tube until the mixture is smooth. Leave to stand for 15 minutes to rest, loosely covered.

2 Lightly grease a 13–15cm/5–6in non-stick frying pan and place over medium heat. When hot, pour in 45–60ml/3–4 tbsp of the batter, tilting the pan to spread the mixture thinly. Cook for about 1½–2 minutes or until the underside of the pancake is pale golden brown, then turn over and cook the other side. Repeat the process until all the batter has been used, stacking the pancakes on a warm plate as you go.

3 For the filling, in a clean bowl mix together well the crumbled feta and Parmesan cheese, the butter and garlic clove. Thoroughly stir in the squeeze-dried spinach.

4 Place 30–45ml/2–3 tbsp of the filling mixture on to the centre of each pancake. Brush a little egg white around the outer edges of the pancakes and then fold them over. Press the edges down well to seal.

5 Fry the pancakes in a little oil on both sides, turning gently, until they are golden brown and the filling is hot. Serve immediately, garnished with Parmesan shavings.

Rice Balls Energy 670kcal/2792kJ; Protein 23.8g; Carbohydrate 73.8g, of which sugars 1.5g; Fat 31.2g, of which saturates 18.2g; Cholesterol 192mg; Calcium 383mg; Fibre 0.7g; Sodium 621mg.
Spinach Pancakes Energy 215kcal/894kJ; Protein 8.7g; Carbohydrate 13g, of which sugars 3.3g; Fat 14.6g, of which saturates 7.7g; Cholesterol 123mg; Calcium 277mg; Fibre 3g; Sodium 297mg.

Ciabatta with Mozzarella and Onions

Serve these tasty, cheese-topped breads as an appetizer. They are ideal to serve with barbecued food and they are just as good cold as hot so can also be taken on a picnic.

Serves 4

1 ciabatta loaf
60ml/4 tbsp red pesto
2 small onions
olive oil, for brushing
225g/8oz mozzarella cheese, sliced
8 black olives, halved and pitted

1 Cut the bread in half horizontally and toast the cut sides lightly on a hot barbecue or under a preheated grill (broiler). Spread the toasted sides with the red pesto.

2 Peel the onions and cut them horizontally into slices. Brush with oil and cook on a hot barbecue or under the grill for 4–5 minutes until the edges are caramelized.

3 Arrange the mozzarella slices on the bread. Add the onion slices and sprinkle some olives over. Cut in half. Return to the barbecue or grill to melt the cheese.

Cook's Tip
Choose mozzarella cheese that is made from water buffalo's milk rather than cow's milk for a superior flavour. It is labelled 'mozzarella di bufala' or 'mozzarella di bufala campana'.

Variation
Ciabatta bread is readily available and is even more delicious when made with spinach, sun-dried tomatoes or chopped olives: you can find these variations in supermarkets and large food stores.

Goat's Cheese and Crostini with Fruit

A sherry marinade accentuates the flavour of the goat's cheese and contrasts beautifully with the fruity tomato, orange and basil salsa.

Serves 4

8 slices of goat's cheese
15ml/1 tbsp sherry
30ml/2 tbsp walnut oil
30ml/2 tbsp olive oil
4 slices of Italian or French bread
1 garlic clove, halved
2 spring onions (scallions), sliced
6 shelled walnut halves, roughly broken
15ml/1 tbsp chopped fresh parsley
salt and ground black pepper
tomatoes and mixed salad leaves, to serve

For the salsa

5 tomatoes, peeled, seeded and chopped
2 oranges, peeled and segmented
15ml/1 tbsp chopped fresh basil
30ml/2 tbsp olive oil
pinch of soft light brown sugar
fresh basil sprig, to garnish

1 Put the goat's cheese slices into a shallow bowl, pour over the sherry, walnut oil and olive oil, then marinate in a cool place for 1 hour.

2 In a bowl, mix together all the ingredients for the salsa. Season to taste and garnish with the basil.

3 Toast the slices of bread on one side, then turn them over and rub the untoasted surfaces with the cut sides of the garlic. Brush with the marinade, then sprinkle the sliced spring onions on top. Arrange two of the marinated slices of cheese on each slice of bread.

4 Pour over any remaining marinade, sprinkle with pepper and cook the crostini under a hot grill (broiler) until the cheese has browned. Sprinkle the walnuts and parsley on top. Serve with the tomatoes, salad leaves and the bowl of salsa.

Cook's Tip
French goat's milk cheese or chèvre is often cylindrical in shape, which makes it perfect for this dish.

Ciabatta Energy 828kcal/3484kJ; Protein 34.8g; Carbohydrate 109.9g, of which sugars 10.4g; Fat 30.7g, of which saturates 11.7g; Cholesterol 40mg; Calcium 562mg; Fibre 6g; Sodium 1664mg.
Crostini Energy 531kcal/2214kJ; Protein 17.4g; Carbohydrate 31.6g, of which sugars 10.1g; Fat 37.8g, of which saturates 11.9g; Cholesterol 47mg; Calcium 175mg; Fibre 3.3g; Sodium 543mg.

Walnut and Goat's Cheese Bruschetta

The combination of toasted walnuts and melting goat's cheese is lovely in this simple appetizer, which can be served with a dressed salad if the occasion calls for it.

Serves 4

50g/2oz/½ cup walnut pieces
4 thick slices walnut bread
120ml/4fl oz/½ cup French dressing
200g/7oz chèvre or other semi-soft goat's cheese

1 Preheat the grill (broiler). Spread out the walnut pieces on a baking sheet. Lightly toast them, shaking the baking sheet once or twice so that they cook evenly, then remove and set them aside, leaving them to cool on the baking sheet.

2 Put the walnut bread on a foil-lined grill rack and lightly toast on one side. Turn the slices over and drizzle the untoasted side of each with 15ml/1 tbsp of the French dressing so that it soaks in a little.

3 Cut the goat's cheese into 12 slices and place three on each piece of bread. Grill (broil) under medium heat for about 3 minutes, until the cheese is melting and beginning to brown and bubble on the surface.

4 Transfer the bruschetta to serving plates, sprinkle with the toasted walnuts and drizzle with the remaining French dressing. Serve the bruschetta immediately.

Cook's Tip

Walnut bread is sold in most large supermarkets and makes an interesting alternative to ordinary crusty bread, although a freshly baked loaf of the latter is fine if speciality breads are not available. If using crusty bread, try to find a slender loaf to slice, so that the portions are not too wide. If you can only buy a large loaf, cut the slices in half to make neat, chunky pieces, perfect for making bruschetta.

Cheese-crusted Party Eggs

Similar to the popular Scotch egg, these whole small eggs are wrapped in a tasty herb-flavoured coating, then deep-fried. Tiny bantam or quail's eggs look dainty and are ideal for dipping into mayonnaise.

Makes 10–20

225g/8oz/4 cups stale white breadcrumbs
1 small leek, very finely chopped
225g/8oz mild cheese, grated
10ml/2 tsp garlic and herb seasoning
60ml/4 tbsp chopped fresh parsley
10ml/2 tsp mild mustard
4 eggs, separated
60–90ml/4–6 tbsp milk
12–20 small spinach or sorrel leaves, stalks removed
12 very small eggs, such as bantam, guinea fowl, or 16–20 quail's eggs, hard-boiled and peeled
50–75g/2–3oz/½–⅔ cup plain (all-purpose) flour, for coating, plus extra for dusting
50g/2oz/4 tbsp sesame seeds
vegetable oil, for deep-frying
salt and ground black pepper
mayonnaise, for dipping

1 Mix the breadcrumbs, leek, cheese, seasoning, parsley and mustard. Beat the egg yolks with the milk and blend into the mixture. Whisk two egg whites until stiff and work enough into the breadcrumb mixture to give a firm, dropping (pourable) consistency. Chill for 1 hour.

2 Divide the mixture into 12 portions. Mould one portion in your hand, place a spinach leaf inside, then an egg and shape the mixture around the egg to enclose it within a thin crust. Seal and dust with flour. Repeat with the remaining portions.

3 Beat the remaining egg white with 30ml/2 tbsp water, then pour into a shallow dish. Mix the flour with salt and pepper and the sesame seeds and place in another dish. Dip the eggs first in the egg white, then in the sesame flour. Chill for 20 minutes.

4 Heat the oil in a pan until a cube of bread browns in 1¼ minutes. Deep-fry the eggs in the hot oil until they are golden brown. Remove, drain on kitchen paper and leave to cool. Serve with a bowl of good mayonnaise for dipping.

Bruschetta Energy 558kcal/2321kJ; Protein 16.7g; Carbohydrate 25.6g, of which sugars 2.2g; Fat 37.2g, of which saturates 12.7g; Cholesterol 47mg; Calcium 137mg; Fibre 1.2g; Sodium 841mg.
Party Eggs Energy 167kcal/694kJ; Protein 6.3g; Carbohydrate 9.3g, of which sugars 0.7g; Fat 11.7g, of which saturates 3.5g; Cholesterol 49mg; Calcium 128mg; Fibre 0.7g; Sodium 183mg.

Cheddar and Chive Scones

These soft scones are delicious warm, split and spread with butter; serve with soup to make a substantial appetizer.

Makes 20

200g/7oz/1¾ cups plain (all-purpose) flour
10ml/2 tsp baking powder
2.5ml/½ tsp bicarbonate of soda (baking soda)
pinch of salt
1.5ml/¼ tsp black pepper
65g/2½oz/5 tbsp unsalted butter, chopped
50g/2oz/½ cup grated mature (sharp) Cheddar cheese
30ml/2 tbsp chopped fresh chives
175ml/6fl oz/¾ cup buttermilk

1 Preheat the oven to 200°C/400°F/Gas 6. Lightly grease two baking sheets.

2 Sift the flour, baking powder, bicarbonate of soda, salt and pepper into a large bowl. Add the butter and rub it into the dry ingredients with your fingertips until the mixture resembles coarse breadcrumbs. Add the grated cheese and chives and stir well to mix.

3 Make a well in the centre of the mixture. Add the buttermilk and stir vigorously until the batter comes away from the sides of the bowl.

4 Drop 30ml/2 tbsp mounds spaced 5–7.5cm/2–3in apart on the prepared baking sheets. Bake for 12–15 minutes, until golden brown.

Variations

- *For Cheddar and Bacon Scones, substitute 45ml/3 tbsp crumbled cooked bacon for the chives.*
- *For Cheese and Ham Scones, substitute grated Parmesan or Pecorino for the Cheddar cheese and 50g/2oz/⅓ cup chopped prosciutto for the chives.*

Cheese Pudding

Old recipes for this classic dish involved cooking layers of toasted bread and cheese in the custard mixture. This version, which uses fresh breadcrumbs, is lighter and more akin to a soufflé. Serve it alone as an appetizer or with a selection of other nibbles and bites.

Serves 4

225g/8oz/2 cups grated mature (sharp) Cheddar-style cheese – Llanboidy or Llangloffan are particularly good
115g/4oz/2 cups fresh breadcrumbs
600ml/1 pint/2½ cups milk
40g/1½oz/3 tbsp butter
3 eggs, beaten
5ml/1 tsp mustard (such as English or wholegrain) or 2.5ml/½ tsp mustard powder
salt and ground black pepper

1 Start by preheating the oven to 200°C/400°F/Gas 6. Then carefully butter the insides of a 1.2 litre/2 pint/5 cup ovenproof soufflé dish.

2 Mix together three-quarters of the grated cheese with the fresh breadcrumbs.

3 Put the remaining ingredients into a pan and stir well. Heat gently, stirring, until the butter has just melted (if the mixture gets too hot then the eggs will start to set).

4 Stir the warm liquid into the cheese mixture and transfer it into the prepared dish. Sprinkle the remaining cheese evenly over the top.

5 Put into the hot oven and cook for about 30 minutes or until golden brown and just set (a knife inserted in the centre should come out clean). Serve immediately.

Variations

Stir a small handful of chopped fresh parsley into the mixture before cooking, or put a layer of soft-cooked leeks in the the bottom of the dish.

Cheddar Scones Energy 124kcal/524kJ; Protein 5.2g; Carbohydrate 21.5g, of which sugars 1.5g; Fat 2.5g, of which saturates 1.4g; Cholesterol 7mg; Calcium 74mg; Fibre 1.9g; Sodium 128mg.
Cheese Pudding Energy 534kcal/2232kJ; Protein 27.5g; Carbohydrate 29.5g, of which sugars 7.9g; Fat 33.9g, of which saturates 20.2g; Cholesterol 227mg; Calcium 656mg; Fibre 0.6g; Sodium 803mg.

Tapenade and Quail's Eggs

A purée made from capers, olives and anchovies, tapenade is popular in Mediterranean cooking. It complements the taste of eggs perfectly, especially quail's eggs. Serve as a snack or appetizer. They also make excellent finger food at a party or gathering.

Serves 8
8 quail's eggs
1 small baguette
45ml/3 tbsp tapenade
frisée lettuce
3 small tomatoes, sliced
black olives, pitted
4 canned anchovy fillets, drained and halved lengthways
a little chopped parsley, to garnish

1 Boil the quail's eggs for 3 minutes, then plunge them straight into cold water to prevent them from cooking further. Crack the shells and remove them.

2 Cut the baguette into slices on the diagonal and spread each one with some of the tapenade.

3 Arrange a little frisée lettuce, torn to fit, and the tomato slices on top. Halve the quail's eggs and place them on top of the tomato slices.

4 Quarter the olives, place one quarter on each and finally add the anchovies. Garnish with parsley.

Cook's Tip
You can make your own tapenade at home, if you prefer. Mix together 1 crushed garlic clove, the juice of 1 lemon, 45ml/3 tbsp chopped capers, 6 chopped anchovy fillets, 250g/9oz pitted black olives and a small bunch of chopped fresh parsley. Add extra virgin olive oil until a paste forms.

Variation
Instead of serving these bites on sliced French bread, you can use savoury crackers or rye bread, if you prefer.

Quail's Eggs in Aspic with Prosciutto

These clever looking eggs in jelly are so easy to make, and are great for summer eating. Serve them with salad leaves and some home-made mayonnaise on the side for a spectacular appetizer at a dinner party.

Serves 4–6
25g/1oz packet aspic powder
45ml/3 tbsp dry sherry
12 quail's eggs
6 slices of prosciutto
12 fresh coriander (cilantro) or flat leaf parsley leaves
salad leaves, to serve

1 Make up the aspic following the packet instructions but replace 45ml/3 tbsp water with the dry sherry, giving a greater depth of flavour. Leave the aspic in the refrigerator until it begins to thicken, but not too thick.

2 Put the quail's eggs in a pan of cold water and bring to the boil. Boil for 1½ minutes only, then pour off the hot water and leave in cold water until cold. This way the yolks should still be a little soft but the whites will be firm enough to peel when really cold.

3 Rinse 12 dariole moulds so they are damp and place them on a tray. Cut the prosciutto into 12 pieces, then roll or fold so they will fit into the moulds.

4 Place a herb leaf in the base of each mould, then put a peeled egg on top. As the jelly begins to thicken, pour in enough to nearly cover each egg, holding it steady. Then put the slice of ham on the egg and pour in the rest of the jelly to fill the mould, so that when you turn them out the eggs will be sitting on the ham.

5 Transfer the tray of moulds to a cold place and then leave for 3–4 hours until set and cold. When ready to serve, run a knife around the top rim of the jelly to loosen. Dip the moulds into warm, not hot, water and shake or tap gently until they appear loose. Invert on to small plates and serve with salad leaves.

Tapenade Eggs Energy 157kcal/666kJ; Protein 6.3g; Carbohydrate 28.4g, of which sugars 1.8g; Fat 2.8g, of which saturates 0.6g; Cholesterol 37mg; Calcium 76mg; Fibre 1.5g; Sodium 523mg.
Quail's Eggs Energy 31kcal/129kJ; Protein 3.9g; Carbohydrate 0.2g, of which sugars 0.2g; Fat 1.2g, of which saturates 0.3g; Cholesterol 36mg; Calcium 8mg; Fibre 0.1g; Sodium 97mg.

Hard-boiled Eggs with Tuna Sauce

A tangy tuna mayonnaise spooned over eggs makes a delicious appetizer.

Serves 6
200g/7oz can tuna in olive oil
3 canned anchovy fillets
15ml/1 tbsp capers, drained
30ml/2 tbsp lemon juice
6 hard-boiled extra-large eggs
60ml/4 tbsp olive oil
salt and ground black pepper
capers and anchovy fillets, to garnish

For the mayonnaise
1 egg yolk
5ml/1 tsp Dijon mustard
5ml/1 tsp white wine vinegar or lemon juice
150ml/¼ pint/⅔ cup olive oil

1 To make the mayonnaise, whisk the egg yolk, mustard and vinegar or lemon juice together in a small bowl. Whisk in the oil a few drops at a time until 3–4 tablespoons have been incorporated. Whisk in the remaining olive oil in a slow and steady stream.

2 Place the tuna with its oil, the anchovies, capers, lemon juice and olive oil in a blender or food processor. Process until the mixture is smooth. Fold into the mayonnaise. Season with black pepper, and salt if necessary. Chill for at least 1 hour.

3 Cut the eggs in half lengthways. Arrange on a platter. Spoon on the mayonnaise and garnish with capers and anchovy fillets.

Cook's Tips

- *If you find that canned anchovies are too salty for your liking, you can reduce their saltiness by soaking them in milk for 20 minutes. Drain off the oil before covering with milk. After soaking, drain and rinse the anchovies in cold water.*
- *When you hard-boil eggs, prevent the greenish discolouration around the yolk by running them under cold water as soon as you take them out of the boiling water.*
- *Peel boiled eggs easily by rolling them firmly under your hand on a chopping board before attempting to take the shells off. The shells will crack evenly and should peel off in one piece.*

Tortilla with Beans

The addition of chopped herbs and a few skinned beans to the classic tortilla makes this a very summery dish. Cut it into small pieces and serve as a tapas dish – it makes a delicious appetizer.

Serves 6–8
45ml/3 tbsp olive oil
2 Spanish (Bermuda) onions, thinly sliced
300g/11oz waxy potatoes, cut into dice
250g/9oz/1¾ cups shelled broad (fava) beans
5ml/1 tsp chopped fresh thyme or summer savory
6 large (US extra large) eggs
45ml/3 tbsp mixed chopped fresh chives and fresh flat leaf parsley
salt and ground black pepper

1 Heat 30ml/2 tbsp of the oil in a 23cm/9in deep non-stick frying pan. Add the onions and potatoes and stir to coat. Cover and cook gently, stirring, for 20–25 minutes until the potatoes are cooked and the onions collapsed.

2 Meanwhile, cook the beans in a pan of boiling salted water for 5 minutes. Drain well and set aside to cool.

3 When the beans are cool enough to handle, peel off and discard the grey outer skins. Add the beans to the frying pan, together with the thyme or summer savory, and season with salt and pepper. Stir well to mix and cook for 2–3 minutes.

4 Beat the eggs with salt and pepper to taste and add the mixed herbs. Pour the egg mixture over the potatoes and onions and increase the heat slightly. Cook gently for about 5 minutes, or until the egg on the bottom sets and browns. During cooking, gently pull the tortilla away from the sides of the pan and tilt to allow the uncooked egg to run underneath.

5 Cover the frying pan with a large, upside-down plate and invert the tortilla on to it. Add the remaining oil to the pan and heat until hot. Slip the tortilla back into the pan, uncooked side down, and cook for 3–5 minutes until the underneath browns. Slide the tortilla out on to a plate. Cut up into wedges or cubes and serve warm rather than piping hot.

Hard-boiled Eggs Energy 369kcal/1529kJ; Protein 16.6g; Carbohydrate 0.1g, of which sugars 0.1g; Fat 33.8g, of which saturates 5.8g; Cholesterol 242mg; Calcium 46mg; Fibre 0g; Sodium 311mg.
Tortilla and Beans Energy 159kcal/666kJ; Protein 8g; Carbohydrate 12.8g, of which sugars 3g; Fat 8.8g, of which saturates 1.8g; Cholesterol 143mg; Calcium 62mg; Fibre 3.2g; Sodium 62mg.

Egg Foo Yung

Hearty and full of flavour, this can be cooked either as one large omelette or as individual omelettes. Either way, it is a clever way of using up leftover roast pork.

Serves 4

6 dried Chinese mushrooms soaked for 20 minutes in warm water
50g/2oz/¼ cup beansprouts
6 drained canned water chestnuts, finely chopped
50g/2oz baby spinach leaves, washed
45ml/3 tbsp vegetable oil
50g/2oz lean roast pork, cut into strips
3 eggs
2.5ml/½ tsp sugar
5ml/1 tsp rice wine or dry sherry
salt and ground black pepper
fresh coriander (cilantro) sprigs, to garnish

1 Drain the mushrooms. Cut off and discard the stems; slice the caps finely and mix with the beansprouts, water chestnuts and spinach leaves.

2 Heat 15ml/1 tbsp oil in a large heavy frying pan. Add the pork and vegetables and toss over the heat for 1 minute.

3 Beat the eggs in a bowl. Add the strips of roast pork and the vegetables and mix well.

4 Wipe the frying pan and heat the remaining oil. Pour in the egg mixture and tilt the pan so that it covers the base. When the omelette has set on the underside, sprinkle the top with salt, pepper and sugar.

5 Invert a plate over the pan, turn both the pan and the plate over, and slide the omelette back into the pan to cook on the other side.

6 Cut the omelette into wedges, drizzle with rice wine or dry sherry and serve immediately, garnished with the sprigs of coriander.

Hard-boiled Eggs in Red Sauce

A perennially popular snack, this spicy egg dish originally came from Indonesia. Served wrapped in a banana leaf, the Malays often eat it with plain steamed rice, sliced chillies, onion and coriander – ideal for a quick, tasty snack or appetizer.

Serves 4

vegetable oil, for deep-frying
8 eggs, hard-boiled and shelled
1 lemon grass stalk, trimmed, quartered and crushed
2 large tomatoes, skinned, seeded and chopped to a pulp
5–10ml/1–2 tsp sugar
30ml/2 tbsp dark soy sauce
juice of 1 lime
fresh coriander (cilantro) and mint leaves, coarsely chopped, to garnish

For the rempah

4–6 fresh red chillies, seeded and chopped
4 shallots, chopped
2 garlic cloves, chopped
2.5ml/½ tsp shrimp paste

1 Using a mortar and pestle or food processor, grind the ingredients for the rempah to form a smooth purée. Set aside.

2 Heat enough oil for deep-frying in a wok or heavy pan and deep-fry the whole boiled eggs until golden brown. Lift them out and drain.

3 Reserve 15ml/1 tbsp of the oil and discard the rest. Heat the oil in the wok or heavy pan and stir in the rempah until it becomes fragrant. Add the lemon grass, followed by the tomatoes and sugar. Cook for 2–3 minutes, until it forms a thick paste. Reduce the heat and stir in the soy sauce and lime juice.

4 Add 30ml/2 tbsp water to thin the sauce. Toss in the eggs, making sure they are thoroughly coated, and serve hot, garnished with chopped coriander and mint leaves.

Cook's Tip
For a fusion twist, serve these with a cucumber raita.

Egg Foo Yung Energy 153kcal/634kJ; Protein 8.1g; Carbohydrate 0.7g, of which sugars 0.5g; Fat 13.1g, of which saturates 2.3g; Cholesterol 151mg; Calcium 46mg; Fibre 0.5g; Sodium 80mg.
Eggs in Red Sauce Energy 266kcal/1104kJ; Protein 15.6g; Carbohydrate 7.1g, of which sugars 6.7g; Fat 19.9g, of which saturates 4.2g; Cholesterol 387mg; Calcium 99mg; Fibre 1g; Sodium 739mg.

Scrambled Eggs with Prawns

The Spanish are particular about eggs, distinguishing between a revuelto, which uses softly set scrambled eggs, and the more solid tortilla that is cooked until set. This revuelto de gambas is an economical way of using a few shellfish and tastes delicious with crusty bread or toast.

Serves 4

1 bunch spring onions (scallions)
25g/1oz/2 tbsp butter
30ml/2 tbsp oil
150g/5oz shelled prawns (shrimp)
8 large (US extra large) eggs
30ml/2 tbsp milk
45ml/3 tbsp chopped fresh parsley
salt and ground black pepper
crusty bread, to serve

1 Chop the spring onions, keeping the white section separate from the green parts. Put the white pieces in a bowl and place about 30ml/2 tbsp of the chopped green pieces in another bowl.

2 Heat the butter and oil in a large frying pan. Add the spring onion white and cook briefly. Add the prawns and heat through. (If the prawns are raw, cook them for 2 minutes or until they turn pink. Do not overcook them or they will toughen.)

3 In a bowl, beat the eggs with the milk and then season with plenty of salt and pepper. Turn the heat to medium-high and pour the egg mixture over the prawns. Cook for about 2 minutes, stirring with a wooden spoon.

4 Sprinkle the creamy scrambled eggs and prawn mixture with parsley and spring onion greens. Divide among four plates and serve immediately with crusty bread.

Variation
The green shoots from garlic bulbs are another very popular spring ingredient for this type of dish and can be used in place of the spring onions (scallions). Called ajetes in Spain, they lend a delicate flavour to scrambled eggs or tortillas.

Herb Omelette

A simple, herb-flavoured omelette is quick and easy to cook and is ideal served as a light opening to a meal to whet the appetite for further courses. Chop the omelette into small squares to serve.

Serves 2

2 eggs
15ml/1 tbsp chopped fresh herbs, such as tarragon, parsley or chives
5ml/1 tsp butter
salt and ground black pepper

1 Lightly beat the eggs in a mixing bowl, add a selection of chosen fresh herbs and season with salt and ground black pepper.

2 Melt the butter in a heavy, non-stick frying pan and swirl it around to coat the base evenly. Heat the butter until hot, but take care not to burn it.

3 Pour in the egg mixture and, as the egg sets, push the edges towards the centre using a spoon, allowing the raw egg to run on to the hot pan.

4 Cook for about 2 minutes, without stirring, until the egg is just lightly set. Quickly fold over the omelette with a metal spatula and serve immediately.

Variation
You can make the omelette more substantial and interesting by frying some chopped mushrooms, diced ham, bacon, diced cooked potato or peas in the pan for a few minutes before adding the egg mixture.

Cook's Tip
Even if you are going to serve more than one, it is better to cook individual omelettes and eat them as soon as they are ready, or keep them warm in a low oven.

Eggs with Prawns Energy 287kcal/1191kJ; Protein 20.1g; Carbohydrate 1.9g, of which sugars 1.9g; Fat 22.4g, of which saturates 7.4g; Cholesterol 468mg; Calcium 126mg; Fibre 0.9g; Sodium 258mg.
Herb Omelette Energy 95kcal/393kJ; Protein 7g; Carbohydrate 0.2g, of which sugars 0.2g; Fat 7.7g, of which saturates 2.9g; Cholesterol 196mg; Calcium 44mg; Fibre 0.4g; Sodium 91mg.

Spanish-style Omelette with Bitter Melon

Bitter melon is often cooked simply in a broth or stew and is frequently combined with pork and shrimps throughout South-east Asia, as in this dish. Made in the style of a Spanish omelette, this dish is often enjoyed as an appetizer or snack served on a banana leaf.

Serves 3–4
450g/1lb bitter melon
30–45ml/2–3 tbsp palm or groundnut (peanut) oil
1 onion, sliced
2–3 garlic cloves, chopped
25g/1oz fresh root ginger, chopped
115g/4oz pork loin, cut into thin, bitesize strips
225g/8oz fresh shrimp or small prawns (shrimp), shelled
2–3 tomatoes, skinned, seeded and chopped
1 small bunch fresh chilli leaves or flat leaf parsley, roughly chopped
3–4 eggs, beaten
salt and ground black pepper

1 Fill a bowl with cold water and stir in 10ml/2 tsp salt. Cut the bitter melon in half, remove the spongy core and seeds, then cut the flesh into bitesize chunks. Put the melon into the salted water and leave to soak for 30 minutes. Drain, rinse well under cold water, then pat dry with kitchen paper.

2 Heat the oil in a pan, stir in the onion, garlic and ginger and fry until beginning to colour. Add the pork and fry for 2 minutes.

3 Add the shrimp and fry until they turn opaque, then add the tomatoes and chilli leaves. Toss in the bitter melon and fry for 3–4 minutes, until tender. Season with salt and pepper.

4 Pour the eggs over the ingredients in the pan, drawing in the sides to let the egg spread evenly. Cover the pan and leave to cook very gently until the eggs have set. Do not allow the bottom of the omelette to burn.

5 Serve the omelette hot, straight from the pan, or leave it to cool and serve it at room temperature.

Smoked Haddock and Cheese Omelette

This creamy, smoked haddock soufflé omelette is also known as Omelette Arnold Bennett, after the famous author who frequently dined in the Savoy Hotel in London. It is now served all over the world, using good Scottish smoked haddock and cheese.

Serves 4
175g/6oz smoked haddock fillet, poached and drained
50g/2oz/½ cup butter, diced
175ml/6fl oz/¾ cup whipping or double (heavy) cream
4 eggs, separated
40g/1½oz/⅓ cup mature (sharp) Cheddar cheese, grated
ground black pepper
watercress, to garnish

1 Remove the skin and any bones from the haddock fillet by carefully pressing down the length of each fillet with your fingertips. Discard them. Using a fork and following the grain of the flesh, flake the flesh into large chunks.

2 Melt half the butter with 60ml/4 tbsp of the cream in a fairly small non-stick pan. Wait until the mixture is hot but not boiling, and then add the chunks of flaked fish. Stir together gently, making sure that you do not break up the flakes of fish. Bring slowly to the boil, stirring constantly. Once it is boiling, cover the pan with a lid, remove from the heat and set aside to cool for at least 20 minutes.

3 Preheat the grill (broiler) to high. Mix the egg yolks with 15ml/1 tbsp of the cream. Season with pepper, then stir into the fish. In a separate bowl, mix the cheese and the remaining cream. Stiffly whisk the egg whites, then fold into the fish mixture.

4 Heat the remaining butter in an omelette pan until it is slightly bubbling. Add the fish mixture and cook until it is browned underneath. Pour the cheese mixture over evenly and grill (broil) until it is bubbling.

5 Serve on a warmed plate immediately, garnished with watercress and with fresh crusty bread to accompany.

Spanish-style Energy 255kcal/1064kJ; Protein 24.3g; Carbohydrate 10.5g, of which sugars 10.1g; Fat 13.2g, of which saturates 2.7g; Cholesterol 318mg; Calcium 149mg; Fibre 2.7g; Sodium 247mg.
Smoked Haddock Energy 410kcal/1698kJ; Protein 18g; Carbohydrate 1.3g, of which sugars 1.3g; Fat 37g, of which saturates 21.3g; Cholesterol 289mg; Calcium 140mg; Fibre 0g; Sodium 561mg.

Smoked Salmon and Chive Omelette

The addition of chopped smoked salmon gives a really luxurious finish to this simple, classic dish, which is an ideal quick and tasty appetizer for four people. The chives add colour and extra flavour.

Serves 4
4 eggs
15ml/1 tbsp chopped fresh chives or spring onions (scallions)
a knob (pat) of butter
50g/2oz smoked salmon, roughly chopped
salt and ground black pepper

1 Break the eggs into a large mixing bowl. Whisk using a fork until the eggs are just combined, then stir in the chopped fresh chives or chopped spring onions. Season with salt and a generous sprinkling of ground black pepper, and set aside.

2 Heat the butter in a medium frying pan until foamy. Pour in the eggs and cook over a medium heat for 3–4 minutes, drawing the cooked egg from around the edge into the centre of the pan from time to time.

3 At this stage, you can either leave the top of the omelette slightly soft or finish it off under a preheated grill (broiler), depending on how you like your omelette. Top with the smoked salmon, carefully fold the omelette over and cut in half to serve.

Variations

- *Use smoked trout instead of smoked salmon. The colour ranges from rose pink to reddish brown and it has very good flavour, especially when it has been hot smoked over oak or birch chippings.*
- *Add a little rocket (arugula) or watercress when folding the omelette. Both have peppery leaves, so use slightly less pepper to season the scrambled egg.*
- *A little crème fraîche or fromage frais, served on the side, makes a good addition. For an extra special occasion, top this with salmon or trout roe.*

Coriander Omelette Parcels

Stir-fried vegetables in black bean sauce make a great omelette filling.

Serves 4
130g/4½oz broccoli, cut into small florets
30ml/2 tbsp groundnut (peanut) oil
1cm/½ in piece fresh root ginger, finely grated
1 large garlic clove, crushed
2 fresh red chillies, seeded and finely sliced
4 spring onions (scallions), sliced diagonally
175g/6oz/3 cups pak choi (bok choy), shredded
50g/2oz/2 cups fresh coriander (cilantro) leaves, plus extra to garnish
100g/4oz/½ cup beansprouts
45ml/3 tbsp black bean sauce
4 eggs
salt and ground black pepper

1 Blanch the broccoli in a pan of boiling salted water for about 2 minutes, drain, then refresh under cold running water and drain again.

2 Meanwhile, heat 15ml/1 tbsp of the oil in a frying pan or wok. Add the ginger, garlic and half the chilli and stir-fry for 1 minute. Add the spring onions, broccoli and pak choi, and stir-fry for 2 minutes more.

3 Chop three-quarters of the coriander and add to the frying pan or wok. Add the beansprouts and stir-fry for about 1 minute, then add the black bean sauce and heat for 1 minute more. Remove the pan from the heat and keep warm.

4 Mix the eggs lightly with a fork and season well. Heat a little of the remaining oil in a small frying pan and add a quarter of the beaten egg. Swirl the egg until it covers the base of the pan, then sprinkle over a quarter of the reserved coriander leaves. Cook until set, then turn out on to a plate and keep warm while you make three more omelettes, adding more oil, when necessary.

5 Spoon the vegetable stir-fry on to the omelettes and roll up. Cut in half crossways and serve garnished with coriander leaves and the remaining chilli.

Smoked Salmon Energy 110kcal/460kJ; Protein 10g; Carbohydrate 0.1g, of which sugars 0.1g; Fat 8.2g, of which saturates 3g; Cholesterol 200mg; Calcium 32mg; Fibre 0g; Sodium 320mg.
Coriander Omelette Energy 148kcal/614kJ; Protein 10.4g; Carbohydrate 6.2g, of which sugars 5.4g; Fat 9.3g, of which saturates 2.2g; Cholesterol 190mg; Calcium 152mg; Fibre 3g; Sodium 323mg.

Rice Omelette Rolls

These tasty rice omelettes make a great supper dish or appetizer and are popular with children, who usually top them with a liberal helping of tomato ketchup.

Serves 4

1 skinless, boneless chicken thigh, about 115g/4oz, cubed
40ml/8 tsp butter
1 small onion, chopped
½ carrot, diced
2 shiitake mushrooms, stems removed and chopped
15ml/1 tbsp finely chopped fresh parsley
225g/8oz/2 cups cooked long grain white rice
30ml/2 tbsp tomato ketchup
6 eggs, lightly beaten
60ml/4 tbsp milk
5ml/1 tsp salt, plus extra to season
ground black pepper
tomato ketchup, to serve

1 Season the chicken with salt and pepper. Melt 10ml/2 tsp butter in a frying pan. Fry the onion for 1 minute, then add the chicken and fry until the cubes are cooked. Add the carrot and mushrooms, stir-fry over a medium heat until soft, then add the parsley. Set this mixture aside.

2 Wipe the frying pan, then add a further 10ml/2 tsp butter and stir in the rice. Mix in the fried ingredients, ketchup and pepper. Stir well, adding salt to taste, if necessary. Keep the mixture warm. Beat the eggs with the milk in a bowl. Stir in the measured salt and add pepper to taste.

3 Melt 5ml/1 tsp of the remaining butter in an omelette pan. Pour in a quarter of the egg mixture and stir it briefly with a fork, then allow it to set for 1 minute. Top with a quarter of the rice mixture.

4 Fold the omelette over the rice and slide it to the edge of the pan to shape it into a curve. Slide it on to a warmed plate, cover with kitchen paper and press neatly into a rectangular shape. Keep the cooked omelette hot while cooking three more from the remaining ingredients. Serve immediately, with tomato ketchup.

Soft Tacos with Spiced Omelette

Served hot, warm or cold, these tacos make a satisfying appetizer to serve with drinks.

Serves 4

30ml/2 tbsp sunflower oil
50g/2oz beansprouts
50g/2oz carrots, cut into thin sticks
25g/1oz Chinese leaves (Chinese cabbage), chopped
15ml/1 tbsp light soy sauce
4 eggs
1 small spring onion (scallion), finely sliced
5ml/1 tsp Cajun seasoning
25g/1oz/2 tbsp butter
4 soft flour tortillas, warmed in the oven or microwave
salt and ground black pepper

1 Heat the oil in a small frying pan and stir-fry the beansprouts, carrot sticks and chopped Chinese leaves until they begin to soften. Add the soy sauce, stir to combine and set aside.

2 Place the eggs, sliced spring onion, Cajun seasoning, salt and ground black pepper in a bowl, and beat together. Melt the butter in a small pan until it sizzles. Add the beaten eggs and cook over a gentle heat, stirring constantly, until almost firm.

3 Divide the vegetables and scrambled egg evenly among the tortillas, fold up into cones or parcels and serve.

Cook's Tip
You can buy fresh soft tortillas in large supermarkets. They freeze well, so keep a packet or two in the freezer.

Variation
Fill warm pitta breads with this spicy omelette mixture. Mini pitta breads are perfect for younger children who may find the folded tacos difficult to handle.

Rice Omelette Rolls Energy 322kcal/1347kJ; Protein 18.1g; Carbohydrate 22.8g, of which sugars 4.9g; Fat 18.5g, of which saturates 8.1g; Cholesterol 337mg; Calcium 80mg; Fibre 1.1g; Sodium 325mg.
Tacos Omelette Energy 280kcal/1168kJ; Protein 9.5g; Carbohydrate 24.2g, of which sugars 2g; Fat 16.7g, of which saturates 5.5g; Cholesterol 204mg; Calcium 80mg; Fibre 1.5g; Sodium 217mg.

Egg Rolls

The title of this recipe could lead to some confusion, especially in the United States, where egg rolls are the same as spring rolls. These egg rolls, however, are wedges of a rolled Thai-style flavoured omelette. They are frequently served as finger food at parties.

Serves 2

3 eggs, beaten
15ml/1 tbsp soy sauce
1 bunch garlic chives, thinly sliced
1–2 small fresh red or green chillies, seeded and finely chopped
small bunch fresh coriander (cilantro), chopped
pinch of sugar
salt and ground black pepper
15ml/1 tbsp groundnut (peanut) oil

For the dipping sauce

60ml/4 tbsp light soy sauce
fresh lime juice, to taste

1 Make the dipping sauce. Pour the soy sauce into a bowl. Add a generous squeeze of lime juice. Taste and add more lime juice if needed. Set the sauce aside.

2 Mix the eggs, soy sauce, chives, chillies and coriander. Add the sugar and season to taste. Heat the oil in a large frying pan, pour in the egg mixture and swirl the pan to cover the base and make an omelette.

3 Cook for 1–2 minutes, until the omelette is just firm and the underside is golden. Slide it out on to a plate and roll up as though it were a pancake. Leave to cool completely.

4 When the omelette is cool, slice it diagonally in 1cm/½in pieces. Arrange the slices on a serving platter and serve with the bowl of dipping sauce.

Cook's Tip

Wear gloves while preparing chillies or cut them up with a knife and fork. Wash your hands afterwards in warm, soapy water.

Smoked Eel with Scrambled Eggs

Smoked eel and eggs makes a pleasant and unusual change from smoked salmon when served as one of the appetizers at a buffet. This dish is a traditional Swedish recipe and makes a great appetizer.

Serves 8

16 slices smoked eel or 8 slices flat smoked eel
10 eggs
a little grated freshly nutmeg
50ml/2fl oz/¼ cup double (heavy) cream
25g/1oz/2 tbsp butter
15ml/1 tbsp chopped fresh chives
salt and ground black pepper
knobs (pats) of butter and a few dill fronds, to garnish

1 Arrange the slices of smoked eel on individual serving plates. Break the eggs into a large bowl and whisk together with the grated nutmeg, double cream and salt and pepper to taste.

2 Melt half the butter in a large, heavy pan over a low heat and add the egg mixture.

3 Stir carefully with a wooden spoon until the mixture starts to set. Mix in the remaining butter and the chopped fresh chives.

4 Serve the eggs immediately with the smoked eel, garnished with a knob of butter to make the scrambled eggs shiny, dill fronds and more black pepper to taste.

Cook's Tip

Smoked eel is a delicacy in Sweden and is often served as an appetizer on special occasions as well as at other times of the year. The eel is smoked in a special way referred to as 'flat smoked eel', and is cut in a similar way to gravlax, sliced thinly at a 45 degree angle. It is smoked without the bone, so it is slightly less gelatinous. If you cannot find smoked eel, substitute smoked salmon or smoked trout.

Egg Rolls Energy 305kcal/1269kJ; Protein 19.2g; Carbohydrate 4.9g, of which sugars 4.5g; Fat 23.6g, of which saturates 5.7g; Cholesterol 275mg; Calcium 48mg; Fibre 0.7g; Sodium 130mg.
Smoked Eel Energy 188kcal/781kJ; Protein 12.1g; Carbohydrate 0.1g, of which sugars 0.1g; Fat 15.7g, of which saturates 6.4g; Cholesterol 291mg; Calcium 44mg; Fibre 0g; Sodium 130mg.

Poached Eggs Florentine

The term 'à la Florentine' means 'in the style of Florence' and refers to dishes cooked with spinach and topped with Mornay sauce. Here is a subtly spiced, elegant starter.

Serves 4

675g/1½lb spinach, washed and drained
25g/1oz/2 tbsp butter
60ml/4 tbsp double (heavy) cream
pinch of freshly grated nutmeg
salt and ground black pepper

For the topping

25g/1oz/2 tbsp butter
25g/1oz/¼ cup plain (all-purpose) flour
300ml/½ pint/1¼ cups hot milk
pinch of ground mace
115g/4oz Gruyère cheese, grated
4 eggs
15ml/1 tbsp freshly grated Parmesan cheese, plus shavings to serve

1 Place the spinach in a large pan with very little water. Cook for 3–4 minutes or until tender, then drain and chop finely.

2 Return the spinach to the pan, add the butter, cream, nutmeg and seasoning and heat through. Place in the base of one large or four small gratin dishes.

3 To make the topping, heat the butter in a small pan, add the flour and cook, stirring constantly, for 1 minute to make a paste. Gradually blend in the hot milk, beating well as it thickens to break up any lumps.

4 Cook for 1–2 minutes, stirring. Remove from the heat and stir in the mace and three-quarters of the Gruyère cheese.

5 Preheat the oven to 200°C/400°F/Gas 6. Poach the eggs in lightly salted water for 3–4 minutes.

6 Make hollows in the spinach with the back of a spoon, and place a poached egg in each one. Cover with the cheese sauce and sprinkle with the remaining Gruyère and Parmesan.

7 Bake in the oven for 10 minutes or until golden brown. Serve immediately with Parmesan shavings.

Chive Scrambled Eggs in Brioches

These creamy scrambled eggs are delicious at any time of day, but when served with France's favourite breakfast bread, they become the ultimate breakfast or brunch treat. Set the brioches at an angle so some filling spills on to the plate.

Serves 4

4 individual brioches
6 eggs, beaten
45ml/3 tbsp chopped fresh chives, plus extra to serve
25g/1oz/2 tbsp butter
45ml/3 tbsp cottage cheese
60–75ml/4–5 tbsp double (heavy) cream
salt and ground black pepper

1 Preheat the oven to 180°C/350°F/Gas 4. Cut the tops off the brioches and set to one side. Carefully scoop out the centre of each brioche, leaving a bread case.

2 Put the brioche cases and lids on a baking sheet and bake in the oven for 5 minutes until they are hot and crisp.

3 Meanwhile, beat the eggs lightly and season to taste. Add about one-third of the chopped chives. Heat the butter in a medium pan until it begins to foam, then add the eggs and cook, stirring constantly with a wooden spoon until they are semi-solid.

4 Stir in the cottage cheese, cream and half the remaining chives. Cook for 1–2 minutes more, making sure that the eggs remain soft and creamy.

5 To serve, put the crisp brioche shells on individual plates, spoon in the creamy scrambled egg and sprinkle with the remaining chives. Top with the lids.

Variation
If you do not happen to have brioches to hand, these wonderful herby eggs taste delicious on top of thick slices of toasted bread. Try them piled high on warm focaccia, or on toasted ciabatta, Granary (whole-wheat) bread or muffins.

Poached Eggs Energy 459kcal/1901kJ; Protein 21.7g; Carbohydrate 11.5g, of which sugars 6.5g; Fat 36g, of which saturates 20.3g; Cholesterol 270mg; Calcium 636mg; Fibre 3.8g; Sodium 626mg.
Scrambled Eggs Energy 414kcal/1731kJ; Protein 16.2g; Carbohydrate 32.5g, of which sugars 10.5g; Fat 25.5g, of which saturates 12g; Cholesterol 322mg; Calcium 154mg; Fibre 1.9g; Sodium 374mg.

Eggs with Chorizo

In Mexico, there are two types of chorizo sausage. The first is freshly made and sold loose; the second is packed in sausage skins and air-dried, like Spanish chorizo. This is a recipe for the former. Freshly made chorizo can be used in a number of savoury dishes, but is particularly good with scrambled egg, as here.

Serves 4

25g/1oz/2 tbsp lard or white cooking fat
500g/1¼lb minced (ground) pork
3 garlic cloves, crushed
10ml/2 tsp dried oregano
5ml/1 tsp ground cinnamon
2.5ml/½ tsp ground cloves
2.5ml/½ tsp ground black pepper
30ml/2 tbsp dry sherry
5ml/1 tsp caster (superfine) sugar
5ml/1 tsp salt
6 eggs
2 tomatoes, peeled, seeded and finely diced
½ small onion, finely chopped
60ml/4 tbsp milk or single (light) cream
fresh oregano sprigs, to garnish
warm corn or wheat flour tortillas, to serve

1 Melt the lard or white cooking fat in a large frying pan over a moderate heat. Add the pork mince and cook until browned, stirring frequently.

2 Stir in the garlic, dried oregano, cinnamon, cloves and black pepper. Cook for 3–4 minutes more.

3 Add the sherry, caster sugar and salt to the mince, stir well and cook for 3–4 minutes until the flavours are blended. Remove from the heat.

4 Put the eggs in a bowl. Beat lightly to mix, then stir in the finely diced tomatoes and chopped onion.

5 Return the chorizo mixture to the heat. Heat it through and pour in the egg mixture. Cook, stirring constantly, until the egg is almost firm.

6 Stir in the milk or single cream and check the seasoning. Garnish with fresh oregano and serve with warm corn or wheat flour tortillas.

Artichokes with Eggs

Artichokes with a tangy spinach filling and poached eggs in hollandaise sauce make a stunning appetizer.

Serves 4

4 large artichokes
500g/1¼lb spinach, washed
50g/2oz/4 tbsp butter
30ml/2 tbsp plain (all-purpose) flour
175ml/6fl oz/¾ cup milk
4 canned anchovy fillets, drained and mashed
Tabasco sauce
salt, ground black pepper and grated nutmeg
4 eggs
200ml/7fl oz/scant 1 cup ready-made hollandise sauce

1 Cut the stems from the artichokes, then cut the top half off each and scoop out the centre leaves and the hairy 'choke'. Put the spinach into a pan with just the water that clings to the leaves. Cover and cook until soft. Drain and, when it is cool, squeeze out the moisture and chop finely.

2 Bring a pan of salted water to the boil. Add the artichokes, cover and cook for 30 minutes or until tender. Lift out with a slotted spoon on to warmed serving plates and keep warm.

3 Melt 50g/2oz/4 tbsp butter in a large pan, mix in the flour and stir for 1 minute over the heat. Remove from the heat and gradually pour in the milk, stirring constantly with a wooden spoon. Return to the heat and stir until the sauce has thickened.

4 Stir the mashed anchovies into the sauce and simmer for about 5 minutes. Add the spinach and simmer. Season with salt and black pepper, nutmeg and Tabasco sauce. Keep warm.

5 Bring a pan of water to a simmer. Break the eggs into individual cups and slide two eggs at a time into the water. Poach for 3 minutes or until the white is set, lift out with a slotted spoon and drain on kitchen paper.

6 Gently warm the hollandaise sauce in a pan. Fill the artichokes with the spinach mixture. Set a poached egg on top of each and spoon hollandaise sauce over the artichokes. Serve.

Eggs and Chorizo Energy 399kcal/1665kJ; Protein 41g; Carbohydrate 6.4g, of which sugars 2.7g; Fat 22.7g, of which saturates 7.5g; Cholesterol 380mg; Calcium 137mg; Fibre 2.9g; Sodium 256mg.
Artichokes Energy 508kcal/2101kJ; Protein 13.6g; Carbohydrate 16g, of which sugars 7.8g; Fat 43.9g, of which saturates 24.1g; Cholesterol 381mg; Calcium 302mg; Fibre 4.7g; Sodium 637mg.

Savoury Scrambled Eggs

Also known as 'Scotch Woodcock', these eggs are flavoured with a hint of anchovy and were popular in England at the beginning of the 20th century. They would have been served as a savoury instead of cheese at the end of a meal but also make a good appetizer.

Serves 2

2 slices bread
40g/1 ½ oz/3 tbsp butter, plus extra for spreading
anchovy paste, such as Gentleman's Relish, for spreading
2 eggs and 2 egg yolks, beaten
60–90ml/4–6 tbsp cream or milk
salt and ground black pepper
anchovy fillets, cut into strips, and paprika, to garnish

1 Toast the bread under a preheated grill (broiler), spread with butter and anchovy paste, then remove the crusts and cut into triangles. Keep warm.

2 Melt the rest of the butter in a medium non-stick pan, then stir in the beaten eggs, cream or milk, and a little salt and pepper. Heat very gently, stirring constantly, until the mixture begins to thicken.

3 Remove the pan from the heat and continue to stir the scrambled eggs until the mixture becomes very creamy, but do not allow it to harden.

4 Divide the scrambled eggs among the triangles of toast and garnish each one with strips of anchovy fillet and a generous sprinkling of paprika. Serve immediately, while still hot.

Cook's Tip
To ensure that your produce perfect scrambled eggs, turn off the heat just before they are fully cooked. The heat of the pan will continue the cooking process.

Eggs Mimosa

Mimosa describes the fine yellow and white grated egg in this dish, which looks very similar to the flower of the same name. The eggs taste delicious when garnished with black pepper and basil leaves. Grated egg yolk can also be used as a garnish for a variety of other savoury dishes, such as sauces, soups and rice dishes.

Serves 4–6

12 eggs
2 ripe avocados, halved and stoned (pitted)
1 garlic clove, crushed
15ml/1 tbsp olive oil

1 Place the eggs in a large pan and pour in enough cold water to cover. Bring the water to simmering point and then cook the eggs for 7 minutes. Remove the eggs from the pan and run them under cold running water.

2 Peel the shells from the eggs. Reserve two of the hard-boiled eggs and halve the remainder. Carefully remove the yolks with a teaspoon and blend them with the avocados, garlic and oil, adding ground black pepper and salt to taste.

3 Spoon or pipe the mixture into the halved egg whites using a piping (pastry) bag with a 1cm/½in or pipe star nozzle.

4 Push the remaining egg whites through a sieve (strainer) and sprinkle over the filled eggs. Strain the yolks and arrange on top. Arrange the filled egg halves on a serving platter.

Cook's Tips
• *Never boil eggs that have come straight out of the refrigerator. Cold eggs may crack when added to hot water.*
• *Always use a kitchen timer when cooking eggs. This will ensure that they are never overcooked, which results in black yolks and a rubbery texture.*

Savoury Eggs Energy 240kcal/995kJ; Protein 12.6g; Carbohydrate 0.1g, of which sugars 0.1g; Fat 21.4g, of which saturates 9.6g; Cholesterol 407mg; Calcium 60mg; Fibre 0g; Sodium 216mg.
Eggs Mimosa Energy 79kcal/327kJ; Protein 4.1g; Carbohydrate 0.5g, of which sugars 0.2g; Fat 6.8g, of which saturates 1.6g; Cholesterol 114mg; Calcium 22mg; Fibre 0.6g; Sodium 43mg.

Son-in-law Eggs

The fascinating name for this dish comes from a story about a prospective bridegroom who very much wanted to impress his future mother-in-law and devised a new recipe based on the only dish he knew how to make – boiled eggs.

Serves 4–6

30ml/2 tbsp vegetable oil
6 shallots, thinly sliced
6 garlic cloves, thinly sliced
6 fresh red chillies, sliced
oil, for deep-frying
6 hard-boiled eggs, shelled
salad leaves, to serve
sprigs of fresh coriander (cilantro), to garnish

For the sauce

75g/3oz/6 tbsp palm sugar (jaggery) or muscovado (brown) sugar
75ml/5 tbsp fish sauce
90ml/6 tbsp tamarind juice

1 To make the sauce, put the sugar, fish sauce and tamarind juice in a pan. Bring to the boil, stirring until the sugar dissolves, lower the heat and simmer for 5 minutes. Taste and add more sugar, fish sauce or tamarind juice, if needed. Transfer the sauce to a bowl and set it aside.

2 Heat the vegetable oil in a frying pan and cook the shallots, garlic and chillies for 5 minutes. Transfer to a bowl.

3 Heat the oil in a deep-fryer or wok to 190°C/375°F or until a cube of bread, added to the oil, browns in about 45 seconds. Deep-fry the eggs in the hot oil for 3–5 minutes, until golden brown. Remove and drain well on kitchen paper.

4 Cut the eggs in quarters and arrange them on a bed of leaves. Drizzle with the sauce and sprinkle over the shallot mixture. Garnish with coriander sprigs and serve immediately.

Cook's Tip
The level of heat varies, depending on which type of chillies are used and whether you include the seeds.

Egg and Salmon Puff Parcels

These crisp elegant parcels hide a mouthwatering collection of flavours and textures and make a delicious appetizer or lunch dish.

Serves 6

75g/3oz/scant ½ cup long grain rice
300ml/½ pint/1¼ cups fish stock
350g/12oz piece salmon tail
juice of ½ lemon
15ml/1 tbsp chopped fresh dill
15ml/1 tbsp chopped fresh parsley
10ml/2 tsp mild curry powder
6 small (US medium) eggs, soft-boiled and cooled
425g/15oz flaky pastry, thawed if frozen
1 small (US medium) egg, beaten
salt and ground black pepper

1 Cook the rice in boiling fish stock for 15 minutes. Drain and set aside to cool. Preheat the oven to 220°C/425°F/Gas 7.

2 Poach the salmon, then remove the bones and skin and flake the fish into the rice. Add the lemon juice, herbs, curry powder and seasoning and mix well. Peel the soft-boiled eggs.

3 Roll out the pastry and cut into six 14–15cm/5½–6in squares. Brush the edges with the beaten egg. Place a spoonful of rice in the middle of each square, push an egg into the middle and top with a little more rice.

4 Pull over the pastry corners to the middle to form a square parcel, squeezing the joins together well to seal. Brush with more egg, place on a baking sheet and bake the puffs in the oven for 20 minutes, then reduce the oven temperature to 190°C/375°F/Gas 5 and cook the puffs for a further 10 minutes, or until golden and crisp underneath.

5 Cool slightly before serving with a curry-flavoured mayonnaise or hollandaise sauce, if you like.

Variation
You can also add a spoonful of cooked chopped fresh or frozen spinach to each parcel.

Son-in-law Eggs Energy 180kcal/752kJ; Protein 7.3g; Carbohydrate 18g, of which sugars 17.1g; Fat 9.4g, of which saturates 2g; Cholesterol 190mg; Calcium 50mg; Fibre 0.5g; Sodium 666mg.
Egg Parcels Energy 494kcal/2063kJ; Protein 23.4g; Carbohydrate 36.9g, of which sugars 1.1g; Fat 29.7g, of which saturates 2.7g; Cholesterol 219mg; Calcium 112mg; Fibre 0.8g; Sodium 326mg.

Grilled Chicken Balls on Skewers

These morsels make a great low-fat appetizer or snack.

Serves 4
300g/11oz skinless chicken, minced (ground)
2 eggs
2.5ml/½ tsp salt
10ml/2 tsp plain (all-purpose) flour
10ml/2 tsp cornflour (cornstarch)
90ml/6 tbsp dried breadcrumbs
2.5cm/1in piece fresh root ginger, grated

For the yakitori sauce
60ml/4 tbsp sake
75ml/5 tbsp shoyu
15ml/1 tbsp mirin
15ml/1 tbsp sugar
2.5ml/½ tsp cornflour (cornstarch) blended with 5ml/1 tsp water

1 Soak eight bamboo skewers for about 30 minutes in water. Put all the ingredients for the chicken balls, except the ginger, in a food processor and process to blend well.

2 Shape the mixture into a small ball about half the size of a golf ball. Make a further 30–32 balls in the same way.

3 Squeeze the juice from the grated ginger into a small mixing bowl. Discard the pulp. Preheat the grill (broiler).

4 Add the ginger juice to a small pan of boiling water. Add the chicken balls, and boil for about 7 minutes, or until the colour of the meat changes and the balls float to the surface. Scoop the balls out using a slotted spoon and drain on kitchen paper.

5 In a small pan, mix all the ingredients for the yakitori sauce, except the cornflour liquid. Bring to the boil, then simmer until the sauce has reduced slightly. Add the cornflour liquid and stir until thickened. Transfer to a small bowl.

6 Drain the skewers and thread three to four balls on each. Grill (broil) for a few minutes, turning frequently until they brown. Brush with sauce and return to the heat. Repeat twice, then serve immediately.

Spicy Chicken Satay with Peanut Sauce

These miniature kebabs are popular all over South-east Asia, and they are especially delicious when cooked over a barbecue. The peanut dipping sauce is a perfect partner for the marinated, grilled chicken.

Serves 4
4 skinless chicken breast fillets

For the marinade
2 garlic cloves, crushed
2.5cm/1in piece fresh root ginger, finely grated
10ml/2 tsp Thai fish sauce
30ml/2 tbsp light soy sauce
15ml/1 tbsp clear honey

For the satay sauce
90ml/6 tbsp crunchy peanut butter
1 fresh red chilli, seeded and finely chopped
juice of 1 lime
60ml/4 tbsp coconut milk
salt

1 First, make the satay sauce. Put all the ingredients in a food processor or blender. Process the mixture until smooth, then check the seasoning and add more salt or lime juice if necessary. Spoon the sauce into a bowl, cover with clear film (plastic wrap) and set aside.

2 Using a sharp knife, slice each chicken breast fillet into four long strips. Put all the marinade ingredients in a large bowl and mix well, then add the chicken strips and toss together until thoroughly coated. Cover and leave for at least 30 minutes in the refrigerator to marinate.

3 Meanwhile, soak 16 wooden satay sticks or kebab skewers in water, to prevent them from burning during cooking.

4 Preheat the grill (broiler) to high or prepare the barbecue. Drain the satay sticks or skewers. Drain the chicken strips. Thread one strip on to each satay stick or skewer.

5 Grill (broil) the chicken skewers for 3 minutes on each side, or until the chicken is golden brown and cooked through. Serve immediately with the satay sauce.

Chicken Balls Energy 332kcal/1398kJ; Protein 30.4g; Carbohydrate 29g, of which sugars 7.4g; Fat 9.7g, of which saturates 2.6g; Cholesterol 339mg; Calcium 84mg; Fibre 0.6g; Sodium 325mg.
Spicy Chicken Energy 375kcal/1564kJ; Protein 42.9g; Carbohydrate 3.9g; of which sugars 2.4g; Fat 20.9g; of which saturates 5.6g; Cholesterol 196mg; Calcium 14mg; Fibre 0g; Sodium 132mg.

Spring Rolls with Chicken, Spring Onions and Almonds

These Moroccan-style spring rolls are delicious dipped in cinnamon-spiced ground almonds and sugar.

Serves 6

30ml/2 tbsp plain (all-purpose) flour
about 30ml/2 tbsp water
12 large spring roll wrappers
sunflower oil, for deep-frying

For the filling

1 small chicken
½ onion, finely chopped
3–4 garlic cloves, finely chopped
25g/1oz/2 tbsp butter
1 cinnamon stick
5ml/1 tsp ground ginger
5ml/1 tsp ras el hanout
pinch of saffron threads
small bunch of flat leaf parsley, chopped
small bunch of fresh coriander (cilantro), chopped
6 eggs, beaten
10ml/2 tsp orange flower water
½ lemon
6–8 spring onions (scallions), thickly sliced
salt and ground black pepper

For the dipping mixture

115g/4oz/1 cup blanched almonds, lightly toasted and coarsely ground
30ml/2 tbsp icing (confectioners') sugar
5–10ml/1–2 tsp ground cinnamon

1 To make the filling, place the chicken in a pan with the onion, garlic, butter, cinnamon, ginger, ras el hanout, saffron and half the herbs. Cover with water and simmer for 1 hour. Lift out the chicken and set aside. Reduce the liquid to 550ml/18fl oz/2½ cups. Remove from the heat and season. Pour the beaten eggs into the hot stock, stirring until the egg has set, then strain. In a bowl, combine the dipping ingredients.

2 Shred the chicken flesh and mix with the cooked eggs and remaining filling ingredients. Mix the flour with the water to form a paste. Sprinkle some almond mixture over each wrapper. Place a tablespoonful of filling in a line 5cm/2in from one corner then roll up, folding in the sides to enclose the filling. Seal with a little flour paste. Heat the oil to 180°C/350°F and cook the rolls three or four at a time until crisp and golden. Drain and serve immediately with the dipping mixture.

Chicken and Vegetable Bundles

Leeks form the wrappers for these enchanting little vegetable bundles. They taste good on their own, but even better as an appetizer accompanied by the soy and sesame dip.

Serves 4

4 skinless, boneless chicken thighs
5ml/1 tsp cornflour (cornstarch)
10ml/2 tsp dry sherry
30ml/2 tbsp light soy sauce
2.5ml/½ tsp salt
large pinch of ground white pepper
4 fresh shiitake mushrooms
1 small carrot
1 small courgette (zucchini)
50g/2oz/½ cup sliced, drained, canned bamboo shoots
1 leek, trimmed
1.5ml/¼ tsp sesame oil

1 Remove any fat from the chicken thighs before cutting each thigh lengthways into eight strips. Place the strips in a bowl. Add the cornflour, sherry and half the soy sauce to the chicken in the bowl. Stir in the salt and pepper and mix well. Cover with clear film (plastic wrap) and leave in a cool place to marinate for 10 minutes.

2 Remove and discard the mushroom stems, then cut each mushroom cap in half (or in slices if very large). Cut the carrot and courgette into eight batons, each about 5cm/2in long, then mix the mushroom halves and bamboo shoots together until well combined.

3 Bring a small pan of water to the boil. Add the leek and blanch until soft. Drain thoroughly, then slit the leek down its length. Separate each layer to give eight long strips.

4 Divide the marinated chicken into eight portions. Do the same with the vegetables. Wrap each strip of leek around a portion of chicken and vegetables to make eight neat bundles. Prepare a steamer.

5 Steam the chicken and vegetable bundles over high heat for 12–15 minutes or until the filling is cooked through. Serve with a sauce made by mixing the remaining soy sauce with the sesame oil.

Spring Rolls Energy 490kcal/2046kJ; Protein 33.3g; Carbohydrate 25.9g, of which sugars 7.2g; Fat 29.1g, of which saturates 4.1g; Cholesterol 249mg; Calcium 126mg; Fibre 2.4g; Sodium 126mg.
Chicken Bundles Energy 450kcal/1891kJ; Protein 46.9g; Carbohydrate 36.2g, of which sugars 16.4g; Fat 14g, of which saturates 2.3g; Cholesterol 105mg; Calcium 131mg; Fibre 10.8g; Sodium 901mg.

Chicken Parcels

These home-made chicken parcels look splendid piled high and golden brown. Flavoured with parsley and nutmeg, they will be an instant success with your dinner guests.

Makes 35

225g/8oz/2 cups strong white bread flour, plus extra for dusting
2.5ml/½ tsp salt
2.5ml/½ tsp caster (superfine) sugar
5ml/1 tsp easy-blend (rapid-rise) dried yeast
25g/1oz/2 tbsp butter, softened
1 egg, beaten, plus a little extra
90ml/6 tbsp warm milk
lemon wedges, to serve
flat leaf parsley, to garnish

For the filling

1 small onion, finely chopped
175g/6oz/1½ cups minced (ground) chicken
15ml/1 tbsp sunflower oil
75ml/5 tbsp chicken stock
30ml/2 tbsp chopped fresh parsley
pinch of grated nutmeg
salt and ground black pepper

1 Sift the flour, salt and sugar into a large bowl. Stir in the dried yeast, then make a well in the centre of the flour. Add the butter, egg and milk and mix to a soft dough. Turn on to a lightly floured surface and knead for 10 minutes, until the dough is smooth and elastic. Put the dough in a clean bowl, cover with clear film (plastic wrap) and then leave in a warm place to rise for 1 hour, or until the dough has doubled in size.

2 Meanwhile, fry the onion and chicken in the oil for about 10 minutes. Add the stock and simmer for 5 minutes. Stir in the parsley, grated nutmeg and salt and ground black pepper. Then leave to cool.

3 Preheat the oven to 220°C/425°F/Gas 7. Knead the dough, then roll it out until it is 3mm/⅛in thick. Stamp out rounds with a 7.5cm/3in cutter. Brush the edges with beaten egg. Put a little filling in the middle, then press the edges together. Leave to rise on oiled baking sheets, covered with oiled clear film (plastic wrap), for 15 minutes. Brush with more egg. Bake for 5 minutes, then for 10 minutes at 190°C/375°F/Gas 5, until well risen. Serve with lemon wedges and garnish with flat leaf parsley.

Chicken and Asparagus Risotto

Use thick asparagus, as fine spears overcook in this risotto. The thick ends of the asparagus are full of flavour and they become beautifully tender in the time it takes for the rice to absorb the stock.

Serves 4

50g/2oz/¼ cup butter
15ml/1 tbsp olive oil
1 leek, finely chopped
115g/4oz/1½ cups oyster mushrooms, sliced
3 skinless chicken breast fillets, cubed
350g/12oz asparagus
250g/9oz/1¼ cups risotto rice
900ml/1½ pints/3¾ cups boiling chicken stock
salt and ground black pepper
Parmesan cheese curls, to serve

1 Heat the butter with the oil in a pan until the mixture is foaming. Transfer the leek to the pan and cook gently until softened, but not coloured. Add the mushrooms and cook for 5 minutes. Remove the vegetables from the pan and set aside.

2 Increase the heat and cook the cubes of chicken until golden on all sides. Do this in batches, if necessary, and then replace them all in the pan.

3 Meanwhile, discard the woody ends from the asparagus and cut the spears in half. Set the fine tips aside. Cut the thick ends in half and add them to the pan. Replace the leek and mushroom mixture and stir in the rice.

4 Pour in a ladleful of boiling stock and cook gently, stirring occasionally, until the stock is absorbed. Continue adding the stock a ladleful at a time, simmering until it is absorbed, the rice is tender and the chicken is cooked.

5 Add the fine aspargus tips with the last ladleful of boiling stock for the final 5 minutes and continue cooking until the asparagus is tender. The whole process should take 25–30 minutes.

6 Season the risotto to taste with salt and lots of ground black pepper and spoon it into individual warm serving bowls. Top each bowl with curls of Parmesan, and serve.

Chicken Parcels Energy 554kcal/2310kJ; Protein 42.5g; Carbohydrate 14.8g, of which sugars 0.5g; Fat 36.6g, of which saturates 22g; Cholesterol 240mg; Calcium 138mg; Fibre 0.6g; Sodium 417mg.
Chicken Risotto Energy 496kcal/2072kJ; Protein 36.1g; Carbohydrate 50g, of which sugars 2.7g; Fat 16.1g, of which saturates 7.4g; Cholesterol 105mg; Calcium 53mg; Fibre 2.7g; Sodium 148mg.

Drunken Chicken

As the chicken is marinated for several days, it is important to use a very fresh bird from a reputable supplier.

Serves 4–6

1 chicken, about 1.4kg/3lb
1cm/½in piece of fresh root ginger, peeled and thinly sliced
2 spring onions (scallions), trimmed
1.75 litres/3 pints/7½ cups water
15ml/1 tbsp salt
300ml/½ pint/1¼ cups dry sherry
spring onions (scallions), shredded, and fresh herbs, to garnish

1 Rinse and dry the chicken inside and out. Place the ginger and spring onions in the body cavity. Put the chicken in a large pan or flameproof casserole and just cover with water. Bring to the boil, skim and cook for 15 minutes.

2 Turn off the heat, cover the pan or casserole tightly and leave the chicken in the cooking liquid for 3–4 hours, by which time it will be cooked. Drain well. Pour 300ml/½ pint/1¼ cups of the stock into a jug (pitcher). Freeze the remaining stock.

3 Remove the skin from the chicken, and joint it neatly. Divide each leg into a drumstick and thigh. Make two more portions from the wings and some of the breast. Finally, cut away the remainder of the breast pieces (still on the bone) and divide each breast into two even portions.

4 Arrange the chicken portions in a shallow dish. Rub salt into the chicken and cover with clear film (plastic wrap). Leave in a cool place for several hours or chill overnight in the refrigerator.

5 Later, lift off any fat from the stock. Mix the sherry and stock and pour over the chicken. Cover again and marinate in the refrigerator for 2 or 3 days, turning occasionally.

6 To serve, cut the chicken into chunky pieces and arrange on a serving platter garnished with spring onion shreds and fresh herbs.

Chicken Chilli Parcels

These fried burritos are a common sight on street stalls and in cafés along the Mexican border with Texas, but are not so well known farther south.

Serves 4

2 skinless chicken breast fillets
1 chipotle chilli, seeded
15ml/1 tbsp vegetable oil
oil, for frying
2 onions, finely chopped
4 garlic cloves, crushed
2.5ml/½ tsp ground cumin
2.5ml/½ tsp ground coriander
2.5ml/½ tsp ground cinnamon
2.5ml/½ tsp ground cloves
300g/11oz/scant 2 cups drained canned tomatillos
400g/14oz/2¾ cups cooked pinto beans
8 X 20–25cm/8–10in fresh wheat flour tortillas
salt and ground black pepper

1 Put the chicken in a large pan, pour over water to cover and add the chilli. Bring to the boil, and then simmer for 10 minutes or until the chicken is cooked and the chilli has softened. Remove the chilli and chop finely. Transfer the chicken on to a plate. Leave to cool slightly, then shred with two forks.

2 Heat the oil in a frying pan. Fry the onions until translucent, then add the garlic and ground spices and cook for 3 minutes. Add the tomatillos and pinto beans. Cook over a moderate heat for 5 minutes, stirring to break up the tomatillos and some of the beans. Simmer for 5 minutes. Add the chicken and season.

3 Wrap the tortillas in foil and place them on a plate. Stand the plate over boiling water for about 5 minutes until they become pliable. Alternatively, wrap them in microwave-safe film and heat them in a microwave on full power for 1 minute.

4 Spoon one-eighth of the bean filling into the centre of a tortilla, fold in both sides, then fold the bottom of the tortilla up and the top down to form a neat parcel. Secure with a cocktail stick (toothpick).

5 Heat the oil in a large frying pan and fry the tortilla parcels in batches until crisp, turning once. Remove them from the oil with a slotted spoon and drain on kitchen paper. Serve hot.

Drunken Chicken Energy 608kcal/2553kJ; Protein 35.4g; Carbohydrate 52.7g, of which sugars 29g; Fat 17.6g, of which saturates 1.9g; Cholesterol 82mg; Calcium 107mg; Fibre 3.7g; Sodium 97mg.
Chicken Chilli Energy 468kcal/1968kj; Protein 27.5g; Carbohydrate 51.1g; of which sugars 6g; Fat 18.5g; of which saturates 2.3g; Cholesterol 61mg; Calcium 105mg; Fibre 3.3g; Sodium 271mg.

Chicken Flautas

Crisp fried tortillas with a chicken and cheese filling make a delicious appetizer. Make sure that the oil is sufficiently hot to prevent the flutes from absorbing too much of it.

Makes 12

2 skinless chicken breast fillets
15ml/1 tbsp vegetable oil
1 onion, finely chopped
2 garlic cloves, crushed
90g/3½oz feta cheese, crumbled
12 corn tortillas, freshly made or a few days old
oil, for frying
salt and ground black pepper

For the salsa

3 tomatoes, peeled, seeded and chopped
juice of ½ lime
small bunch of fresh coriander (cilantro), chopped
½ small onion, finely chopped
3 fresh fresno chillies or similar fresh green chillies, seeded and chopped

1 First make the salsa. Mix the tomatoes, lime juice, coriander, onion and chillies in a bowl. Season with salt and set aside.

2 Put the chicken fillets in a large pan, add water to cover and bring to the boil. Lower the heat and simmer for 15–20 minutes. Remove the chicken and shred into small pieces. Set aside.

3 Heat the oil in a frying pan, add the onion and garlic and fry over a low heat for 5 minutes, or until the onion has softened but not coloured. Add the chicken and season. Mix well, remove from the heat and stir in the feta.

4 Soften the tortillas by steaming three or four at a time on a plate over boiling water. Place a spoonful of the chicken filling on one of the tortillas. Roll up to make a cylinder and secure with a cocktail stick (toothpick). Cover with clear film (plastic wrap) and fill and roll the remaining tortillas.

5 Pour 2.5cm/1in oil into a frying pan. Heat it until a small cube of bread rises to the surface and bubbles at the edges before turning golden. Remove the cocktail sticks, then add the flutes to the pan, a few at a time. Fry for 2–3 minutes until golden all over. Drain on kitchen paper and serve with the salsa.

Caramelized Chicken Wings with Fresh Ginger

Cooked in a wok or in the oven, these caramelized wings are drizzled with chilli oil and eaten with the fingers, so that every bit of tender meat can be gnawed off the bone. Variations of this recipe can be found throughout Vietnam and Cambodia, often served with rice and pickles.

Serves 2–4

75ml/5 tbsp sugar
30ml/2 tbsp groundnut (peanut) oil
25g/1oz fresh root ginger, peeled and finely shredded or grated
12 chicken wings, split in two
chilli oil, for drizzling
mixed pickled vegetables, to serve

1 To make the caramel sauce, gently heat the sugar with 60ml/4 tbsp water in a small, heavy pan until it turns golden. Set aside.

2 Heat the oil in a wok or heavy pan. Add the ginger and stir-fry until fragrant. Add the chicken wings and toss them around the wok to brown.

3 Pour in the caramel sauce and make sure the chicken wings are thoroughly coated in it. Reduce the heat, cover the wok or pan, and cook for about 30 minutes, until the chicken is tender, and the sauce has caramelized.

4 Drizzle chilli oil over the wings and serve from the wok or pan with mixed pickled vegetables.

Cook's Tip

For the pickled vegetables, cut a large carrot and a piece of mooli (daikon) of about the same size into matchsticks. Sprinkle with salt and leave for 30 minutes. Heat 50ml/2fl oz/¼ cup rice vinegar with 100ml/3½fl oz/½ cup water and 15ml/1 tbsp sugar until dissolved and leave to cool. Mix in the rinsed vegetables and marinate for up to 24 hours.

Chicken Flautas Energy 131kcal/553kJ; Protein 9.6g; Carbohydrate 16.8g, of which sugars 1.9g; Fat 3.3g, of which saturates 1.4g; Cholesterol 23mg; Calcium 73mg; Fibre 1.2g; Sodium 209mg.
Caramelized Chicken Energy 393kcal/1641kJ; Protein 30.5g; Carbohydrate 14.4g, of which sugars 14.4g; Fat 24g, of which saturates 6.3g; Cholesterol 134mg; Calcium 16mg; Fibre 0g; Sodium 100mg.

Mexican Chicken Fajitas

The perfect appetizer for casual entertaining, fajitas are a self-assembly dish: warm flour tortillas are brought to the table and everyone adds their own fillings.

Serves 6

3 skinless chicken breast fillets
finely grated rind and juice of 2 limes
30ml/2 tbsp caster (superfine) sugar
10ml/2 tsp dried oregano
2.5ml/½ tsp cayenne pepper
5ml/1 tsp ground cinnamon
2 onions
3 (bell) peppers (1 red, 1 yellow or orange and 1 green)
45ml/3 tbsp vegetable oil
12 ready-made fajitas or soft tortillas, guacamole, salsa and sour cream, to serve

1 Slice the chicken into 2cm/¾in wide strips and place them in a large bowl. Add the lime rind and juice, caster sugar, oregano, cayenne and cinnamon. Mix thoroughly. Set aside to marinate for at least 30 minutes.

2 Cut the onions in half and slice them thinly. Cut the peppers in half, remove the cores and seeds, then slice the flesh into 1cm/½in wide strips.

3 Heat a large frying pan or griddle and warm each tortilla in turn for approximately 30 seconds on each side, or until the surface starts to change colour and begins to blister. Keep the tortillas warm and pliable by wrapping them inside a clean, dry dish towel.

4 Heat the oil in a large frying pan. Stir-fry the marinated chicken for 5–6 minutes, then add the peppers and onions and cook for 3–4 minutes more, until the chicken strips are cooked through and the vegetables are soft and tender, but still juicy. Spoon the chicken mixture into a serving bowl and take it to the table with the warm tortillas and bowls of guacamole, salsa and sour cream.

5 To eat, take a tortilla, spread, it with a little salsa, add a spoonful of guacamole and pile some of the chicken mixture in the centre. The final touch is to add a small dollop of sour cream. The tortilla is then folded and ready to eat.

Panuchos

These stuffed tortillas are a bit fiddly to make, but well worth the effort. Serve as an unusual appetizer topped with onion relish.

Serves 6 (12 panuchos)

150g/5oz/1 cup masa harina (cornmeal)
pinch of salt
120ml/4fl oz/½ cup warm water
2 skinless chicken breast fillets
5ml/1 tsp dried oregano
150g/5oz/about 1 cup Frijoles de Olla, blended to a smooth purée
2 hard-boiled eggs, sliced
oil, for shallow-frying
salt and ground black pepper
onion relish, to serve

1 Mix the masa harina and salt in a bowl. Add the warm water to make a dough. Knead until smooth, wrap in clear film (plastic wrap) and leave for 1 hour.

2 Put the chicken in a pan, add the oregano and cover with water. Bring to the boil, reduce the heat and simmer for 20 minutes, until cooked. Remove the chicken, cool and shred.

3 Roll the dough into 12 balls. Open a tortilla press and line both sides with plastic. Flatten each dough ball in the press into a 6cm/2½in round. Repeat with the remaining dough.

4 Cook each tortilla in a hot frying pan for 15–20 seconds on each side. After a further 15 seconds on one side remove and wrap in a dish towel.

5 Cut a slit in each tortilla, about 1cm/½in deep around the rim. Put a spoonful of the bean purée and a slice of hard-boiled egg in each slit.

6 Heat the oil for shallow-frying in a large frying pan. Fry the tortilla pockets, in batches of two or three, until crisp and golden brown. Keep the first batch warm in a low oven while the remaining tortilla pockets are cooked.

7 Drain the tortillas on kitchen paper, place on individual serving plates and top with chicken and relish. Season to taste with salt and pepper and serve immediately.

Mexican Chicken Fajitas Energy 485kcal/2044kJ; Protein 26g; Carbohydrate 67.4g, of which sugars 15.3g; Fat 14.2g, of which saturates 3.8g; Cholesterol 60mg; Calcium 118mg; Fibre 4g; Sodium 53mg.
Panuchos Energy 258kcal/1080kJ; Protein 19.4g; Carbohydrate 24.9g, of which sugars 0.4g; Fat 9g, of which saturates 1.4g; Cholesterol 98mg; Calcium 20mg; Fibre 1.7g; Sodium 55mg.

Turkey and Avocado Pitta Bread Pizzas

These delectable pizzas are made with pitta breads as the base rather than the usual pizza bases. This makes them extremely quick and easy to make – perfect for a speedy appetizer.

Serves 4

8 plum tomatoes, quartered
45–60ml/3–4 tbsp olive oil
1 large ripe avocado
8 pitta bread rounds
6–7 slices of cooked turkey, chopped
1 onion, thinly sliced
275g/10oz/2½ cups grated Monterey Jack or Cheddar cheese
30ml/2 tbsp chopped fresh coriander (cilantro)
salt and ground black pepper

1 Preheat the oven to 230°C/450°F/Gas 8. Place the tomatoes in a baking dish. Drizzle over 15ml/1 tbsp of the olive oil and season with salt and ground black pepper. Bake in the oven for 30 minutes; do not stir.

2 Remove the baking dish from the oven and mash the coooked tomatoes with a fork, removing the skins as you mash. Set aside.

3 Peel the avocado and remove the stone (pit). Cut the flesh into 16 thin slices.

4 Brush the edges of the pitta breads with oil. Arrange the breads on two baking sheets. Spread each pitta with mashed tomato, almost to the edges.

5 Place two avocado slices on top of the tomato layer on the pitta bases. Sprinkle with the chopped turkey, then add a few onion slices, and salt and black pepper. Sprinkle on the cheese.

6 Place one sheet in the middle of the oven and bake until the cheese begins to melt, 15–20 minutes. Sprinkle with half the coriander and serve. Meanwhile, bake the second batch of pizzas to serve them hot.

Turkey Sticks with Sour Cream Dip

Crisp morsels of turkey, coated in breadcrumbs and served with a quick-to-prepare dip, make excellent appetizers, and even better party food for children.

Serves 4

350g/12oz turkey breast fillets, skinned
50g/2oz/1 cup fine fresh breadcrumbs
1.5ml/¼ tsp paprika
1 small (US medium) egg
salt and ground black pepper

For the sour cream dip
45ml/3 tbsp sour cream
15ml/1 tbsp ready-made tomato sauce
15ml/1 tbsp mayonnaise

1 Preheat the oven to 190°C/375°F/Gas 5. Trim any fat from the turkey breast fillets and cut them into even strips, about 2cm/¾in thick.

2 In a bowl, mix the fresh breadcrumbs and paprika, and season with salt and ground black pepper.

3 Break the egg into a bowl and whisk it with a fork until it is just beaten.

4 Dip the turkey fillet strips into the bowl with the egg, then into the breadcrumbs, turning until evenly coated. Place the coated strips on a greased baking sheet.

5 Cook the turkey at the top of the oven for 20 minutes until crisp and golden. Turn once during the cooking time.

6 To make the dip, mix all the ingredients together and season to taste. Serve the turkey sticks accompanied by the dip.

Variation
If turkey breast fillets are not available then these strips can be made with chicken breast fillets, if you prefer. The cooking time will be about the same as long as the strips are the same size.

Turkey Pizzas Energy 847kcal/3557kJ; Protein 48.2g; Carbohydrate 78.8g, of which sugars 8.7g; Fat 38.4g, of which saturates 17.8g; Cholesterol 104mg; Calcium 641mg; Fibre 5.3g; Sodium 1208mg.
Turkey Sticks Energy 251kcal/1057kJ; Protein 34.1g; Carbohydrate 10.5g, of which sugars 1g; Fat 8.4g, of which saturates 2.8g; Cholesterol 122mg; Calcium 39mg; Fibre 0.3g; Sodium 226mg.

Aubergine with Sesame Chicken

Sweet, delicate-tasting, small aubergines are stuffed with seasoned chicken and deep fried in a crispy sesame seed coating.

Serves 4

175g/6oz chicken, breast portion or thigh, skinned
1 spring onion (scallion), green part only, finely chopped
15ml/1 tbsp dark soy sauce
15ml/1 tbsp mirin or sweet sherry
2.5ml/½ tsp sesame oil
1.5ml/¼ tsp salt
4 small aubergines (eggplants), about 10cm/4in long
15ml/1 tbsp sesame seeds
flour, for dusting
vegetable oil, for deep-frying

For the dipping sauce
60ml/4 tbsp dark soy sauce
60ml/4 tbsp dashi or vegetable stock
45ml/3 tbsp mirin or sweet sherry

1 Remove the chicken meat from the bone and mince (grind) it finely in a food processor or blender. Transfer the minced meat to a mixing bowl.

2 Add the chopped spring onion, soy sauce, mirin or sweet sherry, sesame oil and salt to the minced chicken. Mix together until the ingredients are well combined.

3 Make four slits in each aubergine, leaving them joined at the stem. Spoon the minced chicken mixture into the aubergines, opening them slightly to accommodate the mixture. Dip the fat end of each stuffed aubergine in the sesame seeds, then dust in flour. Set aside.

4 To make the dipping sauce, combine the soy sauce, dashi or vegetable stock and mirin or sweet sherry. Pour into a shallow serving bowl and set aside.

5 Heat the vegetable oil in a deep-fat fryer or heavy pan to 196°C/385°F. Fry the aubergines, in batches of two at a time, for 3–4 minutes.

6 Lift out the aubergines using a slotted spoon. Drain thoroughly on kitchen paper. Serve hot, accompanied by the dipping sauce.

Kabocha Squash with Chicken Sauce

In this appetizer, the mild sweetness of kabocha, similar to that of sweet potato, goes very well with the rich meat sauce.

Serves 4

1 kabocha squash, about 500g/1¼lb
½ yuzu or lime
20g/¾oz mangetouts (snow peas)
salt

For the chicken sauce
100ml/3fl oz/scant ½ cup water
30ml/2 tbsp sake
300g/11oz lean chicken, minced (ground)
60ml/4 tbsp caster (superfine) sugar
60ml/4 tbsp shoyu
60ml/4 tbsp mirin

1 Halve the kabocha, then remove the seeds and fibre around the seeds. Halve again to make four wedges. Trim the stalk end of the kabocha wedge.

2 Remove strips of the peel on each of the wedges, cutting off strips lengthways of about 1–2.5cm/½–1in wide. The kabocha wedges will now have green (skin) and yellow (flesh) stripes.

3 Chop each wedge into large bitesize pieces. Place them side by side in a pan. Pour in enough water to cover, then sprinkle with some salt. Cover and cook for 5 minutes over medium heat, then lower the heat and simmer for 15 minutes until tender. Test the kabocha by pricking with a skewer. When soft enough, remove from heat, cover and leave for 5 minutes.

4 Slice the yuzu or lime into thin discs, then hollow out the inside of the skin to make rings of peel. Cover with a sheet of clear film (plastic wrap) until needed. Blanch the mangetouts in lightly salted water. Drain and set aside.

5 To make the sauce, bring the water and sake to the boil in a pan. Add the chicken for 5 minutes, then add the sugar, shoyu and mirin. Stir constantly until the liquid has almost evaporated.

6 Pile the kabocha on a large plate, then pour over the sauce. Add the mangetouts and serve, garnished with yuzu or lime rings.

Sesame Chicken Energy 248kcal/1026kJ; Protein 11.3g; Carbohydrate 2.3g, of which sugars 1.9g; Fat 21.1g, of which saturates 2.7g; Cholesterol 19mg; Calcium 39mg; Fibre 1.8g; Sodium 249mg.
Kabocha Squash Energy 165kcal/701kJ; Protein 19.2g; Carbohydrate 18.8g, of which sugars 18.1g; Fat 1.1g, of which saturates 0.4g; Cholesterol 53mg; Calcium 51mg; Fibre 1.4g; Sodium 47mg.

Barbecue Chicken

A fragrant marinade of Thai spices and coconut milk gives this chicken a superb flavour. It makes the perfect appetizer for outdoor eating with a delicious difference.

Serves 6

1 chicken, about 1.5kg/3¼lb, cut into 8–10 pieces
lime wedges and fresh red chillies, to garnish

For the marinade

2 lemon grass stalks, roots removed
2.5cm/1in piece fresh root ginger, peeled and thinly sliced
6 garlic cloves, coarsely chopped
4 shallots, coarsely chopped
½ bunch coriander (cilantro) roots, chopped
15ml/1 tbsp palm sugar (jaggery)
120ml/4fl oz/½ cup coconut milk
30ml/2 tbsp Thai fish sauce
30ml/2 tbsp light soy sauce

1 To make the marinade, cut off the lower 5cm/2in of the lemon grass stalks and chop them coarsely. Put into a food processor or blender along with all the other marinade ingredients and process until the mixture has reached a smooth consistency.

2 Place the chicken pieces in a fairly deep dish, pour the marinade over them and stir to mix well, turning the chicken pieces over to coat thoroughly. Cover the dish with clear film (plastic wrap) and leave in a cool place to marinate for at least 4 hours or in the refrigerator overnight.

3 Prepare the barbecue. Cook the chicken over the barbecue for 20–30 minutes, or until the pieces are cooked and golden brown. Alternatively, cook them under a preheated grill (broiler) on medium-high heat. Turn the pieces and brush with the marinade once or twice during cooking. Transfer to a serving platter and garnish with lime wedges and red chillies to serve.

Cook's Tip
You can buy coconut milk fresh, in cans or cartons, or use 50g/2oz creamed coconut, available in packets, and dissolve in 120ml/4fl oz/½ cup warm water.

Chicken Bitki

This is a popular dish in its native country, Poland, and makes an attractive appetizer when offset by deep red beetroot and vibrant green salad leaves.

Makes 12

15g/½ oz/1 tbsp butter, melted
115g/4oz flat mushrooms, finely chopped
50g/2oz/1 cup fresh white breadcrumbs
350g/12oz skinless chicken breast fillets, minced (ground) or finely chopped
2 eggs, separated
1.5ml/¼ tsp grated nutmeg
30ml/2 tbsp plain (all-purpose) flour
45ml/3 tbsp oil
salt and ground black pepper
salad leaves and grated pickled beetroot (beet), to serve

1 Melt the butter in a pan. Cook the mushrooms, stirring occasionally, for about 5 minutes until soft and the juices have evaporated. Set aside to cool.

2 Transfer the cooked mushrooms to a large bowl. Add the fresh breadcrumbs, the chicken, egg yolks and nutmeg. Mix together until the ingredients are well combined. Season with salt and ground black pepper.

3 Whisk the egg whites until they are stiff. Stir half of the egg whites into the chicken mixture to slacken it, then fold in the remainder of the whites.

4 Using your hands, shape the mixture into 12 even meatballs, about 7.5cm/3in long and about 2.5cm/1in wide. If the mixture is sticking to your hands then dampen them slightly with a little water. Roll the shaped bitki in the flour to coat evenly.

5 Heat the oil in a frying pan and fry the bitki, in batches if necessary, for about 10–12 minutes, turning occasionally until they are evenly golden brown and cooked through.

6 Drain the bitki on kitchen paper to remove any excess oil. Serve hot accompanied by some salad leaves and the grated pickled beetroot.

Barbecue Chicken Energy 572kcal/2376kJ; Protein 46.5g; Carbohydrate 9.4g, of which sugars 8.2g; Fat 38.8g, of which saturates 11.3g; Cholesterol 240mg; Calcium 42mg; Fibre 0.7g; Sodium 222mg.
Chicken Bitki Energy 102kcal/426kJ; Protein 8.9g; Carbohydrate 5.2g, of which sugars 0.2g; Fat 5.2g, of which saturates 1.3g; Cholesterol 55mg; Calcium 16mg; Fibre 0.3g; Sodium 69mg.

Tandoori Chicken Sticks

Tender pieces of chicken are marinated and then grilled, with truly excellent results.

Makes about 25
450g/1lb skinless chicken breast fillets

For the coriander yogurt
250ml/8fl oz/1 cup natural (plain) yogurt
30ml/2 tbsp whipping cream
½ cucumber, peeled, seeded and finely chopped
15–30ml/1–2 tbsp fresh chopped mint or coriander (cilantro)
salt and ground black pepper

For the marinade
175ml/6fl oz/¾ cup natural (plain) yogurt
5ml/1 tsp garam masala or curry powder
1.5ml/¼ tsp ground cumin
1.5ml/¼ tsp ground coriander
1.5ml/¼ tsp cayenne pepper (or to taste)
5ml/1 tsp tomato purée (paste)
1–2 garlic cloves, finely chopped
2.5cm/1in piece fresh root ginger, peeled and finely chopped
grated rind and juice of ½ lemon
15–30ml/1–2 tbsp chopped fresh mint

1 Prepare the coriander yogurt. Combine all the ingredients in a bowl and season with salt and pepper. Cover with clear film (plastic wrap) and chill until you are ready to serve.

2 Prepare the marinade. Place all the ingredients in the bowl of a food processor, and process thoroughly until the mixture is smooth. Pour into a shallow dish.

3 Freeze the chicken breast fillets for 5 minutes to firm, then slice in half horizontally. Cut the slices into 2cm/¾in strips and add to the marinade. Toss to coat well. Cover and chill in the refrigerator for 6–8 hours or overnight.

4 Preheat the grill (broiler) and line a baking sheet with foil. Using a slotted spoon, remove the chicken from the marinade and arrange the pieces in a single layer on the baking sheet. Scrunch up the chicken slightly so it makes wavy shapes. Grill (broil) for 4–5 minutes until brown and just cooked, turning once. When cool enough to handle, thread one or two pieces on to cocktail sticks (toothpicks) or short skewers and serve with the coriander yogurt dip.

Balti Chicken in Saffron Sauce

This is a beautifully aromatic chicken dish that is partly cooked in the oven.

Serves 4
50g/2oz/¼ cup butter
30ml/2 tbsp corn oil
1.2–1.3kg/2½–3lb chicken, skinned and cut into 8 pieces
1 medium onion, chopped
5ml/1 tsp crushed garlic
2.5ml/½ tsp crushed black peppercorns
2.5ml/½ tsp crushed green cardamom pods
2.5ml/¼ tsp ground cinnamon
7.5ml/1½ tsp chilli powder
150ml/¼ pint/⅔ cup natural (plain) yogurt
50g/2oz/½ cup ground almonds
15ml/1 tbsp lemon juice
5ml/1 tsp salt
5ml/1 tsp saffron strands
150ml/¼ pint/⅔ cup water
150ml/¼ pint/⅔ cup single (light) cream
30ml/2 tbsp chopped fresh coriander (cilantro)

1 Preheat the oven to 180°C/350°F/Gas 4. Melt the butter with the oil in a karahi, wok or deep pan. Add the chicken pieces and fry until lightly browned, about 5 minutes. Remove the chicken using a slotted spoon, leaving behind the fat.

2 Add the onion to the same pan, and fry over medium heat. Meanwhile, mix together the next 10 ingredients in a bowl. When the onions are lightly browned, pour the spice mixture into the pan and stir-fry for about 1 minute.

3 Add the chicken pieces, and continue to fry for a further 2 minutes, stirring constantly. Pour in the water and bring to a simmer. Transfer the contents of the pan to a casserole and cover with a lid, or, if using a karahi with heatproof handles, cover with foil. Transfer to the oven and cook for 30–35 minutes.

4 Once you are sure that the chicken is cooked right through, remove it from the oven. Transfer the mixture to a frying pan or place the karahi on the stove and stir in the cream.

5 Reheat gently for 2 minutes. Garnish with coriander and serve with naan bread.

Tandoori Chicken Sticks Energy 32kcal/134kJ; Protein 5g; Carbohydrate 1.1g, of which sugars 0.8g; Fat 0.9g, of which saturates 0.4g; Cholesterol 14mg; Calcium 29mg; Fibre 0.2g; Sodium 23mg.
Balti Chicken Energy 554kcal/2321kJ; Protein 75.6g; Carbohydrate 5.1g, of which sugars 4.7g; Fat 25.9g, of which saturates 12.2g; Cholesterol 255mg; Calcium 146mg; Fibre 0.8g; Sodium 792mg.

Chicken with Lemon and Garlic

Extremely easy to cook and delicious to eat, this succulent tapas dish makes an excellent last-minute appetizer and tastes even better served with some home-made aioli.

Serves 4

225g/8oz skinless chicken breast fillets
30ml/2 tbsp olive oil
1 shallot, finely chopped
4 garlic cloves, finely chopped
5ml/1 tsp paprika
juice of 1 lemon
30ml/2 tbsp chopped fresh parsley
salt and ground black pepper
flat leaf parsley, to garnish
lemon wedges, to serve

1 Place the chicken breast fillets between two sheets of clear film (plastic wrap), baking parchment or inside a plastic bag. Bat out with a rolling pin or meat mallet until the fillets are about 5mm/¼in thick.

2 Cut the chicken into strips about 1cm/½in wide. Heat the oil in a large frying pan. Stir-fry the chicken strips with the shallot, garlic and paprika over a high heat for about 3 minutes until lightly browned and cooked through.

3 Add the lemon juice and chopped fresh parsley to the cooked chicken. Season with salt and ground black pepper to taste. Serve immediately with lemon wedges, garnished with flat leaf parsley.

Cook's Tip

To make your own herb aioli, beat together 2 egg yolks in a bowl, whisk in 5ml/1 tsp Dijon mustard and 10ml/2 tsp white wine vinegar. Whisk in 250ml/8fl oz/1 cup light olive oil, a trickle at a time, until the sauce is thick and smooth. Season with salt and pepper and stir in 45ml/3 tbsp chopped mixed fresh herbs, such as chervil, parsley or tarragon, 30ml/2 tbsp watercress and 5 crushed garlic cloves. Cover and chill until ready to serve. If you prefer a more traditional aioli, then simply omit the fresh herbs and watercress.

Chicken Kofta Balti with Paneer

This rather unusual appetizer looks most elegant when served in small individual karahis.

Serves 6

For the koftas
450g/1lb boneless chicken, skinned and cubed
5ml/1 tsp crushed garlic
5ml/1 tsp shredded fresh root ginger
7.5ml/1½ tsp ground coriander
7.5ml/1½ tsp chilli powder
7.5ml/1½ tsp ground fenugreek
1.5ml/¼ tsp ground turmeric
5ml/1 tsp salt
30ml/2 tbsp chopped fresh coriander (cilantro)
2 fresh green chillies, chopped
600ml/1 pint/2½ cups water
corn oil, for frying

For the paneer mixture
1 medium onion, sliced
1 red (bell) pepper, seeded and cut into strips
1 green (bell) pepper, seeded and cut into strips
175g/6oz paneer, cubed
175g/6oz/1½ cups corn
fresh mint sprigs, to garnish

1 Put all the kofta ingredients, apart from the oil, into a medium pan. Bring to the boil slowly over medium heat, and cook until all the liquid has evaporated. Remove from the heat and leave to cool slightly. Put the mixture into a food processor or blender and process for 2 minutes.

2 Transfer the mixture to a large mixing bowl. Taking a little of the mixture at a time, shape it into small balls, using your hands. You should be able to make about 12 koftas.

3 Heat the corn oil in a karahi, wok or deep pan over high heat. Reduce the heat slightly and drop the koftas carefully into the oil. Move them around gently to ensure that they cook evenly. When the koftas are lightly browned, remove them with a slotted spoon and drain on kitchen paper. Set aside.

4 Heat the oil still remaining in the karahi, and flash-fry all the ingredients for the paneer mixture. This should take about 3 minutes over high heat. Divide the paneer mixture evenly between six individual karahis. Add two koftas to each serving, and garnish with mint sprigs.

Chicken with Lemon Energy 119kcal/496kJ; Protein 14.1g; Carbohydrate 1.5g, of which sugars 1.1g; Fat 6.3g, of which saturates 1g; Cholesterol 39mg; Calcium 32mg; Fibre 0.8g; Sodium 38mg.
Chicken Kofta Energy 253kcal/1056kJ; Protein 24.7g; Carbohydrate 10.8g, of which sugars 6.7g; Fat 12.6g, of which saturates 2.2g; Cholesterol 57mg; Calcium 71mg; Fibre 1.8g; Sodium 471mg.

Barbecue-glazed Chicken Skewers

Known as yakitori in Japan, these aromatic chicken and spring onion skewers are popular throughout the country and are often served as an appetizer with drinks or as a snack.

Makes 12 skewers and 8 wing pieces

8 chicken wings
4 chicken thighs, skinned
4 spring onions (scallions), blanched and cut into short lengths

For the basting sauce
60ml/4 tbsp sake
75ml/5 tbsp/⅓ cup dark soy sauce
30ml/2 tbsp tamari sauce
15ml/1 tbsp mirin, or sweet sherry
15ml/1 tbsp sugar

1 If using wooden skewers, soak 12 of them in cold water for about 30 minutes. This will prevent them from getting scorched and burned during the cooking process.

2 Remove the wing tip of the chicken at the first joint. Chop through the second joint, revealing the two narrow bones. Take hold of the bones with a clean cloth and pull, turning the meat around the bones inside out. Remove the smaller bone and discard. Set the wings aside. Bone the chicken thighs and cut the meat into large dice.

3 Drain the 12 skewers and thread the spring onions and the chicken thigh meat on to them. Don't pack the ingredients on too tightly otherwise they may not cook evenly.

4 Measure the basting sauce ingredients into a stainless steel or enamel pan and simmer until the sauce has reduced by about two-thirds. Set aside to cool.

5 Heat the grill (broiler) to a moderately high temperature. Grill (broil) the skewers and wings without applying any oil.

6 When the juices begin to emerge from the chicken, brush the pieces liberally with the basting sauce. Allow a further 3 minutes for the chicken on skewers and not more than 5 minutes for the chicken wings. Serve while hot.

Scented Chicken Wraps

For sheer sophistication, these leaf-wrapped chicken bites take a lot of beating. They are surprisingly easy to make and can be deep-fried in minutes in the wok.

Serves 4

400g/14oz skinless chicken thighs, boned
45ml/3 tbsp soy sauce
30ml/2 tbsp finely grated garlic
15ml/1 tbsp cumin
15ml/1 tbsp ground coriander
15ml/1 tbsp golden caster (superfine) sugar
5ml/1 tsp finely grated fresh root ginger
1 fresh bird's eye chilli
30ml/2 tbsp oyster sauce
15ml/1 tbsp fish sauce
1 bunch of pandanus leaves, to wrap
vegetable oil, for deep-frying
sweet chilli sauce or chilli sambal, to serve

1 Using a cleaver or sharp knife, cut the chicken into bitesize pieces and place in a large mixing bowl.

2 Place the soy sauce, garlic, cumin, coriander, sugar, ginger, chilli, oyster sauce and fish sauce in a blender and process until smooth. Pour over the chicken, cover and leave to marinate in the refrigerator for 6-8 hours.

3 When ready to cook, drain the chicken from the marinade and wrap each piece in a pandanus leaf (you will need to cut the leaves to size) and secure with a cocktail stick (toothpick).

4 Fill a wok one-third full of oil and heat to 180°C/350°F or until a cube of bread, dropped into the oil, browns in 45 seconds. Carefully add the chicken parcels, 3–4 at a time, and deep-fry for 3–4 minutes, or until cooked through. Drain on kitchen paper and serve with the chilli sauce or sambal. (Do not eat the leaves!)

Cook's Tip
Pandanus leaves are usually available from Asian food stores and large supermarkets.

Chicken Skewers Energy 98kcal/415kJ; Protein 20.3g; Carbohydrate 1.9g, of which sugars 1.9g; Fat 0.9g, of which saturates 0.3g; Cholesterol 58mg; Calcium 7mg; Fibre 0.1g; Sodium 417mg.
Chicken Wraps Energy 159kcal/669kJ; Protein 24.5g; Carbohydrate 6.8g, of which sugars 6.6g; Fat 3.9g, of which saturates 0.6g; Cholesterol 70mg; Calcium 10mg; Fibre 0.1g; Sodium 495mg.

Peking Duck

As the Chinese discovered centuries ago, this is quite the best way to eat duck.

Serves 8
1 duck, about 2.25kg/5lb
45ml/3 tbsp clear honey
5ml/1 tsp salt
1 bunch spring onions (scallions), cut into strips
½ cucumber, seeded and cut into matchsticks
24–32 mandarin pancakes

For the dipping sauces
120ml/4fl oz/½ cup hoisin sauce
120ml/4fl oz/½ cup plum sauce

1 Place the duck on a trivet in the sink and scald with boiling water to firm up the skin. Drain the bird thoroughly. Tie kitchen string firmly around the legs of the duck and hang it in a cool place, with a bowl underneath to catch the drips. Leave the duck overnight.

2 Next day, blend the honey, 30ml/2 tbsp water and salt and brush half the mixture over the duck skin. Hang up again for 2–3 hours. Repeat and leave to dry completely for a further 3–4 hours.

3 Preheat the oven to 230°C/450°F/Gas 8. Stand the duck on a rack in a roasting pan, place in the hot oven and reduce the temperature to 180°C/350°F/Gas 4. Roast for about 1¾ hours without basting. After that time, check the skin is crisp; if not, increase the oven temperature to the maximum. Roast for 15 minutes more.

4 Pat the cucumber pieces dry on kitchen paper. Heat the pancakes by steaming them in a foil parcel for 5–10 minutes over boiling water. Pour the dipping sauces into small dishes to share between the guests.

5 Carve the duck into 4cm/1½in pieces. At the table, each guest smears a little sauce on a pancake, tops it with a small amount of crisp duck skin and meat and then adds cucumber and spring onion strips before rolling the pancake up around the filling and eating it.

Asparagus and Prosciutto

Fresh asparagus in season is a delicious vegetable, which can be perfect eaten on its own. It is, however, particularly tasty if it is served with a classic Italian ham, such as proscuitto di Parma. A light herb sauce completes this delicately flavoured dish, which should be served neither too hot nor too cold, but just lukewarm, so that the superior flavour of the asparagus spears can be fully appreciated.

Serves 4
675–900g/1½lb–2lb medium-size asparagus spears, prepared for cooking
175ml/6fl oz clarified butter
10ml/2 tsp lemon juice
30ml/2 tbsp chopped spring onions (scallions)
15ml/1 tbsp chopped fresh parsley
salt and ground black pepper
8 slices prosciutto

1 Half fill a frying pan with salted water. Bring to the boil. Simmer the asparagus spears for 4–5 minutes or until they are just tender. Pierce an asparagus stalk to test if it is cooked. Remove and drain well.

2 Combine the butter, lemon juice, spring onions and parsley in a small saucepan. Season with salt and pepper to taste. Heat the mixture until lukewarm.

3 Divide the asparagus among four warmed plates. Drape two slices of prosciutto over each portion. Spoon over the herb butter and serve.

Cook's Tip
Clarified butter is butter that has had the milk solids removed. Impurities are also removed, which means that the clarified butter will keep for several weeks in the refrigerator. It is made by gently melting the butter, then skimming off all the froth from the surface. There will be a clear yellow layer on top of a milky layer. Pour off the clear fat and discard the milky residue.

Peking Duck Energy 174kcal/734kJ; Protein 16.9g; Carbohydrate 14.9g, of which sugars 4.7g; Fat 5.3g, of which saturates 1.7g; Cholesterol 85mg; Calcium 21mg; Fibre 0.7g; Sodium 334mg.
Asparagus and Prosciutto Energy 82kcal/339kJ; Protein 4.4g; Carbohydrate 1.9g, of which sugars 1.8g; Fat 6.4g, of which saturates 1g; Cholesterol 6mg; Calcium 24mg; Fibre 1.5g; Sodium 121mg.

Melon and Prosciutto Salad

Sections of cool fragrant melon wrapped with slices of air-dried ham make a delicious salad appetizer. If strawberries are in season, serve with a savoury-sweet strawberry salsa.

Serves 4

1 large cantaloupe, Charentais or Galia melon
175g/6oz prosciutto or Serrano ham, thinly sliced

For the salsa
225g/8oz/2 cups strawberries
5ml/1 tsp caster (superfine) sugar
30ml/2 tbsp groundnut (peanut) or sunflower oil
15ml/1 tbsp orange juice
2.5ml/½ tsp finely grated orange rind
2.5ml/½ tsp finely grated fresh root ginger
salt and ground black pepper

1 Halve the melon and scoop the seeds out with a spoon. Cut the rind away with a paring knife, then slice the melon thickly. Chill until ready to serve.

2 To make the salsa, hull the strawberries and cut them into large dice. Place in a small mixing bowl with the sugar and crush lightly to release the juices.

3 Add the oil, orange juice, rind and ginger and mix until all the ingredients are combined. Season to taste with salt and pepper.

4 Arrange the sliced melon on a serving plate, lay the ham over the top and serve with a bowl of salsa, handed round separately for diners to help themselves.

Cook's Tip
Prosciutto means 'ham' in Italian, and is a term generally used to describe seasoned, salt-cured and air-dried hams. Parma ham is the most famed prosciutto. Italian prosciuttos are designated prosciutto cotto, or cooked, and prosciutto crudo, or raw – although edible due to curing. They are labelled according to the place of origin, such as prosciutto di Parma and prosciutto di San Daniele. Buy it in supermarkets and Italian delicatessens.

Figs with Prosciutto and Roquefort

In this easy, stylish dish, figs and honey balance the richness of the ham and cheese. Serve with warm bread for a simple appetizer before any rich main course.

Serves 4
8 fresh figs
75g/3oz prosciutto
45ml/3 tbsp clear honey
75g/3oz Roquefort cheese
ground black pepper

1 Preheat the grill (broiler). Quarter the figs and place on a foil-lined grill rack. Tear each slice of prosciutto into two or three pieces. Crumple the pieces of prosciutto and place them on the foil beside the figs. Brush the figs with 15ml/1 tbsp of the clear honey and cook under the grill until lightly browned.

2 Crumble the Roquefort cheese and divide among four plates, setting it to one side. Add the honey-grilled figs and ham and pour over any cooking juices caught on the foil. Drizzle the remaining honey over the figs, ham and cheese, and serve seasoned with plenty of ground black pepper.

Variations
• Any thinly sliced cured ham can be used instead of prosciutto: Westphalian, Bayonne, Culatello or Serrano.
• The figs could be replaced with fresh pears. Slice 2 ripe but firm dessert pears in quarters and remove the cores. Toss in olive oil and cook on a hot ridged grill or griddle pan for 2 minutes on each side. Drizzle balsamic vinegar over and cook for 1 minute more until nicely coloured.

Cook's Tip
Fresh figs are a delicious treat, whether you choose dark purple, yellowy green or green-skinned varieties. When they are ripe, you can split them open with your fingers to reveal the soft, sweet flesh full of edible seeds. They also taste great stuffed with goat's cheese.

Melon Salad Energy 147kcal/614kJ; Protein 9.2g; Carbohydrate 12.2g, of which sugars 12.2g; Fat 7.1g, of which saturates 1.2g; Cholesterol 25mg; Calcium 29mg; Fibre 1.1g; Sodium 568mg.
Figs Energy 326kcal/1378kJ; Protein 10.7g; Carbohydrate 57.4g, of which sugars 57.4g; Fat 7.5g, of which saturates 3.8g; Cholesterol 25mg; Calcium 324mg; Fibre 6.9g; Sodium 512mg.

Prosciutto with Potato Rémoulade

Rémoulade is a classic piquant dressing based on mayonnaise. The traditional French version is flavoured with mustard, gherkins, capers and herbs, but simpler variations are seasoned only with mustard. Lime juice brings a contemporary twist to this recipe for a cream-enriched dressing.

Serves 4

2 potatoes, each weighing about 175g/6oz, quartered lengthways
150ml/¼ pint/⅔ cup mayonnaise
150ml/¼ pint/⅔ cup double (heavy) cream
5–10ml/1–2 tsp Dijon mustard
juice of ½ lime
30ml/2 tbsp olive oil
12 prosciutto slices
450g/1lb asparagus spears, halved
salt and ground black pepper
25g/1oz wild rocket (arugula), to garnish
extra virgin olive oil, to serve

1 Put the potatoes in a pan. Add water to cover and bring to the boil. Add salt, then simmer for about 15 minutes, or until the potatoes are tender, but do not let them get too soft.

2 Drain the potatoes thoroughly and leave to cool. When cool, cut them into long, thin strips.

3 Beat together the mayonnaise, cream, mustard, lime juice and seasoning in a large bowl. Add the potatoes and stir carefully to coat them with the dressing.

4 Heat the oil in a griddle or frying pan and cook the prosciutto in batches until crisp and golden. Use a draining spoon to remove the ham, draining each piece well.

5 Cook the asparagus in the fat remaining in the pan for about 3 minutes, or until tender and golden.

6 Put a generous spoonful of potato rémoulade on each plate and top with several slices of prosciutto. Add the asparagus and garnish with rocket. Serve immediately, offering olive oil to drizzle over.

Frijoles Charros

These 'cowboy beans' taste rather like Boston baked beans, but with considerably more punch. The flavour improves on keeping, so make the dish the day before you want to serve it.

Serves 6

2 x 400g/14oz cans pinto beans
120ml/4fl oz/½ cup Mexican beer
115g/4oz/⅔ cups drained pickled jalapeño chilli slices
2 tomatoes, peeled and chopped
5ml/1 tsp ground cinnamon
175g/6oz bacon fat
1 onion, chopped
2 garlic cloves, crushed
175g/6oz rindless smoked lean bacon, diced
45ml/3 tbsp soft dark brown sugar
wheat flour tortillas, to serve

1 Put the drained pinto beans in a pan. Stir in the beer and cook over a high heat for 5 minutes, until some of the beer has been absorbed.

2 Lower the heat slightly and stir in the jalapeño chilli slices, then add the tomatoes and cinnamon. Continue to cook, stirring occasionally, for about 10 minutes.

3 Meanwhile, heat the fat bacon in a frying pan until the fat runs. The quantity suggested should yield about 45ml/3 tbsp bacon fat.

4 Lift out the bacon and set aside, then add the onion and garlic to the pan and fry for about 5 minutes, until browned. Using a slotted spoon, lift out the garlic and onions and stir them into the beans.

5 Return the diced smoked bacon to the fat remaining in the frying pan and fry until crisp. Add the bacon and any remaining fat to the beans and mix well.

6 Stir the sugar into the bean and bacon mixture and cook over a low heat, stirring constantly, until the sugar has dissolved. Serve immediately or spoon into a bowl, leave to cool, cover, then chill for reheating next day. Serve with warmed wheat flour tortillas.

Prosciutto Energy 612kcal/2530kJ; Protein 13.1g; Carbohydrate 18.6g, of which sugars 5.4g; Fat 56.5g, of which saturates 16.8g; Cholesterol 99mg; Calcium 74mg; Fibre 3.1g; Sodium 693mg.
Frijoles Charros Energy 235kcal/997kJ; Protein 19.2g; Carbohydrate 37.4g, of which sugars 13g; Fat 2g, of which saturates 0.5g; Cholesterol 18mg; Calcium 92mg; Fibre 9.5g; Sodium 221mg.

Chorizo in Olive Oil

Spanish chorizo sausage has a deliciously pungent taste; its robust seasoning of garlic, chilli and paprika flavours the ingredients it is cooked with. Simply frying chorizo with onions and olive oil is one of its simplest and most delicious uses.

Serves 4
75ml/5 tbsp extra virgin olive oil
350g/12oz chorizo sausage, sliced
1 large onion, thinly sliced
roughly chopped flat leaf parsley, to garnish

1 Heat the oil in a frying pan and fry the chorizo sausage over a high heat until beginning to colour. Remove from the pan with a slotted spoon.

2 Add the sliced onion to the pan and fry until coloured. Return the sausage slices to the pan and heat through for about 2 minutes.

3 Transfer the mixture into a shallow serving dish and sprinkle with the parsley. Serve with warm bread.

Variations

- *Peppers go well with chorizo. Add slices of fresh red (bell) pepper or drained canned pimiento when frying the onion.*
- *A little fresh chilli would be a good addition, but don't overdo it as the chorizo already contains this seasoning. Choose mild fresnos or jalapeños, and remove the seeds.*
- *For those who prefer not to go for the burn, substitute sun-dried tomatoes. Use the ones that come packed in oil, so that you can drain off a little of the oil for frying the chorizo.*

Cook's Tip

Chorizo is usually available in large supermarkets or delicatessens. Other similarly rich, spicy sausages can be used as a substitute.

Chorizo with Garlic Potatoes

A classic tapas recipe, this simple dish can be served in small quantities as a snack or, as here, in slightly larger proportions for an appetizer. The name tapas is derived from *tapa*, a lid, traditionally used by Spanish barmen to cover glasses of cold fino or manzanilla sherry to prevent flies from settling in the drink. The lid usually took the form of a saucer of small canapés or a small portion of a tasty dish to be enjoyed with the sherry.

Serves 4
450g/1lb potatoes
3 eggs, hard-boiled and quartered
175g/6oz chorizo sausage, sliced
150ml/¼ pint/⅔ cup mayonnaise
150ml/¼ pint/⅔ cup sour cream
2 garlic cloves, crushed
salt and ground black pepper
30ml/2 tbsp chopped fresh coriander (cilantro), to garnish

1 Cook the potatoes in a pan of boiling salted water for about 20 minutes, or until tender. Drain and leave to cool.

2 Cut the potatoes into bitesize pieces. Place them in a large serving dish with the eggs and chorizo sausage, and season to taste with salt and pepper.

3 In a small bowl, stir the mayonnaise, sour cream and garlic together with seasoning to taste, then spoon this dressing over the potato mixture.

4 Toss the salad gently to coat the ingredients with dressing, then sprinkle with chopped coriander to garnish.

Variation

To give this dish a more piquant flavour, stir in about 15ml/1 tbsp finely chopped cornichons and 4 finely chopped anchovy fillets. If coriander (cilantro) isn't available, then you can use 15ml/1 tbsp fresh marjoram instead.

Chorizo in Oil Energy 408kcal/1689kJ; Protein 9.2g; Carbohydrate 15.2g, of which sugars 5.1g; Fat 35g, of which saturates 10.7g; Cholesterol 35mg; Calcium 58mg; Fibre 1.3g; Sodium 711mg.
Chorizo with Potatoes Energy 631kcal/2613kJ; Protein 12.8g; Carbohydrate 24.3g, of which sugars 4g; Fat 54.4g, of which saturates 15.5g; Cholesterol 214mg; Calcium 84mg; Fibre 1.4g; Sodium 582mg.

Spicy Chorizo Sausage and Spring Onion Hash

This is a great dish to use up any leftover boiled potatoes, if you have them. The potatoes will absorb some of the delicious spicy flavours of the chorizo.

Serves 4
450g/1lb fresh chorizo sausages
15ml/1 tbsp olive oil
450g/1lb cooked potatoes, cut into small chunks
1 bunch of spring onions (scallions), sliced
salt and ground black pepper

1 Heat a large frying pan over medium heat and add the sausages. Cook for 8–10 minutes, turning occasionally, until cooked through. Remove from the pan and set aside.

2 Add the olive oil to the sausage fat in the pan and then add the potatoes. Cook over a low heat for 5–8 minutes, turning occasionally until golden.

3 Meanwhile, cut the chorizo sausages into bitesize chunks and add to the pan with the potatoes.

4 Add the spring onions to the pan and cook for a couple more minutes, until they are piping hot. Season with salt and pepper, and serve immediately.

Cook's Tips
- *Fresh chorizo sausages are available from good butchers or from Spanish delicatessens and larger supermarkets. They often come in different varieties, with some being hotter and spicier than others – choose those that match your taste.*
- *If you don't have any leftover cooked potatoes then simply boil some from scratch in plenty of salted water until tender. Leave them to cool completely before cutting into small chunks and adding to the frying pan, as specified above.*

Crispy Shanghai Spring Rolls

Crunchy on the outside, succulent in the centre, these crispy Asian rolls are irresistible when served as an appetizer.

Makes 12
12 spring roll wrappers
30ml/2 tbsp plain (all-purpose) flour mixed to a paste with water
sunflower oil, for deep-frying

For the filling
6 Chinese dried mushrooms, soaked for 30 minutes in warm water
150g/5oz fresh firm tofu
30ml/2 tbsp sunflower oil
225g/8oz minced (ground) pork
225g/8oz peeled cooked prawns (shrimp), roughly chopped
2.5ml/½ tsp cornflour (cornstarch), mixed to a paste with 15ml/1 tbsp soy sauce
75g/3oz each shredded bamboo shoot or grated carrot, sliced water chestnuts and beansprouts
6 spring onions (scallions) or 1 young leek, finely chopped
a little sesame oil

1 Make the filling. Drain the mushrooms. Cut off and discard the stems and slice the caps finely. Slice the tofu.

2 Heat the oil in a wok and stir-fry the pork for 2–3 minutes or until the colour changes. Add the prawns, cornflour paste and bamboo shoot or carrot. Stir in the water chestnuts.

3 Increase the heat, add the beansprouts and spring onions or leek and toss for 1 minute. Stir in the mushrooms and tofu. Season, then stir in the sesame oil. Cool quickly on a platter.

4 Separate the spring roll wrappers. Place a wrapper on the work surface with one corner nearest you. Spoon some of the filling near the centre of the wrapper and fold the nearest corner over the filling. Smear a little of the flour paste on the free sides, turn the sides to the middle and roll up. Repeat this procedure with the remaining wrappers and filling.

5 Deep-fry the spring rolls in batches until they are crisp and golden and cooked through. Drain on kitchen paper and serve immediately with a dipping sauce.

Spicy Sausage Energy 522kcal/2172kJ; Protein 14.4g; Carbohydrate 29.6g, of which sugars 3.8g; Fat 39.3g, of which saturates 14.3g; Cholesterol 53mg; Calcium 63mg; Fibre 2.1g; Sodium 869mg.
Crispy Shanghai Spring Rolls Energy 38kcal/161kJ; Protein 1.1g; Carbohydrate 6.6g, of which sugars 0.6g; Fat 1g, of which saturates 0.1g; Cholesterol 0mg; Calcium 15mg; Fibre 0.5g; Sodium 88mg.

Vietnamese Spring Rolls with Pork

These spring rolls from Vietnam make an ideal quick snack or tasty appetizer.

Makes about 30

30 dried rice wrappers
vegetable oil, for deep-frying
1 bunch of fresh mint, stalks removed, and nuoc cham, to serve

For the filling

50g/2oz dried bean thread (cellophane) noodles, soaked in warm water for 20 minutes
25g/1oz dried cloud ear (wood ear) mushrooms, soaked in warm water for 15 minutes
2 eggs
30ml/2 tbsp nuoc mam
2 garlic cloves, crushed
10ml/2 tsp sugar
1 onion, finely chopped
3 spring onions (scallions), finely sliced
350g/12oz/1½ cups minced (ground) pork
175g/6oz/1¾ cups cooked crab meat or raw prawns (shrimp)
salt and ground black pepper

1 To make the filling, squeeze dry the soaked noodles and chop them into small pieces. Squeeze dry the soaked dried cloud ear mushrooms and chop them.

2 Beat the eggs in a bowl. Stir in the nuoc mam, garlic and sugar. Add the onion, spring onions, noodles, mushrooms, pork and crab meat or prawns. Season with salt and black pepper.

3 Have ready a damp dish towel, some clear film (plastic wrap) and a bowl of water. Dip a rice wrapper in the water and place it on the damp towel. Spoon about 15ml/1 tbsp of the filling on to the side nearest to you, just in from the edge. Fold the nearest edge over the filling, fold over the sides, tucking them in neatly, and then roll the whole wrapper into a tight cylinder. Place the roll on a plate and cover with clear film to keep it moist. Continue making rolls, using the remaining wrappers and filling.

4 Heat the vegetable oil in a wok or heavy pan for deep-frying. Make sure it is hot enough by dropping in a small piece of bread; it should foam and sizzle. Cook the spring rolls in batches, turning them in the oil so that they become golden all over. Drain on kitchen paper and serve immediately with mint leaves to wrap around them and nuoc cham for dipping.

Rice Rolls Stuffed with Pork

Steamed rice sheets are very tasty when filled with pork, rolled up, drizzled in herb oil, and then dipped in a hot chilli sauce. Generally, they are eaten as a snack, or served as an appetizer.

Serves 6

25g/1oz dried cloud ear (wood ear) mushrooms, soaked in warm water for 30 minutes
350g/12oz minced (ground) pork
30nl/2 tbsp fish sauce
10ml/2 tsp sugar
15ml/1 tbsp vegetable or groundnut (peanut) oil
2 garlic cloves, finely chopped
2 shallots, finely chopped
2 spring onions (scallions), trimmed and finely chopped
24 fresh rice sheets, 7.5cm/3in square
ground black pepper
herb oil, for drizzling
hot chilli sauce, for dipping

1 Drain the mushrooms and squeeze out any excess water. Cut off and discard the hard stems. Finely chop the rest of the mushrooms and put them in a bowl. Add the minced pork, fish sauce and sugar and mix well.

2 Heat the oil in a wok or heavy pan. Add the garlic, shallots and onions. Stir-fry until golden. Add the pork mixture and stir-fry for 5–6 minutes, until the pork is cooked. Season with pepper.

3 Place the rice sheets on a flat surface. Spoon a tablespoon of the pork mixture on to the middle of a sheet. Fold one side over the filling, tuck in the sides, and roll to enclose the filling, so that it resembles a short spring roll. Repeat this process until all the rice sheets and filling have been used up.

4 Place the filled rice rolls on a serving plate, drizzle with herb oil, and serve with chilli sauce.

Cook's Tip
To make life easy, prepared, fresh rice sheets are available in Asian markets and grocery stores.

Vietnamese Spring Rolls Energy 63Kcal/236kJ; Protein 2g; Carbohydrate 5g, of which sugars 1g; Fat 4g, of which saturates 1g; Cholesterol 20mg; Calcium 10mg; Fibre 0.3g; Sodium 0.06g
Rice Rolls Energy 160kcal/670kJ; Protein 13.8g; Carbohydrate 16g, of which sugars 2.4g; Fat 4.4g, of which saturates 1.1g; Cholesterol 37mg; Calcium 13mg; Fibre 0.6g; Sodium 43mg.

Tortas

The essential ingredients of a torta – a Mexican sandwich – are refried beans and chillies, everything else is subject to change and personal taste. Traditionally they are made using rolls called teleras.

Serves 2

2 fresh jalapeño chillies
juice of ½ lime
2 French bread rolls or 2 pieces of French bread
115g/4oz/⅔ cup refried beans
150g/5oz roast pork
2 small tomatoes, sliced
115g/4oz Cheddar cheese, sliced
small bunch of fresh coriander (cilantro)
30ml/2 tbsp crème fraîche

1 Cut the chillies in half, scrape out the seeds, then cut the flesh into thin strips. Put it in a bowl, pour over the lime juice and leave to stand.

2 If using rolls, slice them in half and remove some of the crumb so that they are slightly hollowed. If using French bread, slice each piece in half lengthways. Set the top of each piece of bread or roll aside and spread the bottom halves with the refried beans.

3 Cut the pork into thin shreds and put these on top of the refried beans. Top with the tomato slices. Drain the jalapeño strips and put them on top of the tomato slices. Add the cheese and sprinkle with coriander leaves.

4 Turn the top halves of the bread or rolls over, so that the cut sides are uppermost, and spread these with crème fraîche. Sandwich back together again and serve.

Variations
Almost any filling can be used in a torta, whether hot or cold. Tempting ingredients to try include chorizo, spicy beef, ham, sliced turkey breast fillets, avocado, fried fish fillets, strips of roast red (bell) peppers, lettuce and sour cream.

Cabbage and Noodle Parcels

The noodles and mushrooms give a delicious Asian flavour to the cabbage rolls.

Serves 6

4 dried Chinese mushrooms, soaked in hot water until soft
50g/2oz cellophane noodles, soaked in hot water until soft
450g/1lb minced (ground) pork
2 garlic cloves, finely chopped
8 spring onions (scallions)
30ml/2 tbsp fish sauce
12 large outer green cabbage leaves

For the sauce
15ml/1 tbsp vegetable oil
1 small onion, finely chopped
2 garlic cloves, crushed
400g/14oz can chopped plum tomatoes
pinch of sugar
salt and ground black pepper

1 Drain the mushrooms, discard the stems and chop the caps. Put them in a bowl. Next, drain the noodles and cut them into short lengths. Add to the bowl with the pork and garlic. Chop two of the spring onions and add to the bowl. Season with the fish sauce and pepper.

2 Blanch the cabbage leaves a few at a time in a pan of boiling, lightly salted water for about 1 minute. Remove the leaves from the pan with a spoon and refresh under cold water. Drain the leaves and dry them well on kitchen paper. Blanch the remaining six spring onions in the same fashion. Drain well.

3 Fill one of the cabbage leaves with a generous spoonful of the pork and noodle filling. Roll up the leaf to enclose the filling, then tuck in the sides and continue rolling to make a tight parcel. Make more parcels in the same way.

4 Split each spring onion lengthways and use to tie the cabbage parcels together.

5 To make the sauce, fry the onion and garlic in the oil in a large pan until soft. Add the tomatoes, season with salt, pepper and a pinch of sugar, then bring to simmering point. Add the cabbage parcels. Cover and simmer for 20–25 minutes. Serve.

Tortas Energy 703kcal/2956kJ; Protein 42.9g; Carbohydrate 72.4g, of which sugars 8.4g; Fat 27.8g, of which saturates 16.4g; Cholesterol 108mg; Calcium 570mg; Fibre 7.8g; Sodium 1329mg.
Cabbage Parcels Energy 159kcal/670kJ; Protein 18g; Carbohydrate 9.8g, of which sugars 3.4g; Fat 5.6g, of which saturates 1.4g; Cholesterol 47mg; Calcium 20mg; Fibre 1.3g; Sodium 238mg.

Savoury Pork Pies

These little pastries come from Spain and are as much fun to eat as they are to make. They will be gone in a flash at a children's party or, serve as an appetizer before a main meal.

Serves 4–6

350g/12oz shortcrust pastry, thawed if frozen

For the filling

15ml/1 tbsp vegetable oil
1 onion, chopped
1 clove garlic, crushed
5ml/1 tsp thyme
115g/4oz/1 cup minced (ground) pork
5ml/1 tsp paprika
1 hard-boiled egg, chopped
1 gherkin, chopped
30ml/2 tbsp chopped fresh parsley
vegetable oil, for deep-frying
salt and ground black pepper

1 To make the filling, heat the vegetable oil in a pan or wok and soften the onion, garlic and thyme without browning, for about 3–4 minutes.

2 Add the pork and paprika to the pan, then brown evenly for 6–8 minutes, stirring frequently. Season well with salt and ground black pepper.

3 Transfer the mixture to a bowl and set aside to cool. When the mixture is cool, add the hard-boiled egg, gherkin and chopped fresh parsley.

4 Turn the pastry out on to a floured work surface and roll out to a 38cm/15in square. Cut out 12 circles about 13cm/5in in diameter. Place 15ml/1 tbsp of the filling on each circle, moisten the edges with a little water, fold over and seal.

5 Heat the vegetable oil in a deep-fryer or heavy pan fitted with a wire basket, to 196°C/385°F. Check the oil is hot enough by dropping in a piece of bread; it should sizzle and brown in about 45 seconds. Place three pies at a time in the basket and deep-fry until golden brown. Frying the pies should take at least 1 minute or the inside filling will not be heated through. Serve warm in a basket covered with a napkin.

Cellophane Noodles with Pork

Simple, speedy and very satisfying, this is an excellent way of using mung bean noodles. It scores high on presentation too, thanks to the contrast between the translucent, thread-like noodles and the vibrant colour of the vegetables.

Serves 2

200g/7oz cellophane noodles
30ml/2 tbsp vegetable oil
15ml/1 tbsp magic paste
200g/7oz minced (ground) pork
1 fresh green or red chilli, seeded and finely chopped
300g/11oz/scant 1½ cups beansprouts
bunch spring onions (scallions), finely chopped
30ml/2 tbsp soy sauce
30ml/2 tbsp fish sauce
30ml/2 tbsp sweet chilli sauce
15ml/1 tbsp light brown sugar
30ml/2 tbsp rice vinegar
30ml/2 tbsp roasted peanuts, chopped, to garnish
small bunch fresh coriander (cilantro), chopped, to garnish

1 Place the noodles in a large bowl, cover with boiling water and soak for 10 minutes. Drain the noodles and set aside until ready to use.

2 Heat the oil in a wok or large, heavy frying pan. Add the magic paste and stir-fry for 2–3 seconds, then add the pork. Stir-fry the meat, breaking it up with a wooden spatula, for 2–3 minutes, until browned all over.

3 Add the chopped chilli to the meat and stir-fry for 3–4 seconds, then add the beansprouts and chopped spring onions, stir-frying for a few seconds after each addition.

4 Snip the noodles into 5cm/2in lengths and add to the wok or pan, with the soy sauce, fish sauce, sweet chilli sauce, sugar and rice vinegar.

5 Toss the ingredients together over the heat until the noodles have warmed through. Pile on to a platter or into a large bowl. Sprinkle the peanuts and coriander over the top and serve.

Pork Pies Energy 209kcal/868kJ; Protein 4.2g; Carbohydrate 14.2g, of which sugars 0.7g; Fat 15.4g, of which saturates 3.8g; Cholesterol 26mg; Calcium 38mg; Fibre 0.9g; Sodium 131mg.
Cellophane Noodles Energy 593kcal/2504kJ; Protein 47.8g; Carbohydrate 72.1g, of which sugars 4.7g; Fat 14.6g, of which saturates 2.8g; Cholesterol 106mg; Calcium 53mg; Fibre 3.2g; Sodium 1461mg.

Tostadas with Shredded Pork and Spices

Crisp fried tortillas topped with refried beans and spiced shredded pork make a delectable treat and they are often sold from stalls in Mexican city streets.

Serves 6
6 corn tortillas, freshly made or a few days old
oil, for frying

For the topping
500g/1¼lb pork shoulder, cut into 2.5cm/1in cubes
2.5ml/½ tsp salt
15ml/1 tbsp oil
1 small onion, halved and sliced
1 garlic clove, crushed
1 pasilla chilli, seeded and ground
5ml/1 tsp ground cinnamon
2.5ml/½ tsp ground cloves
175g/6oz/1 cup refried beans
90ml/6 tbsp sour cream
2 tomatoes, seeded and diced
115g/4oz feta cheese, crumbled
fresh oregano sprigs, to garnish

1 Make the topping. Place the pork in a pan, pour over water to cover and bring to the boil. Lower the heat, cover and simmer for 40 minutes. Drain. Shred the pork, put it in a bowl and season with the salt.

2 Heat the oil in a large frying pan. Add the onion, garlic, chilli and spices. Stir over the heat for 2–3 minutes, then add the shredded meat and cook until the meat is thoroughly heated and has absorbed the flavourings. Heat the refried beans in a separate, small pan.

3 Meanwhile, cook the tortillas. Pour oil into a frying pan to a depth of 2cm/¾in. Heat the oil and fry one tortilla at a time, pressing down with a metal spatula to keep it flat. As soon as a tortilla is crisp, lift out and drain on kitchen paper.

4 Place each tortilla on a plate. Top with refried beans. Add a little of the meat, then spoon over 15ml/1 tbsp of the sour cream. Divide the diced tomato among the tostadas and top each one with the crumbled feta. Serve immediately garnished with fresh oregano.

Carnitas

Use these 'little meats' as part of a main dish or serve with tortillas as an appetizer.

Serves 6–8
2 dried bay leaves
10ml/2 tsp dried thyme
5ml/1 tsp dried marjoram
1.5kg/3⅓lb mixed boneless pork (loin and leg)
3 garlic cloves
2.5ml/½ tsp salt
200g/7oz/scant 1 cup lard or white cooking fat
1 orange, cut into 8 wedges
1 small onion, thickly sliced
warm wheat flour tortillas, to serve

For the salsa
small bunch of fresh coriander (cilantro), stems removed and roughly chopped
1 white onion
8–10 pickled jalapeño chilli slices
45ml/3 tbsp freshly squeezed orange juice

1 Crumble the bay leaves into a mortar. Add the dried thyme and dried marjoram and grind with a pestle to a fine powder.

2 Cut the pork into 5cm/2in cubes and place it in a non-metallic bowl. Add the herbs and salt. Using your fingers, rub the spice mixture into the meat. Cover and marinate for at least 2 hours, preferably overnight.

3 To make the salsa, cut the onion in half, then slice each half thinly. Finely chop the chilli slices. Mix all the salsa ingredients in a bowl, pour over the freshly squeezed orange juice and toss gently to mix. Cover and chill until required.

4 Heat the lard or cooking fat in a flameproof casserole. Add the pork mixture, with the oranges, garlic cloves and onion. Brown the pork cubes on all sides. Using a slotted spoon, lift out the onion and garlic and discard. Cover the casserole and continue to cook over a low heat for about 1½ hours.

5 Remove the lid and lift out and discard the orange wedges. Continue to cook the mixture, uncovered, until all the meat juices have been absorbed and the pork cubes are crisp on the outside and tender and moist inside. Serve with warm tortillas and the salsa.

Tostadas Energy 525kcal/2195kJ; Protein 34.8g; Carbohydrate 37.2g, of which sugars 2.9g; Fat 27.3g, of which saturates 5.9g; Cholesterol 92mg; Calcium 104mg; Fibre 3.4g; Sodium 369mg.
Carnitas Energy 297kcal/1241kJ; Protein 40.8g; Carbohydrate 2.1g, of which sugars 1.9g; Fat 13.9g, of which saturates 5.1g; Cholesterol 124mg; Calcium 37mg; Fibre 0.7g; Sodium 135mg.

Pork-stuffed Green Peppers

Small, thin-skinned peppers are best for this traditional Chinese appetizer.

Serves 4

225g/8oz minced (ground) pork
4–6 drained canned water chestnuts, finely chopped
2 spring onions (scallions), finely chopped
2.5ml/½ tsp finely chopped fresh root ginger
15ml/1 tbsp light soy sauce
15ml/1 tbsp Chinese rice wine or dry sherry
3–4 green (bell) peppers
15ml/1 tbsp cornflour (cornstarch)
oil for deep-frying

For the sauce

30ml/2 tbsp light soy sauce
5ml/1 tsp soft light brown sugar
1–2 fresh red chillies, finely chopped
75ml/5 tbsp ham stock or water

1 Mix the minced pork, chopped water chestnuts, spring onions and ginger. Add the soy sauce and wine or sherry and work them into the pork mixture so that they are evenly distributed and well combined.

2 Cut the peppers in half lengthways and remove the cores and seeds. If the peppers are large, halve them again to make quarters. Stuff the peppers with the pork mixture, pressing it down firmly. Sprinkle a little cornflour over the filled peppers.

3 Heat the oil for deep-frying in a wok, or use a deep-fryer. Using a spider or a large slotted spoon, carefully add the stuffed peppers, meat side down, and fry them for 2–3 minutes. If you have cut the peppers into quarters, you will probably need to do this in batches. Lift out and drain on kitchen paper.

4 Let the oil cool slightly, then pour most of it into a separate pan and set aside. Heat the oil remaining in the wok and add the peppers, this time placing them meat side up. Add the sauce ingredients, shaking the wok so they do not stick to the bottom, and braise the peppers for 2–3 minutes. Lift them out on to a serving dish, meat side up, pour the sauce over and serve immediately.

Pork in Green Sauce with Cactus

The inclusion of cactus pieces, known as nopalitos, gives this appetizer an intriguing flavour which will doubtless be a talking point at the dinner table. Serve with warmed corn tortillas as a snack or appetizer, or with rice and salsa as a more substantial main course.

Serves 4

30ml/2 tbsp vegetable oil
500g/1¼lb pork shoulder, cut in 2.5cm/1 in cubes
1 onion, finely chopped
2 garlic cloves, crushed
5ml/1 tsp dried oregano
3 fresh jalapeno chillies, seeded and chopped
300g/11oz/scant 2 cups drained canned tomatillos
150ml/¼ pint/⅔ cup vegetable stock
300g/11oz jar nopalitos, drained
salt and ground black pepper
warm fresh corn tortillas, to serve

1 Heat the vegetable oil in a large pan. Add the pork cubes and cook over high heat, turning several times until evenly browned all over.

2 Add the onion and garlic to the pan and fry gently until soft, then stir in the oregano and chopped jalapeños. Cook for 2 minutes more.

3 Place the tomatillos into a food processor or blender, add the stock and process until smooth.

4 Transfer the tomatillo mixture to the pork mixture. Cover the pan and cook gently for 30 minutes.

5 While the pork mixture is cooking, soak the nopalitos (pickled strips of cactus paddles) in cold water for 10 minutes.

6 Drain the nopalitos, then add to the pork mixture and continue cooking for about 10 minutes or until the pork pieces are cooked through and tender.

7 Season the mixture with salt and plenty of ground black pepper to taste. Serve this dish with warm corn tortillas.

Pork-stuffed Peppers Energy 198kcal/825kJ; Protein 12.5g; Carbohydrate 4.7g, of which sugars 4.3g; Fat 14.2g, of which saturates 3.1g; Cholesterol 37mg; Calcium 26mg; Fibre 2.3g; Sodium 942mg.
Pork in Green Sauce Energy 522kcal/2194kJ; Protein 41g; Carbohydrate 49.5g, of which sugars 4.8g; Fat 18.6g, of which saturates 7g; Cholesterol 106mg; Calcium 251mg; Fibre 3.1g; Sodium 461mg.

Lion's Head Meat Balls

These larger-than-usual pork balls are first fried, then simmered in stock. They are often served with a fringe of greens such as pak choi to represent the lion's mane.

Serves 2–3

450g/1lb lean pork, minced (ground) finely with a little fat
4–6 drained canned water chestnuts, finely chopped
5ml/1 tsp finely chopped fresh root ginger
1 small onion, finely chopped
30ml/2 tbsp dark soy sauce
beaten egg, to bind
30ml/2 tbsp cornflour (cornstarch), seasoned with salt and ground black pepper
30ml/2 tbsp groundnut (peanut) oil
300ml/½ pint/1¼ cups chicken stock
2.5ml/½ tsp sugar
115g/4oz pak choi (bok choy), stalks trimmed and the leaves rinsed
salt and ground black pepper

1 Mix the pork, water chestnuts, ginger and onion with 15ml/1 tbsp of the soy sauce in a bowl. Add salt and pepper to taste, stir in enough beaten egg to bind, then form into eight or nine balls. Toss a little of the cornflour into the bowl and make a paste with the remaining cornflour and water.

2 Heat the oil in a large frying pan and brown the meat balls all over. Using a slotted spoon, transfer the meat balls to a wok or deep frying pan.

3 Add the stock, sugar and the remaining soy sauce to the oil that is left in the pan. Heat gently, stirring to incorporate the sediment on the bottom of the pan. Pour over the meat balls, cover and simmer for 20–25 minutes.

4 Increase the heat and add the pak choi. Continue to cook for 2–3 minutes or until the leaves are just wilted.

5 Lift out the greens and arrange on a serving platter. Top with the meat balls and keep hot. Stir the cornflour paste into the sauce. Bring to the boil, stirring, until it thickens. Pour over the meat balls and serve immediately.

Sticky Rice Cakes Filled with Pork

These steamed Chinese-style rice cakes are easy to make and are an unusual appetizer.

Serves 2

15ml/1 tbsp vegetable oil
2 garlic cloves, chopped
225g/8oz lean pork, cut into bitesize chunks
30ml/2 tbsp fish sauce
2.5ml/½ tsp sugar
10ml/2 tsp ground black pepper
115g/4oz lotus seeds, soaked for 6 hours and drained
2 lotus or banana leaves, trimmed and cut into 25cm/10in squares
500g/1¼lb/5 cups cooked sticky rice
salt

1 Heat the oil in a heavy pan. Stir in the garlic, until it begins to colour, then add the pork, fish sauce, sugar and pepper. Cover and cook over a low heat for about 45 minutes, or until the pork is tender. Leave to cool, then shred the pork.

2 Meanwhile, cook the lotus seeds in boiling water for about 10 minutes. When soft, drain, pat dry and leave to cool.

3 Place a quarter of the cooked sticky rice in the middle of each lotus or banana leaf. Place half the shredded pork and half the lotus seeds on the rice.

4 Drizzle some of the cooking juices from the pork over the top. Place another quarter of the rice on top, moulding and patting it with your fingers to make sure the pork and lotus seeds are enclosed like a cake. Fold the leaf edge nearest to you over the rice, tuck in the sides, and fold the whole packet over to form a tight, square bundle. Tie it securely with kitchen string. Repeat the process with the second leaf and the remaining ingredients.

5 Fill a wok one-third full of water. Place a double-tiered bamboo steamer, with its lid on, on top. Bring the water to the boil, lift the bamboo lid and place a rice cake on the rack in each tier. Cover and steam for about 45 minutes. Carefully open up the parcels and serve.

Lion's Head Meat Balls Energy 326kcal/1363kJ; Protein 35.2g; Carbohydrate 13.1g, of which sugars 3.3g; Fat 15g, of which saturates 3.4g; Cholesterol 139mg; Calcium 91mg; Fibre 1.1g; Sodium 893mg.
Sticky Rice Cakes Energy 555kcal/2343kJ; Protein 32.3g; Carbohydrate 80.9g, of which sugars 2.6g; Fat 13.6g, of which saturates 3g; Cholesterol 71mg; Calcium 65mg; Fibre 1.1g; Sodium 84mg.

Leek and Bacon Tart

This dish makes an ideal savoury first course served in individual portions. It can also be served in larger proportions with a mixed leaf salad as a light main course for lunch or supper.

Makes 6–8 small tartlets or 1 large tart serving 8–10

275g/10oz/2½ cups plain (all-purpose) flour
pinch of salt
175g/6oz/¾ cup butter
2 egg yolks
about 45ml/3 tbsp very cold water
lettuce leaves and tomatoes, to garnish

For the filling

225g/8oz streaky (fatty) bacon, diced
4 leeks, sliced
6 eggs
115g/4oz/½ cup cream cheese
15ml/1 tbsp mild mustard
pinch of cayenne pepper
salt and ground black pepper

1 Sift the flour and salt into a bowl, and rub in the butter until it resembles fine breadcrumbs. Add the egg yolks and just enough water to combine the dough. Wrap the dough in clear film (plastic wrap) and place in the refrigerator for 30 minutes.

2 Meanwhile, preheat the oven to 200°C/400°F/Gas 6. Roll out the pastry thinly and use to line six to eight tartlet cases or a 28cm/11in tart dish. Remove any air pockets and prick the base with a fork. Line the pastry loosely with baking parchment, weigh down with baking beans and bake the pastry shell blind for 15–20 minutes, or until golden.

3 To make the filling, cook the bacon in a hot pan until crisp. Add the leeks and continue to cook for 3–4 minutes until just softening. Remove from the heat. In a bowl, beat the eggs, cream cheese, mustard, cayenne pepper and seasoning together, then add the leeks and bacon.

4 Remove the paper and baking beans from the tartlet or tart case, pour in the filling and bake for 35–40 minutes.

5 To serve, plate the tartlets on to individual serving plates or cut the tart into narrow wedges and serve warm, with a small salad garnish.

Pork and Bacon Rillettes with Onion Salad

These traditional potted meat rillettes make a great first course.

Serves 8

1.8kg/4lb belly of pork, boned and cut into cubes, bones reserved
450g/1lb rindless streaky (fatty) bacon, finely chopped
5ml/1 tsp salt
1.5ml/¼ tsp ground black pepper
4 garlic cloves, finely chopped
2 fresh parsley sprigs
1 bay leaf
2 fresh thyme sprigs
1 fresh sage sprig
300ml/½ pint/1¼ cups water
crusty French bread, to serve

For the onion salad

1 red onion, halved and thinly sliced
2 spring onions (scallions), cut into fine strips
2 celery sticks, cut into fine strips
15ml/1 tbsp freshly squeezed lemon juice
15ml/1 tbsp light olive oil
ground black pepper

1 Mix together the pork, bacon and salt in a bowl. Cover and leave for 30 minutes. Preheat the oven to 150°C/300°F/Gas 2. Stir the pepper and garlic into the meat. Tie the herbs together and add to the meat.

2 Place the meat mixture in a roasting pan and add the water. Place the bones on top and cover with foil. Cook for 3½ hours.

3 Discard the bones and herbs, and ladle the meat mixture into a metal sieve (strainer) set over a bowl. Leave to drain, then turn the meat into a shallow dish. Reserve the liquid. Use two forks to pull the meat apart into fine shreds.

4 Line a 1.5 litre/2½ pint/6¼ cup terrine or deep, straight-sided dish with clear film (plastic wrap) and spoon in the meat. Strain the reserved liquid and pour it over the meat. Leave to cool. Cover and chill for at least 24 hours, or until set.

5 To make the onion salad, place the onion, spring onions and celery in a bowl. Add the lemon juice and oil and toss gently. Season with a little pepper, but do not add any salt. Serve the rillettes in thick slices, with the salad and crusty French bread.

Leek and Bacon Tart Energy 487kcal/2026kJ; Protein 15.4g; Carbohydrate 28.2g, of which sugars 1.6g; Fat 35.7g, of which saturates 19.1g; Cholesterol 265mg; Calcium 107mg; Fibre 2.1g; Sodium 681mg.
Pork Rillettes Energy 707kcal/2930kJ; Protein 48.7g; Carbohydrate 0.7g, of which sugars 0.6g; Fat 56.5g, of which saturates 19.9g; Cholesterol 183mg; Calcium 23mg; Fibre 0.2g; Sodium 882mg.

Black Pudding with Potato and Apple

This dish makes a deliciously rustic treat. The combination of crisp potato cake, tasty black pudding topped with apples and mushrooms is a real winner. Serve as an appetizer or as a light lunch.

Serves 4
4 large potatoes, peeled
45ml/3 tbsp olive oil
8 slices of black pudding (blood sausage)
115g/4oz cultivated mushrooms, such as oyster or shiitake
2 eating apples, peeled, cored and cut into wedges
15ml/1 tbsp sherry vinegar or wine vinegar
15g/1oz/2 tbsp butter
salt and ground black pepper

1 Grate the potatoes, putting them into a bowl of water as you grate them, drain and squeeze out the excess moisture.

2 Heat 30ml/2 tbsp olive oil in a large non-stick frying pan, add the grated potatoes and seasoning. Press the potatoes into the pan with your hands.

3 Cook the potatoes until golden brown on the underside, then turn over and cook the other side. When cooked, slide on to a warm plate.

4 Heat the remaining oil and fry the black pudding and mushrooms together for a few minutes. Remove from the pan and keep warm.

5 Add the apple wedges to the frying pan and gently cook until golden brown. Add the sherry or wine vinegar to the apples, and boil up the juices. Add the butter, stir with a wooden spatula until it has melted and season to taste with salt and ground black pepper.

6 Cut the potato cake into wedges and divide among four warmed plates. Arrange the black pudding and cooked mushrooms on the bed of potato cake, pour over the apples and the warm juices and serve immediately.

Pork Kebabs

The word kebab comes from Arabic and means 'on a skewer'. Use pork fillet for these kebabs because it is lean and tender, and cooks very quickly. Stuffed into warmed pitta bread with some lettuce leaves, they make a really tasty appetizer or snack.

Serves 4
500g/1¼lb lean pork fillet (tenderloin)
8 large, thick spring onions (scallions), trimmed
120ml/4fl oz/½ cup barbecue sauce
1 lemon
4 warmed pitta breads and lettuce leaves, to serve

1 Cut the pork into 2.5cm/1in cubes. Cut the spring onions into 2.5cm/1in long sticks.

2 Preheat the grill (broiler) to high. Oil the wire rack and spread out the pork cubes on it. Grill (broil) the pork until the juices drip, then dip the pieces in the barbecue sauce and put back under the grill. Grill for a further 30 seconds on each side, repeating the dipping process twice more. Set the cooked pork aside and keep warm.

3 Gently grill (broil) the spring onions until soft and slightly brown outside. Do not dip in the barbecue sauce.

4 Thread about four pieces of pork and three spring onion pieces on to each of eight bamboo skewers.

5 Arrange the skewers on a platter. Cut the lemon into wedges and squeeze a little lemon juice over each skewer. Serve the kebabs immediately, with the remaining lemon wedges, warmed pitta breads and some lettuce leaves.

Cook's Tip
If you are cooking the pork on a barbecue, soak the skewers overnight in water. This prevents them burning. Keep the skewer handles away from the fire and turn them frequently.

Black Pudding Energy 247Kcal/1034kJ; Protein 4.2g; Carbohydrate 28.8g, of which sugars 5.4g; Fat 13.6g, of which saturates 4g; Cholesterol 13mg; Calcium 16mg; Fibre 2.4g; Sodium 132mg.
Pork Kebabs Energy 192kcal/806kJ; Protein 27.6g; Carbohydrate 9.2g, of which sugars 8.8g; Fat 5.1g, of which saturates 1.8g; Cholesterol 79mg; Calcium 21mg; Fibre 0.6g; Sodium 578mg.

Andalusian Mini Kebabs with Spices

The Moors introduced both skewers and the idea of marinating meat to Spain. These little yellow kebabs are a favourite in Andalusia, where many butchers sell the meat ready marinated. The Arab versions used lamb, but pork is used now, because the spicing suits it so perfectly.

Serves 4
2.5ml/½ tsp cumin seeds
2.5ml/½ tsp coriander seeds
2 garlic cloves, finely chopped
5ml/1 tsp paprika
2.5ml/½ tsp dried oregano
15ml/1 tbsp lemon juice
45ml/3 tbsp olive oil
500g/1¼lb lean cubed pork
salt and ground black pepper

1 Starting a couple of hours in advance, grind the cumin and coriander seeds in a mortar and work in the garlic with a pinch of salt. Add the paprika and oregano and mix in the lemon juice. Stir in the olive oil.

2 Cut the pork into small cubes, then skewer them, three or four at a time, on to cocktail sticks (toothpicks).

3 Put the skewered meat in a shallow dish, and pour over the marinade. Spoon the marinade back over the meat to ensure it is well coated. Leave to marinate in a cool place for 2 hours.

4 Preheat the grill (broiler) to high, and line the grill pan with foil. Spread the kebabs out in a row and place them under the grill, close to the heat. Cook for about 3 minutes on each side, spooning the juices over when you turn them, until the meat is cooked through. Sprinkle with a little salt and black pepper, and serve immediately.

Cook's Tip
Leaving the meat in a marinade allows the flavours of the spices to penetrate and also results in tender, juicier meat. If it is convenient, you can assemble the kebabs and put them into the marinade earlier in the day, or the day before you need to cook them.

Barbecued Mini Ribs

These tasty ribs are delicious cooked on a barbecue and almost as good when cooked under a hot grill. They make a fantastically messy appetizer, perfect for adults and children alike. Ensure that you provide plenty of napkins for cleaning up.

Serves 6–8
1 sheet of pork ribs, about 675g/1½lb
90ml/6 tbsp sweet oloroso sherry
15ml/1 tbsp tomato purée (paste)
5ml/1 tsp soy sauce
2.5ml/½ tsp Tabasco sauce
15ml/1 tbsp light muscovado (brown) sugar
30ml/2 tbsp seasoned plain (all-purpose) flour
coarse sea salt

1 Separate the pork ribs, then, using a meat cleaver or heavy knife, carefully cut each rib in half widthways to make approximatley 30 pieces.

2 Mix the sherry, tomato purée, soy sauce, Tabasco and sugar in a bowl. Stir in 2.5ml/½ tsp salt.

3 Put the seasoned flour in a strong plastic bag, then add the ribs and toss to coat. Dip each rib in the sauce. Cook on a hot barbecue or under a hot grill (broiler) for 30–40 minutes, turning occasionally until cooked and a little charred. Sprinkle with salt and serve immediately.

Variation
If you prefer a sweeter flavour, use freshly squeezed orange juice instead of the sweet sherry.

Cook's Tip
Oloroso sherry has a full body and sweet flavour sometimes reminiscent of port.

Andalusian Kebabs Energy 189kcal/793kJ; Protein 30.4g; Carbohydrate 0.8g, of which sugars 0.1g; Fat 7.2g, of which saturates 1.2g; Cholesterol 88mg; Calcium 17mg; Fibre 0.2g; Sodium 77mg.
Barbecued Ribs Energy 202kcal/844kJ; Protein 16.3g; Carbohydrate 6g, of which sugars 3.1g; Fat 11.4g, of which saturates 4.4g; Cholesterol 56mg; Calcium 21mg; Fibre 0.2g; Sodium 133mg.

Five-spice Rib-sticker

Spicy and sweet sticky ribs are a popular choice in Chinese restaurants. Here, you can create your own, but make sure you choose the meatiest spare ribs you can, to make them a real success.

Serves 8

1kg/2¼lb pork spare ribs
10ml/2 tsp Chinese five-spice powder
2 garlic cloves, crushed
15ml/1 tbsp grated fresh root ginger
2.5ml/½ tsp chilli sauce
60ml/4 tbsp muscovado (molasses) sugar
15ml/1 tbsp sunflower oil
4 spring onions (scallions)

1 If the spare ribs are still joined together, cut between them to separate them (or ask your butcher to do this). Place the spare ribs in a large bowl.

2 In a separate small bowl, mix together all the remaining ingredients, except for the spring onions, until they are well combined and blended.

3 Pour the marinade mixture over the ribs. Toss well to coat evenly. Cover the bowl with cling film (platic wrap) and leave to marinate in the refrigerator overnight.

4 Cook the spare ribs under a preheated medium-hot grill (broiler), turning frequently, for 30–40 minutes. Brush the ribs occasionally with the marinade.

5 While the ribs are cooking, finely slice the spring onions on the diagonal. To serve, place the ribs on a serving plate, then sprinkle the spring onions over the top.

Variation
If you want a little more spice in this dish, finely chop a fresh red chilli and add it to the marinade in step 2.

Crispy Fried Pork Belly

This dish is a great treat. Delicious and moreish, the crispy belly pork can be sliced and eaten as an appetizer or snack with salad and pickles, or it can be added to salads, soups and vegetable dishes, making it highly versatile.

Serves 4

3 garlic cloves, chopped
40g/1½oz fresh root ginger, chopped
500g/1¼lb pork belly with the rind, cut into thick slabs
3–4 bay leaves
corn, groundnut (peanut) or vegetable oil, for deep-frying
salt and ground black pepper

To serve
cooked rice (optional)
pickled vegetables (optional)

1 Using a mortar and pestle, grind the garlic and ginger with a little salt and ground black pepper, until the mixture forms a fairly smooth paste.

2 Thoroughly rub the paste all over each of the pork slabs and pile them on to a plate. Cover tightly with clear film (plastic wrap) and place in the refrigerator to marinate for at least 1 hour or overnight.

3 Fill a large pan with water and bring to the boil. Add the bay leaves, reduce the heat to a simmer and slip in the marinated pork slabs. Cook gently for about 1 hour, until the meat is tender but still firm.

4 Put the pork slabs in a colander to drain, cover lightly then leave them there for 30–40 minutes until they have completely dried out.

5 Heat enough oil in a wok or pan for deep-frying. Fry the pork pieces for 5 minutes, until they are golden brown. Using a slotted spoon, lift them out and drain on kitchen paper.

6 If eating the dish straight away, slice the pork thinly and serve with rice and pickled vegetables, if you like.

Five-spice Rib-sticker Energy 309kcal/1297kJ; Protein 38.3g; Carbohydrate 8g, of which sugars 8g; Fat 14g, of which saturates 4.7g; Cholesterol 123mg; Calcium 46mg; Fibre 0.1g; Sodium 75mg.
Crispy Belly Energy 576kcal/2377kJ; Protein 19.2g; Carbohydrate 0.1g, of which sugars 0.1g; Fat 55.4g, of which saturates 17.7g; Cholesterol 90mg; Calcium 14mg; Fibre 0.1g; Sodium 97mg.

Sichuan Pork with Ginger Relish

This dish works best when the pork ribs are grilled in large sections, then sliced to serve, this helps to keep the meat succulent.

Serves 4

4 pork rib slabs, each with 6 ribs, total weight about 2kg/4½lb
40g/1½oz/3 tbsp light muscovado (brown) sugar
3 garlic cloves, crushed
5cm/2in piece fresh root ginger, finely grated
10ml/2 tsp Sichuan peppercorns, finely crushed
2.5ml/½ tsp ground black pepper
5ml/1 tsp finely ground star anise
5ml/1 tsp Chinese five-spice powder
90ml/6 tbsp dark soy sauce
45ml/3 tbsp sunflower oil
15ml/1 tbsp sesame oil

For the relish
60ml/4 tbsp sunflower oil
300g/11oz shallots, chopped
9 garlic cloves, peeled and crushed
7.5cm/3in piece fresh root ginger, finely grated
60ml/4 tbsp seasoned rice wine vinegar
45ml/3 tbsp sweet chilli sauce
105ml/7 tbsp tomato ketchup
90ml/6 tbsp water
60ml/4 tbsp chopped fresh coriander (cilantro) leaves
salt

1 Lay the slabs of pork ribs in a large shallow dish. Mix the remaining ingredients in a bowl and pour the marinade over the ribs. Cover and chill overnight.

2 To make the relish, heat the oil in a heavy pan, add the shallots and cook gently for 5 minutes. Add the garlic and ginger and cook for 4 minutes. Increase the heat and add the rest of the ingredients except the for the coriander. Simmer for about 10 minutes until thickened, then stir in the coriander. Chill.

3 Remove the ribs from the refrigerator 1 hour before cooking. Remove the ribs from the marinade and pat them dry with kitchen paper. Pour the marinade into a pan. Bring it to the boil, then lower the heat and simmer for 3 minutes.

4 Grill (broil) the ribs, turning and basting occasionally with the marinade, until the meat is tender and golden brown all over. Cut into single ribs to serve, with the relish.

Chinese Spare Ribs with Spiced Salt

Fragrant with spices, this authentic Chinese dish makes a great appetizer to an informal meal.

Serves 4

675–900g/1½–2lb meaty pork spare ribs
25ml/1½ tbsp cornflour (cornstarch)
groundnut oil, for deep-frying
coriander (cilantro) sprigs, to garnish

For the spiced salt
5ml/1 tsp Sichuan peppercorns
30ml/2 tbsp coarse sea salt
2.5ml/½ tsp Chinese five-spice powder

For the marinade
30ml/2 tbsp light soy sauce
5ml/1 tsp caster (superfine) sugar
15ml/1 tbsp Chinese rice wine or sherry
ground black pepper

1 Using a heavy sharp cleaver, chop the spare ribs into pieces about 5cm/2in long (or ask your butcher to do this), then place them in a shallow dish.

2 To make the spiced salt, heat a wok to medium heat. Add the Sichuan peppercorns and salt and dry-fry for about 3 minutes, stirring constantly until the mixture colours slightly. Remove from the heat and stir in the five-spice powder. Leave to cool. Using a mortar and pestle grind to a fine powder.

3 Sprinkle 5ml/1 tsp of the spiced salt over the spare ribs and rub in well with your hands. Add the soy sauce, sugar, rice wine or sherry and some ground black pepper, then toss the ribs in the marinade until well coated. Cover and leave to marinate in the refrigerator for about 2 hours, turning occasionally.

4 Pour off any excess marinade. Sprinkle the spare ribs with cornflour and mix well to coat evenly. Half-fill a wok with oil and heat to 180°C/350°F. Deep-fry the spare ribs in batches for 3 minutes until pale golden. Remove and set aside. Reheat the oil to the same temperature. Return the spare ribs to the oil and deep-fry for a second time for 1–2 minutes until crisp and thoroughly cooked. Drain on kitchen paper. Transfer the ribs to a serving plate and sprinkle over 5–7.5ml/1–1½ tsp spiced salt. Garnish with coriander sprigs.

Sichuan Pork Energy 665kcal/2761kJ; Protein 46.6g; Carbohydrate 17g, of which sugars 14.8g; Fat 45.9g, of which saturates 14.2g; Cholesterol 155mg; Calcium 59mg; Fibre 1.4g; Sodium 1111mg.
Chinese Ribs Energy 424kcal/1763kJ; Protein 32.2g; Carbohydrate 2.6g, of which sugars 1.3g; Fat 31.4g, of which saturates 9.8g; Cholesterol 111mg; Calcium 33mg; Fibre 0g; Sodium 345mg.

Roasted Vegetable and Garlic Sausage Loaf

Stuffed with cured meat and roasted vegetables, this crusty cob loaf makes a colourful appetizer for a casual summer lunch or picnic. Serve with fresh green salad leaves.

Serves 6

1 large cob loaf
2 red (bell) peppers, quartered and seeded
1 large leek, sliced
90ml/6 tbsp olive oil
175g/6oz green beans, blanched and drained
75g/3oz garlic sausage, sliced
2 eggs, hard-boiled and quartered
115g/4oz/1 cup cashew nuts, toasted
75g/3oz/⅓ cup soft white (farmer's) cheese with garlic and herbs
salt and ground black pepper

1 Preheat the oven to 220°C/425°F/Gas 7. Slice the top off the loaf and set it aside, then cut out the soft centre, leaving the crust intact. Stand the crusty shell on a baking sheet.

2 Put the red peppers and sliced leek into a roasting pan with the olive oil and cook for 25–30 minutes, or until the peppers have softened, turning occasionally.

3 Spoon half of the pepper and leek mixture into the base of the loaf shell, pressing it down firmly with the back of a spoon. Add the green beans, garlic sausage slices, egg quarters and cashew nuts, packing the layers down well. Season each layer with salt and ground black pepper to taste before adding the next. Dot the soft cheese with garlic and herbs over the filling and top with the remaining pepper and leek mixture.

4 Replace the top of the loaf and bake it for 15–20 minutes, or until the filling is warmed through. Serve, cut into wedges.

Cook's Tip
Do not throw away the soft centre of the loaf. It can be made into breadcrumbs and frozen for use in another recipe.

Beef Satay with a Hot Mango Dip

Strips of tender beef are flavoured with a warmly spiced marinade before being cooked on skewers, then served with a tangy fruit dip, for a delicious introduction to a meal.

Makes 12

450g/1lb sirloin steak, 2cm/¾in thick
15ml/1 tbsp coriander seeds
5ml/1 tsp cumin seeds
50g/2oz/⅓ cup raw cashew nuts
15ml/1 tbsp vegetable oil
2 shallots or 1 small onion, finely chopped
1cm/½in piece fresh root ginger
1 garlic clove, crushed
30ml/2 tbsp each tamarind and soy sauce
10ml/2 tsp sugar
5ml/1 tsp rice or white wine vinegar

For the mango dip

1 ripe mango
1–2 small red chillies, seeded and chopped
15ml/1 tbsp fish sauce
juice of 1 lime
10ml/2 tsp sugar
1.5ml/¼ tsp salt
30ml/2 tbsp fresh coriander (cilantro)

1 Soak 12 bamboo skewers for 30 minutes. Slice the beef into long narrow strips and thread, zigzag-style, on to the skewers. Lay on a flat plate and set aside.

2 For the marinade, dry-fry the seeds and nuts in a large wok or frying pan until evenly brown and the spices have released their fragrances. Transfer to a mortar with a rough surface and crush finely with the pestle. Peel and chop the ginger. Add the oil, shallots or onion, ginger, garlic, tamarind and soy sauces, sugar and vinegar.

3 Spread this marinade over the beef and leave to marinate for up to 8 hours or overnight. Cook the beef under a moderate grill (broiler) or over a barbecue for 6–8 minutes, turning to ensure an even colour.

4 Meanwhile, make the mango dip. Cut away the skin and remove the stone (pit) from the mango. Process the mango flesh with the chillies, fish sauce, lime juice, sugar and salt until smooth, then add the coriander and serve with the beef.

Roasted Loaf Energy 509kcal/2126kJ; Protein 16g; Carbohydrate 42.7g, of which sugars 7.9g; Fat 31.7g, of which saturates 7.8g; Cholesterol 98mg; Calcium 130mg; Fibre 4g; Sodium 578mg.
Beef Satay Energy 62kcal/263kJ; Protein 9g; Carbohydrate 2.9g, of which sugars 2.8g; Fat 1.7g, of which saturates 0.8g; Cholesterol 19mg; Calcium 5mg; Fibre 0.3g; Sodium 205mg.

Bacon-wrapped Beef on Skewers

In northern Vietnam, beef often features on the street menu. Grilled, stir-fried, or sitting majestically in a steaming bowl of pho, beef is used with pride. In Cambodia and southern Vietnam, snacks like this one would normally be made with pork or chicken.

Serves 4

225g/8oz beef fillet (tenderloin) or rump (round) steak, cut across the grain into 12 strips
12 thin rashers (strips) of streaky (fatty) bacon
ground black pepper
chilli sambal, for dipping

For the marinade

15ml/1 tbsp groundnut (peanut) oil
30ml/2 tbsp fish sauce
30ml/2 tbsp soy sauce
4–6 garlic cloves, crushed
10ml/2 tsp sugar

1 To make the marinade, mix all the ingredients in a large bowl until the sugar dissolves. Season generously with black pepper. Add the beef strips, stir to coat them in the marinade, and set aside for about an hour.

2 Preheat a griddle pan over high heat until very hot. Remove the beef strips from the marinade and roll up each strip, then wrap it in a slice of bacon. Thread the rolls on to the skewers, so that you have three rolls on each one.

3 Cook the bacon-wrapped rolls on the hot griddle for 4–5 minutes, turning once, until the bacon is golden and crispy. Serve immediately, with a bowl of chilli sambal for dipping.

Cook's Tip

These tasty skewers can also be cooked under a preheated grill (broiler), or over hot coals on the barbecue. Simply cook for 6–8 minutes, turning every couple of minutes so that the bacon is browned but not burned. Serve them as an appetizer ahead of the main course – they are light enough to whet the appetite without spoiling anticipation of the rest of the meal.

Albondigas

These meatballs are absolutely delicious and the chipotle chilli gives the sauce a distinctive, slightly smoky flavour. Add boiled rice if serving as light meal.

Serves 4

225g/8oz minced (ground) pork
225g/8oz minced (ground) beef
1 onion, finely chopped
50g/2oz/1 cup fresh breadcrumbs
5ml/1 tsp dried oregano
2.5ml/½ tsp ground cumin
2.5ml/½ tsp salt
2.5ml/½ tsp ground black pepper
1 egg, beaten
oil, for frying
fresh oregano sprigs, to garnish
boiled rice, to serve

For the sauce

1 chipotle chilli, seeded
15ml/1 tbsp vegetable oil
1 onion, finely chopped
2 garlic cloves, crushed
175ml/6fl oz/¾ cup beef stock
400g/14oz can chopped tomatoes
105ml/7 tbsp passata (bottled strained tomatoes)

1 Mix the minced pork and beef in a bowl. Add the onion, breadcrumbs, oregano, cumin, salt and pepper. Mix with clean hands until all the ingredients are well combined.

2 Stir in the egg, mix well, then roll into 4cm/1½in balls. Put these on a baking sheet and chill while you prepare the sauce.

3 Soak the dried chilli in hot water for 15 minutes. Heat the oil in a pan and fry the onion and garlic for 3–4 minutes until soft.

4 Drain the chilli, reserving the soaking water, then chop it and add it to the onion mixture. Fry for 1 minute, then stir in the beef stock, tomatoes, passata and soaking water, with salt and pepper to taste. Bring to the boil, lower the heat and simmer, stirring occasionally, while you cook the meatballs.

5 Heat the oil for frying in a frying pan and fry the meatballs in batches for about 5 minutes, turning occasionally, until browned.

6 Drain off the oil and place the meatballs in a shallow pan. Pour over the sauce and simmer for 10 minutes. Garnish with the oregano and serve with boiled rice, if you like.

Bacon-wrapped Beef Energy 282kcal/1172kJ; Protein 21.7g; Carbohydrate 1.1g, of which sugars 1.1g; Fat 21.3g, of which saturates 7.1g; Cholesterol 69mg; Calcium 7mg; Fibre 0g; Sodium 745mg.
Albondigas Energy 412kcal/1717kJ; Protein 26.2g; Carbohydrate 16g, of which sugars 5.9g; Fat 27.6g, of which saturates 7.7g; Cholesterol 118mg; Calcium 50mg; Fibre 1.9g; Sodium 265mg.

Red-hot Meatballs with Roasted Coconut

These Indonesian meatballs are versatile, spicy and delicious. Moulded into small balls, they can be served as an appetizer with a drink; as a snack dipped in kecap manis; or as a main dish with rice and a salad.

Serves 4

5ml/1 tsp coriander seeds
5ml/1 tsp cumin seeds
175g/6oz freshly grated coconut or desiccated (dry unsweetened shredded) coconut
15ml/1 tbsp coconut oil
4 shallots, finely chopped
2 garlic cloves, finely chopped
1–2 red chillies, seeded and finely chopped
350g/12oz minced (ground) beef
beaten egg (if necessary)
rice flour, to coat
corn oil, for shallow frying
salt and ground black pepper

To serve

30–45ml/2–3 tbsp freshly grated coconut or desiccated (dry unsweetened shredded) coconut, dry-fried
1 lime, quartered
kecap manis (Indonesian sweet soy sauce)

1 In a small, heavy pan, dry-fry the coriander and cumin seeds until they give off a nutty aroma. Using a mortar and pestle or electric spice grinder, grind the roasted seeds to a powder. In the same pan, dry-fry the coconut until it begins to colour. Transfer the coconut on to a plate and leave to cool.

2 Heat the coconut oil, stir in the shallots, garlic and chillies and fry until beginning to colour. Transfer to a plate and leave to cool.

3 Put the beef into a bowl and add the ground spices, dry-fried coconut and shallot mixture. Season with salt and pepper. Bind all the ingredients together, adding a little egg if necessary. Knead the mixture with your hands and mould it into little balls, no bigger than a fresh apricot. Coat the balls in rice flour.

4 Heat a thin layer of corn oil in a large frying pan and fry the meatballs for about 5 minutes until they are golden brown. Drain, then arrange on a serving dish. Sprinkle with the coconut and serve with the lime wedges, and kecap manis for drizzling.

Taquitos with Beef

In this Mexican appetizer, home-made corn tortillas are moulded around a tasty filling of tender steak in a spicy, flavoursome sauce.

Serves 12

500g/1½lb rump (round) steak, diced into 1cm/½in pieces
2 garlic cloves, peeled
750ml/1¼ pints/3 cups beef stock
150g/5oz/1 cup masa harina
pinch of salt
120ml/4fl oz/½ cup warm water
7.5ml/1½ tsp dried oregano
2.5ml/½ tsp ground cumin
30ml/2 tbsp tomato purée (paste)
2.5ml/½ tsp caster (superfine) sugar
salt and ground black pepper
shredded lettuce and onion relish, to serve

1 Put the beef and whole garlic cloves in a large pan and cover with the beef stock. Bring to the boil, lower the heat and simmer for 10–15 minutes, until the meat is tender. Using a slotted spoon, transfer the meat to a clean pan and set it aside. Reserve the stock.

2 Mix the masa harina and salt in a large bowl. Add the warm water, a little at a time, to make a dough that can be worked into a ball. Knead this on a lightly floured surface for 3–4 minutes until smooth, then wrap in clear film (plastic wrap) and leave for 1 hour.

3 Divide the dough into 12 small balls. Line the tortilla press with plastic (this can be cut from a new plastic sandwich bag). Put a ball on the press and bring the top down to flatten it into a 5–6cm/2–2½in round. Repeat with the remaining dough balls.

4 Heat a griddle or frying pan until hot. Cook each tortilla for 15–20 seconds on each side, and then for a further 15 seconds on the first side. Keep warm by folding inside a dish towel.

5 Add the oregano, cumin, tomato purée and caster sugar to the pan containing the beef, with a couple of tablespoons of the reserved beef stock. Cook gently for a few minutes to combine the flavour. To assemble, place a little of the lettuce on a warm tortilla, top with a little filling and a little onion relish, and fold in half. Serve immediately.

Red-hot Meatballs Energy 559kcal/2312kJ; Protein 20.2g; Carbohydrate 8g, of which sugars 3.7g; Fat 49.6g, of which saturates 30.4g; Cholesterol 53mg; Calcium 23mg; Fibre 6.3g; Sodium 83mg.
Taquitos with Beef Energy 291kcal/1222kJ; Protein 31.5g; Carbohydrate 26.5g, of which sugars 1.8g; Fat 6.3g, of which saturates 2.1g; Cholesterol 74mg; Calcium 10mg; Fibre 1.1g; Sodium 97mg.

Beef Patties with Onions and Peppers

This is a firm family favourite. It is easy to make and delicious, and it can be varied by adding other vegetables, such as sliced red peppers, broccoli or mushrooms. These patties are very versatile and can be served as an appetizer with salad or a salsa.

Serves 4

500g/1¼ lb lean minced (ground) beef
4 onions, 1 finely chopped and 3 sliced
30ml/2 tbsp garlic-flavoured olive oil or olive oil
2–3 green (bell) peppers, seeded and sliced lengthways into strips
salt and ground black pepper
mixed salad leaves, to serve

1 Place the minced beef, chopped onion and 15ml/1 tbsp garlic-flavoured oil in a bowl and mix well. Season well with salt and ground black pepper and form into four large or eight small patties.

2 Heat the remaining oil in a large non-stick pan, then add the patties and cook on both sides until browned, about 3–4 minutes on each side. Sprinkle over 15ml/1 tbsp water and add a little seasoning.

3 Cover the patties with the sliced onions and peppers. Sprinkle in another 15ml/1 tbsp water and a little seasoning, then cover the pan. Reduce the heat to very low and braise for 20–30 minutes.

4 When the onions are turning golden brown, remove the pan from the heat. Serve the patties with the onions and peppers and some mixed salad leaves.

Variation
These patties can be made with other meat, such as minced (ground) pork, lamb, chicken or turkey if you prefer.

Spicy Shredded Beef

The beef in this tasty appetizer is cut into very fine strips. Freezing the beef briefly before preparation makes it very easy to slice. Serve this appetizer with naan bread or pitta bread.

Serves 2

225g/8oz rump (round) or fillet of beef
15ml/1 tbsp each light and dark soy sauce
15ml/1 tbsp rice wine or medium-dry sherry
5ml/1 tsp soft dark brown sugar or golden granulated sugar
90ml/6 tbsp vegetable oil
1 large onion, thinly sliced
2.5cm/1in piece fresh root ginger, peeled and grated
1 or 2 carrots, cut into matchsticks
2 or 3 fresh or dried chillies, halved, seeded (optional) and chopped
salt and ground black pepper
fresh chives, to garnish

1 Place the beef in the freezer for 30–40 minutes to firm up. With a sharp knife, slice the beef very thinly, then cut each slice into fine strips or shreds.

2 Mix together the light and dark soy sauces with the rice wine or medium-dry sherry and sugar in a bowl. Add the strips of beef and stir well to ensure they are evenly coated with the marinade.

3 Heat a wok and add half the oil. When it is hot, stir-fry the onion and ginger for 3–4 minutes, then transfer to a plate. Add the carrot, stir-fry for 3–4 minutes until slightly softened, then transfer to a plate and keep warm.

4 Heat the remaining oil in the wok, then quickly add the beef, with the marinade, followed by the chillies. Cook over high heat for 2 minutes, stirring all the time.

5 Return the fried onion and ginger to the wok and stir-fry for 1 minute more. Season with salt and pepper to taste, cover and cook for 30 seconds. Spoon the meat into two warmed bowls and add the strips of carrots. Garnish with fresh chives and serve immediately.

Beef Patties Energy 431kcal/1789kJ; Protein 27.9g; Carbohydrate 21.1g, of which sugars 17.2g; Fat 26.6g, of which saturates 9.6g; Cholesterol 75mg; Calcium 60mg; Fibre 4.4g; Sodium 110mg.
Spicy Beef Energy 532Kcal/2207kJ; Protein 27.3g; Carbohydrate 19.3g, of which sugars 15.4g; Fat 38.1g, of which saturates 5.8g; Cholesterol 66mg; Calcium 59mg; Fibre 3.3g; Sodium 1154mg.

Sopes with Picadillo

These small, thick corn tortillas with crimped edges resemble little tarts, filled with spicy beef.

Serves 6

250g/9oz/scant 2 cups masa harina
2.5ml/½ tsp salt
50g/2oz/¼ cup chilled lard or white cooking fat
300ml/½ pint/1¼ cups warm water
15ml/1 tbsp vegetable oil
250g/9oz minced (ground) beef
2 garlic cloves, crushed
1 red (bell) pepper, seeded and chopped
60ml/4 tbsp dry sherry
15ml/1 tbsp tomato purée (paste)
2.5ml/½ tsp ground cumin
5ml/1 tsp ground cinnamon
1.5ml/¼ tsp ground cloves
2.5ml/½ tsp ground black pepper
25g/1oz/3 tbsp raisins
25g/1oz/¼ cup slivered almonds
fresh parsley sprigs, to garnish

1 Put the masa harina and salt in a large bowl. Grate the chilled lard or cooking fat into the bowl and rub it into the dry ingredients. Add the warm water, a little at a time, to make a dough that can be worked into a ball. Knead the dough on a lightly floured surface for 3–4 minutes until smooth. Set aside.

2 Heat the oil in a large pan. Add the beef and brown over a high heat. Add the garlic, and continue cooking for 2–3 minutes.

3 Stir in the red pepper, sherry, tomato purée and spices. Cook for 5 minutes more, then add the raisins and the almonds. Lower the heat and simmer for 10 minutes. The meat should be cooked through and the mixture moist, not wet. Keep hot.

4 Divide the dough into six balls. Open a tortilla press and line both sides with plastic (this can be cut from a new plastic sandwich bag). Put a ball on the press and bring the top down to flatten it into a 10cm/4in round. Make five more rounds.

5 Heat a griddle or frying pan until hot. Add one of the rounds and fry until the underside is beginning to blister. Turn the round over and cook the other side briefly, until the colour is beginning to change. Slide on to a plate and crimp to form a raised edge. Fill with spicy beef and keep hot while cooking and filling the remaining tartlets. Garnish with parsley.

Beef Empanadas

These pastry turnovers make delicious appetizers or perfect finger food.

Serves 4–6

225g/8oz/2 cups plain (all-purpose) flour
2.5ml/½ tsp salt
90g/3½oz/scant ½ cup cold butter, cut into small chunks
juice of ½ lime
50ml/2fl oz/¼ cup lukewarm water
vegetable oil, for deep-frying
chilli salsa, to serve (optional)

For the filling
60ml/4 tbsp olive oil
450g/1lb beef shin or leg (shank), finely diced
1.5ml/¼ tsp ground cumin
1 garlic clove, crushed
10ml/2 tsp paprika
250ml/8fl oz/1 cup light beef stock
450g/1lb potatoes, cubed
2 tomatoes, finely chopped
3 spring onions (scallions), finely chopped
salt and ground black pepper

1 Make the filling. Heat 30ml/2 tbsp of the oil in a large pan over high heat. Fry the beef until golden brown. Push the beef to the side and add the cumin, garlic and paprika. Reduce the heat and cook, stirring, for 2–3 minutes. Stir in the stock and bring to the boil. Cover and cook over low heat for 30 minutes. Stir in the potatoes, tomatoes and spring onions. Cook for 15 minutes, or until the potatoes are tender. Season to taste, then leave to cool.

2 Meanwhile, place the flour and salt in a food processor. Add the butter and process until the mixture resembles breadcrumbs. Combine the lime juice and water and pour into the food processor, with the motor running. Transfer the pastry on to a floured surface and knead to a soft dough. Shape into a ball, wrap in clear film (plastic wrap) and chill for at least 20 minutes.

3 On a floured surface roll out the pastry until it is very thin. Cut out 6cm/2½in circles, using a cutter. Spoon 7.5ml/1½ tsp of the filling into the centre of a circle, then brush the edges with water. Fold to form a half-moon, then press the edges to seal.

4 Pour the oil to a depth of 5cm/2in into a heavy pan. Heat the oil, then add five or six empanadas. Fry for 5 minutes until golden brown, turning halfway through cooking. Remove with a slotted spoon and drain. Serve with a little chilli salsa, if using.

Sopes with Picadillo Energy 197kcal/819kJ; Protein 7g; Carbohydrate 17g, of which sugars 2.4g; Fat 11.3g, of which saturates 5.3g; Cholesterol 24mg; Calcium 82mg; Fibre 0.7g; Sodium 95mg.
Empanadas Energy 638kcal/2658kJ; Protein 22.8g; Carbohydrate 43.6g, of which sugars 2.5g; Fat 42.6g, of which saturates 13.8g; Cholesterol 78mg; Calcium 75mg; Fibre 2.3g; Sodium 174mg.

Golden Beef and Potato Puffs

These crisp, golden pillows of pastry filled with spiced beef and potatoes are delicious served straight from the wok. The light pastry puffs up in the hot oil and contrasts enticingly with the fragrant spiced beef.

Serves 4

15ml/1 tbsp sunflower oil
½ small onion, finely chopped
3 garlic cloves, crushed
5ml/1 tsp fresh root ginger, grated
1 red chilli, seeded and chopped
30ml/2 tbsp hot curry powder
75g/3oz minced (ground) beef
115g/4oz mashed potato
60ml/4 tbsp chopped fresh coriander (cilantro)
2 sheets ready-rolled, fresh puff pastry
1 egg, lightly beaten
vegetable oil, for frying
salt and ground black pepper
fresh coriander (cilantro) leaves, to garnish
tomato ketchup, to serve

1 Heat the oil in a wok, then add the onion, garlic, ginger and chilli. Stir-fry over medium heat for 2–3 minutes. Add the curry powder and beef and stir-fry over high heat for a further 4–5 minutes, or until the beef is browned and just cooked through, then remove from the heat.

2 Transfer the beef mixture to a large bowl and add the mashed potato and chopped fresh coriander. Stir well, then season and set aside.

3 Lay the pastry sheets on a clean, dry surface and cut out eight rounds, using a 7.5cm/3in pastry (cookie) cutter. Place a large spoonful of the beef mixture in the centre of each pastry round. Brush the edges of the pastry with the beaten egg and fold each round in half to enclose the filling. Press and crimp the edges with the tines of a fork to seal.

4 Fill a wok one-third full of oil and heat to 180°C/350°F (or until a cube of bread, dropped into the oil, browns in 15 seconds).

5 Deep-fry the puffs, in batches, for about 2–3 minutes until they turn a golden brown colour. Drain on kitchen paper and serve garnished with fresh coriander leaves. Offer tomato ketchup to diners for dipping.

Oxtail Brawn

This dish uses oxtail to create a mould with herbs.

Serves 9

1.2kg/2½lb oxtail, cut into pieces
2 carrots, scraped
1 onion, halved
2 cloves
bouquet garni, made from 1 thyme sprig, 1 rosemary sprig, 2 parsley sprigs and tied with celery
200ml/7fl oz/scant 1 cup red wine
30ml/2 tbsp red wine vinegar
10g/¼oz gelatine leaves
vegetable oil, for greasing
15ml/1 tbsp chopped fresh parsley
15ml/1 tbsp chopped fresh chives
salt and ground black pepper

1 Cook the oxtail, in batches, in an open pressure cooker. Cook over low heat for 5–10 minutes each side until browned. Add the carrots, onion, cloves, bouquet garni, wine, vinegar and 2.5ml/½ tsp salt and pour in 100ml/3½fl oz/scant ½ cup water. Cover and bring to high pressure, then cook for 2 hours.

2 Remove the meat from the pan with a slotted spoon and reserve the stock. Place the cooked oxtail in a sieve (strainer) and rinse under cold water, then drain and cool. Remove the meat from the bones and chop. Chill for several hours.

3 Strain the stock through muslin (cheesecloth). Add water to make up 500ml/17fl oz/ generous 2 cups, if necessary.

4 Place the gelatine in a bowl of water and soak for 5 minutes. Bring 50ml/2fl oz/¼ cup of stock to the boil, then remove from the heat. Squeeze out the gelatine and dissolve it in the stock. Stir into the rest of the stock and season to taste. Chill until set.

5 Brush a 1 litre/1¾ pint/4 cup mould with oil and ladle a thin layer of half-set stock into it. Sprinkle the stock with half the parsley and chives and chill until fully set.

6 Reserve 150ml/¼ pint/⅔ cup of the stock. Mix the rest with the meat and ladle into the mould. Sprinkle with the remaining herbs. Ladle the reserved stock over the herbs. Chill until set. Turn out the dish, cut into thick slices and serve.

Golden Beef Energy 408kcal/1695kJ; Protein 9g; Carbohydrate 24.2g, of which sugars 1.8g; Fat 31.8g, of which saturates 4.2g; Cholesterol 67mg; Calcium 46mg; Fibre 0.5g; Sodium 202mg.
Oxtail Brawn Energy 163kcal/683kJ; Protein 16.68g; Carbohydrate 2.36g, of which sugars 2.1g; Fat 8.12g, of which saturates 0.1g; Cholesterol 0mg; Calcium 18.7mg; Fibre 0.7g; Sodium 104mg.

Stir-fried Beef in Oyster Sauce

Mouthwatering tender rump steak is cooked here in a delicious combination with shiitake, oyster and straw mushrooms flavoured with garlic, ginger and chilli.

Serves 4–6

450g/1lb rump (round) steak
30ml/2 tbsp soy sauce
15ml/1 tbsp cornflour (cornstarch)
45ml/3 tbsp vegetable oil
15ml/1 tbsp chopped garlic
15ml/1 tbsp chopped fresh root ginger
225g/8oz/3¼ cups mixed mushrooms, such as shiitake, oyster and straw
30ml/2 tbsp oyster sauce
5ml/1 tsp granulated (white) sugar
4 spring onions (scallions), cut into short lengths
ground black pepper
2 fresh red chillies, seeded and cut into strips, to garnish

1 Place the rump steak in the freezer for 30–40 minutes, then use a sharp knife to slice it on the diagonal into thin strips.

2 Mix together the soy sauce and cornflour in a large bowl. Add the steak, turning to coat well, cover with clear film (plastic wrap) and leave to marinate at room temperature for 1–2 hours.

3 Heat half the oil in a wok or large, heavy frying pan. Add the garlic and ginger and cook for 1–2 minutes, until fragrant. Drain the steak, add it to the wok or pan and stir well to separate the strips. Cook, stirring frequently, for a further 1–2 minutes, until the steak is browned all over and tender. Remove from the wok or pan and set aside.

4 Heat the remaining oil in the wok or pan. Add the mushrooms and stir-fry over medium heat until golden brown.

5 Return the steak to the wok and mix it with the mushrooms. Spoon in the oyster sauce and sugar, stir well, then add ground black pepper to taste. Toss over the heat until all the ingredients are thoroughly combined. Stir in the spring onions. Transfer the mixture on to a serving platter, garnish with the strips of red chilli and serve.

Garlic and Chilli Marinated Beef with Corn-crusted Onion Rings

Mexican chillies combine well with garlic in this marinade for grilled steak.

Serves 8

40g/1½oz large mild dried red chillies, such as mulato or pasilla
4 garlic cloves, plain or smoked, finely chopped
10ml/2 tsp ground toasted cumin seeds
10ml/2 tsp dried oregano
120ml/4fl oz/½ cup olive oil
4 beef steaks, rump (round) or rib-eye, 175–225g/6–8oz each
salt and ground black pepper

For the onion rings
4 onions, sliced into rings
475ml/16fl oz/2 cups milk
175g/6oz/1½ cup coarse cornmeal
5ml/1 tsp dried red chilli flakes
10ml/2 tsp ground toasted cumin seeds
10ml/2 tsp dried oregano
vegetable oil, for deep-frying

1 Cut the stalks from the chillies and discard the seeds. Dry-fry the chillies for 2–4 minutes. Place in a bowl, cover with warm water and soak for 20–30 minutes. Drain and reserve the water.

2 Process the chillies to a paste with the garlic, cumin, oregano and oil in a food processor. Add a little soaking water, if needed. Season with pepper.

3 Wash and dry the steaks, drizzle the chilli paste all over them and leave to marinate for up to 12 hours.

4 To make the onion rings, soak the onions in the milk for 30 minutes. Mix the cornmeal, chilli, cumin and oregano and season to taste. Heat the oil for deep-frying to 180°C/350°F, or until a cube of day-old bread turns brown in about 60 seconds.

5 Drain the onion rings and dip each one into the cornmeal mixture, coating it thoroughly. Deep-fry, in batches, for about 2–4 minutes, or until browned and crisp. Lift the onion rings out of the pan with a slotted spoon and drain on kitchen paper.

6 Heat a barbecue or griddle. Season the steaks with salt and cook for 4 minutes on each side for a medium result. Serve.

Beef in Oyster Sauce Energy 282Kcal/1177kJ; Protein 25.4g; Carbohydrate 10.7g, of which sugars 3.4g; Fat 15.5g, of which saturates 4.2g; Cholesterol 69mg; Calcium 16mg; Fibre 0.8g; Sodium 697mg.
Marinated Beef Energy 214kcal/894kJ; Protein 22.1g; Carbohydrate 8.7g, of which sugars 1.5g; Fat 10g, of which saturates 2.7g; Cholesterol 45mg; Calcium 25mg; Fibre 0.4g; Sodium 68mg.

Chilli and Honey-cured Beef

When it comes to ingredients, Asian cooks will dry almost anything – fish, chillies, mushrooms, snake, mangoes, pig's ears and beef are just some of them. Some dried goods are destined for stews, soups and medicinal purposes, whereas others are just for chewing on. This cured beef makes a good nibble or appetizer.

Serves 4

450g/1lb beef sirloin
2 lemon grass stalks, trimmed and chopped
2 garlic cloves, chopped
2 dried Serrano chillies, seeded and chopped
30–45ml/2–3 tbsp honey
15ml/1 tbsp fish sauce
30ml/2 tbsp soy sauce
rice wrappers, fresh herbs and dipping sauce, to serve (optional)

1 Trim the beef and cut it across the grain into thin, rectangular slices, then set aside.

2 Using a mortar and pestle, grind the chopped lemon grass, garlic and chillies to a paste. Stir in the honey, fish sauce and soy sauce. Put the beef into a bowl, add the paste and rub it into the meat. Spread out the meat on a wire rack and place it in the refrigerator, uncovered, for 2 days, or until dry and hard.

3 Cook the dried beef on the barbecue or under a conventional grill (broiler), and serve it as a snack or appetizer on its own or with rice wrappers, fresh herbs and a dipping sauce.

Variation

This recipe also works well with venison. Cut the meat into thin strips and dry exactly as above. The resulting dish will give you a South-east Asian version of the famous biltong, a dish with Dutch roots created by South Africa's European pioneers. Biltong is often likened to beef jerky, but it is more likely to use game meats, including venison and ostrich.

Sweet-and-Sour Tongue with Ginger

Tongue is a favourite ingredient in the Jewish kitchen. It is a cheap but very nutritious meat and although in recent years it has rather gone out of fashion in the West it is now reappearing on the menus of smart restaurants. It is wonderful served hot as an appetizer with the sweet-and-sour sauce in this recipe, and the leftovers are also very good cold, without the sauce, thinly sliced for sandwiches or a salad.

Serves 8

1kg/2¼lb fresh ox tongue
2–3 onions, 1 sliced and 1–2 chopped
3 bay leaves
½–1 stock (bouillon) cube or a small amount of stock powder or bouillon
45ml/3 tbsp vegetable oil
60ml/4 tbsp potato flour
120ml/4fl oz/½ cup honey
150g/5oz/1 cup raisins
2.5ml/½ tsp salt
2.5ml/½ tsp ground ginger
1 lemon, sliced
fresh rosemary sprigs, to garnish

1 Put the tongue, sliced onion and bay leaves in a pan. Pour over cold water to cover and add the stock cube, powder or bouillon. Bring to the boil, reduce the heat, cover and simmer gently for 2–3 hours. Lift the tongue out of the stock, remove the skin and bones and keep the tongue warm. Strain the stock and set aside.

2 In a small frying pan, heat the oil, add the chopped onion and cook for about 5 minutes, until softened.

3 Stir the potato flour into the onions and gradually add about 500ml/17fl oz/2¼ cups of the stock, stirring constantly to prevent lumps forming.

4 Stir the honey, raisins, salt and ginger into the sauce and continue to cook until it has thickened and is smooth. Add the lemon slices and set the sauce aside.

5 Slice the tongue thinly and serve generously coated with the sweet-and-sour sauce. Garnish with rosemary.

Chilli Beef Energy 158kcal/659kJ; Protein 17.3g; Carbohydrate 6.7g, of which sugars 6.6g; Fat 7g, of which saturates 2.9g; Cholesterol 43mg; Calcium 6mg; Fibre 0.1g; Sodium 405mg.
Tongue Energy 446kcal/1864kJ; Protein 21g; Carbohydrate 30.6g, of which sugars 28.1g; Fat 27.6g, of which saturates 0.7g; Cholesterol 98mg; Calcium 34mg; Fibre 1.3g; Sodium 1528mg.

Meatballs with Pine Nuts and Cinnamon

Turkish meatballs, known as kofte, are generally made from lamb or beef, although some contain chicken, and they are shaped into round balls or plump ovals. For a great appetizer, tuck the meatballs into toasted pittas along with sliced red onion, and a spoonful of yogurt.

Serves 4–6

250g/9oz/generous 1 cup lean minced (ground) lamb
1 onion, finely chopped
2 garlic cloves, crushed
10–15ml/2–3 tsp ground cinnamon
30ml/2 tbsp pine nuts
30ml/2 tbsp currants, soaked in warm water for 5–10 minutes and drained
5ml/1 tsp paprika
2 slices of day-old white or brown bread, crusts removed, ground into crumbs
1 egg, lightly beaten
15ml/1 tbsp tomato ketchup
1 bunch each of fresh flat leaf parsley and dill
60ml/4 tbsp plain (all-purpose) flour
sunflower oil, for shallow frying
salt and ground black pepper
lemon wedges, to serve

1 In a bowl, pound the lamb with the onion, garlic and cinnamon. Using your hands, knead the mixture in order to knock out the air, then add the pine nuts with the currants, paprika, breadcrumbs, egg and ketchup. Season with salt and black pepper.

2 Finely chop the herbs, reserving 1–2 sprigs of parsley for the garnish, and knead into the mixture, making sure all the ingredients are mixed well together.

3 Take apricot-sized portions of the mixture in your hands and roll into balls. Flatten each ball so that it resembles a thick disc, then coat lightly in the flour.

4 Heat a thin layer of oil in a heavy pan. Add the meatballs and cook for 8–10 minutes, until browned on all sides. Remove with a slotted spoon and drain on kitchen paper. Serve hot with lemon wedges and garnish with parsley.

Lettuce-wrapped Lamb with Cumin

In this tasty appetizer, lamb is stir-fried with garlic, ginger and spices, then served in crisp lettuce leaves with yogurt, a dab of lime pickle and mint leaves – the contrast of hot and spicy with cool and crisp is excellent and appetizing.

Serves 4

450g/1lb lamb neck fillet
2.5ml/½ tsp chilli powder
10ml/2 tsp ground coriander
5ml/1 tsp ground cumin
2.5ml/½ tsp ground turmeric
30ml/2 tbsp groundnut oil
3–4 garlic cloves, chopped
15ml/1 tbsp grated fresh root ginger
150ml/¼ pint/⅔ cup lamb stock or water
4–6 spring onions (scallions), sliced
30ml/2 tbsp chopped fresh coriander (cilantro)
15ml/1 tbsp lemon juice
lettuce leaves, yogurt, lime pickle and mint leaves, to serve

1 Trim the lamb fillet of any fat and cut into small pieces, then mince (grind) in a blender or food processor, taking care not to overprocess.

2 In a bowl, mix together the chilli powder, ground coriander, cumin and turmeric. Add the lamb and rub the spice mixture into the meat. Cover and leave to marinate for about 1 hour.

3 Heat a wok until hot. Add the oil and swirl it around. When hot, add the garlic and ginger and cook for a few seconds.

4 Add the lamb and continue to stir-fry for 2–3 minutes. Pour in the stock and cook until all the stock has been absorbed and the lamb is tender, adding more stock if necessary.

5 Add the spring onions, fresh coriander and lemon juice, then stir-fry for a further 30–45 seconds. Serve immediately with the lettuce leaves, yogurt, pickle and mint leaves.

Variation
Vegetables, such as cooked diced potatoes or peas, can be added to the lamb.

Meatballs Energy 261kcal/1088kJ; Protein 11.4g; Carbohydrate 15.4g, of which sugars 5.2g; Fat 17.5g, of which saturates 4g; Cholesterol 64mg; Calcium 40mg; Fibre 0.7g; Sodium 129mg.
Lettuce-wrapped Lamb Energy 266kcal/1107kJ; Protein 22.9g; Carbohydrate 1.8g, of which sugars 0.5g; Fat 18.7g, of which saturates 6.7g; Cholesterol 86mg; Calcium 23mg; Fibre 0.3g; Sodium 99mg.

Skewered Lamb with Red Onion Salsa

This summery appetizer is ideal for outdoor eating, although, if the weather fails, the skewers can be cooked indoors rather than barbecued. The refreshing salsa is quick and easy to make and is the ideal accompaniment to the lamb.

Serves 4

225g/8oz lean lamb, cubed
2.5ml/½ tsp ground cumin
5ml/1 tsp paprika
15ml/1 tbsp olive oil
salt and ground black pepper

For the salsa

1 red onion, very thinly sliced
1 large tomato, seeded and chopped
15ml/1 tbsp red wine vinegar
3–4 fresh basil or mint leaves, coarsely torn
small mint leaves, to garnish

1 Place the lamb in a bowl with the cumin, paprika, oil and seasoning. Toss well until the lamb is coated with spices.

2 Cover the bowl with clear film (plastic wrap). Set aside in a cool place for a few hours, or in the refrigerator overnight, so that the lamb absorbs the flavours.

3 Spear the marinated lamb cubes on to four small skewers. Ensure that the cubes are not to tightly packed together.

4 To make the salsa, put the sliced onion, tomato, red wine vinegar and basil or mint leaves in a small bowl and stir together until thoroughly blended. Season to taste with salt, garnish with mint, then set aside while you cook the lamb.

5 Cook the skewers on a barbecue or under a preheated grill (broiler) for 5–10 minutes, turning frequently, until the lamb is well browned. Serve hot, with the salsa.

Cook's Tip

If using wooden or bamboo skewers, soak them first in cold water for at least 30 minutes to prevent them from burning on the barbecue or under the grill (broiler).

Romanian Kebabs

Kebabs are popular worldwide, largely because they are so easily adapted to suit everyone's taste. In this recipe, lean lamb is marinated, then cooked with chunks of vegetables to produce a delicious and healthy appetizer.

Serves 6

675g/1½lb lean lamb, cut into 4cm/1½in cubes
12 button (pearl) onions
2 green (bell) peppers, seeded and cut into 12 pieces
12 cherry tomatoes
12 button (pearl) mushrooms
lemon slices and rosemary sprigs, to garnish
freshly cooked rice and crusty bread, to serve

For the marinade

juice of 1 lemon
120ml/4fl oz/½ cup red wine
1 onion, finely chopped
60ml/4 tbsp olive oil
2.5ml/½ tsp dried sage
2.5ml/½ tsp chopped fresh rosemary
salt and ground black pepper

1 For the marinade, combine the lemon juice, red wine, onion, olive oil, herbs and seasoning in a bowl. Stir the cubes of lamb into the marinade. Cover and chill in the refrigerator for 2–12 hours, stirring occasionally.

2 Remove the lamb pieces from the marinade and thread on to six skewers with the onions, peppers, cherry tomatoes and mushrooms. Preheat the grill (broiler).

3 Brush the kebabs with the marinade and grill (broil) for about 10–15 minutes, turning occasionally, until the meat is evenly browned. Serve the kebabs on cooked rice, with lemon and rosemary.

Variations

- *Use rump (round) steak instead of lamb. Cut it into strips, marinate it as suggested, then interleave the strips on the skewers, with the onions, cherry tomatoes and mushrooms. Omit the green (bell) peppers.*
- *Chicken strips can also be used instead of the lamb.*

Skewered Lamb Energy 135kcal/563kJ; Protein 11.4g; Carbohydrate 2g, of which sugars 1.6g; Fat 9.2g, of which saturates 3.4g; Cholesterol 43mg; Calcium 10mg; Fibre 0.5g; Sodium 51mg.
Romanian Kebabs Energy 322kcal/1340kJ; Protein 23.9g; Carbohydrate 7.6g, of which sugars 6.6g; Fat 20.5g, of which saturates 7g; Cholesterol 86mg; Calcium 28mg; Fibre 2.1g; Sodium 106mg.

Turkish Kebabs with Tomato and Chilli Salsa

The mix of aromatic spices, garlic and lemon gives these kebabs a wonderful flavour – a fiery salsa makes the perfect accompaniment. If you like your salsa really hot, you can leave the seeds in the chilli.

Serves 4

2 garlic cloves, crushed
60ml/4 tbsp lemon juice
30ml/2 tbsp olive oil
1 dried red chilli, crushed
5ml/1 tsp ground cumin
5ml/1 tsp ground coriander
500g/1¼lb lean lamb, cut into 4cm/1½in cubes
8 bay leaves
salt and ground black pepper

For the tomato and olive salsa

175g/6oz/1½ cups mixed pitted green and black olives, roughly chopped
1 small red onion, finely chopped
4 plum tomatoes, peeled and finely chopped
1 fresh red chilli, seeded and finely chopped
30ml/2 tbsp olive oil

1 Mix the garlic, lemon juice, olive oil, chilli, cumin and coriander in a large shallow dish. Add the lamb cubes, with salt and pepper to taste. Mix well. Cover and marinate in a cool place for 2 hours.

2 To make the salsa, put the olives, onion, tomatoes, chilli and olive oil in a bowl. Stir in salt and pepper to taste. Mix well, cover and set aside.

3 Remove the lamb from the marinade and divide the cubes among four skewers, adding the bay leaves at intervals. Grill over a barbecue, on a ridged iron grill pan or under a hot grill (broiler), turning occasionally, for 10 minutes, until the lamb is browned and crisp on the outside and pink and juicy inside. Serve with the salsa.

Cook's Tip
Use meat from the leg for the leanest kebabs.

Shish Kebabs with Sumac

Sumac is a spice, ground from a dried purple berry with a sour, fruity flavour. In this appetizer it complements the richness of the lamb.

Makes 8

675g/1½lb lamb neck fillet, trimmed and cut into 2.5cm/1in pieces
5ml/1 tsp each fennel, cumin and coriander seeds, roasted and crushed
1.5ml/¼ tsp cayenne pepper
5cm/2in piece fresh root ginger
150ml/¼ pint/⅔ cup natural (plain) yogurt
2 small red (bell) peppers
2 small yellow (bell) peppers
300g/11oz small onions
30ml/2 tbsp olive oil
15ml/1 tbsp ground sumac
salt and ground black pepper
8 long metal skewers

To serve

8 Lebanese flatbreads
150ml/¼ pint/⅔ cup natural (plain) yogurt
5ml/1 tsp ground sumac
1 bunch rocket (arugula)
50g/2oz/2 cups fresh parsley
10ml/2 tsp olive oil
juice of ½ lemon

1 Place the lamb pieces in a bowl and sprinkle over the crushed seeds and the cayenne pepper. Grate the ginger and squeeze it over the lamb. Pour over the yogurt. Mix well, cover and marinate overnight in the refrigerator.

2 Prepare the barbecue. Stand a sieve (strainer) over a bowl and pour in the lamb mixture. Leave to drain well. Cut the peppers in half, remove the cores and seeds, then cut the flesh into rough chunks. Place in a bowl. Add the onions and the olive oil. Pat the drained lamb with kitchen paper to remove excess marinade. Add the lamb to the bowl, season and toss well. Thread the lamb, peppers and onions on to the skewers.

3 On a medium-hot barbecue, grill the kebabs for about 10 minutes, turning every 2 minutes. When cooked, transfer to a platter, lightly sprinkle with the sumac, and cover with foil.

4 Place the breads on the barbecue to warm. Place the yogurt in a serving bowl and sprinkle with sumac. Arrange the rocket and parsley in separate bowls and pour over the oil and lemon juice. Serve with the kebabs and the warmed flatbread.

Turkish Kebabs Energy 456kcal/1892kJ; Protein 23.9g; Carbohydrate 7g, of which sugars 6.3g; Fat 37.2g, of which saturates 9.5g; Cholesterol 86mg; Calcium 54mg; Fibre 3.2g; Sodium 1096mg.
Shish Kebabs Energy 361kcal/1515kJ; Protein 22.5g; Carbohydrate 38.4g, of which sugars 8.1g; Fat 14.1g, of which saturates 5.1g; Cholesterol 64mg; Calcium 133mg; Fibre 3g; Sodium 249mg.

Lamb and Ras el Hanout Kebabs

These little round lamb kebabs owe their exotic flavour to ras el hanout, a North African spice blend. Dried rose petals can be found in Moroccan and Middle Eastern stores.

Serves 4–6
30ml/2 tbsp extra virgin olive oil
1 onion, finely chopped
2 garlic cloves, crushed
35g/1¼oz/5 tbsp pine nuts
500g/1¼lb/2½ cups minced (ground) lamb
10ml/2 tsp ras el hanout
10ml/2 tsp dried pink rose petals (optional)
salt and ground black pepper
18 short wooden or metal skewers
150ml/¼ pint/⅔ cup natural (plain) yogurt and 7.5ml/1½ tsp rose harissa, to serve

For the fresh mint chutney
40g/1½oz/1½ cups fresh mint leaves, finely chopped
10ml/2 tsp sugar
juice of 2 lemons
2 apples, peeled and finely grated

1 If using wooden skewers, soak them in cold water for 30 minutes. Heat the oil in a frying pan on the stove. Add the onion and garlic and fry gently for 7 minutes. Stir in the pine nuts. Fry for about 5 minutes more, or until the mixture is slightly golden, then set aside to cool.

2 Make the fresh mint chutney by mixing together all of the ingredients. Set aside.

3 Prepare the barbecue. Place the minced lamb in a large bowl and add the ras el hanout and rose petals, if using. Add the cooled onion mixture and add salt and pepper. Using your hands, mix well, then form into 18 balls. Drain the skewers and mould a ball on to each one. Once the flames have died down, rake a few hot coals to one side. Position a lightly oiled grill rack over the coals to heat.

4 When the coals are cool, or with a thick coating of ash, place the kebabs on the grill over the part with the most coals. If it is easier, cover the barbecue with a lid or tented heavy-duty foil so that the heat will circulate and they will cook evenly all over. Serve with the yogurt, mixed with the rose harissa, if you like.

Lamb Saté

These spicy lamb skewers are traditionally served with dainty diamond-shaped pieces of compressed rice.

Makes 25–30 skewers
1kg/2¼lb leg of lamb, boned
3 garlic cloves, crushed
15–30ml/1–2 tbsp chilli sambal or 5–10ml/1–2 tsp chilli powder
90ml/6 tbsp dark soy sauce
juice of 1 lemon
salt and ground black pepper
groundnut (peanut) or sunflower oil, for brushing

For the sauce
6 garlic cloves, crushed
15ml/1 tbsp chilli sambal or 2–3 fresh chillies, seeded and ground to a paste
90ml/6 tbsp dark soy sauce
25ml/1½ tbsp lemon juice
30ml/2 tbsp boiling water

To serve
thinly sliced onion
cucumber wedges

1 Cut the lamb into neat 1cm/½in cubes. Remove any pieces of gristle, but do not trim off any of the fat because this keeps the meat moist during cooking and enhances the flavour. Spread out the lamb cubes in a single layer in a shallow bowl.

2 Put the garlic, chilli sambal or chilli powder, soy sauce and lemon juice in a mortar. Add salt and pepper and grind to a paste. Alternatively, process the mixture using a food processor.

3 Pour the mixture over the lamb and mix to coat. Cover and leave in a cool place for at least 1 hour. Soak wooden or bamboo skewers in water to prevent them from scorching during cooking.

4 Prepare the sauce. Put the garlic into a bowl. Add the chilli sambal or fresh chillies, soy sauce, lemon juice and boiling water. Stir well.

5 Preheat the grill (broiler). Thread the meat on to the skewers and brush with oil. Grill (broil), turning often. Brush the saté with a little of the sauce and serve hot, with the onion and cucumber wedges. Offer the sauce separately.

Lamb and Ras Energy 257kcal/1070kJ; Protein 17.2g; Carbohydrate 5.1g, of which sugars 4.5g; Fat 18.8g, of which saturates 6g; Cholesterol 64mg; Calcium 33mg; Fibre 0.6g; Sodium 59mg.
Lamb Saté Energy33kcal/139kJ; Protein 3.5g; Carbohydrate 0.6g, of which sugars 0.3g; Fat 1.9g, of which saturates 0.9g; Cholesterol 13mg; Calcium 2mg; Fibre 0.1g; Sodium 86mg.

Shammi Kebabs

These Indian treats are derived from the kebabs of the Middle East. They can be served either as appetizers or side dishes with a raita or chutney.

Serves 5–6

2 onions, finely chopped
250g/9oz lean lamb, boned and cubed
50g/2oz/¼ cup chana dhal or yellow split peas
5ml/1 tsp cumin seeds
5ml/1 tsp garam masala
4–6 fresh green chillies
5cm/2in piece fresh root ginger, grated
175ml/6fl oz/¾ cup water
juice of 1 lemon
a few fresh coriander (cilantro) and mint leaves, chopped, plus extra coriander sprigs to garnish
15ml/1 tbsp gram flour
2 eggs, beaten
vegetable oil, for shallow-frying
salt

1 Put the first seven ingredients and the water into a large pan with salt, and bring to the boil. Simmer, covered, until the meat and dhal are cooked. Remove the lid and continue to cook for a few more minutes, to reduce the excess liquid. Set aside and leave to cool.

2 Transfer the cooled meat mixture to a food processor or blender and process well until the mixture becomes a rough, gritty paste.

3 Put the paste into a large mixing bowl and add the chopped coriander and mint leaves, lemon juice and gram flour. Knead well with your fingers for a good couple of minutes, to ensure that all ingredients are evenly distributed through the mixture, and any excess liquid has been thoroughly absorbed. When the colour appears even throughout, and the mixture has taken on a semi-solid, sticky rather than powdery consistency, the kebabs are ready for shaping into portions.

4 Divide the mixture into 10–12 equal portions and use your hands to roll each into a ball, then flatten slightly. Chill for 1 hour. Dip the kebabs in the beaten egg and shallow-fry each side until golden brown. Pat dry on kitchen paper and serve.

Lamb Tikka

Creamy yogurt and ground nuts go wonderfully with these spices to make a tasty appetizer.

Serves 4–6

450g/1lb lamb fillet
2 spring onions (scallions), chopped

For the marinade

350ml/12fl oz/1½ cups natural (plain) yogurt
15ml/1 tbsp ground almonds, cashewnuts or peanuts
15ml/1 tbsp vegetable oil
2–3 garlic cloves, finely chopped
juice of 1 lemon
5ml/1 tsp garam masala or curry powder
2.5ml/½ tsp ground cardamom
1.5ml/¼ tsp cayenne pepper
15–30ml/1–2 tbsp chopped fresh mint

1 To prepare the marinade, stir together the marinade ingredients. In a separate small bowl, reserve about 120ml/4fl oz/½ cup of the mixture to use as a dipping sauce for the meatballs.

2 Cut the lamb into small pieces and put in the bowl of a food processor with the spring onions. Process, using the pulse action, until the meat is finely chopped. Add 30–45ml/2–3 tbsp of the marinade and process again.

3 Test to see if the mixture holds together by pinching a little between your fingertips. Add a little more marinade, if necessary, but do not make the mixture too wet and soft.

4 With moistened palms, shape the meat mixture into slightly oval balls, about 4cm/1½in long, then arrange them in a shallow dish. Spoon over the remaining marinade, then cover and chill the meatballs in the refrigerator for 8–10 hours or overnight.

5 Preheat the grill (broiler) and line a baking sheet with foil. Thread each meatball on to a skewer and arrange on the baking sheet. Grill (broil) for 4–5 minutes, turning them occasionally, until crisp and golden on all sides. Serve with the reserved marinade as a dipping sauce.

Shammi Kebabs Energy 207kcal/861kJ; Protein 12.8g; Carbohydrate 7.7g, of which sugars 1g; Fat 14.1g, of which saturates 3.6g; Cholesterol 95mg; Calcium 40mg; Fibre 1.1g; Sodium 65mg.
Lamb Tikka Energy 44kcal/182kJ; Protein 4.7g; Carbohydrate 0.4g, of which sugars 0.3g; Fat 2.6g, of which saturates 1.2g; Cholesterol 17mg; Calcium 12mg; Fibre 0.1g; Sodium 25mg.

Fragrant Spiced Lamb on Mini Poppadums

Crisp, melt-in-the-mouth mini poppadums make a great base for these divine little bites. Top them with a drizzle of yogurt and a spoonful of mango chutney, then serve immediately. To make an equally tasty variation, you can use chicken or pork in place of the lamb.

Makes 25

30ml/2 tbsp sunflower oil
4 shallots, finely chopped
30ml/2 tbsp medium curry paste
300g/11oz minced (ground) lamb
90ml/6 tbsp tomato purée (paste)
5ml/1 tsp caster (superfine) sugar
200ml/7fl oz/scant 1 cup coconut cream
juice of 1 lime
60ml/4 tbsp chopped fresh mint leaves
25 mini poppadums
vegetable oil, for frying
salt and ground black pepper
natural (plain) yogurt and mango chutney, to drizzle
red chilli slivers and mint leaves, to garnish

1 Heat the oil in a wok over a medium heat and add the shallots. Stir fry for 4–5 minutes, until softened, then add the curry paste. Stir-fry for 1–2 minutes.

2 Add the lamb and stir-fry over a high heat for 4–5 minutes, then stir in the tomato purée, sugar and coconut cream.

3 Cook the lamb over a gentle heat for 25–30 minutes, or until the meat is tender and all the liquid has been absorbed. Season and stir in the lime juice and mint leaves. Remove from the heat and keep warm.

4 Fill a separate wok one-third full of oil and deep-fry the mini poppadums for 30–40 seconds, until puffed up and crisp. Drain on kitchen paper.

5 Place the poppadums on a serving platter. Put a spoonful of spiced lamb on each one, then top with a little yogurt and mango chutney. Serve immediately, garnished with slivers of red chilli and mint leaves.

Curried Lamb and Potato Cakes

An unusual variation on burgers or rissoles, these little lamb triangles are easy to make. They are really good served hot as an appetizer, but they can also be eaten cold as a snack or taken on picnics.

Makes 12–15

450g/1lb new or small, firm potatoes
3 eggs
1 onion, grated
30ml/2 tbsp chopped fresh parsley
450g/1lb finely minced (ground) lean lamb
115g/4oz/2 cups fresh breadcrumbs
vegetable oil, for frying
salt and ground black pepper
sprigs of fresh mint, to garnish
pitta bread and herby green salad, to serve

1 Cook the potatoes in a large pan of boiling salted water for 20 minutes or until tender, then drain and leave to cool.

2 Beat the eggs in a large bowl. Add the onion, parsley and seasoning and beat together.

3 When the potatoes are cold, grate them coarsely and stir into the egg mixture, together with the minced lamb. Knead the mixture well for 3–4 minutes until all the ingredients are thoroughly blended.

4 Take a handful of the lamb mixture and roll it into a ball. Repeat this process until all the meat is used.

5 Roll the balls in the breadcrumbs and then mould them into fairly flat triangular shapes, about 13cm/5in long. Coat them in the breadcrumbs again.

6 Heat a 1cm/½in layer of oil in a frying pan over medium heat. When the oil is hot, fry the potato cakes for 8–12 minutes until golden brown on both sides, turning occasionally. Drain on kitchen paper.

7 Serve hot, garnished with mint and accompanied by pitta bread and salad.

Fragrant Spiced Lamb Energy 63kcal/260kJ; Protein 2.7g; Carbohydrate 2.7g, of which sugars 1.3g; Fat 4.7g, of which saturates 1.4g; Cholesterol 9mg; Calcium 7mg; Fibre 0.3g; Sodium 45mg.
Curried Lamb Energy 181kcal/760kJ; Protein 10.8g; Carbohydrate 13.9g, of which sugars 1.1g; Fat 9.6g, of which saturates 2.8g; Cholesterol 76mg; Calcium 31mg; Fibre 0.8g; Sodium 128mg.

Curried Lamb Samosas

Filo pastry is perfect for making samosas. Once you've mastered folding them, you'll be amazed at how quick they are to make. These lamb samosas have a simple filling that is tasty and quick to make – perfect for appetizers or party fare.

Serves 4
25g/1oz/2 tbsp butter
225g/8oz/1 cup minced (ground) lamb
30ml/2 tbsp mild curry paste
12 sheets of filo pastry, thawed and wrapped in a damp dish towel
salt and ground black pepper

1 Heat a little of the butter in a large pan and add the lamb. Fry for 5–6 minutes, stirring occasionally until browned.

2 Stir the curry paste into the lamb and cook for 1–2 minutes. Season and set aside. Preheat the oven to 200°C/400°F/Gas 6.

3 Melt the remaining butter in a pan. Cut the pastry sheets in half lengthways. Brush one strip of pastry with butter, then lay another strip on top and brush with more butter.

4 Place a spoonful of lamb in the corner of the strip and fold over to form a triangle at one end. Keep folding over in the same way to form a triangular shape.

5 Brush with butter and place on a baking sheet. Repeat using the remaining pastry and filling. Bake for 10–15 minutes until golden. Serve hot.

Variation
For Cashew Nut Samosas, mix together 225g/8oz cooked and mashed potato, 15ml/1 tbsp chopped cashew nuts, 5ml/1 tsp coconut milk powder, ½ chopped green chilli, 5ml/1 tsp mustard seeds, 5ml/1 tsp cumin seeds, 15ml/1 tbsp chopped fresh coriander (cilantro) and 5ml/1 tsp soft light brown sugar. Use to fill the samosas in place of the lamb filling. If you like, the mustard and cumin seeds can be dry-roasted first.

Grilled Foie Gras

The rich and luxurious texture of the foie gras is teamed here with a sharp, tangy Japanese sauce, ponzu joyu. It takes only seconds to prepare but does need to be made at least 24 hours in advance to give the flavours plenty of time to blend. The caramelized flavour of the pear balances the dish.

Serves 4
2 Asian (nashi) pears
15ml/1 tbsp clear honey mixed with 45ml/3 tbsp water
225g/8oz duck or goose foie gras, chilled and cut into eight 1cm/½in slices

For the ponzu joyu
45ml/3 tbsp mirin
120ml/4fl oz/½ cup tamari
75ml/5 tbsp dried bonito flakes
45ml/3 tbsp rice vinegar
juice of 1 large lemon
4 strips dried kombu seaweed

1 To make the ponzu joyu, place the mirin in a small pan, bring to the boil and cook for about 30 seconds. Pour into a small bowl and add all the remaining ingredients. Cool, then cover and chill for about 24 hours. Strain the mixture into a screw-topped jar and chill until needed.

2 Cut each pear into eight wedges and toss in the honey mixture. Heat a griddle on the stove until a drop of water sprinkled on the surface evaporates instantly. Grill the pear wedges for about 30 seconds on each cut side, or until branded with golden grill marks.

3 Wipe the pan with kitchen paper and heat again. When it is searing hot, grill the foie gras for about 30 seconds on each side. Serve the slices immediately with the ponzu joyu and pear wedges.

Cook's Tip
This can also be cooked on a griddle on the barbecue over hot coals that have a light covering of ash.

Lamb Samosas Energy 101kcal/423kJ; Protein 5g; Carbohydrate 10.4g, of which sugars 0.2g; Fat 4.6g, of which saturates 2.3g; Cholesterol 19mg; Calcium 37mg; Fibre 1g; Sodium 37mg
Grilled Foie Gras Energy 238kcal/988kJ; Protein 7.5g; Carbohydrate 11.1g, of which sugars 10.9g; Fat 18.5g, of which saturates 5.4g; Cholesterol 96mg; Calcium 18mg; Fibre 1.7g; Sodium 692mg.

Devilled Kidneys on Brioche Croûtes

The trick with lamb's kidneys is not to overcook them, so this recipe is a gift for the quick cook. Cream tames the fiery sauce, making a mixture that tastes great on croûtes or as a filling for tartlets.

Serves 4

8 mini brioche slices
25g/1oz/2 tbsp butter
1 shallot, finely chopped
2 garlic cloves, finely chopped
115g/4oz/1½ cups mushrooms, halved
1.5ml/¼ tsp cayenne pepper
15ml/1 tbsp Worcestershire sauce
8 lamb's kidneys, halved and trimmed
150ml/¼ pint/⅔ cup double (heavy) cream
30ml/2 tbsp chopped fresh parsley

1 Preheat the grill (broiler) and toast the brioche slices until golden brown on both sides. Keep warm.

2 Melt the butter in a frying pan. Add the shallot, garlic and mushrooms and cook for 5 minutes, or until the shallot has softened. Stir in the cayenne pepper and Worcestershire sauce and simmer for 1 minute.

3 Add the kidneys to the pan and cook for 3–5 minutes on each side. Finally, stir in the cream and simmer for about 2 minutes, or until the sauce has heated through.

4 Remove the brioche croûtes from the wire rack and place on warmed plates. Top with the kidneys. Sprinkle with chopped parsley and serve with salad.

Cook's Tip
If you can't find mini brioches, you can use a large brioche instead. Slice it thickly and stamp out croûtes using a 5cm/2in round cutter. If you prefer, the brioche croûtes can be fried rather than toasted. Melt 25g/1oz/2 tbsp butter in a frying pan and fry the croûtes until crisp and golden on both sides.

Deep-fried Lamb Patties

These patties are a tasty North African speciality – called kibbeh – of minced meat and bulgur wheat. Moderately spiced, they're good served with yogurt as an appetizer.

Serves 6

450g/1lb lean lamb or lean minced (ground) lamb or beef
salt and ground black pepper
vegetable oil, for deep-frying
avocado slices and fresh coriander (cilantro) sprigs, to serve

For the patties
225g/8oz/1⅓ cups bulgur wheat
1 red chilli, seeded and coarsely chopped
1 onion, coarsely chopped

For the stuffing
1 onion, finely chopped
50g/2oz/⅔ cup pine nuts
30ml/2 tbsp olive oil
7.5ml/1½ tsp ground allspice
60ml/4 tbsp chopped fresh coriander (cilantro)

1 If necessary, coarsely cut up the lamb and process the pieces in a blender or food processor until minced. Divide the minced meat into two equal portions.

2 For the patties, soak the bulgur wheat for 15 minutes in cold water. Drain, then process in a blender or a food processor with the chilli, onion, half the meat and salt and pepper.

3 For the stuffing, cook the onion and pine nuts in the oil for 5 minutes. Add the allspice and remaining meat and cook gently, breaking up the meat with a wooden spoon, until browned. Stir in the coriander and seasoning.

4 Turn the patty mixture out on to a work surface and shape into a cake. Cut into 12 wedges. Flatten one piece and spoon some of the stuffing into the centre. Bring the edges of the patty up over the stuffing, so that the filling is encased.

5 Pour the oil into a large pan to a depth of 5cm/2in and heat until a few crumbs sizzle. Lower half of the filled patties into the oil and deep-fry for about 5 minutes, until golden. Drain well on kitchen paper and keep hot while you are cooking the remainder. Serve, with avocado slices and coriander sprigs.

Devilled Kidneys Energy 575kcal/2412kJ; Protein 37.7g; Carbohydrate 40.7g, of which sugars 13.2g; Fat 30.3g, of which saturates 16.3g; Cholesterol 623mg; Calcium 122mg; Fibre 2g; Sodium 599mg.
Lamb Patties Energy 154kcal/640kJ; Protein 13.6g; Carbohydrate 0.9g, of which sugars 0.8g; Fat 6.2g, of which saturates 3.5g; Cholesterol 211mg; Calcium 44mg; Fibre 0.6g; Sodium 159mg.

Liver and Bacon Varenyky

There is an old Ukrainian superstition that if varenyky are counted, the dough will split and the filling spill out.

Serves 4
200g/7oz/1¾ cups plain (all-purpose) flour
1.5ml/¼ tsp salt
2 eggs, beaten
15g/½oz/1 tbsp butter, melted
beaten egg, for sealing
15ml/1 tbsp sunflower oil

For the filling
15ml/1 tbsp sunflower oil
½ small onion, finely chopped
115g/4oz smoked streaky (fatty) bacon, roughly chopped
225g/8oz chicken or lamb's liver, roughly chopped
30ml/2 tbsp chopped fresh chives, plus extra for garnish
salt and ground black pepper

1 Sift the flour and salt into a bowl. Make a well in the centre. Add the eggs and butter and mix to a dough. Knead the dough on a lightly floured surface for 2–3 minutes, until smooth. Wrap in clear film (plastic wrap) and leave to rest for 30 minutes.

2 For the filling, heat the oil in a pan and cook the onion for 5 minutes. Add the bacon and cook for a further 4–5 minutes. Stir in the liver and cook for 1 minute, until browned.

3 Put the liver mixture in a food processor or blender and process until it is finely chopped, but not smooth. Add the chopped chives and season. Process for a few more seconds.

4 Roll out the dough on a lightly floured surface until 3mm/⅛in thick. Stamp out rounds of dough with a 5cm/2in cutter.

5 Spoon a teaspoon of filling into the middle of each round. Brush the edges of the dough with beaten egg and fold in half to make half-moon shapes. Leave to dry on a floured dish towel for 30 minutes.

6 Bring a pan of salted water to the boil. Add the oil, then add the varenyky, in batches if necessary. Bring back to the boil and cook them at a gentle simmer for 10 minutes, until tender. Drain well and serve hot, garnished with chives.

Chicken Livers in Sherry

This delicious little tapas dish is a particularly good appetizer eaten with bread, toast or French Bread for mopping up the juices.

Serves 4
225g/8oz chicken livers, thawed if frozen
15ml/1 tbsp olive oil
1 small onion, finely chopped
2 small garlic cloves, finely chopped
5ml/1 tsp fresh thyme leaves
30ml/2 tbsp sweet oloroso sherry
30ml/2 tbsp crème fraîche or double (heavy) cream
2.5ml/½ tsp paprika
salt and ground black pepper
fresh thyme, to garnish

1 Carefully trim the chicken livers, removing any green spots and sinews, and discard. Set aside the livers until you are ready to cook them.

2 Heat the olive oil in a large frying pan and fry the onion and garlic, stirring constantly, for 4–6 minutes until the onion begins to soften. Ensure that the garlic doesn't burn, otherwise it will impart a bitter flavour to the dish.

3 Add the chicken livers to the pan along with the thyme and cook for a further 3 minutes.

4 Stir the sherry into the livers, add the crème fraîche and cook briefly until the mixture starts to bubble. Season with salt, ground black pepper and paprika, garnish with fresh thyme and serve immediately.

Cook's Tip
If you can't find any fresh chicken livers then look for frozen ones in the supermarket, but ensure they are fully defrosted before using.

Liver Varenyky Energy 416kcal/1746kJ; Protein 23.3g; Carbohydrate 39.3g, of which sugars 0.8g; Fat 17.4g, of which saturates 6.7g; Cholesterol 336mg; Calcium 99mg; Fibre 1.8g; Sodium 476mg.
Chicken Livers Energy 119kcal/494kJ; Protein 10.3g; Carbohydrate 1.5g, of which sugars 1.1g; Fat 7.1g, of which saturates 2.8g; Cholesterol 222mg; Calcium 13mg; Fibre 0.2g; Sodium 46mg.

Moroccan-spiced Sautéed Chicken Livers

Sautéed offal, such as liver and kidney, is quick and easy to cook and its strong, assertive flavour makes it ideal as an appetizer. It can be cooked simply in olive oil and garlic and served with lemon to squeeze over, or given a more elaborate treatment, as in this dish of spiced chicken livers. This makes a delicious, tangy appetizer, whether you serve the pieces of liver sprinkled over a plate of mixed salad leaves, or spooned on thin slices of toasted bread.

Serves 4

30–45ml/2–3 tbsp olive oil
2–3 garlic cloves, chopped
1 dried red chilli, chopped
5ml/1 tsp cumin seeds
450g/1lb chicken livers, trimmed and cut into bitesize chunks
5ml/1 tsp ground coriander
handful of roasted hazelnuts, roughly chopped
10–15ml/2–3 tsp orange flower water
½ preserved lemon, finely sliced or chopped
salt and ground black pepper
small bunch of fresh coriander (cilantro), finely chopped, to serve

1 Heat the olive oil in a heavy frying pan and stir in the garlic, chilli and cumin seeds. Add the chicken livers and toss over the heat until they are browned on all sides. Reduce the heat a little and continue to cook for 3–5 minutes.

2 When the livers are almost cooked, stir in the ground coriander, hazelnuts, orange flower water and preserved lemon.

3 Season to taste with salt and black pepper and serve immediately, sprinkled with a little fresh coriander.

Variation
Lamb's liver, trimmed and finely sliced, is also good cooked this way. The trick is to sear the outside so that the middle is almost pink and melts in the mouth. If you don't have orange flower water, try a little balsamic vinegar.

Lamb's Liver with Paprika

This is such a delicious way to eat lamb's liver that it is even possible to convert those who don't usually like it. It is a Turkish dish, which was probably adapted from an Albanian recipe as the Ottoman Empire consumed vast expanses of Eastern Europe. Traditionally served as a hot or cold meze dish with sliced red onion and flat leaf parsley, the spiced liver also makes a wonderful dish for supper, served with a salad and a dollop of creamy yogurt, if you like.

Serves 4

500g/1¼lb fresh lamb's liver
30ml/2 tbsp plain (all-purpose) flour
5–10ml/1–2 tsp paprika
45–60ml/3–4 tbsp olive oil
2 garlic cloves, finely chopped
5–10ml/1–2 tsp cumin seeds
sea salt
1 large red onion, cut in half lengthways, in half again crossways, and sliced along the grain
a handful of fresh flat leaf parsley, and 1 lemon, cut into wedges, to serve

1 Place the liver on a chopping board. Using a sharp knife, remove any skin and ducts, then cut the liver into thin strips or bitesize cubes.

2 Mix the flour with the paprika in a shallow bowl and toss the liver in it until well coated.

3 Heat the oil in a heavy pan. Add the garlic and cumin seeds, season with sea salt and cook until the cumin gives off a nutty aroma. Toss in the liver and stir-fry quickly for 2–3 minutes so that it cooks on all sides. Remove and drain on kichen paper.

4 Spread the sliced onion on a serving dish, spoon the liver in the middle and garnish with parsley leaves. Serve hot or cold, with the lemon wedges for squeezing.

Cook's Tip
Don't overcook the liver or it will become tough: the pieces should still be slightly pink inside.

Moroccan-spiced Livers Energy 242kcal/1006kJ; Protein 22.2g; Carbohydrate 1.5g, of which sugars 0.8g; Fat 16.4g, of which saturates 2.2g; Cholesterol 428mg; Calcium 54mg; Fibre 1.5g; Sodium 91mg.
Lamb's Liver Energy 298kcal/1245kJ; Protein 27g; Carbohydrate 11.8g, of which sugars 4.3g; Fat 16.3g, of which saturates 3.3g; Cholesterol 538mg; Calcium 37mg; Fibre 1.3g; Sodium 94mg.

Hot Spicy Prawns with Coriander

This is a quick and easy way of preparing prawns for a snack or appetizer. If you increase the quantities, this dish can also be served as a main course, and is simple enough to make for a tasty midweek dinner. You can select a variety of mushrooms and add them to the pan with the sauce ingredients, if you like. Serve the prawns with bread to mop up the tasty juices.

Serves 2–4

450g/1lb uncooked king prawns (jumbo shrimp),
60ml/4 tbsp olive oil
2–3 garlic cloves, chopped
25g/1oz fresh root ginger, peeled and shredded
1 chilli, seeded and chopped
5ml/1 tsp cumin seeds
5ml/1 tsp paprika
bunch of fresh coriander (cilantro), chopped
salt
1 lemon, cut into wedges, to serve

1 To prepare the prawns, hold each one between two fingers and gently pull off the tail shell. Twist off the head. Peel away the soft body shell and the small claws beneath and rinse thoroughly under cold water.

2 Pour the olive oil into a large, heavy frying pan, and heat the oil over a medium heat. Add the chopped garlic, stirring to ensure it does not burn, or it will taste bitter.

3 Stir in the ginger, chilli and cumin seeds. Cook the mixture briefly, stirring constantly, until the ingredients give off a lovely fragrant aroma. Add the paprika and stir in well.

4 Add the prawns to the pan. Fry them over a fairly high heat, turning them frequently, for 3–5 minutes, until just cooked.

5 Season to taste with salt and add the coriander. Serve immediately, with lemon wedges for squeezing over the prawns.

Variation
This dish is also delicious made with scallops or mussels in place of the prawns.

Prawn Cocktail

There is no nicer appetizer than a good, fresh prawn cocktail – and nothing nastier than one in which soggy prawns swim in a thin, vinegary sauce embedded in limp lettuce. This recipe shows just how good a prawn cocktail can be.

Serves 6

60ml/4 tbsp double (heavy) cream, lightly whipped
60ml/4 tbsp mayonnaise, preferably home-made
60ml/4 tbsp tomato ketchup
5–10ml/1–2 tsp Worcestershire sauce
juice of 1 lemon
½ cos or romaine lettuce or other very crisp lettuce
450g/1lb cooked peeled prawns (shrimp)
salt, ground black pepper and paprika
6 large whole cooked prawns (shrimp) in the shell, to garnish (optional)
thinly sliced, buttered brown bread and lemon wedges, to serve

1 Place the lightly whipped cream, mayonnaise and tomato ketchup in a small bowl and whisk lightly to combine. Add Worcestershire sauce to taste, then whisk in enough of the lemon juice to make a really tangy sauce.

2 Finely shred the lettuce and use to fill six individual glasses one-third full.

3 Stir the prawns into the sauce, check the seasoning and spoon the mixture generously over the lettuce.

4 If you like, drape a whole cooked prawn over the edge of each glass and sprinkle each of the cocktails with ground black pepper and/or paprika. Serve immediately, with thinly sliced brown bread and lemon wedges.

Cook's Tip
Partly peeled prawns make a pretty garnish. To prepare, carefully peel the body shell from the prawns and leave the tail 'fan' for decoration.

Hot Spicy Prawns Energy 382kcal/1591kj; Protein 40.8g; Carbohydrate 1.1g, of which sugars 0.9g; Fat 23.9g, of which saturates 3.4g; Cholesterol 439mg; Calcium 254mg; Fibre 1.9g; Sodium 440mg.
Prawn Cocktail Energy 190kcal/792kJ; Protein 13.8g; Carbohydrate 3.7g, of which sugars 3.6g; Fat 13.5g, of which saturates 4.6g; Cholesterol 167mg; Calcium 74mg; Fibre 0.2g; Sodium 373mg.

Sizzling Prawns

Serve this delicious appetizer as part of a celebration meal.

Serves 4

1–2 dried chillies (to taste)
60ml/4 tbsp olive oil
3 garlic cloves, finely chopped
16 large raw prawns (jumbo shrimp), in the shell
salt and ground black pepper
French bread, to serve

1 Using a knife and fork, split the chillies lengthways and discard the seeds.

2 Heat the oil in a large frying pan and stir-fry the garlic and chilli for 1 minute, until the garlic begins to turn brown.

3 Add the whole prawns and stir-fry for 3–4 minutes, coating them well with the flavoured oil.

4 Remove from the heat and divide the prawns among four dishes. Spoon over the flavoured oil and serve immediately.

Squid with Ginger and Garlic

This quick and tasty recipe can be used for any seafood.

Serves 2

4 ready-prepared and cleaned baby squid, total weight about 250g/9oz
15ml/1 tbsp vegetable oil
2 garlic cloves, peeled and finely chopped
30ml/2 tbsp soy sauce
2.5cm/1in piece fresh root ginger, peeled and finely chopped
juice of ½ lemon
5ml/1 tsp granulated (white) sugar
2 spring onions (scallions), chopped

1 Slice the bodies of the squid and halve the tentacles.

2 Heat the oil in a wok and cook the garlic, stirring, until golden brown. Add the squid and stir-fry for 30 seconds.

3 Add the soy sauce, ginger, lemon juice, sugar and spring onions. Stir-fry for a further 30 seconds, then serve.

Quick-fried Prawns with Spices

These spicy prawns are stir-fried in moments to make a wonderful appetizer. This is fabulous finger food, so be sure to provide your guests with finger bowls.

Serves 4

450g/1lb large raw prawns (shrimp)
2.5cm/1in fresh root ginger, grated
2 garlic cloves, crushed
5ml/1 tsp hot chilli powder
5ml/1 tsp ground turmeric
10ml/2 tsp black mustard seeds
seeds from 4 green cardamom pods, crushed
50g/2oz/¼ cup ghee or butter
120ml/4fl oz/½ cup coconut milk
salt and ground black pepper
30–45ml/2–3 tbsp chopped fresh coriander (cilantro), to garnish
naan bread, to serve

1 Carefully peel the shells from the prawns. Leave the tails attached to the prawns.

2 Using a small, sharp knife, make a slit along the back of each prawn and remove the dark vein. Rinse under cold running water, drain and pat dry.

3 Put the grated ginger, crushed garlic, chilli powder, turmeric, mustard seeds and cardamom seeds in a bowl. Add the peeled prawns and toss until they are coated completely in the spice mixture.

4 Heat a karahi or wok until hot. Add the ghee or butter and swirl it around until foaming.

5 Add the spiced prawns and stir-fry for 1–1½ minutes until they are just turning pink.

6 Stir in the coconut milk and simmer for 3–4 minutes until the prawns are just cooked through. Season to taste with salt and black pepper.

7 Transfer the cooked prawns to serving plates. Garnish with the chopped fresh coriander and serve immediately, accompanied by the naan bread.

Sizzling Prawns Energy 124kcal/511kJ; Protein 5.7g; Carbohydrate 0g, of which sugars 0g; Fat 11.2g, of which saturates 1.6g; Cholesterol 63mg; Calcium 26mg; Fibre 0g; Sodium 62mg.
Squid with Ginger Energy 169kcal/709kJ; Protein 20g; Carbohydrate 5.3g, of which sugars 3.6g; Fat 7.7g, of which saturates 1.2g; Cholesterol 281mg; Calcium 26mg; Fibre 0.2g; Sodium 1207mg.
Prawns with Spices Energy 388kcal/1618kJ; Protein 40.7g; Carbohydrate 5.1g, of which sugars 3.1g; Fat 22.9g, of which saturates 13.4g; Cholesterol 492mg; Calcium 248mg; Fibre 1.7g; Sodium 679mg.

Italian Prawn Skewers

Fresh parsley and lemon are all that is required to create a lovely tiger prawn dish. Grill them or cook them over a barbecue for a tasty and informal al fresco summer appetizer. If you are using wooden skewers, soak them in cold water for half an hour so they will not burn during the cooking process.

Serves 4

900g/2lb raw tiger prawns (jumbo shrimp), peeled
60ml/4 tbsp olive oil
45ml/3 tbsp vegetable oil
75g/3oz/1¼ cups very fine dry breadcrumbs
1 garlic clove, crushed
15ml/1 tbsp chopped fresh parsley
salt and ground black pepper
lemon wedges, to serve

1 Slit the tiger prawns down their backs and, using the point of a sharp knife, remove the dark vein. Rinse the prawns under cold running water and dry them thoroughly between sheets of kitchen paper.

2 Put the olive and vegetable oils in a large bowl and add the prawns. Stir to ensure the oils are combined and the prawns are evenly coated.

3 Add the fine breadcrumbs, crushed garlic and chopped parsley to the bowl of prawns. Season with salt and plenty of ground black pepper. Using your hands, or a wooden spoon, toss the prawns thoroughly to give them an even coating of the breadcrumb mixture.

4 Cover the bowl with clear film (plastic wrap) and leave to marinate for 1 hour in a cool place.

5 Carefully thread the breaded tiger prawns on to four metal or wooden skewers, curling them up as you work, so that the tails of the prawns are skewered neatly in the middle.

6 Preheat the grill (broiler) to a moderate heat. Place the prawn skewers in the grill pan and cook for about 2–3 minutes on each side until they are golden and cooked through. Serve with the lemon wedges.

Butterflied Prawns in Chocolate

There is a tradition in Spain, which originates in Mexico, of cooking savoury dishes with chocolate – and this extends far beyond the classic chilli con carne. This dish is just the kind of culinary adventure that Spanish chefs love.

Serves 4

8 large raw prawns (shrimp), in the shell
15ml/1 tbsp seasoned plain (all-purpose) flour
15ml/1 tbsp pale dry sherry
juice of 1 large orange
15g/½oz dark (bittersweet) chocolate, chopped
30ml/2 tbsp olive oil
2 garlic cloves, finely chopped
2.5cm/1in piece fresh root ginger, finely chopped
1 small dried chilli, seeded and chopped
salt and ground black pepper

1 Peel the prawns, leaving just the tail sections intact. Make a shallow cut down the back of each one and carefully pull out and discard the dark intestinal tract.

2 Turn the prawns over so that the undersides are uppermost, and then carefully slit them open from tail to top, using a small sharp knife, cutting them almost, but not quite, through to the central back line.

3 Press the prawns down firmly to flatten them out. Coat with the seasoned flour and set aside.

4 Gently heat the sherry and orange juice in a small pan. When warm, remove from the heat and stir in the chopped chocolate until melted.

5 Heat the oil in a frying pan. Add the garlic, ginger and chilli and cook for 2 minutes until golden. Remove with a slotted spoon and reserve. Add the prawns, cut side down, and cook for 2–3 minutes until golden brown with pink edges. Turn the prawns and cook for a further 2 minutes.

6 Return the garlic mixture to the pan and pour the chocolate sauce over. Cook for 1 minute, turning the prawns to coat them in the glossy sauce. Season to taste and serve hot.

Italian Skewers Energy 415kcal/1734kJ; Protein 42.2g; Carbohydrate 14.9g, of which sugars 0.8g; Fat 21.1g, of which saturates 2.8g; Cholesterol 439mg; Calcium 227mg; Fibre 1.1g; Sodium 574mg.
Butterflied Prawns Energy 125kcal/520kJ; Protein 8.5g; Carbohydrate 6.5g, of which sugars 3.6g; Fat 6.9g, of which saturates 1.5g; Cholesterol 88mg; Calcium 44mg; Fibre 0.2g; Sodium 88mg.

King Prawns in Sherry

These prawns couldn't be simpler, or quicker, to prepare – yet they're deceptively impressive in terms of flavour and appearance. A winning appetizer for any special celebratory feast.

Serves 4
12 raw king prawns or tiger prawns (jumbo shrimp), peeled
30ml/2 tbsp olive oil
30ml/2 tbsp sherry
a few drops of Tabasco sauce
salt and ground black pepper

1 Make a shallow cut down the back of each prawn, then pull out and discard the dark intestinal tract with a sharp-pointed knife. Leave the tails on the prawns; when they are cooked they will curl and look more decorative.

2 Heat the olive oil in a large frying pan over medium heat. Add the prawns to the pan and fry, stirring frequently, for 2–3 minutes until they turn pink.

3 Pour over the sherry and season with Tabasco sauce, salt and ground black pepper. Transfer the prawns into a large dish and serve immediately.

Cook's Tip
If you prefer more heat in your food, then simply increase the quantity of Tabasco sauce you add to the prawns (shrimp).

Variations
• *Chinese rice wine, known as saki, can be used in place of the sherry, if you prefer.*
• *You can use normal sized prawns (shrimp), if you prefer, but king prawns and tiger prawns are particularly delicious.*

Spicy Shrimp and Scallop Satay

One of the tastiest satay dishes, this is succulent, spicy and extremely moreish. Serve as an appetizer with a fruity salad or pickled vegetables and lime.

Serves 4
250g/9oz shelled shrimp or prawns, deveined and chopped
250g/9oz shelled scallops, chopped
30ml/2 tbsp potato, tapioca or rice flour
5ml/1 tsp baking powder
12–16 wooden, metal, lemon grass or sugar cane skewers
1 lime, quartered, to serve

For the spice paste
2 shallots, chopped
2 garlic cloves, chopped
2–3 red chillies, seeded and chopped
25g/1oz galangal or fresh root ginger, chopped
15g/½oz fresh turmeric, chopped or 2.5ml/½ tsp ground turmeric
2–3 lemon grass stalks, chopped
15–30ml/1–2 tbsp palm or groundnut (peanut) oil
5ml/1 tsp shrimp paste
15ml/1 tbsp tamarind paste
5ml/1 tsp palm sugar (jaggery)

1 Make the paste. In a mortar and pestle, pound the shallots, garlic, chillies, galangal, turmeric and lemon grass to form a paste.

2 Heat the oil in a wok or frying pan, and stir in the paste. Fry until fragrant. Add the shrimp paste, tamarind and sugar and cook, stirring, until the mixture darkens. Set aside to cool.

3 In a bowl, pound the shrimps and scallops together to form a paste, or whizz them in an electric blender or food processor. Add the spice paste, then the flour and baking powder, and beat until blended. Chill in the refrigerator for 1 hour. If using wooden skewers, soak them in water for about 30 minutes.

4 Meanwhile, prepare the barbecue, or, if you are using the grill (broiler), preheat for 5 minutes. Using your fingers, scoop up lumps of the shellfish paste and wrap it around the skewers.

5 Place each skewer on the barbecue or under the grill and cook for 3 minutes on each side, until golden brown. Serve with the lime wedges to squeeze over them.

Prawns in Sherry Energy 79kcal/325kJ; Protein 4.3g; Carbohydrate 0.1g, of which sugars 0.1g; Fat 5.9g, of which saturates 0.9g; Cholesterol 16mg; Calcium 28mg; Fibre 0g; Sodium 306mg.
Spicy Shrimp Satay Energy 220kcal/922kJ; Protein 27.1g; Carbohydrate 11.5g, of which sugars 1g; Fat 7.3g, of which saturates 1g; Cholesterol 151mg; Calcium 99mg; Fibre 1.5g; Sodium 249mg.

Saigon Sizzling Crêpes

These crêpes are made with coconut milk and filled with prawns and vegetables.

Makes 4 large or 8 small

115g/4oz/½ cup minced (ground) pork
15ml/1 tbsp nuoc mam
2 garlic cloves, crushed
175g/6oz/⅔ cup button (white) mushrooms, finely sliced
about 60ml/4 tbsp vegetable oil
1 onion, finely sliced
1–2 green or red Thai chillies, seeded and finely sliced
115g/4oz prawns (shrimp), shelled and deveined
225g/8oz/1 cup beansprouts
1 small bunch of fresh coriander (cilantro), stalks removed, leaves roughly chopped
salt and ground black pepper
nuoc cham, to serve

For the batter

115g/4oz/1 cup rice flour
10ml/2 tsp ground turmeric
10ml/2 tsp curry powder
5ml/1 tsp sugar
2.5ml/½ tsp salt
300ml/½ pint/1¼ cups canned coconut milk
4 spring onions (scallions), trimmed and finely sliced

1 To make the batter, beat the rice flour, spices, sugar and salt with the coconut milk and 300ml/½ pint/1¼ cups water, until smooth and creamy. Stir in the spring onions and then leave to stand for 30 minutes. Meanwhile, in a bowl, mix the pork with the nuoc mam, garlic and seasoning and knead well. Lightly sauté the mushrooms in 15ml/1 tbsp of the oil and set aside.

2 Heat 10ml/2 tsp of the oil in a wide non-stick pan. Stir in a quarter of the onion and chilli, then add a quarter each of the pork mixture and the prawns. Pour in 150ml/¼ pint/⅔ cup of the batter, swirling the pan so that it spreads right to the edges.

3 Pile a quarter of the beansprouts and mushrooms on one side of the crêpe. Reduce the heat, cover and cook for 2–3 minutes. Uncover the pan and cook the crêpe for 2 minutes until brown.

4 Once it is nicely browned, sprinkle some coriander over the empty side of the crêpe and fold it over the beansprouts and mushrooms. Slide the crêpe on to a plate and keep warm while you make the remaining crêpes in the same way. Serve with nuoc cham for dipping.

Braised Turnip with Prawn and Mangetouts

This is an elegant dish in which three colours – the pink of the prawns, the white of the turnips and the green of the mangetouts – look fantastic at the table.

Serves 4

8 small turnips, peeled
600ml/1 pint/2½ cups second dashi stock, or the same amount of water and 7.5ml/1½ tsp dashi-no-moto
10ml/2 tsp shoyu (use the Japanese pale awakuchi soy sauce if available)
60ml/4 tbsp mirin
30ml/2 tbsp sake
16 medium raw tiger prawns (jumbo shrimp), heads and shells removed with tails intact
dash of rice vinegar
90g/3½oz mangetouts (snow peas)
5ml/1 tsp cornflour (cornstarch)
salt

1 Par-boil the turnips for 3 minutes. Drain, then place them side by side in a pan. Add the dashi stock and cover with a saucer to submerge the turnips. Bring to the boil, then add the shoyu, 5ml/1 tsp salt, the mirin and sake. Reduce the heat to low, cover and simmer for 30 minutes.

2 Insert a cocktail stick (toothpick) into the back of each prawn, and remove and discard the black vein. Blanch the prawns in boiling water with the vinegar until the colour just changes. Drain. Cook the mangetouts in lightly salted water for 3 minutes. Drain and set aside.

3 Remove the saucer from the turnips and add the prawns for 4 minutes to warm through. Remove the turnips, drain and place in bowls. Transfer the prawns to a small plate.

4 Mix the cornflour with 15ml/1 tbsp water and add to the pan that held the turnips. Increase the heat a little and shake the pan until the liquid thickens slightly.

5 Place the mangetouts on the turnips and arrange the prawns on top, then pour about 30ml/2 tbsp of the hot liquid from the pan into each bowl.

Saigon Crêpes Energy 379Kcal/1581kJ; Protein 18g; Carbohydrate 37g, of which sugars 9g; Fat 18g, of which saturates 3g; Cholesterol 77mg; Calcium 119mg; Fibre 3.2g; Sodium 0.5g.
Braised Turnip Energy 83kcal/ 351kJ; Protein 6.4g; Carbohydrate 12g, of which sugars 10.4g; Fat 0.6g, of which saturates 0g; Cholesterol 49mg; Calcium 92mg; Fibre 3.5g; Sodium 68mg.

Jumbo Shrimp with Piquant Tomato Sauce

This sauce, from Spain, is served with fish and seafood. It is made with sweet pepper, tomatoes, garlic and almonds, and it is a tasty appetizer.

Serves 4

24 raw king prawns (jumbo shrimp)
30–45ml/2–3 tbsp olive oil
flat leaf parsley, to garnish
lemon wedges, to serve

For the sauce

2 well-flavoured tomatoes
60ml/4 tbsp olive oil
1 onion, chopped
4 garlic cloves, chopped
1 canned pimiento, chopped
2.5ml/½ tsp dried chilli flakes or powder
75ml/5 tbsp fish stock
30ml/2 tbsp white wine
10 blanched almonds
15ml/1 tbsp red wine vinegar
salt

1 To make the sauce, immerse the tomatoes in boiling water for about 30 seconds, then refresh them under cold water. Peel away the skins and roughly chop the flesh.

2 Heat 30ml/2 tbsp of the oil in a pan, add the onion and three garlic cloves and cook until soft. Add the pimiento, tomatoes, chilli, fish stock and wine, then cover and simmer for 30 minutes.

3 Toast the almonds under the grill (broiler) until golden. Transfer to a blender or food processor and grind coarsely. Add the remaining 30ml/2 tbsp of oil, the vinegar and the last garlic clove and process until evenly combined. Add the tomato and pimiento sauce and process until smooth. Season with salt.

4 Remove the heads from the prawns leaving them otherwise unshelled and, with a sharp knife, slit each one down the back and remove the dark vein. Rinse and pat dry on kitchen paper. Preheat the grill.

5 Toss the prawns in olive oil, then spread out in the grill pan. Grill (broil) for about 2–3 minutes on each side, until pink. Arrange on a serving platter with the lemon wedges, and the sauce in a small bowl. Serve immediately, garnished with parsley.

Potted Prawns

The tiny brown prawns that were traditionally used for potting are very fiddly to peel. Since they are rare nowadays, it is easier to use peeled, cooked prawns instead.

Serves 4

225g/8oz/2 cups peeled prawns (shrimp)
225g/8oz/1 cup butter
pinch of ground mace
salt, to taste
cayenne pepper
dill sprigs, to garnish
lemon wedges and thin slices of brown bread and butter, to serve

1 Chop a quarter of the prawns. Melt 115g/4oz/½ cup of the butter slowly in a pan, carefully skimming off any foam that rises to the surface with a metal spoon.

2 Add the prawns, the mace, salt and cayenne pepper to the pan of melted butter and heat gently without boiling. Pour the prawns and butter mixture into four individual pots and set aside to cool.

3 Heat the remaining butter in a clean small pan, then carefully spoon the clear butter over the prawns in the pots, leaving behind the sediment.

4 Leave the pots until the butter is almost set, then place a dill sprig in the centre of each pot. Leave to set completely, then cover and chill.

5 Allow the prawns to come to room temperature, before serving with lemon wedges for squeezing over and thin slices of brown bread and butter.

Variation
If you prefer, gently heat the potted prawns in a low oven before serving. Make sure that the pots are heatpoof, and only heat for a few minutes until the butter starts to run.

Jumbo Shrimp Energy 298kcal/1241kJ; Protein 18.8g; Carbohydrate 28.1g, of which sugars 1.6g; Fat 12.1g, of which saturates 2g; Cholesterol 146mg; Calcium 102mg; Fibre 1.4g; Sodium 587mg.
Potted Prawns Energy 461kcal/1901kJ; Protein 10.3g; Carbohydrate 0.4g, of which sugars 0.4g; Fat 46.6g, of which saturates 29.4g; Cholesterol 230mg; Calcium 55mg; Fibre 0g; Sodium 448mg.

Sautéed Mussels with Garlic and Herbs

These mussels are served without their shells, in a delicious paprika-flavoured sauce. Eat them with cocktail sticks.

Serves 4

900g/2lb fresh mussels
1 lemon slice
90ml/6 tbsp olive oil
2 shallots, finely chopped
1 garlic clove, finely chopped
15ml/1 tbsp chopped fresh parsley
2.5ml/½ tsp sweet paprika
1.5ml/¼ tsp dried chilli flakes
parsley sprigs, to garnish

1 Scrub the mussels, discarding any damaged ones as well as any that are open and which do not close when tapped with the back of a knife.

2 Put the mussels in a large pan with 250ml/8fl oz/1 cup water and the slice of lemon. Bring to the boil and cook for 3–4 minutes, removing the mussels with a slotted spoon as they open and putting them in a bowl.

3 Discard any that remain closed. Using a sharp knife, cut the mussels out of the shells and drain on kitchen paper.

4 Heat the oil in a sauté pan, add the mussels and cook, stirring, for a minute. Remove from the pan.

5 Add the shallots and garlic and cook, covered, over a low heat, for about 5 minutes, until soft and tender. Stir in the parsley, paprika and chilli, then add the mussels with any juices. Cook briefly.

6 Remove the pan from the heat, cover and leave for 1–2 minutes to let the flavours mingle.

7 Pile the mussels into a large warmed bowl or spoon into individual bowls, garnish with parsley and serve immediately.

Mussels with Musselburgh Leeks

Musselburgh is a former fishing port near Edinburgh, famous for its oyster beds and its leeks – a short variety with huge green tops and an excellent flavour.

Serves 4

1.3kg/3lb mussels
1 leek, cut into 5cm/2in lengths
50g/2oz/¼ cup butter
1 onion, finely chopped
pinch of saffron threads
150ml/¼ pint/⅔ cup dry white wine
1 bay leaf
sprig of fresh thyme
6 black peppercorns
100ml/3½fl oz/scant ½ cup double (heavy) cream
ground black pepper
chopped fresh parsley, to garnish

1 Scrub the mussels in plenty of cold water and discard any that are broken or remain open when tapped lightly.

2 Remove the beard from the mussels by pulling hard towards the pointed tip of the mussel. Use a small, sharp knife to scrape off any barnacles.

3 Thoroughly wash the leek, discard any tough outer leaves and cut into fine strips or batons.

4 Melt the butter in a heavy pan, then sweat the onion gently until soft. Add the saffron threads and stir for a few minutes, then add the leek batons and allow to wilt slightly.

5 Add the mussels with the wine, herbs and peppercorns. Cover and steam over medium heat until the mussel shells open, about 5 minutes. Discard any that remain closed.

6 Remove the lid from the pan and add the cream. Simmer rapidly to allow the sauce to thicken slightly. Remove the bay leaf and thyme, and stir well to mix the leek around.

7 Ladle into warmed bowls and serve immediately, with a grind or two of black pepper and garnished with lots of chopped fresh parsley. Provide plenty of hot, crusty bread for mopping up the sauce.

Sautéed Mussels Energy 214kcal/888kJ; Protein 12g; Carbohydrate 1.3g, of which sugars 0.9g; Fat 17.9g, of which saturates 2.6g; Cholesterol 27mg; Calcium 145mg; Fibre 0.4g; Sodium 144mg.
Mussels Energy 332kcal/1379kJ; Protein 17.6g; Carbohydrate 1.9g, of which sugars 1.6g; Fat 25.7g, of which saturates 15.2g; Cholesterol 100mg; Calcium 214mg; Fibre 0.2g; Sodium 288mg.

Gratin of Mussels with Pesto

This is the perfect appetizer for serving when your time is short, since both the pesto and the mussels can be prepared in advance, and the dish assembled and cooked at the last minute.

Serves 4

36 large fresh mussels, scrubbed and bearded
105ml/7 tbsp dry white wine
60ml/4 tbsp finely chopped fresh flat leaf parsley
1 garlic clove, finely chopped
30ml/2 tbsp fresh white breadcrumbs
60ml/4 tbsp olive oil
chopped fresh basil, to garnish
crusty bread, to serve

For the pesto
2 fat garlic cloves, chopped
2.5ml/½ tsp coarse salt
100g/3¾oz/3 cups basil leaves
25g/1oz/¼ cup pine nuts, chopped
50g/2oz/⅔ cup freshly grated Parmesan cheese
120ml/4fl oz/½ cup extra virgin olive oil

1 Put the mussels in a pan with the wine, clamp on the lid and shake over high heat for 3–4 minutes until the mussels have opened. Discard any that remain closed.

2 As soon as the mussels are cool enough to handle, strain the cooking liquid and keep it for another recipe. Discard the empty half-shells. Arrange the mussels in their half-shells in a single layer in four individual gratin dishes. Cover and set aside.

3 To make the pesto, put the chopped garlic and salt in a mortar and pound to a purée with a pestle. Then add the basil leaves and chopped pine nuts and crush to a thick paste. Work in the Parmesan cheese and, finally, gradually drip in enough olive oil to make a smooth and creamy paste. Alternatively, use a food processor.

4 Spoon pesto over the mussels placed in gratin dishes. Mix the parsley, garlic and breadcrumbs. Sprinkle over the mussels. Drizzle with the oil.

5 Preheat the grill (broiler) to high. Stand the dishes on a baking sheet and grill (broil) for 3 minutes. Garnish with basil and serve with crusty bread.

Grilled Green Mussels with Cumin

Green-shelled mussels have a more distinctive flavour than the small, black variety, and turn this appetizer into something extra special.

Serves 4

75ml/5 tbsp fresh parsley leaves
45ml/3 tbsp fresh coriander (cilantro) leaves
1 garlic clove, crushed
pinch of ground cumin
25g/1oz/2 tbsp unsalted butter, softened
25g/1oz/½ cup fresh brown breadcrumbs
12 green mussels or 24 small mussels, on the half-shell
ground black pepper

1 Finely chop the fresh parsley and coriander leaves. Reserve about 30ml/2 tbsp of the chopped parsley to use as a garnish at the end of the preparation.

2 Place the remaining parsley, the coriander, garlic, ground cumin and butter in a mixing bowl and stir together with a wooden spoon until the ingredients are combined.

3 Stir the breadcrumbs into the bowl and season to taste with ground black pepper.

4 Preheat the grill (broiler). Spoon a little of the mixture on to each mussel and grill (broil) for 2 minutes. Serve immediately, garnished with the reserved fresh parsley.

Variation
The herbs can be varied depending on what is available. Either flat leaf parsley or curly parsley can be used. Simply double the amount of parsley if fresh coriander is not available

Cook's Tip
Check with your local fishmonger or fish market to see if they have green-shelled mussels. If unavailable, this dish is just as good made with the more common mussels with black shells.

Gratin Energy 454kcal/1876kJ; Protein 11.7g; Carbohydrate 7.2g, of which sugars 1.4g; Fat 40.4g, of which saturates 7.4g; Cholesterol 22mg; Calcium 277mg; Fibre 2g; Sodium 253mg.
Grilled Mussels Energy 87kcal/361kJ; Protein 3.4g; Carbohydrate 5.6g, of which sugars 0.5g; Fat 5.7g, of which saturates 3.4g; Cholesterol 22mg; Calcium 41mg; Fibre 0.8g; Sodium 147mg.

Steamed Green Mussels in Black Bean Sauce

Large green-shelled mussels are perfect for this delicious dish, although smaller ones will work just as well. Buy the cooked mussels on the half shell, and take care not to overcook them, or they will become tough and rubbery.

Serves 4

15ml/1 tbsp vegetable oil
2.5cm/1in piece fresh root ginger, finely chopped
2 garlic cloves, finely chopped
1 fresh red chilli, seeded and chopped
15ml/1 tbsp black bean sauce
15ml/1 tbsp sake or dry sherry
5ml/1 tsp caster (superfine) sugar
5ml/1 tsp sesame oil
10ml/2 tsp dark soy sauce
20 cooked (New Zealand) green-shelled mussels
2 spring onions (scallions), 1 shredded and 1 cut into fine rings

1 Heat the vegetable oil in a small frying pan until very hot. Fry the ginger, garlic and chilli with the black bean sauce for a few seconds, then add the sake or sherry and caster sugar and cook for 30 seconds more.

2 Remove the sauce from the heat and stir in the sesame oil and soy sauce. Mix thoroughly, using a pair of chopsticks or a wooden spoon.

3 Place a trivet in the base of a heavy pan, then pour in boiling water to a depth of 5cm/2in. Place the mussels on a heatproof plate that will fit over the trivet. Spoon over the sauce.

4 Sprinkle the spring onions over the mussels, cover the plate tightly with foil and place it on the trivet in the pan.

5 Steam the mussels over a high heat for about 10 minutes or until the mussels have heated through.

6 Lift the plate carefully out of the pan, remove the foil and serve immediately.

Mussels and Clams with Lemon Grass and Coconut Cream

Wine is seldom used in green curries but in this recipe it adds depth of flavour to the sauce.

Serves 6

1.8kg/4lb fresh mussels
450g/1lb baby clams
120ml/4fl oz/½ cup dry white wine
1 bunch spring onions (scallions), chopped
2 lemon grass stalks, chopped
6 kaffir lime leaves, chopped
10ml/2 tsp green curry paste
200ml/7fl oz/scant 1 cup coconut cream
30ml/2 tbsp chopped fresh coriander (cilantro)
salt and ground black pepper
garlic chives, to garnish

1 Clean the mussels by pulling off the beards, scrubbing the shells well and scraping off any barnacles with the blade of a knife. Scrub the clams. Discard any mussels or clams that are damaged or broken or which do not close immediately when tapped sharply.

2 Put the wine in a large pan with the spring onions, lemon grass and lime leaves. Stir in the curry paste. Simmer until the wine has almost evaporated.

3 Add the mussels and clams to the pan and increase the heat to high. Cover tightly and steam the shellfish for 5–6 minutes, until they open.

4 Using a slotted spoon, transfer the mussels and clams to a heated serving bowl, cover and keep hot. Discard any shellfish that remain closed. Strain the cooking liquid into a clean pan through a sieve (strainer) lined with muslin (cheesecloth) and simmer briefly to reduce to about 250ml/8fl oz/1 cup.

5 Stir the coconut cream and chopped coriander into the sauce and season with salt and pepper to taste. Heat through. Pour the sauce over the mussels and clams, garnish with the garlic chives and serve immediately.

Green Mussels Energy 218kcal/921kJ; Protein 27.2g; Carbohydrate 5.1g, of which sugars 2.5g; Fat 8.6g, of which saturates 1.2g; Cholesterol 60mg; Calcium 305mg; Fibre 0.5g; Sodium 852mg.
Mussels and Clams Energy 237kcal/993kJ; Protein 22.5g; Carbohydrate 2.8g, of which sugars 1.7g; Fat 13.8g, of which saturates 10.3g; Cholesterol 58mg; Calcium 238mg; Fibre 0.9g; Sodium 606mg.

Scallop and Mussel Kebabs

These delightfully crispy seafood skewers are served with hot toast spread with a lovely fresh herb butter, to make a sumptuous appetizer.

Serves 4

65g/2½oz/5 tbsp butter, at room temperature
30ml/2 tbsp fresh fennel or parsley, finely chopped
15ml/1 tbsp lemon juice
32 small scallops, removed from shells
24 large mussels, in the shell
8 bacon rashers
50g/2oz/1 cup fresh breadcrumbs
50ml/2fl oz/¼ cup olive oil
salt and ground black pepper
hot toast, to serve

1 Make the flavoured butter by combining the butter with the chopped herbs and lemon juice. Add salt and pepper to taste. Mix well and set aside.

2 In a small pan, cook the scallops in their own liquor until they begin to shrink. (If there is no scallop liquor – retained from the shells after shucking – use a little fish stock or white wine.) Drain the scallops well and then pat dry with kitchen paper.

3 Scrub the mussels well and remove their 'beards', then rinse under cold water. Place in a large pan with about 2.5cm/1in of water in the base. Cover and steam the mussels over a medium heat until they open. When cool enough to handle, remove them from their shells, and pat dry using kitchen paper. Discard any mussels that have not opened during cooking.

4 Take eight 15cm/6in wooden or metal skewers. Thread on each one, alternately, four scallops and three mussels. As you are doing this, weave a rasher of bacon between the seafood.

5 Preheat the grill (broiler). Spread the breadcrumbs on a plate. Brush the seafood with olive oil and roll in the crumbs to coat all over.

6 Place the skewers on the grill (broiler) rack. Cook until crisp and lightly browned, about 4–5 minutes on each side. Serve immediately with hot toast and the flavoured butter.

Spiced Clams

This modern appetizer uses Arab spicing to make a hot dip or sauce. Serve with plenty of fresh bread to mop up the delicious juices. Look out for Spanish clams – they tend to be larger than usual clams and go particularly well in this dish.

Serves 3–4

1 small onion, finely chopped
1 celery stick, sliced
2 garlic cloves, finely chopped
2.5cm/1in piece fresh root ginger, grated
30ml/2 tbsp olive oil
1.5ml/¼ tsp chilli powder
5ml/1 tsp ground turmeric
30ml/2 tbsp chopped fresh parsley
500g/1¼lb small clams, in the shell
30ml/2 tbsp dry white wine
salt and ground black pepper
celery leaves, to garnish
fresh bread, to serve

1 Place the onion, celery, garlic and ginger in a large pan, add the olive oil, spices and chopped parsley and stir-fry for about 5 minutes.

2 Add the clams to the pan and cook for 2 minutes. Add the wine, then cover and cook gently for 2–3 minutes, shaking the pan occasionally. Season with salt and pepper. Discard any clams whose shells remain closed.

3 Serve immediately, garnished with celery leaves and accompanied by fresh, crusty bread.

Cook's Tips

- *There are many different varieties of clam fished off the coast of Spain. One of the best is the almeja fina (the carpet shell clam), which is perfect used in this dish. It has a grooved brown shell with a yellow lattice pattern, which gives it its English name. In France it is known as the palourde, and in Italy it is called the vongola.*
- *Before cooking the clams, check that all the shells are closed and discard any that are not. Any clams that do not open during cooking should also be discarded.*

Scallop Kebabs Energy 506kcal/2108kJ; Protein 37.4g; Carbohydrate 14.4g, of which sugars 0.6g; Fat 33.6g, of which saturates 13.7g; Cholesterol 130mg; Calcium 75mg; Fibre 0.6g; Sodium 1414mg.
Spiced Clams Energy 92kcal/381kJ; Protein 6.5g; Carbohydrate 2.2g, of which sugars 1.1g; Fat 5.9g, of which saturates 0.9g; Cholesterol 25mg; Calcium 50mg; Fibre 0.7g; Sodium 458mg.

Grilled Oysters with Highland Heather Honey

Heather honey is very fragrant, because the pollen is gathered by bees late in the season when the heather on the moors is in full flower. Beekeepers in Scotland will take their hives up to the hills once the spring and early summer blossoms are over, so the flavour of the honey becomes more intense.

Serves 4

1 bunch spring onions (scallions), washed
20ml/4 tsp heather honey
10ml/2 tsp soy sauce
16 fresh oysters

1 Preheat the grill (broiler) to medium. Chop the spring onions finely, removing any coarser outer leaves.

2 Place the heather honey and soy sauce in a bowl and mix together. Then add the finely chopped spring onions and mix them in thoroughly.

3 Open the oysters with an oyster knife or a small, sharp knife, taking care to catch the liquid in a small bowl. Leave the oysters attached to one side of the shell. Strain the liquid to remove any pieces of broken shell, and set aside.

4 Place a large teaspoon of the honey and spring onion mixture on top of each oyster.

5 Place under the preheated grill until the mixture bubbles, which will take about 5 minutes. Take care when removing the oysters from the grill as the shells retain the heat quite well. Make sure that you don't lose any of the sauce from inside the oyster shells.

6 Allow the oysters to cool slightly before serving with slices of bread to soak up the juices. Either tip them straight into your mouth or lift them out with a spoon or fork.

Oysters Rockefeller

This is the perfect dish for those who prefer to eat their oysters lightly cooked. As a cheaper alternative, for those who are not as rich as Rockefeller, give mussels or clams the same treatment; they will also taste delicious.

Serves 6

450g/1lb/3 cups coarse sea salt, plus extra to serve
24 oysters, opened
115g/4oz/½ cup butter
2 shallots, finely chopped
500g/1¼lb spinach leaves, finely chopped
60ml/4 tbsp chopped fresh parsley
60ml/4 tbsp chopped celery leaves
90ml/6 tbsp fresh white or wholemeal (whole-wheat) breadcrumbs
10–20ml/2–4 tsp vodka
cayenne pepper
sea salt and ground black pepper
lemon or lime wedges, to serve

1 Preheat the oven to 220°C/425°F/Gas 7. Make a bed of coarse salt on two large baking sheets. Set the oysters in the half-shell in the bed of salt to keep them steady. Set aside.

2 Melt the butter in a large frying pan. Add the chopped shallots and cook them, stirring occasionally, over low heat for about 2–3 minutes until they are softened but not coloured. Stir in the spinach and let it wilt.

3 Add the parsley, celery leaves and breadcrumbs to the pan and fry gently for 5 minutes. Season with salt, ground black pepper and cayenne pepper.

4 Divide the stuffing among the oysters. Drizzle a few drops of vodka over each oyster. Bake in the preheated oven for about 5 minutes until the oysters are bubbling and golden brown. Serve on a heated platter on a shallow salt bed with lemon or lime wedges.

Cook's Tip

Frozen chopped spinach can be used. Thaw it in a colander over a bowl and press out as much liquid as possible.

Grilled Oysters Energy 81kcal/343kJ; Protein 9.2g; Carbohydrate 9.1g, of which sugars 6.9g; Fat 1.2g, of which saturates 0.2g; Cholesterol 46mg; Calcium 121mg; Fibre 0.3g; Sodium 588mg.
Oysters Rockefeller Energy 210kcal/867kJ; Protein 6.4g; Carbohydrate 3.4g, of which sugars 2.1g; Fat 17g, of which saturates 10.1g; Cholesterol 60mg; Calcium 211mg; Fibre 2.3g; Sodium 406mg.

Coquilles St Jacques

A classic French appetizer that calls for the best quality scallops possible to ensure a truly wonderful result. You will need four scallop shells to serve these.

Serves 4

450g/1lb potatoes, chopped
50g/2oz/4 tbsp butter
4 large or 8 small scallops
120ml/4fl oz/½ cup fish stock

For the sauce

25g/1oz/2 tbsp butter
25g/1oz/¼ cup plain (all-purpose) flour
300ml/½ pint/1¼ cups milk
30ml/2 tbsp single (light) cream
115g/4oz/1 cup mature (sharp) Cheddar cheese, grated
salt and ground black pepper
dill sprigs, to garnish
grilled lemon wedges, to serve

1 Preheat the oven to 200°C/400°F/Gas 6. Place the chopped potatoes in a large pan, cover with plenty of water and boil for about 10–15 minutes or until tender. Drain and mash well with the butter.

2 Spoon the mixture into a piping (pastry) bag fitted with a star nozzle. Pipe the potatoes around the outside of a cleaned scallop shell. Repeat the process, making four in total.

3 Simmer the scallops in a little fish stock for 3 minutes or until they are just firm. Drain well and slice the scallops finely. Set them aside.

4 To make the sauce, melt the butter in a small pan, add the flour and cook over a low heat for a couple of minutes. Gradually add the milk and cream, stirring constantly and cook until thickened.

5 Stir in the cheese and cook until melted. Season to taste. Spoon a little sauce in the base of each shell. Divide the scallops between the shells and then pour the remaining sauce over the scallops.

6 Bake the scallops in the preheated oven for approximately 10 minutes or until golden. Garnish with the dill sprigs. Serve with grilled (broiled) lemon wedges.

Garlic Scallops and Prawns

Scallops and prawns provide a healthy meal in next to no time. This particular recipe comes from France and is popular in Provence. It is very quick and easy to make and is perfect for a summer appetizer or a quick meal before a night out in town, as it is lovely and light, and easily digested.

Serves 2–4

6 large shelled scallops
6–8 large raw prawns (jumbo shrimp), peeled
plain (all-purpose) flour, for dusting
30–45ml/2–3 tbsp olive oil
1 garlic clove, finely chopped
15ml/1 tbsp chopped fresh basil
30–45ml/2–3 tbsp lemon juice
salt and ground black pepper

1 Rinse the scallops under cold running water to remove any sand or grit. Drain, then pat dry using kitchen paper. Cut them in half crossways.

2 Season the scallops and prawns with salt and ground black pepper and dust them lightly with flour. Heat the oil in a large, heavy frying pan over high heat. When hot, add the scallops and prawns.

3 Reduce the heat slightly and cook for 2 minutes, then turn the scallops and prawns and add the garlic and basil, shaking the pan to distribute them evenly.

4 Cook for a further 2 minutes, until the scallops are golden and just firm to the touch. Sprinkle over the lemon juice and toss to blend. Spoon into a heated dish or on to individual plates and serve immediately.

Cook's Tips

• Like oysters, scallops are traditionally best when there is an 'r' in the month. Frozen scallops are available, but their quality is not as good as the fresh ones.

• Scallops should be cooked for the shortest possible time, as they become leathery when overcooked. The bright red corals require even less time than the nuggets of white flesh.

Coquilles Energy 466kcal/1948kJ; Protein 24.2g; Carbohydrate 28.8g, of which sugars 5.7g; Fat 28.6g, of which saturates 18.3g; Cholesterol 103mg; Calcium 342mg; Fibre 1.3g; Sodium 496mg.
Garlic Scallops Energy 159kcal/664kJ; Protein 16.4g; Carbohydrate 2.9g, of which sugars 0.2g; Fat 9.2g, of which saturates 1.4g; Cholesterol 72mg; Calcium 51mg; Fibre 0.4g; Sodium 140mg.

King Scallops with Bacon

This is one of the simplest and tastiest appetizers, suitable for any occasion. It combines streaky bacon and scallops with brown butter, which has just begun to burn very slightly. It gives the dish a lovely nutty smell, which is why the French refer to this dish as 'noisette', which means nutty.

Serves 4

12 rashers (strips) streaky (fatty) bacon
12 scallops
225g/8oz/1 cup unsalted butter
juice of 1 lemon
30ml/2 tbsp chopped fresh flat leaf parsley
ground black pepper

1 Preheat the grill (broiler) to high. Wrap a rasher of bacon around each scallop so it goes over the top and not round the side.

2 Cut the butter into chunks and put it in a small pan over low heat.

3 Meanwhile grill (broil) the scallops with the bacon facing up so it protects the meat. The bacon fat will help to cook the scallops. This will take only a few minutes; once they are cooked set aside and keep warm.

4 Allow the butter in the pan to turn a nutty brown colour, gently swirling it from time to time. Just as it is foaming and darkening, take off the heat and add the lemon juice. Be warned, it will bubble up quite dramatically.

5 Place the scallops on warmed serving plates, dress with plenty of chopped fresh parsley and pour the butter over. Serve immediately.

Cook's Tip

Get the scallops on to warmed plates just as the butter is coming to the right colour, then add the lemon juice.

Scallops Wrapped in Prosciutto

This is a delicious summer recipe for an appetizer, which is ideal for cooking over the barbecue. It is also ideal for cooking under the grill if the weather is bad.

Serves 4

24 medium scallops, without corals, prepared for cooking
lemon juice
8–12 slices prosciutto
olive oil, for brushing
ground black pepper
lemon wedges, to serve

1 Preheat the grill (broiler) or prepare a charcoal fire. Sprinkle the scallops with lemon juice. Cut the prosciutto into long strips. Wrap one strip around each scallop. Thread them on to eight metal skewers.

2 Brush the skewers with olive oil. Arrange them on a baking sheet if grilling (broiling). Cook about 10cm/4in from the heat under a preheated grill (broiler) for 3–5 minutes on each side or until the scallops are opaque and tender. Alternatively, cook the skewers over charcoal, turning them once, until the scallops are opaque and tender.

3 Set two skewers on each plate. Sprinkle the scallops with ground black pepper and serve immediately with lemon wedges for squeeezing over.

Cook's Tips

• The edible parts of the scallop are the round white muscle and the coral or roe. When preparing fresh scallops, keep the skirt – the frilly part – for making home-made fish stock.
• Use a good quality Italian prosciutto such as Parma ham. If that is not available, choose a Spanish variety such as Serrano ham, which is dry-cured and air-dried in a similar manner to the Italian prosciuttos.
• Use wooden skewers if you don't have metal ones, but soak them in water for 30 minutes to prevent them burning.

King Scallops Energy 665kcal/2749kJ; Protein 24.4g; Carbohydrate 2.7g, of which sugars 0.6g; Fat 62g, of which saturates 34.7g; Cholesterol 189mg; Calcium 51mg; Fibre 0.5g; Sodium 1240mg.
Scallops Wrapped Energy 224kcal/942kJ; Protein 33.6g; Carbohydrate 4.5g, of which sugars 0.3g; Fat 8.1g, of which saturates 1.6g; Cholesterol 73mg; Calcium 38mg; Fibre 0g; Sodium 525mg.

Crab and Cucumber Wraps with Hoisin Sauce

This dish is a modern twist on the ever-popular Chinese classic, crispy Peking duck with pancakes. In this quick and easy version, crisp, refreshing cucumber and full-flavoured dressed crab are delicious with spicy-sweet hoisin sauce in warm tortilla wraps. Serve the wraps as an appetizer for four people, or as a main course for two.

Serves 2–4
½ cucumber
1 medium dressed crab
4 small wheat tortillas
120ml/8 tbsp hoisin sauce
ground black pepper

1 Cut the cucumber into small even batons and set aside until preparing the wraps. Scoop the dressed crab into a small mixing bowl, add a little ground black pepper and mix lightly to combine.

2 Heat the tortillas gently, one at a time, in a heavy frying pan until they begin to colour on each side. Keep them warm by covering them in a clean dish towel.

3 Spread a tortilla with 30ml/2 tbsp hoisin sauce, then sprinkle with one-quarter of the cucumber.

4 Arrange one-quarter of the seasoned crab meat down the centre of each tortilla and roll up. Repeat with the remaining ingredients. Serve immediately.

Variations
- *Roll up finely sliced spring onions (scallions) in the wraps along with the crab meat and cucumber, if you like.*
- *For a more authentic Chinese dish, use rice wrappers instead of tortillas.*

Dressed Crab with Asparagus

Crab is the juiciest and most flavoursome seafood, possibly better even than lobster and considerably cheaper. This appetizer is a combination of two paragons in the culinary world: crab as the king of seafood and asparagus as a prince among vegetables.

Serves 4
24 asparagus spears
4 dressed crabs
30ml/2 tbsp mayonnaise
15ml/1 tbsp chopped fresh parsley

1 Cut off and discard any woody stems from the asparagus. Heat a pan of water to boiling point. Reduce the heat to a simmer and add the asparagus spears for 4–6 minutes, depending on their size.

2 When cooked, plunge the stems into iced water to stop them from cooking any further. Drain them when cold and pat dry with kitchen paper.

3 Scoop out the white crab meat from the shells and claws and place it in a bowl. If fresh crabs are not available, you can use the same quantity of canned or frozen white crab meat, if you like.

4 Add the mayonnaise and chopped fresh parsley to the bowl of crab meat and combine with a fork. Place the mixture into the crab shells and add six asparagus spears per serving. Serve with crusty bread.

Cook's Tip
Asparagus is highly prized, partly because of its wonderfully delicate and earthy flavour, and partly because in many parts of the world it only has a short growing season. In north-western Europe it is only available for a few weeks in spring, so make the most of it during the season and prepare this delicious appetizer.

Crab Wraps Energy 484kcal/2046kJ; Protein 33.5g; Carbohydrate 74.8g, of which sugars 15.6g; Fat 7.6g, of which saturates 0.9g; Cholesterol 90mg; Calcium 162mg; Fibre 3.2g; Sodium 1559mg.
Dressed Crab Energy 207kcal/859kJ; Protein 19.5g; Carbohydrate 3g, of which sugars 2.8g; Fat 13g, of which saturates 1.9g; Cholesterol 72mg; Calcium 157mg; Fibre 2.6g; Sodium 540mg.

Chilli Crabs

The essential ingredients of this delicious crab dish owe more to South-east Asian cuisine than India, and it is not surprising to discover that it comes from the eastern part of the country.

Serves 4

2 cooked crabs, about 675g/1½lb altogether
1cm/½in cube shrimp paste
2 garlic cloves
2 fresh red chillies, seeded, or 5ml/1 tsp chopped chilli from a jar
1cm/½in fresh root ginger, peeled and sliced
60ml/4 tbsp sunflower oil
300ml/½ pint/1¼ cups tomato ketchup
15ml/1 tbsp soft dark brown sugar
150ml/¼ pint/⅔ cup warm water
4 spring onions (scallions), chopped
cucumber chunks and hot toast, to serve (optional)

1 Remove the large claws of one crab and turn it on to its back, with the head facing away from you. Use your thumbs to push the body up from the main shell. Discard the stomach sac and 'dead men's fingers', that is, lungs and any green matter. Leave the creamy brown meat in the shell, and cut the shell in half with a cleaver or strong knife. Cut the body section in half and crack the claws with a sharp blow from a hammer or cleaver. Avoid splintering the claws. Repeat with the other crab.

2 Grind the shrimp paste, garlic, chillies and ginger to a paste in a food processor or with a pestle and mortar.

3 Heat a karahi or wok and add the oil. Fry the spice paste, stirring constantly, without browning.

4 Stir in the tomato ketchup, sugar and water and mix the sauce well. When just boiling, add all the crab pieces and toss in the sauce until well coated and hot. Serve in a large bowl, sprinkled with the chopped spring onions. Place in the centre of the table for everyone to help themselves. Accompany this dish with cool cucumber chunks and hot toast for mopping up the sauce, if you like.

Soft-shell Crabs with Chilli and Salt

If fresh soft-shell crabs are unavailable, you can buy frozen ones in Asian supermarkets. Allow two small crabs per serving, or one if they are large.

Serves 4

8 small soft-shell crabs, thawed if frozen
50g/2oz/½ cup plain (all-purpose) flour
60ml/4 tbsp groundnut (peanut) or vegetable oil
2 large fresh red chillies, or 1 green and 1 red chilli, seeded and thinly sliced
4 spring onions (scallions) or a small bunch of garlic chives, chopped
sea salt and ground black pepper

To serve

shredded lettuce, mooli (daikon) and carrot
light soy sauce, for dipping

1 Pat the crabs dry with kitchen paper. Season the flour with ground black pepper and coat the dried crabs lightly with the mixture.

2 Heat the oil in a shallow pan until very hot, then put in the crabs (you may need to do this in two batches). Fry for 2–3 minutes on each side, until the crabs are golden brown but still juicy in the middle. Drain the cooked crabs on kitchen paper and keep hot.

3 Add the sliced chillies and spring onions or garlic chives to the oil remaining in the pan and cook gently for about 2 minutes. Sprinkle over a generous pinch of salt, then spread the chilli and onion mixture on to the crabs.

4 Mix the shredded lettuce, mooli and carrot together. Arrange on plates, top each portion with two crabs and serve, with a bowl of light soy sauce for dipping.

Cook's Tip
Look for mooli (daikon) in Asian food stores. If you can't find any, use celeriac instead.

Chilli Crabs Energy 232kcal/971kJ; Protein 8.5g; Carbohydrate 21.8g, of which sugars 21g; Fat 12.9g, of which saturates 1.5g; Cholesterol 19mg; Calcium 28mg; Fibre 0.8g; Sodium 1347mg.
Soft-shell Crabs Energy 306kcal/1280kJ; Protein 37.6g; Carbohydrate 10g, of which sugars 0.5g; Fat 13g, of which saturates 1.5g; Cholesterol 144mg; Calcium 262mg; Fibre 0.5g; Sodium 1101mg.

Asian-style Crab Cakes

You could serve these patties as a simple supper, or an appetizer for eight people. Use a mixture of white and brown crab meat, as the dark adds a depth of flavour and texture. Serve with sweet chilli sauce.

Serves 8

450g/1lb/2⅔ cups fresh crab meat, white and brown
15ml/1 tbsp grated fresh root ginger
15–30ml/1–2 tbsp plain (all-purpose) flour
60ml/4 tbsp sunflower oil
salt and ground black pepper
sweet chilli sauce, to serve

1 Put the white and brown crab meat in a bowl and add the ginger, some salt and ground black pepper and the flour. Stir well until thoroughly mixed.

2 Using your hands, divide the mixture into 16 equal-sized pieces. Shape each piece roughly into patties.

3 Heat the sunflower oil in a frying pan and add the patties, four at a time. Cook for about 2–3 minutes on each side, until golden brown.

4 Remove the cooked cakes from the pan with a metal spatula and leave to drain on kitchen paper for a few minutes.

5 Keep the cooked crab cakes warm in a low oven while you cook the remaining patties in the same way. Serve immediately with a bowl of sweet chilli sauce for dipping.

Cook's Tips
• *The crab mixture may stick to your hands while trying to shape the cakes. If this happens, then keep dampening your hands slightly with a little water.*
• *If fresh crab meat is not available, you can use the same quantity of canned or frozen meat.*

Japanese-style Crab Cakes with Ginger and Wasabi

Wasabi – a traditional Japanese flavouring – is available as a powder or a paste. It is very hot so should be used sparingly.

Serves 6

450g/1lb fresh dressed crab meat (brown and white meat)
30ml/2 tbsp mayonnaise
4 spring onions (scallions), finely chopped, plus extra to garnish
2.5cm/1in piece of fresh root ginger, grated
30ml/2 tbsp chopped fresh coriander (cilantro)
2.5–5ml/½–1 tsp wasabi paste
15ml/1 tbsp sesame oil
salt and ground black pepper
50–115g/2–4oz/1–2 cups fresh breadcrumbs
oil, for frying
lettuce leaves, fresh chilli and lime slices, to serve

For the dipping sauce
5ml/1 tsp wasabi paste
90ml/6 tbsp shoyu

1 Make the dipping sauce by mixing the wasabi and the shoyu in a small bowl. Set aside.

2 Mix the crab meat, mayonnaise, spring onions, ginger, coriander, wasabi paste and sesame oil in a bowl. Stir in a little salt and pepper and add enough fresh breadcrumbs to make a mixture that is firm enough to form patties, but is not too stiff.

3 Chill the crab mixture for 30 minutes, then use your hands to form it into 12 cakes. Heat a shallow layer of oil in a frying pan and fry the crab cakes for about 3–4 minutes on each side, until browned.

4 Serve the crab cakes with lettuce leaves and lime slices, accompanied by the dipping sauce, garnished with chilli and spring onion slices.

Cook's Tip
You can increase the amount of wasabi in the dipping sauce if you prefer a little more heat.

Asian-style Crab Cakes Energy 67kcal/280kJ; Protein 5.7g; Carbohydrate 1.5g, of which sugars 0g; Fat 4.3g, of which saturates 0.5g; Cholesterol 20mg; Calcium 3mg; Fibre 0.1g; Sodium 119mg.
Japanese-style Cakes Energy 190kcal/795kJ; Protein 16.2g; Carbohydrate 7.1g, of which sugars 0.6g; Fat 11g, of which saturates 1.4g; Cholesterol 55mg; Calcium 35mg; Fibre 0.3g; Sodium 388mg.

Potted Salmon with Lemon and Dill

This sophisticated appetizer would be ideal for a dinner party or other special occasion. Preparation is done well in advance, so you can concentrate on making the main course and spending more time with your dinner guests

Serves 6
350g/12oz cooked salmon, skinned
150g/5oz/⅔ cup butter, softened
rind and juice of 1 large lemon
10ml/2 tsp chopped fresh dill
75g/3oz/¾ cup flaked (sliced) almonds, roughly chopped
salt and ground white pepper

1 Flake the cooked salmon into a bowl and then place in a food processor or blender.

2 Add two-thirds of the butter, the lemon rind and juice, half the chopped fresh dill, and plenty of salt and ground black pepper to the salmon in the food processor or blender. Process the mixture until it is quite smooth.

3 Mix the flaked almonds into the salmon mixture. Check the seasoning, adding more salt or pepper if necessary. Spoon the fish mixture into six small ramekins, and pack it down using the back of a spoon.

4 Sprinkle the remaing dill over the top of each ramekin. Clarify the remaining butter by heating it gently and pour over each ramekin to make a seal. Leave to set, then chill in the refrigerator. Serve with crudités, or slices of toasted bread.

Cook's Tip
If you cannot find any fresh dill, then you can substitute the same quantity of dried dill.

Salmon Rice Triangles

These rice shapes – onigiri – are very popular in Japan. You can put anything you like in the rice, so you could invent your own onigiri.

Serves 4
1 salmon steak
15ml/1 tbsp salt
450g/1lb/4 cups freshly cooked sushi rice
¼ cucumber, seeded and cut into matchsticks
½ sheet yaki-nori seaweed, cut into four equal strips
white and black sesame seeds, for sprinkling on the salmon onigiri before serving

1 Grill (broil) the salmon steaks on each side, until the flesh flakes easily when tested with the tip of a sharp knife. Set aside to cool while you make other onigiri. When the salmon is cold, flake it, discarding any skin and bones.

2 Put the salt in a bowl. Spoon an eighth of the cooked rice into a small rice bowl. Make a hole in the middle of the rice and put in a few cucumber matchsticks. Smooth the rice over to cover the cucumber completely.

3 Wet the palms of both hands with cold water, then rub the salt evenly on to your palms.

4 Empty the rice and cucumbers from the bowl on to one hand. Use both hands to shape the rice into a triangular shape, using firm but not heavy pressure, and making sure that the cucumber is encased by the rice. Make three more rice triangles the same way.

5 Mix the flaked salmon into the remaining rice, then shape it into triangles as before.

6 Wrap a strip of yaki-nori around each of the cucumber triangles. Sprinkle sesame seeds on the salmon triangles.

7 Arrange the onigiri on a plate, with alternate triangles inverted for best presentation. Serve immediately.

Potted Salmon Energy 370kcal/1531kJ; Protein 14.8g; Carbohydrate 1.2g, of which sugars 0.9g; Fat 34.1g, of which saturates 14.7g; Cholesterol 82mg; Calcium 64mg; Fibre 1.4g; Sodium 182mg.
Rice Triangles Energy 342kcal/1427kJ; Protein 10.5g; Carbohydrate 29.8g, of which sugars 1.9g; Fat 20.7g, of which saturates 7.8g; Cholesterol 37mg; Calcium 140mg; Fibre 1.1g; Sodium 38mg.

Rice Cakes with Smoked Salmon

These elegant rice cakes are made using a risotto base. You could skip this stage and use leftover risotto, if you have any. Alternatively, use leftover long grain rice and add extra flavour with spring onions.

Serves 4

30ml/2 tbsp olive oil
1 medium onion, chopped
225g/8oz/generous 1 cup risotto rice
about 90ml/6 tbsp white wine
about 750ml/1 1/4 pints/3 cups fish or chicken stock
15g/1/2oz/2 tbsp dried porcini mushrooms, soaked for 10 minutes in warm water to cover
15ml/1 tbsp chopped fresh parsley
15ml/1 tbsp chopped fresh chives
5ml/1 tsp chopped fresh dill
1 egg, lightly beaten
about 45ml/3 tbsp ground rice, plus extra for dusting
oil, for frying
60ml/4 tbsp sour cream
175g/6oz smoked salmon
salt and ground black pepper
radicchio and oakleaf salad, tossed in French dressing, to serve

1 Heat the olive oil in a pan and fry the onion for 3–4 minutes until soft. Add the rice and cook, stirring, until the grains are thoroughly coated in oil. Pour in the wine and stock, a little at a time, stirring constantly over a gentle heat until each quantity of liquid has been absorbed before adding more.

2 Drain the mushrooms and chop them into small pieces. When the rice is tender, and all the liquid has been absorbed, stir in the mushrooms, parsley, chives, dill and seasoning. Remove from the heat and set aside for a few minutes to cool.

3 Add the beaten egg, then stir in enough ground rice to bind the mixture – it should be soft but manageable. Dust your hands with ground rice and shape the mixture into four patties, about 13cm/5in in diameter and about 2cm/3/4in thick.

4 Heat the oil in a shallow pan and fry the rice cakes, in batches if necessary, for 4–5 minutes until evenly browned on both sides. Drain on kitchen paper and cool slightly. Place each rice cake on a plate and top with 15ml/1 tbsp sour cream. Twist two or three thin slices of smoked salmon on top, and serve with a dressed salad garnish.

Smoked Salmon with Warm Potato Cakes

Although the ingredients are timeless, this combination makes an excellent modern dish, which is deservedly popular as a first course or as a substantial canapé to serve with drinks. It also makes a perfect brunch dish, served with lightly scrambled eggs and freshly squeezed orange juice. Choose wild fish if possible.

Serves 6

450g/1lb potatoes, cooked and mashed
75g/3oz/2/3 cup plain (all-purpose) flour
2 eggs, beaten
2 spring onions (scallions), chopped
a little freshly grated nutmeg
50g/2oz/1/4 cup butter, melted
150ml/1/4 pint/2/3 cup sour cream
12 slices of smoked salmon
salt and ground black pepper
chopped fresh chives, to garnish

1 Put the potatoes, flour, eggs and spring onions into a large bowl. Season with salt, black pepper and a little nutmeg, and add half the butter. Mix thoroughly and shape into 12 small potato cakes.

2 Heat the remaining butter in a non-stick frying pan and cook the potato cakes until browned on both sides.

3 To serve, mix the sour cream with some salt and pepper. Fold a piece of smoked salmon and place on top of each potato cake. Top the salmon with the cream and then the chives and serve immediately.

Cook's Tip
If it is more convenient, you can make the potato cakes in advance and keep them overnight in the refrigerator. When required, warm them through in a hot oven 15 minutes before assembling and serving.

Rice Cakes Energy 475kcal/1978kJ; Protein 18.3g; Carbohydrate 55.9g, of which sugars 1.6g; Fat 17.8g, of which saturates 4.1g; Cholesterol 72mg; Calcium 56mg; Fibre 0.6g; Sodium 849mg.
Smoked Salmon Energy 326kcal/1365kJ; Protein 21.9g; Carbohydrate 22.9g, of which sugars 2.3g; Fat 17g, of which saturates 8.6g; Cholesterol 119mg; Calcium 70mg; Fibre 1.2g; Sodium 1315mg.

Smoked Salmon Pancakes with Pesto

These pancakes are easy to prepare and are perfect for an appetizer for a special occasion, or to serve as nibbles at a drinks party.

Serves 4–6

120ml/4fl oz/½ cup milk
115g/4oz/1 cup self-raising (self-rising) flour
1 egg
30ml/2 tbsp pesto sauce
vegetable oil, for frying
200ml/7fl oz/scant 1 cup crème fraîche
75g/3oz smoked salmon, cut into 1cm/½in strips
15g/½oz/2 tbsp pine nuts, toasted
salt and ground black pepper
12–16 fresh basil sprigs, to garnish

1 Pour half of the milk into a medium mixing bowl. Sift in the flour and add the egg, pesto sauce and salt and ground black pepper to taste. Using a wooden spoon, mix the ingredients to a smooth batter.

2 Add the remainder of the milk to the batter and stir until evenly blended.

3 Heat the vegetable oil in a large, heavy frying pan. Spoon the pancake mixture into the heated oil in small heaps. Allow about 30 seconds for the pancakes to rise, then turn them over and cook briefly on the other side until just golden.

4 Remove the cooked pancakes from the pan and keep warm. Continue cooking them in batches until all the batter has been used up. The mixture should make between 12 and 16 pancakes in total.

5 Arrange the pancakes on a large serving plate and top each one with a spoonful of crème fraîche.

6 Cut the smoked salmon into 1cm/½in strips and arrange the pieces on top of each pancake. Sprinkle each pancake with a few pine nuts and garnish with a small sprig of fresh basil. Serve immediately.

Salt-cured Salmon

This is a delicious way of serving salmon as an appetizer. The fish develops a lovely spicy, salty flavour.

Serves 10

50g/2oz sea salt
45ml/3 tbsp caster (superfine) sugar
5ml/1 tsp chilli powder
5ml/1 tsp ground black pepper
45ml/3 tbsp chopped fresh coriander (cilantro)
2 salmon fillets, about 250g/9oz each
sprigs of fresh flat leaf parsley, to garnish
garlic mayonnaise, to serve

1 Mix together the salt, sugar, chilli powder, pepper and coriander in a small bowl. Rub the mixture into the flesh of each salmon fillet with your hands.

2 Place one of the fillets, skin side down, in a shallow glass dish. Place the other fillet on top, with the skin side up. Cover with foil, then place a weight on top.

3 Place the dish in the refrigerator for 48 hours, turning the fish every 8 hours or so and basting it well with the liquid that forms in the dish.

4 Drain the salmon well and transfer to a board. Using a very sharp knife, remove the skin and slice the salmon diagonally, in wafer-thin slices. Arrange on plates and garnish with sprigs of parsley. Serve with garlic mayonnaise.

Cook's Tip

Make the most of the leftover salmon skin by turning it into delicious crunchy strips: after slicing the salt-cured salmon, scrape any remaining fish off the skin and discard. Cut the skin into 1cm/½in wide strips. Cook for 1 minute in hot oil until crisp and browned. Drain thoroughly on kitchen paper and leave to cool. You can then serve the crisp strips of skin as an usual garnish for the slices of salt-cured salmon or as a tapas dish in its own right.

Smoked Salmon Energy 328kcal/1362kJ; Protein 8g; Carbohydrate 16.5g, of which sugars 2.2g; Fat 26g, of which saturates 10.9g; Cholesterol 48mg; Calcium 143mg; Fibre 0.7g; Sodium 350mg.
Salt-cured Salmon Energy 115kcal/479kJ; Protein 9.4g; Carbohydrate 6g, of which sugars 6g; Fat 6.1g, of which saturates 1.1g; Cholesterol 25mg; Calcium 26mg; Fibre 0.2g; Sodium 2016mg.

Smoked Fish Platter

A wide variety of smoked fish is available today – trout, salmon and mackerel feature in this simple appetizer – but any smoked fish can be used.

Serves 4

½ Charentais melon
½ cantaloupe melon
50g/2oz rocket (arugula)
75g/3oz hot-smoked trout fillets
75g/3oz smoked salmon
75g/3oz smoked mackerel with peppercorns

For the dressing

75ml/5 tbsp extra virgin olive oil
15ml/1 tbsp white wine vinegar
5ml/1 tsp wholegrain mustard
5ml/1 tsp clear honey
salt and ground black pepper

1 Scoop out and discard all the seeds from the Charentais and cantaloupe melons and cut each melon into four or eight slices, leaving the skin on. Divide the melon slices among four small serving plates, placing the slices neatly to one side.

2 Add a quarter of the rocket leaves to each plate, arranging them on the opposite side to the melon.

3 Make the honey dressing by combining all the ingredients in a small jug (pitcher). Add plenty of salt and black pepper and whisk well with a fork until the dressing is well blended and emulsified.

4 Divide the smoked fish into four portions, breaking or cutting the trout fillets and smoked salmon into bitesize pieces. Peel the skin from the mackerel, then break up the flesh.

5 Arrange the trout fillets, smoked salmon and mackerel on top of the rocket and melon on each platter. Drizzle the dressing over and serve immediately.

Variation
As long as the total amount of smoked fish is 250g/9oz, any varieties can be used. Try smoked eel for a change.

Smoked Salmon and Rice Salad Parcels

Feta, cucumber and tomatoes give a Greek flavour to the salad in these parcels, a combination which goes well with the rice, especially if a little wild rice is added.

Serves 4

175g/6oz/scant 1 cup mixed wild rice and basmati rice
8 slices smoked salmon, about 350g/12oz total
10cm/4in piece of cucumber, finely diced
about 225g/8oz feta cheese, cubed
8 cherry tomatoes, quartered
30ml/2 tbsp mayonnaise
10ml/2 tsp fresh lime juice
15ml/1 tbsp chopped fresh chervil
salt and ground black pepper
lime slices and fresh chervil, to garnish

1 Cook the rice according to the instructions on the packet. Drain, turn into a bowl and allow to cool.

2 Line four ramekins with clear film (plastic wrap), then line each ramekin with two slices of smoked salmon. Reserve any extra pieces of smoked salmon for the tops of the parcels.

3 Add the cucumber, feta and tomatoes to the rice, and stir in the mayonnaise, lime juice and chervil. Mix together well. Season with salt and pepper to taste.

4 Spoon the rice mixture into the salmon-lined ramekins. (Any leftover mixture can be used to make a rice salad.) Place any extra pieces of smoked salmon on top, then fold over the overlapping pieces of salmon so that the rice mixture is completely encased.

5 Chill the parcels for 30–60 minutes, then invert each parcel on to a plate, using the clear film to ease them out of the ramekins. Carefully peel off the clear film.

6 Garnish each parcel with slices of lime and a sprig of chervil. Serve immediately.

Fish Platter Energy 312kcal/1298kJ; Protein 14.8g; Carbohydrate 15.2g, of which sugars 15.2g; Fat 21.7g, of which saturates 3.5g; Cholesterol 33mg; Calcium 66mg; Fibre 1.3g; Sodium 961mg.
Smoked Salmon Energy 482kcal/2009kJ; Protein 34.9g; Carbohydrate 36.8g, of which sugars 1.8g; Fat 21.4g, of which saturates 9.3g; Cholesterol 76mg; Calcium 256mg; Fibre 0.8g; Sodium 2495mg

Tortilla Cones with Smoked Salmon and Soft Cheese

These quick and easy cones make good appetizers. They are fun to eat and have a very tasty filling.

Serves 4

115g/4oz/½ cup soft white (farmer's) cheese
30ml/2 tbsp roughly chopped fresh dill
juice of 1 lemon
1 small red onion
15ml/1 tbsp drained bottled capers
30ml/2 tbsp extra virgin olive oil
30ml/2 tbsp roughly chopped fresh flat leaf parsley
115g/4oz smoked salmon
8 small or 4 large wheat flour tortillas
salt and ground black pepper
lemon wedges, for squeezing

1 Place the soft cheese in a bowl and mix in half the dill. Add a little salt and pepper and just a dash of the lemon juice to taste. Reserve the remaining lemon juice in a separate mixing bowl.

2 Finely chop the red onion. Add the onion, capers and olive oil to the lemon juice. Add the chopped flat leaf parsley and the remaining dill and gently stir.

3 Cut the salmon into short, thin strips, and add to the red onion mixture. Toss to mix. Season to taste with pepper.

4 If using small tortillas, leave them whole, but large ones need to be cut in half. Spread a little of the soft cheese mixture on each piece of tortilla and top with the smoked salmon mixture.

5 Roll up the tortillas into cones and secure with wooden cocktail sticks (toothpicks). Arrange on a serving plate and add some lemon wedges, for squeezing. Serve immediately.

Cook's Tip
You can also use salted capers in this dish but rinse them thoroughly under cold running water before using.

Marinated Smoked Salmon with Lime and Coriander

If you want an elegant appetizer that is really quick to put together, then this is the one for you. The tangy lime juice and aromatic coriander leaves contrast perfectly with the delicate yet distinct flavour of the smoked salmon. Serve with thinly sliced brown bread and butter.

Serves 6

200g/7oz smoked salmon
a handful of fresh coriander (cilantro) leaves
grated rind and juice of 1 lime
15ml/1 tbsp extra virgin olive oil
ground black pepper
sliced brown bread and butter, to serve

1 Using a sharp knife or pair of kitchen scissors, cut the smoked salmon into even strips and arrange them on a serving platter.

2 Sprinkle the coriander leaves and lime rind over the salmon and squeeze over the lime juice.

3 Drizzle the extra virgin olive oil over the salmon strips and season with plenty of ground black pepper.

4 Cover the serving platter tightly with clear film (plastic wrap) and chill in the refrigerator for 1 hour. Serve the marinated salmon strips accompanied by slices of brown bread and butter so diners can help themselves.

Cook's Tips
- *You can make this dish up to 1 hour before serving. However, do not leave it for longer than this because the lime juice will start to discolour the smoked salmon and spoil the look of the dish.*
- *Choose the more expensive smoked salmon that comes from wild fish for a superior flavour. Farmed salmon, however, makes a good substitute if wild salmon is not available.*

Tortilla Cones Energy 374kcal/1576kJ; Protein 16.6g; Carbohydrate 53.2g, of which sugars 3g; Fat 12g, of which saturates 3.6g; Cholesterol 22mg; Calcium 128mg; Fibre 2.9g; Sodium 783mg.
Marinated Salmon Energy 67kcal/279kJ; Protein 8.7g; Carbohydrate 0.2g, of which sugars 0.2g; Fat 3.4g, of which saturates 0.5g; Cholesterol 12mg; Calcium 23mg; Fibre 0.4g; Sodium 630mg.

Salmon Cakes with Butter Sauce

Salmon fish cakes make a real treat for the start of a dinner party. They are also economical, as you could use any small tail pieces that are on offer from your fishmonger or supermarket.

Makes 6

225g/8oz salmon tail piece, cooked
30ml/2 tbsp chopped fresh parsley
2 spring onions (scallions), trimmed and chopped
grated rind and juice of ½ lemon
225g/8oz mashed potato (not too soft)
1 egg, beaten
50g/2oz/1 cup fresh white breadcrumbs
75g/3oz/6 tbsp butter, plus extra for frying (optional)
oil, for frying (optional)
salt and ground black pepper
courgette (zucchini) and carrot slices and sprig of coriander (cilantro), to garnish

1 Remove all the skin and bones from the fish and mash or flake the flesh in a bowl.

2 Add the parsley, spring onions and 5ml/1 tsp of the lemon rind, and season with salt and lots of black pepper.

3 Gently work the mashed potato into the fish mixture and then shape into six rounds, triangles or croquettes. Chill the salmon cakes for 20 minutes.

4 Preheat the grill (broiler). Place the beaten egg on a plate and the breadcrumbs on a separate plate.

5 Dip the salmon cakes in the beaten egg and then in the breadcrumbs until evenly coated all over. Grill (broil) the fish cakes gently for 5 minutes on each side, or until they are golden. Alternatively, cook them in butter and oil in a frying pan until golden and crisp.

6 To make the butter sauce, melt the butter in a pan, whisk in the remaining lemon rind, the lemon juice and 15–30ml/1–2 tbsp water. Season with salt and black pepper to taste. Simmer the sauce for a few minutes and serve with the hot fish cakes. Garnish with slices of courgette and carrot and a sprig of coriander.

Salmon and Ginger Fish Cakes

These light fish cakes are scented with the exotic flavours of sesame, lime and ginger. They make a tempting appetizer served simply with a wedge of lime for squeezing over, but are also perfect for a light lunch or supper, served with a crunchy, refreshing salad.

Makes 25

500g/1¼lb salmon fillet, skinned and boned
45ml/3 tbsp dried breadcrumbs
30ml/2 tbsp mayonnaise
30ml/2 tbsp sesame seeds
30ml/2 tbsp light soy sauce
finely grated rind of 2 limes
10ml/2 tsp finely grated fresh root ginger
4 spring onions (scallions), finely sliced
vegetable oil, for frying
salt and ground black pepper
spring onions (scallions), to garnish
lime wedges, to serve

1 Finely chop the salmon and place in a bowl. Add the breadcrumbs, mayonnaise, sesame seeds, soy sauce, lime rind, ginger and spring onions and use your fingers to mix until the ingredients are well combined.

2 With wet hands, divide the mixture into about 25 portions and shape each into a small round cake. Place the cakes on a baking sheet lined with baking parchment, cover and chill in the refrigerator for at least two hours. They can be left to chill overnight, if you prefer.

3 When you are ready to cook the fish cakes, heat about 5cm/2in vegetable oil in a wok and fry the fish cakes in batches, over a medium heat, for 2–3 minutes on each side.

4 Drain the fish cakes well on kitchen paper and serve warm or at room temperature, garnished with spring onion slivers and plenty of lime wedges for squeezing over.

Cook's Tip
When chopping the salmon, look out for stray bones and pick these out with tweezers.

Salmon Cakes Energy 188kcal/782kJ; Protein 9.5g; Carbohydrate 6.2g, of which sugars 0.7g; Fat 14.1g, of which saturates 6.8g; Cholesterol 68mg; Calcium 36mg; Fibre 0.9g; Sodium 101mg.
Salmon and Ginger Fish Cakes Energy 83kcal/343kJ; Protein 4.6g; Carbohydrate 1.6g, of which sugars 0.2g; Fat 6.5g, of which saturates 0.9g; Cholesterol 11mg; Calcium 16mg; Fibre 0.2g; Sodium 117mg.

Crispy Salt and Pepper Squid

These delicious morsels of squid look stunning and are perfect served with drinks as an appetizer. The crisp, golden coating contrasts beautifully with the succulent squid inside. Serve them piping hot straight from the wok.

Serves 4

750g/1lb 10oz fresh squid, cleaned
juice of 4–5 lemons
15ml/1 tbsp ground black pepper
15ml/1 tbsp sea salt
10ml/2 tsp caster (superfine) sugar
115g/4oz/1 cup cornflour (cornstarch)
3 egg whites, lightly beaten
vegetable oil, for deep-frying
chilli sauce or sweet-and-sour sauce, for dipping
skewers or toothpicks, to serve

1 Cut the squid into large bitesize pieces and score a diamond pattern on each piece, using a sharp knife or a cleaver.

2 Trim the tentacles. Place the squid flesh in a large mixing bowl and pour over the lemon juice. Cover and marinate for 10–15 minutes. Drain well and pat dry.

3 In a separate bowl, mix together the black pepper, salt, sugar and cornflour. Place the egg whites in a bowl. Dip the squid pieces in the egg whites and then toss lightly in the seasoned flour, shaking off any excess.

4 Fill a wok or large pan one-third full of oil and heat to 180°C/350°F or until a cube of bread, dropped into the oil, browns in 40 seconds. Working in batches, deep-fry the squid for 1 minute. Drain the crispy pieces on kitchen paper and serve immediately, threaded on to skewers, with chilli or sweet-and-sour sauce for dipping.

Cook's Tip
Keep egg whites in a sealed plastic tub in the freezer, ready to thaw for use in dishes such as this.

Eel Wrapped in Bacon

Firm-fleshed and rich in flavour, eel is delicious grilled, braised, or stir-fried. This appetizer is best served with a dipping sauce.

Serves 4–6

2 lemon grass stalks, trimmed and chopped
25g/1oz fresh root ginger, peeled and chopped
2 garlic cloves, chopped
2 shallots, chopped
15ml/1 tbsp palm sugar (jaggery)
15ml/1 tbsp vegetable oil
30ml/2 tbsp fish sauce
1.2kg/2½lb fresh eel, skinned and cut into 2.5cm/1in pieces
12 slices streaky (fatty) bacon
ground black pepper
a small bunch of fresh coriander (cilantro) leaves, to garnish
chilli sambal for dipping

1 Using a mortar and pestle, pound the lemon grass, ginger, garlic and shallots with the sugar to form a paste. Add the oil and fish sauce, mix well and season with black pepper.

2 Place the eel pieces in a shallow dish and smear them thoroughly in the paste. Cover and place in the refrigerator for 2–3 hours to marinate.

3 Wrap each piece of marinated eel in a strip of streaky bacon, including as much of the marinade as possible.

4 To cook the eel parcels, you can use a conventional grill (broiler), a well-oiled griddle pan, or a barbecue. If grilling over charcoal, you can skewer the eel parcels; otherwise, spread them over the grill or griddle pan. Cook the eel parcels until nice and crispy, roughly 2–3 minutes on each side. Serve with fresh coriander leaves and chilli sambal for dipping.

Cook's Tip
When buying fresh eel, it's worth asking the fishmonger to gut it, cut off the head, bone it, skin it and slice it for you – it makes life a lot easier when you get it home.

Eel in Bacon Energy 460kcal/1911kJ; Protein 39.3g; Carbohydrate 0.8g, of which sugars 0.6g; Fat 33.3g, of which saturates 9.1g; Cholesterol 324mg; Calcium 43mg; Fibre 0.1g; Sodium 651mg.
Crispy Squid Energy 346kcal/1462kJ; Protein 31.2g; Carbohydrate 31.3g, of which sugars 2.6g; Fat 11.6g, of which saturates 1.8g; Cholesterol 422mg; Calcium 32mg; Fibre 0g; Sodium 1741mg.

Pan-fried Baby Squid with Moroccan Spices

You need to work quickly to cook this dish, then serve it immediately, so that the squid is just cooked and tender. Baby squid are widely available ready prepared. The flavours of turmeric, ginger and harissa are fabulous with the contrasting sweetness of the squid, which is reinforced by the addition of a spoonful of honey, and the whole dish is sharpened up by the zesty lemon juice.

Serves 4

8 baby squid, prepared, with tentacles
5ml/1 tsp ground turmeric
15ml/1 tbsp olive oil
2 garlic cloves, finely chopped
15g/½ oz fresh root ginger, peeled and finely chopped
5–10ml/1–2 tsp honey
juice of 1 lemon
10ml/2 tsp harissa
salt
small bunch of fresh coriander (cilantro), roughly chopped, to serve

1 Pat dry the squid bodies, inside and out, and dry the tentacles with k tchen paper. Sprinkle the squid and tentacles with the ground turmeric.

2 Heat the olive oil in a large heavy frying pan and stir in the garlic and ginger. Just as the ginger and garlic begin to colour, add the squid and tentacles and fry quickly on both sides over a high heat. (Don't overcook the squid, otherwise it will become rubbery.)

3 Add the honey, lemon juice and harissa and stir to form a thick, spicy, caramelized sauce. Season with salt, sprinkle with the chopped coriander and serve immediately.

Cook's Tip
Harissa, the fiery red paste used in the cuisines of Tunisia, Algeria and Morocco, is made from chillies, olive oil and garlic. The chillies are often smoked, and other flavourings include coriander and cumin.

Squid Stuffed with Garlic Pork

This tasty appetizer calls for tender baby squid to be stuffed with a dill-flavoured pork mixture. The squid can be grilled or fried.

Serves 4

3 dried cloud ear (wood ear) mushrooms
10 dried tiger lily buds
25g/1oz bean thread (cellophane) noodles
8 baby squid, cleaned
350g/12oz minced (ground) pork
3–4 shallots, finely chopped
4 garlic cloves, finely chopped
1 bunch dill fronds, finely chopped
30ml/2 tbsp nuoc mam
5ml/1 tsp palm sugar (jaggery)
ground black pepper
vegetable or groundnut (peanut) oil, for frying
coriander (cilantro) leaves, to garnish
nuoc cham, for drizzling

1 Soak the mushrooms, tiger lily buds and bean thread noodles in lukewarm water for about 15 minutes, until softened. Rinse the squid and pat dry with kitchen paper. Chop the tentacles.

2 Drain the mushrooms, tiger lily buds and bean thread noodles. Squeeze them in kitchen paper to get rid of any excess water, then chop them finely and put them in a bowl. Add the chopped tentacles, minced pork, shallots, garlic and three-quarters of the dill. In a small bowl, stir the nuoc mam with the sugar, until it dissolves completely. Add it to the mixture in the bowl and mix well. Season with black pepper.

3 Using your fingers, stuff the pork mixture into each squid, packing it in firmly. Leave a little gap at the end to sew together with a needle and cotton thread or to skewer with a cocktail stick (toothpick) so that the filling doesn't spill out on cooking.

4 Heat some oil in a large wok or heavy pan, and fry the squid for about 5 minutes, turning them from time to time. Pierce each one several times to release any excess water – this will cause the oil to spit, so take care when doing this; you may wish to use a spatterproof lid. Continue cooking for a further 10 minutes, until the squid are nicely browned. Serve whole or thinly sliced, garnished with the remaining dill and coriander, and drizzled with nuoc cham.

Pan-fried Baby Squid Energy 154kcal/647kJ; Protein 19.8g; Carbohydrate 5.8g, of which sugars 4.3g; Fat 5.9g, of which saturates 1g; Cholesterol 281mg; Calcium 54mg; Fibre 1g; Sodium 144mg.
Squid Stuffed Energy 315kcal/1311kJ; Protein 25g; Carbohydrate 7.9g, of which sugars 1.9g; Fat 20.4g, of which saturates 4.6g; Cholesterol 170mg; Calcium 18mg; Fibre 0.2g; Sodium 110mg.

Fried Whitebait with Cayenne Pepper

These small fish are fried and eaten whole. They are ideal to serve as appetizers.

Serves 4

50g/2oz/½ cup plain (all-purpose) flour
1.5ml/¼ tsp cayenne pepper
250g/9oz whitebait
vegetable oil, for deep-frying
salt and ground black pepper
lime wedges, to serve

1 Sift the flour and cayenne pepper into a deep bowl or large shallow dish. Season the flour with plenty of salt and ground black pepper.

2 Thoroughly coat the whitebait in the seasoned flour, then shake off any excess flour and make sure the whitebait are separate. Do this in batches, placing the coated fish on a plate ready for frying.

3 Pour oil to a depth of 5cm/2in into a deep wide pan. Heat the oil until very hot, then add a batch of whitebait and fry for 2–3 minutes until golden.

4 Remove the cooked whitebait from the pan with a slotted spoon, and drain on kitchen paper and keep warm. Repeat the process with the remaining whitebait.

5 Pile the fried whitebait on a serving plate, season with salt and ground black pepper and serve immediately with the lime wedges for squeezing over.

Variations

- *Small fresh anchovies are also delicious cooked whole in this way. Alternatively, if you find yourself with lots of seafood, you can make up a mixed platter using whitebait, squid and prawns (shrimp).*
- *For a little less spice, replace the cayenne pepper with the same amount of paprika. It is not as hot as cayenne but still imparts a rich, spicy flavour to the fish.*

Marinated Anchovies

The Spanish term for marinated anchovies is boquerones, while anchoas is their word for the canned and salted varieties, which are much used as a flavouring in many parts of the Mediterranean region.

Serves 4

225g/8oz fresh anchovies, heads and tails removed, and split open along the belly
juice of 3 lemons
30ml/2 tbsp extra virgin olive oil
2 garlic cloves, finely chopped
15ml/1 tbsp chopped fresh parsley
flaked sea salt

1 Turn the anchovies on to their bellies, and press down with your thumb.

2 Using the tip of a small, sharp knife, carefully remove the backbones from the flattened fish, and arrange the anchovies skin side down in a single layer on a large plate.

3 Squeeze two-thirds of the lemon juice over the fish and sprinkle them with the salt. Cover and leave to stand for 1–24 hours, basting occasionally with the juices, until the flesh is white and no longer translucent.

4 Transfer the anchovies to a serving plate and drizzle with the olive oil and the remaining lemon juice. Sprinkle the fish with the chopped garlic and parsley, then cover with clear film (plastic wrap) and chill until ready to serve.

Devilled Whitebait

A spicy coating on these small fish gives this appetizer a crunchy bite.

Serves 4

115g/4oz/1 cup plain (all-purpose) flour
2.5ml/½ tsp curry powder
2.5ml/½ tsp ground ginger
2.5ml/½ tsp cayenne pepper
450g/1lb whitebait
oil for deep-frying
salt
lemon wedges, to garnish

1 Mix together the flour, curry powder, ginger, cayenne pepper and a little salt in a large bowl or shallow dish.

2 Coat the fish in the seasoned flour, covering them evenly. Shake off any excess.

3 Heat the oil in a large, heavy pan to 190°C/375°F or until a cube of stale bread, dropped into the oil, browns in about 30 seconds. Fry the whitebait, in batches, for 2–3 minutes, until the fish is golden and crispy.

4 Drain the whitebait well on kitchen paper. Transfer to a dish and keep warm in a low oven until you have cooked all the fish. Serve immediately garnished with lemon wedges.

Fried Whitebait Energy 722kcal/2989kJ; Protein 26.8g; Carbohydrate 7.3g, of which sugars 0.2g; Fat 65.3g, of which saturates 0g; Cholesterol 0mg; Calcium 1183mg; Fibre 0.3g; Sodium 316mg.
Marinated Anchovies Energy 108kcal/449kJ; Protein 14.2g; Carbohydrate 0g, of which sugars 0g; Fat 5.6g, of which saturates 0.9g; Cholesterol 35mg; Calcium 169mg; Fibre 0g; Sodium 2211mg.
Devilled Whitebait Energy 656kcal/2718kJ; Protein 24.4g; Carbohydrate 6.6g, of which sugars 0.1g; Fat 59.4g, of which saturates 0g; Cholesterol 0mg; Calcium 1075mg; Fibre 0.3g; Sodium 288mg.

Seafood Pancakes

Fresh and smoked haddock imparts a wonderful flavour to these appetizers.

Serves 6

For the pancakes

115g/4oz/1 cup plain (all-purpose) flour
pinch of salt
1 egg, plus 1 egg yolk
300ml/½ pint/1¼ cups milk
15ml/1 tbsp melted butter, plus extra for cooking
50–75g/2–3oz Gruyère cheese, grated
frisée lettuce, to serve

For the filling

225g/8oz smoked haddock fillet
225g/8oz fresh haddock fillet
300ml/½ pint/1¼ cups milk
150ml/¼ pint/⅔ cup single (light) cream
40g/1½ oz/3 tbsp butter
40g/1½ oz/¼ cup plain (all-purpose) flour
2 hard-boiled eggs, peeled and chopped
salt and ground black pepper

1 For the pancakes, sift the flour and salt into a bowl. Add the egg and extra yolk. Whisk the egg, and mix in some flour. Add the milk, whisking until smooth. Stir in the melted butter.

2 Melt a little melted butter in a small pan. Add 30ml/2 tbsp of the batter, cook for 30 seconds. Flip the pancake and cook the other side. Repeat to make 12 pancakes, adding melted butter between each. Keep them warm.

3 Poach the fish with the milk for 6–8 minutes. Cool, then remove the skin and bones. Reserve the milk. Measure the cream into a jug (pitcher), strain enough of the milk into the jug to make the quantity up to 450ml/¾ pint/scant 2 cups.

4 Melt the butter, stir in the flour and cook gently for 1 minute. Add the milk mixture, and stir until smooth. Cook for 3 minutes. Season. Add the fish, flaked, to the sauce with the eggs.

5 Preheat the oven to 180°C/350°F/Gas 4. Divide the filling among the pancakes. Roll them up to enclose the filling completely.

6 Add the pancakes to a buttered dish. Bake for 15 minutes, add the Gruyère, cook for 5 minutes and serve with lettuce leaves.

Fish Sausages

This traditional recipe dates from the 17th century. It is still popular today as a satisfying and tasty way of using a variety of fish fillets. The sausages make great appetizers for a dinner party.

Serves 4

375g/13oz fish fillets, such as perch, pike, carp or cod, skinned
1 white bread roll
75ml/5 tbsp milk
25ml/1½ tbsp chopped fresh flat leaf parsley
2 eggs, well beaten
50g/2oz/½ cup plain (all-purpose) flour
50g/2oz/1 cup fine fresh white breadcrumbs
oil, for shallow frying
salt and ground black pepper
deep-fried parsley sprigs and lemon wedges dusted with paprika, to garnish

1 Mince (grind) or process the fish fillets coarsely in a food processor or blender. Soak the white bread roll in the milk for about 10 minutes, then squeeze it out.

2 Mix the minced fish and bread together before adding the chopped fresh parsley and one of the beaten eggs. Season with plenty of salt and ground black pepper. Mix until all the ingredients are well combined.

3 Using your fingers, shape the fish mixture into 10cm/4in long sausage shapes, making them about 2.5cm/1in thick. Place the remaining egg on a plate and the breadcrumbs on a separate plate. Carefully roll the fish sausages in the flour, then in the remaining egg and finally in the breadcrumbs.

4 Heat the oil in a pan, then slowly cook the sausages until golden brown all over. (You may need to work in batches.) Drain well on crumpled kitchen paper. Garnish with the deep-fried parsley sprigs and lemon wedges dusted with paprika.

Variation
If you prefer, the mixture can be formed into the more usual fish cake shape rather than sausages.

Seafood Pancakes Energy 393kcal/1647kJ; Protein 26.7g; Carbohydrate 25.4g, of which sugars 5.7g; Fat 21.2g, of which saturates 11.9g; Cholesterol 203mg; Calcium 273mg; Fibre 0.8g; Sodium 514mg.
Fish Sausages Energy 238kcal/1007kJ; Protein 24.7g; Carbohydrate 25.8g, of which sugars 1.7g; Fat 4.8g, of which saturates 1.4g; Cholesterol 139mg; Calcium 82mg; Fibre 1.2g; Sodium 292mg.

Cinnamon Fish Cakes with Currants, Pine Nuts and Herbs

These spicy Middle Eastern fish cakes are very good to eat as an appetizer. They are flavoured with cinnamon and a classic trio of herbs – parsley, mint and dill.

Serves 4

450g/1lb skinless fresh white fish fillets, such as haddock or sea bass
2 slices of day-old bread, sprinkled with water and left for a few minutes, then squeezed dry
1 red onion, finely chopped
30ml/2 tbsp currants, soaked in warm water for 5–10 minutes and drained
30ml/2 tbsp pine nuts
1 small bunch each of fresh flat leaf parsley, mint and dill, stems removed, leaves finely chopped
1 egg
5–10ml/1–2 tsp tomato purée (paste) or ketchup
15ml/1 tbsp ground cinnamon
45–60ml/3–4 tbsp plain (all-purpose) flour
45–60ml/3–4 tbsp sunflower oil
salt and ground black pepper

To serve

1 small bunch of fresh flat leaf parsley
1–2 lemons or limes, cut into wedges

1 In a bowl, break up the fish with a fork. Add the bread, the chopped onion, currants and pine nuts, then toss in the herbs and mix well.

2 In another small bowl, beat the egg with the tomato purée and 10ml/2 tsp of the cinnamon. Pour the mixture over the fish mixture and season well with salt and pepper, then mix together using your hands and mould into small balls until all the mixture is used up.

3 Mix the flour on a plate with the remaining cinnamon. Press each ball into a flat cake and coat in the flour.

4 Heat the oil in a wide, shallow pan and fry the fish cakes in batches for 8–10 minutes, until golden brown. Lift out and drain on kitchen paper. Serve hot on a bed of parsley, with lemon or lime wedges for squeezing.

Spicy Fish Rösti

The classic Swiss potato pancake, rösti, takes on a new twist with the addition of fish in this deliciously tasty appetizer.

Serves 4

350g/12oz large, firm waxy potatoes
350g/12oz salmon or cod fillet, skinned
3–4 spring onions (scallions), finely chopped
5ml/1 tsp grated fresh root ginger
30ml/2 tbsp chopped fresh coriander (cilantro)
10ml/2 tsp lemon juice
30–45ml/2–3 tbsp sunflower oil
salt and cayenne pepper
coriander (cilantro) sprigs, to garnish
lemon wedges, to serve

1 Cook the potatoes with their skins on in a pan of salted, boiling water for about 10 minutes. Drain and leave to cool for a few minutes.

2 Meanwhile, remove any pin bones from the salmon or cod fillet, finely chop the flesh and place it into a large bowl. Stir in the chopped spring onions, grated root ginger, chopped coriander and lemon juice. Season to taste with salt and cayenne pepper.

3 When the potatoes are cool enough to handle but still warm, peel off the skins and grate the potatoes coarsely. Gently stir the grated potato into the fish mixture.

4 Divide the fish mixture into 12 portions, then shape each into a patty with your hands, pressing the mixture together and leaving the edges slightly rough.

5 Heat the oil in a large frying pan and cook the fish rösti, a few at a time, for about 3–5 minutes on each side, until golden brown and crisp. Remove with a metal spatula and drain well on kitchen paper. Keep the cooked rösti hot while you fry the remaining patties. Serve immediately, garnished with sprigs of coriander and accompanied by lemon wedges for squeezing over the rösti.

Cinnamon Fish Cakes Energy 317kcal/1324kJ; Protein 26.1g; Carbohydrate 17.8g, of which sugars 2.5g; Fat 16.2g, of which saturates 1.9g; Cholesterol 99mg; Calcium 79mg; Fibre 1.6g; Sodium 169mg.
Spicy Fish Röti Energy 208kcal/870kJ; Protein 17.7g; Carbohydrate 14.4g, of which sugars 1.4g; Fat 9.2g, of which saturates 1.2g; Cholesterol 40mg; Calcium 17mg; Fibre 1g; Sodium 63mg.

Grilled Sardines

Fresh sardines have plenty of flavour, so they are really at their best when cooked simply for this appetizer.

Serves 4
8 sardines, about 50g/2oz each
sea salt
2 lemons, halved, to serve

1 Gut the sardines, but leave on the heads and tails. With a sharp knife, slash each side of all the sardines diagonally three times.

2 Place the sardines on a grill (broiler) rack and sprinkle with sea salt. Cook under a preheated high grill for 4 minutes on each side until the flesh is cooked and the skin is blistered and a little charred.

3 Transfer to a serving dish and serve immediately with the lemon halves to squeeze over.

Herbed Fish Fritters

Serve these mini fritters with a tartare sauce if you wish. Simply chop some capers and gherkins, and stir them into home-made or good quality ready-made mayonnaise.

Makes 20
450g/1lb plaice or flounder fillets
300ml/½ pint/1¼ cups milk
450g/1lb cooked potatoes
1 fennel bulb, finely chopped
45ml/3 tbsp chopped fresh parsley
2 eggs
15g/½oz/1 tbsp unsalted butter
250g/9oz/2 cups white breadcrumbs
25g/1oz/2 tbsp sesame seeds
vegetable oil, for deep-frying
salt and ground black pepper

1 Gently poach the fish fillets in the milk for about 15 minutes, until the flesh flakes easily. Drain and reserve the milk.

2 Peel the skin off the fish and remove any stray bones. In a food processor fitted with a metal blade, process the fish, potatoes, fennel, parsley, eggs and butter.

3 Transfer the mixture to a bowl, add 30ml/2 tbsp of the reserved cooking milk and season with salt and plenty of ground black pepper. Mix well.

4 Cover the fish mixture with clear film (plastic wrap) and chill for 30 minutes, then shape into 20 even fritters with your hands.

5 Mix together the breadcrumbs and sesame seeds in a shallow dish, then roll the croquettes in this mixture to form a good coating.

6 Heat the oil in a large, heavy pan until it is hot enough to brown a cube of stale bread in 30 seconds. Deep-fry the croquettes, in small batches, for about 4 minutes, until they are golden brown all over. Drain well on kitchen paper and serve the fritters hot.

Rolled Sardines with Plum Paste

This Japanese dish celebrates the harvest, when the sardine season peaks.

Serves 4
8 sardines, cleaned and filleted
5ml/1 tsp salt
4 umeboshi, about 30g/1¼oz total weight (choose the soft type)
5ml/1 tsp sake
5ml/1 tsp toasted sesame seeds
16 shiso leaves, cut in half lengthways
1 lime, thinly sliced, the centre hollowed out to make rings, to garnish

1 Carefully cut the sardine fillets in half lengthways and place them side by side in a large, shallow container. Sprinkle with salt.

2 Remove the stones (pits) from the umeboshi and put the fruit in a small mixing bowl with the sake and toasted sesame seeds. Mash to form a smooth paste.

3 Wipe the sardine fillets with kitchen paper. With a butter knife, spread some umeboshi paste thinly on to one of the sardine fillets, then press some shiso leaves on top. Roll up the sardine starting from the tail and pierce with a wooden cocktail stick (toothpick). Repeat to make 16 rolled sardines.

4 Preheat the grill (broiler) to high. Lay a sheet of foil on a baking tray, and arrange the sardine rolls on this, spaced well apart. Grill (broil) for 4–6 minutes on each side, turning once.

5 Lay a few lime rings on four individual plates and arrange the rolled sardines alongside. Serve hot.

Cook's Tip
Sardines deteriorate very quickly and must be bought and eaten on the same day. Be careful when buying: the eyes and gills should not be too pink. If the fish 'melts' like cheese when grilled (broiled), throw it away.

Grilled Sardines Energy 327kcal/1362kJ; Protein 35g; Carbohydrate 0.3g, of which sugars 0.3g; Fat 20.5g, of which saturates 8g; Cholesterol 16mg; Calcium 192mg; Fibre 0.5g; Sodium 240mg.
Fish Fritters Energy 149kcal/626kJ; Protein 7.4g; Carbohydrate 14.3g, of which sugars 1.6g; Fat 7.4g, of which saturates 1.4g; Cholesterol 31mg; Calcium 65mg; Fibre 0.9g; Sodium 147mg.
Rolled Sardines Energy 177kcal/740kJ; Protein 20.9g; Carbohydrate 0.7g, of which sugars 0.7g; Fat 9.9g, of which saturates 2.8g; Cholesterol 0mg; Calcium 94mg; Fibre 0.2g; Sodium 121mg.

Smoked Trout with Cucumber and Dill

The trout fillets need no further cooking, making them a great convenience food and a deservedly popular cold appetizer.

Serves 4
1 small cucumber
4–8 smoked trout fillets
sprigs of dill, to garnish
brown bread and butter, to serve

For the dressing
90ml/6 tbsp extra virgin olive oil
30ml/2 tbsp white wine vinegar
15ml/1 tbsp chopped fresh dill
sea salt and ground black pepper

1 To make the dressing, whisk the olive oil and vinegar together vigorously. Alternatively, mix in a screw-top jar and shake until combined.

2 Add the chopped fresh dill to the oil and vinegar and blend in with the whisk, or by shaking the jar. Season with salt and ground black pepper to taste.

3 Peel the cucumber, if you prefer. You can peel off strips, if you like, to give the slices a decorative, ridged effect. Cut the cucumber into slices as thin as possible.

4 Arrange the smoked trout fillets on four serving plates. Lay an equal amount of cucumber slices alongside the trout fillets on the plates.

5 Sprinkle the trout fillets and the cucumber with the dressing, and garnish with sprigs of fresh dill. Serve with brown bread and butter.

Variation
You could make this dish with slices of smoked salmon or cooked salmon fillets if you prefer.

Marinated Smoked Haddock Fillets

This simple but flavourful dish is also excellent made with kipper fillets.

Serves 6
450g/1lb undyed smoked haddock fillet, skinned
1 onion, very thinly sliced into rings
5–10ml/1–2 tsp Dijon mustard
30ml/2 tbsp lemon juice
90ml/6 tbsp olive oil
45ml/3 tbsp dark rum
12 small new potatoes, scrubbed
30ml/2 tbsp chopped fresh dill, plus 6 sprigs to garnish
ground black pepper

1 Cut the fish fillet in half lengthways. Check for and remove any bones by pressing gently with your fingertips and thumb all the way down. Arrange the pieces in a single layer in a shallow non-metallic dish. Sprinkle the onion rings evenly over the top.

2 Whisk together the mustard, lemon juice and some black pepper. Add the oil gradually, whisking constantly. Pour two-thirds of the dressing over the fish. Cover the dish with clear film (plastic wrap) and leave the fish to marinate for 2 hours in a cool place. Sprinkle with the rum and leave for 1 hour more.

3 Cook the potatoes in boiling salted water until tender. Drain, cut in half and place in a bowl. Cool a little, then toss in the remaining dressing. Stir in the chopped fresh dill, cover and set aside.

4 Slice the haddock thinly, as for smoked salmon, or leave whole, if you like. Arrange on small plates and spoon over some marinade and onion rings. Pile the potato halves on one side of each plate and garnish each portion with a sprig of dill. Serve chilled or at room temperature.

Cook's Tip
Try to get a large, thick haddock fillet. If all you can find are small pieces, you can still make the dish, but serve the pieces whole instead of slicing them.

Smoked Trout Energy 467Kcal/1943kJ; Protein 55g; Carbohydrate 0.7g, of which sugars 0.6g; Fat 27g, of which saturates 4.7g; Cholesterol 226mg; Calcium 92mg; Fibre 0.3g; Sodium 206mg.
Marinated Haddock Energy 212kcal/884kJ; Protein 15.3g; Carbohydrate 7.7g, of which sugars 1.3g; Fat 11.7g, of which saturates 1.7g; Cholesterol 27mg; Calcium 37mg; Fibre 0.9g; Sodium 577mg.

Sussex Smokies

England's smokehouses produce some fine products. The flavour and colour of this Sussex dish is best when made with pale, undyed smoked haddock rather than the bright yellow artificially dyed variety. Follow this filling appetizer with a light main course or serve it with crusty bread as a light meal or snack.

Serves 4

350g/12oz smoked haddock
450ml/¾ pint/scant 2 cups milk
25g/1oz/2 tbsp butter
25g/1oz/4 tbsp plain (all-purpose) flour
115g/4oz mature (sharp) Cheddar cheese, grated
60ml/4 tbsp fresh breadcrumbs
salt and ground black pepper
crusty bread, to serve

1 Remove and discard all skin and bones from the smoked haddock and cut the fish into strips.

2 Put the milk, butter, flour and seasoning into a pan. Over a medium heat and whisking constantly, bring to the boil and bubble gently for 2–3 minutes until thick and smooth.

3 Add the haddock and half the grated cheese to the hot sauce, bring it just back to the boil and stir until the cheese has melted.

4 Divide the mixture between individual flameproof dishes or ramekins. Toss together the remaining cheese and the breadcrumbs and sprinkle the mixture over the top of each filled dish.

5 Put the dishes under a hot grill (broiler) until bubbling and golden. Serve immediately with crusty bread.

Cook's Tip

It helps to use a pair of tweezers when removing bones from the smoked haddock fillets. Run your fingers over the fillet to feel for the bones and then pulll them out with the tweezers.

Red Mullet Dolmades

If you cannot find prepared vine leaves, use blanched cabbage or large spinach leaves instead. Plaice, flounder or lemon sole can be substituted in place of the red mullet.

Serves 4

225g/8oz red mullet or red snapper fillets, scaled
45ml/3 tbsp dry white wine
115g/4oz/1 cup cooked long grain rice
25g/1oz/¼ cup pine nuts
45ml/3 tbsp chopped fresh parsley
grated rind and juice of ½ lemon
8 vine (grape) leaves in brine, rinsed and dried
salt and ground black pepper

For the orange butter sauce

grated rind and juice of 2 oranges
2 shallots, very finely chopped
25g/1oz/2 tbsp chilled

1 Preheat the oven to 200°C/400°F/Gas 6. Put the fish fillets in a shallow pan and season with salt and pepper. Pour over the wine, bring to the boil, then lower the heat and poach the fish gently for about 3 minutes, until it is just cooked. Strain, reserving the cooking liquid.

2 Remove the skin from the fish fillets and flake the flesh into a bowl. Gently stir in the rice, pine nuts, the chopped parsley, and lemon rind and juice. Season to taste with salt and pepper.

3 Spoon 30–45ml/2–3 tbsp of the filling into the middle of each vine leaf. Roll up each filled leaf, tucking in the ends to make a secure package. Arrange the dolmades in an ovenproof dish, with the joins underneath. Then pour over the reserved cooking liquid and place the dolmades in the preheated oven for about 5 minutes, until they are thoroughly heated through.

4 Meanwhile, make the sauce. Mix the orange rind and juice and the shallots in a small pan and boil vigorously for a few minutes until the mixture is reduced and syrupy.

5 Strain the sauce into a clean pan, discarding the shallots. Beat in the butter, one piece at a time. Reheat gently, but do not let the sauce boil. Drizzle the sauce over the dolmades and serve.

Sussex Smokies Energy 363kcal/1525kJ; Protein 30.1g; Carbohydrate 21.8g, of which sugars 5.8g; Fat 17.4g, of which saturates 10.8g; Cholesterol 79mg; Calcium 396mg; Fibre 0.5g; Sodium 1073mg.
Red Mullet Energy 185kcal/772kJ; Protein 7.7g; Carbohydrate 12.4g, of which sugars 3.4g; Fat 11.2g, of which saturates 3.6g; Cholesterol 13mg; Calcium 59mg; Fibre 1g; Sodium 74mg.

Monkfish Packages

With its meaty flesh and robust flavour, monkfish is perfect with garlic and chilli in this recipe. You could use a cheaper fish, like eel, but you'll lose the delicious taste of the monkfish.

Serves 4

175g/6oz/1½ cups strong white bread flour
2 eggs
115g/4oz skinless monkfish fillet, diced
grated rind of 1 lemon
1 garlic clove, chopped
1 small red chilli, seeded and sliced
45ml/3 tbsp chopped fresh parsley
30ml/2 tbsp single (light) cream
salt and ground black pepper

For the tomato oil
2 tomatoes, peeled, seeded and finely diced
45ml/3 tbsp extra virgin olive oil
15ml/1 tbsp lemon juice

1 Place the bread flour, eggs and 2.5ml/½ tsp salt in a blender or food processor; pulse until it forms a soft dough. Knead for 2–3 minutes. Wrap in clear film (plastic wrap) and chill for 20 minutes. Clean the food processor.

2 Place the diced monkfish, lemon rind, garlic, chilli and parsley in a blender or food processor; process the mixture until it is very finely chopped. Add the single cream, with plenty of salt and ground black pepper, and process again until a very thick paste is formed.

3 Make the tomato oil by stirring the diced tomatoes with the olive oil and lemon juice in a bowl. Season with salt to taste. Cover and chill.

4 Roll out the dough thinly on a lightly floured surface and cut out 32 rounds, using a 4cm/1½in plain cutter. Divide the filling among half the rounds, then cover with the remaining rounds. Pinch the edges to seal.

5 Bring a pan of water to a simmer and poach the fish packages, in batches, for about 2–3 minutes. Remove with a slotted spoon and drain on some kitchen paper. Serve hot, drizzled with the tomato oil.

Fiery Tuna Spring Rolls

This modern take on the classic spring roll makes a tasty appetizer but is also substantial enough to serve as a main meal.

Serves 4

1 large chunk of very fresh thick tuna steak
45ml/3 tbsp light soy sauce
30ml/2 tbsp wasabi
16 mangetouts (snow peas), trimmed
8 spring roll wrappers
sunflower oil, for deep-frying
soft noodles and stir-fried Asian greens, to serve
soy sauce and sweet chilli sauce, for dipping

1 Place the tuna on a board. Using a sharp knife, cut it into eight slices, each measuring about 12 x 2.5cm/4½ x 1in.

2 Place the tuna in a large, non-metallic dish in a single layer. Mix together the soy sauce and the wasabi and spoon evenly over the fish. Cover and marinate for 10–15 minutes.

3 Meanwhile, blanch the mangetouts in boiling water for about 1 minute, drain and refresh under cold water. Drain and pat dry with kitchen paper.

4 Place a spring roll wrapper on a clean work surface and place a piece of tuna on top, in the centre.

5 Top the tuna with two mangetouts and fold over the sides and roll up. Brush the edges of the wrappers to seal.

6 Repeat the wrapping process with the remaining tuna, mangetouts and wrappers.

7 Fill a large wok one-third full with oil and heat to 180°C/350°F or until a cube of bread browns in 45 seconds. Working in batches, deep-fry the rolls for 1–2 minutes, until crisp and golden.

8 Drain the rolls on kitchen paper and serve immediately with soft noodles and Asian greens. Serve the spring rolls with side dishes of soy sauce and sweet chilli sauce for dipping.

Monkfish Energy 310kcal/1304kJ; Protein 12.9g; Carbohydrate 36.8g, of which sugars 3.4g; Fat 13.5g, of which saturates 3.1g; Cholesterol 103mg; Calcium 112mg; Fibre 2.7g; Sodium 54mg.
Fiery Tuna Spring Rolls Energy 171kcal/717kJ; Protein 14.1g; Carbohydrate 11.4g, of which sugars 1.7g; Fat 8g, of which saturates 1.3g; Cholesterol 14mg; Calcium 36mg; Fibre 0.8g; Sodium 825mg.

Tuna and Wasabi Sashimi

This dish is called maguro butsu in Japan. When preparing big fish such as tuna or swordfish for sashimi, Japanese fishmongers cut the filleted flesh lengthways to make long rectangular shapes, and the trimmings are then sold cheaply. Butsu is a chopped trimming, which has all the quality of the best tuna sashimi. It is dressed with a marinade of wasabi and shoyu.

Serves 4

400g/14oz very fresh tuna, skinned
1 carton mustard and cress (optional)
20ml/4 tsp wasabi paste from a tube, or the same amount of wasabi powder mixed with 10ml/2 tsp water
60ml/4 tbsp shoyu
8 spring onions (scallions), green part only, finely chopped
4 shiso leaves, cut into thin slivers lengthways

1 Cut the tuna into 2cm/¾in cubes. If using mustard and cress, tie into pretty bunches or arrange as a bed in four small serving bowls or plates.

2 Just 5–10 minutes before serving, blend the wasabi paste with the shoyu in a bowl, then add the tuna and spring onions. Mix well and leave to marinate for 5 minutes.

3 Divide the tuna cubes among the bowls and add a few slivers of shiso leaves on top. Serve immediately.

Cook's Tip
Japanese sashimi, a dish of very fresh raw seafood thinly sliced and served with a dipping sauce and simple garnishes, is usually served as the first course of a meal. As it is considered the greatest delicacy in Japanese cuisine, it is served first so that the palate is unaffected by other foods. Shoyu, or Japanese soy sauce, and fiery wasabi are traditional accompaniments, often mixed together in a dipping sauce. The slices of fish are often presented on shiso leaves, which have an aroma rather like apple mint and are also used as a flavouring in Japanese salads and meat and fish dishes.

Tuna Chilli Tacos

Tacos are a useful, quick party snack – but your guests will need to use both hands to eat them. For more civilized dining, serve them as an appetizer at a dinner party.

Serves 8

8 taco shells
400g/14oz can red kidney beans, drained
120ml/4fl oz/½ cup low-fat fromage frais or low-fat cream cheese
2.5ml/½ tsp chilli sauce
2 spring onions (scallions), chopped
5ml/1 tsp chopped fresh mint
½ small crisp lettuce, shredded
425g/15oz can tuna chunks in water, drained
50g/2oz/¾ cup grated reduced-fat Cheddar cheese
8 tomatoes, quartered
mint sprigs, to garnish

1 Preheat the oven to 200°C/400°F/Gas 6. Place the taco shells on a large baking sheet and warm them in the hot oven for a few minutes until crisp.

2 In a bowl, mash the kidney beans lightly with a fork, then stir in the fromage frais or cream cheese, chilli sauce, spring onions, and chopped mint.

3 Fill the taco shells with the shredded lettuce, the bean mixture, and tuna. Top the filled shells with the cheese and serve immediately with the cherry tomatoes, garnished with sprigs of mint.

Variations
- *This tuna chilli mixture would also make an excellent and tasty filling for crisp, grilled potato skins or for a baked jacket potato.*
- *You could use soft, flour tortillas, if you prefer rather than the hard taco shells. Warm the tortillas in a frying pan and then place the lettuce, bean mixture, tuna and cheese on top of the tortilla and fold over to enclose the filling.*

Tuna and Wasabi Energy 145kcal/609kJ; Protein 24.4g; Carbohydrate 1.3g, of which sugars 1.2g; Fat 4.7g, of which saturates 1.2g; Cholesterol 28mg; Calcium 26mg; Fibre 0.4g; Sodium 583mg.
Tuna Chilli Energy 293kcal/1236kJ; Protein 22.7g; Carbohydrate 33.2g, of which sugars 3.7g; Fat 8.6g, of which saturates 1.4g; Cholesterol 41mg; Calcium 77mg; Fibre 2.1g; Sodium 276mg.

Steamed Sole Lettuce Wraps

Lettuce has a delicate texture and subtle flavour that makes it ideal for light fish mixtures such as this.

Serves 4

2 large sole or flounder fillets, skinned
15ml/1 tbsp sesame seeds
15ml/1 tbsp sunflower oil
10ml/2 tsp sesame oil
2.5cm/1in piece of fresh root ginger, peeled and grated
3 garlic cloves, finely chopped
15ml/1 tbsp soy sauce or fish sauce, plus extra, to serve
juice of 1 lemon
1 spring onion (scallion), thinly sliced
8 large soft lettuce leaves
12 large fresh mussels, scrubbed and bearded
salt and ground black pepper
4 lengths of spring onion (scallion) green, blanched and tied in small bows, to garnish (optional)

1 Cut the sole or flounder fillets in half lengthways. Season well and set aside. Prepare a steamer. Heat a heavy frying pan and lightly toast the sesame seeds. Transfer into a bowl and set aside.

2 Heat both oils in the frying pan over medium heat. Add the ginger and garlic and cook until lightly coloured, then stir in the soy sauce or fish sauce with the lemon juice and spring onion. Remove from the heat, add the sesame seeds and stir well.

3 Lay a piece of fish, skin side up, on a board or square of baking parchment. Spread evenly with the ginger mixture, then roll up, starting at the tail end. Repeat with the remaining fish and filling.

4 Plunge the lettuce leaves into the boiling water in the pan below the steamer. Immediately lift them out, using tongs or a slotted spoon. Pat dry with kitchen paper. Wrap each fish roll in two lettuce leaves, making sure that the filling is well covered.

5 Arrange the parcels in the steamer basket, cover and steam for 8 minutes. Add the mussels and steam for 2–4 minutes, until they have opened. Discard any that remain closed.

6 Halve each parcel and arrange two halves on each plate. Drizzle soy sauce or fish sauce around, and place three mussels on each plate. Garnish with spring onion bows, if you like.

Marinated Herrings

Sweet-and-sour and lightly spiced, this classic dish needs to be prepared well in advance to allow for the marinating time. It makes a substantial appetizer when served with pieces of rye bread or slices of crusty French bread.

Serves 4–6

2–3 herrings, filleted
1 onion, sliced
juice of 1½ lemons
30ml/2 tbsp white wine vinegar
25ml/1½ tbsp sugar
10–15 black peppercorns
10–15 allspice berries
1.5ml/¼ tsp mustard seeds
3 bay leaves, torn
salt
rye bread, to serve

1 Soak the herring fillets in a bowl of cold water for 5 minutes, then drain. Pour over fresh water to cover the fish and soak for about 2–3 hours.

2 Drain the soaked fish and, once more, pour over fresh water to cover and leave the fillets to soak overnight.

3 Hold the soaked herrings under cold running water and rinse very well, both inside and out.

4 Cut each fish into bitesize pieces, then place the pieces in a glass bowl or shallow dish.

5 Sprinkle the sliced onion over the fish, then add the lemon juice, white wine vinegar, sugar, peppercorns, allspice, mustard seeds and bay leaves and season with salt. Add enough water to just cover. Cover and chill for 2 days to allow the flavours to blend. Serve with pieces of rye bread.

Cook's Tip
Allspice is a berry native to the West Indies and Central America. It is also known as Jamaica pepper. Look for it in supermarkets and Caribbean food stores.

Steamed Sole Energy 118kcal/492kJ; Protein 15.3g; Carbohydrate 0.9g, of which sugars 0.9g; Fat 5.9g, of which saturates 0.7g; Cholesterol 41mg; Calcium 46mg; Fibre 0.3g; Sodium 359mg.
Marinated Herrings Energy 94kcal/393kJ; Protein 7.7g; Carbohydrate 3.4g, of which sugars 3.2g; Fat 5.6g, of which saturates 1.4g; Cholesterol 21mg; Calcium 29mg; Fibre 0.1g; Sodium 52mg.

Fish Cakes in Banana Leaves

The oily flesh of mackerel is ideal for these spicy cakes. They make a stunning appetizer for a dinner party as the guests open their banana leaves to reveal the delicious contents.

Serves 4–6

4 shallots, chopped
1 lemon grass stalk, trimmed and chopped
25g/1oz galangal, chopped
4 macadamia nuts, roasted
4 dried red chillies, soaked in warm water until soft, squeezed dry and seeded
5ml/1 tsp shrimp paste
5–10ml/1–2 tsp ground turmeric
250ml/8fl oz/1 cup coconut cream
15ml/1 tbsp dark soy sauce
10ml/2 tsp palm sugar (jaggery)
450g/1lb fresh mackerel, cleaned, skinned and flaked
4–6 kaffir lime leaves, finely shredded
2 eggs, lightly beaten
salt and ground black pepper
12 banana leaves, cut into pieces about 20cm/8in square
2 limes, quartered lengthways, and chilli or peanut sambal, to serve

1 Using a food processor, grind the shallots, lemon grass, galangal, nuts and chillies to a paste. Blend in the shrimp paste, turmeric, coconut cream, soy sauce and sugar.

2 Put the flaked mackerel and lime leaves in a bowl. Pour in the spiced coconut cream and the beaten eggs. Season with salt and ground black pepper. Mix the ingredients to evenly coat the fish. Preheat the oven to 200°C/400°F/Gas 6.

3 Lay a square of banana leaf on a flat surface. Place 30ml/2 tbsp of the fish mixture just off centre and fold the sides of the leaf over the top, leaving room for expansion. Secure the package with a cocktail stick (toothpick) threaded through each end. Repeat with the rest of the mixture.

4 Place the banana leaf packages on a baking sheet that is large enough to hold them all; or split between two baking sheets. Bake in the oven for 30 minutes until cooked through.

5 Serve the cakes in the banana leaves with the lime quarters for squeezing and the sambal for dipping.

Spicy Fried Mackerel

This ginger-spiced dish goes down very well with chilled light beer. Try it served hot but it is also excellent cold and is very good served with salad.

Serves 4

675g/1½lb mackerel, filleted
60ml/4 tbsp shoyu
60ml/4 tbsp sake
60ml/4 tbsp caster (superfine) sugar
1 garlic clove, crushed
2cm/¾in piece fresh root ginger, peeled and finely grated
2–3 shiso leaves, chopped into thin strips (optional)
cornflour (cornstarch), for dusting
vegetable oil, for deep-frying
1 lime, cut into thick wedges

1 Using a pair of tweezers, remove any remaining bones from the mackerel. Cut the fillets in half lengthways, then slice diagonally crossways into bitesize pieces.

2 Mix the shoyu, sake, sugar, garlic, grated ginger and shiso in a mixing bowl to make the marinade. Add the mackerel pieces and leave to marinate for 20 minutes.

3 Drain and pat dry gently with kitchen paper. Dust the fillets with cornflour.

4 Heat plenty of vegetable oil in a wok or a deep-fryer. The temperature of the oil must be kept around 180°C/350°F. Deep-fry the mackerel fillets, a few pieces at a time, until they turn a shiny brown colour.

5 Remove the fish pieces as soon as they are done and drain on kitchen paper. Keep them warm while you cook the rest, then serve immediately with wedges of lime.

Cook's Tips
• *Shiso leaves are only sold in Japanese food stores. If you can't find them, use 5–6 chopped basil leaves instead.*
• *Fresh mackerel should be firm and glistening, with shiny eyes. Get the fishmonger to fillet the fish for you.*

Fish Cakes Energy 235kcal/977kJ; Protein 16.7g; Carbohydrate 6.2g, of which sugars 5.9g; Fat 16.1g, of which saturates 3.4g; Cholesterol 104mg; Calcium 44mg; Fibre 0.3g; Sodium 332mg.
Spicy Mackerel Energy 580kcal/2414kJ; Protein 32.2g; Carbohydrate 24g, of which sugars 17g; Fat 38.2g, of which saturates 6.9g; Cholesterol 91mg; Calcium 31mg; Fibre 0g; Sodium 1181mg.

Lemon Sole and Fresh Oyster Salad

Oysters, flavoured with a rice-vinegar dressing, taste wonderful with lemon sole sashimi. In Japan, there is no choice of fish on a menu – it depends on which fish was caught that day.

Serves 4

1 very fresh lemon sole, skinned and filleted into 4 pieces
105ml/7 tbsp rice vinegar
dashi-konbu, in 4 pieces, big enough to cover the fillets
50g/2oz Japanese cucumber, trimmed, or salad cucumber with seeds removed
50g/2oz celery sticks, strings removed
450g/1lb large broad (fava) beans, podded
1 lime, ½ thinly sliced
60ml/4 tbsp walnut oil
seeds from ½ pomegranate
salt

For the oysters

15ml/1 tbsp rice vinegar
30ml/2 tbsp shoyu
15ml/1 tbsp sake
12 large fresh oysters, opened
25g/1oz mooli (daikon) or radishes, peeled and very finely grated
8 chives

1 Sprinkle salt on the sole. Cover and chill for an hour. Mix the rice vinegar and a similar amount of water in a bowl. Wash the fillets in the mixture, then drain. Halve each fillet lengthways.

2 Lay one piece of dashi-konbu on a work surface. Place a pair of sole fillets, skinned sides together, on to it, then lay another piece of konbu on top. Cover all the fillets like this and chill for 3 hours.

3 Halve the cucumber crossways and slice thinly lengthways. Slice diagonally into 2cm/¾in wide pieces. Repeat for the celery. Sprinkle the cucumber with salt and leave for 30–60 minutes. Squeeze to remove moisture. Boil the beans for 15 minutes. Drain, cool, then peel off the skins. Sprinkle with salt. Mix the vinegar, shoyu and sake in a bowl. Slice the sole thinly.

4 Place the cucumber and celery in a mound in the centre of four plates. Lay lime slices on top. Garnish with chives. Place the oysters to one side of the cucumber, topped with broad beans, then season with 5ml/1 tsp of the vinegar and 10ml/2 tsp mooli. Arrange the sole on the other side and drizzle with walnut oil and lime juice. Add the pomegranate seeds and serve.

Ginger and Chilli Steamed Fish Custards

These pretty little custards make an unusual and exotic appetizer for a dinner party. The pandanus leaves impart a distinctive flavour – but don't be tempted to eat them once the custards are cooked: they are inedible.

Serves 4

2 eggs
200ml/7fl oz/scant 1 cup coconut cream
60ml/4 tbsp chopped fresh coriander (cilantro)
1 red chilli, seeded and sliced
15ml/1 tbsp finely chopped lemon grass
2 kaffir lime leaves, finely shredded
30ml/2 tbsp red Thai curry paste
1 garlic clove, crushed
5ml/1 tsp finely grated fresh root ginger
2 spring onions (scallions), finely sliced
300g/11oz mixed firm white fish fillets (cod, halibut or haddock), skinned
200g/7oz raw tiger prawns (shrimp), peeled and deveined
4–6 pandanus (screwpine) leaves
salt and ground black pepper
shredded cucumber, steamed rice and soy sauce, to serve

1 Beat the eggs in a bowl, then stir in the coconut cream, coriander, chilli, lemon grass, lime leaves, curry paste, garlic, ginger and spring onions. Finely chop the fish and roughly chop the prawns and add to the egg mixture. Stir well and season.

2 Grease four ramekins and line them with the pandanus leaves. Divide the fish mixture between them, then arrange in a bamboo steamer.

3 Pour 5cm/2in water into a wok and bring to the boil. Suspend the steamer over the water, cover, reduce the heat to low and steam for 25–30 minutes, or until cooked through. Serve with shredded cucumber and soy sauce.

Cook's Tip
Pandanus leaves are available from Asian markets.

Lemon Sole Energy 264kcal/1105kJ; Protein 22.7g; Carbohydrate 14.8g, of which sugars 1.9g; Fat 13.1g, of which saturates 1.3g; Cholesterol 56mg; Calcium 143mg; Fibre 7.6g; Sodium 295mg.
Ginger and Chilli Energy 150kcal/632kJ; Protein 26.2g; Carbohydrate 2.8g, of which sugars 2.7g; Fat 3.9g, of which saturates 1g; Cholesterol 227mg; Calcium 100mg; Fibre 0.6g; Sodium 234mg.

Fish and Chermoula Mini Pies

These pies are made with ouarka, a fine pastry, but filo pastry will work just as well.

Serves 4
500g/1¼lb firm white fish fillets
225g/8oz uncooked king prawns (jumbo shrimp)
16 sheets of ouarka or filo pastry
60–75ml/4–5 tbsp sunflower oil
1 egg yolk, mixed with a few drops of water
salt

For the chermoula
75ml/5 tbsp olive oil
juice of 1 lemon
5ml/1 tsp ground cumin
5–10ml/1–2 tsp paprika
2–3 garlic cloves, crushed
1 red chilli, seeded and chopped
large bunch of flat leaf parsley, chopped
large bunch of fresh coriander (cilantro), chopped

1 Prepare the chermoula. Combine all the ingredients in a bowl and set aside. Place the fish in a frying pan and add enough water to cover the fillets. Season with a little salt and heat until just simmering, then cook gently for 3 minutes, or until the fish starts to flake. Use a slotted spoon to remove the fish from the liquid and break it up, taking care to remove all bones.

2 Poach the prawns in the fish liquor for 10 minutes, until they turn pink, then drain and shell them. Gently toss the prawns and fish in the chermoula, cover and set aside for 1 hour.

3 Preheat the oven to 180°C/350°F/Gas 4 and grease two baking sheets. To make the pies, open out the sheets of filo pastry but keep them under a damp dish towel. Take two sheets of pastry: brush a sheet with oil and lay the second one on top, then brush it with a little oil. Place some of the fish mixture in the middle of the length of the sheet but to one side of its width. Fold the edge of the pastry over the filling, then fold the long side over to cover the filling completely.

4 Wrap the ends of the pastry around the filling like a collar to make a neat package with the edges tucked in, then brush with egg yolk. Continue in the same way with the rest of the filo and chermoula mixture, then bake the pies for about 20 minutes until the pastry is golden brown.

Thai-style Seafood Turnovers

These elegant appetizer-size turnovers are filled with fish, prawns and fragrant rice.

Makes 18
plain (all-purpose) flour, for dusting
500g/1¼lb puff pastry
1 egg, beaten with a little water
lime twists, to garnish

For the filling
275g/10oz skinned white fish fillets, such as cod or haddock
seasoned plain (all-purpose) flour
8–10 large raw prawns (shrimp)
15ml/1 tbsp sunflower oil
about 75g/3oz/6 tbsp butter
6 spring onions (scallions), sliced
1 garlic clove, crushed
225g/8oz/2 cups cooked Thai fragrant rice
4cm/1½in piece fresh root ginger, grated
10ml/2 tsp finely chopped fresh coriander (cilantro)
5ml/1 tsp finely grated lime rind

1 Preheat the oven to 190°C/375°F/Gas 5. Make the filling. Cut the fish into 2cm/¾in cubes and dust with the flour. Peel the prawns, remove the veins and cut each one into four pieces.

2 Heat half the oil and 15g/½oz/1 tbsp of the butter in a frying pan. Fry the spring onions for 2 minutes. Add the garlic and fry for 5 minutes, until the onions are soft. Transfer to a large bowl.

3 Heat the remaining oil and 25g/1oz/2 tbsp of the butter in a clean pan. Fry the fish pieces briefly. As soon as they begin to turn opaque, use a slotted spoon to transfer them to the bowl with the spring onions. Cook the prawns in the fat remaining in the pan. When they change colour, transfer them to the bowl. Add the cooked rice to the bowl, with the ginger, coriander and grated lime rind. Mix, taking care not to break up the fish.

4 Dust the work surface with a little flour. Roll out the pastry and cut into 10cm/4in rounds. Place spoonfuls of filling just off centre on the rounds. Dot with a little of the remaining butter. Dampen the edges with a little of the egg wash, fold one side of the pastry over the filling and press the edges together firmly.

5 Place the turnovers on two lightly greased baking sheets. Brush them with egg wash. Bake for 12–15 minutes until golden brown all over. Transfer to a plate and garnish with lime twists.

Fish Pies Energy 472kcal/1969kJ; Protein 36.4g; Carbohydrate 19.9g, of which sugars 0.8g; Fat 27.9g, of which saturates 3.9g; Cholesterol 218mg; Calcium 134mg; Fibre 1.7g; Sodium 191mg.
Thai-style Seafood Energy 171kcal/715kJ; Protein 8.6g; Carbohydrate 18.7g, of which sugars 0.9g; Fat 7g, of which saturates 2.3g; Cholesterol 48mg; Calcium 34mg; Fibre 0.4g; Sodium 99mg.

Creamy Cucumber and Walnut Appetizer

In this salad, diced cucumber is bathed in a luscious garlic and yogurt dressing and topped with chopped walnuts for a delicious contrast in texture and flavour. Serve with chunks of rustic bread as a fresh-tasting alternative to a meat or fish pâté.

Serves 6

1 large cucumber
3–5 garlic cloves, finely chopped
250ml/8fl oz/1 cup sour cream or 120ml/4fl oz/½ cup Greek (US strained plain) yogurt mixed with 120ml/4fl oz/½ cup double (heavy) cream
250ml/8fl oz/1 cup yogurt, preferably thick Greek yogurt
2–3 large pinches of dried dill or 30–45ml/2–3 tbsp chopped fresh dill
45–60ml/3–4 tbsp chopped walnuts
salt
sprig of dill, to garnish (optional)

1 Do not peel the cucumber. Using a sharp knife, dice it finely and place in a large mixing bowl.

2 Add the garlic, sour cream or yogurt and cream mixture, Greek yogurt and dill and season with salt. Mix together, then cover and chill.

3 To serve, pile the mixture into a bowl and sprinkle with walnuts. Garnish with dill, if you like.

Cook's Tip
When made with very thick Greek yogurt, this appetizer can be shaped into balls and served on salad leaves.

Variation
For a Greek version, to serve as part of a mezze, add chopped fresh mint instead of dill, omit the walnuts and serve with olives and pitta bread.

Falafel

The secret to making good falafel is to use well-soaked, but not cooked, chickpeas. Do not try to use canned chickpeas for this recipe, as the texture will be mushy and the finished falafel will fall apart.

Serves 6

250g/9oz/generous 1⅓ cups dried chickpeas
1 litre/1¾ pints/4 cups water
45–60ml/3–4 tbsp bulgur wheat
1 large onion, finely chopped
5 garlic cloves, crushed
75ml/5 tbsp chopped fresh parsley
75ml/5 tbsp chopped fresh coriander (cilantro) leaves
45ml/3 tbsp ground cumin
15ml/1 tbsp ground coriander
5ml/1 tsp baking powder
5ml/1 tsp salt
small pinch to 1.5ml/¼ tsp ground black pepper
small pinch to 1.5ml/¼ tsp cayenne pepper
5ml/1 tsp curry powder with a pinch of cardamom seeds
45–60ml/3–4 tbsp gram flour
extra flour, if necessary
vegetable oil, for deep-frying
6 pitta breads, hummus, tahini, chilli sauce, pickles, olives and salads, to serve

1 Place the chickpeas in a large bowl and pour over the water. Leave to soak for 4 hours, drain and grind in a food processor.

2 Put the ground chickpeas in a bowl and stir in the bulgur wheat, onion, garlic, parsley, fresh coriander, ground cumin and coriander, baking powder, salt, black pepper and cayenne pepper, and curry powder, if using. Stir in 45ml/3 tbsp water and leave to stand for about 45 minutes.

3 Stir the gram flour into the falafel batter, adding a little water if it is too thick or a little flour if it is too thin. Using a wet tablespoon and wet hands, shape the mixture into 12–18 balls.

4 In a deep pan or wok, heat the oil for deep-frying to 180°C/350°F. Add the falafel in batches and cook for about 3–4 minutes until golden brown.

5 Serve tucked into warmed pitta bread with a spoonful of hummus and a drizzle of tahini. Accompany with chilli sauce, pickles, olives and some salads.

Creamy Cucumber Energy 167kcal/688kJ; Protein 4.9g; Carbohydrate 5.7g, of which sugars 5.6g; Fat 14g, of which saturates 5.8g; Cholesterol 26mg; Calcium 148mg; Fibre 0.9g; Sodium 56mg.
Falafel Energy 303kcal/1282kJ; Protein 18.5g; Carbohydrate 44.7g, of which sugars 5.2g; Fat 6.9g, of which saturates 1.2g; Cholesterol 0mg; Calcium 88mg; Fibre 7.2g; Sodium 16mg.

Grilled Vegetable Sticks

For this tasty dish, made with tofu, konnyaku and aubergine, you will need 40 bamboo skewers, soaked in water overnight to prevent them burning when grilled.

Serves 4

285g/10¼oz packet tofu block
1 x 250g/9oz packet konnyaku
2 small aubergines (eggplants)
25ml/1½ tbsp toasted sesame oil

For the yellow and green sauces

45ml/3 tbsp shiro-miso
15ml/1 tbsp caster (superfine) sugar
5 young spinach leaves
2.5ml/½ tsp sansho
salt

For the red sauce

15ml/1 tbsp aka-miso
5ml/1 tsp caster (superfine) sugar
5ml/1 tsp mirin

To garnish

pinch of white poppy seeds
15ml/1 tbsp toasted sesame seeds

1 Drain the liquid from the tofu packet and wrap the tofu in three layers of kitchen paper. Set a chopping board on top to press out the remaining liquid. Leave for 30 minutes until the excess liquid has been absorbed by the kitchen paper. Cut into eight 7.5 x 2 x 1cm/3 x ¾ x ½in slices.

2 Drain the liquid from the konnyaku. Cut it in half and put in a small pan with enough water to cover. Bring to the boil and cook for about 5 minutes. Drain and cut the konnyaku into eight 6 x 2 x 1cm/2½ x ¾ x ½in slices.

3 Halve the aubergines lengthways, then halve the thickness to make four flat slices. Soak in cold water for 15 minutes. Drain and pat dry. To make the yellow sauce, mix the shiro-miso and sugar in a pan, then cook over low heat, stirring to dissolve. Remove from the heat. Place half the sauce in a small bowl.

4 Blanch the spinach leaves in rapidly boiling water with a pinch of salt for 30 seconds and drain, then cool under running water. Squeeze out the water and chop finely. Transfer to a mortar and pound to a paste using a pestle. Mix the paste and sansho pepper into the bowl of yellow sauce to make the green sauce.

5 Put the red sauce ingredients in a pan and cook over a low heat, stirring constantly, until the sugar has dissolved. Remove from the heat.

6 Pierce the slices of tofu, konnyaku and aubergine with two bamboo skewers each. Heat the grill (broiler) to high. Brush the aubergine slices with sesame oil and grill (broil) for 7–8 minutes each side. Turn several times.

7 Grill the konnyaku and tofu for 3–5 minutes each side, until lightly browned. Remove from the heat but keep the grill hot.

8 Spread the red miso sauce on the aubergine slices. Spread one side of the tofu slices with green sauce and one side of the konnyaku with the yellow miso sauce from the pan. Grill the slices for 1–2 minutes. Sprinkle the aubergines with poppy seeds and the konnyaku with sesame seeds and serve together.

Stuffed Vine Leaves with Garlic Yogurt

These vine leaves are stuffed with rice that is flavoured with fresh herbs, lemon and a little chilli, before being slowly simmered.

Serves 6

225g/8oz packet preserved vine leaves
1 onion, finely chopped
½ bunch of spring onions (scallions), trimmed and finely chopped
60ml/4 tbsp chopped fresh parsley
10 large mint sprigs, chopped
finely grated rind of 1 lemon
2.5ml/½ tsp crushed dried chillies
7.5ml/1½ tsp fennel seeds, crushed
175g/6oz/scant 1 cup cooked long grain rice
120ml/4fl oz/½cup olive oil
150ml/¼ pint/⅔ cup thick natural (plain) yogurt
2 garlic cloves, crushed
salt
lemon wedges and mint leaves, to garnish (optional)

1 Rinse the vine leaves in cold water. Put in a bowl, cover with boiling water and stand for 10 minutes. Drain thoroughly. Mix together the onion, spring onions, parsley, mint, lemon, chilli, fennel, rice and 25ml/1½ tbsp of the oil. Season with salt.

2 Place a vine leaf, veined side facing upwards, on a work surface and cut off the stalk. Place a heaped teaspoonful of the rice mixture near the stalk end of the leaf. Fold the stalk end over the rice filling, then fold over the sides and carefully roll up into a neat cigar shape.

3 Repeat with the remaining filling to make about 28 stuffed leaves. If some of the vine leaves are quite small, use two and patch them together to make parcels of the same size.

4 Place any remaining leaves in the base of a large, heavy pan. Pack the stuffed leaves in a single layer in the pan. Spoon over the remaining oil, then add 300ml/½ pint/1¼ cups boiling water. Place a plate over the leaves to keep them submerged. Cover the pan and cook over very low heat for 45 minutes.

5 Mix together the yogurt and garlic in a bowl and transfer to a small serving dish. Transfer the stuffed leaves to a serving plate and garnish with lemon wedges and mint, if you like. Serve with the garlic yogurt.

Grilled Vegetable Energy 178kcal/742kJ; Protein 12.9g; Carbohydrate 9.3g, of which sugars 8.6g; Fat 10.2g, of which saturates 1.4g; Cholesterol 0mg; Calcium 761mg; Fibre 1.9g; Sodium 17mg.
Stuffed Vine Leaves Energy 339kcal/1407kJ; Protein 5.8g; Carbohydrate 32.2g, of which sugars 7.3g; Fat 20.9g, of which saturates 2.7g; Cholesterol 0mg; Calcium 95mg; Fibre 3.4g; Sodium 14mg.

Herby Polenta with Tomatoes

Golden polenta flavoured with a selection of fresh summer herbs is pan-fried with seasonal tomatoes for a delicious taste of northern Italian cuisine.

Serves 4

750ml/1¼ pints/3 cups vegetable stock or water
5ml/1 tsp salt
175g/6oz/1 cup polenta
25g/1oz/2 tbsp butter
75ml/5 tbsp chopped mixed fresh parsley, thyme, chives and basil, plus extra, to garnish
olive oil, for greasing and brushing
6 large plum or beefsteak tomatoes
salt and ground black pepper

1 Prepare the polenta in advance: place the stock or water in a heavy pan, with the salt, and bring to the boil. Lower the heat, slowly pour in the polenta, stirring all the time with a wooden spoon.

2 Stir the mixture constantly, using a figure-eight action, over a medium heat for 5 minutes, until the polenta begins to thicken and come away from the sides of the pan.

3 Remove from the heat and continue stirring for another minute or two. Stir in the butter, freshly chopped parsley, thyme, chives and basil, and season with black pepper.

4 Transfer the mixture into a wide, greased tin (pan) or a glass or ceramic dish. Using a flexible spatula, spread the polenta mixture out evenly. Cover the surface closely with baking parchment, then put it in a cool place until it has set completely and is cold.

5 Turn out the polenta on to a board and stamp out eight rounds using a large biscuit or cookie cutter. Or, you can cut the polenta into eight squares with a knife. Brush with oil.

6 Heat a griddle pan and lightly brush it with oil. Cut the tomatoes in two, then brush them with oil and sprinkle with salt and pepper. Cook the tomato halves and polenta patties on the pan for 5 minutes, turning them once. Serve garnished with fresh herbs.

Pickled Broccoli in Miso

Broccoli stem is usually wasted because of the fibrous texture, but you will be surprised how tasty it is when marinated or pickled. In this recipe, miso and garlic give a kick to its subtle flavour. The pickle, which will keep for a few days, also makes a good accompaniment to drinks.

Serves 4

3 broccoli stems (use the florets in another dish, if you wish)
2 Japanese or salad cucumbers, ends trimmed
200ml/7fl oz/scant 1 cup miso (any kind)
15ml/1 tbsp sake
1 garlic clove, crushed

1 Peel the broccoli stems and quarter them lengthways. With a vegetable peeler, peel the cucumber every 5mm/¼in to make green-and-white stripes. Cut in half lengthways. Scoop out the centre with a teaspoon. Slice into 7.5cm/3in lengths.

2 Mix the miso, sake and crushed garlic in a deep, plastic or metal container with a lid. Remove half the miso mix.

3 Lay some of the broccoli stems and cucumber flat in the container and push into the miso mix. Spread a little of the reserved miso over the top of the broccoli and cucumber.

4 Repeat this process to make a few layers of vegetables and miso, filling up the container. Cover with the lid and leave in the refrigerator for 1–5 days.

5 Take out the vegetables, wash off the miso under cold running water, then wipe with kitchen paper. Cut the broccoli stem pieces in half, then slice into thin strips lengthways. Cut the cucumber into 5mm/¼in thick half-moon slices. Serve the vegetables cold.

Variation
Carrot, turnip, kohlrabi, celery, radish or thinly sliced cabbage stems can be used in this way.

Herby Polenta Energy 147kcal/612kJ; Protein 3.2g; Carbohydrate 23.4g, of which sugars 2.1g; Fat 4.2g, of which saturates 1.5g; Cholesterol 5mg; Calcium 6mg; Fibre 1.3g; Sodium 349mg.
Pickled Broccoli Energy 54kcal/227kJ; Protein 5.6g; Carbohydrate 4.9g, of which sugars 3.8g; Fat 1g, of which saturates 0.2g; Cholesterol 0mg; Calcium 66mg; Fibre 2.9g; Sodium 1789mg.

Broccoli Timbales

This elegant but easy-to-make dish is perfect as an appetizer for a dinner party, or could be served as a light main course, if you like. To avoid any last-minute fuss, make the timbales a few hours ahead and cook while the first course is being eaten. Or, serve them on their own as an appetizer with a little white wine butter sauce.

Serves 4

350g/¾lb broccoli florets
45ml/3 tbsp crème fraîche or whipping cream
1 egg, plus 1 egg yolk
15ml/1 tbsp chopped spring onion (scallion)
pinch of freshly grated nutmeg
salt and ground black pepper
white wine butter sauce, to serve (optional)
fresh chives, to garnish

1 Preheat the oven to 190°C/375°F/Gas 5. Lightly butter four 175ml/6fl oz ramekins. Line the bases with baking parchment and butter the parchment.

2 Steam the broccoli in the top of a covered steamer over boiling water for 8–10 minutes until very tender.

3 Put the broccoli in a food processor or blender fitted with the metal blade and process with the cream, egg and egg yolk until smooth.

4 Add the spring onion and season with salt, ground black pepper and nutmeg. Pulse to mix.

5 Spoon the purée into the ramekins and place them in a baking dish. Add boiling water to come halfway up the sides, then bake for 25 minutes, until just set. Invert on to warmed plates and peel off the paper. If serving as an appetizer, pour a little sauce around each timbale and garnish with chives.

Variation
The timbales can be made with other puréed vegetables such as carrot or celeriac, if you like.

Greek Stuffed Vegetables

Colourful peppers and tomatoes make perfect containers for various meat and vegetable stuffings. This rice and herb version uses typically Greek ingredients.

Serves 4

2 large ripe tomatoes
1 green (bell) pepper
1 yellow or orange (bell) pepper
60ml/4 tbsp olive oil, plus extra for sprinkling
2 onions, chopped
2 garlic cloves, crushed
50g/2oz/½ cup blanched almonds, chopped
75g/3oz/scant ½ cup long grain rice, boiled and drained
15g/½oz mint, roughly chopped
15g/½oz fresh parsley, roughly chopped
25g/1oz/2 tbsp sultanas (golden raisins)
45ml/3 tbsp ground almonds
salt and ground black pepper
chopped mixed fresh herbs, to garnish

1 Preheat the oven to 190°C/375°F/Gas 5. Cut the tomatoes in half and scoop out the pulp and seeds using a teaspoon. Leave the tomatoes to drain on kitchen paper with cut sides down. Roughly chop the tomato pulp and seeds.

2 Halve the peppers, leaving the stalks intact. Scoop out the seeds. Brush the peppers with 15ml/1 tbsp of the oil and bake on a baking tray for 15 minutes. Place the peppers and tomatoes in a shallow ovenproof dish and season with salt and pepper.

3 Fry the onions in the remaining oil for 5 minutes. Add the garlic and chopped almonds and fry for a further minute.

4 Remove the pan from the heat and stir in the rice, chopped tomatoes, mint, parsley and golden raisins. Season well then spoon the mixture into the tomatoes and peppers.

5 Pour ⅔ cup boiling water around the tomatoes and peppers and bake, uncovered, for 20 minutes. Scatter with the ground almonds and sprinkle with a little extra olive oil. Return the dish to the oven and bake for about 20 minutes more, or until the top is turning golden. Serve garnished with fresh herbs.

Broccoli Timbales Energy 106kcal/438kJ; Protein 6.4g; Carbohydrate 1.9g, of which sugars 1.6g; Fat 8.1g, of which saturates 4g; Cholesterol 111mg; Calcium 70mg; Fibre 2.3g; Sodium 30mg.
Greek Stuffed Vegetables Energy 234kcal/981kJ; Protein 5.7g; Carbohydrate 32.5g, of which sugars 14.5g; Fat 9.9g, of which saturates 1.2g; Cholesterol 0mg; Calcium 71mg; Fibre 3.6g; Sodium 14mg.

Stuffed Green Chillies

Stuffed chillies are popular all over Mexico. The type of chilli used differs from region to region. Poblanos and Anaheims are quite mild, but you can use hotter chillies if you prefer.

Serves 6

6 fresh poblano or Anaheim chillies
2 potatoes, total weight about 400g/14oz
200g/7oz/scant 1 cup cream cheese
200g/7oz/1¾ cups grated mature (sharp) Cheddar cheese
5ml/1 tsp salt
2.5ml/½ tsp ground black pepper
2 eggs, separated
115g/4oz/1 cup plain (all-purpose) flour
2.5ml/½ tsp white pepper
oil, for frying
chilli flakes to garnish, (optional)

1 Cut a slit down one side of each chilli. Dry-fry the chillies in a pan, turning frequently, until they blister. Place in a plastic bag and tie the top to keep the steam in. Set aside for 20 minutes, then peel off the skins and remove the seeds through the slits, keeping the chillies whole. Dry with kitchen paper and set aside.

2 Scrub or peel the potatoes and cut them into 1cm/½in dice. Bring a large pan of water to the boil, add the potatoes and return to the boil. Lower the heat and simmer for 5 minutes, or until the potatoes are just tender. Drain them thoroughly.

3 Put the cream cheese in a bowl with the mature cheese. Add 2.5ml/½ tsp of the salt and the black pepper. Mix in the potato. Spoon potato filling into each chilli. Put them on a plate, cover with clear film (plastic wrap) and chill for 1 hour to firm up.

4 Put the egg whites in a clean, grease-free bowl and whisk to firm peaks. In another bowl, beat the yolks until pale, then fold in the whites. Scrape the mixture into a large, shallow dish. Spread out the flour in another shallow dish and season it with the remaining salt and the white pepper.

5 Heat the oil for deep-frying to 190°C/375°F. Coat a few chillies in flour and then in egg before frying the chillies in batches until golden and crisp. Drain on kitchen paper and serve hot, garnished with a sprinkle of chilli flakes, if using.

Tomato and Courgette Timbales

Timbales are baked savoury custards typical of the south of France, and mainly made with light vegetables. This combination is delicious as an appetizer. It can be served warm or cool.

Serves 4

butter, for greasing
2 courgettes (zucchini), about 175g/6oz
2 firm, ripe vine tomatoes, sliced
2 eggs plus 2 egg yolks
45ml/3 tbsp double (heavy) cream
15ml/1 tbsp fresh tomato sauce or passata (bottled strained tomatoes)
10ml/2 tsp chopped fresh basil or oregano or 5ml/1 tsp dried oregano
salt and ground black pepper
salad leaves, to serve

1 Preheat the oven to 180°C/350°F/Gas 4. Lightly butter four large ramekins. Trim the courgettes, then cut them into thin slices. Put them into a steamer and steam over boiling water for 4–5 minutes.

2 Drain the courgette slices well in a colander, then layer them in the prepared ramekins, alternating them with the slices of tomatoes.

3 Whisk together the eggs, cream, tomato sauce or passata and basil or oregano in a large bowl. Season to taste with salt and black pepper.

4 Pour the egg mixture into the ramekins. Place them in a roasting pan and half fill the pan with hot water. Bake the ramekins for 20–30 minutes, until the custard is just firm.

5 Cool slightly, then run a knife blade around the rims of the ramekins and carefully turn out on to small plates. Serve with salad leaves.

Cook's Tip
Don't overcook the timbales or the texture of the savoury custard will become rubbery.

Stuffed Chillies Energy 498kcal/2072kJ; Protein 14.9g; Carbohydrate 27.8g, of which sugars 3.2g; Fat 36.5g, of which saturates 18.6g; Cholesterol 127mg; Calcium 322mg; Fibre 1.8g; Sodium 374mg.
Tomato Timbales Energy 72kcal/299kJ; Protein 5.1g; Carbohydrate 2.7g, of which sugars 2.5g; Fat 4.7g, of which saturates 1.3g; Cholesterol 146mg; Calcium 35mg; Fibre 1g; Sodium 55mg.

Roasted Plum Tomatoes with Garlic

This light salad is quick and simple to prepare, and tastes absolutely wonderful. Use a shallow earthenware dish that will allow the tomatoes to sear and char in the hot oven.

Serves 4

8 plum tomatoes, halved
12 garlic cloves, unpeeled
60ml/4 tbsp extra virgin olive oil
3 bay leaves
45ml/3 tbsp fresh oregano leaves, to garnish
salt and ground black pepper

1 Preheat the oven to 230°C/450°F/Gas 8. Place the tomatoes in an ovenproof dish in a single layer and push the whole garlic cloves between them.

2 Brush the tomatoes with oil, add the bay leaves and sprinkle with pepper. Bake for 45 minutes until the tomatoes have softened and are sizzling in the pan. They should be charred around the edges. Season with salt and a little more pepper, if needed. Garnish with fresh oregano and serve.

Griddled Tomatoes on Soda Bread

A drizzle of olive oil and balsamic vinegar, and shavings of Parmesan cheese make this appetizer special.

Serves 4

extra virgin olive oil, for brushing and drizzling
6 tomatoes, thickly sliced
4 thick slices soda bread
balsamic vinegar, for drizzling
salt and ground black pepper
thin shavings of Parmesan cheese, to serve

1 Brush a griddle pan with oil and heat. Add the tomato slices and cook, turning once, for 4 minutes, until slightly blackened.

2 Meanwhile, lightly toast the soda bread. Place the tomatoes on top of the toast and drizzle each portion with a little olive oil and balsamic vinegar. Season to taste with salt and pepper and serve immediately with the shavings of Parmesan cheese.

Spiced Roasted Pumpkin

Pumpkins are favourites for making into pies and pickles. Here chunks of pumpkin are roasted with spices and herbs before being topped with cheese. Serve with a salad of watercress and baby spinach leaves. Minus the cheese, this dish makes a good accompaniment to roast meats, sausages or lamb chops.

Serves 3–4

5ml/1 tsp fennel seeds
30ml/2 tbsp olive oil
1 garlic clove, crushed
5ml/1 tsp ground ginger
5ml/1 tsp dried thyme
pinch of chilli powder (optional)
piece of pumpkin weighing about 1.5kg/3lb 6oz
75g/3oz/¾ cup cheese, such as Caerphilly, grated
salt and ground black pepper

1 Preheat the oven to 200°C/400°F/Gas 6. Lightly crush or bruise the fennel seeds with a mortar and pestle, a rolling pin or the back of a spoon – this helps to release their flavour.

2 Put the oil into a large bowl and stir in the fennel, garlic, ginger, thyme and chilli. Season with salt and pepper and mix.

3 Cut the skin off the pumpkin, scrape out and discard the seeds. Cut the flesh into rough chunks of about 3.5cm/1in. Toss the chunks in the oil mixture until evenly coated, then spread them in a single layer on a large baking tray.

4 Put into the hot oven and cook for about 40 minutes or until tender and golden brown on the edges. It helps to turn them over once during cooking.

5 Sprinkle the cheese over the top and return to the oven for about 5 more minutes. Serve straight from the baking tray, making sure all the golden bits of cheese are scraped up with the pumpkin.

Variation
This works well with other winter squashes too, such as butternut or turban.

Roasted Tomatoes Energy 158kcal/660kJ; Protein 3.1g; Carbohydrate 10.3g, of which sugars 8.4g; Fat 12g, of which saturates 1.9g; Cholesterol 0mg; Calcium 43mg; Fibre 3.6g; Sodium 27mg.
Griddled Tomatoes Energy 172kcal/724kJ; Protein 3.9g; Carbohydrate 25.1g, of which sugars 5.8g; Fat 6.9g, of which saturates 0.9g; Cholesterol 0mg; Calcium 63mg; Fibre 2.3g; Sodium 171mg.
Spiced Pumpkin Energy 171kcal/712kJ; Protein 7.1g; Carbohydrate 8.3g, of which sugars 6.4g; Fat 12g, of which saturates 5g; Cholesterol 17mg; Calcium 238mg; Fibre 3.8g; Sodium 127mg.

Mushroom Caviar

The name caviar refers to the dark colour and texture of this dish of chopped mushrooms. Serve the caviar mixture in individual serving dishes with toasted rye bread rubbed with cut garlic cloves, to accompany. Chopped hard-boiled egg, spring onion and parsley, the traditional garnishes for caviar, can be used here.

Serves 4

45ml/3 tbsp olive or vegetable oil
450g/1lb mushrooms, coarsely chopped
5–10 shallots, chopped
4 garlic cloves, chopped
chopped hard-boiled eggs, sliced spring onion and chopped fresh parsley and toasted bread (optional), to serve

1 Heat the olive or vegetable oil in a large pan, add the mushrooms, shallots and garlic, and cook, stirring occasionally, until browned.

2 Season the mushroom mixture with salt, then continue cooking, stirring occasionally, until the mushrooms give up their liquor.

3 Continue cooking the mixture, stirring frequently, until the liquor from the mushrooms has evaporated and they are brown and dry.

4 Place the mixture in a food processor or blender and process briefly until a chunky paste is formed. Spoon the mushroom caviar into individual dishes and serve accompanied by the hard-boiled eggs, sliced spring onions, parsley and toasted bread, if using.

Variation
For a rich wild mushroom caviar, soak 10–15g/¼–½oz dried porcini in about 120ml/4fl oz/½ cup water for about 30 minutes. Add the porcini and their soaking liquid to the browned mushrooms in step 2. Continue as in the recipe. Serve with wedges of lemon, for their tangy juice.

Slow-cooked Shiitake with Shoyu

Shiitake mushrooms taste unlike other mushrooms. When cooked slowly, they are so rich, meaty and filling, that some people call them 'vegetarian steak'. Serve this dish as an appetizer for a dinner party.

Serves 4

20 dried shiitake mushrooms
30ml/2 tbsp vegetable oil
30ml/2 tbsp shoyu
5ml/1 tsp toasted sesame oil

1 Start soaking the dried shiitake the day before. Put them in a large bowl almost full of water. Cover the shiitake with a plate or lid to stop them floating to the surface of the water. Leave to soak overnight.

2 Remove the shiitake from the soaking water and gently squeeze out the water with your fingers.

3 Measure 120ml/4fl oz/½ cup of the soaking liquid in the bowl, and set aside.

4 Heat the oil in a wok or a large frying pan. Stir-fry the shiitake over a high heat for 5 minutes, stirring constantly.

5 Reduce the heat to the lowest setting, then stir in the reserved soaking liquid and the shoyu.

6 Cook the mushrooms until there is almost no moisture left, stirring frequently. Sprinkle with the toasted sesame oil and remove from the heat.

7 Leave to cool, then slice and arrange the shiitake on a large plate and serve.

Variation
Cut the slow-cooked shiitake into thin strips. Mix with 600g/1lb 6oz/5¼ cups cooked brown rice and 15ml/1 tbsp finely chopped chives. Sprinkle with toasted sesame seeds.

Mushroom Caviar Energy 16kcal/69kJ; Protein 2g; Carbohydrate 1g, of which sugars 0.8g; Fat 0.5g, of which saturates 0.1g; Cholesterol 0mg; Calcium 7mg; Fibre 1.1g; Sodium 539mg.
Shiitake Shoyu Energy 133kcal/553kJ; Protein 1.2g; Carbohydrate 7.4g, of which sugars 7.2g; Fat 11.2g, of which saturates 1.4g; Cholesterol 0mg; Calcium 8mg; Fibre 0.6g; Sodium 537mg.

Stuffed Parsleyed Onions

These stuffed onions are a popular vegetarian appetizer. They are also perfect for a substantial lunch or supper when served with fresh crusty bread and a crisp green salad.

Serves 4

4 large onions
60ml/4 tbsp cooked rice
20ml/4 tsp finely chopped fresh parsley, plus extra to garnish
60ml/4 tbsp strong Cheddar cheese, finely grated
30ml/2 tbsp olive oil
15ml/1 tbsp white wine
salt and ground black pepper

1 Preheat the oven to 200°C/400°F/Gas 6. Cut a slice from the top of each onion and scoop out the centre to leave a fairly thick shell. Combine all the remaining ingredients in a large bowl and stir to mix, moistening with enough white wine to bind the ingredients together well.

2 Use a spoon to fill the onions, then wrap each one in a piece of oiled baking foil. Bake in the preheated oven for 30–40 minutes, until tender, turning the parcels often so they cook evenly. (If you wish you could bake the eggs in the embers of a fire,) Serve the onions garnished with chopped fresh parsley.

Aubergine and Smoked Mozzarella Rolls

Slices of grilled aubergine are stuffed with smoked mozzarella, tomato and basil to make an attractive hors d'oeuvre.

Serves 4

1 large aubergine (eggplant)
45ml/3 tbsp olive oil, plus extra for drizzing (optional)
165g/5½oz smoked mozzarella cheese, cut into 8 slices
2 plum tomatoes, each cut into 4 even slices
8 large basil leaves
balsamic vinegar, for drizzling (optional)
salt and ground black pepper

1 Cut the aubergine lengthways into ten thin slices and discard the two outermost slices. Sprinkle the slices with salt and set them aside for 20 minutes. Rinse well under cold running water to remove all traces of the salt, then drain and pat dry with kitchen paper.

2 Prepare the barbecue or preheat the grill (broiler) and line the rack with foil. Place the aubergine slices on the rack and brush liberally with oil. Cook for 8–10 minutes until tender and golden, turning once.

3 Remove the aubergine slices from the heat, then place a slice of mozzarella, a slice of tomato and a basil leaf in the centre of each aubergine slice. Fold the aubergine over the filling and return to the heat, seam side down, until heated through and the mozzarella begins to melt. Serve drizzled with olive oil and a little balsamic vinegar, if using.

Charred Artichokes with Lemon Oil Dip

This citrus dressing marries particularly well with roasted artichokes. They are usually boiled, but dry-heat cooking also works well.

Serves 4

15ml/1 tbsp lemon juice or white wine vinegar
2 globe artichokes, trimmed
12 garlic cloves, unpeeled
90ml/6 tbsp olive oil
1 lemon
sea salt
sprigs of flat leaf parsley, to garnish

1 Preheat the oven to 200°C/400°F/Gas 6. Add the lemon juice or vinegar to a bowl of cold water. Cut each artichoke into wedges. Pull the hairy choke out from the centre, then drop them into the acidulated water until needed.

2 Drain the artichoke wedges and place in a roasting tin with the garlic. Add half the oil and toss well to coat. Sprinkle with salt and roast for 40 minutes, stirring once or twice, until the artichoke wedges are tender and a little charred.

3 Next, begin to make the dip. Using a small, sharp knife, thinly pare away two strips of rind from the lemon. Lay the strips on a board and carefully scrape away any remaining pith. Place the rind in a small pan with water to cover. Bring to the boil, then simmer for 5 minutes. Drain the rind, refresh it in cold water, then chop it roughly. Set aside.

4 Arrange the cooked artichokes on a serving plate and set aside to cool for 5 minutes. Using the back of a fork, gently flatten the garlic cloves so that the flesh squeezes out of the skins. Transfer the garlic flesh to a bowl, mash to a purée, then add the lemon rind.

5 Squeeze the juice from the lemon and, using the fork, whisk it into the garlic mixture, together with the remaining oil. Serve the artichokes warm with the lemon dip. Garnish with a few sprigs of flat leaf parsley.

Stuffed Onions Energy 324kcal/1349kJ; Protein 12.5g; Carbohydrate 28.9g, of which sugars 11.8g; Fat 18.5g, of which saturates 5.4g; Cholesterol 49mg; Calcium 303mg; Fibre 3.6g; Sodium 338mg.
Aubergine Rolls Energy 283kcal/1185kJ; Protein 8.9g; Carbohydrate 24.7g, of which sugars 6.7g; Fat 17.3g, of which saturates 6.6g; Cholesterol 25mg; Calcium 56mg; Fibre 3.3g; Sodium 125mg.
Charred Artichokes Energy 158kcal/651kJ; Protein 0.7g; Carbohydrate 1.3g, of which sugars 1.3g; Fat 16.7g, of which saturates 2.4g; Cholesterol 0mg; Calcium 52mg; Fibre 1.4g; Sodium 75mg.

Pears and Stilton

Stilton is the classic British blue cheese, but you could use other blue cheeses. Comice pears are a good choice for this dish, but for a dramatic colour contrast, select the excellent Red Williams pear.

Serves 4

4 ripe pears, lightly chilled
75g/3oz blue Stilton
50g/2oz curd (farmer's) cheese
ground black pepper
watercress sprigs or rocket (arugula), to garnish

For the dressing

45ml/3 tbsp light olive oil
15ml/1 tbsp lemon juice
10ml/2 tsp toasted poppy seeds
salt and ground black pepper

1 First make the dressing: place the olive oil and lemon juice, poppy seeds and seasoning in a screw-top jar and then shake together until emulsified.

2 Cut the pears in half lengthways, then scoop out the cores and cut away the calyx from the rounded end.

3 Beat together the Stilton, curd cheese and a little pepper. Divide this mixture among the cavities in the pears.

4 Shake the jar containing the dressing to mix it again, then spoon it over the pears. Serve garnished with some watercress sprigs or rocket leaves.

Variation

Other blue cheese to try in place of the Stilton include Gorgonzola, Roquefort, Danish blue and Dolcelatte.

Cook's Tip

Place unripe pears in a brown paper bag to speed up the ripening process. If you need to slow down the speed of ripening, keep the pears in the refrigerator.

Cheese and Leek Sausages

These tasty sausages, which are flavoured with herbs and mustard, are the ideal appetizer for vegetarians as they are made from cheese and leeks rather than the usual meat.

Makes 8

150g/5oz/2½ cups fresh breadcrumbs
150g/5oz generous cup grated Caerphilly cheese
1 small leek, very finely chopped
15ml/1 tbsp chopped fresh parsley
leaves from 1 thyme sprig, chopped
2 eggs
7.5ml/1½ tsp English (hot) mustard powder
about 45ml/3 tbsp milk
plain (all-purpose) flour, for coating
15ml/1 tbsp oil
15g/½ oz/1 tbsp butter, melted
salt and ground black pepper
salad leaves and tomato halves, to serve

1 Mix together the breadcrumbs, cheese, leek and herbs in a large bowl. Season with salt and ground black pepper.

2 In another bowl, whisk the two eggs with the English mustard and reserve 30ml/2 tbsp. Stir the rest into the bowl with the cheese mixture. Pour in enough milk to bind the mixture together.

3 Divide the cheese mixture into eight portions and then form them into sausage shapes with your hands.

4 Dip the sausages in the reserved egg to coat. Season the flour, then roll the sausages in it to give a light, even coating. Chill for about 30 minutes until they are firm.

5 Preheat the grill (broiler) and oil the rack. Mix the oil and melted butter together and use to brush over the sausages.

6 Cook the sausages under the grill for 5–10 minutes, turning them carefully every now and then, until golden brown all over. Serve the sausages hot or cold, with some salad leaves and tomato halves.

Pears and Stilton Energy 243kcal/1007kJ; Protein 7.2g; Carbohydrate 15.5g, of which sugars 15.5g; Fat 17.2g, of which saturates 6.4g; Cholesterol 21mg; Calcium 109mg; Fibre 3.5g; Sodium 208mg.
Sausages Energy 193kcal/809kJ; Protein 8.8g; Carbohydrate 15.1g, of which sugars 0.9g; Fat 10.9g, of which saturates 5.7g; Cholesterol 70mg; Calcium 179mg; Fibre 0.8g; Sodium 309mg.

Caramelized Mushrooms with Allspice and Herbs

Button mushrooms caramelize beautifully in their own juice, but still keep their moistness and nutty flavour. They are perfect served as an appetizer on their own or as part of a hot or cold mezze dish. You can use whatever herbs and spices you enjoy and have available to flavour this dish.

Serves 4

45ml/3 tbsp olive oil
15ml/1 tbsp butter
450g/1lb button (white) mushrooms, wiped clean
3–4 garlic cloves, peeled and finely chopped
10ml/2 tsp allspice berries, crushed
10ml/2 tsp coriander seeds
5ml/1 tsp dried mint
1 small bunch each of fresh sage and flat leaf parsley, chopped
salt and ground black pepper
lemon wedges, to serve

1 Heat the oil and butter in a wide, heavy pan, then stir in the mushrooms with the garlic, allspice and coriander. Cover and cook for about 10 minutes, shaking the pan from time to time, until the mushrooms start to caramelize.

2 Remove the lid and toss in the mint with some of the sage and parsley. Cook for a further 5 minutes, until most of the liquid has evaporated, then season with salt and pepper.

3 Transfer the mushrooms into a serving dish and sprinkle the rest of the sage and parsley over the top. Serve hot or at room temperature, with lemon wedges for squeezing.

Cook's Tip

Keep the mushrooms whole, trimming the stalks if necessary. Avoid washing them before cooking as they absorb a lot of water. Instead, wipe the caps with a clean damp cloth.

Lemon and Bean Stuffed Mushrooms

Portabello mushrooms have a rich flavour and a meaty texture that go well with this herb-and-lemon stuffing.

Serves 4–6

400g/14oz/2 cups drained, canned aduki beans
45ml/3 tbsp olive oil, plus extra for brushing
1 onion, finely chopped
2 garlic cloves, crushed
30ml/2 tbsp chopped fresh thyme or 5ml/1 tsp dried thyme
8 large field mushrooms, such as portabello mushrooms, stalks finely chopped
50g/2oz/1 cup fresh wholemeal (whole-wheat) breadcrumbs
juice of 1 lemon
185g/6½ oz/¾ cup goat's cheese, crumbled
salt and ground black pepper

For the pine nut sauce

50g/2oz/½ cup pine nuts, toasted
50g/2oz/1 cup cubed white bread
2 garlic cloves, chopped
200ml/7fl oz/scant 1 cup milk
45ml/3 tbsp olive oil
15ml/1 tbsp chopped fresh parsley, to garnish (optional)

1 Rinse the canned beans, drain well, then set aside. Preheat the oven to 200°C/400°F/Gas 6. Heat the oil in a large, heavy frying pan, add the onion and garlic and cook for 5 minutes, until softened. Add the thyme and the mushroom stalks and cook for a further 3 minutes, stirring occasionally, until tender.

2 Stir in the beans, breadcrumbs and lemon juice, season well, then cook for 2 minutes, until heated through. Mash about two-thirds of the beans with a fork or potato masher.

3 Brush an ovenproof dish and the base and sides of the mushrooms with oil, then top each one with a spoonful of the bean mixture. Place the mushrooms in the dish, cover with foil and bake for 20 minutes. Remove the foil. Top each mushroom with goat's cheese and bake for a further 15 minutes, or until the cheese is melted and the mushrooms are tender.

4 Place all the ingredients for the sauce in a food processor and blend until smooth. Add more milk if it appears too thick. Sprinkle with parsley, if using, and serve with the mushrooms.

Caramelized Mushrooms Energy 125kcal/517kJ; Protein 2.8g; Carbohydrate 1.2g, of which sugars 0.8g; Fat 12.2g, of which saturates 3.3g; Cholesterol 8mg; Calcium 58mg; Fibre 2.5g; Sodium 37mg.
Stuffed Mushrooms Energy 403kcal/1680kJ; Protein 17g; Carbohydrate 25.8g , of which sugars 5.8g; Fat 26.5g, of which saturates 8g; Cholesterol 31mg; Calcium 158mg; Fibre 5.8g; Sodium 572mg.

Marquis Potatoes

These crispy potato treats are finished with a deliciously tangy tomato mixture set in the centre of the potato nest.

Serves 6
900g/2lb floury potatoes
450g/1lb ripe tomatoes
15ml/1tbsp olive oil
2 shallots, finely chopped
25g/1oz/2 tbsp butter
3 egg yolks
60ml/4 tbsp milk
chopped fresh parsley, to garnish
sea salt and ground black pepper

1 Peel and cut the potatoes into small chunks, then boil in a pan of lightly salted water for about 15–20 minutes or until they are very tender.

2 Meanwhile, blanch the tomatoes in boiling water and then plunge into a bowl of cold water. Peel the skins and then scoop the seeds out. Chop the tomato flesh.

3 Heat the olive oil in a large frying pan and fry the shallots for 2 minutes, stirring constantly.

4 Add the chopped tomatoes to the pan and fry for a further 10 minutes until the moisture has evaporated. Set aside.

5 Drain the potatoes through a colander and return to the pan and allow the steam to dry off. Set them aside to allow to cool slightly.

6 Mash the potatoes thoroughly with the butter and two of the egg yolks and the milk. Season with plenty of salt and ground black pepper.

7 Grease a baking sheet. Spoon the potato into a piping (pastry) bag fitted with a medium star nozzle. Pipe six oval nests on to the sheet. Beat the remaining egg with a little water and brush over the potato. Grill (broil) for 5 minutes or until golden.

8 Spoon the tomato mixture inside the nests and top with a little parsley. Serve them immediately.

Yorkshire Potato Puffs

Mini Yorkshire puddings with a soft centre of herby potato mash will make an unusual first course before the Sunday roast.

Serves 6
275g/10oz floury potatoes
creamy milk and butter, for mashing
5ml/1 tsp chopped fresh parsley
5ml/1 tsp chopped fresh tarragon
75g/3oz/⅔ cup plain (all-purpose) flour
1 egg
120ml/4fl oz/½ cup milk
vegetable oil or sunflower fat, for baking
salt and ground black pepper

1 Cook the potatoes in a large pan of boiling water until tender, then mash with a little creamy milk and butter. Stir in the chopped parsley and tarragon and season well to taste. Preheat the oven to 200°C/400°F/Gas 6.

2 Process the flour, egg, milk and a little salt in a food processor fitted with the metal blade or a blender to make a smooth batter.

3 Place about 2.5ml/½ tsp of oil or a small knob of sunflower fat in each of six ramekin dishes and place in the oven on a baking tray for 2–3 minutes until the oil or fat is very hot.

4 Working quickly, pour a small amount of batter (about 20ml/4 tsp) into each ramekin dish. Add a heaped tablespoon of the mashed potatoes and then pour an equal amount of the remaining batter in each dish. Bake for 15–20 minutes until the puddings are puffy and golden brown.

5 Using a metal spatula, ease the puddings out of the ramekin dishes and arrange on a large serving dish. Serve immediately.

Cook's Tip
Cook and mash the potatoes the day before to save time before you need to make the puffs, or to prepare for a dinner party in advance.

Marquis Potatoes Energy 204kcal/857kJ; Protein 5g; Carbohydrate 27.8g, of which sugars 5.3g; Fat 8.9g, of which saturates 3.6g; Cholesterol 111mg; Calcium 41mg; Fibre 2.4g; Sodium 65mg.
Potato Puffs Energy 146kcal/614kJ; Protein 3.7g; Carbohydrate 18.1g, of which sugars 1.8g; Fat 7.1g, of which saturates 1.1g; Cholesterol 33mg; Calcium 52mg; Fibre 0.9g; Sodium 29mg.

Mini Baked Potatoes with Blue Cheese

These mini baked potatoes are perfect as finger food for a party or as an appetizer, especially as you can prepare them in advance.

Makes 20

20 small new or salad potatoes
60ml/4 tbsp vegetable oil
coarse salt
120ml/4fl oz/½ cup sour cream
25g/1oz blue cheese, such as Roquefort or Stilton, crumbled
30ml/2 tbsp chopped fresh chives, for sprinkling

1 Preheat the oven to 180°C/350°F/Gas 4. Wash and dry the potatoes. Pour the oil into a bowl. Add the potatoes and toss to coat thoroughly.

2 Dip the potatoes in the coarse salt to coat lightly. Spread out the potatoes in one layer on a baking sheet. Bake for about 45–50 minutes until tender.

3 Put the sour cream into a small bowl and add the blue cheese. Blend together until well combined.

4 Cut a cross in the top of each cooked potato with a sharp knife. Press the sides of each potato gently with your fingers to make them open up.

5 While the potatoes are still hot, top each one with a generous dollop of the blue cheese mixture. It will melt down into the potato nicely. Sprinkle with chives on a serving dish and serve hot or at room temperature.

Variation
This dish works just as well as a light snack. If you don't want to be bothered with lots of fiddly small potatoes, simply bake one large floury potato per person. Use whatever blue cheese is available to make the creamy topping.

Deep-fried New Potatoes with Saffron Aioli

Serve these crispy little golden potatoes dipped into a wickedly garlicky mayonnaise – then watch them disappear in a matter of minutes. They make a tasty appetizer or are equally good as a snack.

Serves 4

2.5ml/½ tsp saffron strands
20 baby, new or salad potatoes
vegetable oil, for deep frying
salt and ground black pepper

For the aioli
1 egg yolk
2.5ml/½ tsp Dijon mustard
300ml/½ pint/1¼ cups extra virgin olive oil
15–30ml/1–2 tbsp lemon juice
1 garlic clove, crushed

1 For the aioli, put the egg yolk in a small mixing bowl with the mustard and a pinch of salt. Mix until combined. Beat in the olive oil very slowly, drop by drop, then in a thin stream. Add the lemon juice.

2 Season the aioli with salt and ground black pepper, then add the crushed garlic and beat the mixture thoroughly until well combined.

3 Place the saffron in a small bowl and add 10ml/2 tsp hot water. Press the saffron with the back of a teaspoon, to extract the colour and flavour, and leave to infuse (steep) for 5 minutes. Beat the saffron and the liquid into the aioli.

4 Cook the potatoes in their skins in boiling salted water for 5 minutes, then turn off the heat. Cover the pan and leave for 15 minutes. Drain the potatoes, then dry them thoroughly in a clean dish towel.

5 Heat a 1cm/½in layer of oil in a deep pan. When the oil is very hot, add the potatoes and fry quickly, turning occasionally, until crisp and golden brown all over. Drain them thoroughly on kitchen paper and serve hot with the saffron aioli.

Mini Baked Potatoes Energy 63kcal/262kJ; Protein 1.1g; Carbohydrate 6.3g, of which sugars 0.7g; Fat 3.9g, of which saturates 1.3g; Cholesterol 5mg; Calcium 14mg; Fibre 0.4g; Sodium 22mg.
Deep-fried Potatoes Energy 788kcal/3266kJ; Protein 5g; Carbohydrate 40.3g, of which sugars 3.3g; Fat 68.6g, of which saturates 9.7g; Cholesterol 50mg; Calcium 21mg; Fibre 2.5g; Sodium 30mg.

Stuffed Potato Skins

These stuffed potato skins are ideal for a quick snack or as an appetizer for an informal gathering.

Serves 6

3 baking potatoes, about 350g/12oz each, scrubbed and patted dry
15ml/1 tbsp vegetable oil
40g/1½oz/3 tbsp butter
1 onion, chopped
1 green (bell) pepper, seeded and coarsely chopped
5ml/1 tsp paprika
115g/4oz/1 cup grated Monterey Jack or Cheddar cheese
salt and ground black pepper

1 Preheat the oven to 230°C/450°F/Gas 8. Brush the potatoes with the vegetable oil. Prick them in several places on all sides with a fork. Place in a baking dish. Bake until tender, about 1½ hours.

2 Meanwhile, heat the butter in a large non-stick frying pan. Add the onion and a little salt and cook over medium heat until softened, about 5 minutes. Add the pepper and continue cooking until just tender but still crunchy, 2–3 minutes more. Stir in the paprika and set aside.

3 When the potatoes are done, halve them lengthways. Scoop out the flesh, keeping the pieces coarse. Keep the potato skins warm. Preheat the grill (broiler).

4 Add the potato flesh to the vegetables in the frying pan and cook over high heat, stirring, until the potato is lightly browned. Season with ground black pepper.

5 Divide the vegetable mixture between the potato skins. Sprinkle the cheese on top. Grill (broil) until the cheese just melts, about 3–5 minutes. Serve immediately.

Variation
For Bacon-stuffed Potato Skins, add 130g/4½oz/¾ cup chopped cooked bacon to the cooked potato flesh and vegetables. Stuff as above.

Potato Skewers with Mustard Dip

These potatoes are cooked on the barbecue and have a great flavour and a deliciously crisp skin. Try these tasty kebabs served with a thick, garlic-rich dip.

Serves 4

For the dip
4 garlic cloves, crushed
2 egg yolks
30ml/2 tbsp lemon juice
300ml/½ pint/1¼ cups extra virgin olive oil
10ml/2 tsp wholegrain mustard
salt and ground black pepper

For the skewers
1kg/2¼lb small new potatoes
200g/7oz shallots, halved
30ml/2 tbsp olive oil
15ml/1 tbsp sea salt

1 Prepare the barbecue for cooking the skewers before you begin. To make the dip, place the garlic, egg yolks and lemon juice in a blender or a food processor fitted with the metal blade and process for a few seconds until the mixture is throughly combined and smooth.

2 Keep the blender motor running and add the oil very gradually, pouring it in a thin stream, until the mixture forms a thick, glossy cream. Add the mustard and stir the ingredients together, then season with salt and pepper. Chill until needed.

3 Par-boil the potatoes in their skins in boiling water for about 5 minutes. Drain well and then thread them on to metal skewers alternating with the shallots.

4 Brush the skewers with oil and sprinkle with salt. Cook over a barbecue for 10–12 minutes, turning occasionally. Serve immediately accompanied by the dip.

Cook's Tip
Early or 'new' potatoes and salad potatoes have a firmness necessary to stay on the skewer. Don't be tempted to use other types of small potato, they will probably split or fall off the skewers during cooking.

Potato Skins Energy 283kcal/1184kJ; Protein 8.4g; Carbohydrate 30.9g, of which sugars 4.6g; Fat 14.4g, of which saturates 8.2g; Cholesterol 34mg; Calcium 161mg; Fibre 2.3g; Sodium 211mg.
Potato Skewers Energy 488kcal/2024kJ; Protein 4.3g; Carbohydrate 29.5g, of which sugars 4.1g; Fat 40g, of which saturates 6.1g; Cholesterol 65mg; Calcium 28mg; Fibre 2.2g; Sodium 49mg.

Straw Potato Cake

This dish gets its name from its interesting straw-like texture. Serve cut into wedges as a hearty appetizer or as part of a selection of snacks.

Serves 4

450g/1lb firm baking potatoes
25ml/1½ tbsp butter, melted
15ml/1 tbsp vegetable oil
salt and ground black pepper

1 Peel and grate the potatoes, then toss with melted butter and season with salt and pepper.

2 Heat the oil in a large heavy frying pan. Add the potato and press down to form an even layer that covers the base of the pan. Cook over medium heat for 7–10 minutes until the base is well browned.

3 Loosen the cake if it has stuck to the bottom by shaking the pan or running a knife under it. To turn the cake, invert a large baking tray over the frying pan and, holding it tightly against the pan, turn them both over together. Lift off the frying pan, return it to the heat and add a little more oil if it looks dry.

4 Slide the potato cake back into the frying pan, browned side uppermost, and continue cooking until the underside is crisp and golden. Serve the cake hot, cut into individual wedges.

Orange Candied Sweet Potatoes

A true taste of America – no Thanksgiving table is complete unless sweet potatoes are on the menu.

Serves 8

900g/2lb sweet potatoes
250ml/8fl oz/1 cup orange juice
50ml/2fl oz/¼ cup maple syrup
5ml/1 tsp freshly grated ginger
7.5ml/1½ tsp ground cinnamon
6.5ml/1¼ tsp ground cardamom
7.5ml/1½ tsp salt
ground black pepper
ground cinnamon, to garnish
orange segments, to serve

1 Preheat the oven to 180°C/350°F/Gas 4. Peel and dice the potatoes. Put the chunks into a large pan. Add water to cover and bring to the boil. Add salt, then simmer for about 5–8 minutes, or until the potatoes are tender, but do not let them get too soft.

2 Meanwhile, stir all the remaining ingredients together in a large mixing bowl. Spread out on to a non-stick shallow ovenproof dish.

3 Drain the diced sweet potatoes thoroughly and sprinkle over the other ingredients in the dish.

4 Place the dish in the preheated oven and bake for about 1 hour, stirring the potatoes every 15 minutes until the potatoes are tender and they are well coated.

5 Serve as an appetizer before a main dish, with orange segments and ground cinnamon, and with some fresh crusty bread and butter.

Onion and Potato Cake

Serve this ever-popular dish as an appetizer with a salad accompaniment. The slow cooking time will vary a little depending on the potatoes and how thinly they are sliced: use a food processor or mandoline (if you have one) to make paper-thin slices. The mound of potatoes will cook down to make a thick buttery cake.

Serves 6

900g/2lb new potatoes, peeled and thinly sliced
2 medium onions, very finely chopped
salt and ground black pepper
115g/4oz/½ cup butter

1 Preheat the oven to 190°C/375°F/Gas 5. Lightly butter a 20cm/8in round cake tin (pan) and line the base with a circle of baking parchment.

2 Arrange some of the potato slices evenly in the bottom of the tin and then sprinkle some of the onions over them. Season with salt and pepper. Reserve 25g/1oz/2 tbsp of the butter and dot the mixture with tiny pieces of the remaining butter.

3 Repeat these layers, using up all the ingredients and finishing with a layer of potatoes. Melt the reserved butter and brush it over the top.

4 Cover the potatoes with foil, put in the hot oven and cook for 1–1½ hours, until tender and golden. Remove from the oven and leave to stand, still covered, for 10–15 minutes.

5 Carefully turn out the onion cake on to a warmed plate and serve with a salad or as an accompaniment to a main meal.

Cook's Tip

If using old potatoes, cook and serve in an earthenware or ovenproof glass dish. Then remove the cover for the final 10–15 minutes to lightly brown the top.

Potato Cake Energy 146kcal/610kJ; Protein 2g; Carbohydrate 18.2g, of which sugars 1.5g; Fat 7.7g, of which saturates 3.4g; Cholesterol 12mg; Calcium 8mg; Fibre 1.1g; Sodium 47mg.
Candied Sweet Potatoes Energy 124kcal/529kJ; Protein 1g; Carbohydrate 31.6g, of which sugars 26.1g; Fat 0.2g, of which saturates 0g; Cholesterol 0mg; Calcium 22mg; Fibre 0.9g; Sodium 461mg.
Onion and Potato Cake Energy 272kcal/1133kJ; Protein 3.5g; Carbohydrate 29.5g, of which sugars 5.8g; Fat 16.3g, of which saturates 10.1g; Cholesterol 41mg; Calcium 29mg; Fibre 2.4g; Sodium 135mg.

Bombay Potatoes

This authentic dish belongs to the Gujarati, a totally vegetarian sect and the largest population group in the city of Mumbai. It makes a tasty appetizer served with fruit chutney and poppadums.

Serves 4–6

2 onions
2 fresh green chillies
50g/2oz/2 cups fresh coriander (cilantro)
450g/1lb new potatoes
5ml/1 tsp turmeric
60ml/4 tbsp vegetable oil
2 dried red chillies
6–8 curry leaves
1.5ml/¼ tsp asafoetida
2.5ml/½ tsp each cumin, mustard, onion, fennel and nigella seeds
lemon juice, to taste
salt

1 Chop the onions and chillies finely, and coarsely chop the fresh coriander.

2 Scrub the potatoes under cold running water and cut them into small pieces.

3 Boil the potatoes in water with a little salt and 2.5ml/½ tsp of the turmeric for 10–15 minutes, or until tender. Drain the potatoes well, then mash them and set aside.

4 Heat the oil in a frying pan and fry the dried chillies and curry leaves until the chillies are nearly burnt.

5 Add the sliced onions, green chillies, fresh coriander and remaining turmeric to the pan, add the asafoetida, cumin, mustard, onion, fennel and nigella seeds. Cook, stirring occasionally, until the onions are soft.

6 Fold in the potatoes and add a few drops of water. Cook over a low heat for about 10 minutes, stirring well to ensure the spices are evenly mixed.

7 Stir in lemon juice to taste into the potatoes, and serve immediately while piping hot.

Twice Baked Gruyère and Potato Soufflés

This appetizer can be prepared in advance if you are entertaining and given its second baking just before you serve it up.

Serves 4

225g/8oz floury potatoes
2 eggs, separated
175g/6oz/1½ cups Gruyère cheese, grated
50g/2oz/½ cup self-raising (self-rising) flour
50g/2oz spinach leaves
butter, for greasing
salt and ground black pepper
salad leaves, to serve

1 Preheat the oven to 200°C/400°F/Gas 6. Cook the potatoes in lightly salted boiling water for 20 minutes until very tender. Drain and mash with the two egg yolks.

2 Stir in half of the Gruyère cheese and all of the flour. Season to taste with salt and pepper.

3 Finely chop the spinach and fold into the potato mixture.

4 Whip the egg whites until they form soft peaks. Fold a little of the egg white into the mixture to loosen it slightly. Using a large spoon, fold the remaining egg white into the mixture.

5 Grease four large ramekin dishes. Pour the mixture in and place on a baking sheet and bake for 20 minutes. Remove from the oven and leave to cool.

6 Turn the soufflés out on to a baking sheet and sprinkle with the remaining cheese. Bake again for 5 minutes and serve immediately with salad leaves.

Variation
For a different flavouring, try replacing the Gruyère with a crumbled blue cheese, such as Stilton or Shropshire Blue, which have a more intense taste than the Gruyère.

Bombay Potatoes Energy 143kcal/595kJ; Protein 2.1g; Carbohydrate 17.4g, of which sugars 4.7g; Fat 7.7g, of which saturates 0.9g; Cholesterol 0mg; Calcium 21mg; Fibre 1.7g; Sodium 10mg.
Baked Gruyère Energy 304kcal/1270kJ; Protein 16.7g; Carbohydrate 19g, of which sugars 1.2g; Fat 17.5g, of which saturates 10.4g; Cholesterol 138mg; Calcium 380mg; Fibre 1.2g; Sodium 376mg.

Spicy Peanut Balls

Tasty rice balls, rolled in chopped peanuts and deep-fried, make a delicious appetizer. Serve them simply as they are, or with a chilli sauce for dipping.

Serves 4

1 garlic clove, crushed
1cm/½in piece fresh root ginger, peeled and finely chopped
1.5ml/¼ tsp turmeric
5ml/1 tsp sugar
2.5ml/½ tsp salt
5ml/1 tsp chilli sauce
10ml/2 tsp Thai fish sauce or soy sauce
30ml/2 tbsp chopped fresh coriander (cilantro)
juice of ½ lime
225g/8oz/2 cups cooked white long grain rice
115g/4oz/1 cup peanuts, chopped
vegetable oil, for deep-frying
lime wedges and chilli dipping sauce, to serve (optional)

1 Process the garlic, ginger and turmeric in a food processor or blender until the mixture forms a paste.

2 Add the sugar, salt, chilli sauce and fish sauce or soy sauce, with the chopped coriander and lime juice. Process briefly to mix the ingredients.

3 Add three-quarters of the cooked rice to the paste and process until smooth and sticky. Scrape into a mixing bowl and stir in the remainder of the rice.

4 Divide the rice mixture into 16 pieces. Wet your hands and shape each piece into a ball.

5 Place the chopped peanuts on a plate. Roll the rice balls in the peanuts, making sure they are evenly coated.

6 Heat the oil in a deep-fryer or wok to 190°C/375°F. Check the oil is hot enough by dropping in a piece of bread; it should sizzle and brown within about 40 seconds. Deep-fry the peanut balls, in batches if necessary, until crisp.

7 Drain the cooked balls on kitchen paper and then pile on to a serving platter. Serve the balls while hot with lime wedges and a chilli dipping sauce, if you like.

Deep-fried Onion Rings

These are a very popular appetizer and they make a great accompaniment for grilled meats, especially steaks and burgers. They also provide a crisp contrast when served with sliced hard-boiled eggs or fried mushrooms.

Serves 4

2 Spanish (Bermuda) onions, thickly sliced
1 large egg white, lightly beaten
60ml/4 tbsp plain (all-purpose) flour
groundnut oil for deep-frying
salt and ground black pepper

1 Separate the onion slices into rings. Dip them into the egg white and stir to coat on all sides.

2 Season the flour with salt and pepper, then dip the onion rings into it, one at a time, until evenly coated.

3 Heat the oil for deep-frying to 190°C/375°F, or until a cube of day-old bread browns in 30–40 seconds. Fry the onion rings for 3–4 minutes, until browned and crisp. Drain on kitchen paper and serve immediately.

Variations

- *For corn-crusted onion rings, soak red onion rings in milk for about 30 minutes. Drain, then dip into coarse cornmeal (polenta), mixed with a pinch each of dried red chilli flakes, paprika and ground toasted cumin seeds. Deep-fry.*
- *For spicy onion rings, mix 90ml/6 tbsp chickpea flour (besan or gram flour) with 2.5ml/½ tsp each of ground cumin, ground coriander, chilli powder and garam masala. Season and add 1 chopped green chilli and 30ml/2 tbsp chopped fresh coriander (cilantro). Mix with 45–60ml/3–4 tbsp cold water to make a fairly thick batter. Dip the onion rings into the batter, then deep-fry until crisp.*
- *For onion tempura, beat 2 egg yolks with 150ml/¼ pint/⅔ cup iced sparkling water. Lightly mix in 115g/4oz sifted self-raising (self-rising) flour and a pinch of salt, leaving the batter lumpy. Dip onion rings into the batter and deep-fry.*

Spicy Peanut Balls Energy 123kcal/512kJ; Protein 2.9g; Carbohydrate 12.4g, of which sugars 0.8g; Fat 6.8g, of which saturates 1g; Cholesterol 0mg; Calcium 7mg; Fibre 0.4g; Sodium 45mg.
Deep-fried Onion Energy 214kcal/880kJ; Protein 1.4g; Carbohydrate 8.9g, of which sugars 6.3g; Fat 19.5g, of which saturates 2.3g; Cholesterol 0mg; Calcium 28mg; Fibre 1.6g; Sodium 4mg.

Onion Bhajias

A favourite snack in India, bhajias consist of a savoury vegetable mixture in a crisp and spicy batter. They can be served as an appetizer or as a side dish with curries.

Serves 6–8

2 large onions
225g/8oz/2 cups gram flour
2.5ml/½ tsp chilli powder
5ml/1 tsp ground turmeric
5ml/1 tsp baking powder
1.5ml/¼ tsp asafoetida
2.5ml/½ tsp each nigella, fennel, cumin and onion seeds, coarsely crushed
2 fresh green chillies, finely chopped
50g/2oz/2 cups fresh coriander (cilantro), chopped
vegetable oil, for deep-frying
salt

1 Using a sharp knife, slice the onions into thin rounds. Separate the slices and set them aside on a plate.

2 In a bowl, mix together the flour, chilli powder, ground turmeric, baking powder and asafoetida. Add salt to taste. Sift the mixture into a large mixing bowl.

3 Add the coarsely crushed seeds, onion slices, green chillies and fresh coriander and toss together well. Add enough cold water to make a paste, then stir in more water to make a thick batter that coats the onions and spices.

4 Heat enough oil in a wok or pan for deep-frying. Drop spoonfuls of the mixture into the oil and fry until they are golden brown, turning occasionally. Drain well and serve hot.

Cook's Tip
Gram flour, also known as besan, is made from ground chickpeas. It is available in Asian food stores and supermarkets.

Variation
This versatile batter can be used with other vegetables, including okra, cauliflower and broccoli.

Vegetable Samosas

A selection of highly spiced vegetables in a pastry casing makes these samosas a delicious snack or appetizer at any time of the day.

Serves 6–8

14 sheets of filo pastry, thawed and wrapped in a damp dish towel
oil, for brushing the pastries

For the filling
3 large potatoes, boiled and roughly mashed
75g/3oz/¾ cup frozen peas, thawed
50g/2oz/⅓ cup canned corn, drained
5ml/1 tsp ground coriander
5ml/1 tsp ground cumin
5ml/1 tsp dry mango powder (amchur)
1 small onion, finely chopped
2 fresh green chillies, finely chopped
30ml/2 tbsp coriander (cilantro) leaves, chopped
30ml/2 tbsp chopped fresh mint leaves
juice of 1 lemon
salt

1 Preheat the oven to 200°C/400°F/Gas 6. Cut each sheet of filo pastry in half lengthways and fold each piece in half lengthways to give 28 thin strips. Lightly brush with oil.

2 Toss all the filling ingredients together in a large mixing bowl until they are well blended. Adjust the seasoning with salt and lemon juice if necessary.

3 Using one strip of the pastry at a time, place 15ml/1 tbsp of the filling mixture at one end and fold the pastry diagonally over. Continue folding to form a triangle shape.

4 Brush the samosas with oil. Bake in the oven for about 10–15 minutes, until golden brown. Serve while hot or leave to cool and serve cold.

Cook's Tip
Work with one or two sheets of filo pastry at a time and keep the rest covered with a damp dish towel to prevent it drying out.

Onion Bhajias Energy 284kcal/1181kJ; Protein 5.1g; Carbohydrate 27g, of which sugars 4.7g; Fat 18g, of which saturates 1.9g; Cholesterol 0mg; Calcium 38mg; Fibre 3.3g; Sodium 5mg.
Vegetable Samosas Energy 160kcal/675kJ; Protein 3.9g; Carbohydrate 28.7g, of which sugars 2.2g; Fat 4.1g, of which saturates 0.5g; Cholesterol 0mg; Calcium 45mg; Fibre 2g; Sodium 23mg.

Crunchy Summer Rolls

These delightful rice paper rolls filled with crunchy raw summer vegetables and fresh herbs are light and refreshing, either as a snack or an appetizer to a meal.

Serves 4

12 rice-paper roll wrappers
1 lettuce, leaves separated and ribs removed
2–3 carrots, cut into julienne strips
1 small cucumber, peeled, halved lengthways and seeded, and cut into julienne strips
3 spring onions (scallions), trimmed and cut into julienne strips
225g/8oz/1 cup beansprouts
1 bunch fresh mint leaves
1 bunch coriander (cilantro) leaves
dipping sauce, to serve

1 Pour some lukewarm water into a shallow dish. Soak the rice papers, 2–3 at a time, for about 5 minutes until they are pliable. Place the soaked papers on a clean dish towel and cover with a second dish towel to keep them moist.

2 Work with one paper at a time. Place a lettuce leaf towards the edge nearest to you, leaving about 2.5cm/1in to fold over. Place a mixture of the vegetables on top, followed by some mint and coriander leaves.

3 Fold the edge nearest to you over the filling, tuck in the sides, and roll tightly to the edge on the far side. Place the filled roll on a plate and cover with clear film (plastic wrap), so it doesn't dry out. Repeat with the remaining rice papers and vegetables.

4 Serve with a dipping sauce of your choice. If you are making these rolls ahead of time, keep them in the refrigerator, under a damp dish towel, so that they remain moist.

Cook's Tip
Rice paper wrappers can be bought in Chinese and South-east Asian markets. You can also add pre-cooked shredded pork or prawn to summer rolls.

Spinach Empanadillas

Little pies like these are part of the Moorish tradition in Spain. The Arabs brought spinach to Europe, and pine nuts and raisins are typical Arab flavourings.

Makes 20

25g/1oz/¼ cup raisins
25ml/1½ tbsp olive oil
450g/1lb fresh spinach leaves, washed, drained and chopped
6 canned anchovies, drained and chopped
2 garlic cloves, finely chopped
25g/1oz/¼ cup pine nuts, roughly chopped
350g/12oz puff pastry
1 egg, beaten
salt and ground black pepper

1 To make the filling, soak the raisins in a little warm water for 10 minutes. Drain well, then chop roughly.

2 Heat the olive oil in a large pan, add the spinach, stir, then cover and cook over a low heat for about 2 minutes until the spinach starts to wilt. Remove the lid, turn up the heat and cook until any liquid has evaporated.

3 Add the chopped anchovies, garlic and seasoning to the spinach and cook, stirring, for about 1 minute.

4 Remove the pan from the heat, then stir in the soaked raisins and pine nuts, and set aside to cool.

5 Meanwhile, preheat the oven to 180°C/350°F/Gas 4. Roll out the pastry on a lightly floured surface to a 3mm/⅛ in thickness.

6 Using a 7.5cm/3in pastry cutter, cut the pastry into 20 rounds, re-rolling any scraps if necessary. Place about 10ml/2 tsp filling in the middle of each round, then brush the edges with a little water.

7 Bring up the sides of the pastry and seal well. Press the edges together with the back of a fork. Brush with egg.

8 Place the pies, slightly apart, on a lightly greased baking sheet and bake for about 15 minutes, until puffed and golden brown. Transfer to a wire rack to cool and serve warm.

Crunchy Summer Rolls Energy 106kcal/445kJ; Protein 3.5g; Carbohydrate 21.2g, of which sugars 4.7g; Fat 0.7g, of which saturates 0.2g; Cholesterol 0mg; Calcium 44mg; Fibre 2.2g; Sodium 15mg.
Spinach Empanadillas Energy 95kcal/396kJ; Protein 2.4g; Carbohydrate 7.8g, of which sugars 1.5g; Fat 6.4g, of which saturates 0.3g; Cholesterol 10mg; Calcium 53mg; Fibre 0.5g; Sodium 125mg.

Tempeh Cakes with Dipping Sauce

These tasty little rissoles go very well with the light dipping sauce that accompanies them.

Makes 8

1 lemon grass stalk, outer leaves removed and inside finely chopped
2 garlic cloves, chopped
2 spring onions (scallions), finely chopped
2 shallots, finely chopped
2 fresh red chillies, seeded and finely chopped
2.5cm/1in piece fresh root ginger, finely chopped
60ml/4 tbsp chopped fresh coriander (cilantro), plus extra to garnish
250g/9oz/2¼ cups tempeh, thawed if frozen, sliced
15ml/1 tbsp fresh lime juice
5ml/1 tsp sugar
45ml/3 tbsp plain (all-purpose) flour
1 large (US extra large) egg, lightly beaten
salt and ground black pepper
vegetable oil, for frying

For the dipping sauce
45ml/3 tbsp mirin
45ml/3 tbsp white wine vinegar
2 spring onions (scallions), thinly sliced
15ml/1 tbsp sugar
2 fresh red chillies, seeded and finely chopped
30ml/2 tbsp chopped fresh coriander (cilantro)
large pinch of salt

1 Make the dipping sauce. Mix together the mirin, vinegar, spring onions, sugar, chillies, coriander and salt in a small bowl. Cover with clear film (plastic wrap) and set aside.

2 Place the lemon grass, garlic, spring onions, shallots, chillies, ginger and coriander in a food processor or blender, then process to a coarse paste. Add the tempeh, lime juice and sugar and process until combined, then add the flour and egg, with salt and pepper to taste. Process to a coarse, sticky paste.

3 Scrape the paste into a bowl. Take one-eighth of the mixture at a time and form it into rounds with your hands.

4 Fry the tempeh cakes in a wok for 5–6 minutes, turning once, until golden. Drain, then serve with the sauce.

Spiced Chickpea Rissoles Coated with Sesame Seeds

Sesame seeds are used to give a crunchy coating to these spicy patties. Serve with the tahini yogurt dip and warm pitta bread as a tasty appetizer.

Serves 4

250g/9oz/1⅓ cups dried chickpeas
2 garlic cloves, crushed
1 red chilli, seeded and sliced
5ml/1 tsp ground coriander
5ml/1 tsp ground cumin
15ml/1 tbsp chopped fresh mint
15ml/1 tbsp chopped fresh parsley
2 spring onions (scallions), finely chopped
1 large egg, beaten
sesame seeds, for coating
sunflower oil, for frying
salt and ground black pepper

For the tahini yogurt dip
30ml/2 tbsp light tahini
200g/7oz/scant 1 cup natural (plain) yogurt
5ml/1 tsp cayenne pepper, plus extra for sprinkling
15ml/1 tbsp chopped fresh mint
1 spring onion (scallion), finely sliced

1 Place the chickpeas in a bowl, cover with cold water and leave to soak overnight. Drain and rinse the chickpeas, then place in a pan and cover with cold water. Bring to the boil and boil rapidly for 10 minutes, then reduce the heat and simmer for 1½–2 hours until tender.

2 Meanwhile, make the tahini yogurt dip. Mix together the tahini, yogurt, cayenne pepper and mint in a small bowl. Sprinkle with the spring onion, extra cayenne pepper and mint, then chill in the refrigerator.

3 Combine the chickpeas with the garlic, chilli, ground spices, herbs, spring onions and seasoning, then mix in the egg. Place in a food processor and blend until the mixture forms a coarse paste. If the paste seems too soft, chill it for 30 minutes.

4 Form the chilled chickpea paste into 12 patties with your hands, then roll each one in the sesame seeds to coat. Heat enough oil to cover the base of a frying pan. Fry the rissoles, in batches, for 6 minutes, turning once. Serve with the dip.

Tempeh Cakes Energy 79kcal/332kJ; Protein 4.5g; Carbohydrate 9.1g, of which sugars 4.3g; Fat 2.3g, of which saturates 0.4g; Cholesterol 26mg; Calcium 192mg; Fibre 0.8g; Sodium 15mg.
Spiced Rissoles Energy 552kcal/2312kJ; Protein 21.3g; Carbohydrate 63.7g, of which sugars 8.2g; Fat 25.3g, of which saturates 3.6g; Cholesterol 48mg; Calcium 234mg; Fibre 10.8g; Sodium 95mg.

Spinach and Chickpea Pancakes

These pancakes have a tasty spinach and chickpea filling.

Serves 4–6

15ml/1 tbsp olive oil
1 large onion, chopped
250g/9oz fresh spinach
400g/14oz can chickpeas, drained, skins removed and coarsely mashed
2 courgettes (zucchini), grated
30ml/2 tbsp chopped fresh coriander (cilantro)
2 eggs, beaten
salt and ground black pepper
fresh coriander (cilantro) leaves, to garnish

For the pancake batter

150g/5oz/1¼ cups plain (all-purpose) flour
1 egg
350ml/12fl oz/1½ cups milk
15ml/1 tbsp sunflower or olive oil
butter or oil, for greasing

For the sauce

25g/1oz/2 tbsp butter
30ml/2 tbsp plain (all-purpose) flour
300ml/½ pint/1¼ cups milk

1 First make the pancakes. Whisk together the flour, a little salt, the egg, milk and 75ml/5 tbsp water to make a thin batter. Stir in the oil. Heat a frying pan, grease lightly and fry the pancakes on one side only, to make eight large pancakes. Set aside.

2 Heat the oil in a frying pan and fry the onion for 4–5 minutes until soft. Wash the spinach, place in a pan and cook until wilted, shaking the pan occasionally. Chop the spinach roughly and place in a bowl. Add the mashed chickpeas, onion, courgette and coriander. Stir in the beaten eggs, season and mix well.

3 Place the pancakes, cooked side up, on a work surface and place spoonfuls of filling down the centre. Fold one half of the pancake over the filling and roll it up. Place in a large, buttered ovenproof dish and preheat the oven to 180°C/350°F/Gas 4.

4 Melt the butter for the sauce in a pan, stir in the flour, and then gradually add the milk. Heat gently, stirring constantly, until the sauce thickens. Simmer gently for 2–3 minutes, stirring. Season with salt and pepper and pour over the pancakes.

5 Bake the pancakes in the oven for 15 minutes, until golden and then serve garnished with coriander leaves.

Spicy Corn Patties

Serve these spicy treats with fresh lime wedges and a dollop of chilli sambal to give that extra fiery kick.

Serves 4

2 fresh corn on the cob
3 shallots, chopped
2 garlic cloves, chopped
25g/1oz galangal or fresh root ginger, chopped
1–2 chillies, seeded and chopped
2–3 candlenuts or macadamia nuts, ground
5ml/1 tsp ground coriander
5ml/1 tsp ground cumin
15ml/1 tbsp coconut oil
3 eggs
45–60ml/3–4 tbsp grated fresh coconut or desiccated (dry unsweetened shredded) coconut
2–3 spring onions (scallions), white parts only, finely sliced
corn or groundnut (peanut) oil, for shallow frying
1 small bunch fresh coriander (cilantro) leaves, chopped
salt and ground black pepper
1 lime, quartered, for serving
chilli sambal, for dipping

1 Put the corn on the cob into a large pan of water, bring to the boil and boil for about 8 minutes, until cooked but still firm. Drain the cobs and refresh under running cold water. Using a sharp knife, scrape all the corn off the cob and set aside.

2 Using a mortar and pestle, grind the shallots, garlic, galangal and chillies until they form a paste. Add the candlenuts, ground coriander and cumin and beat well together.

3 Heat the coconut oil in a small wok or heavy pan, stir in the spice paste and stir-fry until the paste becomes fragrant and begins to colour. Transfer on to a plate and leave to cool.

4 Beat the eggs in a large bowl. Add the coconut and spring onions and beat in the corn and the paste. Season the mixture.

5 Heat a thin layer of corn oil in a heavy frying pan. Working in batches, drop spoonfuls of the corn mixture into the oil and fry the patties for 2–3 minutes, until golden brown on both sides.

6 Drain the patties on kitchen paper and arrange on a serving dish on top of the coriander. Serve hot or at room temperature with wedges of lime to squeeze over and a chilli sambal.

Spinach Pancakes Energy 560Kcal/2351kJ; Protein 26.2g; Carbohydrate 68.2g, of which sugars 14.8g; Fat 22.1g, of which saturates 7.5g; Cholesterol 166mg; Calcium 473mg; Fibre 8.6g; Sodium 472mg.
Spicy Corn Patties Energy 368kcal/1531kJ; Protein 10.8g; Carbohydrate 18.1g, of which sugars 8.2g; Fat 28.7g, of which saturates 9.7g; Cholesterol 143mg; Calcium 68mg; Fibre 4.1g; Sodium 196mg.

Spaghettini with Roasted Garlic

If you have never tried roasting garlic, then this is the recipe that will convert you to its delicious mellowed sweetness. Spaghettini is very fine spaghetti, but any long thin pasta can be used in this dish – try spaghetti, linguine, tagliatelle or capellini. This simple pasta dish is very good served as an appetizer before a light meal.

Serves 4

1 whole head of garlic
120ml/4fl oz/½ cup extra virgin olive oil
400g/14oz fresh or dried spaghettini
coarsely shaved Parmesan cheese
crusty bread, to serve

1 Preheat the oven to 180°C/350°F/Gas 4. Place the garlic in an oiled roasting pan and roast it for 30 minutes.

2 Leave the garlic to cool, then lay it on its side and slice off the top one-third with a sharp knife.

3 Hold the garlic over a bowl and dig out the flesh from each clove with the point of the knife. When all the flesh has been added to the bowl, pour in the oil and add plenty of black pepper. Mix well.

4 Cook the pasta in a pan of salted boiling water according to the instructions on the packet. Drain the pasta and return it to the clean pan. Pour in the oil and garlic mixture and toss the pasta vigorously over a medium heat until all the strands are thoroughly coated. Serve immediately, with shavings of Parmesan cheese and some crusty bread.

Variation

For a fiery finish, sprinkle crushed, dried red chillies over the pasta when tossing it with the oil and garlic. Or, for a milder finish, remove the seeds from a fresh green chilli then chop it very finely. Toss with the pasta, oil and garlic.

Spaghetti with Lemon

This is the dish to make as an appetizer to an Italian feast, or as a quick midweek supper. If you keep spaghetti and olive oil in the kitchen cupboards, and garlic and lemons in the vegetable rack, you can prepare this delicious meal in minutes. You can also add some freshly grated Parmesan cheese if you have some.

Serves 4

350g/12oz dried spaghetti
90ml/6 tbsp extra virgin olive oil
juice of 1 large lemon
2 garlic cloves, cut into very thin slivers

1 Cook the pasta in a pan of salted boiling water according to the instructions on the packet, then drain well and return to the pan.

2 Pour the olive oil and lemon juice over the cooked pasta, sprinkle in the slivers of garlic and add seasoning to taste. Toss the pasta over a medium to high heat for 1–2 minutes. Serve immediately in four warmed bowls.

Tagliatelle with Vegetable Ribbons

Narrow strips of courgette and carrot mingle well with tagliatelle to resemble coloured pasta. Serve with freshly grated Parmesan cheese handed round separately. Children may prefer grated Cheddar or Edam cheese.

Serves 4

2 large courgettes (zucchini)
2 large carrots
250g/9oz fresh egg tagliatelle
60ml/4 tbsp garlic-flavoured olive oil
salt and ground black pepper
freshly grated Parmesan cheese, to serve

1 With a vegetable peeler, cut the courgettes and carrots into long thin ribbons.

2 Bring a large pan of lightly salted water to the boil, and then add the courgette and carrot ribbons. Bring the water back to the boil and blanch the vegetables for 30 seconds, then take out the courgettes and carrots with a slotted spoon and set them aside in a bowl.

3 Bring the water back to boiling point and cook the pasta for 3 minutes. Drain well and return it to the pan.

4 Add the vegetable ribbons, garlic-flavoured oil and seasoning to the pan and toss over medium to high heat until the pasta and vegetables are glistening with oil. Serve immediately in warmed pasta bowls.

Cook's Tip

Garlic-flavoured olive oil is used in this dish. Flavoured oils such as chilli or basil are a quick way of adding flavour to pasta.

Spaghetti with Garlic Energy 545kcal/2296kJ; Protein 14.5g; Carbohydrate 84.9g, of which sugars 4.1g; Fat 18.7g, of which saturates 2.6g; Cholesterol 0mg; Calcium 55mg; Fibre 4.2g; Sodium 8mg.
Lemon Spaghetti Energy 448kcal/1886kJ; Protein 10.5g; Carbohydrate 64.9g, of which sugars 3g; Fat 18.1g, of which saturates 2.5g; Cholesterol 0mg; Calcium 22mg; Fibre 2.6g; Sodium 3mg.
Tagliatelle Energy 397kcal/1663kJ; Protein 11.5g; Carbohydrate 52.4g, of which sugars 8.3g; Fat 17.1g, of which saturates 3.3g; Cholesterol 19mg; Calcium 80mg; Fibre 4.8g; Sodium 127mg.

Wild Mushroom and Fontina Tarts

Fontina cheese gives these tarts a creamy, nutty flavour.

Serves 4

25g/1oz/½ cup dried wild mushrooms
30ml/2 tbsp olive oil
1 red onion, chopped
2 garlic cloves, chopped
30ml/2 tbsp medium-dry sherry
1 egg
120ml/4fl oz/½ cup single (light) cream
25g/1oz fontina cheese, thinly sliced
salt and ground black pepper
rocket (arugula) leaves, to serve

For the pastry

115g/4oz/1 cup wholemeal (whole-wheat) flour
50g/2oz/4 tbsp unsalted butter
25g/1oz/¼ cup walnuts, roasted and ground
1 egg, lightly beaten

1 To make the pastry, rub the flour and butter together until the mixture resembles fine breadcrumbs. Add the nuts, then the egg and mix to a soft dough. Wrap, then chill for 30 minutes.

2 Meanwhile, soak the mushrooms in 300ml/½ pint/1¼ cups boiling water for 30 minutes. Drain and reserve the liquid. Cook the onion in the oil over a low heat for 5 minutes, then add the garlic and cook for about 2 minutes, stirring frequently.

3 Add the soaked mushrooms and cook for 7 minutes over high heat until the edges become crisp. Add the sherry and the reserved soaking liquid. Cook over a high heat for 10 minutes, until the liquid evaporates. Season to taste and set aside to cool.

4 Preheat the oven to 200°C/400°F/Gas 6. Lightly grease four 10cm/4in tartlet tins (muffin pans). Roll out the pastry on a lightly floured work surface and use to line the tartlet tins.

5 Prick the pastry, line with baking parchment and baking beans and bake blind for 10 minutes. Remove the paper and the beans.

6 Whisk the egg and cream to mix, add to the mushroom mixture, then season to taste. Spoon into the pastry cases, top with cheese slices and bake for 20 minutes, until the filling is set. Serve warm with rocket.

Tomato and Tapenade Tarts

These delicious individual tarts look and taste fantastic, despite the fact that they demand very little time or effort. The mascarpone cheese topping melts as it cooks to make a smooth, creamy sauce. Cherry tomatoes have a delicious sweet flavour with a low acidity, but plum tomatoes or the vine-ripened variety are also suitable for these tarts and will give delicious results. Red pesto can be used instead of the tapenade if you prefer a subtler flavour.

Serves 4

500g/1¼lb puff pastry, thawed if frozen
60ml/4 tbsp black or green olive tapenade
500g/1¼lb cherry tomatoes
90g/3½oz/scant ½ cup mascarpone cheese

1 Preheat the oven to 220°C/425°F/Gas 7. Lightly grease a large baking sheet and sprinkle it with water.

2 Roll out the pastry on a lightly floured surface and cut out four 16cm/6½in rounds, using a bowl or small plate as a guide.

3 Transfer the pastry rounds to the prepared baking sheet. Using the tip of a sharp knife, mark a shallow cut 1cm/½in in from the edge of each round to form a rim.

4 Reserve half the tapenade and spread the rest over the pastry rounds, keeping the paste inside the marked rim.

5 Cut half the tomatoes in half. Pile all the tomatoes, whole and halved, on the pastry, again keeping them inside the rim. Season lightly.

6 Place the baking sheet in the oven and bake the tarts for 20 minutes, until the pastry is well risen and golden.

7 Dot with the remaining tapenade. Spoon a little mascarpone on the centre of the tomatoes and season with black pepper. Bake for a further 10 minutes, until the mascarpone has melted to make a sauce. Serve the tarts warm.

Mushroom Tarts Energy 409kcal/1701kJ; Protein 10.2g; Carbohydrate 21.9g, of which sugars 2.3g; Fat 31g, of which saturates 13.4g; Cholesterol 143mg; Calcium 121mg; Fibre 2.3g; Sodium 199mg.
Tomato Tarts Energy 543kcal/2269kJ; Protein 10.2g; Carbohydrate 50.8g, of which sugars 6.2g; Fat 35.9g, of which saturates 2.4g; Cholesterol 9mg; Calcium 91mg; Fibre 1.7g; Sodium 736mg.

Risotto Frittata

Half omelette, half risotto, this makes a delightful appetizer or snack.

Serves 4

250g packet instant risotto, mushroom flavour
40g/1½oz/3 tbsp butter
1 small onion, finely chopped
1 garlic clove, crushed
1 large red (bell) pepper, seeded and cut into thin strips
175g/6oz/2½ cups button (white) mushrooms, thinly sliced
60ml/4 tbsp freshly grated Parmesan cheese
6–8 eggs
30ml/2 tbsp water
salt and ground black pepper
lamb's lettuce (corn salad), to garnish

1 Make the instant risotto, following the instructions on the packet. Timings will vary from 2 minutes for the extra-fast varieties to 12 minutes for 'pronto'.

2 Meanwhile, melt 30ml/2 tbsp of the butter in a large pan. Fry the onion and garlic over low heat for 3–4 minutes until the onion has softened. Add the red pepper strips to the pan and fry for 2–3 minutes, then stir in the mushroom slices. Cook for 4–5 minutes, then stir in the risotto with the Parmesan cheese. Spoon the mixture into a bowl and set aside.

3 Break the eggs into a bowl and add the water. Beat lightly, then add salt and pepper to taste.

4 Preheat the grill (broiler). Melt the remaining butter with the oil in a large omelette pan. Add the risotto mixture. Spread the mixture out to cover the base of the pan evenly.

5 Pour the beaten egg carefully over the risotto mixture in the pan, distributing it as evenly as possible. Cook over high heat for 1 minute, then lower the heat to medium and cook until the frittata is set underneath, but still slightly moist on top.

6 Put the pan under the grill (broiler) until the frittata finishes cooking and turns a golden brown. Loosen it and slide it on to a heated plate. Serve in wedges, garnished with lamb's lettuce.

Risotto with Four Cheeses

This is a very rich dish. Serve it for a special dinner-party first course, with a light, dry sparkling white wine to accompany it.

Serves 4–6

40g/1½oz/3 tbsp butter
1 small onion, finely chopped
1.2 litres/2 pints/5 cups vegetable or chicken stock
350g/12oz/1¾ cups risotto rice
200ml/7fl oz/scant 1 cup dry white wine
50g/2oz/½ cup grated Gruyère cheese
50g/2oz/½ cup diced taleggio cheese
50g/2oz/½ cup diced Gorgonzola cheese
50g/2oz/⅔ cup freshly grated Parmesan cheese
salt and ground black pepper
chopped fresh flat leaf parsley, to garnish

1 Melt the butter in a large, heavy pan or deep frying pan and cook the onion over a gentle heat for about 4–5 minutes, stirring frequently, until softened and lightly browned. Pour the stock into a separate pan and heat it to simmering point.

2 Add the rice to the onion mixture, stir until the grains start to swell and burst, then add the wine. Stir until it stops sizzling and most of it has been absorbed by the rice.

3 Pour a little of the hot stock into the pan. Add salt and black pepper to taste. Stir the rice over low heat until the stock has been absorbed.

4 Gradually add the remaining stock, a little at a time, allowing the rice to absorb the liquid before adding more, and stirring constantly. After about 20–25 minutes the rice will be al dente and the risotto will have a creamy consistency.

5 Turn off the heat under the pan, then add the Gruyère, taleggio, the Gorgonzola and 30ml/2 tbsp of the Parmesan. Stir gently until the cheeses have melted, then taste for seasoning. Spoon into a serving bowl and garnish with parsley. Serve the remaining Parmesan separately.

Risotto Frittata Energy 434kcal/1804kJ; Protein 19.5g; Carbohydrate 34.1g, of which sugars 3.6g; Fat 24.5g, of which saturates 9.5g; Cholesterol 314mg; Calcium 241mg; Fibre 1.4g; Sodium 311mg.
Risotto with Cheeses Energy 420kcal/1749kJ; Protein 13.7g; Carbohydrate 47.6g, of which sugars 0.8g; Fat 16.4g, of which saturates 10.4g; Cholesterol 45mg; Calcium 282mg; Fibre 0.1g; Sodium 355mg.

Red-hot Mexican Rice

Versions of this dish – a relative of Spanish rice – are popular all over South America. It is a delicious medley of rice, tomatoes and aromatic flavourings.

Serves 6

200g/7oz/1 cup long grain rice
200g/7oz can chopped tomatoes in tomato juice
½ onion, roughly chopped
2 garlic cloves, roughly chopped
30ml/2 tbsp vegetable oil
450ml/¾ pint/scant 2 cups chicken stock
2.5ml/½ tsp salt
3 fresh fresno chillies or other fresh green chillies, trimmed
150g/5oz/1 cup frozen peas (optional)
ground black pepper

1 Put the rice in a large heatproof bowl and pour over boiling water to cover. Stir once, then leave to stand for 10 minutes. Transfer into a strainer over the sink, rinse under cold water, then drain again. Set aside to dry slightly.

2 Pour the tomatoes and juice into a food processor or blender, add the onion and garlic and process until smooth.

3 Heat the oil in a large, heavy pan, add the rice and cook over a moderate heat until it turns a delicate golden brown. Stir occasionally to ensure that the rice does not stick to the pan.

4 Add the tomato mixture and stir over a moderate heat until all the liquid has been absorbed. Stir in the stock, salt, whole chillies and peas, if using. Continue to cook, stirring occasionally, until all the liquid has been absorbed and the rice is just tender.

5 Remove the pan from the heat, cover it with a tight-fitting lid and leave it to stand in a warm place for 5–10 minutes. Remove the chillies, fluff up the rice lightly and serve, sprinkled with black pepper. The chillies may be used as a garnish, if liked.

Cook's Tip
Do not stir the rice too often after adding the stock or the grains will break down and the mixture will become starchy.

Artichoke Rice Cakes with Manchego

These unusual little snacks contain artichoke in the rice mixture, and they break open to reveal a melting cheese centre. Manchego is made from sheep's milk and has a tart flavour that goes wonderfully with the taste of the rice cakes.

Serves 6

1 large globe artichoke
50g/2oz/¼ cup butter
1 small onion, finely chopped
1 garlic clove, finely chopped
115g/4oz/⅔ cup paella rice
450ml/¾ pint/scant 2 cups hot chicken stock
50g/2oz/⅔ cup grated fresh Parmesan cheese
150g/5oz Manchego cheese, very finely diced
45–60ml/3–4 tbsp fine cornmeal
olive oil, for frying
salt and ground black pepper
fresh flat leaf parsley, to garnish

1 Remove the stalks, leaves and choke to leave just the heart of the artichoke; chop the heart finely.

2 Melt the butter in a pan and gently fry the chopped artichoke heart, onion and garlic for 5 minutes until softened. Stir in the rice and cook for about 1 minute.

3 Keeping the heat fairly high, gradually add the stock, stirring occasionally until all the liquid has been absorbed and the rice is cooked – this should take about 20 minutes. Season well, then stir in the Parmesan cheese. Transfer the mixture to a bowl. Leave to cool, then cover and chill for at least 2 hours.

4 Spoon about 15ml/1 tbsp of the mixture into the palm of one hand, flatten slightly, and place a few pieces of diced cheese in the centre. Shape the rice around the cheese to make a small ball. Flatten slightly with your hand, then roll in the cornmeal, shaking off any excess. Repeat with the remaining mixture to make about 12 cakes.

5 Shallow fry the rice cakes in hot olive oil for 4–5 minutes until they are crisp and golden brown. Drain on kitchen paper and serve hot, garnished with flat leaf parsley.

Red-hot Rice Energy 162kcal/676kJ; Protein 2.8g; Carbohydrate 28.4g, of which sugars 1.6g; Fat 4g, of which saturates 0.5g; Cholesterol 0mg; Calcium 11mg; Fibre 0.5g; Sodium 167mg.
Artichoke Cakes Energy 354kcal/1469kJ; Protein 12g; Carbohydrate 21.8g, of which sugars 0.8g; Fat 23.6g, of which saturates 12.3g; Cholesterol 50mg; Calcium 299mg; Fibre 0.5g; Sodium 331mg.

Semolina and Pesto Gnocchi

These gnocchi are cooked rounds of semolina paste, which are brushed with melted butter, topped with cheese and baked.

Serves 4–6

750ml/1¼ pints/3 cups milk
200g/7oz/generous 1 cup semolina
45ml/3 tbsp pesto sauce
60ml/4 tbsp finely chopped sun-dried tomatoes, patted dry if oily
50g/2oz/¼ cup butter
75g/3oz/1 cup freshly grated Pecorino cheese
2 eggs, beaten
freshly grated nutmeg
salt and ground black pepper
tomato sauce, to serve
basil, to garnish

1 Heat the milk in a pan. When it is on the point of boiling, sprinkle in the semolina, stirring constantly until the mixture is smooth and thick. Lower the heat and simmer for 2 minutes.

2 Remove from the heat and stir in the pesto and sun-dried tomatoes, with half the butter and half the Pecorino. Add the eggs, with nutmeg, salt and pepper to taste. Spoon on to a clean shallow baking dish or tin (pan) to a depth of 1cm/½in and level the surface. Leave to cool, then chill.

3 Preheat the oven to 190°C/375°F/Gas 5. Lightly grease a shallow baking dish. Using a 4cm/1½in cutter, stamp out as many rounds as possible from the semolina pasta.

4 Place the leftover semolina paste on the base of the greased dish and arrange the rounds on top in overlapping circles. Melt the remaining butter and brush it over the gnocchi. Sprinkle over the remaining Pecorino. Bake for 30–40 minutes until golden. Serve with tomato sauce and garnish with basil.

Variations

- *Substitute any mature (sharp) hard grating cheese for the Pecorino, such as the Spanish cheeses Manchego or Mahon.*
- *Instead of pesto, use a small pack of chopped frozen spinach that has been thawed and squeezed to remove any excess water, or use 90ml/6 tbsp mixed chopped herbs.*

Malfatti with Grilled Pepper Sauce

The Italians use ricotta, which is a rich but light cream cheese, in sweet and savoury dishes, such as this appetizer.

Serves 4

500g/1¼lb young leaf spinach
1 onion, finely chopped
1 garlic clove, crushed
15ml/1 tbsp extra virgin olive oil
350g/12oz/1½ cups ricotta cheese
3 eggs, beaten
50g/2oz/½ cup natural-coloured dried breadcrumbs
50g/2oz/½ cup plain (all-purpose) flour
50g/2oz/⅔ cup freshly grated Parmesan cheese
freshly grated nutmeg
25g/1oz/2 tbsp butter, melted
salt and ground black pepper

For the sauce

2 red (bell) peppers, quartered and cored
30ml/2 tbsp extra virgin olive oil
1 onion, chopped
400g/14oz can chopped tomatoes
150ml/¼ pint/⅔ cup water

1 Make the sauce. Grill the pepper quarters, skin side up, until they blister and blacken. Cool slightly, then peel and chop. Heat the oil in a frying pan and lightly fry the onion and peppers for 5 minutes. Add the tomatoes and water, with salt and pepper to taste. Bring to the boil, then simmer for 15 minutes. Purée in a food processor, return to the clean pan and set aside.

2 Trim any thick stalks from the spinach, wash well if necessary, then blanch in a pan of boiling water for 1 minute. Drain, refresh under cold water and drain again. Squeeze dry, then chop finely.

3 Put the onion, garlic, oil, ricotta, eggs and breadcrumbs in a bowl. Mix in the spinach. Stir in the flour and 5ml/1 tsp salt with half the Parmesan, then season with pepper and nutmeg. Roll the mixture into 12 small logs and chill lightly.

4 Bring a large pan of water to the boil. Carefully drop in the malfatti in batches and cook for 5 minutes. Remove with a slotted spoon and toss with the melted butter.

5 To serve, reheat the sauce and divide it among four plates. Arrange four malfatti on each, sprinkle with Parmesan and serve.

Gnocchi Energy 560kcal/2348kJ; Protein 25.8g; Carbohydrate 47.8g, of which sugars 9g; Fat 31.1g, of which saturates 15.3g; Cholesterol 159mg; Calcium 566mg; Fibre 1.1g; Sodium 484mg.
Malfatti Energy 563kcal/2345kJ; Protein 25.8g; Carbohydrate 35.2g, of which sugars 15.3g; Fat 36.4g, of which saturates 16.5g; Cholesterol 205mg; Calcium 440mg; Fibre 6.1g; Sodium 511mg.

Rice Noodles with Fresh Herbs

These rice noodles are simply tossed with crunchy salad vegetables, fresh herbs and sharp flavourings to make a delicious and satisfying vegetarian snack. They also make a refreshing and sophisticated first course as part of an Asian-inspired dinner party.

Serves 4
half a small cucumber
4–6 lettuce leaves
1 bunch mixed fresh basil, coriander (cilantro), mint and oregano
225g/8oz dried rice sticks (vermicelli)
115g/4oz/½ cup beansprouts
juice of half a lime
soy sauce, to drizzle (optional)

1 Peel the cucumber, cut it in half lengthways, remove the seeds, and cut into even matchsticks. Using a sharp knife, cut the lettuce into fine shreds. Remove the stalks from the herbs and shred the leaves.

2 Add the rice sticks to a pan of boiling water, loosening them gently, and cook for 3–4 minutes, or until white and just tender. Drain, rinse under cold water, and drain again.

3 In a bowl, toss the shredded lettuce, beansprouts and cucumber together, then toss in the shredded herbs.

4 Add the cooked rice noodles to the bowl and mix well. Pour in the lime juice and toss the ingredients together. Drizzle the salad with a little soy sauce, if using, and serve the noodles immediately in individual bowls.

Cook's Tip
Look out for rice noodles in Asian food stores and supermarkets.

Variation
You can use mung bean noodles in place of the rice noodles, if you prefer. They become very translucent when cooked.

Borek

Versions of these crisp, cheese-filled pastries are a common feature of street food throughout much of the Mediterranean. They are easy to make at home as a tasty appetizer.

Serves 5
250g/9oz feta cheese, crumbled
2.5ml/½ tsp freshly grated nutmeg
30ml/2 tbsp each chopped fresh parsley, dill and mint
10 filo pastry sheets, each about 30 × 18cm /12 × 7in
75g/3oz/6 tbsp melted butter or 90ml/6 tbsp olive oil
ground black pepper

1 Preheat the oven to 190°C/375°F/Gas 5. Mix the feta, nutmeg and herbs in a bowl. Add pepper to taste and mix to a creamy filling.

2 Brush a sheet of filo lightly with butter or oil, place another on top of it and brush that too.

3 Cut the buttered sheets in half lengthways to make 10 strips, each 30 × 9cm/12 × 3½in. Place 5ml/1 tsp of the cheese filling at the base of a long strip, fold the corners in diagonally to enclose it, then roll the pastry up into a cigar shape.

4 Brush the end with a little butter or oil to seal, then place join side down on a non-stick baking sheet. Repeat with the remaining pastry and filling. Brush the borek with more butter or oil and bake for 20 minutes or until crisp and golden. Cool on a wire rack and serve at room temperature.

Cook's Tip
When using filo pastry, it is important to keep unused sheets covered so that they don't dry out. The quantities for filo pastry in the recipe above are approximate, as the size of filo sheets varies. Any unused pastry will keep in the refrigerator for a week or so, if it is well wrapped.

Rice Noodles Energy 217kcal/908kJ; Protein 6.4g; Carbohydrate 46.1g, of which sugars 1.5g; Fat 0.6g, of which saturates 0.1g; Cholesterol 0mg; Calcium 51mg; Fibre 1.3g; Sodium 11mg.
Borek Energy 238kcal/996kJ; Protein 6g; Carbohydrate 27.4g, of which sugars 4.4g; Fat 12.4g, of which saturates 1.9g; Cholesterol 40mg; Calcium 102mg; Fibre 1.3g; Sodium 174mg.

Vegetable Pancakes with Tomato Salsa

These little spinach and egg pancakes can be prepared in advance, to avoid too much last-minute cooking, and served as an appetizer with the spicy salsa.

Serves 4–6
225g/8oz spinach
1 small leek
a few sprigs of fresh coriander (cilantro) or parsley
3 large eggs
50g/2oz/½ cup plain (all-purpose) flour, sifted
oil, for frying
25g/1oz/⅓ cup freshly grated Parmesan cheese
salt, ground black pepper and grated nutmeg

For the tomato salsa
2 tomatoes, peeled and chopped
¼ fresh red chilli, finely chopped
2 pieces sun-dried tomato in oil, drained and chopped
1 small red onion, chopped
1 garlic clove, crushed
60ml/4 tbsp good olive oil
30ml/2 tbsp sherry
2.5ml/½ tsp soft light brown sugar

1 Shred or chop the spinach with the leek and coriander or parsley until fine but not puréed. Alternatively, chop them in a food processor but do not over-process. Beat in the eggs and seasoning to taste. Gradually blend in the flour and 30–45ml/2–3 tbsp water and set aside for 20 minutes.

2 To prepare the tomato salsa, mix together all the ingredients in a bowl, then cover and leave for 2–3 hours for the flavours to mingle together.

3 To cook, drop small spoonfuls of the batter into a lightly oiled non-stick frying pan and fry until golden underneath. Turn and cook briefly on the other side. Drain on kitchen paper. Sprinkle with Parmesan and serve hot with the tomato salsa.

Variation
Use watercress, sorrel or chard or a mixture of sorrel and chard in place of the spinach, if you like.

Mushrooms on Spicy Toast

Dry-panning is a quick way of cooking mushrooms that makes the most of their flavour. It works well with large, flat mushrooms. The juices run when they are heated, so they become really moist and tender.

Serves 4
8–12 large flat field (portabello) mushrooms
50g/1oz/2 tbsp butter
5ml/1 tsp curry paste
salt
4 slices thickly sliced white bread, toasted, to serve

1 Preheat the oven to 200°C/400°F/Gas 6. Peel the field mushrooms, if necessary, and remove the stalks. Heat a dry frying pan until very hot.

2 Place the mushrooms in the hot frying pan, with the gills facing upward. Using half the butter, add a piece the size of a hazelnut to each one, then sprinkle all the mushrooms lightly with salt. Cook over a medium heat until the butter begins to bubble and the mushrooms are juicy and tender.

3 Meanwhile, mix the remaining butter with the curry paste to get a smooth mixture. Spread over the toasted bread. Bake the toasts in the oven for about 10 minutes, pile the mushrooms on top and serve.

Variations
Using a flavoured butter makes these mushrooms even more special. Try one of the following:
- ***Herb butter*** *Mix softened butter with chopped fresh herbs such as parsley and thyme, or marjoram and chopped chives.*
- ***Olive butter*** *Mix softened butter with diced green olives and spring onions (scallions).*
- ***Tomato butter*** *Mix softened butter with sun-dried tomato purée (paste).*
- ***Garlic butter*** *Mix softened butter with finely chopped garlic.*
- ***Pepper and paprika butter*** *Mix softened butter with 2.5ml/½ tsp paprika and 2.5ml/½ tsp black pepper.*

Vegetable Pancakes Energy 153kcal/635kJ; Protein 4.6g; Carbohydrate 6.2g, of which sugars 2.1g; Fat 11.8g, of which saturates 2.2g; Cholesterol 63mg; Calcium 92mg; Fibre 1.3g; Sodium 84mg. **Mushrooms on Toast** Energy 350kcal/1460kJ; Protein 6.8g; Carbohydrate 25.7g, of which sugars 2.1g; Fat 25.3g, of which saturates 14.2g; Cholesterol 57mg; Calcium 78mg; Fibre 2g; Sodium 318mg.

Spinach and Nutmeg Spring Rolls

In Morocco, these little savoury pastries may be filled with minced lamb or beef, cheese with herbs, or, as in this recipe, spinach fragrant with freshly grated nutmeg. Easy to make, they are always shaped into cigars or triangles. The filling can be prepared ahead of time but the pastry should not be unwrapped until you are ready to make the pastries, otherwise it will dry out.

Makes 32

8 sheets of ouarka or filo pastry
sunflower oil, for deep-frying

For the spinach filling

50g/2oz/¼ cup butter
1 onion, finely chopped
275g/10oz fresh spinach, cooked, drained and chopped
small bunch of fresh coriander (cilantro), finely chopped
pinch of freshly grated nutmeg
salt and ground black pepper

1 To make the spinach filling, melt the butter in a small heavy pan. Add the chopped onion and cook over a low heat for 15 minutes, stirring occasionally, until softened but not browned. Stir in the spinach and coriander. Season with nutmeg, salt and pepper, then set aside to cool.

2 Lay a sheet of ouarka or filo pastry on a work surface, keeping the other sheets covered with a damp cloth or in a plastic bag. Cut the sheet widthways into four strips.

3 Spoon a little of the filling mixture on to the first strip, at the end nearest to you. Fold the corners of the pastry over the mixture to seal it, then roll up the pastry and filling away from you into a tight cigar. As you reach the end of the strip, brush the edges with a little water and continue to roll up the cigar to seal in the filling. Repeat, placing the finished rolls under a damp cloth.

4 Heat the sunflower oil for deep-frying to 180°C/350°F, or until a cube of day-old bread browns in 30 seconds. Add the rolls to the oil in batches and fry over a medium heat until golden brown. Drain on kitchen paper. Serve the rolls while they are still warm.

Aubergine, Tomato and Mozzarella Wraps

Robust vegetables such as aubergines make ideal wraps. Next time you are looking for something a little out of the ordinary, try these flavourful parcels.

Serves 4

2 large, long aubergines (eggplant)
225g/8oz mozzarella cheese
2 plum tomatoes
16 large fresh basil leaves
30ml/2 tbsp extra virgin olive oil
salt and ground black pepper
toasted pine nuts and torn fresh basil leaves, to garnish

For the dressing

60ml/4 tbsp extra virgin olive oil
5ml/1 tsp balsamic vinegar
15ml/1 tbsp sun-dried tomato paste
15ml/1 tbsp lemon juice

1 Cut each aubergine lengthways into eight thin slices, about 5mm/¼in thick. Bring a large pan of water to the boil, add the slices and cook for 2 minutes, until softened. Drain in a colander, then pat dry with kitchen paper.

2 Cut the mozzarella cheese into eight slices. Trim the top and base of each tomato, then slice each into eight slices.

3 Lay an aubergine slice on a chopping board and place another slice on top of it so that they form a cross. Place a slice of tomato in the centre, season with salt and pepper, then add a basil leaf followed by a slice of mozzarella, another basil leaf, a slice of tomato and a little more seasoning, if you like.

4 Bring up the ends of the aubergine slices around the filling to form a neat parcel. Repeat with the remaining ingredients to make another seven parcels. Cover with clear film (plastic wrap) and chill for at least 20 minutes.

5 Meanwhile, make the dressing by whisking all the ingredients together in a small bowl. Brush the parcels with the olive oil and grill (broil) under a medium heat for about 5 minutes on each side, or until golden. Serve hot, sprinkled with the toasted pine nuts and basil leaves. Offer the dressing separately.

Spinach Rolls Energy 41kcal/171kJ; Protein 0.6g; Carbohydrate 2.8g, of which sugars 0.3g; Fat 3.1g, of which saturates 1g; Cholesterol 3mg; Calcium 23mg; Fibre 0.4g; Sodium 22mg.
Aubergine Wraps Energy 317kcal/1311kJ; Protein 11.7g; Carbohydrate 3.8g, of which sugars 3.6g; Fat 28.5g, of which saturates 10.2g; Cholesterol 33mg; Calcium 217mg; Fibre 2.5g; Sodium 229mg.

Tortilla Wrap with Tabbouleh and Avocado

Tabbouleh needs lemon juice and lots of fresh herbs and ground black pepper.

Serves 6

salt and ground black pepper
4 wheat tortillas, to serve
flat leaf parsley, to garnish (optional)

For the tabbouleh

175g/6oz/1 cup bulgur wheat
30ml/2 tbsp chopped fresh mint
30ml/2 tbsp chopped fresh flat leaf parsley
1 bunch spring onions (scallions), sliced
½ cucumber, diced
50ml/2fl oz/¼ cup olive oil
juice of 1 large lemon

For the avocado

1 ripe avocado, stoned (pitted), peeled and diced
juice of ½ lemon
½ red chilli, seeded and sliced
1 garlic clove, crushed
½ red (bell) pepper, seeded and finely diced

1 To make the tabbouleh, place the bulgur wheat in a large heatproof bowl and pour over enough boiling water to cover. Leave for 30 minutes until the grains are tender but still retain a little resistance to the bite. Drain thoroughly in a sieve (strainer), then transfer back into the bowl.

2 Add the mint, parsley, spring onions and cucumber to the bulgur wheat and mix thoroughly. Blend together the olive oil and lemon juice in a jug (pitcher) and pour over the tabbouleh, season to taste with salt and pepper and toss well to mix. Cover with clear film (plastic wrap) and chill in the refrigerator for 30 minutes to allow the flavours to mingle.

3 To make the avocado mixture, place the avocado in a bowl and add the lemon juice, chilli and garlic. Season to taste with salt and pepper and mash with a fork to form a smooth purée. Stir in the red pepper.

4 Warm the tortillas in a dry frying pan and serve either flat, folded or rolled up with the tabbouleh and avocado mixture. Garnish with parsley, if using.

Red Onion and Goat's Cheese Pastries

Fresh thyme adds a tasty edge to the mellow red onion in these scrumptious pastries, which are topped with luscious goat's cheese. The puff pastry rises around the fillng to create attractive individual tarts.

Serves 4

15ml/1 tbsp olive oil
450g/1lb red onions, sliced
30ml/2 tbsp fresh thyme or 10ml/2 tsp dried
15ml/1 tbsp balsamic vinegar
425g/15oz packet ready-rolled puff pastry, thawed if frozen
115g/4oz goat's cheese, cubed
1 egg, beaten
salt and ground black pepper
fresh oregano sprigs, to garnish (optional)
mixed green salad leaves, to serve

1 Heat the oil in a large, heavy frying pan, add the onions and fry over a gentle heat for 10 minutes, or until softened, stirring occasionally. Add the thyme, seasoning and vinegar, and cook for another 5 minutes. Remove the pan from the heat and leave the onions to cool.

2 Preheat the oven to 220°C/425°F/Gas 7. Unroll the puff pastry and, using a 15cm/6in plate as a guide, cut four rounds. Place the pastry rounds on a dampened baking sheet and, using the point of a knife, score a border, 2cm/¾in inside the edge of each round. (Do not cut through the pastry.)

3 Divide the onions among the pastry rounds and top with the goat's cheese. Brush the edge of each round with beaten egg.

4 Bake the pastries for 25–30 minutes, or until they are golden. Garnish with oregano sprigs, if you like, before serving with mixed salad leaves.

Variation
Ring the changes by spreading the pastry base with pesto or tapenade before you add the filling.

Tortilla Wrap Energy 259kcal/1081kJ; Protein 5.1g; Carbohydrate 35g, of which sugars 1.9g; Fat 11.5g, of which saturates 1.9g; Cholesterol 0mg; Calcium 55mg; Fibre 1.7g; Sodium 52mg.
Red Onion Pastries Energy 595kcal/2482kJ; Protein 15.4g; Carbohydrate 50.8g, of which sugars 8.1g; Fat 39.4g, of which saturates 5.9g; Cholesterol 74mg; Calcium 139mg; Fibre 1.6g; Sodium 543mg.

Herbed Greek Pies

Mixed fresh herbs give these little pies a delicate flavour. They are delicious served warm as a first course, but are equally delicious eaten cold as part of a buffet or picnic feast.

Serves 4

115g/4oz/1 cup plain (all-purpose) flour
50g/2oz/4 tbsp butter, diced
15–25ml/1–1½ tbsp water

For the filling

45–60ml/3–4 tbsp tapenade or sun-dried tomato paste
1 large (US extra large) egg
100g/3¾oz/scant ½ cup thick Greek (US strained plain) yogurt
90ml/6 tbsp milk
1 garlic clove, crushed
30ml/2 tbsp chopped mixed herbs, such as thyme, basil and parsley
salt and ground black pepper

1 To make the pastry, mix together the flour, a pinch of salt and the diced butter. Using your fingertips or a pastry blender, rub the butter into the flour until the mixture resembles fine breadcrumbs. Mix in the water using a round-bladed knife and knead the mixture lightly to form a firm dough. Wrap the dough in clear film (plastic wrap) and chill in the refrigerator for 30 minutes.

2 Preheat the oven to 190°C/375°F/Gas 5. Roll out the pastry thinly and cut out eight rounds using a 7.5cm/3in cutter. Line deep patty tins (muffin pans) with the pastry rounds, then line each one with a piece of baking parchment.

3 Place the tins in the oven and bake blind for 15 minutes. Remove the baking parchment and bake the pastry for a further 5 minutes, or until the cases are crisp.

4 To make the filling, spread a little tapenade or tomato paste in the base of each pastry case. Whisk together the egg, yogurt, milk, garlic, herbs and seasoning.

5 Spoon the filling into the pastry cases and bake for about 25–30 minutes, or until the filling is just firm and the pastry golden. Leave the pies to cool slightly before carefully removing from the tins and serving.

Red Onion and Black Olive Pissaladière

For a taste of the Mediterranean, try this French-style pizza – it makes a delicious and easy snack or appetizer. Cook the sliced red onions slowly until they are caramelized and sweet before piling them into the pastry cases. To prepare the recipe in advance, pile the cooled onions on to the pastry round and chill the pissaladière until you are ready to bake it.

Serves 6

75ml/5 tbsp extra virgin olive oil
500g/1¼lb small red onions, thinly sliced
500g/1¼lb puff pastry, thawed if frozen
75g/3oz/¾ cup small pitted black olives
salt and ground black pepper
salad leaves, to serve

1 Preheat the oven to 220°C/425°F/Gas 7. Heat the oil in a large, heavy frying pan and cook the onions gently, stirring frequently, for 15–20 minutes, until they are soft and golden. Season to taste with salt and pepper.

2 Roll out the pastry thinly on a floured surface. Cut out a 33cm/13in round and transfer it to a large, lightly dampened baking sheet.

3 Spread the onions over the pastry in an even layer to within 1cm/½in of the edge. Sprinkle the olives on top. Bake the tart in the oven for about 20–25 minutes, until the pastry is risen and deep golden. Cut into wedges and serve warm or cold with salad leaves.

Variation
Like Italian pizzas, the toppings for a pissaladière can vary depending on your taste. Possible additions include anchovy fillets, sliced tomatoes and a sprinkling of fresh herbs.

Herbed Pies Energy 193kcal/806kJ; Protein 5.2g; Carbohydrate 18.8g, of which sugars 3.7g; Fat 11.4g, of which saturates 3.8g; Cholesterol 50mg; Calcium 93mg; Fibre 0.9g; Sodium 190mg.
Pissaladière Energy 436kcal/1815kJ; Protein 5.9g; Carbohydrate 37.4g, of which sugars 5.8g; Fat 31.1g, of which saturates 1.5g; Cholesterol 0mg; Calcium 77mg; Fibre 1.5g; Sodium 542mg.

Parsnip, Carrot and Chèvre Cheese Fricassée

This excellent vegetarian appetizer can also be served as a fine accompaniment for roast or grilled meats or fish.

Serves 4–6

4 parsnips
4 carrots
1 red onion, sliced
30ml/2 tbsp pine nuts or flaked (sliced) almonds, lightly toasted
sprigs of tarragon, to garnish

For the sauce

40g/1½oz/3 tbsp unsalted butter
40g/1½oz/⅓ cup plain (all-purpose) flour
300ml/½ pint/1¼ cups milk
130g/4½oz chèvre (goat's cheese)
15ml/1 tbsp chopped fresh or 2.5ml/½ tsp dried tarragon
salt and ground black pepper

1 Cut the parsnips and carrots into sticks. Put them in a pan and add the onion. Season, cover with cold water and bring to the boil.

2 Lower the heat and simmer for 10 minutes or until the vegetables are just tender. Drain, reserving 200ml/7fl oz/scant 1 cup of the cooking water in a measuring jug (cup). Put the vegetables in a dish and keep hot.

3 Make the sauce. Melt the butter in a clean pan and stir in the flour. Cook for 1 minute, stirring, then gradually whisk in the reserved vegetable water and the milk. Heat, whisking, until the sauce boils and thickens. Lower the heat and simmer the sauce gently for 2 minutes.

4 Remove the sauce from the heat and stir in the chèvre, tarragon and salt and pepper.

5 Pour the sauce over the vegetables and sprinkle with the pine nuts or almonds. Garnish with the sprigs of tarragon and serve. Triangles of wholemeal (whole-wheat) toast make a good accompaniment.

Baked Mediterranean Vegetables

Crisp and golden crunchy batter surrounds these vegetables, turning them into a substantial appetizer. Make sure the fat is really hot before adding the batter or it will not rise well.

Serves 10–12

1 small aubergine (eggplant), trimmed, halved and thickly sliced
1 egg
115g/4oz/1 cup plain (all-purpose) flour
300ml/½ pint/1¼ cups milk
30ml/2 tbsp fresh thyme leaves, or 10ml/2 tsp dried
1 red onion, quartered
2 large courgettes (zucchini)
1 each red and yellow (bell) pepper, seeded and quartered
60–75ml/4–5 tbsp sunflower oil
salt and ground black pepper
30ml/2 tbsp freshly grated Parmesan cheese and fresh herbs, to garnish

1 Place the sliced aubergine in a colander or sieve (strainer), sprinkle generously with salt and leave for 10 minutes. Drain and pat dry on kitchen paper.

2 Meanwhile, to make the batter, beat the egg, then gradually beat in the flour and a little milk to make a smooth thick paste. Blend in the rest of the milk, add the thyme leaves and seasoning to taste and blend until smooth. Leave in a cool place until required.

3 Put the sunflower oil in a roasting pan and heat in the oven at 220°C/425°F/Gas 7. Add the vegetables, coat them well with the oil and return to the oven for 20 minutes until they are beginning to turn tender.

4 Whisk the batter, pour over the vegetables in the roasting pan and return to the oven for 30 minutes.

5 When the pastry is puffed up and golden all over, lower the oven temperature to 190°C/375°F/Gas 5 for 10–15 minutes until crisp around the edges. Sprinkle with the Parmesan and herbs and serve while warm.

Fricassée Energy 268kcal/1118kJ; Protein 9.5g; Carbohydrate 21.8g, of which sugars 10.7g; Fat 16.5g, of which saturates 8.3g; Cholesterol 37mg; Calcium 145mg; Fibre 5.1g; Sodium 209mg.
Baked Vegetables Energy 113kcal/473kJ; Protein 4.3g; Carbohydrate 11.9g, of which sugars 4.3g; Fat 5.7g, of which saturates 1.4g; Cholesterol 17mg; Calcium 89mg; Fibre 1.5g; Sodium 45mg.

Spiced Vegetables with Coconut

This spicy and substantial stir-fry could be served as an appetizer, or as a vegetarian main course for two. Eat it with spoons and forks, and provide hunks of fresh Granary bread for mopping up the delicious coconut milk.

Serves 2–4

1 red chilli
2 large carrots
6 celery sticks
1 fennel bulb
30ml/2 tbsp grapeseed oil
2.5cm/1in fresh root ginger, grated
1 garlic clove, crushed
3 spring onions (scallions), sliced
400ml/14fl oz can coconut milk
15ml/1 tbsp chopped fresh coriander (cilantro)
salt and ground black pepper
fresh coriander (cilantro) sprigs, to garnish

1 Halve, seed and finely chop the chilli. If necessary, wear rubber gloves to protect your hands.

2 Thinly slice the carrots and the celery sticks on the diagonal. Trim the fennel bulb and slice roughly, using a sharp knife.

3 Heat the wok, then add the oil. When the oil is hot, add the chilli, fennel, carrots, celery, ginger, garlic and spring onions and stir-fry for 2 minutes.

4 Stir in the coconut milk with a large spoon and bring the mixture to the boil.

5 Stir in the coriander, and salt and pepper, and serve garnished with coriander sprigs.

Cook's Tip
When buying fennel, look for well-rounded bulbs; flatter ones are immature and will not have developed their full aniseed-like flavour. The bulbs should be white with overlapping ridged layers. Avoid any that look damaged or bruised. The fennel should be dry, but not desiccated.

Summer Vegetables with Yogurt Pesto

Chargrilled summer vegetables make a delicious appetizer when served Mediterranean-style with Greek (US strained plain) yogurt.

Serves 8

4 small aubergines (eggplants)
4 large courgettes (zucchini)
2 red (bell) peppers
2 yellow (bell) peppers
2 fennel bulbs
2 red onions
300ml/½ pint/1¼ cups Greek (US strained plain) yogurt
90ml/6 tbsp pesto
olive oil, for brushing
salt and ground black pepper

1 Cut the aubergines into 1cm/½in slices. Sprinkle with salt and leave to drain for about 30 minutes. Rinse well in cold running water and pat dry.

2 Use a sharp kitchen knife to cut the courgettes in half lengthways. Cut the peppers in half, removing the seeds but leaving the stalks in place. Slice the fennel bulbs and the red onions into thick wedges, using a sharp kitchen knife.

3 Prepare the barbecue. Stir the yogurt and pesto lightly together in a bowl, to make a marbled sauce. Spoon the yogurt pesto into a serving bowl, cover and set aside.

4 Arrange the vegetables on the barbecue, brush generously with oil and sprinkle with plenty of salt and black pepper.

5 Cook the vegetables until golden brown and tender, turning occasionally. The aubergines and peppers will take 6–8 minutes to cook, the courgettes, onion and fennel 4–5 minutes. Serve the cooked vegetables with the yogurt pesto.

Cook's Tip
Baby vegetables are excellent for cooking whole on the barbecue, so look for baby aubergines (eggplants) and (bell) peppers, in particular. There's no need to salt the aubergines if they are small.

Spicy Vegetables Energy 59kcal/248kJ; Protein 2.2g; Carbohydrate 11.3g, of which sugars 10.9g; Fat 0.9g, of which saturates 0.3g; Cholesterol 0mg; Calcium 105mg; Fibre 4.8g; Sodium 175mg.
Summer Vegetables Energy 107kcal/447kJ; Protein 5.7g; Carbohydrate 13g, of which sugars 12.1g; Fat 4g, of which saturates 1g; Cholesterol 2mg; Calcium 133mg; Fibre 4.5g; Sodium 56mg.

Iced Melon Soup

Use different varieties of melon for this cool soup and ice sorbet to create subtle contrast. Try a mix of Charentais and Ogen or cantaloupe and Galia.

Serves 6–8

2.25kg/5–5¼lb very ripe melon
45ml/3 tbsp orange juice
30ml/2 tbsp lemon juice
mint leaves, to garnish

For the melon and mint sorbet

25g/1oz/2 tbsp sugar
120ml/4fl oz/½ cup water
2.25kg/5–5¼lb very ripe melon
juice of 2 limes
30ml/2 tbsp chopped fresh mint

1 To make the melon and mint sorbet, put the sugar and water into a pan and heat gently until the sugar dissolves. Bring to the boil and simmer for 4–5 minutes, then remove from the heat and leave to cool.

2 Halve the melon. Scrape out the seeds, then cut it into large wedges and cut the flesh out of the skin. Weigh about 1.5kg/3–3½lb melon.

3 Purée the melon in a food processor or blender with the cooled syrup and lime juice.

4 Stir in the mint and pour the melon mixture into an ice-cream maker. Churn, following the manufacturer's instructions, or until the sorbet is smooth and firm. Alternatively, pour the mixture into a suitable container and freeze until icy around the edges. Transfer to a food processor or blender and process until smooth. Repeat the freezing and processing two or three times or until smooth and holding its shape, then freeze until firm.

5 To make the chilled melon soup, prepare the melon as in step 2 and purée it in a food processor or blender. Pour the purée into a bowl and stir in the orange and lemon juice. Place the soup in the refrigerator for 30–40 minutes, but do not chill it for too long as this will dull its flavour.

6 Ladle the soup into bowls and add a large scoop of the sorbet to each. Garnish with mint leaves and serve immediately.

Chilled Coconut Soup

Refreshing, cooling and not too filling, this soup is the perfect antidote to hot weather. For a formal meal, it would be excellent after the first course, to refresh diners' palates before the main course.

Serves 6

1.2 litres/2 pints/5 cups milk
225g/8oz/2⅔ cups desiccated (dry unsweetened shredded) coconut
400ml/14fl oz/1⅔ cups coconut milk
400ml/14fl oz/1⅔ cups chicken stock
200ml/7fl oz/scant 1 cup double (heavy) cream
2.5ml/½tsp salt
2.5ml/½ tsp ground white pepper
5ml/1 tsp caster (superfine) sugar
small bunch of fresh coriander (cilantro)

1 Pour the milk into a large pan. Bring it to the boil, stir in the coconut, lower the heat and allow to simmer for 30 minutes. Spoon the mixture into a food processor and process until smooth. This may take a while – up to 5 minutes – so pause frequently and scrape down the sides of the bowl.

2 Rinse the pan to remove any coconut that remains, pour in the processed mixture and add the coconut milk. Stir in the chicken stock (home-made, if possible, which gives a better flavour than a stock cube), cream, salt, pepper and sugar. Bring the mixture to the boil, stirring occasionally, then lower the heat and cook for 10 minutes.

3 Reserve a few coriander leaves to garnish, then chop the rest finely and stir into the soup. Pour the soup into a large bowl, let it cool, then cover and place in the refrigerator to chill. Before serving, taste the soup and adjust the seasoning, if necessary. Serve in chilled bowls, garnished with the coriander leaves.

Cook's Tip

Avoid using sweetened desiccated coconut, which would spoil the flavour of this soup.

Iced Melon Soup Energy 150kcal/636kJ; Protein 2.9g; Carbohydrate 35.3g, of which sugars 35.3g; Fat 0.6g, of which saturates 0g; Cholesterol 0mg; Calcium 75mg; Fibre 2.3g; Sodium 175mg.
Coconut Soup Energy 597kcal/2474kJ; Protein 10.8g; Carbohydrate 16.9g, of which sugars 16.9g; Fat 54.7g, of which saturates 40.8g; Cholesterol 69mg; Calcium 317mg; Fibre 6.7g; Sodium 188mg.

Classic Gazpacho

This classic chilled soup is deeply rooted in the region of Andalusia, southern Spain. The soothing blend of tomatoes, sweet peppers and garlic is sharpened with sherry vinegar, and enriched with olive oil. Serving it with saucerfuls of garnishes has virtually become a tradition.

Serves 4

1.3–1.6kg/3–3½lb ripe tomatoes
1 green (bell) pepper, seeded and roughly chopped
2 garlic cloves, finely chopped
2 slices day-old bread, crusts removed
60ml/4 tbsp extra virgin olive oil
60ml/4 tbsp sherry vinegar
150ml/¼ pint/⅔ cup tomato juice
300ml/½ pint/1¼ cups iced water
salt and ground black pepper
ice cubes, to serve (optional)

For the garnishes
30ml/2 tbsp olive oil
2–3 slices day-old bread, diced
1 small cucumber, peeled and finely diced
1 small onion, finely chopped
1 red (bell) and 1 green (bell) pepper, seeded and finely diced
2 hard-boiled eggs, chopped

1 Skin the tomatoes, then quarter them and remove the cores and seeds, saving the juices. Put the pepper in a food processor or blender and process for a few seconds. Add the tomatoes, reserved juices, garlic, bread, oil and vinegar and process. Add the tomato juice and blend to combine.

2 Season the soup to taste with salt and ground black pepper, then pour into a large bowl, cover with clear film (plastic wrap) and chill for at least 12 hours.

3 Prepare the garnishes. Heat the olive oil in a frying pan and fry the bread cubes for about 4–5 minutes until golden brown and crisp all over. Drain well on kitchen paper, then arrange in a small dish. Place each of the remaining garnishes in separate small dishes.

4 Just before serving, dilute the soup with the ice-cold water. The consistency should be thick but not too stodgy. If you like, stir a few ice cubes into the soup, then spoon into bowls and serve with the garnishes.

Chilled Tomato and Sweet Pepper Soup

This delicious soup is made in the slow cooker before being chilled. Grilling the peppers gives a mild smoky flavour, but you can leave out this step, if you like.

Serves 4

2 red (bell) peppers
30ml/2 tbsp olive oil
1 onion, finely chopped
2 garlic cloves, crushed
675g/1½lb ripe tomatoes
120ml/4fl oz/½ cup red wine
450ml/¾ pint/scant 2 cups vegetable or chicken stock
2.5ml/½ tsp caster (superfine) sugar
salt and ground black pepper
chopped fresh chives, to garnish

For the croûtons
2 slices white bread, crusts removed
45ml/3 tbsp olive oil

1 Cut each pepper into quarters and remove the core and seeds. Place each quarter, skin side up, on a grill (broiler) rack. Grill (broil) until the skins are blistered and charred, then transfer to a bowl and cover with a plate.

2 Heat the oil in a frying pan. Add the onion and garlic and cook gently for about 10 minutes until soft, stirring occasionally. Meanwhile, remove the skin from the peppers and roughly chop the flesh. Cut the tomatoes into chunks.

3 Transfer the onions to the ceramic cooking pot and add the peppers, tomatoes, wine, stock and sugar. Cover and cook on high for 3–4 hours, or until the vegetables are very tender. Leave the soup to stand for about 10 minutes to cool slightly.

4 Ladle the soup into a food processor or blender and process until smooth. Press through a sieve (strainer) into a bowl. Leave to cool before chilling in the refrigerator for at least 3 hours.

5 Make the croûtons. Cut the bread into cubes. Heat the oil in a frying pan and fry the bread until golden. Drain on kitchen paper.

6 Season the soup to taste with salt and pepper, then ladle into chilled bowls. Top with croûtons and chopped chives and serve.

Classic Gazpacho Energy 356kcal/1494kJ; Protein 7.6g; Carbohydrate 41.9g, of which sugars 21.5g; Fat 18.8g, of which saturates 2.9g; Cholesterol 0mg; Calcium 90mg; Fibre 6.7g; Sodium 346mg.
Chilled Tomato Soup Energy 262kcal/1090kJ; Protein 3.5g; Carbohydrate 17.6g, of which sugars 11.5g; Fat 18g, of which saturates 2.6g; Cholesterol 0mg; Calcium 47mg; Fibre 3.4g; Sodium 499mg.

Fresh Tomato Soup

Choose the ripest-looking tomatoes and add sugar and balsamic vinegar to taste. The quantity will depend on the natural sweetness of the fresh tomatoes. On a hot day, this soup is also delicious chilled.

Serves 6

1.3–1.6kg/3–3½lb ripe tomatoes
400ml/14fl oz/1⅔ cups vegetable stock
45ml/3 tbsp sun-dried tomato purée (paste)
30–45ml/2–3 tbsp balsamic vinegar
10–15ml/2–3 tsp sugar
a small handful of fresh basil leaves, plus extra to garnish
salt and ground black pepper

For serving
toasted cheese croûtes
crème fraîche

1 Plunge the tomatoes into boiling water for 30 seconds, then drain. Peel off the skins and quarter the tomatoes.

2 Put the tomatoes in a large pan and pour over the vegetable stock. Bring just to the boil, reduce the heat, cover and simmer gently for 10 minutes until the tomatoes are pulpy.

3 Stir in the tomato purée, vinegar, sugar and basil. Season with salt and pepper, then cook gently, stirring, for 2 minutes.

4 Process the soup in a food processor or blender, then return it to a clean pan and reheat gently.

5 Serve in bowls, topping each portion with one or two toasted cheese croûtes and a spoonful of crème fraîche. Garnish with basil leaves.

Cook's Tip
Use a sharp knife to cut a cross in the base of each tomato before plunging it into the boiling water. The skin will then peel back easily from the crosses.

Garlic Soup

This interesting and surprisingly subtly flavoured soup makes good use of an ingredient that is not only delicious but also has great health-giving properties. It certainly brings a great sense of well-being and is a real treat for garlic-lovers.

Serves 8

12 large garlic cloves, crushed
15ml/1 tbsp olive oil
15ml/1 tbsp melted butter
1 small onion, finely chopped
15g/½oz/2 tbsp plain (all-purpose) flour
15ml/1 tbsp white wine vinegar
1 litre/1¾ pints/4 cups vegetable stock
2 egg yolks
croûtons, to serve

1 Heat the oil and butter in a pan, add the garlic and onion, and cook them gently for 20 minutes, stirring occasionally.

2 Stir in the flour and make a smooth paste. Cook for a few minutes, stirring, without letting the mixture brown. Then stir in the wine vinegar, stock and 1 litre/1¾ pints/4 cups water. Bring to the boil, reduce the heat and cover the pan. Simmer gently for 30 minutes.

3 Just before serving, lightly whisk the egg yolks in a bowl. Remove the pan from the heat and add a ladleful of soup to the yolks. Stir with the whisk until the yolks are well mixed with the soup, then pour the mixture into the pan.

4 Heat the soup over low heat, stirring, for a few seconds but do not allow it to simmer or boil or the yolks will curdle. Put the croûtons into soup bowls and pour the hot soup over them, then serve immediately.

Cook's Tip
Once the yolks are added the soup is difficult to reheat from cold. If the whole batch is not going to be served, pour half into a pan and add just 1 egg yolk. Finish the rest when required.

Fresh Tomato Soup Energy 49kcal/210kJ; Protein 1.9g; Carbohydrate 9.5g, of which sugars 9.5g; Fat 0.7g, of which saturates 0.2g; Cholesterol 0mg; Calcium 19mg; Fibre 2.4g; Sodium 38mg.
Garlic Soup Energy 55kcal/229kJ; Protein 1.3g; Carbohydrate 3g, of which sugars 0.5g; Fat 4.4g, of which saturates 1.6g; Cholesterol 54mg; Calcium 12mg; Fibre 0.3g; Sodium 50mg.

Squash Soup with Hot Horseradish Cream

The partnering of squash and apple in this curried soup is superb. For fans of horseradish, the cream topping is an absolute must.

Serves 6

1 butternut squash
1 cooking apple
25g/1oz/2 tbsp butter
1 onion, finely chopped
5–10ml/1–2 tsp curry powder, plus extra to garnish
900ml/1½ pints/3¾ cups vegetable stock
5ml/1 tsp chopped fresh sage
150ml/¼ pint/⅔ cup apple juice
salt and ground black pepper
lime shreds, to garnish (optional)

For the horseradish cream (optional)
60ml/4 tbsp double (heavy) cream
10ml/2 tsp horseradish sauce
2.5ml/½ tsp curry powder

1 Peel the squash, remove the seeds and chop the flesh. Peel, core and chop the apple.

2 Heat the butter in a large pan. Add the onion and cook, stirring occasionally, for 5 minutes until soft. Stir in the curry powder. Cook to bring out the flavour, stirring constantly, for about 2 minutes.

3 Add the stock, squash, apple and sage. Bring to the boil, lower the heat, cover and simmer for 20 minutes until the squash and apple are soft.

4 If making the horseradish cream, whip the cream in a bowl until stiff, then stir in the horseradish sauce and curry powder. Cover and chill until required.

5 Purée the soup in a food processor or blender. Return to the clean pan and add the apple juice, with salt and pepper to taste. Reheat gently, without boiling.

6 Serve the soup in bowls, topped with a spoonful of horseradish cream, if liked, and a dusting of curry powder. Garnish with a few lime shreds.

Spicy Carrot Soup

Garlic croûtons are very easy to make, and, once you know how, they can of course be used to top all kinds of soups.

Serves 6

15ml/1 tbsp olive oil
1 large onion, chopped
675g/1½lb carrots, sliced
5ml/1 tsp each ground coriander, ground cumin and hot chilli powder
900ml/1½ pints/3¾ cups vegetable stock
salt and ground black pepper
sprigs of fresh coriander (cilantro), to garnish

For the garlic croûtons
a little olive oil
2 garlic cloves, crushed
4 slices bread, crusts removed, cut into 1cm/½in cubes

1 Heat the oil in a large pan, add the onion and carrots and cook gently for 5 minutes, stirring occasionally. Add the ground spices and cook gently for 1 minute, continuing to stir.

2 Stir in the stock, bring to the boil, then cover and cook gently for about 45 minutes until the carrots are tender.

3 Meanwhile, make the garlic croûtons. Heat the oil in a frying pan, add the garlic and cook gently for 30 seconds, stirring. Add the bread cubes, turn them over in the oil and fry over medium heat for a few minutes until crisp and golden brown all over, turning frequently. Drain on kitchen paper and keep warm.

4 Purée the soup in a food processor or blender until smooth, then season to taste with salt and pepper. Return the soup to the rinsed-out pan and reheat gently. Serve hot, sprinkled with garlic croûtons and garnished with coriander sprigs.

Cook's Tip
There is a confusing array of curry powders and pastes available. Many of the pastes are too complicated in flavour for a simple soup, but a basic, good-quality curry powder can be used instead of the three separate spices.

Squash Soup Energy 118kcal/489kJ; Protein 1.3g; Carbohydrate 7.7g, of which sugars 6.7g; Fat 9.3g, of which saturates 5.7g; Cholesterol 23mg; Calcium 50mg; Fibre 1.7g; Sodium 44mg.
Spicy Carrot Soup Energy 124kcal/517kJ; Protein 2.5g; Carbohydrate 19.7g, of which sugars 10.6g; Fat 4.4g, of which saturates 0.6g; Cholesterol 0mg; Calcium 55mg; Fibre 3.4g; Sodium 116mg.

Pumpkin and Parsnip Soup

The textures of carrot, parsnip and pumpkin go so very well together, making a soup that is wonderfully rich in texture and flavour.

Serves 4

15ml/1 tbsp olive or sunflower oil
15g/½oz/1 tbsp butter
1 onion, chopped
225g/8oz carrots, chopped
225g/8oz parsnips, chopped
225g/8oz pumpkin
about 900ml/1½ pints/3¾ cups vegetable stock
lemon juice, to taste
salt and ground black pepper

For the garnish

7.5ml/1½ tsp olive oil
½ garlic clove, finely chopped
45ml/3 tbsp chopped fresh parsley and coriander (cilantro), mixed
a good pinch of paprika

1 Heat the oil and butter in a large pan and fry the onion for about 3 minutes until softened, stirring occasionally. Add the carrots and parsnips, stir well, cover and cook over a gentle heat for a further 5 minutes.

2 Cut the pumpkin into chunks, discarding the skin and pith, and stir into the pan. Cover and cook for a further 5 minutes, then add the stock and seasoning, and slowly bring to the boil. Reduce the heat if necessary. Cover the pan and simmer the soup for 35–40 minutes until the vegetables are tender.

3 Allow the soup to cool slightly, then pour it into a food processor or blender and purée until smooth. Add a little extra stock or water if the soup seems too thick. Pour the soup back into the rinsed-out pan and reheat gently.

4 To make the garnish, heat the olive oil in a small pan and fry the chopped garlic and herbs for 1–2 minutes. Add the paprika and stir well.

5 Taste the soup and adjust the seasoning, then stir in lemon juice to taste. Pour the soup into bowls and spoon a little of the prepared garnish on each portion. Carefully swirl the garnish through the soup using a skewer or cocktail stick (toothpick), or the point of a knife. Serve immediately.

Quick Pistou Soup

A delicious chunky vegetable soup served with tomato pesto. Serve in small portions as an appetizer.

Serves 6

1 courgette (zucchini), diced
1 small potato, diced
1 shallot, chopped
1 carrot, diced
400g/14oz can chopped tomatoes
1.2 litres/2 pints/5 cups vegetable stock
50g/2oz green beans, cut into 1cm/½in lengths
50g/2oz/½ cup frozen petits pois (baby peas)
50g/2oz/½ cup small pasta shapes
30ml/2 tbsp pesto sauce
10ml/2 tsp tomato purée (paste)
salt and ground black pepper
freshly grated Parmesan or Pecorino cheese, to serve

1 Place the courgette, potato, shallot, carrot and tomatoes in a large pan. Add the vegetable stock and season with salt and plenty of black pepper. Bring to the boil over a medium heat, then reduce the heat, cover the pan and simmer for 20 minutes.

2 Add the green beans and petits pois to the pan and bring the soup back to the boil. Boil the mixture briefly for about 1 minute.

3 Add the pasta. Simmer the soup for a further 10 minutes, or until the pasta is tender. Taste and adjust the seasoning.

4 Ladle the soup into bowls. Mix together the pesto and tomato purée; stir a little into each serving and sprinkle with grated cheese.

Variations

- *To strengthen the tomato flavour, try using tomato-flavoured spaghetti, broken into small lengths, instead of pasta shapes.*
- *Sun-dried tomato purée (paste) can be used instead of the regular kind if you prefer.*

Pumpkin Soup Energy 137kcal/568kJ; Protein 2.3g; Carbohydrate 14.3g, of which sugars 9.5g; Fat 8.2g, of which saturates 2.7g; Cholesterol 8mg; Calcium 83mg; Fibre 5.3g; Sodium 47mg.
Quick Pistou Soup Energy 96kcal/406kJ; Protein 4.1g; Carbohydrate 15g, of which sugars 5.3g; Fat 2.7g, of which saturates 0.7g; Cholesterol 2mg; Calcium 47mg; Fibre 2.5g; Sodium 37mg.

French Onion Soup

This is perhaps the most famous of all onion soups.

Serves 6

50g/2oz/¼ cup butter
15ml/1 tbsp olive or groundnut (peanut) oil
2kg/4½lb onions, sliced
5ml/1 tsp chopped fresh thyme
5ml/1 tsp caster (superfine) sugar
15ml/1 tbsp sherry vinegar
1.5 litres/2½ pints/6¼ cups good vegetable stock
25ml/1½ tbsp plain (all-purpose) flour
150ml/¼ pint/⅔ cup dry white wine
45ml/3 tbsp brandy
salt and ground black pepper

For the croûtes

6–12 thick slices day-old French bread, about 2.5cm/1in thick
1 garlic clove, halved
15ml/1 tbsp French mustard
115g/4oz Gruyère cheese, grated

1 Heat the butter and oil in a large pan. Add the onions and stir. Cook over medium heat for 5–8 minutes, stirring once or twice, until the onions begin to soften. Stir in the thyme. Reduce the heat to very low, cover and cook the onions for 20–30 minutes, stirring frequently, until very soft and golden.

2 Uncover the pan and increase the heat slightly. Stir in the sugar and cook for 5–10 minutes, until the onions start to brown. Add the sherry vinegar and increase the heat again, then continue cooking, stirring frequently, until the onions turn a deep, golden brown – this could take up to 20 minutes.

3 Bring the stock to the boil in another pan. Stir the flour into the onions and cook for 2 minutes, then gradually stir in the stock, wine, brandy and seasoning to taste. Bring to the boil, stirring, reduce the heat and simmer for 10–15 minutes.

4 For the croûtes, preheat the oven to 150°C/300°F/Gas 2. Place the bread on a greased baking tray and bake for 15–20 minutes, until lightly browned. Rub with the garlic and spread with mustard, then sprinkle with the cheese.

5 Preheat the grill (broiler) on the hottest setting. Ladle the soup into six flameproof bowls. Add the croûtes and grill (broil) until the cheese melts, bubbles and browns. Serve immediately.

Cheese and Celeriac Soup

Cheese and celeriac are brilliant together, especially in this Dutch Gouda soup.

Serves 4

40g/1½oz/3 tbsp butter
1 onion, chopped
50g/2oz/½ cup plain (all-purpose) flour
1.2 litres/2 pints/5 cups milk
150g/5oz/1¼ cups grated mature (sharp) Gouda cheese
1 small celeriac
salt
chopped fresh chives, to garnish
toast, to serve

1 Melt the butter in a pan. Add the onion and cook over low heat, stirring occasionally, for 5 minutes, until softened.

2 Stir in the flour and cook, stirring constantly, for 2 minutes, then gradually stir in the milk.

3 Continue to cook, stirring, until slightly thickened. Add 50g/2oz/½ cup of the grated Gouda and cook, stirring occasionally, for about 15 minutes.

4 Meanwhile, peel and finely dice the celeriac, then cook it in boiling water for about 10 minutes, or until tender.

5 Drain the celeriac and add to the soup with the remaining cheese. Stir until the cheese has melted.

6 Season to taste with salt, then ladle the soup into warm bowls and garnish with chives. Serve immediately with hot crisp toast and butter.

Variations

- *For a smooth soup, purée the cooked celeriac and soup, then return it to the pan and stir in the remaining cheese.*
- *Use half and half celeriac and swede (rutabaga), and add a carrot to the soup.*
- *Try other cheeses: strong Cheddar or Spanish manchego are suitable, or add Stilton or Danish blue for a punchy flavour.*

French Onion Soup Energy 415kcal/1745kJ; Protein 13g; Carbohydrate 61.6g, of which sugars 12.6g; Fat 14.1g, of which saturates 6.7g; Cholesterol 25mg; Calcium 240mg; Fibre 4.1g; Sodium 1022mg.
Cheese Soup Energy 407kcal/1703kJ; Protein 21.5g; Carbohydrate 25.7g, of which sugars 15.9g; Fat 25.2g, of which saturates 16.1g; Cholesterol 71mg; Calcium 704mg; Fibre 1.4g; Sodium 582mg.

Wild Mushroom Soup

Wild mushrooms are expensive. Dried porcini have an intense flavour, so only a small quantity is needed. Meat stock may seem odd in a vegetable soup, but it helps to strengthen the earthy flavour of the mushrooms.

Serves 4

25g/1oz/2 cups dried porcini mushrooms
250ml/8fl oz/1 cup warm water
30ml/2 tbsp olive oil
15g/½oz/1 tbsp butter
2 leeks, thinly sliced
2 shallots, coarsely chopped
1 garlic clove, coarsely chopped
225g/8oz fresh wild mushrooms
1.2 litres/2 pints/5 cups meat stock, such as beef or chicken
2.5ml/½ tsp dried thyme
150ml/¼ pint/⅔ cup double (heavy) cream
salt and ground black pepper
fresh thyme sprigs, to garnish

1 Put the dried porcini in a bowl, add the warm water and leave to soak for 20–30 minutes. Lift the porcini out of the liquid and squeeze to remove as much of the soaking liquid as possible. Strain all the liquid and reserve to use later. Finely chop the porcini.

2 Heat the oil and butter in a large pan until foaming. Add the leeks, shallots and garlic and cook gently for about 5 minutes, stirring frequently, until softened but not coloured.

3 Chop or thinly slice the fresh mushrooms and add to the pan. Stir over medium heat for a few minutes until they begin to soften. Pour in the meat stock and bring to the boil. Add the porcini, soaking liquid, dried thyme and salt and pepper. Lower the heat, half-cover the pan and simmer gently for 30 minutes, stirring occasionally.

4 Pour about three-quarters of the soup into a blender or food processor and process until smooth. Return to the soup remaining in the pan, stir in the double cream and heat through. Check the consistency, adding more stock or water if the soup is too thick. Taste and adjust the seasoning. Serve hot, garnished with sprigs of fresh thyme.

Leek and Potato with Heart of Palm Soup

This delicate soup has a luxurious, creamy, almost velvety texture. The subtle yet distinctive flavour of the palm hearts is like no other, although it is mildly reminiscent of artichokes and asparagus. Serve with fresh bread for a really satisfying lunch.

Serves 4

25g/1oz/2 tbsp butter
10ml/2 tsp olive oil
1 onion, finely chopped
1 large leek, finely sliced
15ml/1 tbsp plain (all-purpose) flour
1 litre/1¾ pints/4 cups well-flavoured chicken stock
350g/12oz potatoes, peeled and cubed
2 x 400g/14oz cans hearts of palm, drained and sliced
250ml/8fl oz/1 cup double (heavy) cream
salt and ground black pepper
cayenne pepper and chopped fresh chives, to garnish

1 Heat the butter and oil in a large pan over a low heat. Add the onion and leek and stir well until coated in butter. Cover and cook for 5 minutes until softened and translucent.

2 Sprinkle the flour into the pan over the vegetables. Stir and cook, still stirring, for 1 minute.

3 Pour in the stock and add the potatoes. Bring to the boil, stirring, then lower the heat and simmer for 10 minutes. Stir in the hearts of palm and the cream, and simmer gently for a further 10 minutes.

4 Process the soup in a food processor or blender until smooth. Pour it back into the rinsed-out pan and heat gently, adding a little water if necessary. The consistency should be thick but not too heavy. Do not allow to boil. Season with salt and ground black pepper.

5 Ladle the soup into warm bowls and garnish each portion with a pinch of cayenne pepper and a sprinkling of fresh chives. Serve immediately.

Mushroom Soup Energy 149kcal/618kJ; Protein 3.1g; Carbohydrate 9g, of which sugars 0.5g; Fat 11.4g, of which saturates 6.9g; Cholesterol 28mg; Calcium 25mg; Fibre 1.5g; Sodium 79mg.
Leek and Potato Energy 486kcal/2013kJ; Protein 5.2g; Carbohydrate 25.1g, of which sugars 7.9g; Fat 41.2g, of which saturates 24.5g; Cholesterol 99mg; Calcium 147mg; Fibre 4.9g; Sodium 184mg.

Miso Soup with Wakame

Essential to any Japanese meal is a bowl of rice. Next is miso soup, served in a lacquered bowl.

Serves 4
5g/⅛oz dried wakame
115g/4oz fresh soft tofu or long-life silken tofu
400ml/14fl oz/1⅔ cups dashi stock
45ml/3 tbsp miso
2 spring onions (scallions), finely chopped
shichimi togarashi or sansho (optional), to serve

1 Soak the wakame in cold water for 15 minutes. Drain and chop into stamp-size pieces if using the long or broad type.

2 Cut the tofu into 1cm/½in strips, then cut horizontally through the strips. Cut the thin strips into squares.

3 Bring the dashi stock to the boil. Put the miso in a small cup and mix with 60ml/4 tbsp hot stock. Reduce the heat to low and pour two-thirds of the miso back into the pan of stock.

4 Taste the soup and add more miso if required. Add the wakame and the tofu and increase the heat. Just before the soup comes to the boil again, add the spring onions and remove the pan from the heat. Do not boil.

5 Serve the soup ladled into bowls and sprinkled with shichimi togarashi or sansho, if liked.

Cook's Tips
- *Buy a pack of dried konbu for making dashi stock. If liked, for additional flavour in a vegetarian stock, add shredded spring onion to the water when soaking the konbu. (Fine shreds of dried fish are used in non-vegetarian dashi.)*
- *Sansho is a spice, known as Japanese pepper. It is part of the seven-spice mixture known as shichimi togarashi. Look out for Japanese spices in specialist stores or among the Japanese ingredients on deli counters in larger supermarkets.*

Hot and Sour Soup

This spicy, warming soup really whets the appetite and is the perfect introduction to a simple Chinese meal.

Serves 4
10g/¼oz dried cloud ear (wood ear) mushrooms
8 fresh shiitake mushrooms
900ml/1½ pints/3¾ cups vegetable stock
75g/3oz firm tofu, cubed
50g/2oz/½ cup canned sliced bamboo shoots
15ml/1 tbsp caster (superfine) sugar
45ml/3 tbsp rice vinegar
15ml/1 tbsp light soy sauce
1.5ml/¼ tsp chilli oil
2.5ml/½ tsp salt
large pinch of ground white pepper
15ml/1 tbsp cornflour (cornstarch)
1 egg white
5ml/1 tsp sesame oil
2 spring onions (scallions), sliced into fine rings
white pepper, to serve

1 Soak the dried cloud ear mushrooms in hot water for 20 minutes or until soft. Drain, trim off and discard the hard base from each cloud ear and then chop the fungus roughly.

2 Remove and discard the stems from the shiitake mushrooms. Cut the caps into thin strips.

3 Place the stock, both types of mushroom, tofu and bamboo shoots in a large pan. Bring the stock to the boil, lower the heat and simmer for about 5 minutes.

4 Stir in the sugar, vinegar, soy sauce, chilli oil, salt and pepper. Mix the cornflour to a paste with a little cold water. Add to the soup, stirring constantly, and bring to the boil, stirring until it thickens slightly.

5 Lightly whisk the egg white with a fork, just enough to break it up, then pour it slowly into the soup in a steady stream, stirring constantly so that it forms threads. Add the sesame oil.

6 Ladle the soup into heated bowls and garnish with spring onion rings. Serve immediately, offering white pepper at the table for anyone who wants a hotter soup.

Miso Soup with Wakame Energy 40kcal/167kJ; Protein 3.8g; Carbohydrate 3.4g, of which sugars 1.3g; Fat 1.3g, of which saturates 0.2g; Cholesterol 0mg; Calcium 156mg; Fibre 0.9g; Sodium 892mg.
Hot and Sour Soup Energy 102kcal/429kJ; Protein 7.3g; Carbohydrate 7.3g, of which sugars 0.3g; Fat 5.1g, of which saturates 1g; Cholesterol 44mg; Calcium 135mg; Fibre 0.7g; Sodium 208mg.

Beetroot Soup with Ravioli

Beetroot and pasta are a delicious duo. With bought ravioli and ready cooked beetroot, this substantial soup is ready in minutes. Ideal for a tasty supper or speedy first course.

Serves 4

225g/8oz fresh mushroom ravioli
1 small onion or shallot, finely chopped
2 garlic cloves, crushed
5ml/1 tsp fennel seeds
600ml/1 pint/2½ cups chicken or vegetable stock
225g/8oz cooked beetroot (beet)
30ml/2 tbsp fresh orange juice
fresh fennel or dill leaves, to garnish
crusty bread, to serve

1 Bring a large pan of salted water to the boil. Add the ravioli and bring back to the boil. Cook for 3–5 minutes or according to the packet instructions, until the ravioli are tender, but not soft. Drain well and rinse under cold running water, then set aside in a colander.

2 Put the onion, garlic and fennel seeds into a pan. Then pour in 150ml/¼ pint/⅔ cup of the stock. Bring to the boil, cover and simmer for 5 minutes, or until the onion is tender.

3 Peel and finely dice the beetroot, reserving 60ml/4 tbsp for the garnish. Add the rest of the beetroot to the pan and pour in the remaining stock. Bring to the boil.

4 Add the orange juice and cooked ravioli and simmer for 2 minutes. Ladle into shallow soup bowls. Garnish with the reserved diced beetroot and fresh fennel or dill leaves. Serve hot, with crusty bread.

Cook's Tip
Polish-style beetroot soup is often served with pasta filled with dried mushrooms. Cheese-filled pasta is also excellent. Plain pasta shapes can be used and a little diced cooked ham added, then Parmesan cheese sprinkled over when serving.

Brown Rice and Mushrooms in Clear Soup

This is a good and quick way of using up left-over rice. Short grain Japanese or Italian brown rice are best for this recipe.

Serves 4

1 litre/1¾ pints/4 cups second dashi stock, or the same amount of water and 20ml/4 tsp dashi-no-moto
60ml/4 tbsp sake
5ml/1 tsp salt
60ml/4 tbsp shoyu
115g/4oz fresh shiitake mushrooms, thinly sliced
600g/1lb 6oz cooked brown rice
2 large (US extra large) eggs
30ml/2 tbsp chopped fresh chives

For the garnish
15ml/1 tbsp sesame seeds
shichimi togarashi (seven-spice powder), optional

1 Mix together the dashi stock, sake, salt and shoyu in a large pan. Bring to the boil, then add the sliced shiitake. Cook for 5 minutes over medium heat.

2 Add the cooked rice to the pan and stir over medium heat. Break up any large chunks with a wooden spoon, and heat until the rice is thoroughly warmed through.

3 Break the eggs into a medium bowl and beat together with a fork until combined.

4 Pour the eggs into the pan. Lower the heat and cover. Do not stir. Remove from the heat after 3 minutes and leave to stand for 3 minutes more. Sprinkle in the chives. Serve immediately garnished with sesame seeds and shichimi togarashi.

Cook's Tip
Although Japanese recipes often include exotic ingredients, which aren't always readily available, this delicious soup is well worth hunting them down. Try large supermarkets or Asian food stores, such as Chinese markets.

Beetroot Soup Energy 141kcal/589kJ; Protein 4.4g; Carbohydrate 13.3g, of which sugars 3.5g; Fat 7.9g, of which saturates 2.2g; Cholesterol 6mg; Calcium 86mg; Fibre 1.1g; Sodium 79mg.
Brown Rice Soup Energy 280kcal/1180kJ; Protein 8.4g; Carbohydrate 50g, of which sugars 2.4g; Fat 4.7g, of which saturates 1.3g; Cholesterol 95mg; Calcium 48mg; Fibre 2.1g; Sodium 1111mg.

Cellophane Noodle Soup

The noodles used in this soup go by various names: glass, cellophane, bean thread or transparent.

Serves 4

4 large dried shiitake mushrooms
15g/½oz dried lily buds
½ cucumber, coarsely chopped
2 garlic cloves, halved
90g/3½oz white cabbage, coarsely chopped
1.2 litres/2 pints/5 cups boiling water
115g/4oz cellophane noodles
30ml/2 tbsp soy sauce
15ml/1 tbsp palm sugar (jaggery) or light muscovado (brown) sugar
90g/3½oz block silken tofu, diced
fresh coriander (cilantro) leaves, to garnish

1 Soak the shiitake mushrooms in warm water for 30 minutes. In a separate bowl, soak the dried lily buds in warm water, also for 30 minutes.

2 Meanwhile, put the cucumber, garlic and cabbage in a food processor and process to a smooth paste. Scrape the mixture into a large pan and add the measured boiling water.

3 Bring to the boil. Reduce the heat and cook for 2 minutes, stirring occasionally. Strain this stock into another pan, return to a low heat and bring to simmering point.

4 Drain the lily buds, rinse under cold running water, then drain again. Cut off any hard ends. Add the lily buds to the stock with the noodles, soy sauce and sugar and cook for 5 minutes more.

5 Strain the mushroom soaking liquid into the soup. Discard the mushroom stems, then slice the caps. Divide them and the tofu among four bowls. Pour the soup over the mushrooms and tofu, garnish and serve immediately.

Cook's Tip
Tough and brittle, it is better not to try to break or chop cellophane noodles before adding to a hot stock, soup or stew.

Tortilla and Tomato Soup

There are several tortilla soups. This one is an aguada – or liquid – version, and is intended for serving as an appetizer or light meal. The crisp tortilla pieces add an unusual texture.

Serves 4

4 corn tortillas, freshly-made or a few days old
15ml/1 tbsp vegetable oil, plus extra, for frying
1 small onion, finely chopped
2 garlic cloves, crushed
400g/14oz can plum tomatoes, drained
1 litre/1¾ pints/4 cups vegetable stock
small bunch of fresh coriander (cilantro), chopped
salt and ground black pepper

1 Cut each tortilla into four or five strips, each about 2cm/¾in wide. Pour oil to a depth of 2cm/¾in into a frying pan. Heat until a small piece of tortilla floats and bubbles at the edges. Fry the tortilla strips in batches, until golden, turning occasionally. Remove with a slotted spoon and drain on kitchen paper.

2 Heat the 15ml/1 tbsp vegetable oil in a large heavy-based pan. Add the onion and garlic and cook gently for 2–3 minutes, stirring, until the onion is soft and translucent. Do not let the garlic turn brown or it will give the soup a bitter taste.

3 Chop the tomatoes and add them to the onion mixture. Stir in the stock. Bring to the boil, then lower the heat and simmer for about 10 minutes, until the liquid has reduced slightly.

4 Add the coriander, reserving a little for garnish, and season to taste. Place a few of the crisp tortilla pieces in the bottom of four warmed soup bowls. Ladle the soup on top. Sprinkle each portion with the reserved chopped coriander and serve.

Cook's Tip
An easy way to chop the coriander (cilantro) is to put the leaves in a mug and cut with a pair of scissors. Hold the scissors vertically in both hands and work the blades back and forth until the coriander is finely chopped.

Cellophane Noodle Soup Energy 148kcal/618kJ; Protein 4.1g; Carbohydrate 29.7g, of which sugars 5.7g; Fat 1.1g, of which saturates 0.1g; Cholesterol 0mg; Calcium 139mg; Fibre 0.7g; Sodium 546mg.
Tortilla Soup Energy 270kcal/1135kJ; Protein 8.3g; Carbohydrate 36.9g, of which sugars 7.2g; Fat 10.7g, of which saturates 3.6g; Cholesterol 12mg; Calcium 164mg; Fibre 3.3g; Sodium 248mg.

Tortellini Chanterelle Broth

The savoury-sweet quality of chanterelle mushrooms combines well in a simple broth with spinach-and-ricotta-filled tortellini. The addition of a little sherry creates a lovely warming effect.

Serves 4

350g/12oz fresh spinach and ricotta tortellini, or 175g/6oz dried
1.2 litres/2 pints/5 cups chicken stock
75ml/5 tbsp dry sherry
175g/6oz fresh chanterelle mushrooms, trimmed and sliced, or 15g/½oz/¼ cup dried chanterelles
chopped fresh parsley, to garnish

1 Cook the spinach and ricotta tortellini according to the packet instructions. Fresh tortellini will cook much more quickly than the dried variety.

2 Place the chicken stock in a large pan over high heat and bring to the boil. Add the dry sherry and fresh or dried mushrooms and simmer for 10 minutes.

3 Strain the tortellini, add to the stock, and heat for a minute to warm through. Ladle the hot broth into four warmed soup bowls, making sure each contains the same proportions of tortellini and mushrooms. Garnish with the chopped parsley and serve.

Cook's Tip

Chanterelles are plentiful in the wild in many regions and are a firm favourite of mushroom pickers. If there are any growing in woodlands near your home, then go exploring and you may come back with a tasty haul of free mushrooms. Ensure that you know exactly what you are looking for as there are poisonous varieties to avoid. Picked mushrooms should be carried in a basket rather than a bag so their spores will drop on to the forest floor as you search.

Clam and Pasta Soup

This soup is a variation of the pasta dish spaghetti alle vongole, using store-cupboard ingredients. Serve it with hot focaccia or ciabatta for a tasty and filling first course.

Serves 4

30ml/2 tbsp olive oil
1 large onion, finely chopped
2 garlic cloves, crushed
400g/14oz can chopped tomatoes
15ml/1 tbsp sun-dried tomato purée (paste)
5ml/1 tsp granulated (white) sugar
5ml/1 tsp dried mixed herbs
about 750ml/1¼ pints/3 cups fish or vegetable stock
150ml/¼ pint/⅔ cup red wine
50g/2oz/½ cup small dried pasta shapes
150g/5oz jar or can clams in natural juice
30ml/2 tbsp finely chopped fresh flat leaf parsley, plus a few whole leaves to garnish
salt and ground black pepper

1 Heat the olive oil in a large, heavy pan. Add the chopped onion and cook gently for 5 minutes, stirring frequently, until translucent and softened.

2 Add the garlic, tomatoes, sun-dried tomato purée, sugar, herbs, stock and wine to the pan. Season with salt and ground black pepper to taste.

3 Bring the soup to the boil. Lower the heat, half-cover the pan and simmer, stirring occasionally, for 10 minutes.

4 Add the pasta and continue simmering, uncovered, for about 10 minutes, or until the pasta is al dente. Stir occasionally to prevent the pasta shapes from sticking together.

5 Add the clams and their juice to the soup and heat through for 3–4 minutes, adding more stock if required. Do not allow it to boil, or the clams will become tough.

6 Remove the soup from the heat, stir in the chopped parsley and adjust the seasoning. Serve hot, sprinkled with coarsely ground black pepper and parsley leaves.

Tortellini Broth Energy 204kcal/859kJ; Protein 7.6g; Carbohydrate 23.4g, of which sugars 1.5g; Fat 4.3g, of which saturates 0.1g; Cholesterol 0mg; Calcium 106mg; Fibre 1.6g; Sodium 185mg.
Clam Soup Energy 196kcal/821kJ; Protein 9.3g; Carbohydrate 20.2g, of which sugars 8.9g; Fat 6.5g, of which saturates 1g; Cholesterol 25mg; Calcium 67mg; Fibre 2.6g; Sodium 466mg.

Spicy Beef and Mushroom Soup

Ginger gives this satisfying soup a delightful tang.

Serves 4

10g/½oz dried porcini mushrooms
6 spring onions (scallions)
115g/4oz carrots
350g/12oz lean rump (round) steak
about 30ml/2 tbsp oil
1 garlic clove, crushed
2.5cm/1in fresh root ginger, grated
1.2 litres/2 pints/5 cups beef stock
45ml/3 tbsp light soy sauce
60ml/4 tbsp sake or dry sherry
75g/3oz dried thin egg noodles
75g/3oz spinach, shredded
salt and ground black pepper

1 Break up the dried porcini, place them in a bowl and pour over 150ml/¼ pint/⅔ cup boiling water. Cover and leave the mushrooms to soak for 15 minutes.

2 Cut the spring onions and carrots into fine 5cm/2in long strips. Trim any fat from the meat and slice into thin strips.

3 Heat the oil in a large pan and cook the beef in batches until browned. Remove and drain on kitchen paper. Add the garlic, ginger, spring onions and carrots to the pan and stir-fry for 3 minutes.

4 Add the beef stock, the mushrooms and their soaking liquid, the soy sauce, sherry and plenty of seasoning. Bring to the boil, reduce the heat and simmer, covered, for 10 minutes.

5 Break up the noodles slightly and add to the pan with the spinach. Simmer gently for 5 minutes, or until the beef is tender. Adjust the seasoning before serving in warmed bowls.

Cook's Tips
• *Chilling the beef briefly in the freezer will make it much easier to slice into thin strips.*
• *Dried mixed mushrooms are also available to buy and can be used in this recipe.*

Red Pepper and Pasta in Broth

This simple soup is ideal for a light supper when served with ciabatta bread and also makes a delicious first course for an al fresco supper. Soup pasta is called pastini in Italian and is now widely available. Choose one particular shape or use a mixture of different shapes and colours for a more interesting result.

Serves 4

1.2 litres/2 pints/5 cups well-flavoured vegetable or chicken stock
75g/3oz/¾ cup tiny soup pasta
2 pieces bottled roasted red (bell) pepper, about 50g/2oz
coarsely shaved Parmesan cheese, to serve

1 Bring the stock to the boil in a large pan. Add seasoning to taste, then drop in the dried soup pasta. Stir well and bring the stock back to the boil.

2 Reduce the heat so that the soup simmers and cook for 7–8 minutes, until the pasta shapes are al dente, or tender but still firm to the bite.

3 Drain the pieces of roasted pepper and dice them finely. Place them in the base of four warmed soup plates. Taste the soup for seasoning before ladling it into the soup plates. Serve immediately, topped with shavings of Parmesan.

Cook's Tip
There are many different pastini to choose from, including stellette (stars), anellini (tiny thin rounds), risoni (rice-shaped) and farfalline (little butterflies). You could also use the fine 'angel hair' pasta, capellini, broken into smaller pieces.

Variation
Use fresh (bell) peppers instead of bottled: first roast them until charred, then remove the skins and seeds and dice.

Spicy Beef Soup Energy 315kcal/1316kJ; Protein 23.4g; Carbohydrate 17.4g, of which sugars 4g; Fat 15.5g, of which saturates 4.5g; Cholesterol 56mg; Calcium 57mg; Fibre 1.9g; Sodium 713mg.
Red Pepper Broth Energy 79kcal/334kJ; Protein 2.9g; Carbohydrate 15.9g, of which sugars 2.4g; Fat 0.8g, of which saturates 0.1g; Cholesterol 0mg; Calcium 10mg; Fibre 1g; Sodium 426mg.

Snapper and Tamarind Soup

Tamarind gives this light, fragrant noodle soup a slightly sour taste.

Serves 4

2 litres/3½ pints/8 cups water
1kg/2¼lb red snapper (or other red fish such as mullet)
1 onion, sliced
50g/2oz tamarind pods
15ml/1 tbsp fish sauce
15ml/1 tbsp sugar
30ml/2 tbsp vegetable oil
2 garlic cloves, finely chopped
2 lemon grass stalks, very finely chopped
4 ripe tomatoes, peeled and coarsely chopped
30ml/2 tbsp yellow bean paste
225g/8oz rice vermicelli, soaked in warm water until soft
115g/4oz/½ cup beansprouts
8–10 fresh basil or mint sprigs
25g/1oz/¼ cup roasted peanuts, ground
salt and ground black pepper

1 Bring the water to the boil in a pan. Lower the heat and add the fish and onion, with 2.5ml/½ tsp salt. Simmer gently until the fish is cooked through.

2 Remove the fish from the stock with a slotted spoon and set aside to cool slightly. Add the tamarind, fish sauce and sugar to the stock. Cook for 5 minutes, then strain the stock into a large bowl. Carefully remove all of the bones from the fish, keeping the flesh in big pieces.

3 Heat the oil in a large frying pan. Add the garlic and lemon grass and cook for a few seconds. Stir in the tomatoes and bean paste. Cook gently for 5–7 minutes, until the tomatoes are soft. Add the stock, bring back to a simmer and adjust the seasoning. Stir to mix.

4 Drain the vermicelli and divide among individual serving bowls. Add the beansprouts, fish and basil or mint, and sprinkle the ground peanuts on top. Top up each bowl with the hot soup.

Cook's Tip
Use about 15ml/1 tbsp prepared tamarind paste instead of the pods, if you prefer.

Hearty Fish Chowder

Hand around freshly made brown bread with this soup.

Serves 4–6

50g/2oz/¼ cup butter
1 large onion, chopped
115g/4oz bacon, rind removed, diced
4 celery sticks, diced
2 large potatoes, diced
450g/1lb ripe, juicy tomatoes, chopped
450ml/¾ pint/2 cups fish stock
450g/1lb white fish fillets, such as cod, flounder or haddock, skinned and cut into chunks
225g/8oz shellfish, such as prawns (shrimp), scallops or mussels
about 300ml/½ pint/1¼ cups milk
25g/1oz/¼ cup cornflour (cornstarch)
salt and ground black pepper
lightly whipped cream and chopped parsley, to garnish

1 Melt the butter in a large pan, add the onion, bacon, celery and potatoes and coat with the butter. Cover and sweat over a very gentle heat for 5–10 minutes, without colouring.

2 Meanwhile purée the tomatoes in a food processor or blender, and strain them to remove the skin and pips. Add with the fish stock to the pan. Bring to the boil, cover and leave to simmer gently until the potatoes are tender, skimming the top occasionally as required.

3 Prepare fresh prawns by plunging briefly in a pan of boiling water. Remove from the pan as the water boils. Cool and peel.

4 If using mussels, scrub the shells and discard any that do not open when tapped. Put the mussels into a shallow, heavy pan, without adding any liquid. Cover tightly and cook over a high heat for a few minutes, shaking occasionally, until all the mussels have opened. Discard any that fail to open. Remove the cooked mussels from their shells. Leave raw shelled scallops whole.

5 Add the shellfish to the soup. Blend the milk and cornflour together in a jug (pitcher), stir into the soup and bring to the boil. Reduce the heat, cover and simmer for a few minutes until the fish is tender. Add extra milk or stock if necessary and seasoning. Serve garnished with cream and some parsley.

Snapper Soup: Energy 495kcal/2079kJ; Protein 43.1g; Carbohydrate 55.5g, of which sugars 9.1g; Fat 11.4g, of which saturates 1.9g; Cholesterol 65mg; Calcium 108mg; Fibre 2.4g; Sodium 165mg.
Hearty Fish Chowder: Energy 488kcal/2050kJ; Protein 46g; Carbohydrate 36.2g, of which sugars 11.3g; Fat 18.7g, of which saturates 9.6g; Cholesterol 127mg; Calcium 163mg; Fibre 3.5g; Sodium 771mg.

Malayan Prawn Laksa

This spicy prawn and noodle soup tastes just as good when made with fresh crab meat or any flaked cooked fish.

Serves 3–4

115g/4oz rice vermicelli or stir-fry rice noodles
15ml/1 tbsp vegetable or groundnut oil
600ml/1 pint/2½ cups fish stock
400ml/14fl oz/1⅔ cups thin coconut milk
30ml/2 tbsp Thai fish sauce
½ lime
16–24 cooked peeled prawns (shrimp)
salt and cayenne pepper
60ml/4 tbsp fresh coriander (cilantro) sprigs and leaves, chopped, to garnish

For the spicy paste

2 lemon grass stalks, finely chopped
2 fresh red chillies, seeded and chopped
2.5cm/1in piece fresh root ginger, peeled and sliced
2.5ml/½ tsp shrimp paste
2 garlic cloves, chopped
2.5ml/½ tsp ground turmeric
30ml/2 tbsp tamarind paste

1 Cook the rice vermicelli or noodles in a large pan of boiling salted water according to the instructions on the packet. Drain into a large sieve (strainer) or colander, then rinse under cold water and drain. Set aside and keep warm.

2 To make the spicy paste, place all the ingredients in a mortar and pound with a pestle. Or, if you prefer, put the ingredients in a food processor or blender and process to a smooth paste.

3 Heat the oil in a large pan, add the spicy paste and fry, stirring constantly, for a few moments to release all the flavours, but be careful not to let it burn.

4 Add the fish stock and coconut milk and bring to the boil. Stir in the Thai fish sauce, then simmer for 5 minutes. Season with salt and cayenne to taste, adding a squeeze of lime. Add the prawns and heat through for a few seconds.

5 Divide the noodles among three or four soup plates. Pour the soup over, making sure that each bowl has an equal number of prawns. Garnish with coriander and serve piping hot.

Crab, Coconut and Coriander Soup

Quick and easy to cook, this soup has all the flavours associated with the Bahia region of Brazil: creamy coconut, palm oil, coriander and, of course, chilli.

Serves 4

30ml/2 tbsp olive oil
1 onion, finely chopped
1 celery stick, finely chopped
2 garlic cloves, crushed
1 fresh red chilli, seeded and chopped
1 large tomato, peeled and chopped
45ml/3 tbsp chopped fresh coriander (cilantro)
1 litre/1¾ pints/4 cups fresh crab or fish stock
500g/1¼lb crab meat
250ml/8fl oz/1 cup coconut milk
30ml/2 tbsp palm oil
juice of 1 lime
salt

For serving

hot chilli oil
lime wedges

1 Heat the olive oil in a pan over low heat. Stir in the onion and celery, and sauté gently for 5 minutes, until softened and translucent. Stir in the garlic and chilli and cook for a further 2 minutes.

2 Add the tomato and half the coriander and increase the heat. Cook, stirring, for 3 minutes, then add the stock. Bring to the boil, then reduce the heat and simmer for 5 minutes.

3 Stir the crab, coconut milk and palm oil into the pan and simmer over a very low heat for a further 5 minutes. The consistency should be thick, but not stew-like, so add some water if needed.

4 Stir in the lime juice and remaining coriander, then season with salt to taste. Serve in warmed bowls with the chilli oil and lime wedges on the side.

Variation
Try chunks of white fish fillet instead of crab for a change.

Prawn Laksa Energy 194kcal/814kJ; Protein 12.1g; Carbohydrate 28.1g, of which sugars 5.2g; Fat 3.8g, of which saturates 0.6g; Cholesterol 98mg; Calcium 108mg; Fibre 0.9g; Sodium 217mg.
Crab Soup: Energy 228kcal/951kJ; Protein 23.6g; Carbohydrate 5.4g, of which sugars 5g; Fat 12.6g, of which saturates 3.7g; Cholesterol 90mg; Calcium 199mg; Fibre 1.1g; Sodium 767mg.

Monkfish Broth

Lemon grass, chillies and galangal are among the flavourings used in this fragrant soup.

Serves 2–3

1 litre/1¾ pints/4 cups fish or light chicken stock
4 lemon grass stalks
3 limes
2 small fresh hot red chillies, seeded and thinly sliced
2cm/¾in piece fresh galangal, peeled and thinly sliced
6 coriander (cilantro) stalks, with leaves
2 kaffir lime leaves, coarsely chopped (optional)
350g/12oz monkfish fillet, skinned and cut into 2.5cm/1in pieces
15ml/1 tbsp rice vinegar
45ml/3 tbsp fish sauce
30ml/2 tbsp chopped coriander (cilantro) leaves, to garnish

1 Pour the stock into a pan and bring it to the boil. Meanwhile, slice the bulb end of each lemon grass stalk diagonally into pieces about 3mm/⅛in thick.

2 Peel off four wide strips of lime rind with a potato peeler, taking care to avoid the white pith underneath which would make the soup bitter. Squeeze the limes and reserve the juice.

3 Add the sliced lemon grass, lime rind, chillies, galangal and coriander stalks to the stock, with the kaffir lime leaves, if using. Simmer for 1–2 minutes.

4 Add the monkfish, rice vinegar and fish sauce to the pan, with half the reserved lime juice. Simmer for about 3 minutes, until the fish is just cooked.

5 Lift out and discard the coriander stalks, taste the broth and add more lime juice if necessary; the soup should taste quite sour. Sprinkle with the coriander leaves and serve.

Variation
Prawns (shrimp), scallops, squid, sole or flounder can be substituted for the monkfish. If you use kaffir lime leaves, you will need the juice of only two limes.

Saffron-flavoured Mussel Soup

This creamy soup, with the jet black shells and plump mussels, tastes as delicious and colourful as it looks. The flavours are subtle yet distinctive – just right for shellfish soup.

Serves 4

1.5kg/3–3½lb fresh mussels
600ml/1 pint/2½ cups white wine
few fresh parsley stalks
50g/2oz/¼ cup butter
2 leeks, finely chopped
2 celery sticks, finely chopped
1 carrot, chopped
2 garlic cloves, chopped
large pinch of saffron threads
600ml/1 pint/2½ cups double (heavy) cream
3 tomatoes, peeled, seeded and chopped
salt and ground black pepper
30ml/2 tbsp chopped fresh chives, to garnish

1 Scrub the mussels and pull away the beards. Put into a large pan with the wine and parsley stalks. Cover, bring to the boil and cook for 4–5 minutes, shaking the pan occasionally, until the mussels have opened. Discard the stalks and any mussels that refuse to open.

2 Drain the mussels over a large bowl, reserving the cooking liquid. When cool enough to handle, remove about half of the cooked mussels from their shells. Set aside with the remaining mussels in their shells.

3 Melt the butter in a large pan and add the leeks, celery, carrot and garlic, and cook for 5 minutes until softened. Strain the reserved mussel cooking liquid through a fine sieve (strainer) or muslin (cheesecloth). Add to the pan and cook over a high heat for 8–10 minutes to reduce slightly. Strain into a clean pan, add the saffron strands and cook for 1 minute.

4 Add the cream and bring back to the boil. Season well. Add all the mussels and the tomatoes and heat gently to warm through. Ladle the soup into four bowls, then sprinkle with the chopped chives and serve immediately.

Monkfish Broth Energy 92kcal/394kJ; Protein 19.8g; Carbohydrate 1.8g, of which sugars 1.6g; Fat 0.8g, of which saturates 0.1g; Cholesterol 16mg; Calcium 50mg; Fibre 0.8g; Sodium 1096mg.
Saffron Soup Energy 441kcal/1825kJ; Protein 9.6g; Carbohydrate 3.1g, of which sugars 3.1g; Fat 39.1g, of which saturates 23.9g; Cholesterol 116mg; Calcium 137mg; Fibre 0.6g; Sodium 156mg.

Fish Soup with Rouille

Although simple to make, the flavour is quite complex.

Serves 6

1kg/2¼lb mixed fish, skinned
30ml/2 tbsp olive oil
1 onion, chopped
1 carrot, chopped
1 leek, chopped
2 large ripe tomatoes, chopped
1 red (bell) pepper, seeded and chopped
2 garlic cloves, peeled
150g/5oz/⅔ cup tomato purée (paste)
1 large fresh bouquet garni, with 3 parsley sprigs, 3 small celery sticks and 3 bay leaves
300ml/½ pint/1¼ cups dry white wine
salt and ground black pepper

For the rouille

2 garlic cloves, coarsely chopped
5ml/1 tsp coarse salt
1 thick slice of white bread, crust removed, soaked in water and then squeezed dry
1 fresh red chilli, seeded and coarsely chopped
45ml/3 tbsp olive oil
salt
pinch of cayenne pepper (optional)

For the garnish

12 slices of baguette, toasted
50g/2oz/½ cup finely grated Gruyère cheese

1 Cut the fish into 7.5cm/3in chunks, removing any bones. Heat the oil in a large pan. Fry the chunks of fish, onion, carrot, leek, tomatoes, pepper and garlic over medium heat for 5 minutes. Add the tomato purée, bouquet garni and wine, then pour in cold water to cover the mixture. Season well and bring to the boil. Lower the heat, cover and simmer very gently for 1 hour.

2 Meanwhile, make the rouille. Crush the garlic and salt in a mortar and pestle. Add the bread and chilli and pound until smooth, or process in a food processor to a purée. Whisk in the oil, a drop at a time, to make a smooth, shiny sauce. Season with salt and add a pinch of cayenne, if you like. Set aside.

3 Lift out and discard the bouquet garni. Process the soup, in batches, in a food processor, then push through a sieve (strainer) into a clean pan. Reheat the soup but do not allow it to boil. Taste and adjust the seasoning, if necessary, and ladle into individual bowls. Top each with two slices of toasted baguette, a spoonful of rouille and some grated Gruyére.

Cappuccino of Puy Lentils, Lobster and Tarragon

Adding cold butter is key to whipping up a froth in this unusual soup.

Serves 6

450–675g/1–1½lb live lobster
150g/5oz/⅔ cup Puy lentils
1 carrot, 1 celery stick, and 1 small onion, halved
1 garlic clove
1 bay leaf
large bunch of tarragon, tied firmly
1 litre/1¾ pints/4 cups fish stock
120ml/4fl oz/½ cup double (heavy) cream
25g/1oz/2 tbsp butter, finely diced and chilled until ice cold
salt and ground black pepper
lobster claws (optional) and tarragon sprigs, to garnish

1 Bring a large stockpot of water to the boil. Lower the live lobster into the water and cover the pan. Cook for 15–20 minutes, then drain the lobster and leave to cool.

2 Put the Puy lentils in a large pan and pour in enough cold water to cover. Add the carrot, celery, onion, garlic and herbs. Bring the water to the boil and simmer for 20 minutes.

3 Drain the lentils and discard the herbs and vegetables. Process the lentils in a food processor until smooth. Set aside.

4 Break the claws off the lobster, crack them open and remove all the meat from inside. Reserve claws for garnish, if liked. Break off the tail, split it open and remove the meat. Cut all the meat into bitesize pieces.

5 Pour the fish stock into a large clean pan and bring to the boil. Lightly stir in the lentil purée and cream, but do not mix too much otherwise you will not be able to create the frothy effect. The mixture be quite watery in places. Season well.

6 Using a hand-held blender or electric beater, whisk the soup mixture, adding the butter, a piece at a time, until it is very frothy.

7 Divide the lobster meat among the bowls and pour in the soup. Garnish with tarragon and lobster claws, if liked. Serve.

Fish Soup Energy 554kcal/2334kJ; Protein 42.7g; Carbohydrate 56.8g, of which sugars 11.4g; Fat 15.2g, of which saturates 3.7g; Cholesterol 85mg; Calcium 210mg; Fibre 4.7g; Sodium 748mg.
Cappuccino of Puy Energy 232kcal/969kJ; Protein 12.4g; Carbohydrate 12.6g, of which sugars 0.7g; Fat 15.1g, of which saturates 9g; Cholesterol 66mg; Calcium 45mg; Fibre 2.2g; Sodium 123mg.

Chicken, Leek and Barley Soup

This recipe is based on the traditional Scottish soup, cock-a-leekie.

Serves 6

115g/4oz/⅔ cup pearl barley
1 chicken, weighing about 2kg/4¼lb
900g/2lb leeks
1 bouquet garni
1 large carrot, thickly sliced
2.4 litres/4 pints/10 cups chicken or beef stock
400g/14oz ready-to-eat prunes
salt and ground black pepper
chopped fresh parsley, to garnish

1 Rinse the pearl barley in a sieve (strainer) under cold water, then cook it in a large pan of boiling water for 10 minutes. Drain, rinse well and drain thoroughly. Set aside in a cool place.

2 Cut the breast portions from the chicken and set aside, then place the remaining carcass in the pan. Cut half the leeks into 5cm/2in lengths and add them to the pan with the bouquet garni, carrot and stock.

3 Bring the stock to the boil, then reduce the heat and cover the pan. Simmer gently for 1 hour, skimming occasionally. Add the chicken breasts and cook for another 30 minutes until they are just cooked. Leave until cool enough to handle.

4 Strain, and skim the fat from, the stock. Reserve the chicken breasts and the meat from the carcass. Discard the skin, bones, cooked vegetables and herbs. Return the stock to the pan.

5 Add the barley. Bring to the boil, then lower the heat and cook very gently for 15–20 minutes, until the barley is just tender. Season the soup to taste and add the prunes. Thinly slice the remaining leeks and add them to the pan. Bring to the boil, cover and simmer gently for 10 minutes, or until the leeks are cooked.

6 Slice the chicken breast portions and then add them to the soup with the remaining chicken meat from the carcass, sliced or cut into neat pieces. Reheat the soup, if necessary, then ladle it into warm, deep soup plates and sprinkle with plenty of chopped parsley to garnish.

Chicken and Ginger Soup

This aromatic soup is rich with coconut milk and intensely flavoured with galangal, lemon grass and kaffir lime leaves.

Serves 4–6

4 lemon grass stalks, roots trimmed
2 x 400ml/14fl oz cans coconut milk
475ml/16fl oz/2 cups chicken stock
2.5cm/1in piece root ginger, peeled and thinly sliced
10 black peppercorns, crushed
10 kaffir lime leaves, torn
300g/11oz skinless chicken breast fillets, cut into thin strips
115g/4oz/1 cup button (white) mushrooms
50g/2oz/½ cup baby corn cobs, quartered lengthways
60ml/4 tbsp lime juice
45ml/3 tbsp fish sauce
chopped fresh red chillies, spring onions (scallions) and fresh coriander (cilantro) leaves, to garnish

1 Cut off the lower 5cm/2in from each lemon grass stalk and chop it finely. Bruise the remaining pieces of the stalk with a rolling pin.

2 Bring the coconut milk and chicken stock to the boil in a large pan. Add all the lemon grass, the ginger, peppercorns and half the lime leaves, lower the heat and simmer gently for 10 minutes. Strain into a clean pan.

3 Return the soup to the heat, then add the chicken strips, mushrooms and corn. Simmer for 5–7 minutes or until the chicken is cooked through.

4 Stir the lime juice and fish sauce into the soup, then add the remaining lime leaves. Serve hot, garnished with chillies, spring onions and coriander.

Cook's Tip
Pieces of fresh root ginger can be stored in the freezer. They thaw out quickly when needed, or can even be shaved or grated while still frozen.

Chicken and Barley Soup Energy 326kcal/1383kJ; Protein 33.7g; Carbohydrate 44.4g, of which sugars 27.2g; Fat 2.7g, of which saturates 0.5g; Cholesterol 82mg; Calcium 73mg; Fibre 7.5g; Sodium 85mg.
Chicken and Ginger Soup Energy 87kcal/371kJ; Protein 13.1g; Carbohydrate 6.8g, of which sugars 6.7g; Fat 1.1g, of which saturates 0.4g; Cholesterol 35mg; Calcium 42mg; Fibre 0.3g; Sodium 620mg.

Chunky Chicken Minestrone

This is a special minestrone made with fresh chicken. Served with crusty Italian bread, it makes a hearty meal in itself.

Serves 4–6

15ml/1 tbsp olive oil
2 chicken thighs
3 rindless streaky (fatty) bacon rashers (strips), chopped
1 onion, finely chopped
a few fresh basil leaves, shredded
a few fresh rosemary leaves, finely chopped
15ml/1 tbsp chopped fresh flat leaf parsley
2 potatoes, cut into 1cm/½in cubes
1 large carrot, cut into 1cm/½in cubes
2 small courgettes (zucchini), cut into 1cm/½in cubes
1–2 celery sticks, cut into 1cm/½in cubes
1 litre/1¾ pints/4 cups chicken stock
200g/7oz/1¾ cups frozen peas
90g/3½oz/scant 1 cup stellette or other small soup pasta
salt and ground black pepper
Parmesan cheese shavings, to serve

1 Heat the oil in a large frying pan, add the chicken thighs and fry for about 5 minutes on each side. Remove with a slotted spoon and set aside.

2 Add the bacon, onion and herbs to the pan and cook gently, stirring constantly, for about 5 minutes. Add the potatoes, carrot, courgettes and celery and cook for 5–7 minutes more.

3 Return the chicken thighs to the pan, add the stock and bring to the boil. Reduce the heat. Cover and cook over a low heat for 35–40 minutes, stirring the soup occasionally, until the chicken pieces are cooked. Remove the chicken thighs with a slotted spoon and place them on a board.

4 Stir the peas and pasta into the soup and bring it back to the boil. Reduce the heat and simmer, stirring frequently, for 7–8 minutes until the pasta is cooked.

5 Cut the meat off the chicken, discarding the bones and skin. Dice the meat and add it to the soup. Taste for seasoning and serve sprinkled with Parmesan cheese shavings.

Duck Consommé

This soup is a good example of the influence the Vietnamese community in France has had on modern French cooking.

Serves 4

1 duck carcass (raw or cooked), plus 2 legs or any giblets, trimmed of fat
1 large onion, unpeeled, root off
2 carrots, cut into chunks
1 parsnip, cut into chunks
1 leek, cut into chunks
2–4 garlic cloves, crushed
2.5cm/1in piece fresh root ginger, peeled and sliced
15ml/1 tbsp black peppercorns
4–6 sprigs of fresh thyme
small bunch of coriander (cilantro), leaves and stems separated

For the garnish
1 small carrot
1 small leek, halved lengthways
4–6 shiitake mushrooms, sliced
soy sauce
2 spring onions, sliced
watercress or finely shredded Chinese leaves (Chinese cabbage)
ground black pepper

1 Put the duck carcass and legs or giblets, onion, carrots, parsnip, leek and garlic in a large, heavy pan or flameproof casserole. Add the ginger, peppercorns, thyme and coriander stems, cover with cold water and bring to the boil, skimming off any foam that rises to the surface.

2 Reduce the heat and simmer gently for 1½–2 hours, then strain through a sieve (strainer) lined with muslin (cheesecloth) into a bowl, discarding the bones and vegetables. Cool the stock and chill for several hours or overnight. Skim off congealed fat and blot with kitchen paper.

3 For the garnish, cut the carrot and leek into 5cm/2in pieces and slice into thin strips. Place in a pan with the mushrooms.

4 Pour in the stock and add a few dashes of soy sauce and some pepper. Bring to the boil, skimming any foam that rises to the surface. Taste and adjust the seasoning. Stir in the spring onions and watercress or Chinese leaves. Ladle the consommé into warmed bowls and sprinkle with the coriander leaves before serving.

Chunky Minestrone Energy 198kcal/833kJ; Protein 15.6g; Carbohydrate 23.3g, of which sugars 3.9g; Fat 5.4g, of which saturates 1.4g; Cholesterol 30mg; Calcium 31mg; Fibre 3.2g; Sodium 224mg.
Duck Consommé Energy 12kcal/51kJ; Protein 1.4g; Carbohydrate 1.9g, of which sugars 1.6g; Fat 0.6g, of which saturates 0.2g; Cholesterol 0mg; Calcium 13mg; Fibre 1g; Sodium 550mg.

Lamb and Cucumber Soup

This is a very simple soup to prepare, but it tastes delicious nevertheless.

Serves 4

225g/8oz lamb steak
15ml/1 tbsp light soy sauce
10ml/2 tsp Chinese rice wine or dry sherry
2.5ml/½ tsp sesame oil
7.5cm/3in piece cucumber
750ml/1¼ pints/3 cups chicken or vegetable stock
15ml/1 tbsp rice vinegar
salt and ground white pepper

1 Trim off any excess fat from the lamb. Thinly slice the lamb into small pieces and place in a bowl. Add the soy sauce, wine or sherry and sesame oil. Mix well, then cover and set aside to marinate for 25–30 minutes. Discard the marinade.

2 Halve the cucumber lengthways (do not peel), then cut it into thin slices diagonally.

3 In a wok or pan, bring the stock to a rolling boil, add the lamb and stir to separate.

4 Bring the soup back to the boil, then add the cucumber slices, vinegar and seasoning. Bring back to the boil, remove from the heat and serve immediately.

Variations

- *Use fine cut, lean boneless pork instead of lamb. Add a little chopped fresh root ginger to spice up the soup.*
- *For a sweet-sour soup, stir in honey to taste – it is delicious with the lamb or with pork.*
- *For a punchy flavour, thinly slice a milld to medium fresh green chilli and add it to the soup with a good handful of chopped fresh mint. Sprinkle in a little sugar for a sweet-sour, piquant minted soup.*
- *For additional crunch, cut some celery and spring onions (scallions) into fine shreds and soak them in iced water until they curl. Drain, dry and use as a garnish.*

Split Pea and Ham Soup

This soup is another fabulous variation on the popular pea and ham favourite. The main ingredient for this dish is bacon hock, which is the narrow piece of bone cut from a leg of ham. You could use a piece of pork belly instead, if you prefer, and remove it with the herbs before serving.

Serves 4

450g/1lb/2½ cups green split peas
4 rindless bacon rashers (strips)
1 onion, roughly chopped
2 carrots, sliced
1 celery stick, sliced
1 sprig of fresh thyme
2 bay leaves
1 large potato, roughly diced
1 bacon hock
ground black pepper

1 Put the split peas into a bowl, cover with plenty of cold water and leave to soak overnight.

2 Cut the bacon into small pieces. In a large pan, dry fry the bacon for 4–5 minutes or until crisp. Remove from the pan with a slotted spoon.

3 Add the chopped onion, carrots and celery to the fat in the pan and cook for 3–4 minutes or until the onion is softened but not browned.

4 Return the fried bacon to the pan and stir, then pour in 2.4 litres/4¼ pints/10½ cups water.

5 Drain the split peas and add to the pan with the thyme, bay leaves, potato and bacon hock. Bring to the boil, reduce the heat, cover and cook gently for 1 hour.

6 Remove the thyme, bay leaves and hock. Process the soup in a blender or food processor until smooth. Then pour it back into a clean pan.

7 Cut the meat from the hock, discarding the fat and skin. Dice the meat and add it to the soup. Heat gently, stirring to prevent the soup from sticking to the pan. Season with plenty of pepper. Ladle into warm soup bowls and serve.

Lamb and Cucumber Soup Energy 105kcal/438kJ; Protein 11.2g; Carbohydrate 0.4g, of which sugars 0.3g; Fat 6.6g, of which saturates 3g; Cholesterol 43mg; Calcium 6mg; Fibre 0g; Sodium 316mg.
Split Pea Soup Energy 466kcal/1974kJ; Protein 32.2g; Carbohydrate 75.6g, of which sugars 6.2g; Fat 5.9g, of which saturates 1.9g; Cholesterol 13mg; Calcium 75mg; Fibre 7g; Sodium 443mg.

Wonton Soup

In China, wonton soup is served as a snack, or dim sum, rather than as a soup course during a large meal. However, in the Western tradition, this soup makes an ideal first course as part of a Chinese-inspired feast.

Serves 4

175g/6oz pork, not too lean, roughly chopped
50g/2oz peeled prawns (shrimp), finely chopped
5ml/1 tsp soft light brown sugar
15ml/1 tbsp Chinese rice wine or dry sherry
15ml/1 tbsp light soy sauce
5ml/1 tsp finely chopped spring onions (scallions)
5ml/1 tsp finely chopped fresh root ginger
24 ready-made wonton skins
about 750ml/1 ¼ pints/3 cups stock
15ml/1 tbsp light soy sauce
finely chopped spring onions (scallions), to garnish

1 In a bowl, thoroughly mix the chopped pork and prawns with the sugar, rice wine or sherry, soy sauce, spring onions and ginger. Set the mixture aside for 25–30 minutes to allow all the flavours to mingle.

2 Lay the wonton skins out on a flat surface. Place 5ml/1 tsp of the pork mixture in the centre of each wonton skin.

3 Wet the edges of each filled wonton skin with a little water and press them together with your fingers to seal. Fold each wonton parcel over.

4 To cook, bring the stock to a rolling boil in a wok, add the wontons and cook for 4–5 minutes. Season with the soy sauce and add the spring onions.

5 Place an equal number of cooked wontons in individual soup bowls, pour over the soup and serve immediately.

Cook's Tip
Ready-made wonton skins are available in packs from large supermarkets and Asian food stores.

Tomato and Beef Soup

Another wholesome and much-loved classic, the tomatoes and spring onions give this light beef broth a superb flavour. It is quick and easy to make, and ideal as an appetizer or light lunch.

Serves 4

75g/3oz rump (round) steak
900ml/1 ½ pints/3¾ cups beef stock
30ml/2 tbsp tomato purée (paste)
6 tomatoes, halved, seeded and chopped
10ml/2 tsp caster (superfine) sugar
15ml/1 tbsp cornflour (cornstarch)
1 egg white
2.5ml/½ tsp sesame oil
salt and ground black pepper
2 spring onions (scallions), finely shredded

1 Cut the beef into thin strips and place in a pan. Pour over boiling water to cover. Cook for 2 minutes, then drain thoroughly and set aside.

2 Bring the stock to the boil in a clean pan. Stir in the tomato purée, then the tomatoes and sugar.

3 Add the beef strips, allow the stock to boil again, then lower the heat and simmer for 2 minutes.

4 Mix the cornflour to a paste with 15ml/1 tbsp water in a small bowl. Add the mixture to the soup, stirring constantly. Bring to the boil, stirring, and cook for a few minutes, until the soup thickens slightly.

5 Lightly beat the egg white in a cup and then stir it into the soup. When the egg white changes colour, season the soup with salt and pepper to taste. Ladle the soup into individual bowls. Drizzle with the sesame oil, sprinkle with spring onions and serve immediately.

Variation
It's tempting to use canned rather than fresh tomatoes to cut down on preparation time, but the flavour will not be the same.

Wonton Soup Energy 134kcal/568kJ; Protein 13.6g; Carbohydrate 16.3g, of which sugars 1.9g; Fat 2.1g, of which saturates 0.7g; Cholesterol 52mg; Calcium 42mg; Fibre 0.6g; Sodium 589mg.
Tomato and Beef Soup Energy 79kcal/337kJ; Protein 6.2g; Carbohydrate 11.1g, of which sugars 7.6g; Fat 1.5g, of which saturates 0.5g; Cholesterol 11mg; Calcium 16mg; Fibre 1.5g; Sodium 58mg.

Panzanella Salad

If sliced, juicy tomatoes layered with day-old bread sounds strange for a salad, don't be deceived – it's quite delicious. A popular Italian salad, this dish is ideal for serving as an appetizer.

Serves 4–6

4 thick slices day-old bread, either white, brown or rye
1 small red onion, thinly sliced
450g/1lb ripe tomatoes, thinly sliced
115g/4oz mozzarella cheese, thinly sliced
5ml/1 tbsp fresh basil, shredded, or fresh marjoram
120ml/4fl oz/½ cup extra virgin olive oil
45ml/3 tbsp balsamic vinegar
juice of 1 small lemon
salt and ground black pepper
pitted and sliced black olives or salted capers, to garnish

1 Dip the slices of bread briefly in cold water, then carefully squeeze out the excess water.

2 Arrange the bread slices in the base of a shallow salad bowl or other shallow dish.

3 Soak the onion slices in cold water for about 10 minutes while you prepare the other ingredients. Drain thoroughly and set aside.

4 Layer the tomatoes, cheese, onion, basil or marjoram on top of the bread. Season with salt and ground black pepper in between each layer. Sprinkle over the olive oil, vinegar and lemon juice.

5 Top with the olives or capers, cover with clear film (plastic wrap) and chill in the refrigerator for at least 2 hours or overnight, if possible.

Cook's Tip
Balsamic vinegar can be expensive but has an exquisite flavour, achieved through being aged in wooden barrels like a wine.

Green Bean and Sweet Red Pepper Salad

Serrano chillies are very fiery, so they give this salad a wickedly spicy kick. Use a milder variety of chilli, if you prefer a little less heat.

Serves 4

350g/12oz green beans
2 red (bell) peppers, seeded and chopped
2 spring onions (scallions), chopped
1 or more drained pickled serrano chillies, rinsed, seeded and chopped
1 iceberg lettuce, coarsely shredded
olives, to garnish

For the dressing
45ml/3 tbsp red wine vinegar
135ml/9 tbsp olive oil
salt and ground black pepper

1 Cook the green beans in a pan of boiling water for about 4–6 minutes until just tender. Drain the beans, rinse under cold running water and drain again. Cut into quarters and set aside to cool.

2 Combine the cooked green beans, chopped red peppers, chopped spring onions and serrano chillies in a salad bowl.

3 Make the salad dressing. Pour the red wine vinegar into a bowl or jug (pitcher). Add salt and ground black pepper to taste, then gradually whisk in the olive oil until well combined.

4 Pour the salad dressing over the prepared vegetables and toss lightly together to mix and coat thoroughly.

5 Line a large serving platter with the shredded iceberg lettuce leaves and arrange the salad vegetables attractively on top. Garnish with the olives and serve immediately.

Cook's Tip
Wash your hands thoroughly after chopping the chillies and make sure you don't touch your eyes.

Panzanella Salad Energy 237kcal/987kJ; Protein 6.3g; Carbohydrate 15.4g, of which sugars 3.5g; Fat 17.1g, of which saturates 4.5g; Cholesterol 11mg; Calcium 105mg; Fibre 1.3g; Sodium 213mg.
Green Bean Energy 280kcal/1153kJ; Protein 3.1g; Carbohydrate 9.4g, of which sugars 8.4g; Fat 25.8g, of which saturates 3.8g; Cholesterol 0mg; Calcium 55mg; Fibre 3.9g; Sodium 5mg.

Green Salad with Raspberry Dressing

Adding a splash of raspberry vinegar to the dressing enlivens a simple green salad, turning it into a sophisticated side dish or appetizer.

Serves 4
45ml/3 tbsp olive oil
2 garlic cloves, finely sliced
4 handfuls of green salad leaves
15ml/1 tbsp raspberry vinegar
salt and ground black pepper

1 Heat the oil in a small pan and add the garlic. Fry gently for 1–2 minutes, or until just golden: do not burn the garlic. Remove the garlic with a slotted spoon and drain on kitchen paper. Pour the oil into a small bowl.

2 Arrange the salad leaves in a serving bowl. Whisk the vinegar into the reserved oil and season with salt and pepper. Pour the dressing over the salad, toss and sprinkle with the fried garlic.

Spinach and Roast Garlic Salad

Don't worry about the amount of garlic in this salad. During roasting, the garlic cloves become deliciously sweet and subtle and lose much of their pungent taste.

Serves 4
12 garlic cloves, unpeeled
60ml/4 tbsp extra virgin olive oil
450g/1lb baby spinach leaves
50g/2oz/½ cup pine nuts, toasted
juice of ½ lemon
salt and ground black pepper

1 Preheat the oven to 190°C/375°F/Gas 5. Place the garlic in a small roasting pan, add 30ml/2 tbsp of the olive oil, tossing well to coat all over, and roast in the oven for about 15 minutes, until the garlic cloves are softened and slightly charred around the edges.

2 While still warm, tip the garlic into a salad bowl. Add the spinach, pine nuts, lemon juice, remaining olive oil and a little salt. Toss well and add black pepper to taste. Serve immediately, inviting guests to squeeze the softened garlic purée out of the skin to eat.

Mixed Leaf and Herb Salad with Toasted Seeds

This simple salad is the perfect antidote to a rich, heavy meal as it contains fresh herbs that can aid the digestion.

Serves 4
115g/4oz/4 cups salad leaves
50g/2oz/2 cups mixed salad herbs, such as coriander (cilantro), parsley, basil and rocket
25g/1oz/2 tbsp pumpkin seeds
25g/1oz/2 tbsp sunflower seeds

For the dressing
60ml/4 tbsp extra virgin olive oil
15ml/1 tbsp balsamic vinegar
2.5ml/½ tsp Dijon mustard
salt and ground black pepper

1 Start by making the dressing. Combine the olive oil, balsamic vinegar and mustard in a screw-top jar. Add salt and ground black pepper to taste. Close the jar tightly, then shake the dressing vigorously.

2 Place the salad and herb leaves in a large salad bowl and toss lightly together.

3 Toast the pumpkin and sunflower seeds in a dry frying pan over medium heat for 2 minutes, until golden, tossing frequently to prevent them from burning otherwise they will taste bitter and ruin the salad. Allow the seeds to cool slightly before sprinkling over the salad.

4 Pour the dressing over the salad in the bowl and toss until all the leaves are thoroughly coated. Serve immediately.

Variations
- *Balsamic vinegar adds a rich, sweet taste to the dressing, but red or white wine vinegar could be used instead.*
- *A few nasturtium flowers would look very pretty in this salad, as would borage flowers.*

Green Salad Energy 78kcal/320kJ; Protein 0.2g; Carbohydrate 0.4g, of which sugars 0.4g; Fat 8.4g, of which saturates 1.2g; Cholesterol 0mg; Calcium 7mg; Fibre 0.2g; Sodium 1mg.
Spinach Salad Energy 209kcal/866kJ; Protein 7.2g; Carbohydrate 9.2g, of which sugars 6.7g; Fat 16.2g, of which saturates 5.5g; Cholesterol 18mg; Calcium 218mg; Fibre 3.9g; Sodium 170mg.
Mixed Leaf Salad Energy 178kcal/737kJ; Protein 2.9g; Carbohydrate 3.1g, or which sugars, 1g; Fat: 17.2g, or which saturates 2.2g; Cholesterol 0mg; Caclium 26mg; Fibre 1.1g; Sodium 20mg.

Spinach with Raisins and Pine Nuts

Raisins and pine nuts are frequent partners in recipes, especially ones that originate in the Iberian peninsula. Here, tossed with wilted spinach and croûtons, they make a delicious appetizer or a main meal accompaniment.

Serves 4
50g/2oz/⅓ cup raisins
1 thick slice crusty white bread
45ml/3 tbsp olive oil
25g/1oz/⅓ cup pine nuts
500g/1¼lb young spinach, stalks removed
2 garlic cloves, crushed
salt and ground black pepper

1 Put the raisins in a small bowl with boiling water and leave to soak for 10 minutes.

2 Meanwhile, cut the crusts from the slice of bread and discard them. Cut the bread into neat cubes. Heat 30ml/2 tbsp of the oil in a large frying pan and fry the bread until golden. Drain on kitchen paper and set aside.

3 Heat the remaining oil in the frying pan. Fry the pine nuts, stirring constantly, until just beginning to colour. Add the spinach and garlic to the pan and cook quickly, turning the spinach until it has just wilted.

4 Toss in the raisins and season lightly with salt and pepper. Transfer to a warmed serving dish. Sprinkle the spinach mixture with croûtons and serve hot.

Cook's Tip
Make sure that the oil in the frying pan is hot when adding the bread cubes, so that they are quickly sealed on all sides, otherwise they will absorb oil rather than cooking in it.

Variation
Use the leaves of Swiss chard or spinach beet instead of the spinach, cooking them for a little longer if necessary.

Sweet-and-sour Artichoke Salad

A sweet-and-sour sauce, poured over lightly cooked summer vegetables, works perfectly in this delicious salad. Serve as an appetizer or as a side dish.

Serves 4
6 small globe artichokes
juice of 1 lemon
30ml/2 tbsp olive oil
2 medium onions, roughly chopped
175g/6oz/1½ cups fresh or frozen broad (fava) beans (shelled weight)
175g/6oz/1½ cups fresh or frozen peas (shelled weight)
salt and ground black pepper
fresh mint leaves, to garnish

For the sweet-and-sour sauce
120ml/4fl oz/½ cup white wine vinegar
15ml/1 tbsp caster (superfine) sugar
a handful of fresh mint leaves, roughly torn

1 Peel the outer leaves from the artichokes and discard. Cut the artichokes into quarters and place them in a bowl of water with the lemon juice.

2 Heat the olive oil in a large pan and add the onions. Cook, stirring occasionally, until the onions are golden.

3 Add the beans and stir, then drain the artichokes and add to the pan. Pour in about 300ml/½ pint/1¼ cups water and cook, covered, for a further 10–15 minutes.

4 Add the peas to the pan, season with salt and ground black pepper and cook for a further 5 minutes, stirring from time to time, until the vegetables are tender. Pour through a sieve (strainer) or colander and place all the vegetables in a bowl. Leave to cool, then cover and chill.

5 To make the sweet-and-sour sauce, mix all the ingredients in a small pan. Heat gently for 2–3 minutes, until the sugar has dissolved. Simmer gently for 5 minutes, stirring occasionally. Leave to cool. To serve, drizzle the sauce over the vegetables and garnish with mint leaves.

Spinach Salad Energy 198kcal/824kJ; Protein 5.2g; Carbohydrate 14.3g, of which sugars 11g; Fat 13.7g, of which saturates 1.6g; Cholesterol 0mg; Calcium 226mg; Fibre 3.1g; Sodium 218mg.
Sweet-and-Sour Salad Energy 172kcal/717kJ; Protein 8g; Carbohydrate 21g, of which sugars 10.8g; Fat 6.8g, of which saturates 1g; Cholesterol 0mg; Calcium 106mg; Fibre 7.3g; Sodium 82mg.

Mixed Seaweed Salad

Seaweed is a nutritious, alkaline food which is rich in fibre. Its unusual flavours are a great complement to fish and tofu dishes. This salad is extremely low in fat.

Serves 4

5g/⅛oz each dried wakame, dried arame and dried hijiki seaweeds
about 130g/4½oz fresh enokitake mushrooms
15ml/1 tbsp rice vinegar
6.5ml/1¼ tsp salt
2 spring onions (scallions)
a few ice cubes
½ cucumber, cut lengthways
250g/9oz mixed salad leaves

For the dressing

60ml/4 tbsp rice vinegar
7.5ml/1½ tsp toasted sesame oil
15ml/1 tbsp shoyu
15ml/1 tbsp water with a pinch of instant dashi powder
2.5cm/1in piece fresh root ginger, finely grated

1 Soak the dried wakame seaweed for 10 minutes in one bowl of water and, in a separate bowl of water, soak the dried arame and hijiki seaweeds together for 30 minutes.

2 Trim the hard end of the enokitake mushroom stalks, then cut the bunch in half and separate the stems.

3 Cook the wakame and enokitake in boiling water for 2 minutes, then add the arame and hijiki for a few seconds. Immediately remove from the heat.

4 Drain in a sieve (strainer) and sprinkle over the vinegar and salt while still warm. Chill until needed.

5 Slice the spring onions into long, thin, strips, then soak in a bowl of cold water with a few ice cubes added to make them curl up. Drain. Slice the cucumber into thin, half-moon shapes.

6 Mix the dressing ingredients in a bowl. Arrange the mixed salad leaves in a large bowl with the cucumber on top, then add the seaweed and enokitake mixture. Decorate the salad with spring onion curls and serve with the dressing.

Beansprout and Mooli Salad

Ribbon-thin slices of fresh, crisp vegetables mixed with beansprouts make the perfect foil for an unusual Asian-style dressing.

Serves 4

225g/8oz/1 cup beansprouts
1 cucumber
2 carrots
1 small mooli (daikon)
1 small red onion, thinly sliced
2.5cm/1in fresh root ginger, peeled and cut into thin matchsticks
1 small red chilli, seeded and thinly sliced
handful of fresh coriander (cilantro) or mint leaves

For the dressing

15ml/1 tbsp rice wine vinegar
15ml/1 tbsp light soy sauce
15ml/1 tbsp Thai fish sauce
1 garlic clove, finely chopped
15ml/1 tbsp sesame oil
45ml/3 tbsp groundnut (peanut) oil
30ml/2 tbsp sesame seeds, lightly toasted

1 To make the dressing, place all the dressing ingredients in a screw-top jar and shake well.

2 Wash the beansprouts under cold running water and drain thoroughly in a colander.

3 Peel the cucumber, cut in half lengthwise and scoop out the seeds. Peel the cucumber flesh into long ribbon strips using a potato peeler.

4 Peel the carrots and radish into long strips in the same way as the cucumber.

5 Put the beansprouts in a shallow serving dish and add the carrots, radish and cucumber strips. Add the red onion, ginger, chilli and coriander or mint leaves and toss to mix. Pour the dressing over the salad just before serving.

Cook's Tip
The dressing can be made in advance. It will keep well for a couple of days if stored in the refrigerator or a cool place.

Mixed Seaweed Salad Energy 26kcal/107kJ; Protein 1.5g; Carbohydrate 2.1g, of which sugars 2g; Fat 1.3g, of which saturates 0.2g; Cholesterol 0mg; Calcium 28mg; Fibre 1.2g; Sodium 272mg.
Beansprout Salad Energy 176kcal/728kJ; Protein 3.8g; Carbohydrate 6.7g, of which sugars 5.2g; Fat 15.1g, of which saturates 1.6g; Cholesterol 0mg; Calcium 82mg; Fibre 2.6g; Sodium 371mg.

Pumpkin Salad

Red wine vinegar brings out the sweetness of the pumpkin. No salad leaves are used, just plenty of fresh parsley. A great dish for a cold appetizer.

Serves 4

1 large red onion, peeled and very thinly sliced
200ml/7fl oz/scant 1 cup olive oil
60ml/4 tbsp red wine vinegar
675g/1 ½lb pumpkin, peeled and cut into 4cm/1 ½in pieces
40g/1 ½oz/¾ cup fresh flat leaf parsley leaves, chopped
salt and ground black pepper
fresh flat leaf parsley sprigs, to garnish (optional)

1 Mix the sliced red onion, olive oil and vinegar in a large salad bowl. Season with salt and ground black pepper, then stir well to combine.

2 Put the pumpkin pieces in a large pan of cold salted water. Bring to the boil, then lower the heat and simmer gently for 15–20 minutes. Drain.

3 Immediately add the drained pumpkin to the bowl containing the dressing and toss lightly with your hands. Leave to cool.

4 Stir the chopped parsley into the pumpkin mixture, cover the bowl tightly with clear film (plastic wrap) and chill in the refrigerator until needed.

5 Allow the salad to come back to room temperature before serving. Garnish with fresh parsley sprigs, if you like.

Cook's Tip
Fresh parsley is simple to grow yourself at home. Buy an established plant and keep it on a sunny windowsill in your kitchen. Ensure it is kept moist but don't over-water it – it will handle periods of little water better than too much water. Pull off the leaves as and when you need them. They will regrow in a matter of days.

Asparagus and Orange Salad

This is a slightly unusual combination of ingredients with a simple dressing based on good-quality olive oil.

Serves 4

225g/8oz asparagus, trimmed and cut into 5cm/2in lengths
2 large oranges
2 well-flavoured tomatoes, cut into eighths
50g/2oz cos lettuce leaves
30ml/2 tbsp extra virgin olive oil
2.5ml/½ tsp sherry vinegar
salt and ground black pepper

1 Cook the asparagus in boiling, salted water for 3–4 minutes, until just tender. The cooking time may vary according to the size of the asparagus stems. Drain and refresh under cold water, then leave on one side to cool.

2 Grate (shred) the rind from half one orange and reserve.

3 Cut a slice off the top and bottom of one orange to reveal the flesh. Place the orange upright on a board and, using a small sharp knife, cut off the skin, taking care to remove all the bitter white pith. Repeat with the second orange, reserving any juice.

4 Holding one orange over a bowl to catch the juices, cut between the membrane to release the segments. Repeat with the second orange. Reserve the juices.

5 Put the asparagus, orange segments, tomatoes and lettuce in a salad bowl.

6 Mix together the oil and vinegar, and add 15ml/1 tbsp of the reserved orange juice and 5ml/1 tsp of the grated rind. Season with salt and pepper to taste. Just before serving, pour the dressing over the salad and mix gently to coat the ingredients.

Cook's Tip
Take care not to overcook the asparagus; it should still be quite firm when bitten into. Overcooked spears will lose flavour and many of the healthy nutrients.

Pumpkin Salad Energy 404kcal/1663kJ; Protein 1.7g; Carbohydrate 5.2g, of which sugars 4g; Fat 42g, of which saturates 6.1g; Cholesterol 0mg; Calcium 73mg; Fibre 2.4g; Sodium 4mg.
Asparagus and Orange Salad Energy 92kcal/384kJ; Protein 2.6g; Carbohydrate 7.2g, of which sugars 7.1g; Fat 6.1g, of which saturates 0.9g; Cholesterol 0mg; Calcium 46mg; Fibre 2.4g; Sodium 8mg.

Black and Orange Salad

This dramatically colourful salad is ideal to serve in a selection of appetizers.

Serves 4
3 oranges
115g/4oz/1 cup pitted black olives
15ml/1 tbsp chopped fresh coriander (cilantro)
15ml/1 tbsp chopped fresh parsley

For the dressing
30ml/2 tbsp olive oil
15ml/1 tbsp lemon juice
2.5ml/½ tsp paprika
2.5ml/½ tsp ground cumin

1 Cut a slice off the top and bottom of one orange to reveal the flesh. Place the orange upright on a board and, using a small sharp knife, cut off the skin, taking care to remove all the bitter white pith. Repeat with the remaining oranges, then cut between the membranes to release the segments.

2 Place the orange segments in a salad bowl and add the black olives, coriander and parsley.

3 To make the dressing, blend together the olive oil, lemon juice, paprika and cumin.

4 Pour the dressing over the salad and toss gently until the ingredients are well coated. Chill in the refrigerator for about 30 minutes and serve immediately.

Variation
The strong flavours and vivid colours of this salad work brilliantly with couscous. Adapt the recipe by chopping the orange segments and olives quite finely (using a mandoline makes this a quick and easy job). Mix the finely chopped olives and oranges with the herbs and dressing into a bowl of cooked couscous while it is still warm. Either chill the salad or serve it immediately. It's delicious cold or warm – and it is perfect as part of a mezze.

Carrot and Orange Salad

This classic fruit and vegetable combination makes a wonderful, fresh-tasting salad. It makes a great first-course dish for the winter months, and it is also particularly good with hot or cold poultry dishes.

Serves 4
450g/1lb carrots
2 large oranges
15ml/1 tbsp olive oil
30ml/2 tbsp lemon juice
pinch of sugar (optional)
30ml/2 tbsp chopped pistachio nuts or toasted pine nuts
salt and ground black pepper

1 Peel the carrots, if necessary, and grate them into a large serving bowl.

2 Cut a slice off the top and bottom of one orange. Place the orange upright on a chopping board and cut off the skin, taking care to remove all the bitter white pith. Repeat with the second orange, reserving any juice.

3 Working over a bowl to catch the juices, cut between the membranes to release the orange segments.

4 Whisk together the olive oil, lemon juice and reserved orange juice in a bowl. Season with a little salt and pepper to taste, and add sugar, if you like.

5 Toss the orange segments together with the carrots and pour the dressing over. Sprinkle the salad with the pistachio nuts or pine nuts before serving.

Cook's Tip
If the carrots are very young and fresh then they shouldn't need peeling – a thorough wash with a scrubbing brush will be fine. The older they get, the tougher the skin will be and they will need peeling before grating.

Black and Orange Salad Energy 129kcal/537kJ; Protein 1.8g; Carbohydrate 11.1g, of which sugars 10.6g; Fat 9g, of which saturates 1.3g; Cholesterol 0mg; Calcium 79mg; Fibre 3g; Sodium 654mg.
Carrot and Orange Salad Energy 137kcal/571kJ; Protein 2.9g; Carbohydrate 15.9g, of which sugars 15.1g; Fat 7.3g, of which saturates 1.1g; Cholesterol 0mg; Calcium 72mg; Fibre 4.4g; Sodium 72mg.

Orange and Red Onion Salad with Cumin

Cumin and mint give this refreshing, quick-to-prepare salad a very Middle-Eastern flavour. Small, seedless oranges are most suitable, if available, as they will involve less preparation.

Serves 6
6 oranges
2 red onions
15ml/1 tbsp cumin seeds
5ml/1 tsp coarsely ground black pepper
15ml/1 tbsp chopped fresh mint
90ml/6 tbsp olive oil
salt
fresh mint sprigs and pitted black olives, to garnish

1 Slice the oranges thinly, catching any juices. Holding each orange slice in turn over a bowl, cut round with scissors to remove the peel and pith. Reserve the juice.

2 Peel the red onions, keeping them whole, and then thinly slice them and separate into rings.

3 Arrange the orange and onion slices in layers in a shallow dish, sprinkling each layer with cumin seeds, black pepper, chopped mint, olive oil and salt to taste. Pour over the reserved orange juice.

4 Toss the salad to ensure the ingredients are coated and leave to marinate in a cool place for about 2 hours. Garnish with the fresh mint sprigs and sprinkle over the pitted black olives, and serve immediately.

Cook's Tip
Whole cumin seeds are available from large supermarkets and Asian food stores. Store them in a cool, dark place in an airtight jar and use within a few months of buying otherwise they will begin to lose their excellent flavour – the same applies to most other dried spices and herbs in the kitchen.

Vietnamese Table Salad

Simple and attractive, this arranged salad makes a delightful appetizer with lightly spiced finger food.

Serves 4–6
1 crunchy lettuce, leaves separated
½ cucumber, peeled and thinly sliced
1–2 carrots, finely sliced
200g/7oz/scant 1 cup beansprouts
1–2 unripe star fruit, finely sliced
1–2 green bananas, finely sliced
1 firm papaya, halved, seeded, peeled and finely sliced
1 bunch each fresh mint and basil, stalks removed
juice of 1 lime

1 Arrange all the salad ingredients attractively on a plate, with the lettuce leaves on one side to use as wrappers.

2 Squeeze the lime juice over the fruits, particularly the bananas to help them retain their colour, and place the salad in the middle of the table.

Green Mango Salad

This exotic salad, served with stir-fried prawns, is delicious as an appetizer. Green mangoes have dark skins and light green flesh.

Serves 4
450g/1lb green mangoes
rind and juice of 2 limes
30ml/2 tbsp sugar
30ml/2 tbsp nuoc mam
2 green Thai chillies, seeded and finely sliced
1 small bunch fresh coriander (cilantro), stalks removed, finely chopped
salt
stir-fried prawns, to serve

1 Peel, halve and stone (pit) the mango, then slice into thin strips.

2 In a bowl, mix together the lime juice and rind, sugar and nuoc mam. Add the mango strips with the chillies and coriander, then add salt to taste and stand for 20 minutes to allow the flavours to mingle before serving with prawns.

Orange salad Energy 199kcal/825kJ; Protein 1.6g; Carbohydrate 11.52g, of which sugars 11.3g; Fat 16.6g, of which saturates 2.4g; Cholesterol 0mg; Calcium 68mg; Fibre 2.3g; Sodium 7mg.
Vietnamese salad Energy 108kcal/455kJ; Protein 4g; Carbohydrate 21g, of which sugars 12g; Fat 1g, of which saturates 0g; Cholesterol 0mg; Calcium 110mg; Fibre 42g; Sodium 0.02mg.
Green mango salad Energy 92kcal/391kJ; Protein 1g; Carbohydrate 22g, of which sugars 15g; Fat 0g, of which saturates 0g; Cholesterol 0mg; Calcium 32mg; Fibre 33g; Sodium 0.5mg.

Brown Bean Salad

Brown beans, sometimes called ful medames, are available from health-food stores and Middle-Eastern grocery stores. Dried broad beans or black or red kidney beans will make a good substitute.

Serves 6

350g/12oz/1½ cups dried brown beans
3 fresh thyme sprigs
2 bay leaves
1 onion, halved
4 garlic cloves, crushed
7.5ml/1½ tsp crushed cumin seeds
3 spring onions (scallions), finely chopped
90ml/6 tbsp chopped fresh parsley
20ml/4 tsp lemon juice
90ml/6 tbsp olive oil
3 hard-boiled eggs, roughly chopped
1 pickled cucumber, roughly chopped
salt and ground black pepper

1 Put the dried brown beans in a bowl with plenty of cold water and leave to soak overnight. Drain, transfer to a pan and cover with fresh cold water. Bring to the boil and boil rapidly for 10 minutes.

2 Reduce the heat and add the thyme, bay leaves and onion. Simmer very gently for about 1 hour, until tender. Drain and discard the herbs and onion.

3 Place the beans in a large bowl. Mix together the garlic, cumin seeds, spring onions, parsley, lemon juice and oil in a small bowl, and add a little salt and pepper. Pour over the beans and toss the ingredients lightly together.

4 Gently stir in the chopped hard-boiled eggs and pickled cucumber. Transfer the bean salad to a serving dish and serve immediately.

Variation
To ring the changes, try using crumbled feta cheese or goat's cheese instead of the hard-boiled egg.

Quinoa Salad with Citrus Dressing

Quinoa is a type of grain grown in the Andes. A staple food of the region, it has been cultivated since the time of the Incas and Aztecs. Quinoa is packed with protein and is also gluten free, so it is ideal for vegetarians and those who are gluten intolerant.

Serves 6

175g/6oz/1 cup quinoa
90ml/6 tbsp olive oil
juice of 2 limes
juice of 1 large orange
2 fresh green chillies, seeded and finely chopped
2 garlic cloves, crushed
½ cucumber, peeled
1 large tomato, seeded and cubed
4 spring onions (scallions), sliced
30ml/2 tbsp chopped fresh mint
15ml/1 tbsp chopped fresh flat leaf parsley
salt

1 Put the quinoa in a sieve (strainer), rinse thoroughly under cold water, then transfer into a large pan. Add just enough cold water to cover and bring to the boil. Lower the heat and gently simmer for 10–12 minutes, until tender. Drain and leave to cool.

2 Make the dressing by whisking the olive oil with the lime and orange juices. Stir in the chopped green chillies and the garlic and season with salt.

3 Cut the cucumber in half lengthways and, using a teaspoon, scoop out and discard the seeds. Cut into 5mm/¼in slices and add to the cooled quinoa with the cubed tomato, spring onions and herbs. Toss well to combine.

4 Whisk the dressing again, then pour over the salad and toss again until well mixed and the ingredients are well coated in the dressing. Check the seasoning and serve.

Cook's Tip
Quinoa can also be eaten plain as an accompaniment to meat or fish dishes.

Brown Bean Salad Energy 300kcal/1258kJ; Protein 16.6g; Carbohydrate 27.1g, of which sugars 2.5g; Fat 14.8g, of which saturates 2.5g; Cholesterol 95mg; Calcium 99mg; Fibre 9.9g; Sodium 50mg.
Quinoa Salad Energy 213kcal/885kJ; Protein 3.4g; Carbohydrate 24.3g, of which sugars 2g; Fat 11.6g, of which saturates 1.6g; Cholesterol 0mg; Calcium 26mg; Fibre 0.5g; Sodium 5mg.

Couscous Salad

Couscous has become an extremely popular salad ingredient, and there are many variations on the classic theme. This salad comes from Morocco.

Serves 4

275g/10oz/1⅔ cups couscous
550ml/18fl oz/2½ cups boiling vegetable stock
16–20 pitted black olives, halved
2 small courgettes (zucchini), cut into matchstick strips
25g/1oz/¼ cup flaked almonds, toasted
60ml/4 tbsp olive oil
15ml/1 tbsp lemon juice
15ml/1 tbsp chopped fresh coriander (cilantro)
15ml/1 tbsp chopped fresh parsley
good pinch of ground cumin
good pinch of cayenne pepper
salt
sprigs of coriander (cilantro), to garnish

1 Place the couscous in a bowl and pour over the boiling stock. Stir with a fork, then set aside for 10 minutes to allow all of the stock to be absorbed. Fluff up with a fork.

2 Add the olives, courgettes and almonds to the couscous and mix in gently.

3 Whisk the olive oil, lemon juice, coriander, parsley, cumin, cayenne and a pinch of salt in a bowl. Pour the dressing over the salad and toss to mix. Transfer to a serving dish and garnish with coriander sprigs.

Cook's Tip
This salad benefits from being made several hours ahead, which allows the flavours to thoroughly mingle together.

Variations
- *You can substitute ½ cucumber for the courgettes (zucchini) and pistachios for the almonds.*
- *For extra heat, add a pinch of chilli powder to the dressing.*

Caesar Salad

This famous salad of crisp lettuce tossed with a fresh egg dressing and crunchy croûtons is always popular.

Serves 4

2 large garlic cloves, halved
45ml/3 tbsp extra virgin olive oil
4 slices wholemeal (whole-wheat) bread
1 small romaine or 2 Little Gem (Bibb) lettuces
50g/2oz piece of Parmesan cheese, shaved or coarsely grated (shredded)

For the dressing
1 egg
10ml/2 tsp French mustard
5ml/1 tsp Worcestershire sauce
30ml/2 tbsp fresh lemon juice
30ml/2 tbsp extra virgin olive oil
salt and ground black pepper

1 Preheat the oven to 190°C/375°F/Gas 5. Rub the inside of a salad bowl with one of the half cloves of garlic.

2 Heat the olive oil gently with the remaining garlic in a frying pan for 3 minutes, stirring constantly, then remove and discard the garlic.

3 Remove the crusts from the bread and cut the bread into small cubes. Toss these in the garlic-flavoured oil, making sure they are well coated. Spread out the bread cubes on a baking sheet and bake for about 10 minutes, until crisp. Remove from the oven, then leave to cool.

4 Separate the lettuce leaves, wash and dry them and arrange in a shallow salad bowl. Chill until ready to serve.

5 To make the dressing, bring a small pan of water to the boil, lower the egg into the water and boil for 1 minute only. Crack it into a bowl. Use a teaspoon to scoop out and discard any softly set egg white. Using a balloon whisk, beat in the French mustard, Worcestershire sauce, lemon juice and olive oil, then season with salt and pepper to taste.

6 Sprinkle the Parmesan over the salad and then drizzle the dressing over. Sprinkle with the croûtons. Take the salad to the table, toss lightly and serve immediately.

Couscous Salad Energy 324kcal/1344kJ; Protein 7.1g; Carbohydrate 37.4g, of which sugars 1.8g; Fat 17g, of which saturates 2.1g; Cholesterol 0mg; Calcium 80mg; Fibre 2.1g; Sodium 287mg.
Caesar Salad Energy 261kcal/1083kJ; Protein 9.2g; Carbohydrate 11.5g, of which sugars 1.5g; Fat 20.1g, of which saturates 5g; Cholesterol 60mg; Calcium 190mg; Fibre 1.9g; Sodium 305mg.

Roasted Tomatoes and Mozzarella with Basil Oil

The basil oil needs to be made just before serving to retain its fresh colour.

Serves 4

olive oil, for brushing
6 large plum tomatoes
350g/12oz fresh mozzarella cheese, cut into 8–12 slices
fresh basil leaves, to garnish

For the basil oil

25 fresh basil leaves
60ml/4 tbsp extra virgin olive oil
1 garlic clove, crushed

For the salad

90g/3½ oz/4 cups salad leaves
50g/2oz/2 cups mixed salad herbs, such as coriander (cilantro), basil and rocket (arugula)
25g/1oz/3 tbsp pumpkin seeds
25g/1oz/3 tbsp sunflower seeds
60ml/4 tbsp extra virgin olive oil
15ml/1 tbsp balsamic vinegar
2.5ml/½ tsp Dijon mustard

1 Preheat the oven to 200°C/400°F/Gas 6 and oil a baking sheet. Cut the tomatoes in half lengthways and remove the seeds. Place skin side down on a baking sheet and roast for 20 minutes or until the tomatoes are tender.

2 Meanwhile, make the basil oil. Place the basil leaves, olive oil and garlic in a food processor and process until smooth. Transfer to a bowl and chill.

3 Put the salad leaves and herbs in a large bowl and toss lightly to mix. Toast the pumpkin and sunflower seeds in a dry frying pan over medium heat for about 2 minutes until golden, tossing frequently. Allow the seeds to cool before sprinkling over the salad.

4 Whisk together the oil, vinegar and mustard, then pour the dressing over the salad and toss until the leaves are well coated.

5 For each serving, place the tomato halves on top of two or three slices of mozzarella and drizzle over the basil oil. Season well. Garnish with basil leaves and serve with the salad.

Salad with Watermelon and Feta Cheese

The combination of sweet and juicy watermelon with salty feta cheese was inspired by the Turkish tradition of eating watermelon with salty white cheese in the hot summer months. It is ideal for a cold appetizer.

Serves 6–8

30–45ml/2–3 tbsp extra virgin olive oil
juice of ½ lemon
5ml/1 tsp vinegar of choice
sprinkling of fresh thyme
pinch of ground cumin
4 large slices of watermelon, chilled
1 frisée lettuce, core removed
130g/4½oz feta cheese, preferably sheep's milk feta, cut into bitesize pieces
handful of lightly toasted pumpkin seeds
handful of sunflower seeds
10–15 black olives

1 Pour the extra virgin olive oil, lemon juice and vinegar into a bowl or jug (pitcher).

2 Add the fresh thyme and ground cumin to the bowl or jug, and whisk until the ingredients are well combined. Set the dressing aside until you are ready to serve the salad.

3 Cut the rind off the watermelon and remove as many seeds as possible from inside the fruit. Cut the flesh into bitesize triangular-shaped chunks.

4 Put the lettuce leaves in a salad bowl, pour over the dressing and toss together. Arrange the leaves on a serving dish or individual plates and top with the watermelon pieces, feta cheese, pumpkin and sunflower seeds and black olives. Serve the salad immediately.

Cook's Tip
Use plump black Mediterranean olives, such as kalamata, for this recipe, or other shiny, dry-cured black olives.

Roasted Tomatoes Energy 525kcal/2174kJ; Protein 20.2g; Carbohydrate 7g, of which sugars 4.8g; Fat 46.4g, of which saturates 15.9g; Cholesterol 51mg; Calcium 371mg; Fibre 2.8g; Sodium 381mg.
Salad with Watermelon Energy 256kcal/1006kJ; Protein 7.7g; Carbohydrate 12.9g, of which sugars 11.6g; Fat 19.7g, of which saturates 6.2g; Cholesterol 23mg; Calcium 165mg; Fibre 1.4g; Sodium 616mg.

Marinated Feta Cheese Salad with Capers

Marinating cubes of feta cheese with herbs and spices gives a marvellous flavour. Serve this salad as an appetizer with chunky slices of toast.

Serves 6

350g/12oz feta cheese
2 garlic cloves
2.5ml/½ tsp mixed peppercorns
8 coriander seeds
1 bay leaf
15–30ml/1–2 tbsp drained capers
fresh oregano or thyme sprigs
olive oil, to cover
hot toast, to serve

1 Cut the feta cheese into cubes. Thickly slice the garlic. Put the mixed peppercorns and coriander seeds in a mortar and crush lightly with a pestle.

2 Pack the feta cubes into a large preserving jar with the bay leaf, interspersing layers of cheese with garlic, crushed peppercorns and coriander, capers and the fresh oregano or thyme sprigs.

3 Pour in enough olive oil to cover the feta cheese. Close the jar tightly and leave to marinate for 2 weeks in the refrigerator.

4 Lift out the feta cubes and serve on hot toast, with some chopped tomatoes and a little of the flavoured oil from the jar drizzled over.

Cook's Tip
Rinse the capers thoroughly before use as they can be very salty.

Variation
Add pitted black or green olives to the feta cheese in the marinade, if you like.

Watercress Salad with Pear and Dunsyre Blue Dressing

A refreshing light salad, this appetizer combines lovely peppery watercress, soft juicy pears and a tart dressing. Dunsyre Blue has a wonderfully sharp flavour with a lovely crumbly texture.

Serves 4

25g/1oz Dunsyre Blue cheese
30ml/2 tbsp walnut oil
15ml/1 tbsp lemon juice
2 bunches watercress, thoroughly washed and trimmed
2 ripe pears
salt and ground black pepper

1 Crumble the Dunsyre Blue into a bowl, then mash into the walnut oil, using a fork.

2 Whisk in the lemon juice to create a thickish mixture. If you need to thicken it further, add a little more cheese. Season to taste with salt and ground black pepper.

3 Arrange a pile of watercress on the side of four plates.

4 Peel and slice the two pears then place the pear slices to the side of the watercress, allowing half a pear per person. You can also put the pear slices on top of the watercress, if you prefer. Drizzle the dressing over the salad. The salad is best served immediately at room temperature.

Cook's Tips
- *Choose ripe Comice or similar pears that are soft and juicy.*
- *If you want to get things ready in advance, peel and slice the pears then rub with some lemon juice; this will stop them discolouring so quickly.*

Variations
- *For a milder, tangy dressing use Dolcelatte cheese instead.*
- *Use rocket (arugula) in place of the watercress, if you like.*

Marinated Feta Energy 165kcal/683kJ; Protein 9.3g; Carbohydrate 1.3g, of which sugars 0.9g; Fat 13.6g, of which saturates 8.3g; Cholesterol 41mg; Calcium 211mg; Fibre 0.1g; Sodium 840mg.
Watercress Salad Energy 106Kcal/849kJ; Protein 7.8g; Carbohydrate 16.2g, of which sugars 14.8g; Fat 12.4g, of which saturates 5.2g; Cholesterol 23mg; Calcium 148mg; Fibre 1.1g; Sodium 754mg.

French Goat's Cheese Salad

This is a French salad and cheese course all on one plate. It makes a quick and satisfying appetizer or a light lunch.

Serves 4
200g/7oz bag of prepared mixed salad leaves
4 rashers (strips) back bacon
115g/4oz full-fat goat's cheese
16 thick slices crusty white bread

For the dressing
60ml/4 tsp olive oil
15ml/1 tbsp tarragon vinegar
10ml/1 tsp walnut oil
5ml/1 tsp Dijon mustard
5ml/1 tsp wholegrain mustard

1 Preheat the grill (broiler) to medium heat. Rinse and dry the salad leaves, then arrange them in four individual bowls. Place the ingredients for the dressing in a screw-topped jar, shake together well, and reserve.

2 Lay the bacon rashers on a board, then stretch them with the back of a knife and cut each into four crossways. Roll each piece up and grill (broil) for 2–3 minutes.

3 Slice the goat's cheese into eight and then halve each slice. Top each slice of bread with a piece of goat's cheese and place under the grill. Turn over the bacon and continue cooking with the toasts until the cheese is golden and bubbling.

4 Arrange the bacon rolls and toasts on top of the prepared salad leaves, shake the dressing well and pour a little of it over each. Serve immediately.

Variations
- *If you prefer, just slice the goat's cheese and place it on toasted crusty white bread.*
- *Use wholewheat toast for a deliciously nutty flavour that complements the walnut oil in the dressing.*
- *Vegetarians and vegans could replace the bacon rolls with halved, ripe cherry tomatoes, and the goat's cheese with slices of avocado.*

Leek and Egg Salad

Smooth-textured leeks are especially delicious warm when partnered with an earthy-rich sauce of parsley, olive oil and walnuts. Serve as an appetizer or a side salad with grilled fish and new potatoes.

Serves 4
675g/1½lb young leeks
1 egg
fresh parsley sprigs, to garnish

For the dressing
25g/1oz fresh parsley
30ml/2 tbsp olive oil
juice of ½ lemon
50g/2oz/½ cup shelled, broken walnuts, toasted
5ml/1 tsp caster (superfine) sugar
salt and ground black pepper

1 Bring a pan of salted water to the boil. Cut the leeks into 10cm/4in lengths and rinse well to flush out any grit or soil. Cook the leeks for 8 minutes. Drain and part-cool under running water.

2 Lower the egg into boiling water and cook for 12 minutes. Cool under cold running water, shell and set aside.

3 To make the dressing, finely chop the parsley in a food processor. Add the olive oil, lemon juice and toasted walnuts. Blend for 1–2 minutes, until smooth.

4 Adjust the consistency with about 90ml/6 tbsp water. Add the sugar and season to taste with salt and pepper.

5 Place the leeks on an serving plate, then spoon on the sauce. Finely grate the hard-boiled egg and sprinkle over the sauce. Garnish with the fresh parsley sprigs and serve while the leeks are still warm.

Cook's Tip
Toast the walnuts by dry-frying them in a non-stick pan. Keep them moving so that they don't burn.

French Salad Energy 667kcal/2806kJ; Protein 24.5g; Carbohydrate 85.6g, of which sugars 5.4g; Fat 27.8g, of which saturates 9g; Cholesterol 40mg; Calcium 240mg; Fibre 4.1g; Sodium 1483mg.
Leek and Egg Salad Energy 197kcal/817kJ; Protein 6.3g; Carbohydrate 6.5g, of which sugars 5.2g; Fat 16.4g, of which saturates 2.1g; Cholesterol 48mg; Calcium 73mg; Fibre 4.5g; Sodium 24mg.

Halloumi and Grape Salad

Sweet, juicy grapes really complement the distinctive salty flavour of halloumi cheese in this delectable warm salad from Cyprus.

Serves 4

150g/5oz mixed green salad leaves
75g/3oz seedless green grapes
75g/3oz seedless black grapes
250g/9oz halloumi cheese
45ml/3 tbsp olive oil
fresh young thyme leaves or dill, to garnish

For the dressing

60ml/4 tbsp olive oil
15ml/1 tbsp lemon juice
2.5ml/½ tsp caster (superfine) sugar
15ml/1 tbsp chopped fresh thyme or dill
salt and ground black pepper

1 To make the dressing, mix together the olive oil, lemon juice and sugar. Season with salt and pepper to taste. Stir in the thyme or dill and set aside.

2 Toss together the salad leaves and the green and black grapes, then transfer to a large serving plate.

3 Thinly slice the cheese. Heat the oil in a large frying pan. Add the cheese and fry briefly until turning golden on the underside. Turn the cheese with a fish slice or metal spatula and cook the other side until golden.

4 Arrange the cooked cheese slices on top of the salad. Pour over the dressing and toss to combine. Garnish with thyme or dill and serve immediately.

Cook's Tips

- *Most supermarkets sell ready-mixed bags of prepared salad leaves, which are ideal for use in this recipe. Experiment with various combinations to find the lettuce flavours that you like best. A mix of rocket (arugula), spinach and watercress is good. or try a mix with fresh herbs included.*
- *Halloumi cheese is now widely available from most large supermarkets and Greek delicatessens.*

Halloumi with Rocket Salad

This delicious salad has a robust flavour and a salty tang. Traditionally, it is brought to the table in a cast-iron frying pan, but this modern version accompanies it with a peppery rocket salad.

Serves 4

30ml/2 tbsp olive oil, for frying
8 slices Greek Kefalotyri or Greek Cypriot Haloumi cheese, each about 1cm/1/2in thick
ground black pepper
lemon wedges, to serve

For the salad

15ml/1 tbsp red wine vinegar
60ml/4 tbsp extra virgin olive oil
a handful of rocket (arugula) leaves

1 Start by making the salad. Whisk the vinegar and extra virgin olive oil in a small bowl and use to dress the rocket leaves. Spread them out on a platter.

2 Heat the olive oil for frying in a large griddle pan or non-stick frying pan and lay the slices of cheese, side by side, on the base. Do not allow the slices to touch as they might stick together. Let them sizzle for a couple of minutes, turning each one over using tongs or a metal spatula as it starts to get crisp at the sides.

3 Sprinkle the cheese slices with pepper. As soon as the bases turn golden, remove them from the pan and arrange them on the dressed rocket. Serve immediately, with the lemon wedges to squeeze over the top.

Cook's Tips

- *Halloumi is a good cheese for frying or grilling (broiling) because it can be cooked without melting.*
- *Any salad leaves can be used in this dish instead of the rocket (arugula). Try an equal mix of watercress and lamb's lettuce.*
- *Halloumi is often eaten with fruit, such as watermelon, which helps to offset the salty taste. Herbs, particularly mint, are also good served with this cheese.*

Halloumi and Grape Energy 365kcal/1513kJ; Protein 12.2g; Carbohydrate 7.2g, of which sugars 7.2g; Fat 32.2g, of which saturates 11.4g; Cholesterol 36mg; Calcium 250mg; Fibre 0.8g; Sodium 250mg.
Halloumi and Rocket Energy 284kcal/1173kJ; Protein 9.7g; Carbohydrate 0.9g, of which sugars 0.9g; Fat 26.9g, of which saturates 9.2g; Cholesterol 29mg; Calcium 195mg; Fibre 0.5g; Sodium 199mg.

Herring Salad with Beetroot and Sour Cream

Sweet, earthy beetroot and tangy sour cream team up with robustly flavoured herrings to make a salad with lots of character. Serve alone as an appetizer or with slices of rye bread as a substantial light lunch.

Serves 8

2 beetroot (beets)
1 large tangy cooking apple
500g/1 ¼lb matjes herrings (schmaltz herrings), drained and cut into slices
2 small pickled cucumbers, diced
10ml/2 tsp caster (superfine) sugar, or to taste
10ml/2 tsp cider vinegar or white wine vinegar
300ml/½ pint/1 ¼ cups sour cream
lettuce, to serve
sprigs of fresh dill and chopped onion or onion rings, to garnish

1 Bring a large pan of water to the boil. Drop in the whole beetroot and lower the heat to a simmer. Cook the beetroot until tender, about 1 hour depending on size. Set aside to cool.

2 Peel, core and dice the apple. Put in a bowl and add the herrings, cucumbers, sugar and cider or white wine vinegar.

3 Gently mix the ingredients, then stir in the sour cream. Dice the cooked beetroot and add to the herring mixture. Chill.

4 Serve the salad on a bed of lettuce leaves, garnished with fresh dill and chopped onion or onion rings.

Cook's Tip
Always cook beetroot (beet) whole. Never top and tail, chop or peel before cooking. This prevents the red dye from 'leaching' out, which not only stains, it impairs flavour. Trim off the stalks at least an inch above the beetroot, and wash gently in cold water without breaking the skin.

Aubergine Salad with Shrimp and Egg

An appetizing and unusual salad that you will find yourself making over and over again. Roasting the aubergines really brings out their flavour.

Serves 4–6

2 aubergines (eggplants)
15ml/1 tbsp vegetable oil
30ml/2 tbsp dried shrimp, soaked in warm water for 10 minutes
15ml/1 tbsp coarsely chopped garlic
1 hard-boiled egg, chopped
4 shallots, thinly sliced into rings
fresh coriander (cilantro) leaves and 2 fresh red chillies, seeded and sliced, to garnish

For the dressing

30ml/2 tbsp fresh lime juice
5ml/1 tsp palm sugar (jaggery) or light muscovado (brown) sugar
30ml/2 tbsp Thai fish sauce

1 Preheat the oven to 180°C/350°F/Gas 4. Prick the aubergines several times with a skewer, then place them directly on the shelf of the oven for about 1 hour, turning at least twice. Remove the aubergines. Set aside until cool enough to handle.

2 Meanwhile, make the dressing. Put the lime juice, sugar and fish sauce in a small bowl. Whisk well with a fork or balloon whisk. Cover with clear film (plastic wrap) and set aside.

3 Remove the skin from the cooled aubergines and cut the flesh into medium slices.

4 Heat the oil in a small frying pan. Drain the dried shrimp thoroughly and add them to the pan with the garlic. Cook over medium heat for about 3 minutes, until golden. Remove from the pan and set aside.

5 Arrange the aubergine slices on a serving dish. Top with the chopped hard-boiled egg, shallot rings and dried shrimp mixture. Drizzle over the dressing and garnish with the fresh coriander and red chillies. Serve immediately.

Herring Salad Energy 212kcal/878kJ; Protein 9.6g; Carbohydrate 6.5g, of which sugars 6.2g; Fat 16.5g, of which saturates 4.7g; Cholesterol 51mg; Calcium 72mg; Fibre 0.6g; Sodium 266mg.
Aubergine Salad Energy 58kcal/242kJ; Protein 4.6g; Carbohydrate 3.1g, of which sugars 2.8g; Fat 3.2g, of which saturates 0.6g; Cholesterol 57mg; Calcium 74mg; Fibre 1.5g; Sodium 230mg.

Fresh Tuna Salad Niçoise

Fresh tuna transforms this famous salad from the south of France into something really special.

Serves 4

4 tuna steaks, about 150g/5oz each
30ml/2 tbsp olive oil
225g/8oz fine green beans
1 small cos or romaine lettuce or 2 Little Gem (Bibb) lettuces
4 new potatoes, boiled
4 ripe tomatoes or 12 cherry tomatoes
2 red (bell) peppers, seeded and cut into thin strips
4 hard-boiled eggs, sliced
8 drained anchovy fillets in oil, halved lengthwise
16 large black olives
salt and ground black pepper
12 fresh basil leaves, to garnish

For the dressing

15ml/1 tbsp red wine vinegar
90ml/6 tbsp olive oil
1 fat garlic clove, crushed

1 Brush the tuna on both sides with a little olive oil and season with salt and ground black pepper. Heat a ridged griddle or the grill (broiler) until very hot, then grill (broil) the tuna steaks for 1–2 minutes on each side; they should still be pink and juicy in the middle. Set aside.

2 Cook the beans in a pan of lightly salted boiling water for 4–5 minutes or until just tender. Drain, refresh under cold water and drain again.

3 Separate the lettuce leaves and arrange them on four individual serving plates. Slice the potatoes and tomatoes, if large (leave cherry tomatoes whole), and divide them among the plates. Arrange the fine green beans and red pepper strips on top of them.

4 Shell the eggs and cut into thick slices. Place two slices on each plate with an anchovy fillet draped over. Sprinkle four olives on to each plate.

5 To make the dressing, whisk together the vinegar, olive oil and garlic and season to taste. Drizzle over the salads. Arrange the tuna steaks on top, sprinkle over the basil and serve.

Avocado and Smoked Fish Salad

Avocado and smoked fish make a good combination and, flavoured with herbs and spices, create a delectable and elegant appetizer. Smoked haddock or cod can also be used in this salad.

Serves 4

15g/½oz/1 tbsp butter or margarine
½ onion, finely sliced
5ml/1 tsp mustard seeds
225g/8oz smoked mackerel, flaked
30ml/2 tbsp fresh chopped coriander (cilantro)
2 firm tomatoes, peeled and chopped
15ml/1 tbsp lemon juice

For the salad

2 avocados
½ cucumber
15ml/1 tbsp lemon juice
2 firm tomatoes
1 green chilli
salt and ground black pepper

1 Melt the butter or margarine in a frying pan, add the sliced onion and mustard seeds and fry for 5 minutes until the onion is soft but not browned.

2 Add the fish, chopped coriander, tomatoes and lemon juice and cook over low heat for about 2–3 minutes. Remove from the heat and leave to cool.

3 To make the salad, slice the avocados and cucumber thinly. Place together in a bowl and sprinkle with the lemon juice to prevent discoloration. Slice the tomatoes and seed them, and finely chop the chilli.

4 Place the cooled fish mixture in the centre of a large serving plate.

5 Arrange the avocado slices, cucumber and tomatoes decoratively around the outside of the fish. Or, spoon a quarter of the fish mixture on to each of four serving plates.

6 Divide the avocado, cucumber and tomato slices equally among the plates. Then sprinkle with the chopped fresh chilli and season with a little salt and ground black pepper, and serve immediately.

Fresh Tuna Salad Energy 542kcal/2260kJ; Protein 46.8g; Carbohydrate 14.3g, of which sugars 9.8g; Fat 33.7g, of which saturates 6.5g; Cholesterol 236mg; Calcium 132mg; Fibre 4.4g; Sodium 671mg.
Avocado Energy 386kcal/1596kJ; Protein 12.8g; Carbohydrate 4.6g, of which sugars 3.1g; Fat 35.2g, of which saturates 8.6g; Cholesterol 67mg; Calcium 32mg; Fibre 3.4g; Sodium 455mg.

Smoked Trout and Noodle Salad

It is important to use ripe juicy tomatoes for this salad.

Serves 4

225g/8oz somen noodles
2 smoked trout, skinned and boned
30ml/2 tbsp snipped chives
2 hard-boiled eggs, chopped
lime halves, to serve

For the dressing

6 ripe plum tomatoes
2 shallots, finely chopped
30ml/2 tbsp tiny capers, rinsed
30ml/2 tbsp chopped fresh tarragon
finely grated (shredded) rind and juice of ½ orange
60ml/ 4 tbsp extra virgin olive oil
salt and ground black pepper

1 To make the dressing, cut the tomatoes into chunks. Place in a bowl with the shallots, capers, tarragon, orange rind and juice and olive oil. Season with salt and pepper and mix well. Leave at room temperature for 1–2 hours.

2 Cook the noodles until just tender. Drain, rinse them and drain again. Toss the noodles into the dressing, season with salt and ground black pepper to taste, and divide between the serving plates.

3 Flake the trout over the noodles, then sprinkle the chives and chopped egg over the top. Add the lime halves and serve.

Smoked Trout and Horseradish Salad

In the summer, when lettuce leaves are sweet and crisp, partner them with fillets of smoked trout, warm new potatoes and a creamy horseradish dressing.

Serves 4

675g/1½lb new potatoes
4 smoked trout fillets
115g/4oz mixed lettuce leaves
4 slices dark rye bread, cut into fingers
salt and ground black pepper

For the dressing

60ml/4 tbsp creamed horseradish
60ml/4 tbsp groundnut (peanut) oil
15ml/1 tbsp white wine vinegar
10ml/2 tsp caraway seeds

1 Put the potatoes in a pan of salted water and bring to the boil. Simmer for about 15 minutes until tender. Remove the skin from the trout fillets and lift the flesh from the bone.

2 To make the dressing, place all the ingredients in a jar and shake vigorously. Season the lettuce with salt and pepper and moisten them with the dressing. Divide the salad among four plates.

3 Flake the trout fillets and cut the potatoes in half. Scatter them together with the rye bread fingers over the salad leaves and toss to mix. Season the salad to taste and serve.

Cook's Tip
In some cases it is better to season the leaves rather than the dressing when making a salad.

Warm Chicken and Tomato Salad with Hazelnut Dressing

This simple, warm salad combines pan-fried chicken and spinach with a light, nutty dressing. Serve it as an appetizer on an autumn day.

Serves 4

45ml/3 tbsp olive oil
30ml/2 tbsp hazelnut oil
15ml/1 tbsp white wine vinegar
1 garlic clove, crushed
15ml/1 tbsp chopped fresh mixed herbs
225g/8oz baby spinach leaves
250g/9oz cherry tomatoes, halved
1 bunch spring onions (scallions), chopped
2 skinless chicken breast fillets, cut into thin strips
salt and ground black pepper

1 To make the dressing, place 30ml/2 tbsp of the olive oil with the hazelnut oil, vinegar, garlic and chopped herbs in a small bowl and whisk together until thoroughly mixed. Set aside.

2 Trim any long stalks from the spinach leaves, then place in a large serving bowl with the tomatoes and spring onions, and toss together to mix.

3 Heat the remaining olive oil in a frying pan, and stir-fry the chicken over high heat for 7–10 minutes until it is cooked, tender and lightly browned.

4 Arrange the cooked chicken pieces over the salad. Give the dressing a quick whisk to blend, then drizzle it over the salad. Add salt and ground black pepper to taste, toss lightly and serve immediately.

Variations
- *Use other meat or fish, such as steak, pork fillet or salmon fillet, in place of the chicken breasts. Simply stir-fry until cooked and add to the salad as described.*
- *Any salad leaves can be used in this dish instead of the baby spinach. Try an equal mix of rocket (arugula), watercress and lamb's lettuce.*

Trout and Noodle Energy 474kcal/1979kJ; Protein 26g; Carbohydrate 51.5g, of which sugars 5.3g; Fat 17.6g, of which saturates 3.1g; Cholesterol 121mg; Calcium 49mg; Fibre 1.5g; Sodium 1464mg.
Smoked Trout Energy 428kcal/1797kJ; Protein 25.3g; Carbohydrate 41.8g, of which sugars 5.4g; Fat 18.9g, of which saturates 2.6g; Cholesterol 28mg; Calcium 84mg; Fibre 3.7g; Sodium 1712mg.
Warm Chicken Energy 260kcal/1081kJ; Protein 20.7g; Carbohydrate 3.7g, of which sugars 3.6g; Fat 18.1g, of which saturates 2.6g; Cholesterol 53mg; Calcium 124mg; Fibre 2.3g; Sodium 140mg.

Chicken Liver Salad

This delicious salad may be served as a tasty first course on individual plates or as a main course for a summer lunch party.

Serves 4

mixed salad leaves such as frisée, oak leaf lettuce, radicchio
1 avocado, diced
30ml/2 tbsp lemon juice
2 pink grapefruit
350g/12oz chicken livers
30ml/2 tbsp olive oil
1 garlic clove, crushed
salt and ground black pepper
whole fresh chives, to garnish

For the dressing

30ml/2 tbsp lemon juice
60ml/4 tbsp olive oil
2.5ml/½ tsp wholegrain mustard
2.5ml/½ tsp clear honey
15ml/1 tbsp chopped fresh chives
salt and ground black pepper

1 To make the dressing, put the lemon juice, olive oil, mustard, honey and chopped fresh chives into a screw-top jar, and shake vigorously. Season to taste with salt and ground black pepper.

2 Arrange the previously washed and well-drained mixed salad leaves attractively on a large serving plate. Peel and dice the avocado and mix with the lemon juice to prevent browning. Add to the plate of mixed leaves.

3 Peel the grapefruit, removing as much of the white pith as possible. Split into segments and arrange with the leaves and avocado on the serving plate.

4 Dry the chicken livers on kitchen paper and remove any unwanted pieces. Using a sharp knife, cut the larger chicken livers in half. Leave the smaller ones whole.

5 Heat the oil in a large frying pan. Stir-fry the chicken livers and garlic briskly until the livers are brown all over (they should be slightly pink inside). Season to taste with salt and black pepper, remove from the pan and drain on kitchen paper.

6 Place the chicken livers, while still warm, on to the salad leaves and spoon over the dressing. Garnish with the whole chives and serve immediately.

Warm Duck Salad with Poached Eggs

Golden duck skewers look and taste wonderful.

Serves 4

3 skinless duck breast portions, thinly sliced
30ml/2 tbsp soy sauce
30ml/2 tbsp balsamic vinegar
30ml/2 tbsp groundnut (peanut) oil
1 shallot, finely chopped
115g/4oz/1½ cups chanterelle mushrooms
4 eggs
50g/2oz mixed salad leaves
salt and ground black pepper
30ml/2 tbsp extra virgin olive oil, to serve

1 Put the duck in a shallow dish and toss with the soy sauce and balsamic vinegar. Cover and chill for 30 minutes. Meanwhile, soak 12 bamboo skewers (about 13cm/5in long) in water to help prevent them from burning during cooking.

2 Preheat the grill (broiler). Thread the marinated duck slices on to the bamboo skewers, pleating them neatly. Place the skewers on a grill pan and cook for 3–5 minutes, then turn them and cook for a further 3 minutes, or until the duck pieces are golden brown.

3 Meanwhile, heat the groundnut oil in a frying pan and cook the chopped shallot until softened. Add the mushrooms and cook over a high heat for 5 minutes, stirring occasionally.

4 While the chanterelles are cooking, half fill a frying pan with water, add a little salt and heat until simmering. Break the eggs one at a time into a cup, then gently tip into the water. Poach the eggs gently for about 3 minutes, or until the whites are set. Use a slotted spoon to transfer the eggs to a warm plate, pat them dry with kitchen paper, then trim off any untidy white.

5 Arrange the salad leaves on four individual plates, then add the chanterelles and skewered duck. Place the poached eggs on the plates. Drizzle the salad with olive oil, season with pepper and serve immediately.

Chicken Liver Salad Energy 313kcal/1299kJ; Protein 17g; Carbohydrate 8.3g, of which sugars 8g; Fat 23.7g, of which saturates 4.1g; Cholesterol 333mg; Calcium 42mg; Fibre 2.4g; Sodium 72mg.
Warm Duck Salad Energy 271kcal/1132kJ; Protein 29.2g; Carbohydrate 1.5g, of which sugars 1.1g; Fat 18.6g, of which saturates 3.9g; Cholesterol 314mg; Calcium 51mg; Fibre 0.7g; Sodium 196mg.

Sesame Duck and Noodle Salad

This salad is complete in itself and makes a lovely summer appetizer, or serve as a light lunch.

Serves 4

2 skinless duck breast fillets
15ml/1 tbsp oil
150g/5oz sugar snap peas
2 carrots, cut into 7.5cm/3in batons
225g/8oz medium egg noodles
6 spring onions (scallions), sliced
salt
30ml/2 tbsp coriander (cilantro) leaves, to garnish

For the marinade

15ml/1 tbsp sesame oil
5ml/1 tsp ground coriander
5ml/1 tsp five-spice powder

For the dressing

15ml/1 tbsp garlic vinegar or white wine vinegar
5ml/1 tsp soft light brown sugar
5ml/1 tsp soy sauce
15ml/1 tbsp toasted sesame seeds
45ml/3 tbsp sunflower oil
30ml/2 tbsp sesame oil
ground black pepper

1 Slice the duck breast fillets thinly across and put them in a shallow dish. Mix the ingredients for the marinade, pour over the duck and coat thoroughly. Cover and leave to marinate in a cool place for 30 minutes.

2 Heat the oil in a frying pan, add the slices of duck breast and stir-fry for 3-4 minutes until cooked. Set aside.

3 Bring a pan of lightly salted water to the boil. Place the sugar snap peas and carrots in a steamer that will fit on top of the pan. When the water boils, add the noodles.

4 Place the steamer on top and steam the vegetables, while cooking the noodles for the time suggested on the packet. Set the steamed vegetables aside. Drain the noodles, refresh them under cold running water and drain again. Place them in a serving bowl.

5 Make the dressing by whisking all the ingredients in a bowl. Pour over the noodles and mix well. Add the sugar snap peas, carrots, spring onions and duck slices and toss to mix. Garnish with the coriander leaves and serve.

Carpaccio with Rocket

Invented in Venice, carpaccio is named in honour of the Renaissance painter. In this sophisticated Italian dish, raw beef is lightly dressed with lemon juice and olive oil, and it is traditionally served with shavings of Parmesan cheese. Use very fresh meat of the best quality and ask the butcher to slice it very thinly.

Serves 4

1 garlic clove, peeled and cut in half
1½ lemons
50ml/2fl oz/¼ cup extra virgin olive oil
2 bunches rocket (arugula)
4 very thin slices of beef fillet
115g/4oz Parmesan cheese, shaved
salt and ground black pepper

1 Rub the cut side of the garlic over the inside of a bowl. Squeeze the lemons into the bowl, then whisk in the olive oil. Season with salt and black pepper, then leave to stand for at least 15 minutes.

2 Carefully wash the bunches of rocket and tear off any thick stalks. Spin dry or pat dry with kitchen paper. Arrange the rocket around the edge of a serving platter or divide among four individual plates.

3 Place the sliced beef in the centre of the platter and pour the dressing over, ensuring that the meat gets an even covering.

4 Arrange the Parmesan shavings on top of the meat slices and serve immediately.

Variation
You can also serve meaty fish, such as tuna, in the same way. Place a fresh tuna steak between sheets of clear film (plastic wrap) and pound with a rolling pin to flatten it out. Then roll it up tightly and wrap in clear film. Place in the freezer for about 4 hours until firm. Unwrap the fish and, using a very sharp knife, cut the fish crossways into slices as thin as possible. Serve in the same way.

Duck Noodle Salad Energy 550kcal/2301kJ; Protein 25.3g; Carbohydrate 47g, of which sugars 4.2g; Fat 31.6g, of which saturates 5.2g; Cholesterol 99mg; Calcium 70mg; Fibre 4.5g; Sodium 192mg.
Carpaccio with Rocket Energy 244kcal/1013kJ; Protein 17.3g; Carbohydrate 0.1g, of which sugars 0.1g; Fat 19.4g, of which saturates 7.9g; Cholesterol 44mg; Calcium 384mg; Fibre 0.4g; Sodium 336mg.

Index

Aduki beans: lemon and bean stuffed mushrooms 189
Aioli: deep-fried new potatoes with saffron aioli 191
 tapenade and aioli with vegetables 28
Albondigas 127
Allspice: caramelized mushrooms with allspice and herbs 189
Almonds: spring rolls with chicken, spring onions and almonds 99
 tapas of almonds, olives and cheese 28
Anchovies: anchovy and caper bites 29
 anchovy terrine 68
 bruschetta with anchovies, quail's eggs and roasted cumin 31
 crostini with tomato, red pepper and mozzarella toppings 33
 marinated anchovies 168
 olive and anchovy bites 29
 tapenade and aioli with vegetables 28
 tapenade with quail's eggs and crudités 16
Angels on horseback 30
Apples: black pudding with potato and apple 122
Arame seaweed: mixed seaweed salad 235
Arbroath smokies: smoked haddock pâté 63
Artichokes: artichoke and cumin dip 10
 artichoke rice cakes with Manchego 203
 artichokes with eggs 95
 charred artichokes with lemon oil dip 187
 sweet-and-sour artichoke salad 234
Asparagus: asparagus and egg terrine 70
 asparagus and prosciutto 110
 chicken and asparagus risotto 100
 crackling rice paper seafood rolls 49
 dressed crab with asparagus 157
 salmon rolls with asparagus and butter sauce 40
 smoked fish and asparagus mousse 72
 tapenade and aioli with vegetables 28
Aspic: quail's eggs in aspic with Parma ham 86
Aubergines: aubergine and pepper spread 9
 aubergine and smoked mozzarella rolls 187
 aubergine salad with shrimp and egg 245
 aubergine, tomato and mozzarella wraps 207
 aubergine with sesame chicken 105
 baba ganoush with Lebanese flatbread 15
 baked Mediterranean vegetables 210
 crisp fried aubergine 54
 grilled vegetable sticks 181
 grilled vegetable terrine 67
 summer vegetables with yogurt pesto 211
 vegetable tempura 55
Avocados: avocado and smoked fish salad 248
 eggs mimosa 96
 fiery guacamole 16
 shrimp, egg and avocado mousses 73
 tortilla wrap with tabbouleh and avocado 208
 turkey and avocado pitta bread pizzas 104

Baba ganoush with Lebanese flatbread 15
Baby peas see Petits pois
Bacon: angels on horseback 30
 bacon-rolled enokitake mushrooms 38
 bacon-wrapped beef on skewers 127
 chunky chicken minestrone 229
 devils on horseback 31
 eel wrapped in bacon 166
 frijoles charros 112
 king scallops with bacon 156
 leek and bacon tart 121
 liver and bacon Varenyky 142
 popiah 49
 pork and bacon rillettes with onion salad 121
Bamboo shoots: chicken and vegetable bundles 99
Banana leaves: fish cakes in banana leaves 177
Bananas: Vietnamese table salad 238
Basil: basil and lemon dip 11
 herbed Greek pies 209
 herby polenta with tomatoes 182
 mixed leaf and herb salad with toasted seeds 233
 rice noodles with fresh herbs 205
 roast tomatoes and mozzarella with basil oil 241
Beans: brown bean salad 239
 cannellini bean and rosemary bruschetta 32
 cannellini bean pâté 63
 chilli bean dip 10
 frijoles charros 112
 garlic-infused spicy bean dip 14
 green bean and sweet red pepper salad 232
 lemon and bean stuffed mushrooms 189
 mushroom and bean pâté 65
 quick pistou soup 216
 roasted vegetable and garlic sausage loaf 126
 tapenade and aioli with vegetables 28
 tortas 116
 tortilla with beans 87
Beansprouts: beansprout and mooli salad 235
 Vietnamese table salad 238
Beef: albondigas 127
 bacon-wrapped beef on skewers 127
 beef empanadas 130
 beef patties with onions and peppers 129
 beef satay with a hot mango dip 126
 carpaccio with rocket 251
 chilli and honey-cured beef 133
 garlic and chilli marinated beef with corn-crusted onion rings 132
 golden beef and potato puffs 131
 red-hot meatballs with roasted coconut 128
 sopes with picadillo 130
 spicy beef and mushroom soup 223
 spicy koftas 37
 spicy shredded beef 129
 stir-fried beef in oyster sauce 132
 taquitos with beef 128
 tomato and beef soup 231
Beer: frijoles charros 112
Beet see Beetroot
 Beetroot: beetroot soup with ravioli 220
 chicken bitki 106
 herring salad with beetroot and sour cream 245
 sweet and salty beetroot crisps 25
Bell peppers see Green peppers; Orange peppers; Red peppers; Yellow peppers
Bitter melon: Spanish-style omelette with bitter melon 90
Black bean sauce: steamed green mussels in black bean sauce 152
Black pudding: black pudding with potato and apple 122
 paprika-spiced black pudding crostini 34
Blue cheese: blue cheese and chive pennies 78
 blue cheese dip 19
 mini baked potatoes with blue cheese 191
Borek 205
Brandy: chicken liver and brandy pâté 64
Bread: angels on horseback 30
 Baba ganoush with Lebanese flatbread 15
 bread sticks 20
 Caesar salad 240
 cheese and potato bread twists 22
 classic gazpacho 213
 crispy pork balls 37
 devils on horseback 31
 griddled tomatoes on soda bread 185
 home-made crisp rye breads 21
 Monte Cristo triangles 21
 muhammara 9
 mushrooms on spicy toast 206
 Navajo fried bread 20
 panzanella salad 232

 prawn toasts with sesame seeds 27
 pretzels 22
 roasted vegetable and garlic sausage loaf 126
 spicy toasts 32
 taramasalata 17
 see also Brioches; Bruschetta; Ciabatta; Crostini; Pitta bread
Brioches: chive scrambled eggs in brioches 94
 devilled kidneys on brioche croûtes 141
Broad beans: garlic-infused spicy bean dip 14
 tortilla with beans 87
Broccoli: broccoli timbales 183
 pickled broccoli in miso 182
Broths: monkfish broth 226
 red pepper and pasta in broth 223
 tortellini chanterelle broth 222
Brown beans: brown bean salad 239
Bruschetta: bruschetta with anchovies, quail's eggs and roasted cumin 31
 cannellini bean and rosemary bruschetta 32
 walnut and goat's cheese bruschetta 84
Butter: salmon cakes with butter sauce 165
 salmon rolls with asparagus and butter sauce 40
Butterfly prawn skewers with chilli and raspberry dip 30
Butternut squash: squash soup with hot horseradish cream 215

Cabbage and noodle parcels 116
Cacik 14
Cactus: pork in green sauce with cactus 119
Caerphilly cheese: cheese and leek sausages 188
Calamari with two-tomato stuffing 61
Cannellini beans: cannellini bean pâté 63
 cannellini bean and rosemary bruschetta 32
Capers: anchovy and caper bites 29
 marinated feta cheese salad with capers 242
Cardamom chicken mousselines 71
Carnitas 118
Carp: fish sausages 169
Carpaccio with rocket 251
Carrots: carrot and orange salad 237
 chicken and vegetable bundles 99
 chunky chicken minestrone 229
 crunchy summer rolls 197
 deep-fried tofu balls 36
 parsnip, carrot and chèvre cheese fricassée 210
 quick pistou soup 216
 spiced vegetables with coconut 211
 spicy carrot dip 12
 spicy carrot soup 215
 sushi 38
 tagliatelle with vegetable ribbons 200
 tapenade and aioli with vegetables 28
 vegetable tempura 55
 Vietnamese table salad 238
Cashew nuts: roasted coconut cashew nuts 23
Cayenne pepper: fried whitebait with cayenne pepper 168
Celeriac: celeriac fritters with mustard dip 56
 cheese and celeriac soup 217
Celery: chunky chicken minestrone 229
 spiced vegetables with coconut 211
Chanterelle mushrooms: tortellini chanterelle broth 222
Cheddar cheese: bitesize cheese brioches 77
 Cheddar and chive scones 85
 cheese and chilli tortillas 79
 cheese pudding 85
 smoked haddock and cheese omelette 90
 spicy toasts 32
Cheese
 cheese-crusted party eggs 84
 chilli yogurt cheese in olive oil 75
 see also individual cheese names
Chévre cheese: parsnip, carrot and chèvre cheese fricassée 210
Chicken: aubergine with sesame chicken 105
 balti chicken in saffron sauce 107
 barbecue chicken 106
 barbecue-glazed chicken skewers 109
 caramelized chicken wings with fresh ginger 102
 cardamom chicken mousselines 71
 chicken and asparagus risotto 100
 chicken and ginger soup 228
 chicken and sticky rice balls 36
 chicken and vegetable bundles 99
 chicken bitki 106
 chicken chilli parcels 101
 chicken croquettes 56
 chicken flautas 102
 chicken kofta balti with paneer 108
 chicken, leek and barley soup 228
 chicken parcels 100
 chicken with lemon and garlic 108
 chunky chicken minestrone 229
 drunken chicken 101
 golden Parmesan chicken 57
 grilled chicken balls on skewers 98
 kabocha squash with chicken sauce 105
 Mexican chicken faijitas 103
 Monte Cristo triangles 21
 paella croquettes 60
 panuchos 103
 rice omelette rolls 92
 scented chicken wraps 109
 smoked chicken with peach mayonnaise in filo tartlets 44
 spicy chicken satay with peanut sauce 98
 spring rolls with chicken, spring onions and almonds 99
 tandoori chicken sticks 107
 warm chicken and tomato salad with hazelnut dressing 249
Chicken livers: chicken liver and brandy pâté 64
 chicken liver salad 250
 chicken livers in sherry 142
 liver and bacon Varenyky 142
Chickpeas: falafel 180
 hummus 15
 spiced chickpea rissoles coated with sesame seeds 198
 spinach and chickpea pancakes 199
Chicory: smoked eel and chicory salad 247
Chillies: butterfly prawn skewers with chilli and raspberry dip 30
 cheese and chilli tortillas 79
 chicken chilli parcels 101
 chilli and honey-cured beef 133
 chilli bean dip 10
 chilli crabs 158
 chilli yogurt cheese in olive oil 75
 feta and roast pepper dip with chillies 19
 fiery guacamole 16
 frijoles charros 112
 garlic and chilli marinated beef with corn-crusted onion rings 132
 ginger and chilli steamed fish custards 178
 hard-boiled eggs in red sauce 88
 pepitas 23
 soft-shell crabs with chilli and salt 158
 spicy toasts 32
 stuffed green chillies 184
 tortas 116
 tuna chilli tacos 175
 Turkish kebabs with tomato and chilli salsa 136
Chinese chives: crab dim sum with Chinese chives 52
Chives: blue cheese and chive pennies 78
 Cheddar and chive scones 85
 chive scrambled eggs in brioches 94
 herb omelette 89
 herby polenta with tomatoes 182
 smoked salmon and chive omelette 91
Chocolate: butterflied prawns in chocolate 146
Chorizo sausage: chorizo in olive oil 113
 chorizo pastry puffs 48
 chorizo with garlic potatoes 113
 eggs with chorizo 95
 spicy chorizo sausage and spring onion hash 114
Ciabatta: ciabatta with mozzarella and onions 83
 crostini with tomato, red pepper and mozzarella toppings 33
 prawn and vegetable crostini 34
Cilantro *see* Coriander
Cinnamon: cinnamon fish cakes with currants, pine nuts and herbs 170
 meatballs with pine nuts and cinnamon 134
Clams: clam and pasta soup 222
 mixed seafood salad 247
 mussels and clams with lemon grass and coconut cream 152
 spiced clams 153

Cloud ear mushrooms, dried: hot and sour soup 219
Coconut: chilled coconut soup 212
coconut chips 24
red-hot meatballs with roasted coconut 128
roasted coconut cashew nuts 23
Coconut cream: lemon and coconut dhal dip 13
mussels and clams with lemon grass and coconut cream 152
pea and potato pakoras with coconut and mint chutney 35
Coconut milk: crab, coconut and coriander soup 225
spiced vegetables with coconut 211
Cod: brandade of salt cod 17
eggy Thai fish cakes 42
fish sausages 169
ginger and chilli steamed fish custards 178
hearty fish chowder 224
Parmesan fish goujons 61
salt cod and potato fritters 58
spicy fish rösti 170
Thai fish cakes with cucumber relish 42
Thai-style seafood turnovers 179
Three-fish terrine 69
Cod roe, smoked: taramasalata 17
Coppa: leek terrine with deli meats 70
Coquilles St Jacques 155
Coriander: caramelized mushrooms with allspice and herbs 189
coriander omelette parcels 91
crab, coconut and coriander soup 225
fiery guacamole 16
hot spicy prawns with coriander 144
marinated smoked salmon with lime and coriander 164
mixed leaf and herb salad with toasted seeds 233
rice noodles with fresh herbs 205
corn: cheese tamales 80
corn griddle cakes 76
garlic and chilli marinated beef with corn-crusted onion rings 132
spicy corn patties 199
tung tong 46
vegetable samosas 196
Courgettes: Asian-style courgette fritters 55
baked Mediterranean vegetables 210
chicken and vegetable bundles 99
chunky chicken minestrone 229
grilled vegetable terrine 67
quick pistou soup 216
summer vegetables with yogurt pesto 211
tagliatelle with vegetable ribbons 200
tomato and courgette timbales 184
vegetable tempura 55
Couscous salad 240
Crab: Asian-style crab cakes 159
chilli crabs 158
crab and cucumber wraps with hoisin sauce 157
crab and ricotta tartlets 45
crab and tofu dumplings 52
crab, coconut and coriander soup 225
crab dim sum with Chinese chives 52
crab egg rolls 41
crab meat and water chestnut wontons 53
crisp-fried crab claws 58
dressed crab with asparagus 157
hot crab soufflés 73
Japanese-style crab cakes with ginger and wasabi 159
popiah 49
seafood wontons 53
soft-shell crabs with chilli and salt 158
Croquettes: chicken croquettes 56
meat croquettes 57
paella croquettes 60
Stilton croquettes 78
Crostini: crostini with tomato, red pepper and mozzarella toppings 33
egg crostini with rouille 33
goat's cheese and crostini with fruit 83
paprika-spiced black pudding crostini 34
prawn and vegetable crostini 34
Cucumbers: cacik 14
crab and cucumber wraps with hoisin sauce 157
creamy cucumber and walnut appetizer 180
crunchy summer rolls 197
lamb and cucumber soup 230
smoked trout with cucumber and dill 172
Thai fish cakes with cucumber relish 42
tsatziki 13
Vietnamese table salad 238
yogurt with cucumber and mint 11
Cumin: artichoke and cumin dip 10
bruschetta with anchovies, quail's eggs and roasted cumin 31
grilled green mussels with cumin 151
lettuce-wrapped lamb with cumin 134
orange and red onion salad with cumin 238

Daikon *see* Mooli
Danish blue cheese: blue cheese dip 19
Devils on horseback 31
Dill: cinnamon fish cakes with currants, pine nuts and herbs 170
filo cigars filled with feta, parsley, mint and dill 46
potted salmon with lemon and dill 160
smoked trout with cucumber and dill 172
Dips: artichoke and cumin dip 10
baba ganoush with Lebanese flatbread 15
basil and lemon dip 11
beef satay with a hot mango dip 126
blue cheese dip 19
butterfly prawn skewers with chilli and raspberry dip 30
celeriac fritters with mustard dip 56
charred artichokes with lemon oil dip 187
chilli bean dip 10
feta and roast pepper dip with chillies 19
garlic-infused spicy bean dip 14
hummus 15
lemon and coconut dhal dip 12
Libyan spicy pumpkin dip 12
melting cheese dip 74
potato skewers with mustard dip 192
salmon dip 18
saucy tomato dip 8
sesame and lemon dip 11
spicy carrot dip 12
tapenade with quail's eggs and crudités 16
taramasalata 17
thousand island dip 18
turkey sticks with sour cream dip 104
Duck: duck consommé 229
duck wontons with mango sauce 51
grilled foie gras 140
Peking duck 110
sesame duck and noodle salad 251
warm duck salad with poached eggs 250
Duck egg nests 48
Duck liver pâté and redcurrant sauce 65
Dumpling wrappers: crab dim sum with Chinese chives 52
Dunsyre Blue cheese: watercress salad with pear and Dunsyre Blue dressing 242

Eels: eel wrapped in bacon 166
smoked eel and chicory salad 247
smoked eel with scrambled eggs 93
Eggplants *see* Aubergines
Eggs: artichokes with eggs 95
asparagus and egg terrine 70
aubergine salad with shrimp and egg 245
Caesar salad 240
cheese-crusted party eggs 84
chive scrambled eggs in brioches 94
coriander omelette parcels 91
crab egg rolls 41
curry crackers 25
deep-fried tofu balls 36
duck egg nests 48
egg and salmon puff parcels 97
egg crostini with rouille 33
egg foo yung 88
egg rolls 93
eggs mimosa 96
eggy Thai fish cakes 42
hard-boiled eggs in red sauce 88
hard-boiled eggs with tuna sauce 87
herb omelette 89
leek and egg salad 243
Monte Cristo triangles 21
poached eggs Florentine 94
rice omelette rolls 92
risotto frittata 202
savoury scrambled eggs 96
scrambled eggs with prawns 89
seafood pancakes 169
shrimp, egg and avocado mousses 73
smoked eel with scrambled eggs 93
smoked haddock and cheese omelette 90
smoked salmon and chive omelette 91
soft tacos with spiced omelette 92
son-in-law eggs 97
Spanish-style omelette with bitter melon 90
spicy toasts 32
spinach and cheese pancakes 82
spinach and chickpea pancakes 199
tortilla with beans 87
twice-baked Gruyère and potato soufflés 194
vegetable pancakes with tomato salsa 206
warm duck salad with poached eggs 250
Emmenthal cheese: Monte Cristo triangles 21
Enokitake mushrooms: bacon-rolled enokitake mushrooms 38

Fajitas: Mexican chicken faijitas 103
Falafel 180
Fava beans *see* Broad beans
Fennel: herbed fish fritters 171
herbed plaice fritters 59
tapenade with quail's eggs and crudités 16
Feta cheese: borek 205
cheese scrolls 77
cheese tamales 80
chicken flautas 102
feta and roast pepper dip with chillies 19
filo cigars with feta, parsley, mint and dill 46
marinated feta cheese salad with capers 242
polpettes 81
salad with watermelon and feta cheese 241
spinach and cheese pancakes 82
Figs with prosciutto and Roquefort 111
Filo pastry: borek 205
filo cigars with feta, parsley, mint and dill 46
garlic prawns in filo tartlets 45
smoked chicken with peach mayonnaise in filo tartlets 44
Firecrackers 54
Fish: fish and chermoula mini pies 179
fish soup with rouille 227
see also individual fish names
Five-spice powder: five-spice and ginger pork wontons 50
five-spice rib-sticker 124
Flaky pastry: egg and salmon puff parcels 97
Flounder: hearty fish chowder 224
herbed fish fritters 171
steamed sole lettuce wraps 176
Foie gras: grilled foie gras 140
Fonduta 74
Fontina cheese: cheese fritters in wonton wrappers 80
fonduta 74
wild mushrooms and fontina tarts 201
French stick: paprika-spiced black pudding crostini 34
Fromage frais: thousand island dip 18

Fruit chutney: devils on horseback 31
Fruit conserve: baked sausage terrine with fruity conserve 69

Garam masala: curry crackers 25
Garlic: chicken with lemon and garlic 108
chorizo with garlic potatoes 113
garlic and chilli marinated beef with corn-crusted onion rings 132
garlic prawns in filo tartlets 45
garlic scallops and prawns 155
garlic soup 214
garlic-infused spicy bean dip 14
hummus 15
roasted plum tomatoes with garlic 185
sautéed mussels with garlic and herbs 150
spaghettini with roasted garlic 200
spinach and roast garlic salad 233
squid stuffed with garlic pork 167
squid with ginger and garlic 145
stuffed vine leaves with garlic yogurt 181
Garlic sausage: roasted vegetable and garlic sausage loaf 126
Ginger: caramelized chicken wings with fresh ginger 102
chicken and ginger soup 228
five-spice and ginger pork wontons 50
ginger and chilli steamed fish custards 178
Japanese-style crab cakes with ginger and wasabi 159
salmon and ginger fish cakes 165
Sichuan pork with ginger relish 125
squid with ginger and garlic 145
sweet and sour tongue with ginger 133
Gnocchi: semolina and pesto gnocchi 204
Goat's cheese: French goat's cheese salad 243
goat's cheese and crostini with fruit 83
goat's cheese soufflé 76
red onion and goat's cheese pastries 208
walnut and goat's cheese bruschetta 84
Goose: grilled foie gras 140
Gorgonzola cheese: risotto with four cheeses 202
Gouda cheese: cheese and celeriac soup 217
Grapes: halloumi and grape salad 244
Green beans: green bean and sweet red pepper salad 232
quick pistou soup 216
roasted vegetable and garlic sausage loaf 126
tapenade and aioli with vegetables 28
Green curry paste: green curry puffs 47
Green peppers: aubergine and pepper spread 9
beef patties with onions and peppers 129
classic gazpacho 213
feta and roast pepper dip with chillies 19
Greek stuffed vegetables 183
pork-stuffed green peppers 119
Gruyère cheese: cheese aigrettes 79
melting cheese dip 74
Monte Cristo triangles 21
risotto with four cheeses 202
twice-baked Gruyère and potato soufflés 194
Guinness: cheese and Guinness fondue 75

Haddock: cinnamon fish cakes with currants, pine nuts and herbs 170
eggy Thai fish cakes 42
ginger and chilli steamed fish custards 178
haddock and smoked salmon terrine 68
hearty fish chowder 224
marinated smoked haddock fillets 172
mini saffron fish cakes 43
Parmesan fish goujons 61
seafood pancakes 169
smoked haddock and cheese omelette 90
smoked haddock pâté 63
Sussex smokies 173
Thai-style seafood turnovers 179
three-fish terrine 69
Halibut: ginger and chilli steamed fish custards 178
Halloumi cheese: halloumi and grape salad 244
halloumi with rocket salad 244
Ham: asparagus and prosciutto 110
egg crostini with rouille 33
figs with prosciutto and Roquefort 111
herbed liver pâté pie 66
leek terrine with deli meats 70
melon and prosciutto salad 111
Monte Cristo triangles 21

prosciutto and mozzarella parcels 20
prosciutto with potato rémoulade 112
quail's eggs in aspic with prosciutto 86
scallops wrapped in prosciutto 156
split pea and ham soup 230
Hazelnut oil: warm chicken and tomato salad with hazelnut dressing 249
Hearts of palm: leek and potato with heart of palm soup 218
Herrings: herring salad with beetroot and sour cream 245
marinated herrings 176
Hijiki seaweed: mixed seaweed salad 235
Hoisin sauce, crab and cucumber wraps with hoisin sauce 157
Honey: chilli and honey-cured beef 133
grilled oysters with highland heather honey 154
Horseradish: smoked trout and horseradish salad 249
squash soup with hot horseradish cream 215
Hummus 15

Irish 'melting' cheese: cheese and Guinness fondue 75

Juniper: turkey, juniper and green peppercorn terrine 67

Kabocha squash with chicken sauce 105
Kebabs: lamb and ras el hanout kebabs 137
Romanian kebabs 135
scallop and mussel kebabs 153
shammi kebabs 138
shish kebab with sumac 136
Turkish kebabs with tomato and chilli salsa 136
Kidney beans: chilli bean dip 10
Konnyaku: grilled vegetable sticks 181

Lamb: curried lamb and potato cakes 139
curried lamb samosas 140
deep-fried lamb patties 141
devilled kidneys on brioche croûtes 141
fragrant spiced lamb on mini poppadums 139
lamb and cucumber soup 230
lamb and ras el hanout kebabs 137
lamb saté 137
lamb tikka 138
lettuce-wrapped lamb with cumin 134
meatballs with pine nuts and cinnamon 134
Romanian kebabs 135
shammi kebabs 138
shish kebab with sumac 136
skewered lamb with red onion salsa 135
Turkish kebabs with tomato and chilli salsa 136
Lamb's liver: lamb's liver with paprika 143
liver and bacon Varenyky 142
Leeks: cheese and leek sausages 188
chicken and vegetable bundles 99
chicken, leek and barley soup 228
leek and bacon tart 121
leek and egg salad 243
leek and potato with heart of palm soup 218
leek, saffron and mussel tartlets 44
leek terrine with deli meats 70
mussels with Musselburgh leeks 150
roasted vegetable and garlic sausage loaf 126
vegetable pancakes with tomato salsa 206
Lemon grass: mussels and clams with lemon grass and coconut cream 152
Lemon sole: breaded sole batons 60
lemon sole and fresh oyster salad 178
Lemons: basil and lemon dip 11
charred artichokes with lemon oil dip 187
chicken with lemon and garlic 108
lemon and bean stuffed mushrooms 189
lemon and coconut dhal dip 13
potted salmon with lemon and dill 160
sesame and lemon dip 11
spaghetti with lemon 200
Lettuces: Caesar salad 240
lettuce-wrapped lamb with cumin 134
steamed sole lettuce wraps 176
Vietnamese table salad 238
Limes: deep-fried tofu balls 36
fiery guacamole 16
marinated smoked salmon with lime and coriander 164
quinoa salad with citrus dressing 239
Ling: mini saffron fish cakes 43
Lion's head meat balls 120
Lobster: cappuccino of Puy lentils, lobster and tarragon 227

Mackerel: avocado and smoked fish salad 248
fish cakes in banana leaves 177
smoked fish platter 163
smoked mackerel pâté 64
spicy fried mackerel 177
Malfatti with grilled pepper sauce 204
Mallard pâté 66
Manchego cheese: artichoke rice cakes with Manchego 203
tapas of almonds, olives and cheese 28
Mangetouts: braised turnip with prawn and mangetouts 148
Mangoes: beef satay with a hot mango dip 126
duck wontons with mango sauce 51
green mango salad 238
Mascarpone: thousand island dip 18
Mayonnaise: prosciutto with potato rémoulade 112
smoked chicken with peach mayonnaise in filo tartlets 44
measurements 4
Melons: iced melon soup 212
melon and prosciutto salad 111
salad with watermelon and feta cheese 241
Mint: caramelized mushrooms with allspice and herbs 189
cinnamon fish cakes with currants, pine nuts and herbs 170
filo cigars filled with feta, parsley, mint and dill 46
pea and potato pakoras with coconut and mint chutney 35
rice noodles with fresh herbs 205
yogurt with cucumber and mint 11
Miso: miso soup with wakame 219
pickled broccoli in miso 182
Monkfish: monkfish broth 226
monkfish packages 174
Monterey Jack cheese: cheese and chilli tortillas 79
Mooli: beansprout and mooli salad 235
Mousse: salmon and pike mousse 72
sea trout mousse 71
shrimp, egg and avocado mousses 73
smoked fish and asparagus mousse 72
Mozzarella cheese: aubergine and smoked mozzarella rolls 187
aubergine, tomato and mozzarella wraps 207
cheese and chilli tortillas 79
ciabatta with mozzarella and onions 83
crostini with tomato, red pepper and mozzarella toppings 33
fried rice balls stuffed with mozzarella 82
prosciutto and mozzarella parcels 20
roast tomatoes and mozzarella with basil oil 241
spicy toasts 32
Muhammara 9
Mullet roe, smoked: taramasalata 17
Mushrooms: bacon-rolled enokitake mushrooms 38
caramelized mushrooms with allspice and herbs 189
chicken and vegetable bundles 99
hot and sour soup 219
lemon and bean stuffed mushrooms 189
mushroom and bean pâté 65
mushroom caviar 186
mushrooms on spicy toast 206
prawn and vegetable crostini 34
shiitake and scallop bundles 41
slow-cooked shiitake with shoyu 186
spicy beef and mushroom soup 223
stuffed mushrooms with spinach 81
tortellini chanterelle broth 222
wild mushroom soup 218
wild mushrooms and fontina tarts 201
Mussels: gratin of mussels with pesto 151
grilled green mussels with cumin 151
leek, saffron and mussel tartlets 44
mixed seafood salad 247
mussels and clams with lemon grass and coconut cream 152
mussels with Musselburgh leeks 150
potato, mussel and watercress salad 246
saffron-flavoured mussel soup 226
sautéed mussels with garlic and herbs 150
scallop and mussel kebabs 153
steamed green mussels in black bean sauce 152
Mustard: celeriac fritters with mustard dip 56
potato skewers with mustard dip 192

Noodles: cabbage and noodle parcels 116
cellophane noodle soup 221
cellophane noodles with pork 117
firecrackers 54
Malayan prawn laksa 225
rice noodles with fresh herbs 205
sesame duck and noodle salad 251
smoked trout and noodle salad 249
Nopalitos: pork in green sauce with cactus 119
Nori: seaweed-wrapped prawn rolls 39
sushi 38
Nutmeg: spinach and nutmeg spring rolls 207
nutritional analysis 4

Olive oil: charred artichokes with lemon oil dip 187
chilli yogurt cheese in olive oil 75
chorizo in olive oil 113
roast tomatoes and mozzarella with basil oil 241
Olives: black and orange salad 237
olive and anchovy bites 29
red onion and black olive pissaladière 209
spicy Moroccan olives 27
tapas of almonds, olives and cheese 28
tapenade and aioli with vegetables 28
tapenade with quail's eggs and crudités 16
Omelettes: coriander omelette parcels 91
herb omelette 89
rice omelette rolls 92
smoked haddock and cheese omelette 90
smoked salmon and chive omelette 91
soft tacos with spiced omelette 92
Spanish-style omelette with bitter melon 90
Onions: beef patties with onions and peppers 129
ciabatta with mozzarella and onions 83
deep-fried onion rings 195
French onion soup 217
garlic and chilli marinated beef with corn -crusted onion rings 132
onion and potato cake 193
onion bhajias 196
orange and red onion salad with cumin 238
pork and bacon rillettes with onion salad 121
red onion and black olive pissaladière 209
red onion and goat's cheese pastries 208
skewered lamb with red onion salsa 135
stuffed parsleyed onions 187
Orange peppers: Greek stuffed vegetables 183
Oranges: asparagus and orange salad 236
black and orange salad 237
carrot and orange salad 237
goat's cheese and crostini with fruit 83
orange and red onion salad with cumin 238
orange candied sweet potatoes 193
quinoa salad with citrus dressing 239
Oregano: rice noodles with fresh herbs 205
Oregon Blue cheese: blue cheese and chive pennies 78
oven temperatures 4
Ox tongue: sweet and sour tongue with ginger 133
Oxtail terrine 131

Oyster sauce: stir-fried beef in oyster sauce 132
Oysters: angels on horseback 30
grilled oysters with highland heather honey 154
lemon sole and fresh oyster salad 178
oysters Rockefeller 154

Pancetta: leek terrine with deli meats 70
Pandanus leaves: scented chicken wraps 109
Paneer: chicken kofta balti with paneer 108
Panuchos 103
Panzanella salad 232
Papaya: Vietnamese table salad 238
Paprika: lamb's liver with paprika 143
paprika-spiced black pudding crostini 34
Parmesan cheese: cheese aigrettes 79
cheese fritters in wonton wrappers 80
golden Parmesan chicken 57
mini sausage rolls 47
Parmesan fish goujons 61
Parmesan thins 26
risotto with four cheeses 202
spinach and cheese pancakes 82
Parsley: caramelized mushrooms with allspice and herbs 189
cinnamon fish cakes with currants, pine nuts and herbs 170
filo cigars filled with feta, parsley, mint and dill 46
herb omelette 89
herbed fish fritters 171
herbed Greek pies 209
herbed liver pâté pie 66
herbed plaice fritters 59
herby polenta with tomatoes 182
mixed leaf and herb salad with toasted seeds 233
sautéed mussels with garlic and herbs 150
stuffed parsleyed onions 187
Parsnips: parsnip, carrot and chèvre cheese fricassée 210
pumpkin and parsnip soup 216
Pasta: clam and pasta soup 222
red pepper and pasta in broth 223
Pâtés: cannellini bean pâté 63
chicken liver and brandy pâté 64
duck liver pâté and redcurrant sauce 65
mallard pâté 66
mushroom and bean pâté 65
smoked haddock pâté 63
smoked mackerel pâté 64
smoked salmon pâté 62
spiced pork pâté 62
Peaches: smoked chicken with peach mayonnaise in filo tartlets 44
Peanut butter: pork and peanut wontons with plum sauce 50
spicy chicken satay with peanut sauce 98
Peanuts: peanut crackers 26
spicy peanut balls 195
Pearl barley: chicken, leek and barley soup 228
Pears: pears and Stilton 188
watercress salad with pear and Dunsyre Blue dressing 242
Peas: chunky chicken minestrone 229
pea and potato pakoras with coconut and mint chutney 35
vegetable samosas 196
see also Mangetouts; Petits pois
Pepitas 23
Pepper: crispy salt and pepper squid 166
fried whitebait with cayenne pepper 168
turkey, juniper and green peppercorn terrine 67
Peppers *see* Green peppers; Orange peppers; Red peppers; Yellow peppers
Perch: fish sausages 169
Pesto: gratin of mussels with pesto 151
semolina and pesto gnocchi 204
smoked salmon pancakes with pesto 162
summer vegetables with yogurt pesto 211
Petits pois: green curry puffs 47
paella croquettes 60
quick pistou soup 216
Pig's liver: baked sausage terrine with fruity conserve 69